SPEECH PLANNING (page 57)

STEP 1 — Action

Using Brainstorming and Concept Mapping to Identify Speech Topics

The goal of this activity is to help you identify prospective topics for speeches.

1. Develop a subject list.
   a. Divide a sheet of paper into three columns. Label column 1 "major and career interests," label column 2 "hobbies and activities," and label column 3 "concerns and issues."
   b. Working on one column at a time, identify subjects of interest to you. Try to identify at least three subjects in each column.
   c. Place a check mark next to the one subject in each list that you would most enjoy speaking about.
   d. Keep the lists for future use in choosing a topic for an assigned speech.
2. For each subject you have checked, brainstorm a list of topics that relate to that subject.
3. Look at the topics you have brainstormed. In which do you have the most interest and expertise? Place a check mark beside one or two of these.
4. Then, for each item on the brainstorm list that you have checked, develop a concept map to identify smaller topic areas and related ideas that might be developed into future speeches.

CourseMate You can go online to print a worksheet that will help you complete this activity. Go to your CourseMate for *Challenge* to access Action Step 1 Activity 1A.

SPEECH PLANNING (page 64)

STEP 1 — Action

Analyzing Your Audience

1. Decide on a method for gathering audience data.
2. Collect the data.
3. Copy or duplicate the Audience Analysis Summary Form (Exhibit 4.5).
4. Use the information you have collected to complete the form.
5. Write two short paragraphs to describe your initial impression of audience demographics, knowledge, and attitudes toward your subject.
6. Save the completed form. You will refer to this audience analysis information to address listener relevance throughout the speech-planning process.

CourseMate You can download an online copy of this form. Go to your CourseMate for *Challenge* to access the chapter resources for Chapter 4 and then click Audience Analysis Summary Form.

Speech Planning Action Steps

PULL OUT SECTION ☞

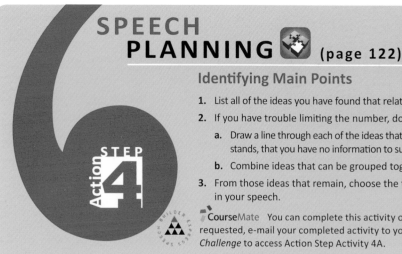

SPEECH PLANNING (page 122)

Identifying Main Points

1. List all of the ideas you have found that relate to the specific purpose of your speech.
2. If you have trouble limiting the number, do the following:
   a. Draw a line through each of the ideas that you believe the audience already understands, that you have no information to support, or that just seems too complicated.
   b. Combine ideas that can be grouped together under a single heading.
3. From those ideas that remain, choose the two to four you will use as main points in your speech.

CourseMate You can complete this activity online with Speech Builder Express and, if requested, e-mail your completed activity to your instructor. Go to your CourseMate for *Challenge* to access Action Step Activity 4A.

SPEECH PLANNING (page 125)

Writing a Thesis Statement

The goal of this activity is to use your general and specific goals and the main points you have identified to develop a well-worded thesis statement for your speech.

1. Write the general and specific goals you developed in Activity 4A.
2. List the main points you identified in Activity 4A.
3. Now write one or two complete sentences that combine your specific goal with your main point ideas.

CourseMate You can complete this activity online with Speech Builder Express, view a student sample of this activity, and, if requested, e-mail your completed activity to your instructor. Go to your CourseMate for *Challenge* to access Action Step Activity 4B.

SPEECH PLANNING (page 132)

Developing the Main Points of Your Speech

The goal of this activity is to help you phrase and order your main points.

1. Write your thesis statement.
2. Underline the two to four main points identified in your thesis statement.
3. For each underlined item, write one sentence that summarizes what you want your audience to know about that idea.
4. Review the main points as a group.
   a. Is the relationship between each main point statement and the goal statement clearly specified? If not, revise.
   b. Are the main points parallel in structure? If not, consider why and revise.
5. Choose an organizational pattern for your main points.
6. Identify the pattern you have used.

CourseMate You can complete this activity online with Speech Builder Express, view a student sample of this activity, and, if requested, e-mail your completed activity to your instructor. Go to your CourseMate for *Challenge* to access Activity 4C.

SPEECH PLANNING (page 72)

Action STEP 1

Writing a Specific Goal

Type of speech: _____

1. Write a draft of your general speech goal using a complete sentence that specifies the type of response you want from the audience.
2. Revise the infinitive to make it reflect the specific audience response you desire.
3. Check the number of ideas expressed in the statement. If the statement contains more than one idea, select one and rewrite the statement.
4. Improve the statement so that it describes the precise focus of your speech as it relates to your intended audience.

Write the final draft of the specific goal:

_____
_____
_____

You can complete this activity online with Speech Builder Express, a speech outlining and development tool that will help you complete the action steps in this book to develop your speech. You can access Speech Builder Express through your CourseMate for *Challenge.*

SPEECH PLANNING (page 89)

Action STEP 2

Recognizing Opportunities for Audience Adaptation

To identify opportunities for audience adaptation and lay a groundwork for applying information from the next several chapters, state your potential topic and then answer the following questions.

Potential topic: _____

1. How relevant will the audience find this material? How can I demonstrate that the material is timely, proximate, and has personal impact on the members of this audience?
2. What is my audience's initial disposition toward my speech topic likely to be?
3. What common ground do audience members share with each other and with me?
4. What can I do to enhance my credibility?
5. How can I make it easier for audience members to comprehend and remember the information I will share?
6. What language or cultural differences do audience members have with each other and with me?

CourseMate You can complete this activity online, view another student sample of this activity, and, if requested, e-mail your completed activity to your instructor. Go to your CourseMate for *Challenge* to access Action Step 2, Activity 2.

SPEECH
PLANNING (page 159)

Action STEP 4

Compiling a List of Sources

The goal of this activity is to help you record the list of sources you used in your speech.

1. Review your research cards, separating those whose information you have used in your speech from those whose information you have not used.

2. Note on your research card or your outline where you'll reference the source during your speech.

3. List the sources whose information was used in the speech by copying the bibliographical information recorded on the research card.

4. For short lists, organize your list alphabetically by the last name of the first author. Be sure to follow a form given in the text. If you did not record some of the bibliographical information on your notecard, you will need to revisit the library, database, or other source to find it.

CourseMate You can complete this activity online with Speech Builder Express, view a student sample of this activity, and, if requested, e-mail your completed activity to your instructor. Go to your CourseMate for *Challenge* to access Activity 4G.

SPEECH
PLANNING (page 166)

Action STEP 4

Completing the Formal Speech Outline

CourseMate Write and review a complete-sentence outline of your speech using material you've developed so far with the Action Steps in Chapters 4 through 8. You can complete this activity online with Speech Builder Express, view a student sample of this activity, and, if requested, e-mail your completed activity to your instructor. Go to your CourseMate for *Challenge* to access Activity 4H.

SPEECH
PLANNING (page 186)

Action STEP 5

Choosing, Preparing, and Using Presentational Aids

The goal of this activity is to identify information where a presentational aid would increase audience interest, understanding, and retention.

1. Identify the key ideas in your speech for which you believe a presentational aid would increase audience interest, facilitate understanding, or increase retention.

2. For each idea you have identified, list the type of presentational aid you think would be most appropriate to develop and use.

3. For each aid you have identified, decide how you will design it.

4. For each aid you have identified, decide on the method you will use to display it and how you will reference it during the speech.

CourseMate You can complete this activity online with Speech Builder Express, download a Presentational Aids Planning Chart to help you organize your aids, and, if requested, e-mail your completed activity to your instructor. Go to your Speech Communication CourseMate for *Challenge* to access Activity 5A.

SPEECH
PLANNING (page 136)

STEP
Action 4

Outlining the Speech Body

The goal of this exercise is to help you get started on the outline for the body of your first speech. Using complete sentences, write the following:

1. The specific speech goal you developed in Activity 4A.
2. The thesis statement you developed in Activity 4B.
3. A transition to the first main point.
4. The first main point you developed in Activity 4C.
5. The outline of the listener relevance link, subpoints, and support for your first main point, similar to the sample shown earlier, under "Outlining Subpoints."
6. A transition from your first main point to your second.
7. The other points, subpoints, support, section transitions, and signposts. Use the format for numeration, spacing, and so on shown in the Student Response to Activity 4D. (Note that the labels Introduction, Conclusion, and Sources are included just to help you understand the requirements for your final outline.) For a sample of a completed outline, see pages 162–166 of Chapter 8.

 CourseMate You can complete this activity online with Speech Builder Express and, if requested, e-mail your completed activity to your instructor. Go to your CourseMate for *Challenge* to access Activity 4D.

SPEECH
PLANNING (page 152)

STEP
Action 4

Creating Speech Introductions

The goal of this activity is to create choices for how you will begin your speech.

1. For the speech body you outlined earlier, write three different introductions— using different rhetorical devices (startling statement, a question, a story, a personal reference, a joke, a quotation, action, or suspense) to get attention— that you believe meet the primary goals of effective introductions and would be appropriate for your speech goal and audience.
2. Of the three introductions you drafted, which do you believe is the best? Why?
3. Write that introduction in outline form, indicating in parentheses where you are meeting each goal.

 CourseMate You can complete this activity online with Speech Builder Express, view a student sample of this activity, and, if requested, e-mail your completed activity to your instructor. Go to your CourseMate for *Challenge* to access Activity 4E.

SPEECH
PLANNING (page 156)

STEP
Action 4

Creating Speech Conclusions

The goal of this activity is to help you create choices for how you will conclude your speech.

1. For the speech body you outlined earlier, write three different conclusions that review important points you want the audience to remember, and include a clincher that provides closure by leaving the audience with a vivid impression.
2. Which do you believe is the best? Why?
3. Write that conclusion in outline form.

CourseMate You can complete this activity online with Speech Builder Express, view a student sample of this activity, and, if requested, e-mail your completed activity to your instructor. Go to your CourseMate for *Challenge* to access Activity 4F.

SPEECH PLANNING 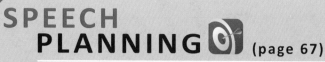 (page 67)

Analyzing the Occasion

The goal of this activity is to help you understand your speech occasion. Fill in answers to the following questions:

1. What are the special expectations for the speech? _____
2. What is the appropriate length for the speech? _____
3. How large will the audience be? _____
4. Where will the speech be given? _____
5. When will the speech be given? _____
6. Where in the program does the speech occur? _____
7. What equipment is necessary to give the speech? _____

Write a short paragraph mentioning which aspects of the setting are most important for you to consider in speech preparation and why.

CourseMate You can complete this activity online, print it, and, if requested, e-mail it to your instructor. Go to your CourseMate for *Challenge* to access Action Step 1, Activity 1C.

SPEECH PLANNING 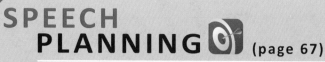 (page 69)

Selecting a Topic

Use your responses to Action Step Activities 1A, 1B, and 1C to complete this activity.

1. Look over the concept map you prepared in Activity 1A. List each of the specific topics that you generated:

   _____   _____   _____
   _____   _____   _____
   _____   _____   _____

2. Using the information you compiled in Activity 1B, the audience analysis, compare each topic to your audience profile. Eliminate topics that seem less appropriate for this specific audience. Write each of the topics that remain:

   _____   _____   _____
   _____   _____   _____

3. Using the information you compiled in Activity 1C, your analysis of the occasion, compare each of the remaining topics to your setting profile. Eliminate topics that seem less appropriate. Write each of the topics that remain:

   _____   _____   _____

4. The remaining topics are appropriate to your public speaking situation; you can be confident that you can develop an appropriate speech from any of these. So, from this list, select the one that you are most excited about sharing with others. My topic will be: _____

CourseMate You can go online to the CourseMate for *Challenge* to complete this activity and print out a worksheet that will help you select your topic.

SPEECH PLANNING (page 225)

Rehearsing Your Speech

The goal of this activity is to rehearse your speech, analyze it, and rehearse it again. One complete rehearsal includes (1) a practice, (2) an analysis, and (3) a second practice.

1. Find a place where you can be alone to practice your speech. Follow the six points of the first rehearsal.

2. Watch and listen to the recording. Review your outline as you do so and then complete a speech evaluation checklist to see how well you presented your speech during this rehearsal. (You can find the Speech Evaluation Checklist: General Criteria on page 14 in Chapter 1, a more detailed checklist in this chapter, and checklists for informative and persuasive speeches in later chapters.)

   List three specific changes you will make in your next practice session.

   One: _____

   Two: _____

   Three: _____

3. Go through the six steps outlined for the first rehearsal again. Then assess: Did you achieve the goals you set for the second rehearsal?

   Reevaluate the speech using the checklist and continue to practice until you are satisfied with all of your presentation.

CourseMate You can complete this activity online, print copies of this rehearsal analysis sheet, see a student sample of a practice round, and, if requested, e-mail your work to your instructor. Go to your CourseMate for *Challenge* to access Activity 6.

SPEECH PLANNING (page 299)

Speech Planning Action Step for Persuasive Speeches

Writing a Specific Goal as a Persuasive Proposition

1. Tentatively phrase your goal as a proposition.

2. Check whether you believe that your target audience is opposed to, has no opinion of, or is in favor of your proposition. Why?

3. Check whether you believe that the degree of your target audience's attitude makes your goal too difficult to meet or your audience is already convinced of your goal. If you've checked either of these, then rephrase your goal to adapt to that audience attitude.

4. Check whether your proposition, as stated or revised, is one of fact, value, or policy.

CourseMate You can complete this activity online with Speech Builder Express. Go to your CourseMate for *Challenge* to access Action Step Activity 7.

SPEECH PLANNING (page 105)

Action STEP 3

Gathering and Evaluating Information Sources

The goal of this activity is to help you compile a list of potential sources for your speech.

1. Brainstorm a list of keywords that are related to your speech goal.
2. Identify gaps in your current knowledge that you would like to fill.
3. Using a search engine, identify sponsored and personal websites that may be sources of information for your speech.
4. Work with a library database (either physically located at the library or electronically) to list specific resources that appear to provide information for your speech.
5. Gather and skim the resources you have identified to decide which are likely to be the most useful.
6. Evaluate each resource to determine how much faith you can place in the information.
7. Determine what primary research you might conduct to fill gaps in the information you have collected.

CourseMate

You can complete this activity online, print it, and, if requested, e-mail it to your instructor. Go to your CourseMate for *Challenge* to access Action Step 3, Activity 3A.

SPEECH PLANNING (page 112)

Action STEP 3

Record Relevant Information on Research Cards

The goal of this activity is to review the source material that you identified in Action Step Activity 3A and to record on research cards specific items of information that you might wish to use in your speech.

1. Carefully read all print and electronic sources (including website material) that you have identified and evaluated as appropriate sources for your speech. Review your notes and tapes from all interviews and observations.
2. As you read an item (fact, opinion, example, illustration, statistic, anecdote, narrative, comparison–contrast, quotation, definition, or description) that you think might be useful in your speech, record the item on a research card or on the appropriate electronic research card form available at your CourseMate for *Challenge*. (If you are using an article that appeared in a periodical source that you read online, use the periodical research card form.)

CourseMate You can complete this activity online and, if requested, e-mail it to your instructor. You can also use online forms to prepare your own research cards and print them for use in preparing your speech. Go to your CourseMate for *Challenge* to access Action Step Activity 3B.

SPEECH PLANNING (page 115)

Action STEP 3

Citing Sources

On the back of each research card, write a short phrase that you can use in your speech as an oral footnote for the material on this card.

The *Challenge* of *Effective* Speaking

Rudolph F. Verderber
University of Cincinnati

Deanna D. Sellnow
University of Kentucky

Kathleen S. Verderber
Northern Kentucky University

15th Edition

Australia • Brazil • Japan • Korea • Mexico • Singapore
Spain • United Kingdom • United States

WADSWORTH
CENGAGE Learning

WADSWORTH
CENGAGE Learning™

The Challenge of Effective Speaking,
Fifteenth Edition

Rudolph F. Verderber, Deanna D. Sellnow, Kathleen S. Verderber

Senior Publisher: Lyn Uhl

Executive Editor: Monica Eckman

Senior Development Editor: Greer Lleuad

Development Editor: Angela Kao

Assistant Editor: Rebekah Matthews

Editorial Assistant: Colin Solan

Media Editor: Jessica Badiner

Senior Marketing Manager: Amy Whitaker

Marketing Coordinator: Gurpreet S. Saran

Marketing Communications Manager:
   Caitlin Green

Senior Content Project Manager:
   Rosemary Winfield

Art Director: Linda Helcher

Print Buyer: Justin Palmeiro

Text and Cover Designer: Pronk Design

Composition and Production Services: Integra
   Software Services, Inc.

For product information and technology assistance, contact us at
Cengage Learning Customer & Sales Support, 1-800-354-9706.
For permission to use material from this text or product,
submit all requests online at **www.cengage.com/permission.**
Further permissions questions can be emailed to
permissionrequest@cengage.com.

Library of Congress Control Number: 2010936949

ISBN-13: 978-0-495-91134-0

ISBN-10: 0-495-91134-8

Wadsworth
20 Channel Center Street
Boston, MA 02210
USA

Cengage Learning is a leading provider of customized learning solutions with office locations around the globe, including Singapore, the United Kingdom, Australia, Mexico, Brazil and Japan. Locate your local office at **international.cengage.com/region**.

Cengage Learning products are represented in Canada by Nelson Education, Ltd.

For your course and learning solutions, visit **www.cengage.com**.

Purchase any of our products at your local college store or at our preferred online store **www.cengagebrain.com**.

Printed in the U.S.A
2 3 4 5 6 7 14 13 12

Brief Contents

part one

Orientation

part two

Principles

part three

Informative and Persuasive Speaking

part four

Adapting to Other Occasions and Formats

contents

part one

Orientation

Principles

Informative and Persuasive Speaking
part three

part four   Adapting to Other Occasions and Formats

preface

We are really excited about this new edition of *The Challenge of Effective Speaking,* and we believe you will be too. As you will see, we do three important things in this revision. First, we ground public speaking firmly in its roots—rhetorical theory—beginning in Chapter 1 and then throughout the book. Doing so reminds readers that public speaking concepts and skills are based on a rhetorical tradition that has stood the test of time for over 2,000 years!

Second, in this edition we worked hard to make the relevance of ethical public speaking in contemporary life transparent to students. For instance, we replaced all the Spotlight on Speakers features with Putting Speaking Skills to Work vignettes, which highlight the important role public speaking has played in the lives of real people in a variety of professions. We also replaced many of the sample student speeches with ones based on topics that today's students are grappling with, such as prescription drug abuse, cyber-bullying, civic engagement, and "hooking up." Regarding ethical public speaking, we updated many of the Reflect on Ethics features so that they now describe real-life speaking scenarios, such as the incident between Kanye West and Taylor Swift (Chapter 3), Jon Stewart's criticisms of Jim Cramer (Chapter 4), and John McCain's self-identification as a maverick (Chapter 5). In addition, we made ethics a focal point of all of the chapter opening vignettes and embedded discussions of ethics within every chapter.

Third, we revamped Chapters 13 and 14 on persuasion to reflect, initially, the nature of persuasive messages and then, with that in mind, how to construct persuasive speeches. Chapter 13 now focuses specifically on how people process persuasive messages and the role of logos, ethos, and pathos in persuasion. Chapter 14 describes in detail how to phrase a persuasive speech goal as a proposition; how to frame persuasive arguments when attempting to convince others to agree with you, to act, or both; and what ethical guidelines to follow when attempting to persuade.

While we are excited about the changes we have made to update and improve the text, we have worked hard to make sure that this book continues to focus on the hallmarks that have made it a classic. We are thrilled to have heard both students and instructors confirm that what has become known as the Verderber method for speech preparation really works! So we continue to organize the heart of the book around the six Speech Planning Action Steps. These steps guide you from topic selection to the rehearsal process to delivery. After we discuss the concepts and rationale for each step, we provide a sequence of easy-to-complete activities that will help students prepare an effective speech quickly. From both research and our experience as instructors, we know that speakers who are well prepared feel more confident about speaking, and they usually deliver great speeches. So we advocate that instructors assign the activities as part of the assessment of student speeches, and we encourage students to use the activities even when they are not assigned. Why? Because we know that they are efficient, they work, and we want students who are reading our book to be successful. That's why we wrote it!

New to This Edition

There are many exciting changes to this edition.

Major Content Changes

- We made a conscious decision to incorporate a **stronger emphasis on rhetoric and rhetorical theory** so that students understand why public speaking is a liberal art. We worked hard to make this theory student-friendly through the use of clear definitions and interesting examples.

- In response to faculty requests, we have **increased the discussion of speech anxiety**. For example, Chapter 2 now includes tips for using breathing techniques and progressive muscle relaxation exercises to reduce anxiety. In addition, the chapter also provides more specific techniques for managing anxiety.

- We have completely **reorganized the two chapters on persuasive speaking**. In previous editions Chapter 13 focused on reasoning and culminated in the speech-to-convince assignment. Chapter 14 then described the role of emotions in persuasion, speaker credibility, and audience motivation, and finished with the speech-to-motivate/actuate assignment. Although this organization had pedagogical merit, it left many students with the mistaken impression that we either persuade through logical reasoning *or* through emotional and motivational arguments. In this edition we have clarified content so that students better understand how to create speeches in which reasoning, emotion, and speaker credibility work together to convince an audience or motivate it to act. In Chapter 13, "Understanding Persuasive Messages," we focus on understanding what makes a speech persuasive. In this chapter we present the theory, concepts, and skills associated with logos, ethos, and pathos, including an extended explanation of Toulmin's model for forming arguments. In Chapter 14, "Persuasive Speaking," we concentrate on how to adapt the basic speech planning process to persuasive speeches.

- **All new Putting Speaking Skills to Work boxes** in each chapter highlight how people routinely use public speaking skills at work. Examples include Saejean Oh, a 22-year-old artist who uses her speaking skills to market herself and her work (Chapter 3); Stephen Strieby, a 24-year-old Marine who adapts his speaking skills to multiple audiences and situations (Chapter 8); and Edwin C. Goldberg, a 47-year-old rabbi who uses technology to make his sermons more appealing to his congregation (Chapter 16). These boxes demonstrate that in most of the occupations today's students are preparing for, public speaking skills are critical to effective job performance.

- Our discussion of **ethics in public speaking** has been extensively revised and is interwoven throughout the text. In Chapter 1, the section on ethics introduces five fundamental ethical standards: honesty, integrity, fairness, respect, and responsibility. Chapter-opening photos and their captions reinforce one specific standard per chapter. **New Reflect on Ethics boxes** in each chapter use contemporary "ripped from the headlines" situations to help students think through ethical challenges and the choices people face in public communication settings today. Examples include Coldplay's admitted plagiarism of other musicians' work (Chapter 6) and lobbyists who use social media to shape public opinion without revealing their corporate affiliations (Chapter 13).

- End-of-chapter activities now include two **new assignment options: Impromptu Speech Exercises and Assessment Activities.** Although students may only give three or four graded speeches per term, the new impromptu speech exercises challenge students to practice speaking more often with short, quickly prepared speeches related to chapter material. Assessment activities are also tied to chapter content so that students and instructors can measure how well students understand and can apply the concepts and skills in each chapter.

■ **Two bonus chapters**, available through Cengage Learning's Flex-Text customization program, present a more detailed look at impromptu speaking and a workbook for students who are completing service learning assignments. (For more information about the Flex-Text program, see the Instructor Resources section later in this preface.)

Chapter Revisions of Note

■ **Chapter 1, "Foundations of Public Speaking,"** has been extensively revised. It begins with a brief discussion of the general process of human communication, whether one is engaged in formal public speaking or an interpersonal communication interaction in a face-to-face or online setting. After a discussion of the elements in the process and the general communication contexts that situate public speaking among intrapersonal, interpersonal, group, and mass communication, the chapter focuses on the empowering role of public speaking as a liberal art and in a democratic society. Next, we introduce the ethical principles of public speaking that are addressed throughout the book. After this, we describe the foundational theoretical concept of the rhetorical situation as it grounds effective public speaking. Finally, the major principles of effective speechmaking are discussed. The chapter ends by explaining and providing an example of a speech of self-introduction, which instructors often choose to assign during the first days of class.

■ **Chapter 2, "Developing Confidence through the Speech-Planning Process,"** includes an expanded discussion of public speaking apprehension, including symptoms, causes, and methods for managing it effectively. These methods include communication orientation motivation, visualization, relaxation, systematic desensitization, cognitive restructuring, and skills training techniques. This chapter also introduces the six-step speech planning process we believe to be the key to confident public speaking, and it closes with an example of the process applied to a narrative/personal experience speech.

■ **Chapter 3, "Listening and Responding Effectively,"** now begins by addressing why it is important to study listening in a public speaking course and then differentiates hearing from listening. Based on reviewer suggestions, the chapter then discusses the different types of listening before addressing specific strategies for improving listening skills. The chapter concludes with a comprehensive discussion of how to listen to and constructively critique a speech, including how to prepare feedback for the speaker.

■ **Chapter 4, "Selecting an Appropriate Speech Goal,"** has been rewritten so that students understand how the speech goal must be grounded in the rhetorical public speaking situation. Now students will understand that an effective speech goal comes from not only what the speaker wants to talk about, but also the specific needs of the audience. The discussion of audience analysis has been expanded so that students not only learn how to collect demographic data, but also how to use that data to inform them as they prepare their speeches. Moreover, we describe the ethical use of audience data.

■ **Chapter 5, "Adapting to Audiences,"** has had minor revisions and continues to present information in the order in which a speaker will encounter specific issues and need to make decisions. We continue to explain the need to adapt to diverse learning styles to aid information comprehension and retention. The section on language and cultural differences now describes specific adaptation strategies a speaker should use when speaking in a second (or third) language.

- **Chapter 6, "Gathering and Evaluating Information,"** has been updated to reflect the way that college students and working professionals use the Internet to find useful information. So when we discuss how to find secondary sources, we begin by explaining how to locate sources with the Internet. We then describe how to locate the same resources offline. Our emphasis is on using electronic databases to search for print resources, identifying relevant and reliable websites and web pages, and evaluating both online and offline information sources. We expanded the section on primary research to now include fieldwork observations, surveys, interviews, original artifact examinations, and experiments. We continue to propose research cards as an effective means for recording information and how you can adapt this proven method to electronic files.

- **Chapter 7, "Organizing and Outlining the Speech Body,"** features a new extended example to demonstrate each substep in the organizing process. The new topic of this example, on the uses and abuses of the drug Adderall, is a timely one on most college campuses.

- **Chapter 8, "The Introduction and Conclusion,"** begins by emphasizing the importance of audience-centered introductions and conclusions. This chapter also includes updated examples of the rhetorical devices you can use to ethically get the audience's attention and clinch the speech in a way that will help them remember your speech. In addition, we expanded the discussion of generating speaker credibility by grounding it in ethos. Finally, we continue to use the speech on Adderall as our extended example in this chapter.

- **Chapter 9, "Presentational Aids,"** has been updated to reflect the increased expectations for audio and visual material to accompany any speech. We begin the chapter by discussing how the ability to make computerized presentation aids has changed speech making in professional settings. After describing the various types of visual, audio, and audiovisual aids that might be used in a speech, we focus on the ubiquitous computerized slideshow. We catalog the uses and abuses of computerized slideshows before explaining how to effectively create and use them.

- **Chapter 10, "Language and Oral Style,"** has a new title that reflects the extensive revision of the chapter. We begin with a discussion of how oral style differs from written style, and then describe how to choose language that is appropriate, accurate, clear, and vivid. We introduce the concept of *verbal immediacy* to underscore the importance of adapting our language to the needs of the rhetorical situation. We discuss the ethical issues associated with humor, profanity, vulgarity, and hate speech. The semantic triangle is used to explain the need to speak accurately. We conclude the chapter with guidelines for dealing with dialects.

- **Chapter 11, "Practicing Delivery,"** has been lightly revised. The section on use of body has been reorganized so that it begins with a discussion of eye contact, audience contact, and facial expression before describing gestures, movement, posture, poise, and appearance. We have expanded our discussion of gestures to include specific gestures that can be used to emphasize points or clarify structure. When describing rehearsal strategies, we now include a discussion specifically about how to rehearse with presentational aids. Finally, there is a new sample speech on volunteering and civic engagement.

- **Chapter 12, "Informative Speaking,"** has also been lightly revised. It now includes a brief discussion of the nature of informative speaking and describes the importance of developing material that is suited to different learning styles. The chapter also highlights the important role of using listener relevance links to gain and maintain audience interest throughout the speech. The chapter also includes a new sample expository speech about hurricanes.

- **Chapter 13, "Understanding Persuasive Messages,"** focuses on the nature of persuasion, how people process persuasive messages, and the role of logos, ethos, and pathos in persuasion. We expanded our discussion of logos to include both inductive and deductive reasoning, as well as Toulmin's model for forming arguments. We also added arguing from sign to the types and tests of argument, as well as a section on evaluating evidence. We reorganized the section on ethos to focus specifically on how conveying good character, goodwill, competence, and credibility function to persuade. Finally, the discussion on pathos describes how to ethically use specific positive and negative emotions to persuade.

- **Chapter 14, "Persuasive Speaking,"** builds on Chapter 13 and focuses on planning a persuasive speech. The chapter explains how to use audience analysis data to detect an audience's attitude toward a persuasive topic. It describes how to frame a persuasive speech goal as a proposition of fact, value, or policy. We then identify some common patterns used to organize speeches to convince and provide a sample speech to convince that uses a comparative advantages framework. This is followed by a section describing the common frameworks used to organize speeches to actuate and, again, we provide a sample speech to actuate. Finally, we emphasize the special duty that persuasive speakers have to maintain high ethical standards, and we provide several ethical guidelines to follow when speaking to persuade.

- **Chapter 15, "Ceremonial Speaking: Speeches for Special Occasions,"** now inlcudes a description of roasts as a type of tribute speech.

- **Chapter 16, "Developing and Delivering Group Presentations,"** has two new sections. The first addresses the benefits and the problems associated with group conflict, as well as strategies for conflict management. The second section briefly introduces electronic conferencing and how streaming video and slideshows are being used in group discussions, problem solving, and group presentations.

Continuing Features

- **Speech Plan Action Steps** guide students through a step-by-step preparation process that results in significantly better speeches. These Action Step activities are supplemented by in-text and online examples of each activity prepared by other students.

- **Sample student speeches** in Chapters 1, 11, 12, and 14 include adaptation plans, outlines, and transcripts with accompanying analyses. **Three new speeches** are featured in Chapters 11 and 14. In addition, video of these and other student speeches—including an impromptu speech—are featured in this book's online resources.

- **Speech Snippet boxes** throughout the book provide "snippets" of speeches by student speakers working through the myriad issues they must face when preparing a speech. For example, in the Chapter 5 discussions about adapting to an audience, the Speech Snippet boxes highlight how speakers demonstrated personal impact in a speech, addressed timeliness and acknowledged listener attitudes, demonstrated their direct expertise, established their trustworthiness, and more.

In addition, the fifteenth edition includes the following new and updated technological features:

- The **Speech Communication CourseMate for** *The Challenge of Effective Speaking* provides students with easy access to the integrated technology resources that accompany the book. These resources include learning, study, and exam preparation tools such as *Challenge*'s interactive eBook, Audio Study Tools, flashcards, chapter notepads, and the Speech Planning Action Steps activities and Applying What You've Learned activities that support the printed textbook. Watch comprehension soar as your class works with the printed textbook and the textbook-specific website. In addition, CourseMate's Engagement Tracker tracking tools allow instructors to monitor the progress of the class as a whole or of individual students. Engagement Tracker helps you identify students at risk early in the course, uncover which concepts are most difficult for your class, monitor time on task, and keep your students engaged. The CourseMate for *Challenge* goes beyond the book to deliver what you need!

- The *Challenge* **Interactive Video Activities** feature videos of all the sample student speeches featured in the text, as well as evaluation worksheets and critical thinking questions for each speech.

- The book's **Web Resource web links** are easily accessed from the CourseMate for *Challenge*. These links have been integrated into the text to expand skills practice and learning online—they are highlighted in the text with colored text and icons. All the links are monitored to ensure that they remain active.

If you want your students to have access to the online resources for *Challenge*, please be sure to order them for your course. These resources can be bundled with every new copy of the text or ordered separately. If you do not order them, your students will not have access to these resources. *Contact your local Wadsworth Cengage Learning sales representative for more details.*

Supplementary Materials

In addition to the *Challenge* online textbook resources just described, the fifteenth edition can be packaged with a suite of integrated resources for students and instructors.

Student Resources

- **Student Workbook for** *The Challenge of Effective Speaking* by Larry Edmonds, Arizona State University. The student workbook has been updated for the fifteenth edition and offers chapter-by-chapter skill-building exercises, vocabulary lists, quizzes, and copies of the speech evaluation checklists featured in the text.

- Many of the Speech Planning Action Steps can be completed with **Speech Builder Express 3.0 organization and outlining program**. This interactive web-based tool coaches students through the speech organization and outlining process. By completing interactive sessions based on the in-text Action Steps, students can prepare and save their outlines—including a plan for visual aids and a Works Cited section—formatted according to the principles presented in the text. Text models of speech elements reinforce students' interactive practice.

- Practice and present with **Speech Studio**™. With Speech Studio, students can upload video files of practice speeches or final performances, comment on their peers' speeches, and review their grades and instructor feedback. Speech Studio's flexibility lends itself to use in traditional, hybrid, and online courses.

It allows instructors to save valuable in-class time by conducting practice sessions and peer review work virtually; combine the ease of a course management tool with a convenient way to capture, grade, and review videos of live, in-class performances; and simulate an in-class experience for online courses.

- **Audio Study Tools for *The Challenge of Effective Speaking*.** This text's mobile content provides a fun and easy way for students to review chapter content whenever and wherever. For each chapter of the text, students will have access to a 5- to 7-minute review consisting of a brief summary of the main points in the text and review questions. Students can purchase the Audio for *Challenge* through CengageBrain.com (see below) and download files to their computers, iPods, or MP3 players.

- **InfoTrac College Edition with InfoMarks.** Access this virtual library's more than 18 million reliable, full-length articles from 5,000 academic and popular periodicals, and retrieve results almost instantly. They also have access to InfoMarks—stable URLs that can be linked to articles, journals, and searches to save valuable time when doing research—and to the InfoWrite online resource center, where students can access grammar help, critical-thinking guidelines, guides to writing research papers, and much more.

- **CengageBrain Online Store.** CengageBrain.com is a single destination for more than 15,000 new print textbooks, textbook rentals, eBooks, single eChapters, and print, digital, and audio study tools. CengageBrain.com provides the freedom to purchase Cengage Learning products à-la-carte—exactly what you need, when you need it. Visit www.CengageBrain.com for details.

- ***Service Learning in Communication Studies: A Handbook*** by Rick Isaacson and Jeff Saperstein. This is an invaluable resource for students in the basic course that integrates, or will soon integrate, a service learning component. This handbook provides guidelines for connecting service-learning work with classroom concepts and advice for working effectively with agencies and organizations. It also provides model forms and reports, as well as a directory of online resources.

- ***A Guide to the Basic Course for ESL Students*** by Esther Yook, Mary Washington College. This guide for non-native speakers includes strategies for accent management and overcoming speech apprehension, in addition to helpful web addresses and answers to frequently asked questions.

Instructor Resources

- **Instructor's Resource Manual with Test Bank** by Brian L. Heisterkamp, California State University, San Bernardino. This indispensable manual features changes from the fourteenth edition to the fifteenth edition, sample syllabi, chapter-by-chapter outlines, summaries, vocabulary lists, suggested lecture and discussion topics, classroom exercises, assignments, and a comprehensive test bank with answer key and rejoinders.

- **PowerLecture CD-ROM.** Updated for the fifteenth edition, this CD-ROM contains an electronic version of the Instructor's Resource Manual, ExamView® Computerized Testing, predesigned Microsoft® PowerPoint® presentations, and JoinIn® classroom quizzing. The PowerPoint presentations contain text, images, and videos of the case studies and can be used as they are or customized to suit your course needs.

- **Public Speaking: An Online Approach; Public Speaking: A Problem Based Learning Approach; and Public Speaking: A Service-Learning Approach for Instructors** by Deanna Sellnow, University of Kentucky. Each of these instructor workbooks includes a course syllabus and icebreakers; relevant discussions of basic public speaking topics such as coping with anxiety, learning cycles and styles, outlining, and ethics; and informative, persuasive, and ceremonial (special occasion) speeches.

- **The Teaching Assistant's Guide to the Basic Course** by Katherine G. Hendrix, University of Memphis. Based on leading communication teacher training programs, this guide covers general teaching and course management topics as well as specific strategies for communication instruction—for example, providing effective feedback on performance, managing sensitive class discussions, and conducting mock interviews.

- **Student Speeches for Critique and Analysis.** This multivolume video series offers both imperfect and award-winning sample student speeches. The speeches presented in *Challenge* are available in this series.

- **ABC News DVD: Speeches by Barack Obama.** This DVD includes nine famous speeches by President Barack Obama, from 2004 to present day, including his speech at the 2004 Democratic National Convention; his 2008 speech on race, "A More Perfect Union"; and his 2009 inaugural address. Speeches are divided into short video segments for easy, time-efficient viewing. This instructor supplement also features critical thinking questions and answers for each speech, designed to spark class discussion.

- **Videos for Speech Communication 2010: Public Speaking, Human Communication, and Interpersonal Communication.** This DVD provides footage of news stories from BBC and CBS that relate to current topics in communication, such as teamwork and how to interview for jobs, as well as news clips about speaking anxiety and speeches from contemporary public speakers, such as Michelle Obama and Senator Hillary Clinton.

- **Turn-It-In.** This proven online plagiarism-prevention software promotes fairness in the classroom by helping students learn to correctly cite sources and allowing instructors to check for originality before reading and grading papers and speeches. Turn-It-In quickly checks student work against billions of pages of Internet content, millions of published works, and millions of student papers and speeches; within seconds the program generates a comprehensive originality report.

- **TeamUP Technology Training and Support.** Get trained, get connected, and get the support you need for the seamless integration of technology resources into your course. This unparalleled technology service and training program provides robust online resources, peer-to-peer instruction, personalized training, and a customizable program you can count on. Visit http://www.cengage.com/teamup/training/ to sign up for online seminars, first days of class services, technical support, or personalized, face-to-face training. Our online and onsite trainings are frequently led by one of our Lead Teachers, faculty members who are experts in using Wadsworth Cengage Learning technology and can provide best practices and teaching tips.

- **Flex-Text Customization Program.** With this program you can create a text as unique as your course: quickly, simply, and affordably. As part of our flex-text program, you can add your personal touch to *Challenge* with a course-specific cover and up to 32 pages of your own content—at no additional cost.

Contact your local Cengage Learning representative or go to http://www.cengage.com/highered/ for more information, user names and passwords, examination copies, or a demonstration of these ancillary products. These items are available to qualified adopters.

Acknowledgements

The book you are holding is the result of a team effort, and we have been privileged to work with the best. First, we want to acknowledge the wonderful students whose speeches appear in this book. We also want to thank our colleagues around the world who have used previous editions of the book and have graciously shared with us their experiences teaching from these texts. We would like to single out the following people who participated in the review process for this edition: Diane Badzinski, Colorado Christian University; Benjamin Cline, Culver-Stockton College; Ginni Jurkowski, State University of New York, Geneseo; Susan Lichtman, Miami Dade College, Kendall Campus; Kimberly Rosenfeld, Cerritos College; Yasmin Shenoy, University of Hartford; Amy Trombley, Collin College; Jamie Ward, University of Michigan, Dearborn; Angelique Wood, Westwood College; Pamela Xanthopoulos, Jackson State Community College; and Wendy Yarberry, Florida State College.

As we prepared this revision, we worked with some familiar faces and welcomed several new editorial, marketing, and production team members. We have enjoyed working with our senior publisher, Lyn Uhl; assistant editor, Rebekah Matthews; editorial assistant, Colin Solan; marketing manager, Amy Whitaker; marketing coordinator, Gurpreet S. Saran; media editor, Jessica Badiner; production manager, Samantha Ross Miller; senior content project manager, Rosemary Winfield; and project manager, Amanda Hellenthal. Special thank yous are due for two people. First, to Monica Eckman, our executive editor, whose belief in this book is only outweighed by her enthusiasm and hard work on our behalf. Her responsiveness to our needs as authors is above and beyond. And second, to Greer Lleuad, our senior developmental editor, who tried to turn us over to another development editor but found that we were the proverbial bad pennies who kept showing up. Her wisdom, wit, and gentle touch continue to make her a joy to work with and make our jobs so much easier.

We'd also like to thank Karen S. Davis for helping us research and write the new Putting Speaking Skills to Work boxes, as well as the professionals we profiled: Sean Daly, Raj Gaur, Edwin C. Goldberg, Frances James, Jaime Koepsell, Jeff McGuire, Stacey L. McKeever, Sally A. Morrison, Saejean Oh, Beth Richey-Sullivan, Brittany Smith, Kendra Smith, Stephen Strieby, Jon Sweeten, Stella Trip, and Charlene Williams.

Finally, we are indebted to our families, who put up with us when we are writing and not always available to attend to their needs. During the writing of this edition, the Verderbers welcomed new granddaughter Madeleine Kathleen Herriott, and the Sellnow family celebrated the fiftieth wedding anniversary of Deanna's parents, John and Delores Miller, to whom we dedicate this edition. As always, to God be the glory!

IndexStock/SuperStock

1

Ethical communicators are honest, fair, responsible, and demonstrate integrity and respect for others.

foundations of
public speaking

What's the Point?
QUESTIONS YOU'LL BE ABLE TO ANSWER AFTER READING THIS CHAPTER:

1. How does the communication process work?
2. What are the contexts in which communication occurs?
3. What is public speaking, and why is it important to study?
4. What does it mean to be an ethical speaker?
5. How does understanding the rhetorical situation help you prepare a speech?

When Sean Jones, a candidate for council, was invited to speak at the Riverside Community Center, he prepared and delivered a talk on his views about the proposed recreation center.

Chen Chen had been awarded "server of the month" three times since she began working at the restaurant. So at her annual performance review, she felt a bit nervous, but she compellingly presented her case for a raise to her manager.

Jediah had landed an interview for his dream job as an electrical engineer. The interview would be conducted via teleconferencing software, and Jediah was asked to begin with a 10- to 15-minute webinar explaining why he was the best candidate for the position.

As Marquez, Bill, and Gianna drove home from the movie they had seen, Bill said he thought the movie deserved an Academy Award nomination for Best Picture and asked the others if they agreed. Marquez listened carefully and then gave two reasons he thought the movie didn't deserve the honor.

Nancy Bauer, a purchasing clerk, came to the monthly meeting of the engineering group to give a short multimedia-aided presentation on how to use the new online requisition system for ordering parts for newly designed machines. She had previously given similar presentations to other departments in the company.

In each of the five situations described above, one person was talking to others. But in which of these situations was someone giving a "speech"? You probably recognized that Sean and Nancy were giving speeches because they both prepared beforehand, and you probably visualized them standing in front of their audiences. But what about Chen, Jediah, and Marquez? Hadn't they also thought about what they were saying and organized their thoughts in an effort to persuade their "audiences"? In the broadest sense, they were also giving speeches. In this course, you will learn how to give speeches to an audience. But these skills will actually apply across a variety of personal, business, and community situations. In fact, **public speaking**, a sustained formal presentation by a speaker to an audience, is simply one form of human communication. So learning to be an effective public speaker will help you to be more effective in other communication settings as well.

We begin this book by presenting some foundational communication concepts. In the first section of the chapter, we describe a basic model of human communication to help you understand how public speaking is similar to and different from other communication contexts. Because public speaking is one of the oldest liberal arts, we then provide a brief overview of the historical origins of the study of public address. Next, we present five principles that guide ethical

public speaking:
a sustained formal presentation by a speaker to an audience

communicators. Then, we introduce the concept of the rhetorical situation as a tool for analyzing a particular public speaking occasion. We conclude with a discussion of what makes a speech effective by previewing a speech-planning and -making process designed to help you become a confident effective public speaker.

The Human Communication Process

Communication is the process of creating shared meaning. To understand how this process works, let's look at its essential elements: participants (who), messages (what), channels (how), interference/noise (distractions), feedback (reaction), and contexts (what kind).

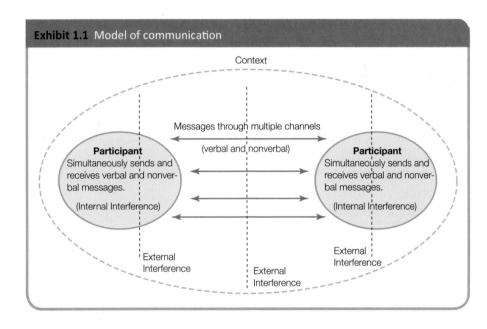

Exhibit 1.1 Model of communication

Participants

Participants are the individuals who assume the roles of senders and receivers during an interaction (see Exhibit 1.1). As **senders**, participants form and transmit messages using verbal symbols (words) and nonverbal behaviors. **Receivers** interpret the messages sent by others. Although all participants serve as both senders and receivers, in public speaking contexts, one participant acts primarily as sender and presents an extended message to which the other participants listen, interpret, and provide mostly nonverbal feedback.

Messages

Messages are the verbal utterances, visual images, and nonverbal behaviors to which meaning is attributed during communication. In public speaking situations, messages are typically speeches that are prepared beforehand and presented by one participant. **Meanings** are the interpretations participants make of the messages they send and receive. Messages are meant to convey the thoughts of the speaker but are easy to misinterpret. So the meaning that the sender intends may not be the meaning that the receiver understands. **Encoding** is the process of putting our thoughts and feelings into words and nonverbal behaviors, while **decoding** is the process of interpreting the verbal and nonverbal messages sent by others. **Feedback messages** sent by receivers are intended to let the sender know how the receiver made sense of the original

communication: the process of creating shared meaning

participants: the individuals who assume the roles of senders and receivers during an interaction

senders: participants who form and transmit messages using verbal symbols and nonverbal behaviors

receivers: participants who interpret the messages sent by others

messages: the verbal utterances and nonverbal behaviors to which meaning is attributed during communication

meanings: the interpretations participants make of the messages they send and receive

encoding: the process of putting our thoughts and feelings into words and nonverbal behaviors

decoding: the process of interpreting the verbal and nonverbal messages sent by others

feedback messages: messages sent by receivers intended to let the sender know how the receiver made sense of the original message

message. As you can imagine, when you give a speech, you have to carefully encode many thoughts and pay attention to how you organize these so that your audience—the receivers of this complex message—will be able to decode it and understand as you intend.

Channels

Channels are both the route traveled by a message and the means of transportation. Messages are transmitted through sensory channels. We send and receive messages primarily through auditory (speaking and hearing) and visual (seeing) channels.

Interference/Noise

Interference, also referred to as **noise**, is any stimulus that interferes with the process of sharing meaning. Noise can be physical or psychological. Physical noise is any external sight or sound that distracts us from the message. For example, when someone enters the room while a speaker is talking or when a fire engine's siren roars by, a listener might not hear the message. Psychological noise refers to the thoughts and feelings you experience that compete with the sender's message for your attention. So when you daydream about what you have to do at work today or when you feel offended when a speaker uses foul language, you are essentially distracted based on psychological noise.

Feedback

Feedback is the reactions and responses to messages that indicate to the sender whether and how a message was heard, seen, and interpreted. We can express feedback verbally by telling the sender what we understood or thought about a message, or we may simply indicate our understanding and reaction through nonverbal behavior, like nodding our heads to indicate agreement, raising eyebrows to register our surprise, or cocking our head and furrowing our eyebrows to indicate that we do not understand. When audiences listen to a speech, most of their feedback is usually nonverbal.

Contexts

Communication research reveals that there are specific contexts in which communication occurs. These differ by the number of participants and the balance of roles among them.[1] Let's briefly look at four of these.

Intrapersonal communication (a.k.a. self-talk) is communicating with yourself. Usually this is done by thinking through choices, strategies, and the possible consequences of taking action. When you sit in class and consider what you'll have for dinner tonight, you are communicating intrapersonally. Much of our intrapersonal communication occurs subconsciously.[2] When you drive into your driveway "without thinking," you're communicating intrapersonally but at a subconscious level. When you are giving a speech and notice confused looks on your listeners' faces, you might communicate intrapersonally as you recognize the need to rephrase your explanation.

Interpersonal communication is communication between two people.[3][4] When you stop to chat with a friend between classes about weekend plans, how your family is, or what you did last night, you are engaging in interpersonal communication. You are also communicating interpersonally when you have a heart-to-heart talk with a close friend or family member. Interpersonal communication sometimes occurs in a public speech setting when, during a question-and-answer session, a speaker directs remarks to one audience member.

Small group communication is communication that occurs among approximately three to ten people.[5] There are many kinds of small groups; examples include a family, a group of friends, a group of classmates working together on a class project, and a management team in the workplace.[6] Some research suggests there are more small groups in the United States than there are people. Small group communication occurs in a public speech setting when a team is asked to work together to research, prepare, and deliver a presentation on a particular topic.

Public communication is communication that occurs among more than ten people and where one message is presented to the participants who function as receivers and whose own messages are limited primarily to feedback. One form of public communication is **mass communication**, which is communication produced and transmitted via media to massive audiences. Newspapers, magazines, e-zines, books, blogs, listservs, television programs, movies, websites, Facebook pages, tweets on Twitter, and YouTube are all examples of mass communication. Public speaking has been considered a separate type of public communication because the intended audience is usually physically present to witness the speech. As media become more pervasive, however, the distinction between mass communication and public speaking has been somewhat blurred. For example, when President Obama gives a State of the Union address, he does so in the physical presence of the U.S. Congress, the Supreme Court justices, and other invited guests, but his speech is televised to a mass audience, as well.

As media become more pervasive, the distinction between mass communication and public speaking is becoming blurred.

Fabrizio Costantini / The New York / Redux Pictures

Public Speaking as a Liberal Art

When we say that public speaking is a **liberal art**, we mean that the knowledge and skills you gain by studying public speaking are general knowledge and essential skills that will help you participate effectively as an engaged citizen in our democratic society. This differs from the specialized knowledge you acquire when you study material in your major or when you develop skills specific to your profession. So that's why a course devoted in part or entirely to public speaking is often required in a general education curriculum.[7]

The Role of Public Speaking Education in Democracies

Since ancient times, liberal arts education has been at the center of study for free people in democracies. In fact, the word "liberal" means "free," and in ancient Greece it was the type of general education offered to free men (yes, back then it was restricted to men). Public speaking was central to a liberal education because it was the means by which free men conducted business, made public decisions, and gained and maintained power.[8] Today, effective public speakers continue to reap rewards in personal relationships, the work world, and the public sphere.[9]

Certainly, the formal study of public speaking equips you to give effective presentations; however, the process of preparing these speeches accomplishes something much more important. The study of public speaking teaches you not

small group communication: the interaction that occurs in a group of approximately three to ten people

public communication: communication that occurs among more than ten people where one message is presented to the participants who function as receivers whose own messages are limited to feedback

mass communication: communication produced and transmitted via media to large audiences

liberal art: a body of general knowledge needed to effectively participate in a democratic society *what* to think but *how* to think—a central skill for a responsible citizen living in a democracy, especially the sound-bite-saturated, image-managed, political environment we live in today. Essentially, you learn to think critically and question what you read, see, and hear. You also learn how to behave ethically as both a sender and receiver of messages.

As you struggle to choose a topic, you must consider why you are speaking and what you know well enough and think is important enough to present to others. You must assess how much you know about a topic and augment that knowledge with further study. When collecting additional information, you must critically evaluate the credibility of the information, the validity and reliability of the facts presented, and the logical reasoning offered. As you prepare your speeches, you must consider how to best organize your ideas and what words to use to be both clear and compelling. And, as you present your speeches, you must attend to the nonverbal behaviors of your listeners and adjust your message as needed to ensure they are getting the meaning you intend.

Learning to think critically and behave ethically as you prepare and present your own speeches also equips you to analyze the messages offered by others. You will be able to critically judge the information and arguments of others and to identify flaws in their reasoning. You will be able to identify how others use emotion to try to persuade you. And you will be better equipped to realize when others are communicating unethically.

All of these activities are critical mental disciplines you can apply to a wide variety of issues and settings. Democracies only thrive in settings where citizens are capable of fulfilling their civic responsibilities to analyze, think about, and eloquently speak out about important issues. So public speaking is a liberal art—an essential skill for free, engaged citizens.

The Power of Effective Public Speaking for Free People

Just as the democratic civilizations throughout history have understood the importance of public speaking education, so do we know that being able to effectively present your ideas in a speech empowers you in several ways.

First, public speaking skills empower you to participate in democratic processes. Free speech is a hallmark of democracy. The strategies and policies our government adopts are a direct result of the debate that occurs across the nation: in living rooms; over pizza at the local hangout; on blogs and social networking sites; in the media; as well as in our executive, legislative, and judicial branches of government. When equipped with effective public speaking skills, you have the confidence to speak out and voice your ideas on important public issues.

Second, public speaking skills empower you to communicate complex ideas and information in ways that all audience members can understand. Most of us have had an unfortunate experience with a teacher who "talked over our heads." The teacher understood the material but was unable to express it clearly to us. When we can express our ideas clearly, we are more likely to share them. When others understand our ideas, they learn from us. This confidence equips us to share our knowledge to the benefit of others.

Third, public speaking skills empower you to achieve your career goals and be self-sufficient. Research shows that, for almost any job, one of the most highly sought-after skills in new hires is oral communication skills.[10] So, whether you aspire to a career in business, industry, government, the arts, or education, good communication skills are a prerequisite to your success. Although you might be hired on the basis of your technical competence, your success will depend on your ability to communicate what you know to others, including your manager, your clients, and your colleagues.

Ethical Principles for Public Speaking

Ethics are moral principles that a society, group, or individual hold that differentiate right from wrong and good behavior from bad behavior. In other words, ethics reflect what we believe we "ought to" and "ought not to" think and do. As audience members, we expect speakers to behave ethically. Likewise, as speakers, we expect audience members to behave ethically. What standards should we conform to as ethical communicators? Five generally agreed-upon ethical standards are honesty, integrity, fairness, respect, and responsibility. Let's look at each of these principles more closely as they relate to public speaking situations:

1. **Ethical communicators are honest.** In other words, ethical public speakers tell the truth. An audience expects that what you tell them will be true—not made up, not your personal belief presented as fact, and not an exaggeration. If, during or after your speech, members of your audience doubt the accuracy of something you have said, they are likely to reject all of your ideas. To make sure that what you say is truthful, you will want to research your topic carefully and present both sides of controversial issues accurately.

   Honest speakers credit the ideas of others they use in their speech and do not try to pass those ideas off as their own. **Plagiarism** is passing off the ideas, words, or created works of another as one's own. It is intellectual theft—stealing another's idea. Sadly, plagiarism is now commonplace. According to a 2002–2003 survey of 3,500 graduate students at U.S. and Canadian universities, "23 percent to 25 percent of students acknowledged one or more instances of 'cutting and pasting' from Internet sources and/or published documents."[11] And results of a survey conducted by the Center for Academic Integrity indicate that as many as 80 percent of college students admit to having plagiarized.[12] As a result, many colleges and universities now use plagiarism-detection software programs regularly when grading student papers. In most colleges, plagiarism can result in failing an assignment or the entire course, and it can even lead to being suspended from school. In the world beyond the classroom, plagiarism has led to lawsuits and has ruined promising careers. How can you recognize if you are plagiarizing?

   - If you change a few words at the beginning, in the middle, or at the end of a material, but copy much of the rest, you are plagiarizing.
   - If you completely paraphrase the unique ideas of another person and do not credit that person, you are plagiarizing.
   - If you purchase, borrow, or use a speech or essay in part or in whole that was prepared by another and present it as original, you are plagiarizing.[13]

   Honest speakers provide the sources for their material so audience members have the information they need to evaluate the truthfulness of what is being said. Where ideas originate is often as important as the ideas themselves. For example, if a statistic about global warming comes from an article by a renowned scientist in a respected peer-reviewed journal, it is likely to have more credibility than if it comes from a celebrity's blog.

2. **Ethical communicators have integrity.** In other words, they practice what they preach. A speaker who gives a speech on the need to quit smoking and who then goes outside and lights up lacks integrity. A listener who espouses

ethics: moral principles that a society, group, or individual hold that differentiate right from wrong and good behavior from bad behavior

plagiarism: passing off the ideas, words, or created works of another as one's own by failing to credit the source

Ethical speakers embody the behaviors they advocate for others. Ed Begley Jr., an avid environmentalist, shows up at Hollywood events on a bicycle and lives "off the grid" in a green home powered by solar energy.

Ron Galella, Ltd./WireImage/Getty Images

the importance of civil dialogue but who interrupts the speech of someone who takes the opposite side of an issue lacks integrity.

3. **Ethical communicators are fair.** For speakers, behaving fairly means researching and accurately reporting all sides of an issue, even if some of the information runs contrary to your stand on a controversial issue. For listeners, it means considering all of the evidence that a speaker presents, even when that evidence contradicts what they believe.

4. **Ethical communicators demonstrate respect for others.** Behaving respectfully means being considerate of others and their feelings. For example, speakers show respect for their audience by choosing language and humor that is bias free, inoffensive, and inclusive. Listeners demonstrate respect by giving their undivided attention to the speaker. It is disrespectful to a speaker for audience members to send or read text or e-mail messages, read any other materials during the speech, hold side conversations, or in any other way "multitask" during a speech.

5. **Ethical communicators are responsible.** Being responsible means being accountable for your actions or your words. A well-settled point of law is that, if someone yells "FIRE" in a crowded theater when there is no fire and someone is injured in the stampede for the door, the person who yelled is responsible for the injury caused. So, too, are speakers responsible for the foreseeable outcomes of what they advocate. Ethical speakers only advocate for things that are in the best interest of audience members. When the organizers of the Hope for Haiti Now concert decided to only ask for small donations, they were being responsible. They recognized that many in the audience might be swept up in the moment and donate more than they could really afford. So they limited texted donations to $5 or $10. Similarly, listeners have the responsibility for critically evaluating the positions that speakers advocate so they do not blindly accept what may be inaccurate, dishonest information, or positions that are not in their best interest.

Throughout this book, we will elaborate on how these ethical principles should guide you as you prepare your speeches and listen to the speeches of others. We will also challenge you to reflect on ethical choices presented in the feature "Reflect on Ethics," which you will find in most chapters. To learn more about ethics, use your CourseMate for *Challenge* to access **Web Resource 1.1: The Basics of Ethics** and **Web Resource 1.2: Ethics Connection**. The first links to The Internet Encyclopedia of Philosophy, which provides an easy-to-read, thorough discussion about ethics. The second links to the website for the Markkula Center for Applied Ethics at Santa Clara University, a forum for research and discussion on ethical issues in American life.

CourseMate

rhetorical situation: the composite of the occasion, speaker, and the audience that influences the speech that is given

Understanding the Rhetorical Situation

Public speaking is rooted in what we refer to as the rhetorical tradition.[14] The rhetorical tradition was conceived more than 2,000 years ago. Way back then, the Greek philosopher Aristotle observed, "The audience is the end

Reflect on Ethics

CELEBRITY CHEF CONCOCTS IMPRESSIVE PAST

Celebrity chef Robert Irvine came to St. Petersburg in 2007 with a plan to turn it into "the next Monaco." He claimed to be a royal knight and asked to be introduced as Sir Robert Irvine. He said he owned a castle in Scotland and had cooked for presidents and royalty.[15]

Today, however, it's difficult to separate fact from fiction when it comes to Sir Robert Irvine. What is known to be true is that he is an excellent chef and star of the Food Network's, *Dinner: Impossible*, which is now in its eighth season. He published a cookbook with Harper Collins in 2007. He lives in Abescon, N.J., in a modestly priced house with his wife and two children.

But from there, the "facts" get murky:

- On his Web page, Irvine lists a B.S. degree in food and nutrition from the University of Leeds. Officials from the University of Leeds have no record of Robert Irvine having been a student there.

- In his book, Irvine claims to have worked on the wedding cake for Prince Charles and Princess Diana. He was at the school where the cake was made, but did he actually help make it? Does "picking fruit and things like that" count?

- On his resume, Irvine says he received several Five Star Diamond Awards from the American Academy of Hospitality Sciences. The "academy" is actually housed in a Manhattan apartment, and recipients pay for the honor.

- On being a royal knight, according to Jenn Stebbing, press officer at Buckingham Palace: "He is not a KCVO Knight Commander of the Royal Victorian Order and he wasn't given a castle by the queen of England." Irvine now admits that was a lie.

- Irvine claims to have trained White House military cooks and served presidents and heads of state. White House spokespersons claim he has never had anything to do with planning, preparing, or serving at any public or private White House food function.

1. What, if any, ethical communication principles did Irvine violate and, if so, how?

2. When, if ever, is it ok to stretch the truth about your qualifications?

3. Is it ok to exaggerate the facts about yourself if you're famous? If "everyone else does it" too? Explain.

---

and object of the speech."[16] What he meant was that the eloquence of your words is irrelevant if the words are not heard by, are not understood by, or do not affect the people to whom you are speaking. Today, we recognize that the effectiveness of any speech depends not just on understanding the audience but also on how well the speaker gives a speech that fits the rhetorical situation. In one sense, the rhetorical situation is the composite of the speaker, audience, and occasion. In Exhibit 1.2, you can see the **rhetorical situation** depicted in a Venn diagram. As you can see, the rhetorical situation is the place where the speaker, audience, and occasion overlap. But Lloyd Bitzer, the rhetorical scholar who introduced the concept of the rhetorical situation, believed that the particular speech given by an individual to an audience on a specific occasion is the result of some real or perceived specific need that a speech might help to address.[17] Bitzer referred to this as the **"exigence."**[18] According to the Encarta dictionary, exigence is "something that a situation demands or makes urgently necessary and that puts pressure on the people involved."[19] On January 12, 2010, a massive earthquake in Haiti created an exigence that led many people to speak out about the dire need for aid. In the United States, from President Obama's televised speech to the nation to the simple calls to action heard in grade school classrooms across the country, individuals felt compelled to speak out and

exigence: some real or perceived need that a speech might help address.

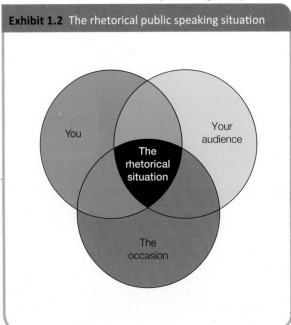

Exhibit 1.2 The rhetorical public speaking situation

speaker: the source or originator of the speech

audience: the specific group of people to whom your speech is directed

audience analysis: a study made to learn about the diverse characteristics of audience members and then, based on these characteristics, to predict how audience members are apt to listen to, understand, and be motivated to act on your speech

occasion: the setting in which the speech is given

speech effectiveness: the extent to which audience members listen to, understand, remember, and are motivated to act on what a speaker has said

audience-centered: offering ideas in ways that respond to a felt need, are appropriate to the occasion, reflect careful research, make sense, and sound interesting

to help the victims of this disaster. The earthquake created an exigence that motivated speakers to seek an occasion and audience where a speech they would give could accomplish something. Juanita, a sophomore in a California high school, recognized that neither she nor her classmates knew what to do if they were to experience an earthquake while at school. So she did some research and delivered a three-minute public service announcement over the P.A. system during morning announcements. At his place of work, Brian gave a two-minute speech at the department's monthly meeting urging his coworkers to join him on Saturday at a local church where people were preparing boxes of essential items to ship to Haiti.

Speaker

The **speaker** is the source or originator of the speech. As the speaker, what you discuss and the language you use to express those ideas will depend on your interests, beliefs, background, and public speaking skills. You will choose topics that you care about, know something about, and want to inform or persuade others about. Your personal experiences will influence the attitudes and beliefs you express, so what you say will be unique to you. For example, after her son was killed in Iraq, Cindy Sheehan began speaking out about the legitimacy of war and became a leader in the anti-war movement. Her speeches are informed by her experience as a grieving mother. Leah Bolger, a leader of the Veterans for Peace organization, retired from the U.S. Navy after 20 years of service. Her military experiences influence her anti-war speeches. Each woman brings her own uniqueness to bear on what she says, so while both women share the same exigence, the speeches they give are informed by their unique backgrounds.

Audience

The **audience** is the specific group of people to whom your speech is directed. **Audience analysis** is a study made to learn about the diverse characteristics of audience members and then, based on these characteristics, to predict how audience members are apt to listen to, understand, and be motivated to act on your speech. Armed with an understanding of your specific audience, you are in a better position to develop a speech tailored to that audience and designed to motivate that specific audience to address the exigence as far as the audience is able. For example, the organizers of the Hope for Haiti Now concert recognized that a large part of their audience would be teens and young adults who were tech savvy, so they encouraged the audience to donate small amounts of money immediately via text messages. But because the organizers also expected a significant number of people in the audience to be encouraged to give larger donations and that many in this group were not tech savvy, they also had celebrities staffing toll-free phone lines.

Organizers of the Hope for Haiti Now concert demonstrated ethical respect for the different levels of giving their audience could afford.

AP Photo/Mark Davis, Hope for Haiti Now

The Occasion

The **occasion** is the setting in which the speech is given. It encompasses the purpose for which the audience is gathered, their shared expectations about what is to happen there. The physical location and layout of the event, as well as potential constraints arising from any of these.

When the congregation assembles at a church, synagogue, or mosque, they expect to hear sermons that elaborate on religious texts or principles. When physicians attend a professional meeting on "new treatment options for multiple sclerosis," they expect to hear a scientific presentation about the efficacy of new treatments. Imagine what would happen if the local rabbi were to present his sermon to the physicians. Or if the physician were to present her findings to a service at the local synagogue.

What expectations does this occasion create for the speeches that will be given?

Jeff Malet/Newscom

The location and the layout of the room where a speech is given are also important parts of the occasion. The speech you prepare to give in a large auditorium for an audience of more than a thousand is likely to be different than the speech you would prepare to give in a restaurant to an audience of twenty. Suppose that you had prepared to address twenty people but arrived at the event to discover that your audience would number in the hundreds. Instead of walking around the room while you talked, you were expected to be on a stage with a handheld microphone. How would you change your plan for delivering the speech?

Principles of Effective Public Speaking

When you give a speech, your goal is to communicate with your audience members. **Speech effectiveness** is the extent to which audience members listen to, understand, remember, and are motivated to act on what a speaker has said. Therefore, all effective public speakers and speeches are audience-centered.

Effective Speakers Are Audience-Centered

Audience-centered speakers offer their ideas in ways that respond to a felt need, are appropriate to the occasion, reflect careful research, make sense, and sound interesting. You do so through the rhetorical appeals of ethos, pathos, and logos.[20] **Ethos** includes everything you say and do to convey competence and good character. Dressing professionally, being poised as you speak, citing credible sources, and speaking within the time parameters allotted, for instance, convey ethos. **Pathos** consists of everything you say and do to appeal to emotions, which can range from negative emotions such as fear or dread to positive emotions such as adventure or joy. **Logos** includes everything you say and do to appeal to logic and sound reasoning. Essentially, you are audience-centered when you demonstrate honesty and respect for your listeners by selecting an appropriate topic, developing your points in ways that reflect careful research and sound reasoning, organizing the content in a way that is easy for your audience to follow, rehearsing your delivery to be fluent and compelling, and presenting your speech so that it meets the expectations of the rhetorical situation.

ethos: everything you say and do to convey competence and good character

pathos: everything you say and do to appeal to emotions

logos: everything you say and do to appeal to logic and sound reasoning

Content

Kris decided to talk about how growing up in a resort town influenced her plans to study hospitality management; how being an identical twin contributed to her decision to attend this college; and how she hoped to use her major to work in a ski resort where she could help children with disabilities learn to snowboard. She made sure her content was audience-centered by focusing on the importance of pursuing one's dreams when selecting a major and a career goal.

macrostructure: the overall framework you use to organize your speech content

microstructure: the specific language and style choices you use as you frame your ideas and verbalize them to your audience

Macrostructure

Kris decided that the most logical way to present her main ideas was chronologically. She would begin by talking about being a twin, then discuss how her upbringing influenced her choice of majors, and then she'd conclude with her dream of teaching kids with disabilities to snowboard. She planned to use people's curiosity about twins to pique interest during her introduction, and she planned a conclusion that would challenge her audience to pursue their passions.

An Effective Speech Includes Audience-Appropriate Content

The content of a speech is the information and ideas you present. It encompasses your purpose for giving the speech, the main ideas you will present, and the evidence you use to develop your main ideas. Evidence clarifies, explains, or supports your main ideas. It includes facts, expert opinions, and elaborations, and it comes from your own experiences as well as from research materials you collect. Effective evidence has sufficient breadth and depth. *Breadth* refers to the amount and types of evidence you use. *Depth* is the level of detail you provide from each piece of evidence. Evidence is effective when it is logically linked to the main idea it supports. The ideas you choose to present depend on what is appropriate for your audience and the occasion, and you adapt your content so that it includes listener-relevance links, which are statements of how and why the ideas you offer are of interest to your listeners. Doing so makes the exigence of your ideas transparent.

An Effective Speech Is Well Structured

The structure of a speech is the framework that organizes the content. Clear structure helps your listeners follow your ideas so they can understand the points you are making.[21] Clear structure includes both macrostructure and microstructure.

Macrostructure is the overall framework you use to organize your speech content. It has four elements: the introduction, body, conclusion, and transitions. The introduction is the beginning segment of the speech and should be structured so that you build audience interest in your topic and preview what you are going to say (you tell them what you are going to tell them). The speech body contains the main ideas and supporting material you have decided to present; it is organized into a pattern that makes the ideas easy for the audience to understand and remember (you tell them). The conclusion ends the speech, reminds the audience of your main ideas, and motivates them to remember or act upon what you have said (you tell them what you told them). The macrostructure of your speech also includes transitions, which are the phrases you use to move from one main point to the next.

You have studied macrostructure throughout your education as you learned to write. Now, however, you will be learning how to adapt it to oral messages. You'll see that careful attention to macrostructure is more important when you craft a speech than when you write an essay. A reader can easily reread a poorly written essay to try to understand your intent, but an audience does not usually have the opportunity to rehear your speech. So, as you prepare each of your speeches, you will need to develop an organizational framework that enables your audience to quickly understand and easily remember the ideas you present.

Whereas macrostructure is the overall framework you design for your speech, **microstructure** is the specific language and style choices you use as you frame your ideas and verbalize them to your audience. Pay careful attention to microstructure while practicing and delivering your speech so that you can present your ideas with words that are instantly intelligible and guide your audience to thoughts that are consistent with your own. Practicing and using words that are appropriate, accurate, clear and vivid will help you accomplish your speaking goal.

As your practice wording, you can also plan to use **rhetorical devices**. These language techniques are designed to create audience attention, hold interest, and aid memory. Again, from your composition classes, you may be familiar with techniques such as alliteration, onomatopoeia, personification, and other rhetorical devices. In Chapter 10, you will learn how to frame your ideas using effective rhetorical devices that make it easy for your audience to understand and remember the ideas in your speech.

An Effective Speech Is Delivered Expressively

Delivery is how you use your voice and body to present your message. The manner in which a speech is delivered can dramatically affect the audience's ability to listen to, understand, remember, and act on the ideas presented. Speakers whose voice and body actions have a conversational quality encourage audience members to listen. When speakers use appropriate volume, rate, pronunciation, and enunciation, they make their message easier for the audience to understand. When speakers are expressive and enthusiastic, listeners are more likely to remember and act on what has been said. In fact, listeners often are more persuaded by the manner in which a speech is delivered than by the words used.[22]

Speaking conversationally means sounding as though you are having a spontaneous conversation with your audience rather than simply reading to them or performing in front of them. Speaking expressively means using various vocal techniques so you sound a bit more dramatic than you would in casual conversation. Some common vocal techniques used in speeches include speaking more quickly or loudly to underscore your attitudes or emotional convictions, stressing key words or phrases, and pausing strategically to call attention to important ideas.

PUTTING SPEAKING SKILLS TO WORK

Do, Play, Create

Beth Richey-Sullivan, Choral Music Teacher Hoover High School, Glendale, California

Photo courtesy of Beth Richey-Sullivan

Beth Richey-Sullivan, 29, has always enjoyed speaking in public—even after experiencing one or two speaking mishaps. For instance, one time in high school "I stood up to give a speech, in a suit and heels, and tripped and fell. Boom! I hit the floor. So I got up, dusted myself off, and kept going."

In her Missouri high school forensics club, Richey-Sullivan was involved in acting, debating, and writing and delivering speeches. Her interest in performance led to her earning a Bachelor of Music Education at the University of Missouri, Kansas City, Conservatory of Music and Dance. When she was 19 years old and still an undergrad, she took her first conducting job with a church choir. Around that time she saw a video of acclaimed choral conductor Donald Neuen and knew she wanted to study with him at the University of California, Los Angeles. She went on to get her Master of Music in choral conducting there.

Now Richey-Sullivan puts the speaking skills she learned in school to work teaching grades seven through twelve and conducting the school marching band and choirs. She's learned to overcome any nervousness she feels about speaking by being prepared. "The only time I'm ever nervous is when I'm not prepared. . . . Be

> **Don't be afraid to let your personality come out. Be yourself.**

confident in your subject matter and there's nothing to be afraid of." She's also learned that being well prepared doesn't mean you have to know *every possible thing* about your topic. "Don't ever be afraid to say, 'I don't know.' You're not expected to be perfect. You can say, 'Let me find that out for you' or 'I've never thought of that.'"

One of her principal speaking engagements recently was teaching a workshop on choral conducting for band teachers at the Music Teachers' Association of California annual convention. She took a smart approach to her speaking situation, considering her audience's needs while at the same time speaking in a way that felt comfortable to her. "I prepared syllabi, outlines, and handouts, and we talked about the literature. But I ran the workshop like the participants were my class—I had them do things as though they were a choir. It was interactive. . . . The more you do, play, [and] create, the more you'll remember. I prepare things that are fun."

"One thing I learned at UKC," says Richey-Sullivan, "was *don't waste anybody's time*. . . . Stay on top of your subject matter. You'll be confident in what you know. And don't be afraid to let your personality come out. Be yourself."

delivery: how you use your voice and body to present your message

As you may already know, nonverbal communication is just as important as verbal communication in conveying messages. Effective speakers know this and use their eyes, face, stance, and hands to help them deliver a speech. For example, they make eye contact with audience members rather than focus solely on their notes, and they use appropriate facial expressions to reflect their conviction about their topic. They stand with poise and confidence, they avoid fidgeting, and they use gestures to reinforce important points.

For an example of a speech of self-introduction, read Kris's outline for her entire speech at the end of this chapter. There you'll see the culmination of her efforts to make her speech audience-centered and well structured.

SPEECH ASSIGNMENT

Speech of Self-Introduction

Prepare a two- to three-minute speech of self-introduction. Tell us about the following:

1. Your personal background
2. Something that makes you unique
3. Why you chose your major

As you prepare your speech, use the Speech Evaluation Checklist that follows to check that your speech includes all the elements of an effective speech.

SPEECH EVALUATION CHECKLIST

General Criteria

You can use this checklist to critique a speech of self-introduction that you hear in class. (You can also use it to critique your own speech.) As you listen to the speaker, consider what makes a speech effective. Then answer the following questions.

Content

_____ 1. Were all main points addressed per the assignment?

_____ 2. Were two to three pieces of evidence provided for each main point (breadth)?

_____ 3. Was one extended piece of evidence provided for each main point (depth)?

_____ 4. Were listener-relevance links provided for each main point?

_____ 5. Did the speech fall within the time constraints of the assignment?

Structure

1. Did the speech provide all the basic elements of an effective speech: introduction, body, conclusion, and transitions? (macrostructure)

2. Did the introduction catch the audience's interest? _____ state the topic of the speech? _____ preview the main points of the speech? _____

CONTINUED

3. Were the main points organized in a way that helped the audience understand and remember the ideas in the speech? _____

4. Were transitions provided between each main point? _____

5. Did the conclusion remind the audience of the main points? _____ motivate the audience to remember the main ideas of the speech? _____

6. Did the speaker use words that were accurate and clear? _____ vivid and emphatic? _____ appropriate and inclusive? *(microstructure)*

7. Did the speaker use rhetorical devices that gained the audience's attention? _____ held the audience's interest? *(microstructure)* _____

Delivery

1. Did the speaker use the appropriate volume? _____ rate of speaking? _____

2. Did the speaker use proper pronunciation? _____ enunciation? _____

3. Was the speaker's voice intelligible? _____ conversational? _____ expressive? _____

4. Did the speaker look up from his or her notes most of the time and make eye contact with the audience? _____

5. Did the speaker use appropriate facial expressions and gestures to reinforce important points? _____

6. Did the speaker appear poised and confident? _____

CourseMate You can use your Speech Communication CourseMate to access this checklist, complete it online and compare your feedback to that of the authors, or print a copy to use in class.

SAMPLE SPEECH

Speech of Self-Introduction

Mirror Image

by Kris Treinen[23]

CourseMate Use your CourseMate for *Challenge* to watch a video clip of Kris presenting her speech in class.

INTRODUCTION

I. Have you ever looked into a mirror and seen your reflection and realized that the reflection in the mirror wasn't really you? I have, many times.

Attention getter

II. As you listen to my speech today, I believe you'll begin to understand how important I believe it is to believe in yourself, your family and friends, and, most important, your dreams.

Listener relevance link

III. Today, I'd like to introduce myself to you by talking about why my mirror image makes me unique, how where I grew up influenced my choice of majors, and how, ultimately, my major has helped shape my career goal.

Thesis statement with main point preview

CONTINUED

Body

Main Point I

When I was a child, I had a mirror image that wasn't really me and I still have it today.

Listener-relevance link

Thinking of my mirror image reminds me how important it is to have family and friends who love me.

A. My mirror image isn't really an "it" but a "her."
  1. Her name is Karla, and she is my identical "mirror image" twin sister.
  2. Every day I am away from her, I realize how easy it was to take her and my family for granted.

B. My sister and I were born right here at a local hospital in Fargo, North Dakota.
  1. We were born three minutes apart.
  2. I was born first, so I'm the oldest.

C. We were known as the "good" twin and the "evil" twin.
  1. Here is a story about me as the "good" twin.
  2. Here is a story about her as the "evil" twin.

Transition: Now that you know how having my own mirror image—my twin—makes me unique, let's talk a bit about how where I grew up influenced my choice of a major.

Main Point II

I spent most of my life growing up in the lakes area of Brainerd, Minnesota.

Listener-relevance link

Perhaps you'll want to visit this area after you hear about it today.

A. I grew up in a small town called Nisswa, Minnesota.
  1. I moved to Nisswa when I was three years old.
  2. We lived in a house that was very special to me.

B. As I grew up in an area known for lots of snow in the winter, I got involved in snowboarding.
  1. I started snowboarding recreationally.
  2. Then I competed as a snowboarder.
  3. Eventually, I taught snowboarding as a part-time job.

Transition: So my upbringing led me to realize I love to snowboard and to teach snowboarding, which is why I chose to come to school here at North Dakota State University (NDSU).

Main Point III

I chose to further my education with a major in hospitality management.

Listener-relevance link

I feel lucky every time I realize I can get a major and eventually earn a living doing something I love—working with people in the hospitality and recreation fields.

A. NDSU has a reputable program.
B. The winters in the Fargo area allow me to continue to pursue snowboarding.
C. Ultimately, my degree will help me pursue my goal to work in a ski resort area and help children with disabilities learn to snowboard.

Conclusion

Thesis restatement with main point summary
Clincher

I. Now that you know a little bit about me as a twin and why I chose to major in hospitality management, I hope you'll be inspired to also follow your career dreams.

II. I hope you now see why I have learned to look beyond the reflection I see in the mirror to understand who I really am on the way to who I will one day become.

Summary

Public speaking is important to achieving success in nearly every walk of life. It is one form of human communication, which consists of participants, messages, channels, noise, and feedback. Public speaking occurs within the public communication context. Intrapersonal, interpersonal, and group communication are additional contexts within which we communication regularly.

Effective public speaking skills are a liberal art that make it possible for us to enact our civic responsibility to participate actively as a member of a democratic society. To do so, however, we must adhere to five essential ethical principles: to be honest, to have integrity, to behave fairly, to demonstrate respect for others, and to act responsibly. Public speaking challenges us to behave ethically.

Public speaking is an audience-centered process that occurs within a rhetorical situation comprised of speaker, audience, and occasion and is guided by exigence. How effective a speech is depends on how well audience members listen to, understand, remember, and are motivated to act on what the speaker has said. The audience-centered speaker demonstrates honesty and respect for listeners by employing ethos, pathos, and logos throughout the speech-planning and -presenting process and adhering to principles of effective content, structure, and delivery.

Challenge Resource and Assessment Center

CourseMate Now that you have read Chapter 1, use your Speech Communication CourseMate for *The Challenge of Effective Speaking* for quick access to the electronic resources that accompany this text. These resources include:

- **Study tools** that will help you assess your learning and prepare for exams (*digital glossary, key term flash cards, review quizzes*).
- **Activities and assignments** that will help you hone your knowledge and build your public speaking skills throughout the course (*Speech Snippets, Speech Assignments, Action Step*

Activities). Many of these activities allow you to compare your answers with those provided by the author, and, if requested, submit your answers to your instructor.

- **Media resources** that will help you explore communication concepts online (*Web Resources*), develop your speech outlines (*Speech Builder Express 3.0*), watch and critique videos of sample speeches (*Interactive Video Activities*), upload your speech videos for peer reviewing and critique other students' speeches (*Speech Studio online speech review tool*), and download chapter reviews so you can study when and where you'd like (*Audio Study Tools*).

This chapter's application activities and video resources are featured in this end-of-chapter section.

Applying What You've Learned

1. **Impromptu Speech Activity:** Identify one of your "heroes." Your hero may or may not be famous. Identify one of the five ethical principles this hero's life adheres to and why. In your two- to three-minute impromptu speech, provide at least two incidents that serve as evidence regarding how this person demonstrates/demonstrated the principle.

2. **Assessment Activity A:** Visit the homepage on Facebook. If you don't have an account, you might make one to observe while completing this course. Read through the postings on the "news

feed" and identify which of them adhere to and do not adhere to the ethical communication principles proposed in this chapter.

3. **Assessment Activity B:** Visit a local retail store in a nearby mall. Spend time observing what you see. Describe what you observe according to the elements of the rhetorical situation (occasion, speaker, and audience). Do you think the sales clerk you observed was effective? Again, based on what you observed regarding the rhetorical situation, why or why not?

Web Resources

1.1 The Basics of Ethics (8)

1.2 Ethics Connection (8)

Video Resources

1. Use your Interactive Video Activities to watch, analyze, and see the transcript and outlines for Kris Treinen's speech of self-introduction, "Mirror Image."

2. Use Speech Studio to upload a video of your own speech of self-introduction for feedback from your instructor and classmates. Or search for other students' first speeches—do their speeches give you ideas for how you could make your speech more effective? ☑Speech Studio

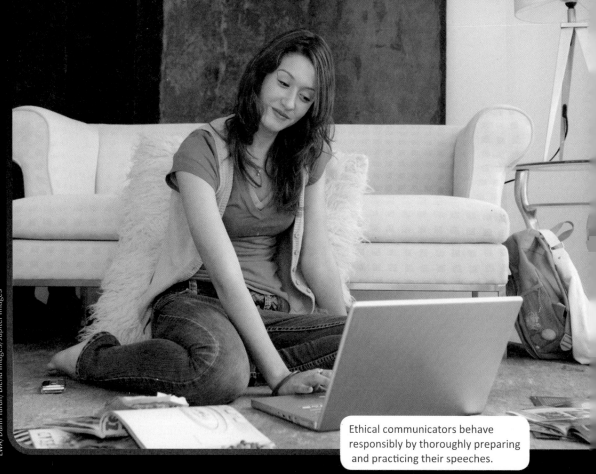

LWA/Dann Tardif/Blend Images/Jupiter Images

Ethical communicators behave
responsibly by thoroughly preparing
and practicing their speeches.

2

developing confidence through the speech-planning process

Professor Montrose begins class by saying, "Let's look at some of the key points of the chapter that you were assigned to read for today." He then points to Paul and asks, "What were the keys to solving the Kingston problem effectively?" Paul, sputtering and turning red, begins to sweat and stammers, "Well, uh, I guess that, well . . ." Professor Montrose then points to the next student and asks, "Sylvia, what would you say about this?" Sylvia looks at Professor Montrose and answers, "According to the text, there are three steps involved." She goes on to list the steps and then discusses each of the three.

Y ou might think, "Poor, Paul. He just got so nervous when Professor Montrose pointed at him and asked him the question that he couldn't remember a thing." And perhaps he did suffer from severe public speaking apprehension—or stage fright. But then why was Sylvia able to look Professor Montrose in the eye, tell him there are three steps, and then discuss each? One answer might be, "Well, she doesn't suffer stage fright, so she was able to answer the question." Although that might well be true, there's another answer as well: Paul hadn't prepared well for class, while Sylvia had not only read the text but had also outlined the key points and reviewed them over a cup of coffee before class.

Recall the title of this chapter: "Developing Confidence through the Speech-Planning Process." Although stage fright is normal in public settings, even the most frightened person whose heart is pounding will perform better when he or she is well prepared. In fact, as many as 76 percent of experienced public speakers claim to feel fearful before presenting a speech.[1] For example, did you know that award-winning actors Meryl Streep and Kim Basinger, singer Barbra Streisand, singer/actor Donny Osmond, professional football player Ricky Williams, and evangelist Billy Graham all experience fear about speaking in front of others? In spite of their fear, all are effective public speakers because they employ the strategies for managing nervousness that we will share with you in this chapter.

We begin this chapter by explaining what scholars call public speaking apprehension. Then we discuss the causes and benefits of public speaking apprehension, as well as how you can manage anxiety successfully. And, finally, we explain how careful preparation can help you develop and display confidence when you speak. At the end of the chapter, we introduce the narrative/personal experience speech, a common early speech assignment.

Understanding Public Speaking Apprehension

public speaking apprehension: the level of fear a person experiences when anticipating or actually speaking to an audience

Public speaking apprehension is the level of fear a person experiences when anticipating or actually speaking to an audience. Almost all of us have some level of public speaking apprehension, but about 15 percent of the U.S. population experiences high levels of apprehension.[2] Yet this apprehension hardly ever stops people from speaking!

In fact, having some public speaking apprehension makes one a better public speaker than having none at all. Why? Because those feelings we label as fear are really a sign of the adrenaline boost that will help us perform at our best.

Just as an adrenaline boost helps us perform better as athletes, musicians, and actors, it also helps us deliver better public speeches when we manage it effectively.[3] So, if you are lackadaisical about giving a speech, you probably will not do a good job.[4] Because at least some tension is constructive, the goal is not to eliminate nervousness but to learn how to manage it.[5]

Now that we understand that some public speaking apprehension can actually help, let's identify the symptoms you may experience and the causes for speaking apprehension. Then we'll describe specific techniques you can use to manage public speaking in ways that will make you a more effective public speaker.

Symptoms of Public Speaking Apprehension

The symptoms of public speaking apprehension vary from individual to individual and range from mild to debilitating. Symptoms can be cognitive, physical, or emotional. Cognitive symptoms include negative self-talk (a.k.a. negative intrapersonal communication), which is also the most common cause of public speaking apprehension.[6] For example, a highly apprehensive person might dwell on thoughts such as "I'm going to make a fool of myself" or "I just know that I'll blow it." Physical symptoms may be stomach upset (or butterflies), flushed skin, sweating, shaking, lightheadedness, rapid or pounding heartbeats, stuttering, and vocalized pauses ("like," "you know," "ah," "um"). Emotional symptoms include feeling anxious, worried, or upset.

Luckily, public speaking apprehension gradually decreases for most of us as we speak. Researchers have identified three phases we proceed through: anticipation, confrontation, and adaptation.[7] Exhibit 2.1 depicts this cycle visually.

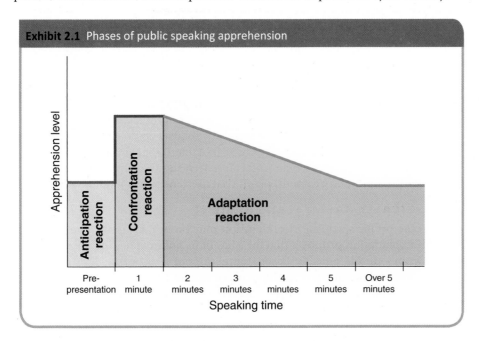

Exhibit 2.1 Phases of public speaking apprehension

The **anticipation phase** is the anxiety we experience before giving the speech, both while preparing it and waiting to speak. The **confrontation phase** is the surge of anxiety we feel as we begin delivering the speech. This begins to fall about a minute or so into the speech. The **adaptation phase** is the period during which our anxiety level gradually decreases. It typically begins about one minute into the presentation and tends to level off after about five minutes.[8] So, it's normal to be nervous before you speak and, when understood and managed effectively, can result in a better speech than having no nervousness at all.

anticipation phase: the anxiety you experience prior to giving the speech, including the nervousness you feel while preparing and waiting to speak

confrontation phase: the surge of anxiety you feel as you begin delivering your speech

adaptation phase: the period during which your anxiety level gradually decreases

There are many ways to measure your level of public speaking apprehension. Exhibit 2.2 presents one short survey that is widely used by researchers. You can complete the six questions and score them to gauge your level of apprehension.

Exhibit 2.2 Personal Report of Public Speaking Apprehension*

These statements give you a chance to express how you feel about speaking in public. Please indicate in the space provided the degree to which each statement applies to you by marking whether you:

1 = strongly agree; 2 = agree; 3 = are undecided; 4 = disagree; 5 = strongly disagree

_____ **1.** I have no fear of giving a speech.
_____ **2.** Certain parts of my body feel very tense and rigid while giving a speech.
_____ **3.** I feel relaxed while giving a speech.
_____ **4.** My thoughts become confused and jumbled when I am giving a speech.
_____ **5.** I face the prospect of giving a speech with confidence.
_____ **6.** While giving a speech, I get so nervous I forget the facts I really know.
_____ **TOTAL**

SCORING: Begin by reversing the numbers you assigned to statements 2, 4, and 6 (1 = 5, 2 = 4, 3 = 3, 4 = 2, 5 = 1). Then, add all six numbers.

INTERPRETING: If your total is more than 24, you may experience a high level of public speaking apprehension. People who are highly apprehensive will benefit most from applying the techniques designed to reduce anxiety.

---

*Taken from the PRCA-24, subscale Public Speaking. See Rich, V. P., & McCroskey, J. C. (1997). *Communication apprehension, avoidance, and effectiveness*. Scottsdale, AZ: Gorsuch Scarisbrick.

Causes of Public Speaking Apprehension

Public speaking apprehension is most commonly caused by negative self-talk.[9] **Self-talk** is defined as intrapersonal communication regarding perceived success or failure in a particular situation. Negative self-talk about giving a speech increases anxiety. Negative self-talk generally focuses on a fear of being stared at, a fear of the unknown, a fear of failure, or a fear of becoming fearful. Where do these negative thoughts come from? Research suggests three common roots: biologically based temperament, previous experience, and level of skills.

BIOLOGICALLY BASED TEMPERAMENT

First, some public speaking apprehension may be inborn. This "communibiological" explanation proposes that for a few of us public speaking apprehension stems from our biologically based temperament. According to this theory, people who are extroverted tend to experience lower levels of public speaking apprehension than people who are introverted. Similarly, people who naturally experience elevated levels of general anxiety and shyness tend to experience higher levels of public speaking anxiety than people who do not.[10] Does this mean that, if you are temperamentally predisposed toward high public speaking apprehension, you are doomed to be ineffective in your speaking efforts? Of course not. Remember the successful celebrities we mentioned earlier? Many of them are introverted and generally anxious and shy, yet all of them enjoy a great deal of public speaking success.

PREVIOUS EXPERIENCE

Second, our level of apprehension may also result from our experiences with public speaking while growing up. In other words, some of us actually learned to fear public speaking! Research tells us that most public speaking apprehension

self-talk: intrapersonal communication regarding success or failure in a particular situation stems from such socialization.[11] We are socialized in two main ways: through modeling and reinforcement. **Modeling** is learning by observing and then imitating those you admire or are close to.[12] **Reinforcement** is learning from personal experiences so that past responses to our behavior shape our expectations about how our future behavior will be received.[13]

Consider your past. How did modeling affect your current communication behavior? What was oral communication like in your home when you were a child? What was it like in your community? Did your parents talk freely with each other in your presence? Did family or community members talk with each other a great deal, or were they quiet and reserved? What was it like around the dinner table or at community events? Did any of your family members do much public speaking? What were their experiences? Did they avoid public speaking if they could? If your family tended to be quiet and reserved and avoided speaking in public or showed fear about it, your own preferences and fears may stem from modeling. Modeling an aversion to speaking freely in public influenced noted *Boston Globe* columnist Diana White, who remarked, "In my family, looking for attention was one of the worst sins a child could commit. 'Don't make a spectacle of yourself' was a familiar phrase around our house."[14]

How you have been reinforced by others in your speaking efforts also influences how well you believe you performed in the past and affects how apprehensive you feel about future speaking occasions. We have all had many "public speaking" experiences, from reading aloud during second grade, to giving an oral report in science class, to accepting a sports award at a banquet. If the responses to your speaking in the past were generally positive, you probably learned to feel confident of your ability. If, on the other hand, the responses were negative, you probably learned to feel fearful of public speaking. So, if your second-grade teacher humiliated you when you read aloud, if you flubbed that science report, or if friends laughed at your acceptance speech, you will probably be more apprehensive about speaking in public than if you had been praised for your efforts. The public speaking apprehension you feel because of negative past experiences, though uncomfortable, does not have to influence your future performances. There are strategies you can use as you prepare to speak that will help you reduce your apprehension and be more effective. We will discuss some of these strategies in the next section.

LEVEL OF SKILLS

An important source of public speaking apprehension comes from having underdeveloped speaking skills. This "skill deficit" theory was the earliest explanation for apprehension and continues to receive the attention of researchers. It suggests that most of us become apprehensive because we don't know how to (or choose not to) plan or prepare effectively for a public presentation.

Effective speech planning is an orderly process based on a set of skills. If you do not know or apply these skills, you are likely to have higher anticipation reaction levels. On

modeling: learning by observing and then imitating those you admire or are close to

reinforcement: learning from personal experiences and past responses to our behavior

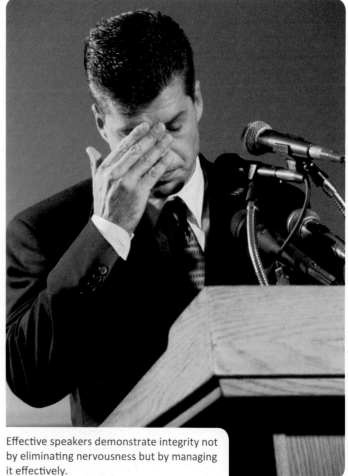
Chuck Savage/Corbis

Effective speakers demonstrate integrity not by eliminating nervousness but by managing it effectively.

the other hand, as you become skilled at using the six-step speech-planning process previewed later in this chapter, your preparation will give you confidence and your anticipation reaction will be lower than if you were ill prepared. The goal of this course is to help you become skilled and, in so doing, help you become a more confident public speaker.

Managing Public Speaking Apprehension

Because public speaking apprehension has multiple causes, there are both general methods and specific techniques that can help us reduce our anxiety and manage our nervousness.

General Methods

Some methods are targeted at reducing the apprehension that results from our worrisome thoughts and negative self-talk. Other methods are aimed at reducing our physical symptoms of anxiety. Still others focus on helping us overcome the skill deficiencies that lead to our anxiety. In this section, we consider six common methods for reducing public speaking apprehension.

communication orientation motivation (COM) techniques: designed to reduce anxiety by helping the speaker adopt a "communication" rather than a "performance" orientation toward the speech

performance orientation: viewing public speaking as a situation demanding special delivery techniques to impress an audience aesthetically or viewing audience members as hypercritical judges who will not forgive even minor mistakes

communication orientation: viewing a speech as just an opportunity to talk with a number of people about an important topic

visualization: a method that reduces apprehension by helping speakers develop a mental picture of themselves giving a masterful speech

1. **Communication orientation motivation (COM) techniques** are designed to reduce anxiety by helping us adopt a "communication" rather than a "performance" orientation toward our speeches.[15] According to communication researcher Michael Motley, public speaking anxiety increases when we hold a **performance orientation**, viewing public speaking as demanding special delivery techniques to impress our audience "aesthetically"[16] or viewing audience members as hypercritical judges who will not forgive even our minor mistakes. When we approach public speaking with a performance orientation, our self-talk tends to focus on our fear of failing, which increases our anxiety. On the other hand, if we approach public speaking from a **communication orientation**, we view our speech as just an opportunity to talk with a number of people about an important topic. When we have a communication orientation, we focus on getting our message across to people in our audience rather than on how the people in our audience are judging us as a performer.

    So, one way to reduce public speaking apprehension is to view public speaking as a conversation with a group of people where we focus on getting our message across, not on how they might be judging our performance.

2. **Visualization** is a method that reduces apprehension by helping us develop a mental picture of ourselves giving a masterful speech. Doing so counters the fear of failure and the fear of becoming fearful. Like COM techniques, visualization helps us overcome the cognitive and emotional symptoms of apprehension. Joe Ayres and Theodore S. Hopf, two scholars who have conducted extensive research on visualization, have found that if people can visualize themselves going through an entire speech-preparation and speech-making process, they will have a much better chance of succeeding when they are speaking.[17]

    Visualization has been used extensively to improve athletic performances. In a study of basketball players trying to improve their foul-shooting percentages, players were divided into three groups. One group never practiced, another group practiced making foul shots, and a third group "practiced" by visualizing themselves making foul shots. As we would expect, those who physically practiced improved far more than those who didn't practice at all. But those who simply *visualized* practicing improved almost as much as those who actually practiced.[18] Imagine what happens when you both visualize *and* practice!

By visualizing the process of speech making, not only do people seem to lower their general apprehension, but they also report fewer negative thoughts when they actually speak.[19] So, you will want to use visualization activities as part of your speech preparation. Go to your CourseMate for *Challenge* to access **Web Resource 2.1: Visualizing Your Success**. This audio activity will guide you through a visualization in which you will imagine that you successfully accomplish the complete speech preparation and presentation process.

3. **Relaxation exercises** include breathing techniques and progressive muscle relaxation exercises. For these exercises to be effective, you must learn how to do them and practice them regularly. With consistent practice, these will eventually become habitual, and you will be able to use them to calm yourself in the moments before your speech.

If people can visualize themselves going through an entire process, they will have a much better chance of succeeding when they are in the situation.

Corbis/PhotoLibrary

Let's take a closer look at breathing techniques. We were all born breathing correctly; using the muscles in our abdomen to draw air into and push air out of our lungs. But when we become anxious, the muscles in our abdomens tense and so we take shallower breaths, often raising our shoulders to get air into our lungs and dropping them to expel the air. Shallow breathing contributes to anxiety, depression, and fatigue.[20] Think of your lungs as balloons that fill up with air. Have you ever seen someone making balloon animals? If so, you probably noticed that, when the artist wanted part of the balloon to remain uninflated, he or she squeezed that area off with the hand. Shallow breathing is like filling only the top half of the balloon because, when your abdominal muscles tighten, you stop air from filling the bottom half of your lungs. Fortunately, we can retrain ourselves to breath from the abdomen and thereby reduce our anxiety. Exhibit 2.3 offers some suggestions.

Similarly, we can train our bodies to relax by practicing progressive muscle relaxation exercises. Essentially, you systematically tense certain muscle groups for about ten seconds and then relax them for another ten seconds while focusing on what the relaxed state feels like.[21] Once you teach your body to relax on command, you can call it to do so before beginning to give your speech, again allowing the adrenaline rush to work for you.

CourseMate

relaxation exercises: breathing techniques and progressive muscle relaxation exercises that help reduce anxiety

---

Exhibit 2.3 Breathing and relaxation exercises

1. **Abdominal breathing:** Lie on the floor and place your hand on your abdomen. Consciously focus on filling your abdomen with air when you inhale by watching your hand rise. Then, as you release the air, watch your hand lower again.

2. **Sighing:** By sighing right before it is your turn to speak, you can release tension and lower your anxiety level, allowing the inevitable rush of adrenaline to work for you, not against you.[22]

3. **Progressive muscle relaxation exercises:** Consciously tense and relax each of these muscle groups twice and then move on to the next group: hands, arms, shoulders, neck, lips, tongue, mouth, eyes and forehead, abdomen, back, midsection, thighs, stomach, calves, feet, and toes.

---

4. **Systematic desensitization** is a method that reduces apprehension by gradually having people visualize and perform increasingly more frightening events while remaining in a relaxed state. Individuals first learn procedures

systematic desensitization: a method that reduces apprehension by gradually having people visualize and perform increasingly more frightening events while remaining in a relaxed state for relaxation and then learn to apply these to each of the anxiety-producing events that they visualize. Thus, they learn to remain relaxed when they encounter these anxiety-producing situations in real life.[23] This method is used to help people overcome the physical symptoms of public speaking apprehension. Research tells us that more than 80 percent of those who try this method reduce their level of anxiety.[24] Essentially, once you are in a relaxed state, you imagine yourself in successively more stressful speech-planning and speech-making situations—for example, researching a speech topic in the library, practicing the speech out loud in front of a roommate, and delivering the final speech to your audience. Once you can maintain a relaxed state while visualizing yourself in each event, you try performing each event while maintaining the learned state of calmness. The ultimate goal of systematic desensitization is to transfer the calm feelings we attain while visualizing to the actual speaking event. Calmness on command—and it works.

cognitive restructuring: a process designed to help you systematically change your intrapersonal communication (self-talk) about public speaking

5. **Cognitive restructuring** is a process designed to help you change your intrapersonal communication about public speaking. The goal is to replace anxiety-arousing negative self-talk with anxiety-reducing positive self-talk. Effective speakers do so with regard to each of the fears we mentioned earlier: the fear of being stared at, the unknown, failure, and of becoming fearful. The process consists of four steps.

   - Identify your fears. Write down all the fears that come to mind when you know you must give a speech.
   - Analyze how rational these fears are. Most fears about public speaking are, in fact, irrational because public speaking is not life threatening.
   - Develop positive coping statements to replace each negative self-talk statement. There is no list of coping statements that will work for everyone; you can develop positive coping statements to replace negative self-talk. Psychologist Richard Heimberg of the State University of New York at Albany asks his clients to consider just how many listeners in an audience of 100 would even notice or care if the clients did what they're afraid of doing when giving a speech. Ultimately, he concludes with the question, "Can you cope with the one or two people who [notice or criticize or] get upset?"[25]
   - Incorporate your positive coping statements into your life so that they're second nature. You can do this by writing your statements down and reading them aloud to yourself each day, as well as before you give a speech. The more you repeat your coping statements to yourself, silently and aloud, the more natural they will become and the more unnatural your negative thoughts will seem.

   Exhibit 2.4 is an example of how one student used this process to help her. For an activity that will help you develop positive coping statements to replace negative self-talk, go to your CourseMate for *Challenge* to access **Web Resource 2.2: Restructure Your Expectations**.

CourseMate

public speaking skills training: systematic practicing of the skills associated with the processes involved in preparing and delivering an effective public speech with the intention of improving speaking competence and reducing public speaking apprehension

6. **Public speaking skills training** is the systematic practicing of the skills associated with preparing and delivering an effective public speech, with the intention of reducing public speaking apprehension. Skills training is based on the assumption that some of our anxiety about speaking in public is due to not knowing how to be successful—we lack the knowledge and behaviors to be effective. Therefore, if we learn the processes and behaviors associated with effective speech making, then we will be less anxious.[26] Public speaking skills include those associated with the processes of goal analysis, audience and situation analysis, organization, delivery, and self-evaluation.[27]

   All six of these methods for reducing public speaking apprehension have successfully helped people reduce their anxiety. If you think you'll

Exhibit 2.4 Negative self-talk versus positive coping statements

Beth decided to try cognitive restructuring to reduce her anxiety about giving speeches in front of her classmates. Here is how she worked through the process:

Negative self-talk
1. I'm afraid I'll stumble over my words and look foolish.
2. I'm afraid everyone will be able to tell that I'm nervous.
3. I'm afraid my voice will crack.
4. I'm afraid I'll sound boring.

Positive coping statements
1. Even if I stumble, I will have succeeded as long as I get my message across.
2. They probably won't be able to tell I'm nervous, but as long as I focus on getting my message across, that's what matters.
3. Even if my voice cracks, as long as I keep going and focus on getting my message across, I'll succeed at what matters most.
4. I won't sound bored if I focus on how important this message is to me and to my audience. I don't have to do somersaults to keep their attention because my topic is relevant to them.

experience public speaking apprehension in this course, which of these techniques do you think might help you? Have you already tried some of them in other situations? If they helped, do you think you could apply them to reduce your anxiety about giving a speech? For most people, using several of them yields the best results.[28]

Specific Techniques

Along with the six general methods just discussed, we recommend several specific anxiety-reducing techniques to employ in the days before you deliver your speech and on the day you actually give it.

1. **Allow sufficient time to prepare.** As soon as you know the day you are to give your speech and the expectations for it, identify the topic and begin to prepare. Ideally, you should spend at least a week or ten days researching, organizing, and practicing your speech.

2. **Use presentational aids.** Recall that one of the major fears that increase public speaking anxiety is the fear of being stared at. Although it is human nature to enjoy being recognized for things we've done well, it is not human nature to be the constant center of attention for a prolonged amount of time.[29] When giving a public speech, that is exactly what happens. All eyes are focused constantly on us, and we can feel conspicuous. Using presentational aids allows you to direct your audience's attention to something else at carefully placed points during the speech, which can diminish the sense of being constantly stared at and the anxiety that can accompany it.

3. **Practice your speech aloud.** When you practice your speech aloud, you get comfortable hearing yourself talk about your topic. You identify sections of the speech where your ideas may not flow and where you need to do additional preparation. By the third or fourth time you have practiced aloud, you will notice your delivery becoming easier, and you will gain confidence in your ability to present your ideas to others.

   Many successful speakers not only practice aloud alone but also practice in front of trusted friends who serve as a "practice" audience and give the speaker feedback. If possible, practice your speech in the room where you'll ultimately deliver it. Hearing your voice in the room where you'll speak reduces anxiety that can arise as a result of the fear of the unknown because you now know what it will feel like to present your speech in that room. Finally, on the night before your speech, review your speech plan immediately before you go to sleep. That way, as you sleep, your mind will continue to prepare.[30]

4. **Dress up.** We tend to feel more confident when we know we look good. By dressing up for your speech, you'll reduce anxiety about being stared at because you feel good about how you look. Not only that, dressing up demonstrates good character and enhances credibility (ethos) because doing so sends a message that you care about the audience, the occasion, and the message you want to get across to your listeners.

5. **Choose an appropriate time to speak.** If you have a choice about whether you will give your speech first, last, or somewhere in between, pick the time that works best for you. Some speakers become more nervous when they sit and listen to others, so they are better off speaking early in the class period. Others find that listening to their peers calms them, so they are better off speaking later in the class period. If given a chance, choose to speak at the time that is optimal for you.

6. **Use positive self-talk.** Immediately prior to getting up to speak, coach yourself with a short "pregame pep talk." Remind yourself about the importance of what you have to say. Remember all the hard work you have done to be prepared and recall how good you are when you are at your best. Remind yourself that nervousness is normal and useful. Tell yourself that you are confident and ready.

7. **Face the audience.** Face the audience with confidence. When it is time, walk purposefully to the front. Plant yourself firmly yet comfortably, and take a second or two to look at the audience. Take a deep breath (you might even silently count to five while reviewing the first lines of your speech in your head) and begin your well-rehearsed introduction.

8. **Focus on sharing your message.** Although you may feel nervous, your audience rarely "sees" it. Continue to focus on sharing your ideas with the audience rather than focusing on your nerves.

Effective Speech Planning: The Key to Confidence

Whether you are a marketing account manager presenting an advertising campaign idea to your corporate clients, a coach trying to motivate your team for its game with your arch rival, or a student giving a speech in class, you will have more confidence in your likelihood of success when you have developed an effective **speech plan**—a strategy for achieving your goal.

speech plan: a strategy for achieving your goal

In this text, you will learn a six-step process for planning your speeches that is grounded in the works of major speech scholars across the ages. Ancient Roman philosophers actually clarified the five general rules for effective public speeches more than 2,000 years ago. These rules, known as the **canons of rhetoric**, which are commonly attributed to Cicero, still hold true today.[31] These five canons are invention (an effective speech has convincing content), arrangement (an effective speech is clearly organized), style (an effective speech uses appropriate language), delivery (an effective speaker delivers the oration with confidence, fluency, and strategic retention aids), and memory (an effective speaker delivers the oration with confidence, fluency, and strategic retention aids). While classical approaches to speech planning were speaker-focused, later public speaking scholars recognized that effective speeches were

canons of rhetoric: five general rules for effective public speeches audience-centered and addressed the rhetorical situation.32 In the chapters to come, you will be learning a process for speech planning that is both rooted in ancient wisdom and informed by contemporary understanding of how to prepare effective speeches. The steps in this process are

1. Select a speech goal that is appropriate to the rhetorical situation.
2. Understand your audience and adapt to it.
3. Gather and evaluate information to use in the speech.
4. Organize and develop ideas into a well-structured outline.
5. Choose, prepare, and use appropriate presentational aids.
6. Practice oral language and delivery style.

As you practice the skills, you will gain confidence in your ability to present your ideas effectively. Let's briefly preview what you will learn in each step.

Step 1: Select a Speech Goal That Is Appropriate to the Rhetorical Situation

Your **speech goal** is a specific statement of what you want your audience to know, believe, or do. To arrive at an appropriate speech goal, you need to consider yourself as the speaker, the audience, and the occasion. Doing so will encourage your audience to pay attention because they will perceive it as relevant and timely.

> **speech goal:** a specific statement of what you want your listeners to know, believe, or do

You begin by selecting a topic that you know something about and that interests you or is important to you. Although there could be times in your life when you must speak on a topic that is unfamiliar to you, in the great majority of speaking experiences, you will speak on topics that meet these tests.

Because your speech will be given to a particular audience, before you get very far you need to think about your audience: Who are they? What do they need to know about your topic? What do they already know? To answer these questions, you need to make a preliminary audience analysis based on their gender, culture, average age, education level, occupation, income level, and group affiliation. Then, you can assess the kinds of material the audience is likely to know and the information they are likely to respond to.

Likewise, you need to consider the occasion: What is the size of the audience? When will the speech be given? Where will the speech be given? Are there any peculiarities of the room? What is the time limit for the speech? What are the audience expectations for the speech?

Once you determine a topic based on your interest and expertise, the audience, and the occasion, you are ready to phrase your speech goal. Every speech has a general and a specific goal. For most classroom speeches, the general goal is usually either to inform, where your goal is shared understanding, or to persuade, where your goal is to convince your audience believe something or persuade them to take action. Some other general goals, which Aristotle called ceremonial speeches, are called for on specific special occasions (e.g., to introduce, to entertain, and to celebrate).33

Your specific speech goal articulates exactly what you want your audience to understand, believe, or do. For instance, Gina, who is majoring in health and nutrition, might phrase her informative speech goal as, "I want the audience to understand three methods for ridding our bodies of harmful toxins." And Glen, a bioengineering major, might phrase his persuasive speech goal as, "I want to convince my audience of the value of genetic engineering."

Step 2: Understand Your Audience and Adapt to It

Once you have a clear and specific speech goal based on the speaker, audience, and occasion, you begin the task of understanding your audience more fully and how to adapt your speech to it. **Audience adaptation** is the process of

> **audience adaptation:** the process of tailoring your speech's information to the needs, interests, and expectations of your listeners

Suppose you were giving a speech on genetic engineering. Your adaptation challenges would differ between the audience pictured here and an audience composed of young college students.

Bill Aron/PhotoEdit

tailoring your speech's information to the needs, interests, and expectations of your listeners. As you prepare for a speech, you will consider your specific audience's needs and seek to meet these needs continually throughout the speech-planning and -practicing process.

For any speech, it is important to consider the audience's initial level of interest in your goal, their ability to understand the content of the speech, and their attitude toward you and your topic.

If you believe your audience has very little interest in your speech topic, you will need to adapt to them so that they understand why the topic is important. For instance, if Glen is talking with an audience that he believes has very little interest in genetic engineering, he may pique their interest by talking about some of the genetically modified foods they probably eat without knowing it.

Not only will you need to adapt your speech by piquing audience interest, but if you believe that your audience doesn't know much about your topic, you will want to provide the basic information they need to understand your speech. For instance, Glen may need to begin by talking about how genetic engineering differs from organically grown foods.

Finally, you will need to adapt to your audience's initial attitudes toward your topic. Glen should do some research to learn where his audience stands on this topic before he begins. If the majority of his audience is against genetic engineering, he will adapt by selecting arguments and evidence that can be accepted by the audience.

Step 3: Gather and Evaluate Information to Use in the Speech

When you select a topic, although you already know something about it, you will usually need additional information. In addition to drawing on material from your own knowledge and experiences, you can draw on the expertise of others by reading printed materials, as well as by conducting interviews and surveys. Regardless of the sources of your information, you will need to evaluate the information you gather and select the items you deem valid and truthful. The more you know about your topic, the easier it is to evaluate the information you uncover in your research. For instance, Nora, who is a member of the local volunteer Life Squad, will be able to give a better speech on CPR than a person with no practical experience who has learned about CPR from reading and interviewing others. Why? Because, as a volunteer, Nora has actually used this skill and has real experiences to draw from. Likewise, as a student of bioengineering, Glen is able to explain the process of genetic engineering because he has studied it in his classes.

Step 4: Organize and Develop Ideas into a Well-Structured Outline

You begin the process of organizing your speech by identifying the two to four major ideas you want your audience to remember. You then turn each major idea into a complete sentence. These sentences will become the main points for the body of your speech. Next you combine your speech goal with each major idea into a succinct thesis statement with main point preview that describes specifically what you want your audience to understand, believe, or do when you have finished speaking. This process provides the initial framework, or macro-structure, of your speech.

Main points must be carefully worded, and then they must be arranged in an organizational framework that helps the audience understand and remember them. Two of the most basic organizational frameworks are chronological and topical order. In later chapters, we'll consider several frameworks you may want to use in your speeches. Chronological means following an order that moves from first to last. So, Nora, who is planning to speak on how to perform CPR on a child, will organize her speech following the steps (what is done first, second, and third) involved in administrating CPR. In some circumstances, you may find that your speech is best presented topically. Topical means following an order of headings. For instance, Gina, who decides to inform her audience about the three proven methods for removing harmful toxins from the body, may begin with the simplest one—keeping hydrated—and ending with the most difficult one—eating more natural whole foods.

Having identified, phrased, and ordered the main points, you are now ready to outline the body of the speech. Although it is tempting to work out a speech as it comes to mind, speeches are not essays, and you will be more effective if you prepare a thorough outline.

After you have outlined the body of the speech, which includes noting elaborations, you can outline your introduction and conclusion. Your introduction should get attention, establish listener relevance and speaker credibility, and lead into the body of the speech. Because there are never any guarantees that your audience is ready to pay full attention to the speech, an effective introduction draws the audience into what you are saying.

In your conclusion, you will want to remind the audience of your main points and speech goal. You should do this in a creative way with a clincher that ties back to the attention catcher, which helps the audience remember.

When you think you are finished, review the outline to make sure that the parts are relevant to your goal. The length of your outline will depend on the length of your speech. In a speech of three to five minutes, the outline may contain up to 50 percent or more of the words in the speech; for a five- to eight-minute speech, up to 33 to 50 percent may be included. And in speeches of 30 to 45 minutes, the outline may contain as few as 20 percent of the words.

Although an expert who speaks frequently on a topic may be able to speak effectively from a mental outline or a few notes, most of us benefit from the discipline of organizing and developing a formal speech outline.

Step 5: Choose, Prepare, and Use Appropriate Presentational Aids

"A picture is worth a thousand words" is an old saying with a lot of wisdom. So, even for a very short speech, you may decide to use a visual or other presentational aid that will help clarify, emphasize, or dramatize what you say. Because audiences understand and retain information better when they have received that information through more than one sense, objects, models, charts, pictorial representations, projections, and computer graphics that are constructed well and integrated smoothly maximize the effect of a speech. As you get ready to practice your speech, make sure you consider when to use presentational aids, how long to use them, and how to integrate them so that everyone can see and/or hear them.

Step 6: Practice Oral Language and Delivery Style

In your practice sessions, you need to choose the wording of main points and supporting materials carefully. If you have not practiced various ways of phrasing your key ideas, you run the risk of missing a major opportunity for communicating your ideas effectively. In practice sessions, work on the appropriateness, accuracy, clarity, and vividness of your wording. Recall that these language choices make up the microstructure of your speech.

Although a speech is composed of words, how effective you will be is also largely a matter of how well you use your voice and body in delivering your speech. You will want to present the speech intelligibly (understandably), conversationally, and expressively. You will also want to use good posture and eye contact (look at members of the audience while you are speaking) to appear confident and comfortable, as well as facial expressions and gestures that emphasize emotional intentions and clarify structure.

Very few people can present speeches effectively without considerable practice. Practicing out loud gives you confidence that you can talk conversationally and comfortably with your audience and accomplish your speech goal within the time limit. Don't try to memorize the speech. Trying to memorize your speech is likely to add to your public speaking anxiety because you may also fear forgetting what you planned to say. Instead, deliver your speech extemporaneously—that is, practiced until the ideas of the speech are firmly in mind, even though the wording varies a bit from practice to practice and during the actual presentation.

Exhibit 2.5 summarizes the six action steps of an effective speech plan in outline form. These steps will be explained in more detail in later chapters of this book. As you read, you will see specific speech-preparation activities that are related to each action step. By completing all of these activities, you will gain confidence in your ability to be effective when you give your speech.

Preparing a Narrative/Personal Experience Speech

Walter R. Fisher, a professor of communication at the University of Southern California, claims that human beings understand and interpret the world around us through storytelling.[34] He and others propose narrative theory as a primary way in which we make sense of the world around us, that is, through stories. The **narrative/personal experience speech** is a presentation in which you recount an experience or experiences you have had and the significance you attach to it or them. In it, you talk about the setting, characters, and events as they serve as "good reasons" for accepting a moral you deem important. A **moral** is simply a life lesson about right and wrong. This speech is an excellent opportunity for you to try out the basic speech preparation action steps we have

narrative/personal experience speech: a presentation in which you recount an experience or experiences you have had and the significance you attach to it or them

moral: a life lesson about right and wrong

Exhibit 2.5 An effective speech plan is the product of these six action steps

Goals

I. Select a speech goal that is appropriate to the rhetorical situation.

I. Select a speech goal that is appropriate to the rhetorical situation (Chapter 4).
   A. Brainstorm and concept map to select a topic you know something about and that is important to you.
   B. Analyze your audience to assess their familiarity with and interest in your topic.
   C. Consider how the occasion affects what is appropriate for you to talk about.
   D. Develop a speech goal statement tailored to your audience and the occasion.

Audience

II. Understand your audience and adapt to it.

II. Understand your audience and adapt to it (Chapter 5).
   A. Understand audience diversity.
   B. Understand audience initial interest in and attitude toward your topic.
   C. Adjust content to be appropriate for your audience's current understanding of, interest in, and attitude toward your topic.
   D. Determine how you will establish your credibility with your audience.

Research

III. Gather and evaluate information

III. Gather and evaluate information to use in the speech (Chapter 6).
   A. Examine what you know already about your topic and where you need additional information.
   B. Locate, evaluate, and select types and sources.
   C. Record relevant information on research cards.
   D. Cite sources.

Organization

IV. Organize and develop ideas into a well-structured outline.

IV. Organize and develop ideas into a well-structured outline (Chapters 7 and 8).
   A. Identify the two to four major ideas you want your audience to remember.
   B. Combine your speech goal with these major ideas to form a thesis statement with main point preview.
   C. Develop your main points.
   D. Develop and outline the speech body.
   E. Create an introduction that gets attention, establishes listener relevance and credibility, and states your thesis with main point preview.
   F. Create a conclusion that both summarizes your goal and main points and that leaves your audience with a vivid impression that provides a sense of closure.
   G. Compile a list of sources.
   H. Review and revise the outline as needed.

Presentational Aids

V. Choose, prepare, and use appropriate presentational aids.

V. Choose, prepare, and use appropriate presentational aids (Chapter 9).
   A. Consider visual or other presentational aids that will help clarify, emphasize, or dramatize what you say.
   B. Make sure your aids use another symbol system (beyond just words alone).
   C. Make sure your visual aids are large enough to be seen.
   D. Make sure your audio aids are loud enough to be heard in the back of the room.
   E. Plan when to use presentational aids and how to integrate them during the speech.

Delivery

VI. Practice oral language and delivery style.

VI. Practice oral language and delivery style (Chapters 10 and 11).
   A. Practice until the wording is accurate, clear, vivid, and appropriate.
   B. Practice until the delivery is intelligible, conversational, and expressive.
   C. Practice integrating presentational aids until you can do so confidently and smoothly.
   D. Continue practicing until you can deliver it extemporaneously within the time limit.

When Digital-Speak Won't Do

Stella Tripp, Fellowship Coordinator, Department of Medicine, Division of Cardiology, University of California, Los Angeles

Stella Tripp, 29, is naturally shy and would rather e-mail than talk—and even then to just one person. "I call it digital-speak. Even with e-mail, if a lot of people are copied, I'll often delete them and write only to the original sender." She's more comfortable in one-on-one settings.

Despite her shyness, Tripp communicates with and manages all the medical graduate students, or fellows, who are pursuing cardiology training at University of California, Los Angeles (UCLA). She meets with them twice a week to see that their training adheres to the guidelines of the Accreditation Council for Graduate Medical Education. "I maintain their portfolios—their training, the research they do, the presentations they make. I coordinate their schedules, the educational conferences they attend, their meetings. And I answer a lot of questions."

This sort of management requires effective communication skills, and Tripp certainly has them. But she still gets nervous asking senior physicians for clarifying information about, say, grant proposals that affect the graduate students. One of her greatest challenges is when the physicians send her the wrong paperwork or details. "I have difficulty talking to people so far above me, especially when I need to tell them they're incorrect about something. I don't feel like it's my place." To help overcome this challenge, she's developed strategies that help her reduce her anxiety and get the information she needs. For example, she

> "I was diligent about knowing everything I had to speak on. I couldn't feel unprepared."

might enhance her credibility by backing up her request with a more authoritative source. "Sometimes I'll ask my boss for advice and tell the doctors 'my boss advises . . . .' Or I might cite a [UCLA] website, maybe on grant policies."

Over time, Tripp has fine-tuned the public speaking skills she began acquiring in college. She earned her B.A. in sociology and black studies at the University of California, Santa Barbara. Although public speaking made her nervous, she was required to give presentations in some of her classes. She was careful to do the research she needed to do to feel prepared. "I was diligent about knowing everything I had to speak on. I couldn't feel unprepared [because, if] I got a question I didn't know the answer to, I froze." But she's learned that, although you want to be as fully prepared for your speech as possible, it's okay if you don't know *everything* about your topic. You can get back to audience members with more information later. "Now, in my job, if someone asks me something I don't know, I'll say so."

Whether she's asking for grant information, necessary data, or just the meaning of a particularly obscure medical acronym, Tripp has had to overcome her natural reticence. She has risen above many of her challenges by creating solutions that are comfortable for her and that encourage others to listen. "When I have trouble getting what I need from senior doctors, I have a method: be polite, thankful, and 'remindful'!"

just introduced. Let's look at how Danelle applied these steps to prepare her speech "Me and My Aunt Barb."

The first step is to develop a speech goal appropriate to the public speaking situation. For her narrative/personal experience speech assignment, Danelle considered several experiences but finally chose the story of her and her aunt Barb.

She knew that the speech would be for an audience of about fifteen classmates who were all traditional-age college students, that the assignment was a narrative/personal experience speech, and that the time limit was three to five minutes.

Her general goal was to inform. Specifically, Danelle wanted the audience to appreciate how her experiences with her aunt Barb as her babysitter shaped Danelle's morals.

Her strategy for audience adaptation included using personal pronouns and other means of creating common ground by telling about her personal experiences. She also planned to use main points and statements within them that would encourage listeners to relate.

Because it was a personal experience narrative, Danelle didn't need additional research; she only needed to reconstruct the details of the stories she would share about her experiences growing up with her aunt Barb.

Danelle began her speech with a description of her aunt Barb, then recounted the story of her aunt as her babysitter, and concluded by reinforcing the point of her story.

When you use narratives/personal experiences as a speech or in a speech, remember the following elements:

- A narrative has a point to it, usually a life lesson about right and wrong. Think carefully about the point of your story and make sure it is appropriate.

- A narrative is developed with supporting details that give background to and embellish the story so that the point has maximum effect. Be sure to describe the character(s), setting(s), and events with vivid details to which listeners can relate.

- Narrative drama can be increased by using dialogue. Dialogue gives an audience the experience of "being there" and increases their interest and involvement.

- Most narratives dramatize because they recount emotional incidents. They may be funny, tragic, or frightening, but effectively told personal experiences establish an emotional bond between speaker and audience.

Danelle enhanced her speech with two photographs she displayed using the multimedia projector and screen in the front of the room. The first was of her and her aunt Barb playing at the park when Danelle was a little girl. The second was a picture of her with her aunt Barb, which was taken at a recent family reunion. Danelle used clear and vivid language to tell her story. She also practiced her speech several times until she was comfortable with her ability to tell the story.

Reflect on Ethics
WHAT WOULD *YOU* DO?

FOOTBALL COACH FORCED TO RESIGN OVER INACCURATE RESUME

After taking the Georgia Tech football team to five straight bowl games and earning a 52–33 win-loss record there, George O'Leary was delighted to be selected as the new football coach at the University of Notre Dame. However, after admitting he lied on his resume, he resigned five days later.[35] O'Leary's resume claimed he had earned a master's degree in education from New York University in 1972 and that he was a three-time letter winner in football at the University of New Hampshire. In fact, O'Leary was a student at NYU but never earned a degree from there. In addition, he was on the football team at UNH, but he never played in a game.

He justified his lies by saying that "many years ago, as a young married father," he was pursuing his dream to become a college football coach and that these inaccuracies were never removed from his resume or biographical statement "in later years." Some said he did the right thing by resigning, because Notre Dame needs a coach they can trust—his actions must demonstrate honesty and loyalty. Others, like UNH football coach

Sean McDonnell, were "surprised and shocked that he had to resign because of something like this," claiming he "was a guy with great integrity."

1. What, if any, ethical principles did George violate and how?

2. Some people justify exaggerating, or even lying, on their resumes by saying that everybody does it. And if they don't also do it, they will hurt their chances of getting a good job. In fact, according to CareerBuilder.com, 38 percent of those surveyed admitted to embellishing their job responsibilities on their resumes, and 18 percent admitted to lying about their skill sets. Given these numbers, are the justifications reasonable? Why or why not?

3. If you believe stretching the truth is acceptable in certain circumstances, how far can you go before you cross the line into unacceptable behavior?

4. Do you think O'Leary should have resigned over this issue? Why or why not?

SPEECH ASSIGNMENT

Preparing a Narrative/Personal Experience Speech

Prepare a three- to five-minute narrative/personal experience speech. Think about experiences you have had that shaped your morals in some way.

NARRATIVE/PERSONAL EXPERIENCE SPEECH EVALUATION CHECKLIST

General Criteria

You can use this checklist to critique a narrative/personal experience speech that you hear in class. (You can also use it to critique your own speech.) As you listen to the speaker, consider what makes a speech effective. Then, answer the following questions.

Content

1. Did the speaker's narrative make an important point (moral of the story)? _____
2. Did the speaker provide sufficient details about the setting(s), character(s), and event(s)? _____
3. Did the speaker dramatize the story with dialogue or emotional incidents? ____
4. Did the speaker offer listener-relevance links? _____
5. Did the speech fall within the time constraints of the assignment? _____

Structure

1. Did the speech provide all the basic elements of an effective speech: introduction, body, conclusion, and transitions? *(macrostructure)* _____
2. Did the introduction catch the audience's interest? _____ state the goal of the speech? _____ preview the main points of the speech? _____
3. Were transitions provided between each main point? _____
4. Did the conclusion remind the audience of the main points? _____ motivate the audience to remember the main points of the speech? _____
5. Did the speaker use words that were accurate and clear? _____ vivid and emphatic? _____ appropriate and inclusive? *(microstructure)* _____

Delivery

1. Was the speaker's voice intelligible? _____ conversational? _____ expressive? _____
2. Did the speaker look up from his or her notes most of the time and make eye contact with the audience? _____
3. Did the speaker use appropriate facial expressions to convey emotion? _____
4. Did the speaker use appropriate gestures to reinforce important points? _____
5. Did the speaker appear to be poised and confident? _____

CourseMate You can use your CourseMate for *Challenge* to access this checklist, complete it online and compare your feedback to that of the authors, or print a copy to use in class.

Summary

This chapter discusses public speaking apprehension, how careful preparation can help you develop confidence when you speak in public, and how to prepare a narrative/personal experience speech.

Public speaking apprehension is the level of fear a person experiences when speaking. Symptoms include cognitive, physical, and emotional reactions that vary from person to person. The level of apprehension varies over the course of speaking. The root of apprehension, negative self-talk, has three causes: biologically based temperament, previous experience, and level of skill.

Several methods are available for managing public speaking apprehension. General methods include communication orientation motivation (COM) techniques, visualization, relaxation, systematic desensitization, cognitive restructuring, and public speaking skills training. Specific techniques include allowing sufficient time to prepare, using presentational aids, practicing the speech aloud, dressing up, choosing an appropriate time to speak, using positive self-talk, facing the audience with confidence, and focusing on sharing your message.

Gaining confidence through effective speech planning reduces public speaking apprehension and increases speaking effectiveness. An effective speech plan is the product of six action steps. The first step is to select a speech goal that is appropriate to the rhetorical situation. The second step is to understand your audience and adapt to it. The third step is to gather and evaluate information to use in the speech. The fourth step is to organize and develop ideas into a well-structured outline. The fifth step is to choose appropriate presentational aids. And the sixth step is to practice oral language and delivery style of the speech until you sound confident and fluent.

A good opening assignment is a narrative/personal experience speech in which you recount an experience you have had and the significance you attach to it. A narrative is a speech told in story form that makes an important point (moral) and is developed with supporting details about the setting, characters, and events.

Challenge Resource and Assessment Center

CourseMate Now that you have read Chapter 2, use your Speech Communication CourseMate for *The Challenge of Public Speaking* for quick access to the electronic resources that accompany this text. These resources include:

- **Study tools** that will help you assess your learning and prepare for exams (*digital glossary, key term flash cards, review quizzes*).

- **Activities and assignments** that will help you hone your knowledge and build your public speaking skills throughout the course (*Speech Snippets, Speech Assignments, Action Step Activities*). Many of these activities allow you to compare your answers with those provided by the authors, and, if requested, submit your answers to your instructor.

- **Media resources** that will help you explore communication concepts online (*Web Resources*), develop your speech outlines (*Speech Builder Express 3.0*), watch and critique videos of sample speeches (*Interactive Video Activities*), upload your speech videos for peer reviewing and critique other students' speeches (*Speech Studio online speech review tool*), and download chapter reviews so you can study when and where you'd like (*Audio Study Tools*).

This chapter's application activities and video resource are featured in this end-of-chapter section.

Applying What You've Learned

1. **Impromptu Speech Activity:** Identify a character from the *Peanuts* comic strip who communicates either ethically or unethically toward Charlie Brown. Prepare a two- to three-minute narrative speech explaining why. Be sure to tell your story with details about the setting, the characters, and the event(s) that support the life lesson or moral of your story.

2. **Assessment Activity A:** Practice a calming sigh to reduce anxiety right before you get up to give your speech. (1) Inhale deeply but gently through your nose. (2) Slowly let the air out while saying "Ahhhh." (3) Let your body go limp for a couple of moments. (4) Repeat. Do you feel more relaxed as you get up to speak?

3. **Assessment Activity B:** Prepare and practice your personal cognitive restructuring by following this five-step process. (1) Create your own negative self-talk list by writing down four or five fears that come to mind when you know you must give a speech. (2) Identify why that fear is irrational, that is, how you're blowing it out of proportion. (3) Create a positive self-talk statement to replace each negative one. (4) Place these statements on a small notecard you can keep in your pocket or wallet. (5) Practice your positive self-talk statements daily until they become second nature.

Web Resources

2.1 Visualizing Your Success (25)

2.2 Restructure Your Expectations (27)

Video Resource

1. Use Speech Studio to upload a video of your own narrative/personal experience speech for feedback from your instructor and classmates. Or search for other students' narrative speeches—do their speeches give you ideas for how you could make your speech more effective?

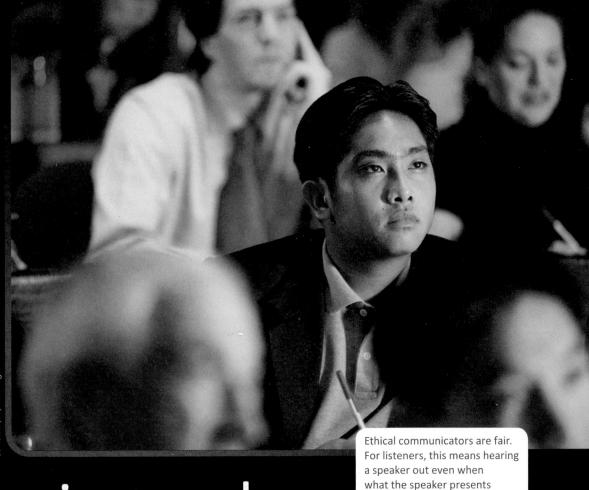
Comstock/Jupiter Images

3

listening and responding effectively

Ethical communicators are fair. For listeners, this means hearing a speaker out even when what the speaker presents contradicts what you believe.

What's the Point?

QUESTIONS YOU'LL BE ABLE TO ANSWER AFTER READING THIS CHAPTER:

1. Why is it important to study listening in a public speaking course?

2. What is the difference between listening and hearing?

3. What are five different types of listening?

4. What strategies can you employ to improve your listening skills?

5. How can you constructively critique speeches you hear?

As Ms. Fisher finished her remarks about improving restaurant service, she said, "And remember, the goal is to encourage customers to perceive their overall dining experience positively, not to move in and out too quickly. Return business is what is most important for success."

As Brady, Jill, and Max were leaving the workshop, Brady said, "I was glad to hear that Ms. Fisher recognized the importance of moving customers in and out quickly."

"That wasn't her point," said Jill. "She said that return business is the goal."

"I'm sure she emphasized efficiency," responded Brady. "Max, what do you think she said?"

"I don't have a clue. I was thinking about how I'm going to pay rent tomorrow because it cost a lot more to repair my car than I thought it would."

Does this conversation sound familiar? Have you had times when you'd swear that you heard right when you didn't? If your answer is "Not me," then we congratulate you, for this example illustrates two of the three most common listening problems: hearing what was said but misunderstanding, not remembering what was said, and missing what was said.

Recall that communication is the process of creating shared meaning. For communication to be effective, the *speaker* must present the message clearly and compellingly. Equally important, however, is that the *listener* understands and accurately remembers what was said.

Obviously, before you can listen, you must first hear what is said. Although listening depends on hearing, the two are not the same. **Hearing** is simply the biological process that occurs when the brain detects sound waves. Sometimes people do not hear well, for example, when a person is deaf or hard of hearing or when the messages are transmitted at a very low volume or when external interference/noise competes for the brain's attention—such as a passing fire engine or someone talking on a cell phone.

In contrast to hearing, listening occurs after the brain has detected the sound waves and is sorting out what those waves mean. According to the International Listening Association, "**Listening** is the process of receiving, attending to, constructing meaning from, and responding to spoken or nonverbal messages."[1] Listening is important because, of our time spent communicating, 50 percent or more is spent listening.[2] Although all of us have spent a great deal of time learning to read and write, fewer than 2 percent of us have had any formal listening training.[3] In fact, even when they try to listen carefully, most people remember only about 50 percent of what they hear shortly after hearing it and only about 25 percent two days later.[4]

Yet effective listening is a key to success in most occupations. One survey of top-level North American executives revealed that 80 percent believe listening is one of the most important skills needed in the corporate environment.[5] Frankly, listening skill (or lack thereof) is often at the root of company success or failure. To clarify, when employees fail to listen effectively to instructions,

hearing: the biological process that occurs when the brain detects sound waves

listening: the process of receiving, attending to, constructing meaning from, and responding to spoken or nonverbal messages they usually make mistakes. Mistakes cost the organization time and money. And when supervisors don't listen effectively to employees when they share concerns about potential problems or their creative ideas and solutions, again, the result may be lost time and money. Results of one huge study of more than 6,000 organizational crisis events revealed that, in nearly every instance, employees and others had warned management repeatedly about potential problems. Had management listened effectively, the crises may have been avoided.[6] And, of course, when the employees of a company do not listen and respond to customers, they are bound to fail. So it simply makes sense to improve listening skills.

To be an effective communicator, you must understand and practice effective listening skills. During this course, you might give as many as six speeches, but you will probably listen to more than sixty. As you listen, you can practice the skills you learn in this chapter.

In this chapter, we discuss five different types of listening, how you can improve your listening skills, and guidelines for providing a constructive and ethical speech critique.

Types of Listening

Although we spend most of the time we are communicating listening, the type of listening we engage in varies based on the situation. So in order to be an effective listener in different situations, you must consider your purpose for listening. Scholars have identified five types of listening based on five different purposes.[7] Each type requires a different degree of psychological processing.

In an **appreciative listening** situation, your goal is simply to enjoy the thoughts and experiences of others. You do not have to focus as closely on specifics as you do in other listening situations. When we listen to music for enjoyment and to speakers because we like their style, we are engaged in appreciative listening. In a **discriminative listening** situation, your goal is to understand the speaker's meaning conveyed in other ways than the words themselves, for example, nonverbal cues such as rate, pitch, inflection, and gestures. So when a doctor is explaining the results of a test, a patient listens carefully not only to what the doctor is saying but also to the nonverbal cues that indicate whether the results are troubling or routine. In a **comprehensive listening** situation, your goal is to understand, remember, and recall what has been said. We listen comprehensively, for example, to professors giving lectures, speakers at training seminars, and television broadcasters projecting weather forecasts. In an **empathic listening** situation, your goal is to be a sounding board to help another sort through feelings. We listen empathically, for example, when we listen to a close friend grieve over the death of a loved one. Finally, in a **critical listening** situation, your ultimate goal is to evaluate the worth of a message. When we listen to salespeople trying to convince us that their brand is better than the others, we are listening critically. Because you need to hear, understand, evaluate, and assign worth to the message, as well as remember and recall it, critical listening requires more psychological processing than the others. We turn now to some techniques you can employ to improve your listening skills in both face-to-face and virtual settings.

appreciative listening: your goal is to enjoy the thoughts and experiences of others

discriminative listening: your goal is to understand the speaker's meaning conveyed in other ways than the words themselves

comprehensive listening: your goal is to understand, remember, and recall what was said

empathic listening: your goal is to be a sounding board to help another sort through feelings

critical listening: your goal is to evaluate the worth of a message

Improving Your Listening Skills

Effective listening is a complex psychological process made up of five steps. These steps are attending, understanding, remembering, evaluating, and responding to the message (see Exhibit 3.1 on page 45). In this section, we offer some techniques for improving your skills related to each step.

Peanuts: 2010 Peanuts Worldwide LLC., dist. UFS., Inc.

Effective listeners attend to the speaker by getting physically ready to listen, resisting distractions, hearing the speaker out, and identifying benefits of focusing on the speaker's message.

Attending

attending: paying attention to what the speaker is saying regardless of extraneous interference

Attending is paying attention to what the speaker is saying regardless of extraneous interferences. Poor listeners have difficulty exercising control over what they attend to, often letting their mind drift to thoughts totally unrelated to the speech. One reason for this stems from the fact that people typically speak at a rate of about 120 to 150 words per minute, but our brains can process between 400 and 800 words per minute.[8] This means we usually assume we know what a speaker is going to say before he or she finishes saying it. That gives our minds time to wander from the message. Remember Max's response to the question of which interpretation was more on target: *"I don't have a clue. I was thinking about how I'm going to pay rent tomorrow because it cost a lot more to repair my car than I thought it would."*

Not only does the gap between speaking rate and processing create opportunities for inattention, but research suggests that the average attention span for adults today is twenty minutes or less.[9] Some reports even claim that, thanks to the Internet, satellite TV, DVR, and smart phone technology, our attention spans have become considerably shorter.[10] Consider your own experiences listening to speeches, class lectures, and other extended presentations. Do you ever find yourself daydreaming, reading a text message, or checking e-mail or Facebook? Do you find yourself multitasking in similar ways when participating in a teleconference, webinar, or other online presentation? If you want to find out how long your attention span is, go to your CourseMate for *Challenge* to access **Web Resource 3.1: Attention Span Self-Test**.

To be an effective listener, then, you need to train yourself to focus on what people are saying regardless of potential distractions. Let's consider four techniques for doing so.

1. **Get physically ready to listen.** Good listeners create a physical environment that reduces potential distractions and adopt a listening posture. For example, you might turn off background music, your cell phone, and your computer so you won't be tempted to turn your attention to them when you are trying to listen. You can also adopt a listening posture by sitting upright in your chair, leaning slightly forward, stopping any random physical movement, and looking directly at the speaker or screen.[11]

2. **Resist mental distractions while you listen.** Block out wandering thoughts when they creep into your head while you listen. These thoughts may stem from a visual distraction (such as someone entering the room while the speaker is talking), an auditory distraction (such as people chatting beside you during a speech), or a physical distraction associated with body aches, pains, or discomfort (such as wondering what you'll eat for lunch because your stomach is growling). Consciously attending to these mental distractions will help you focus on the message and improve your listening skill.

3. **Suspend judgment while you hear the speaker out.** Far too often, we let a person's mannerisms and words "turn us off." If you find yourself upset by a speaker's ideas on gay marriage, abortion, or any controversial topic, instead of tuning out or getting ready to argue, work that much harder to listen objectively so that you can understand the speaker's position before you react.

At the 2009 MTV Video Music Awards, Kanye West jumped on stage while Taylor Swift was delivering her acceptance speech and interrupted her by saying, "Yo, Taylor. I'm happy for ya. I'm gonna let you finish. But Beyonce had one of the best videos of all time. One of the best videos of all time."[12] Many have offered their opinions about how West was an unethical communicator at that moment because he violated the ethical principle of demonstrating respect for others. Similarly, many have commented about how Swift and Beyonce reacted to the situation ethically because they adhered to that same principle. West has retorted that his actions were okay because he was adhering to the ethical principle of honesty—he believed he was telling the truth. One commenter, "Down n TX," posted a comment on Alison Bonaguro's CMT blog that he or she wished Swift had hit West over the head with the award. Another commenter, "Bree," said "As for Pink, and all the other celebs bad-mouthing Kanye, more power to you!! What he did was cold, and he deserves everything he's gonna get."

1. How would you respond to West's contention?
2. Do you support Down n TX's and Bree's reactions? Why or why not?
3. What advice would you give to someone who disagreed as vehemently as West did to a public message?

Likewise, even when a speaker uses language that is offensive to you, you need to persevere and not be distracted. If we are not careful, we may become distracted when a speaker mumbles, stumbles over words, or fumbles with his or her notes. We need to focus instead on what is being said to be effective listeners.

4. **Identify the benefits of attending to the speaker's words.** At times, we do this almost automatically, especially when your professor says something like, "Pay attention to this because it will be on the test." But you can also provide your own motivation. As you listen, ask yourself why and how you might use the information to improve some aspect in your own life, for instance, to help you solve a work-related problem or to improve personally.

Understanding and Remembering

Understanding is the ability to assign accurate meaning to what was said. Sometimes we may not fully understand a speaker's message because the speaker uses words that are not in our vocabulary or discusses complex technical concepts that are new to us, and sometimes we might miss the emotional intent of the message. **Remembering** is being able to retain and recall information we have heard. Sometimes we have difficulty remembering because we fail to realize personal relevance while the message is being communicated. We can also have difficulty remembering because we are bombarded with so many messages all the time every day. Let's consider five listening techniques that can help you understand and remember the messages you hear.

understanding: the ability to assign accurate meaning to what was said

remembering: being able to retain and recall information we have heard

Ethical listeners demonstrate respect for others by refraining from texting, answering e-mails, or chatting with others during a speech.

1. **Determine the speaker's organization.** Determining the organization helps you establish a framework for understanding and remembering the information.[13] In any extended message, an effective speaker has an overall organizational macrostructure, which includes a goal, main points that develop the goal, and details that develop each main point. Effective listeners mentally (or physically) outline the

i love images/Jupiter Images

organization so that, when the speech is over, they can cite the goal, the main points, and some of the key details.

For instance, during a PTA meeting, Gloria Minton, a teacher, gives a short presentation on the problem of bullying. Her goal is to explain what can be done in school to deter this behavior. In her speech, she presents two main ideas: what teachers can do and what students who are harassed can do. She gives examples, statistics, and specific recommendations to develop each of the points she makes. When she is finished, audience members who have listened carefully can remember her goal and state steps that both teachers and harassed students can take even though they may not remember the specific examples and statistics that she used to develop each point. To be an effective listener, ask yourself, "What does the speaker want me to know or do?" (goal); then ask, "What are each of the main points?"; and finally ask, "What details explain or support each of the main points?"

2. **Ask questions.** Although ethical listeners demonstrate respect by waiting until the speaker is finished to ask questions, you can make notes of any questions you have as you listen. Some of these questions may eventually be answered as the speaker moves through the presentation. However, others may not. Then, you can pose these remaining questions during the question-and-answer period following the presentation, privately approach the speaker after the presentation, or use the questions to do additional research about the topic yourself later.

3. **Silently paraphrase key information.** A **paraphrase** is putting into your own words the meaning you have assigned to a message. It is not simply repeating what has been said. After you have listened to a message, you should be able to summarize your understanding of it. So, after the speaker explains the criteria for selecting the best cell phone plan, you might say to yourself, "In other words, the key to deciding whether an unlimited plan is cost effective depends on how many minutes I'm likely to spend talking on the phone each month."

4. **Observe nonverbal cues.** We interpret messages more accurately when we observe the nonverbal behaviors that accompany the words. Good speakers use their tone of voice, facial expressions, and gestures to emphasize important points and clarify structure. You can improve your listening skills by noticing where and how the speaker is attempting to emphasize or clarify points and then keying in on those comments.

5. **Take good notes.** Note taking is a powerful method for improving your memory of what you have heard in a speech. Not only does note taking provide a written record that you can go back to, but also by taking notes, you take a more active role in the listening process.[14, 15]

What constitutes good notes varies by situation. For a short speech, good notes may consist of a statement of the goal, a brief list of main points, and a few of the most significant details. For a lengthy and rather detailed presentation, good notes will also include more detailed statements of supporting material, as well as questions that arise while listening. Review the basics of effective listening and note taking by going to your CourseMate for *Challenge* to access **Web Resource 3.2: Effective Listening and Note Taking**.

CourseMate

Evaluating and Responding

Evaluating is critically analyzing what is said to determine its truthfulness, utility, and trustworthiness. Critical analysis is especially important when the speaker expects you to believe, support, or act on what was said. If you don't critically analyze what you hear, you risk going along with ideas that violate your values. **Responding** is providing feedback to the speaker about what is being said. Responding to a speech usually occurs nonverbally through behaviors, such as smiling, nodding one's head in agreement, and applauding after the speaker finishes, though in some cultures audience members may give short verbal responses, as well. Sometimes, however, you need to prepare a formal written evaluation, or critique, of a presentation by a classmate, colleague, or employee. Typically, a critique is based on your critical analysis of how well the speech and speaker performed on specific key criteria.

Preparing a Constructive Critique

A **constructive critique** is an analysis of a presentation that evaluates how well a speaker meets a specific speaking goal while following the norms for good speaking and that recommends how the presentation could be improved. Essentially, a critique allows you to provide a speaker with *meaningful* feedback. Constructive critiques follow four guidelines.

First, effective critiques communicate specific observations. Comments like "great job" or "slow down" are too vague to truly help a speaker improve. Instead, describe specific things the speaker did to make you conclude that the speech was great. For example, did she use transitions in a way that helped you follow her train of thought? Or point out specific places where you would have liked the speaker to present the material at a slower pace.

constructive critique: an analysis of a speech or presentation that evaluates how well a speaker meets a specific speaking goal while following the norms for good speaking and that recommends how the presentation could be improved

Exhibit 3.1 Effective and ineffective listening behaviors

	Effective listening behavior	Ineffective listening behavior
Attending to the speech	Physically and mentally focusing on what is being said, even when information doesn't seem relevant	Seeming to listen but looking out the window and letting your mind wander
	Adjusting listening behavior to the specific requirements of the situation	Listening the same way regardless of type of material
Understanding/ remembering speech information	Determining organization by identifying goals, main points, and supporting information	Listening to individual bits of information without regard for structure
	Asking yourself questions to help you identify key aspects of the speech	Seldom or never reconsidering what was said
	Silently paraphrasing to solidify understanding	Seldom or never paraphrasing
	Seeking out subtle meanings based on nonverbal cues	Ignoring nonverbal cues
	Taking good notes	Relying on memory alone
Evaluating and Responding	Assessing quality of content, structure, and delivery	Relying on gut reactions

Second, effective critiques begin with observations about what a speaker did well before turning to observations about what the speaker could do better. Begin with positive observations so that you reinforce what the speaker did well. When we are reinforced for what we have done, we are more likely to continue doing it. By the same token, there is room for improvement in any speech. Because the goal of a critique is to help the speaker improve, describe the specific problems you observe in the speech and then offer suggestions for overcoming them.

Third, effective critiques follow observation statements with explanations about how and why the observed behavior affected the speech. For example, if you suggest that the speaker slow down while previewing the speech's main points, your statement will be more helpful if you also explain that the speaker's rate did not allow the audience time to remember the points.

Finally, effective critiques are phrased so that it's clear they reflect your personal perceptions, not "truth." You can ensure this by using "I" rather than "you" language. For example, instead of using "you" language to say, "You need to slow down," use "I" language. For example, "During the preview of main points, I had trouble listening because they were presented faster than I could understand and remember them."

A Blend of Business and Friendship

Saejean Oh, Artist
Los Angeles, California

Saejean Oh, 22, is a recent graduate of the Art Center College of Design in Pasadena, California. She has a BFA degree in Illustration. Like many artists, Oh feels she isn't suited to an office environment. She'd much rather live a freelance life and dictate her own schedule.

One of the challenges she's had to deal with in her personal life is her shyness, especially in today's world of professional art, which is all about making contacts and marketing yourself. "It's a myth about the artist being Van Gogh hiding in his studio—or, today, hiding online. You have to get out there, go to gallery shows, talk about your work." She knew she'd have to push her work and make a name for herself, but her shyness prevented her from taking a public speaking class in school. Nonetheless, her college experiences provided the lessons she needed to survive in the art industry. "I learned not to be intimidated by others. I think of them as peers. Networking opportunities [in the art world consist of] hanging out and making friends. The art world is a blend between business and friendship."

Her college experience also gave her multiple opportunities to speak before her peers. These speaking

> **"Just being objective opens up a dialogue—there's room for connection with people."**

opportunities helped her learn to accept critique. "We continually had group critique sessions. We set up our work in real-life situations, the way we wanted people to view it. In the beginning I was *very* nervous." But these opportunities allowed Oh to discover a comfortable way of communicating. "Beforehand I would run through the process in my head. I'd be clear about my intent, deciding what I wanted to convey, [such as] why I used a certain color." When it was her turn to speak, she made an effort to be honest and try to connect with people. "I'd talk about the positive first, then talk about the negative objectively. Just being objective opens up a dialogue—there's room for connection with people."

These experiences taught Oh an important lesson about public speaking and life in general: "It's okay if you're not the best. You don't have to be perfect. You'll do better if you don't have that pressure on you." Rather, she says, "be well rounded. Be aware of what's going on in the world. Keep educating yourself—*especially* after you're out of school, when you have to be self-motivated. Keep learning!"

Content of Constructive Critiques

A constructive critique offers observations about a speech's content, structure, and delivery. Comments on content focus on *what* the speaker said and an analysis of the topic and supporting material. For example, you might comment on how effectively the speaker used reasoning, or you might comment on the breadth and depth of the information used to develop each main idea. You might observe how relevant, recent, or credible the speaker's evidence seemed to be. Exhibit 3.2 illustrates ineffective and effective constructive critique comments regarding content.

Exhibit 3.2 Ineffective and effective comments about the content of a narrative/personal experience speech

Ineffective	Effective
• Interesting stories.	• I liked the story about your trip to the carnival. The many details you provided made it sound really fun!
• Too short.	• I would have liked to hear another example for each main point. This would have helped me better understand why the carnival was so significant to you.

Comments on structure may be addressed to both the overall organization (macrostructure) and wording (microstructure) of the speech. You might provide feedback on the clarity of the speaker's goal, transitions, summary, or ordering of main ideas. You might also talk about the speaker's language and style choices. Exhibit 3.3 offers some examples of ineffective and effective constructive critique comments regarding structure.

Exhibit 3.3 Ineffective and effective comments about the structure of a narrative/personal experience speech

Ineffective	Effective
• Nice transitions.	• Your transitions reminded me of the main point.
• Boring introduction.	• Because you finished one main point and introduced the upcoming main point in your transition. I found it easy to follow your ideas.
	• I would have tuned in to the speech more quickly if you had begun with a great story about the carnival to capture my attention before stating your thesis.

Comments on delivery focus on how the speaker used his or her voice and body. In commenting on voice, you might consider how intelligible, conversational, and emotionally expressive the speaker was. You may also comment on the speaker's use of body, poise, gestures, facial expressions, and eye contact. Consider if the speaker's mannerisms distracted you from the speech's message or enhanced it. Comment on the specific behaviors that contributed to your opinion of the speaker's use of body. Exhibit 3.4 provides a couple of examples of ineffective and effective constructive critique comments regarding delivery.

Exhibit 3.4 Ineffective and effective comments about the delivery of a narrative/personal experience speech

Ineffective	Effective
• Great gestures!	• I really liked how you gestured while you stated your transitions. It made it even clearer to me that we were moving to the next main point.
• Slow down.	• When you previewed your main points, you were speaking so quickly that I didn't catch them. For me, it would be helpful if you had spoken more slowly so I could have processed the main points. That way, I would have followed along better throughout the speech.

Certainly, you can help other speakers improve by offering effective constructive critiques. You can also help yourself by completing a self-critique after each speech you give using the same approach you use to critique others. Begin by noting one or two specific things you did well in terms of content, structure, and delivery. Then, consider one thing you'll focus on improving for your next speech. This self-critique approach is actually a form of cognitive restructuring that can help reduce your anxiety because it forces you to temper negative self-talk with positive self-talk immediately after your speech. Exhibit 3.5 presents

Exhibit 3.5 General criteria for a constructive critique

1. **Content of the speech**
   - Does the speaker establish common ground and adapt the content to the audience's interests, knowledge, and attitudes?
   - Does the speaker seem to have expertise in the subject areas?
   - Does the speaker have high-quality sources for the information given in the speech?
   - Does the speaker reveal the sources of the information?
   - Are the sources relevant? recent? varied? distributed throughout the speech?
   - Does the information presented explain or support each of the main points?
   - Are presentational aids appropriate and well used?
   - Is each main point supported with breadth? depth? listener relevance?

2. **Structure of the speech**
   - Does the introduction of the speech get attention, establish listener relevance and credibility, and lead into the topic?
   - Has the speaker stated a clear goal for the speech?
   - Are the main points of the speech clearly stated, parallel, and meaningful?
   - Do transitions lead smoothly from one point to another?
   - Does the information presented explain or support each of the main points?
   - Does the speaker use language that is appropriate, accurate, clear and vivid?
   - Does the speaker use a compelling style?
   - Does the conclusion summarize the main points and end with a clincher?

3. **Delivery of the speech**
   - Does the speaker sound intelligible? conversational? expressive?
   - Is the presentation fluent?
   - Does the speaker look at the audience?
   - Does the speaker use appropriate facial expressions?
   - Were the pronunciation and articulation acceptable?
   - Does the speaker have good posture?
   - Does the speaker have sufficient poise?

a list of general criteria that you may draw upon when preparing a constructive critique. You can use these criteria as a starting point for giving feedback to a speaker or critiquing your own speech.

As we will see later in this text, there are additional aspects of content, delivery, and structure you will want to consider in your constructive critique. We will provide additional criteria in speech-specific checklists you can use to evaluate each type of speech you study in this text. These customized critique sheets will include the primary criteria (specific skills) your instructor is expecting speakers to demonstrate in the particular speech as well as general criteria in Exhibit 3.5, skills that speakers will attempt to meet in all speeches.

SPEECH EVALUATION CHECKLIST

General Criteria Checklist for Providing Constructive Critique

_____ 1. Did you offer specific comments about your observations? (Consider what, where, and how.)

_____ 2. Did you begin with observations about what the speaker did well, reinforcing positive behavior?

_____ 3. Did you offer specific suggestions for what the speaker could do to improve? (Consider what, where, and how.)

_____ 4. Did you provide an explanation for each comment you made?

_____ 5. Did you focus on the *speech,* using "I" language to phrase each statement as a personal perception?

_____ 6. Did you avoid focusing on the *speaker personally* and avoid using "you" language, which can sound like a personal attack?

SPEECH ASSIGNMENT

Preparing a Constructive Critique

CourseMate Use your CourseMate for *Challenge* to access and watch Tiffany's speech, "Meat Free and Me." Prepare a constructive critique of this speech, using the general criteria offered in this chapter. Be sure to offer specific comments about positive aspects of the speech, provide specific suggestions for improvement, explain your observations, and use nonthreatening "I" language.

Summary

Listening is the process of receiving, attending to, constructing meaning from, and responding to spoken or nonverbal messages. Scholars have identified five different types of listening based on five different purposes. These are appreciative, discriminative, comprehension, empathic, and critical listening. Effective listening is an active process that requires the skills of attending, understanding, remembering, evaluating, and responding.

The process of attending to a message is sharpened by getting ready to listen, resisting mental distractions while you listen, hearing the speaker out regardless of your thoughts or feelings, and identifying benefits of attending to the speaker.

Understanding and remembering are enhanced by determining the speaker's organization, asking questions, silently paraphrasing, paying attention to nonverbal cues, and taking good notes.

Evaluating is the process of critically analyzing how truthful, useful, and trustworthy you judge a speaker and the speaker's information to be. Critical analysis requires you to judge the quality of the content, structure, and delivery of the speech.

In public speaking situations, effective listeners respond nonverbally in the form of smiles, head nods, and applause, as well as verbally by critiquing the speeches of others. Because overall speaking effectiveness is complex, effective critics base their evaluation on how well the speaker meets the specific criteria related to the type of speech that has been given. Constructive critiques cite specific strengths of speeches, suggest ways in which speakers can improve, provide clear explanations of observations, and use nonthreatening "I" language.

Challenge Resource and Assessment Center

CourseMate Now that you have read Chapter 3, use your Speech Communication CourseMate for *The Challenge of Effective Speaking* for quick access to the electronic resources that accompany this text. These resources include:

- **Study tools** that will help you assess your learning and prepare for exams (*digital glossary, key term flash cards, review quizzes*).
- **Activities and assignments** that will help you hone your knowledge and build your public speaking skills throughout the course (*Speech Snippets, Speech Assignments, Action Step*

Activities). Many of these activities allow you to compare your answers with those provided by the authors, and, if requested, submit your answers to your instructor.

- **Media resources** that will help you explore communication concepts online (*Web Resources*), develop your speech outlines (*Speech Builder Express 3.0*), watch and critique videos of sample speeches (*Interactive Video Activities*), upload your speech videos for peer reviewing and critique other students' speeches (*Speech Studio online speech review tool*), and download chapter reviews so you can study when and where you'd like (*Audio Study Tools*).

This chapter's application activities and video resources are featured in this end-of-chapter section.

1. **Impromptu Speech Activity:** Consider the last time you listened to music. Prepare and present a two- to three-minute impromptu speech describing the situation, the type of listening you engaged in, and what you remember about the song(s) you heard.

2. **Assessment Activity A:** Dale Carnegie once said "You can make more friends in two months by becoming interested in other people than you can in two years by trying to get other people interested in you."[16] Try this experiment at your workplace: Ask a coworker his or her opinion about something and really listen to the response. Follow up with a "why" or "how" question, and really listen again. Write a short one- to two-page reflection paper about how you are received.

3. **Assessment Activity B:** Keep a log of three conversations you have with a friend, family member, or coworker. Try to limit how much talking you do. Keep the other person talking by asking "how" and "why" questions. Assess the experience in written form by answering the following questions: (a) How much of the conversations can you describe here? (b) Was it difficult to keep quiet? Why or why not? (c) Were you able to stay focused? If so, how? If not, why? (d) Do you think the other person noticed your efforts to listen rather than speak? Explain.

Web Resources

3.1   Attention Span Self-Test (42)

3.2   Effective Listening and Note Taking (44)

Video Resources

1. Use your Interactive Video Activities to watch, analyze, and see the transcript and outlines for Tiffany's speech, "Meat Free and Me."

2. Use Speech Studio to upload a video of an impromptu speech you've given in class for feedback from your instructor and classmates. Or search for other students' impromptu speeches—do their speeches give you ideas for how you could make your next impromptu speech more effective?

James Marshall/Documentary Value/Corbis

Ethical communicators demonstrate respect by selecting a speech goal that is appropriate for the audience and occasion.

4

selecting an appropriate speech goal

What's the Point?

QUESTIONS YOU'LL BE ABLE TO ANSWER AFTER READING THIS CHAPTER:

1. What strategies can you use to brainstorm for speech topics?

2. What should you consider about your audience when determining your speech goal?

3. How can you find out about your audience before giving your speech?

4. In what ways might the occasion for your speech influence your speech goal?

5. How should you phrase your specific speech goal?

Action STEP 1 Select a speech goal that is appropriate to the rhetorical situation.

A. Brainstorm and concept map for topics.

B. Analyze your audience.

C. Analyze the rhetorical situation.

D. Develop a speech goal statement tailored to your audience and the occasion.

Donna Montez is a marine biologist. She knows that her audience wants to hear her talk about marine biology, but she doesn't know what aspect of the topic she should focus on.

Romeo Brown has been invited to speak to a student assembly at the inner-city middle school he attended. He has a lot he could say to these students who are so much like him, but he really wants them to understand what they need to do now to have a shot at going to college.

Dan Wong is taking a public speaking class. His first speech is scheduled for two weeks from tomorrow. As of today, he doesn't have the foggiest idea what he is going to talk about.

In real-life settings, people are invited to speak because they have expertise on a particular subject or have some relationship to the audience. Nevertheless, choosing exactly what to speak about is usually left in the hands of the speaker. So, although Donna and Romeo may have an idea about what the audience expects, they, like Dan, will need to take the first action step, which is to determine a specific speech goal that is appropriate to the rhetorical situation.

You must determine your specific speech goal in light of the rhetorical situation, the reason your speech needs to be given (exigence). Recall from Chapter 1, and as Exhibit 4.1 reiterates, these circumstances include the speaker (you), the audience, and the occasion (the setting, including the purpose, audience, expectations, and location). Because the audience is a crucial component of the speaking situation, your specific speech goal must be based on **audience analysis**, the study of the intended audience for your speech, and **audience adaptation**, the process of tailoring your speech's information to the needs, interests, and expectations of your listeners. This step in the speech-making process is rooted in what communication scholars refer to as uncertainty reduction theory.[1] Of course, effective speakers continually adjust their analysis of their audience and adapt their speech accordingly throughout the speech-planning and speech-making process, but these steps begin at the point of determining your specific speech goal.

audience analysis: the study of the intended audience for your speech

audience adaptation: the process of tailoring your speech's information to the needs, interests, and expectations of your listeners

Exhibit 4.1 The rhetorical situation

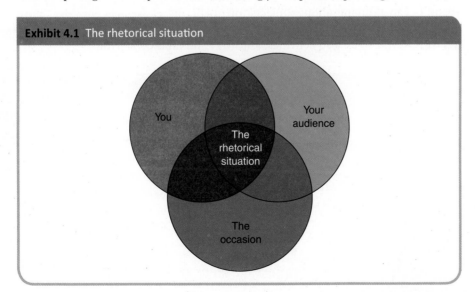

In this chapter, we explain each of the five substeps that help speakers determine a specific speech goal that is appropriate to the rhetorical situation. These five substeps are identifying possible topics, analyzing your audience, understanding the occasion, choosing a topic, and, finally, developing a specific speech goal statement. Although we discuss each task separately, in practice they overlap and can be completed in a different order.

Identifying Potential Topics

What do you know a lot about? What has interested you enough that you have gained some expertise in it? Our speech topics should come from subject areas in which we already have some knowledge and interest. What is the difference between a subject and a topic? A **subject** is a broad area of expertise, such as movies, renewable energy, computer technology, or the Middle East. A **topic** is a narrow, specific aspect of a subject. So, if your broad area of expertise is movies, you might feel qualified to speak on a variety of topics such as how the Academy Awards nomination process works; the relationships among movie producers, directors, and distributors; or how technology is changing movie production.

In this section, you will learn how to identify subject areas that interest you and then, from those subject areas, to identify and select potential specific topics that you can use for the speeches you will present.

subject: a broad area of expertise, such as movies, renewable energy, computer technology, or the Middle East

topic: some specific aspect of a subject

Listing Subjects

You can identify potential subjects for your speeches simply by listing those areas that (1) are important to you and (2) you know something about. These areas will probably include such things as your probable vocations or areas of formal study (major, prospective profession, or current job), your hobbies or leisure activities, and your special interests (social, economic, educational, or political concerns). So, if sales and marketing are your actual or prospective vocations, skateboarding and snowboarding are your favorite activities, and problems of illiteracy, substance abuse, and obesity are your special concerns, then these are subject areas from which you can identify topics for your speeches.

At this point, it is tempting to think, "Why not just talk on a subject I know an audience wants to hear about?" But in reality, all subject areas can interest an audience when speakers use their expertise or insight to enlighten the audience on a particular subject. If you speak on a topic that really interests you, you will find it easier to prepare for and be enthusiastic about presenting.

Exhibit 4.2 contains subjects that Holly, a beginning speech student, listed as she began thinking about subjects for upcoming class speeches. She chose to organize her subjects by using three broad headings: (1) major and career interests, (2) hobbies and activities, and (3) issues and concerns.

Exhibit 4.2 Holly's subject lists

Major and career interests	Hobbies and activities	Issues and concerns
teaching	social networking	endangered birds
website design	rowing	child pornography on the Internet and child abuse
information systems	Big Brothers Big Sisters organizations	personal privacy and the Internet
technology training	birding	water pollution
computer-aided design	photography	global warming

Gentle Dental Persuasion

Charlene Williams,
Dental Hygienist
Gentle Dental
Pasadena, California

For many people, the mere mention of going to the dentist—even for a routine cleaning—is frightening. And taking care of their teeth day to day seems unachievable. But a dental office in Pasadena, California, has changed those feelings for a lot of patients. Charlene Williams, 45, is the dental hygienist everyone wishes they had. Her approach with her patients is to assess her primary goal for their care. "I try not to make people feel bad. Nine out of ten patients aren't doing what they should, and they know it. Why make them feel bad? If I can get them to come in and see me twice a year, we've made progress."

Informing her patients about proper oral hygiene is an important part of Williams's job. She takes a holistic approach to this task, again considering her overall goal of persuading her patients to take better care of their teeth. "When I spend time learning about a person, I find out about their general health. What's going on in the whole body affects the mouth. If I know they're under stress or are diabetic, if I see bleeding or puffiness, I can communicate to the dentist better and also give the patient instructions on how to help that condition." She uses compassion and kindness to slowly move patients to good oral health. "Life isn't ideal. Not everybody wakes up and brushes and flosses and rinses. We have to be realistic. If they never floss, can I get them to do it two days a week? If they don't rinse, can I get them to go out and buy a bottle of mouthwash?"

> **It's challenging. You want to get the information out there accurately—you're impacting lives.**

Williams started out studying accounting at California State University, Fullerton, but after two years she switched her focus to get a two-year associate in science degree at Pasadena City College. She then passed the California State Board and got her Registered Dental Hygiene license. Her decision to pursue a different degree was mainly practical. "I couldn't get the courses I wanted. But I knew dental hygiene was something I was interested in."

In addition to working in the dental office with her patients, Williams gives educational presentations. She demonstrates oral hygiene in elementary schools to groups of twenty or thirty children, from kindergarten to sixth grade. "I use visual aids—charts, toothbrushes, pictures of teeth with grime. It's fun. The kids chew little color tablets that show them where plaque is hiding. My challenge is to make the terminology suitable to the age group. I tell them about the 'tooth bug' that can lead to cavities." Every year or two she also speaks at Pasadena City College's Women in Careers Day. "[The college opens its] doors to high school girls from all different backgrounds [who are] seeking education options. I talk about my education and career. It's challenging. You want to get the information out there accurately—you're impacting young girls' lives."

But Williams prefers the "intimate sessions" with her patients. "I'm more of a one-on-one person. And it's good for me. I benefit more than my patients. I learn so much."

Photo courtesy of Charlene Williams

Brainstorming for Topic Ideas

Recall that a topic is a specific aspect of a subject, so from one subject you can list numerous topics by **brainstorming**—an uncritical, nonevaluative process of generating associated ideas. When you brainstorm, you list as many ideas as you can without evaluating them. Brainstorming allows you to take advantage of the basic commonsense principle that just as it is easier to select a correct answer to a multiple-choice question than to think of the answer to the same question without the choices, so too is it easier to select a topic from a list than to come up with a topic out of the blue.

Holly decided she wanted to give a speech on the subject of birding. By brainstorming, she was able to come up with a list of possible topics that included: what is birding, how to identify birds, endangered birds, choosing and using binoculars for birding, keeping a bird list, and backyard birding. For practice brainstorming, go to your CourseMate for *Challenge* to access **Web Resource 4.1: Brainstorming**.

brainstorming: an uncritical, nonevaluative process of generating associated ideas

CourseMate

Concept Mapping for Topic Ideas

You can use concept mapping to identify specific topics and related areas. **Concept mapping** is a visual means of exploring connections between a subject and related ideas.[2] To generate connections, you might ask yourself questions about your subject, focusing on who, what, where, when, and how. Holly decided that she wanted to give her speech on the topic of endangered birds, but then she felt that even that topic was too broad, so she used concept mapping to help her further identify possible topics on endangered birds. In Exhibit 4.3, you can see an example of what Holly's concept map looked like. Notice how concept mapping allowed Holly to think more deeply about a general topic idea that she had brainstormed and develop several more specific topics that could be used in shorter speeches or in speeches with different audiences.

Speech Planning Action Step 1, Activity 1A will help you develop a list of topic ideas to use for your speeches in this course. See the Student Response box immediately following the activity for a sample of how one student completed this exercise.

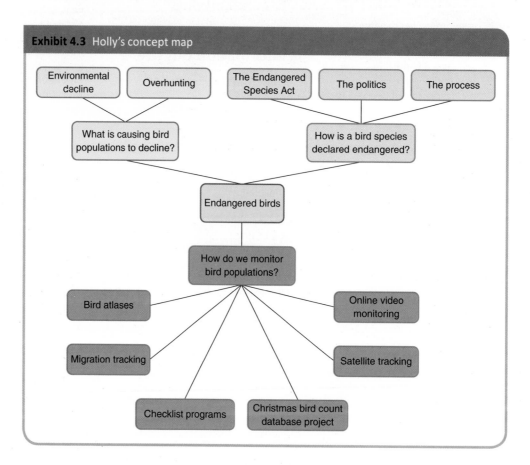

Exhibit 4.3 Holly's concept map

Analyzing the Audience

Because speeches are presented to a particular audience, before you can finally decide on your topic, you need to understand who will be in your prospective audience. Recall that audience analysis is the study of the intended audience for your speech. During your audience analysis, you will want to develop a demographic profile of your audience that includes age, gender, socioeconomic background, race, ethnicity, religion, geographic uniqueness, and language. You will also want to understand audience members' knowledge of and attitudes toward your topic. This information will help you choose from your topic list one that is appropriate for most audience members. You will use your audience analysis to tailor your speech to meet the needs, interests, and expectations of your listeners. To read an interesting article on the importance of careful audience analysis, go to your CourseMate for *Challenge* to access **Web Resource 4.2: Defining Your Audience**.

CourseMate

Types of Audience Data Needed

The first step in analyzing the audience is to gather audience demographic data and subject-specific information to determine in what ways audience members are similar to and different from you and from one another.

DEMOGRAPHIC AUDIENCE DATA

Helpful demographic information about your audience includes each member's age, education, gender, income, occupation, race, ethnicity, religion, geographic uniqueness, and language. It is also important to know about your audience members' level of knowledge and attitude toward your subject (see Exhibit 4.4 on page 59). You will use the demographic information you collect for several purposes.

First, demographic information helps you choose a specific topic and the main ideas you will present. The information you collect about your audience helps you make educated inferences about what they know about your subject area and what their attitudes are toward it. These inferences can then help you narrow your focus and choose an appropriate specific topic. For example, imagine that you want to talk about some aspect of the Internet, which is a very broad subject. Your audience analysis reveals that your audience is composed of college students, most of whom are under 21 years old, so you decide to talk about the dangers of blogging. You choose this topic based on the reasonable assumption that traditional-age college students are web savvy and understand what blogging is.

SPEECH PLANNING

ACTIVITY 1A

Action STEP 1

Using Brainstorming and Concept Mapping to Identify Speech Topics

The goal of this activity is to help you identify prospective topics for speeches.

1. Develop a subject list.
   a. Divide a sheet of paper into three columns. Label column 1 "major and career interests," label column 2 "hobbies and activities," and label column 3 "concerns and issues."
   b. Working on one column at a time, identify subjects of interest to you. Try to identify at least three subjects in each column.
   c. Place a check mark next to the one subject in each list that you would most enjoy speaking about.
   d. Keep the lists for future use in choosing a topic for an assigned speech.
2. For each subject you have checked, brainstorm a list of topics that relate to that subject.
3. Look at the topics you have brainstormed. In which do you have the most interest and expertise? Place a check mark beside one or two of these.
4. Then, for each item on the brainstorm list that you have checked, develop a concept map to identify smaller topic areas and related ideas that might be developed into future speeches.

CourseMate   You can go online to print a worksheet that will help you complete this activity. Go to your CourseMate for *Challenge* to access Action Step 1 Activity 1A.

Using Brainstorming and Concept Mapping to Identify Speech Topics

Step 1: Subject List

Major and career interests	Hobbies and activities	Issues and concerns
teaching	*tennis*	*literacy*
√ early childhood education	*√ volunteering*	*√ childcare*
curriculum development	*reading*	*abstinence education*
coaching	*soccer*	*obesity*
motherhood	*photography*	*cancer research funding*

Step 2: Brainstorm List for "Childcare"

parental care
family care
nannies
in-home group care
parent cooperatives
day care

Step 3: Concept Map for "Day Care"

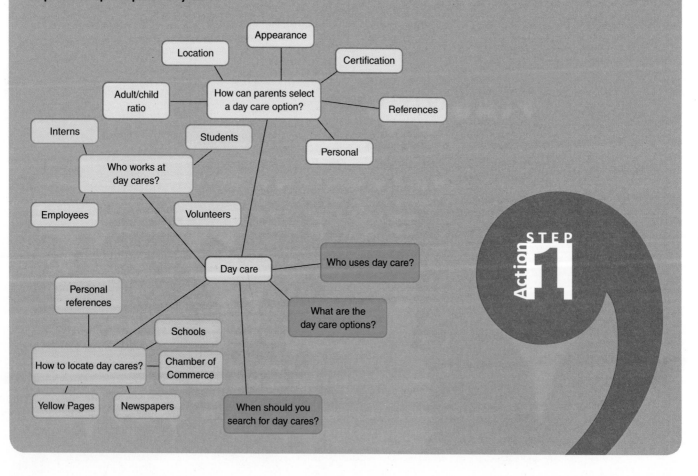

Second, demographic information can help you discover the ways in which your audience members are similar to and different from one another and from you. This information will help you tailor your speech to your audience. In planning your speech, it is just as important to recognize and adapt to differences as it is to acknowledge similarities. For example, while the majority of your classroom audience may be composed of traditional-age college students, you may have several audience members who are "nontraditional" students and somewhat older. If you begin your speech on the dangers of blogging with the assumption that everyone in the audience is familiar with blogging and base all your examples on today's youth culture, audience members who grew up in an earlier era may not understand your cultural references or be familiar with the practice of blogging.

Third, understanding who is in your audience will help later when you develop appropriate **listener-relevance links**, which are statements of how and why the ideas you offer are of interest to your listeners. If your audience research indicated that about half of your audience has blogged, a fourth have not blogged but have read blogs, and another fourth have never really seen a blog, then during your speech on the dangers of blogging, you would use listener-relevance links that were appropriate for both those who are savvy and those who aren't. So, for example, you might pique everyone's interest with this link: "If you have blogged, you may not be aware of the long-term potential dangers in this practice. And if you have not yet blogged, you probably know and care about someone who has. So what I am about to say might prevent you or someone you care about from making a costly mistake." Exhibit 4.4 presents a list of questions to answer when acquiring demographic information about an audience.

listener-relevance links: statements of how and why the ideas you offer are of interest to your listeners

SUBJECT-RELATED AUDIENCE DATA

Not only will you want to understand the demographic makeup of your audience, but you will also want to learn about the average knowledge level that your audience members have on your subject, their interest in the subject, their attitudes

---

Exhibit 4.4 Demographic audience analysis questions

Age. What is the age range of your audience, and what is the average age?

Education. What percentage of your audience has a high school, college, or postgraduate education?

Sex. What percentage of your audience is male? female?

Socioeconomic background. What percentage of your audience comes from high-, middle-, or low-income families?

Occupation. Is a majority of your audience from a single occupational group or industry, or do audience members come from diverse occupational groups?

Race. Are most members of your audience of the same race, or is there a mixture of races?

Ethnicity. What ethnic groups are in the audience? Are most audience members from the same cultural background?

Religion. What religious traditions are followed by audience members?

Geographic uniqueness. Are audience members from the same state, city, or neighborhood?

Language. What languages do a significant number of members of the audience speak as a first language? What language (if any) is common to all audience members?

Knowledge of subject. What can I expect the audience already knows about my subject? How varied is the knowledge level of audience members?

Attitude toward subject. What can I expect my audience's feelings to be about my subject?

CourseMate

credibility: the perception that you are knowledgeable, trustworthy, and personable

toward the subject, and their perceptions of your credibility. Knowing this information will help you reach your goals of (1) forming reasonable generalizations about your audience and (2) adapting your speech to embrace subject-related diversity. Let's take a closer look at each of these pieces of information.

1. **Audience knowledge.** What can you expect your average audience member to already know about your subject? What topics are likely to provide new information for most of them? It is important that you choose a topic geared to the background knowledge you can expect audience members to have. When you choose a topic that most audience members already know about, you will bore them if you are not really creative. On the other hand, if you choose a topic for which your audience has insufficient background, you will have to provide the background or risk confusing them. For instance, if your subject is music, you can expect that an audience of traditional-age college students will know the general history of rock 'n' roll, including the major performers. So the topic "A Brief History of Rock 'n' Roll" is unlikely to offer them much new information. However, a speech on the contributions of girl bands to the development of rock 'n' roll would draw on the audience's background knowledge but offer new information to most audience members.

2. **Audience interest.** How attracted are audience members likely to be to your subject? For instance, suppose you would like to speak on the subject of cancer drugs. If your audience is made up of health-care professionals, you can assume that because of their vocations they will be curious about the subject. But if your audience is this beginning public speaking class, then unless they have had a personal experience with cancer, they may not naturally relate to your subject. So you can either choose another topic or make an extra effort to determine why cancer drugs are important to your audience and articulate this relevance in your speech.

3. **Audience attitude toward the subject.** How does your audience feel about your subject? This is especially important when you want to influence their beliefs or move the audience members to action. You can determine your audience's attitudes toward your subject directly by surveying them, which we will discuss in the next section. If you cannot survey the audience directly, you might try to see if published opinion polls related to your subject are available. Then you can estimate your audience members' attitudes by studying these opinion polls and extrapolating their results to your audience. To access links to one of the world's most respected polling organizations, go to your CourseMate for *Challenge* to access **Web Resource 4.3: Public Opinion Polls**.

   Finally, in some cases, you will be forced to estimate the audience's attitudes from the speaking occasion and the demographic information you have acquired. Once you understand your audience's attitude toward your subject, you can choose a topic that will allow you to influence rather than alienate the audience. For example, a speech calling for strict gun control is likely to be perceived differently by classmates who grew up in an urban environment where gang violence is a problem than by those who grew up in a suburb where gun crimes are relatively rare or in a rural area where many people are hunters.

4. **Audience attitude toward you as a speaker.** Will your audience recognize you as a subject matter expert? Will they know that beforehand, or will you have to establish your credibility as you speak? **Credibility** is based on the perception that you are knowledgeable (have the necessary understanding that allows you to explain the topic well), trustworthy (are honest, dependable, and ethical), and personable (show enthusiasm, warmth, friendliness,

and concern for audience members). You will want to choose a topic that allows the audience to perceive you as credible and to believe that you know what you are talking about.

Methods for Gathering Audience Data

1. **You can collect data through surveys.** Although it is not always possible, the most direct way to collect audience data is to survey the audience. A **survey** is a questionnaire designed to gather information directly from people. Some surveys are done as interviews; others are written forms that are completed by the participants. The four kinds of items or questions most likely to be used in a survey are called two-sided, multiple-response, scaled, and open-ended.

   ■ **Two-sided items** force the respondent to choose between two answers, such as yes/no, for/against, or pro/con. Suppose you wanted to understand your audience members' attitudes on the subject of TV. You might phrase several questions with two-sided answers, such as:

   Andrew Wallace/Reters/Corbis

   Even Conan O'Brien must consider his audience's knowledge of, interest in, and attitudes toward various subjects when he plans his opening monologue.

   Do you believe prime-time TV shows contain too much violence?

   _____ Yes _____ No

   Do you watch any of the *Law and Order* TV shows?

   _____ Yes _____ No

   Two-sided items are easy to use in an interview, and the answers are easy to sort during analysis.

   ■ **Multiple-response items** give the respondent several alternative answers from which to choose. These items are especially useful for gathering demographic data. For example:

   Which best describes your religious tradition?

   _____ Protestant   _____ Evangelical   _____ Catholic
   _____ Jewish   _____ Buddhist   _____ Muslim
   _____ Atheist   _____ Other

   Multiple-response items can also be used to assess the extent of knowledge that audience members have about a topic. For example, a speaker might assess audience members' knowledge about diamonds with the following question:

   Please indicate what you know about diamonds by placing an X next to each topic you already know about.

   _____ How to value a diamond
   _____ How diamonds are made
   _____ How to tell the difference between a diamond and a fake
   _____ Blood diamonds

survey: a canvassing of people to get information about their ideas and opinions, which are then analyzed for trends

two-sided items: survey items that force the respondent to choose between two answers, such as yes/no, for/against, or pro/con

multiple-response items: survey items that give the respondent several alternative answers from which to choose

- **Scaled items** measure the direction or intensity of an audience member's feeling or attitude toward something. For example:

  Indicate the extent to which you agree or disagree with the following statement:

  There is too much violence on prime-time TV.

  _____ Strongly agree _____ Agree _____ Neutral _____ Disagree _____ Strongly disagree

  Scaled items can also be used to assess audience interest in a subject. For example:

  Please indicate, by checking the appropriate response, how interested you are in learning about each of the following.

  How to value diamonds:

  _____Very interested _____Somewhat interested_____Uninterested

  How diamonds are cut:

  _____Very interested _____Somewhat interested_____Uninterested

  Blood diamonds:

  _____Very interested _____Somewhat interested_____Uninterested

- **Open-ended items** encourage respondents to elaborate on their opinions without forcing them to answer in a predetermined way. These items yield rich information, but the wide variety of responses make them difficult to analyze. For example, to determine what you would need to do to establish your credibility on the subject of TV violence, you might ask: How can you tell if someone is an expert on TV violence?

2. **You can gather data through informal observation.** If you are familiar with members of your audience (as you are with members of your classroom audience), you can get much of the important data about them through informal observation. For instance, after being in class for even a couple of sessions, you should be able to estimate the approximate age or age range and the ratio of men to women. Because you are all in college, you know the educational level. As you listen to your classmates talk, you will learn more about their interest in, knowledge of, and attitudes about many issues.

3. **You can gather data by questioning the person who invited you to speak.** When you are invited to speak to a group you are unfamiliar with, ask your contact person to answer the demographic questions in Exhibit 4.5. Even when the person cannot provide answers to all of the questions, the information you get will be helpful. If necessary, probe your contact person to at least estimate answers for those demographics that are likely to be most important for your topic.

4. **You can make educated guesses about audience demographics and attitudes.** If you can't get information in any other way, you will have to make educated guesses based on such indirect information as the general makeup of the people who live in a specific community and belong to a group like this or the kinds of people who are likely to attend the event or occasion. Suppose, for example, that you are asked by a nonprofit group you support to give a speech on volunteer opportunities with this charity to a meeting of high school guidance counselors who oversee community service projects for students. You can infer a number of things about audience members. First, all will be college-educated high school counselors from your city. They will all speak English. There are likely to be more women than men, and their ethnic backgrounds can be assumed to be similar to that of your community. They will be interested in your topic, but their knowledge of the specific opportunities at your agency will vary.

Whether you survey your audience, rely on informal observation, question the person who invited you to speak, or make educated guesses about audience demographics and subject-related information, you will want to record the information in a form that is convenient to use. Exhibit 4.5 presents an audience analysis summary form you can use to summarize your findings.

Now that you understand audience analysis, you can complete Speech Planning Action Step 1, Activity 1B. See the Student Response box immediately following the activity for a sample of how one student completed this exercise.

Exhibit 4.5 Audience analysis summary form

My subject is _____

Data were collected:

_____ by survey
_____ by direct observation
_____ by questioning the person who invited me
_____ by educated guessing

Demographic Data

1. The average audience member's education level is _____ high school _____ college _____ postgraduate.

2. The ages range from _____ to _____. The average age is about _____.

3. The audience is approximately _____ percent male and _____ percent female.

4. My estimate of the average income level of the audience is _____ upper _____ middle _____ lower.

5. Most audience members are of _____ the same occupation/major (which is _____) _____ different occupations/majors.

6. Most audience members are of _____ the same race (which is _____) _____ a mixture of races.

7. Most audience members are of _____ the same religion (which is _____) _____ a mixture of religions.

8. Most audience members are of _____ the same nationality (which is _____) _____ a mixture of nationalities.

9. Most audience members are from _____ the same state _____ the same city _____ the same neighborhood _____ different areas.

10. Most audience members _____ speak English as their first language _____ English as a second language (ESL).

Subject-Specific Data

1. The average audience member's knowledge of the subject is likely to be _____ extensive _____ moderate _____ limited because

   _____.

2. The average audience member's interest in this subject is likely to be _____ high _____ moderate _____ low because _____

   _____.

3. The average audience member's attitude toward my subject is likely to be _____ positive _____ neutral _____ negative because

   _____.

4. My initial credibility with the audience is likely to be _____ high _____ medium _____ low because _____

   _____

   _____

SPEECH SNIPPET

Making Educated Guesses about Your Audience

Karlie was asked to give a speech on universal health care to a local service club composed of business professionals. It wasn't practical for her to gather data about her audience before her speech, but she inferred that most of them probably received medical insurance through the companies they worked for. She made her topic relevant to them by talking about the advantages and disadvantages of universal health care relative to private insurance options. In that way, she was able to acknowledge the value of private insurance for those who have it and then move on to compare the two options for society overall.

Conclusion

Based on these data _____
_____
_____ ,

which relate to my speech topic in the following ways: _____
_____
_____ ,

I will tailor my speech in the following ways: _____
_____
_____

marginalizing: ignoring the values, needs, and interests of certain audience members, leaving them feeling excluded from the speaking situation

stereotyping: assuming all members of a group have similar behaviors or beliefs simply because they belong to the group

demographic diversity: the range of demographic characteristics represented in an audience

Using Audience Data Ethically

Once you have collected demographic and subject-related data from audience members, you can use what you have learned to tailor your speech to their interests, needs, and expectations. To demonstrate respect for everyone in your audience, you will want to avoid making inappropriate or inaccurate assumptions based on demographic or subject-related information you have collected. Two potential pitfalls you'll want to avoid are marginalizing and stereotyping.

Marginalizing is the practice of ignoring the values, needs, and interests of certain audience members, leaving them feeling excluded from the speaking situation. **Stereotyping** is assuming all members of a group have similar knowledge levels, behaviors, or beliefs simply because they belong to the group. For example, general demographic information like age and education can help you make reasonable assumptions about your audience. But if I find out most of my audience members are 20–25 and have blogged, I might marginalize the few members who have never blogged if I proceed as though everyone has done so. Similarly, if I find out that the average age of my audience is 65, I might stereotype and assume that most of the audience knows nothing about blogging when, in fact, several of them have done so.

You can minimize your chances of marginalizing or stereotyping by recognizing and acknowledging the demographic diversity your audience analysis reveals. **Demographic diversity** is the range of demographic characteristics

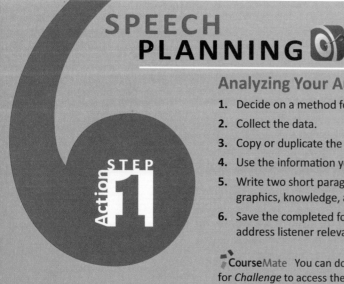

SPEECH PLANNING

ACTIVITY 1B

Action STEP 1

Analyzing Your Audience

1. Decide on a method for gathering audience data.
2. Collect the data.
3. Copy or duplicate the Audience Analysis Summary Form (Exhibit 4.5).
4. Use the information you have collected to complete the form.
5. Write two short paragraphs to describe your initial impression of audience demographics, knowledge, and attitudes toward your subject.
6. Save the completed form. You will refer to this audience analysis information to address listener relevance throughout the speech-planning process.

CourseMate You can download an online copy of this form. Go to your CourseMate for *Challenge* to access the chapter resources for Chapter 4 and then click Audience Analysis Summary Form.

ACTIVITY 1B

STUDENT RESPONSE

Analyzing Your Audience

Audience Analysis Summary Form

Demographic Data

1. The average audience member's education level is _____ high school _X_ college _____ postgraduate.

2. The ages range from _19_ to _24_. The average age is about _20_.

3. The audience is approximately _65_ percent male and _35_ percent female.

4. My estimate of the average income level of the audience is _____ upper _X_ middle _____ lower.

5. Most audience members are of _X_ the same occupation/major (which is _communication students_) _____ different occupations/majors.

6. Most audience members are of _X_ the same race (which is _white_) _____ a mixture of races.

7. Most audience members are of _X_ the same religion (which is _Judeo-Christian tradition_) _____ a mixture of religions.

8. Most audience members are of _X_ the same nationality (which is _American_) _____ a mixture of nationalities.

9. Most audience members are from _____ the same state _____ the same city _____ the same neighborhood _X_ different areas.

10. Most audience members speak _X_ English as their first language _____ English as a second language (ESL).

Summary description of key audience characteristics: *From these data, I conclude that most audience members are similar to one another and to me. We are all students at U.C. Most of us are around 20 years old, which suggests that we have a common generational view. Because U.C. is a commuter school, most of us are probably in the middle to lower socioeconomic class. There are more men than women in the class, and we are mostly white middle-class Americans. Although we have some religious diversity, most of us come from Judeo-Christian religious traditions.*

Subject-Specific Data

1. The average audience member's knowledge of the subject is likely to be _____ extensive _____ moderate _X_ limited because *my audience members are mostly communication students, not geology or mineralogy students* .

2. The average audience member's interest in this subject is likely to be _____ high _X_ moderate _____ low because *without encouragement, they have no need without encouragement, they have no need to know about this subject. Mineralogy is hardly a trendy subject* .

3. The average audience member's attitude toward my subject is likely to be _____ positive _X_ neutral _____ negative because *the audience doesn't really have any information about the topic*.

4. My initial credibility with the audience is likely to be _____ high _____ medium _X_ low because *this is our first speech and they don't know I am a geology major whose family owns a jewelry store*.

Summary: *Most audience members don't know a lot about diamonds and have only a moderate interest in the subject, although it is not a controversial subject. So I will need to make sure to address listener relevance and include listener-relevance links throughout the speech to maintain my audience's interest during the entire speech.*

represented in an audience. So while the average age of your audience may be 65, there may also be some in the audience who are much younger. Second, collecting audience data that are directly related to your subject can help you minimize stereotyping. For example, to gauge what your audience knows about blogging, you might include a few questions when collecting subject-related data that address what they know about this topic.

Analyzing the Occasion

occasion: the setting, which includes the purpose, audience expectations, and location

The **occasion** is essentially the setting, which includes the purpose, audience expectations, and location. The answers to several questions about the occasion should guide your topic selection and other parts of your speech planning.

1. **What are the special expectations (i.e., the exigence) for the speech?** Why is this speech being given? Every speaking occasion is surrounded by expectations. At an Episcopalian Sunday service, for example, the congregation expects the minister's sermon to have a religious theme. At a national sales meeting, the field representatives expect to hear about new products. For your classroom speeches, a major expectation is that your speech will meet the assignment requirements. Whether the speech assignment is defined by purpose (to inform or to persuade), by type (expository or demonstration), or by subject (book analysis or current event), your topic should reflect the nature of that assignment.

2. **What is the appropriate length for the speech?** The time limits for classroom speeches are usually quite short, so you will want to choose a topic that is narrow enough to be accomplished in the time allotted. "Three Major Causes of the Declining Honey Bee Population" can be presented in five minutes, but "A History of Human Impact on the Environment" cannot. Problems with time limits are not peculiar to classroom speeches. For example, the expected length for the sermon in a Protestant Sunday service may be twenty to thirty minutes; the expected length for a homily in a Roman Catholic Mass may be only ten minutes. It is important to understand and adhere to audience expectations regarding time limits—this demonstrates respect for your listeners. For example, consider when you attended a concert or other public event that required an expensive ticket. If the main event was too short, it probably failed to meet your expectations about how much entertainment you should get for your money, and you probably felt cheated. Or consider when a teacher kept you in class longer than the allotted time. You were likely frustrated because it seemed the instructor failed to respect your other classes, your job, or the other commitments you juggled along with that particular course.

3. **How large will the audience be?** If you will be speaking to a small audience (fewer than fifty people), you will be physically close enough to them to talk in a normal voice and to move about. In contrast, if you will be speaking to a large audience, you will probably need a microphone, and you'll be less likely to be able to move about.

4. **Where will the speech be given?** Because rooms vary in size, lighting, seating arrangements, and the like, consider the factors that may affect your presentation. In a long, narrow room, you may need to speak louder than usual to reach the back row. In a dark room, make sure the lights are on and that the blinds or shades are open to bring in as much light as possible.

   Venues outside school settings offer even greater variations in conditions. Ask for specific information about seating capacity, shape, number of rows, nature of lighting, existence of a speaking stage or platform, distance between speaker and first row, and so on before you speak. If possible, visit the place and see it for yourself.

tag at top right

5. **When will the speech be given?** A speech given early in the morning requires a different approach from one given right after lunch or in the evening. If a speech is scheduled after a meal, for instance, the audience may be lethargic, mellow, or even on the verge of sleep. As a result, it helps to insert more "attention getters" (examples, illustrations, and stories) to counter potential lapses of attention.

Ethical speakers select a topic that is appropriate to the rhetorical situation.

FB-Fischer FB-Fischer/imagebroker.net/PhotoLibrary

6. **Where in the program does the speech occur?** If you are the only speaker or the featured speaker, you have an obvious advantage: You are the focal point of audience attention. In the classroom, however, and at some rallies, hearings, and other events, there are many speeches, and your place on the schedule may affect how you are received. For example, if you go first, you may need to "warm up" the listeners and be prepared to meet the distraction of a few audience members' strolling in late. If you speak last, you must counter the tendency of the audience to be weary from listening to several speeches.

7. **What equipment is necessary to give the speech?** For some speeches, you may need a microphone, a flip chart, an LCD projector and screen, or a hookup for your laptop computer. In most instances, speakers have some kind of speaking stand, but it is wise not to count on it. If the person who has invited you to speak has any control over the location and equipment, be sure to explain what you need, but always have alternative plans in case what you have asked for is unavailable. It is frustrating to plan a computer PowerPoint presentation, for example, and then discover that there's no place to plug in the computer!

Speech Planning Action Step 1, Activity 1C will help you understand the occasion so that you take into consideration your purpose, audience expectations,

SPEECH PLANNING

STEP
Action 1

Analyzing the Occasion

The goal of this activity is to help you understand your speech occasion. Fill in answers to the following questions:

1. What are the special expectations for the speech? _____
2. What is the appropriate length for the speech? _____
3. How large will the audience be? _____
4. Where will the speech be given? _____
5. When will the speech be given? _____
6. Where in the program does the speech occur? _____
7. What equipment is necessary to give the speech? _____

Write a short paragraph mentioning which aspects of the setting are most important for you to consider in speech preparation and why.

CourseMate You can complete this activity online, print it, and, if requested, e-mail it to your instructor. Go to your CourseMate for *Challenge* to access Action Step 1, Activity 1C.

STUDENT RESPONSE

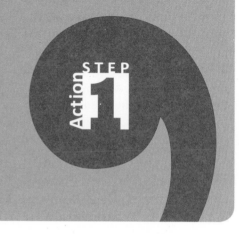

Analyzing the Occasion

1. What are the special expectations for the speech? *an informative speech*
2. What is the appropriate length for the speech? *4–6 minutes*
3. How large will the audience be? *13–15 people*
4. Where will the speech be given? *614 Dyer Hall*
5. When will the speech be given? *9:30 a.m., Tuesday*
6. Where in the program does the speech occur? *I will try to go first.*
7. What equipment is necessary to give the speech?
   LCD projector, computer, and screen

Time is certainly important: Four to six minutes is not very long. I plan to time my speech when I practice to make sure I stay within the expected time limits. Also, I want to make sure that I am one of the first speakers.

Action STEP 1

and location as you choose your topic and develop your speech. See the Student Response box immediately following the activity for a sample of how one student completed this exercise.

Selecting a Topic

Armed with your topic lists and the information you have collected on your audience and the occasion, you are ready to select a topic that will be appropriate to the public speaking situation.

As you review your list of topics, compare each to your audience profile. Are there some topics that are too simple for this audience's knowledge base? Too

Reflect on Ethics

WHAT WOULD *YOU* DO?

JIM CRAMER AND CNBC'S MAD MONEY

Jim Cramer hosts CNBC's *Mad Money*, a program devoted to providing financial advice to its viewers. In an interview on Comedy Central's *The Daily Show*, Jon Stewart claimed both Stewart and Cramer are "snake oil salesmen" but that *The Daily Show* is labeled as such. Stewart was essentially arguing that his program on Comedy Central admits to being satire whereas CNBC's *Mad Money* is duping viewers by claiming to offer sound financial advice, when actually it is not. For example, Stewart showed footage of Cramer recommending that his viewers buy Bear Stearns stock just before it collapsed. If you are personally unfamiliar with the show, watch at least one episode before answering the following questions. Then, with regard to *Mad Money*, consider the elements of the audience and the occasion we've discussed in this chapter (purpose, audience expectations, and location).

1 How would you respond to Stewart's claim that *Mad Money's* host is being unethical?

2 How might Cramer be demonstrating or violating the ethical principle of honesty in terms of the program's purpose?

3 How might Cramer be demonstrating or violating the ethical principle of integrity with regard to audience expectations?

4 Why might the fact that *Mad Money* is shown on CNBC (and not Comedy Central) influence your decision about its host as an ethical communicator?

5 Given that many people now rely on *The Daily Show* to get their news, was Jon Stewart behaving ethically when he made his charge? How does the fact that he made the claim on *The Daily Show* influence your decision?

difficult? Are some topics likely to be more interesting to the audience? How do the audience's age, ethnicity, and other demographic features mesh with each topic? By asking these and similar questions, you will be able to identify topics that are appropriate for the audience. Then consider the occasion. Are some topics too broad for the time allotted? Are there topics that won't meet the special expectations? Answers to these and other questions will help you identify the topics that are appropriate to your setting.

Speech Planning Action Step 1, Activity 1D will help you select your topic. See the Student Response box immediately following the activity for a sample of how one student completed this exercise.

Writing a Speech Goal Statement

Once you have chosen your topic, you are ready to identify and write the general speech goal you hope to achieve in the speech and then the specific goal that is tailored to the public speaking situation.

Understanding General and Specific Speech Goals

The **general goal** is the overall intent of the speech. Most speeches intend to entertain, to inform, or to persuade, even though each type of speech may include elements of other types. Consider the following examples: Conan

general goal: the overall intent of the speech

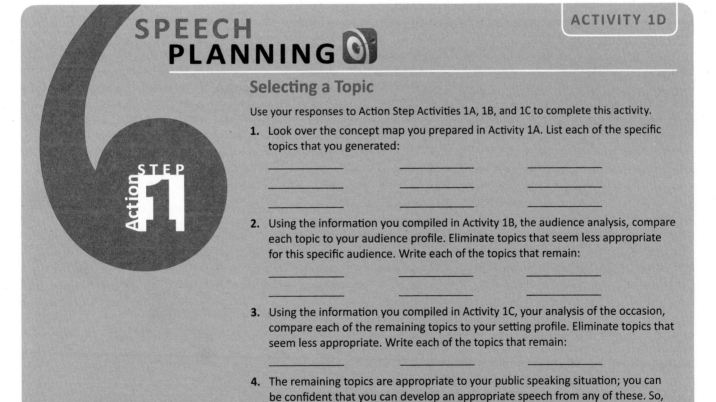

SPEECH PLANNING

ACTIVITY 1D

Action STEP 1

Selecting a Topic

Use your responses to Action Step Activities 1A, 1B, and 1C to complete this activity.

1. Look over the concept map you prepared in Activity 1A. List each of the specific topics that you generated:

   _____   _____   _____
   _____   _____   _____

2. Using the information you compiled in Activity 1B, the audience analysis, compare each topic to your audience profile. Eliminate topics that seem less appropriate for this specific audience. Write each of the topics that remain:

   _____   _____   _____
   _____   _____   _____

3. Using the information you compiled in Activity 1C, your analysis of the occasion, compare each of the remaining topics to your setting profile. Eliminate topics that seem less appropriate. Write each of the topics that remain:

   _____   _____   _____

4. The remaining topics are appropriate to your public speaking situation; you can be confident that you can develop an appropriate speech from any of these. So, from this list, select the one that you are most excited about sharing with others. My topic will be: _____

   CourseMate You can go online to the CourseMate for *Challenge* to complete this activity and print out a worksheet that will help you select your topic.

STUDENT RESPONSE

Selecting a Topic

1. Write each of the topics that appeared on your concept map in Activity 1A:

    Low-cost ways to travel   *Study abroad programs*

    Youth hostels   *Working on cruise ships*

    Organizing alternative spring   *Elderhostel*
    break group trips

2. Using the information you compiled in Activity 1B, the audience analysis, compare each topic to your audience profile. Eliminate topics that seem less appropriate. Write each of the topics below:

    Low-cost ways to travel   *Study abroad programs*

    Youth hostels   *Organizing alternative spring*
            break group trips

3. Using the information you compiled in Activity 1C, your analysis of the occasion for this speech, compare each of the remaining topics to your setting profile. Eliminate topics that seem less appropriate. Write each of the topics that remain below:

    Study abroad programs   *Youth hostels*

    Organizing alternative spring
    break group trips

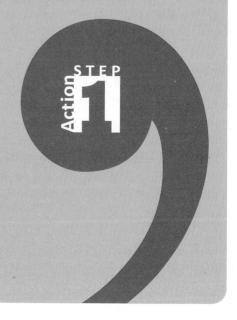

Action **STEP 1**

4. Each of the remaining topics is appropriate to your public speaking situation; you can be confident that you can develop an appropriate speech from any of these. So, from the topics that remain, select the one that you are most excited about sharing with others.

    My topic will be organizing alternative spring break group trips.

O'Brien's opening monologue is intended to entertain, even though it may include material that is seen as persuasive. Likewise, President Obama's campaign speeches were intended to persuade, even though they also may have been very informative.

The general goal is usually dictated by the occasion. (In this course, your instructor is likely to specify it.) Most speeches given by adults as part of their job or community activities have the general goal of informing or persuading.

Whereas the general goal is often determined by the setting in which a speech is given, the **specific goal**, or specific purpose of a speech, is a single statement that identifies the exact response the speaker wants from the audience. For a speech on the topic "Vanishing Honeybees," one might state the specific goal as, "I would like the audience to understand the four reasons honeybees are vanishing." For a speech on "Supporting the United Way," a specific goal might be stated as, "I would like the audience to donate money to the United Way."

In the first example, the goal is informative: The speaker wants the audience to understand the reasons. In the second example, the goal is

specific goal: a single statement that identifies the exact response the speaker wants from the audience persuasive: The speaker wants to persuade the audience to donate money.

Phrasing a Specific Speech Goal

The occasion (or in the case of this class, the assignment) usually dictates the nature of your general speech goal. A specific speech goal, however, must be carefully crafted because it lays the foundation for organizing the speech.

The following guidelines can help you craft a well-worded specific goal.

1. **Write a draft of your general speech goal using a complete sentence that specifies the type of response you want from the audience.** Julia, who has been concerned with and is knowledgeable about the subject of illiteracy, drafts the following statement of her general speech goal.

   I want my audience to understand the effects of illiteracy.

   Julia's draft is a complete sentence, and it specifies the response she wants from the audience: *to understand* the effects of illiteracy. Her phrasing tells us that she is planning to give an informative speech.

2. **Revise the statement (and the infinitive phrase) until it indicates the specific audience reaction desired.** If your objective is to explain (to inform), the infinitive that expresses your desired audience reaction could be "to understand," "to recognize," "to distinguish," or "to identify." If you see the goal of your speech as changing a belief or calling the audience to action, then your general goal is persuasive and can be reflected by the use of such infinitives as "to believe," "to accept," "to change," or "to do." If Julia wanted to convince her audience, her specific goal might be worded:

   I want my audience to believe that illiteracy is a major problem.

3. **Make sure that the goal statement contains only one idea.** Suppose Julia had first written

   I would like the audience to understand the nature of illiteracy and its effects on the individual and society.

   This statement is not a good specific goal because it includes two distinct ideas: understanding the nature of illiteracy and understanding the specific effects that may follow from being illiterate. Either one is a worthy goal—but not both in one speech. Julia needs to choose one of these ideas. If your goal statement includes the word *and*, you have more than one idea.

4. **Revise your statement until it describes the precise focus of your speech (the infinitive phrase articulates the complete response you want from your audience).** Julia's draft "I want my audience to understand the effects of illiteracy" is a good start, but the infinitive phrase "to understand the effects of illiteracy" is vague. Exactly what about illiteracy is it that Julia wants her audience to understand? Here is where you need to consider your audience analysis and adapt your specific goal in ways that address listener relevance. What is it about illiteracy your particular audience should know and why?

   At this point, Julia may need to begin doing some research to focus her ideas and refine her goal statement. Because Julia knows her classmates all

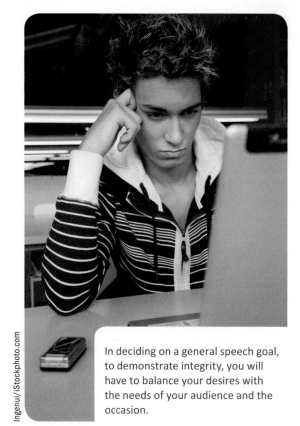

Ingenui/iStockphoto.com

In deciding on a general speech goal, to demonstrate integrity, you will have to balance your desires with the needs of your audience and the occasion.

Exhibit 4.6 General and specific speech goals

Informative Goals

General goal: To inform the audience about e-books
Specific goal: I want the audience to understand the differences between the Kindle and the Sony/iPad approaches to electronic books.
General goal: To inform the audience about forms of mystery stories
Specific goal: I want the audience to be able to identify the three basic forms of mystery stories.

Persuasive Goals

General goal: To persuade the audience that saving for retirement is important
Specific goal: I want the audience to begin a personal ROTH IRA funded this year with at least 2 percent of their income.
General goal: To persuade the audience to get involved with the food bank
Specific goal: I want to persuade the audience to volunteer to work on the campus food drive for our local food bank.

have the goal of becoming gainfully employed after graduating, and because she knows how illiteracy places people in the workplace at a disadvantage, she might rephrase her specific goal to read:

> I want the audience to understand three ways illiteracy hinders a person's effectiveness in the workplace.

This statement meets the criteria for a good specific goal statement because it indicates the specific desired audience reaction and it contains only one explicit idea that is the focus of the speech.

A good specific goal statement is important because it will guide your research as you prepare the speech. Once you have completed your research, you will

SPEECH PLANNING

ACTIVITY 1E

Action STEP 1

Writing a Specific Goal

Type of speech: _____

1. Write a draft of your general speech goal using a complete sentence that specifies the type of response you want from the audience.
2. Revise the infinitive to make it reflect the specific audience response you desire.
3. Check the number of ideas expressed in the statement. If the statement contains more than one idea, select one and rewrite the statement.
4. Improve the statement so that it describes the precise focus of your speech as it relates to your intended audience.

Write the final draft of the specific goal:

_____
_____
_____

 You can complete this activity online with Speech Builder Express, a speech outlining and development tool that will help you complete the action steps in this book to develop your speech. You can access Speech Builder Express through your CourseMate for *Challenge.*

ACTIVITY 1E

STUDENT RESPONSE

Writing a Specific Goal

Type of speech: *informative*

1. Write a draft of your general speech goal using a complete sentence that specifies the type of response you want from the audience.

    I want the audience to understand how a fire is lit without a match.

2. Revise the infinitive to make it reflect the specific audience response you desire.

    I want the audience to be able to light a fire without a match.

3. Check the number of ideas expressed in the statement. If the statement contains more than one idea, select one and rewrite the statement.

    I want my audience to recognize the basic steps necessary in lighting a fire without a match.

4. Improve the statement so that it describes the precise focus of your speech as it relates to your intended audience.

    I want my audience to recognize the three basic steps involved in lighting a fire without a match.

Write the final draft of the specific goal:

I want my audience to recognize the three basic steps involved in lighting a fire without a match.

expand your specific goal statement into a thesis statement, which will be the foundation on which you will organize the speech. Exhibit 4.6 gives several additional examples of general and specific informative and persuasive goals.

Speech Planning Action Step 1, Activity 1E will help you develop a well-written specific goal statement for your speech. See the Student Response box immediately following the activity for a sample of how one student completed this exercise.

Summary

The first step of effective speech preparation is to identify a topic. You begin by selecting a subject that is important to you and that you know something about, such as a job, a hobby, or a contemporary issue that concerns you. To arrive at a specific topic, brainstorm a list of related words under each subject. When you have brainstormed at least fifteen topics under each heading, you can check two or three specific topics under each heading that are most meaningful to you. Then, develop a concept map to come up with a variety of smaller topic areas and related ideas.

The second step is to analyze the audience to decide how to shape and direct your speech. Audience analysis is the study of the intended audience for your speech. You will want to gather demographic data and subject-related data. To ensure that you don't unintentionally marginalize or stereotype your listeners based on demographic characteristics, you may survey your audience using two-sided, multiple-response, scaled, or open-ended questions. You may also gather data through informal observation, by questioning the person who invited you to speak, and by making educated guesses about audience demographics and attitudes. Finally, you'll want to use the information ethically by demonstrating respect for the demographic diversity represented in your audience. You can do so by not marginalizing or stereotyping.

The third step is to analyze the occasion, which will affect your overall speech plan, by asking such questions as: What are the special expectations for the speech? What is the appropriate length for the speech? How large will the audience be? Where will the speech be given? When will the speech be given? Where in the program does the speech occur? What equipment is necessary to give the speech?

The fourth step is to select a topic that is appropriate for the rhetorical situation.

The final step is to write your speech goal. The general goal of a speech (the overarching purpose) is to entertain, to inform, or to persuade. The specific goal is a single statement that identifies the exact response the speaker wants from the audience. Writing a specific speech goal involves the following four-step procedure: (1) Write a first draft of your speech goal using a complete sentence that specifies the type of response you want from your audience. (2) Revise the statement (and the infinitive phrase) until it indicates the specific audience reaction desired. (3) Make sure that the goal statement contains only one idea. (4) Revise your statement until it describes the precise focus of your speech as it relates to the knowledge, interests, and values of your listeners.

Challenge Resource and Assessment Center

CourseMate Now that you have read Chapter 4, use your Speech Communication CourseMate for *The Challenge of Effective Speaking* for quick access to the electronic resources that accompany this text. These resources include:

- **Study tools** that will help you assess your learning and prepare for exams (*digital glossary, key term flash cards, review quizzes*).

- **Activities and assignments** that will help you hone your knowledge and build your public speaking skills throughout the course (*Speech Snippets, Speech Assignments, Action Step*

Activities). Many of these activities allow you to compare your answers with those provided by the authors, and, if requested, submit your answers to your instructor.

- **Media resources** that will help you explore communication concepts online (*Web Resources*), develop your speech outlines (*Speech Builder Express 3.0*), watch and critique videos of sample speeches (*Interactive Video Activities*), upload your speech videos for peer reviewing and critique other students' speeches (*Speech Studio online speech review tool*), and download chapter reviews so you can study when and where you'd like (*Audio Study Tools*).

This chapter's application activities and video resources are featured in this end-of-chapter section.

Applying What You've Learned

1. **Impromptu Speech Activity:** Identify a pet peeve and prepare a two- to three-minute impromptu speech describing the pet peeve and why it bothers you. Include in your reasons which ethical communication principle(s) it violates in your opinion and why.

2. **Assessment Activity A:** Complete Action Steps 1A through 1E for one of the speeches you may give this semester.

3. **Assessment Activity B:** Suppose you were asked to give a speech about some aspect of your work to a group of your coworkers and managers. Explain what demographic and subject-specific information you would need, how you would collect it, and how you might use it in your speech planning. How would your approach differ if your audience were your speech classmates?

Speech-Planning Action Steps

1A: Use Brainstorming and Concept Mapping to Identify Speech Topics (58)

1B: Analyzing Your Audience (64)

1C: Analyzing the Occasion (68)

1D: Selecting a Topic (70)

1E: Writing a Specific Goal (72)

Web Resources

4.1 Brainstorming (55)

4.2 Defining Your Audience (57)

4.3 Public Opinion Polls (60)

Video Resources

1. Go to Speech Studio and browse the speeches posted there. Do any of the topics of the speeches you see give you ideas for your own classroom speeches? Do some of the topics inspire you to brainstorm for more topics?

2. Use Speech Studio to upload a video of a speech you're working on. Ask your instructor and classmates for feedback on the statement of your specific goal. Or look through other students' speeches to see how effectively they state their specific goals—do their statements give you ideas for how you could make your statement more effective?

SPEECH
Studio

5

Ethical communicators demonstrate respect for their listeners by adapting their message to them at all points in the speech-making process.

adapting to audiences

What's the Point?

QUESTIONS YOU'LL BE ABLE TO ANSWER AFTER READING THIS CHAPTER:

1. Why is it important to articulate the relevance of your speech to your audience?

2. What should you do if your audience does not share your attitude about the topic of your speech?

3. What can you do to help your audience see you as trustworthy and knowledgeable about your topic?

4. Why is it important to address diverse learning styles in your speech?

5. What can you do to overcome language and cultural differences between you and your audience?

Action STEP 2
Understand your audience and adapt to it.

A. Understand audience diversity.

B. Understand audience initial interest and attitude.

C. Adjust content to be appropriate for your audience.

D. Determine how you will establish your credibility with the audience.

Suzanne entered the studio to anchor the 5:00 evening news for the first time, thinking, "I can't believe I've landed my dream job of anchoring the nightly news in a major metropolitan market." Within moments of the start of the broadcast, however, telephones at the studio began ringing off the hook. Unfortunately, she had unintentionally offended a majority of the viewers before she even said a word. You see, Suzanne's post was with a television station in Boston, and she was wearing an orange suit on Saint Patrick's Day.

After the broadcast, the assistant news director explained to Suzanne, "Orange is associated with Northern Irish Protestants who deposed the Roman Catholic King James II in 1690. So by wearing orange today, Saint Patrick's Day, you outraged and offended many of our Irish Catholic viewers."

This true story of award-winning news anchor Suzanne Bates illustrates how important it is to understand and adapt to your specific audience.[1] In the previous chapter, we saw how audience and occasion considerations help you to choose a speech topic and goal. In this chapter, we describe how you can use audience analysis to tailor what you say to the audience throughout the speech. The second Speech Planning Action Step is to understand your audience and adapt your speech to it.

Audience adaptation is the process of tailoring your speech's information to the needs, interests, and expectations of your listeners. Your concerns about adapting to your audience will inform your research efforts, your choice of main points, the supporting material that you will use to develop those points, and even the jokes you might want to tell. So recognizing audience adaptation needs during Action Step 2 lays the foundation for the work that follows. In the rest of this chapter, we describe the issues of adaptation, including demonstrating the relevance of your topic, acknowledging initial audience disposition toward your topic, establishing common ground, gaining credibility, ensuring information comprehension and retention, and managing language and cultural differences. Your consideration of these issues will enable you to formulate a specific blueprint to use as you plan your speech.

> **audience adaptation:** the process of tailoring your speech's information to the needs, interests, and expectations of your listeners

Relevance

The first issue you face is demonstrating **relevance**—adapting the information in a speech so that audience members realize its importance to them. Listeners pay attention to and are interested in ideas that have a personal impact ("What does this have to do with me?") and are bored when they don't see how a speech relates to them. Effective speakers demonstrate the timeliness, proximity, and personal impact that the ideas in their speech have for their audience.

> **relevance:** adapting the information in a speech so that audience members view it as important to them

Effective speakers adapt to their audience early and often by establishing relevance. J. J. did this in his speech about the dangers of texting or talking on a cell phone while driving by noting that most of his audience probably were guilty of driving while phoning.

Michael Ventura/Alamy

timeliness: showing how information on is useful now or in the near future

proximity: the relevance of information to personal life space

initial audience disposition: the knowledge of and opinions about your topic that your listeners have before they hear you speak

Demonstrate Timeliness

Information has **timeliness** when it is useful now or in the near future. You can increase the relevance of the information you present by showing how it is timely for a particular audience. For example, in a speech about the hazards of talking on cell phones while driving, J. J. established the topic's relevance to the audience with this introduction:

> *Most of us in this room, as many as 90 percent of us in fact, are a danger to society. Why? Because we talk or text message on our cell phones while driving. Although driving while phoning (DWP) seems harmless, a recent study conducted by the Nationwide Mutual Insurance Company reports that DWP is the most common cause of accidents today—even more common than driving under the influence (DUI). Did you know that when you talk on the phone when you're driving—even if you do so on a hands-free set—you're four times more likely to get into a serious crash than if you're not doing so? That's why several states have actually made doing so illegal. So this issue is far from harmless and is certainly one each of us should take seriously.*

To see an excellent example of how timeliness can affect a message—President Ronald Reagan's 1986 speech on the *Challenger* space shuttle disaster—go to your CourseMate for *Challenge* to access **Web Resource 5.1: Demonstrating Timeliness**. ⚡**CourseMate**

Demonstrate Proximity

Listeners are more likely to be interested in information that has **proximity**, a relationship to their personal "space." Psychologically, we pay more attention to information that is related to our "territory"—to us, our family, our neighborhood, or our city, state, or country. You have probably heard speakers say, "Let me bring this close to home for you . . ." and then make their point by using a local example. As you research your speech, you will want to look for statistics and examples that have proximity for your audience. For example, J. J. used the latest DWP accident statistics in his state and a story reported in the local paper of a young mother who was killed while DWPing.

Demonstrate Personal Impact

When you present information on a topic that can have a serious physical, economic, or psychological impact on audience members, they will be interested in what you have to say. For example, notice how your classmates' attention picks up when your instructor states that what is said next "will definitely be on the test." Your instructor understands that this "economic impact" (not paying attention can "cost") is enough to refocus most students' attention on what is said. As you prepare your speech, incorporate ideas that create personal impact for your audience.

Initial Audience Disposition

Initial audience disposition is the knowledge of and opinions about your topic that your listeners have before they hear you speak. Adapting to the initial audience disposition means creating a speech that takes into account how much audience members already know about your topic and what their attitudes are toward it. As part of your audience analysis, you identified the initial attitude you expected most of your audience members to have toward your topic. During your speech preparation, choose specific supporting material with these initial attitudes in mind.

Adapting to listeners' attitudes is obviously important for persuasive speeches, but it is also important for informative speeches. For example, a speech on refinishing wood furniture is meant to be informative. However, you may face an audience whose initial attitude is that refinishing furniture is difficult, uninteresting, or complicated. On the other hand, you may face an audience of young homeowners who are addicted to HGTV and who are really looking forward to your talk. Although the refinishing process you describe in both situations would be the same, your approach to explaining the steps would differ somewhat. If you know your audience thinks refinishing furniture is complicated and boring, you will need to pique their interest and convince them that the process is really simpler than they initially thought. And if you know you have an audience of new homeowners and have found out through a simple show of hands that most of them enjoy watching HGTV, you can play upon their interest as you speak—by making reference to some of the most popular shows on HGTV.

Common Ground

People in the audience are unique, with different knowledge, attitudes, philosophies, experiences, and ways of perceiving the world. They may or may not know others in the audience. So it is easy for them to assume that they have nothing in common with you or with other audience members. Yet when you speak, you will be giving one message to that diverse group. **Common ground** is the background, knowledge, attitudes, experiences, and philosophies that are shared by audience members and the speaker. Effective speakers use audience analysis to identify areas of similarity and then use the adaptation techniques of personal pronouns, rhetorical questions, and common experiences to create common ground.

Use Personal Pronouns

The simplest way to establish common ground is to use **personal pronouns**—"we," "us," and "our." For example, in a speech to an audience whose members are known to be sympathetic to legislation limiting violence in children's programming on TV, notice the effect of using a personal pronoun:

> I know that most people worry about the effects that violence on TV is having on young children.

> I know that most of us worry about the effects that violence on TV is having on young children.

By using "us" instead of "people," the speaker includes the audience members and thus gives them a stake in listening to what follows.

Ask Rhetorical Questions

A second way of developing common ground is to pose **rhetorical questions**—questions phrased to stimulate a mental response rather than an actual spoken response on the part of the audience. Rhetorical questions create common ground by alluding to information that is shared by audience members and the speaker. They are often used in speech introductions but can also be effective as transitions and in other parts of the speech. For instance, notice how this transition, phrased as a rhetorical question, creates common ground:

SPEECH SNIPPET

Demonstrating Personal Impact

To drive home the impact of DWP, J. J. talked about John, his high school friend, who is now paralyzed and wheelchair-bound because his girlfriend crashed into another car while she was texting.

SPEECH SNIPPET

Acknowledging Listener Attitudes

In her introductory remarks, Tiffany acknowledged listener attitudes in her speech "Meat Free and Me": "With Thanksgiving just around the corner, many of you are probably anticipating a feast complete with a flavorful, juicy turkey as the main course. I am too, but many of you would find my menu bizarre—I'm planning to feast on rice pilaf with grilled vegetables and garlic-roasted tofu." In this way, Tiffany acknowledges that her audience will find her alternative menu for Thanksgiving dinner odd.

common ground: the background, knowledge, attitudes, experiences, and philosophies audience members and the speaker share

personal pronouns: "we," "us," and "our"—pronouns that directly link the speaker to members of the audience

---

Drawing on Common Experiences

In his speech about skydiving, Kyron related the sensation of falling out of a plane to something most listeners could probably relate to in this way: "The first thing you feel when you finally jump is that stomach-in-the-mouth sensation that is similar to something we've all experienced when we have lurched because we've missed a step going down a staircase or when we have momentarily gone airborne in a car from approaching the crest of a hill too fast."

When you have watched a particularly violent TV program, have you ever asked yourself, "Did they really need to be this graphic to make the point?"

Rhetorical questions are meant to have only one answer that highlights similarities between the speaker and audience members and leads them to be more interested in the content that follows.

Draw from Common Experiences

You can also develop common ground by sharing personal experiences, examples, and illustrations that embody what you and the audience have in common. For instance, in a speech about the effects of television violence, you might allude to a common viewing experience:

You know how sometimes at a key moment when you're watching a really frightening scene in a movie you quickly shut your eyes? I vividly remember slamming my eyes shut over and over again during the scariest scenes in Texas Chainsaw Massacre, The Blair Witch Project, *and* Halloween.

To create material that draws on common experiences, you must first analyze how you and audience members are similar in the exposure you have had to the topic or in other areas that you can then compare to your topic.

PUTTING SPEAKING SKILLS TO WORK

Adapting to Success

Jeff McGuire,
Cellular retail sales consultant
Naples, Florida

Jeff McGuire will tell you that the public speaking course he took as part of his degree requirements at Florida Gulf Coast University changed his life. When probed, he explains that he used to talk too fast and lose his words. He'd fill the spaces with "ums," "ya knows," and awkward pauses. As a cellular retail sales consultant, these verbal tics made it difficult for his clients to see that he really had a lot of product expertise. He says, "You can know everything there is to know about your product. But if you can't apply the principles of public speaking to what you are trying to say, it doesn't really matter because your clients aren't going to see you as competent."

Jeff knew that he had mastered public speaking skills when, one day at work, his manager ask him to do an impromptu presentation of their store to a group of visiting company executives. Quickly organizing his thoughts and tailoring what he said to the specific executives, he made a good impression on his audience and the other people in his store. When the presentation was over he thought, "Wow, if I hadn't had that public speaking course, I couldn't have done that." And shortly after that he got a promotion, which

"My public speaking course changed my life!"

he believes came from being able to demonstrate his mastery of the products.

Jeff believes that the key to success in sales is to understand the specific needs of your customer and then to find the product that fills those needs. This means being able to give the client valid reasons for choosing your product. So he puts the skills of audience analysis and persuasion to work each day.

Raised on Big Pine Key in Florida, Jeff is an avid and accomplished scuba diver. In fact, his demonstration speech for speech class was how to put on scuba gear. Like many students, Jeff took a year off from school to make money for tuition and is now finishing his degree in marketing. He plans to work in advertising, and his goal is to produce commercials—his dream is to work with his twin brother, who is studying film production. Reflecting on the future, Jeff commented, "I know that whatever I do, I'll always view my public speaking class as being a life-changer for me, and I would encourage other people to take the course seriously. You may change jobs and careers, but you're going to need public speaking skills in whatever you do."

Speaker Credibility

Credibility is the confidence that an audience places in the truthfulness of what a speaker says. The impact of credibility on speaker success has been a fundamental concept in public speaking since Aristotle described it as *ethos* more than 2,000 years ago. Having been understood as a key concept for so long, it is no wonder that several theories exist about how speakers develop credibility. You can read a summary of these theories by going to your CourseMate for *Challenge* to access **Web Resource 5.2: Holistic Theory of Speaker Credibility**.

Some people are widely known as experts in a particular area and have proven to be trustworthy and likable. When these people give a speech, they don't have to adapt their remarks to establish their credibility. For example, in November 2008 Nancy Nielsen, president of the American Medical Association, spoke to fellow physicians on the subject of standing up for patients when health plans don't—no one listening would have questioned her credibility.

However, most of us, even if we are given a formal introduction that attempts to acquaint the audience with our credentials and character, will still need to adapt our remarks to build audience confidence in the truthfulness of what we are saying. Three adaptation techniques can affect how credible we are perceived to be: demonstrating knowledge and expertise, establishing trustworthiness, and displaying personableness.

Demonstrate Knowledge and Expertise

When listeners perceive you to be a knowledgeable expert, they will perceive you as credible. Their assessment of your **knowledge and expertise** depends on how well you convince them that you are qualified to speak on this topic. You can demonstrate your knowledge and expertise through direct and indirect means.

You establish your expertise directly when you disclose your experiences with your topic, including formal education, special study, demonstrated skill, and your "track record." For example, in a speech on DWP, J. J. explained:

> *I became interested in the issue of driving while phoning (DWP) after being involved personally in an accident caused by a driver who was talking on the phone. Since then, I've done a great deal of research on the subject and am involved in a grassroots organization devoted to passing legislation to ban driving while phoning in our state.*

Of course, to make claims like this, you must have had experiences that give you "standing" to speak on your topic. This is why it is critical for you to choose a topic you know something about. When you can demonstrate your personal involvement with your topic, your audience begins to trust that you understand the material you are presenting.

Audience members will also assess your expertise through indirect means, such as how well prepared you seem and how much you demonstrate firsthand involvement by using personal examples and illustrations. Audiences have an almost instinctive sense of when a speaker is "winging it," and most audiences distrust a speaker who does not appear to have command of the material. Speakers who are overly dependent on their notes or who hem and haw fumbling to find ways to express their ideas undermine the confidence of the audience. On the other hand, when your ideas are easy to follow and clearly expressed, audience members perceive you to be more credible.

Similarly, when your ideas are developed through specific statistics, high-quality examples, illustrations, and personal experiences, audience members

rhetorical questions: questions phrased to stimulate a mental response rather than an actual spoken response from the audience

credibility: the perception that you are knowledgeable, trustworthy, and personable

CourseMate

knowledge and expertise: how well you convince your audience that you are qualified to speak on the topic

SPEECH SNIPPET

Demonstrating Direct Expertise

Tiffany demonstrated direct expertise with her topic when she declared, "About five years ago, I made a decision to stop eating meat, which has changed my life in several ways. Living a vegetarian lifestyle is an important aspect of who I am today."

Establishing Trustworthiness

Tiffany established trustworthiness in her speech by framing it as an explanation about why she chose to live a vegetarian lifestyle rather than trying to persuade her listeners to make that same choice: "In the next few minutes, we'll talk about how I made this choice to live meat-free, some of the family issues I've dealt with as a result of this choice, and some of the specific ways this choice continues to affect my life today."

trustworthiness: the extent to which the audience can believe that what you say is accurate, true, and in their best interests

are more likely to view you as credible. Think about how impressed you are with instructors who always seem to have two or three perfect examples and illustrations and who are able to recall statistics without looking at their notes. Compare this with your experiences with instructors who seem tied to the textbook and don't appear to know much about the subject beyond their prepared lecture. In which instance do you perceive the instructor to be more knowledgeable?

Establish Trustworthiness

Your **trustworthiness** is the extent to which the audience can believe that what you say is accurate, true, and in their best interests. The more your audience sees you as trustworthy, the more credible you will be. People assess others' trustworthiness by judging their character and their motives. So you can establish yourself as trustworthy by following ethical standards and by honestly explaining what is motivating you to speak.

As you plan your speech, you need to consider how to demonstrate your character—that you are honest, industrious, dependable, and a morally strong person. For example, when you credit the source of your information as you speak, you confirm that the information is true—that you are not making it up—and you signal your honesty by not taking credit for someone else's ideas. Similarly, if you present the arguments evenly on both sides of an issue, instead of just the side you favor, audience members will see you as fair-minded.

How trustworthy you appear to be will also depend on how the audience views your motives. If people believe that what you are saying is self-serving rather than in their interests, they will be suspicious and view you as less trustworthy. Early in your speech, then, it is important to show how audience members will benefit from what you are saying. For example, in his speech on toxic waste, Brandon might describe how one community's ignorance of toxic waste disposal allowed a toxic waste dump to be located in their community, which led to serious health issues. He can then share his motive by saying something like this: "My hope is that this speech will give you the information you need to thoughtfully participate in decisions like these that may face your community."

Display Personableness

We have more confidence in people that we like. **Personableness** is the extent to which you project an agreeable or pleasing personality. The more your listeners like you, the more likely they are to believe what you tell them. We quickly decide how much we like a new person based on our first impressions. This fact is actually based on a concept we refer to in the communication field as impression formation and management, which is rooted in the theory of symbolic interactionism.[2] These first impressions are based on what we infer about people from what we see, such as how they dress, how physically attractive we find them, how well they speak, whether they smile and appear friendly, and even how they carry themselves. Although first impressions are not always correct, we still use them. That's why a successful business professional

"Tell me about yourself, Kugelman—your hopes, dreams, career path, and what that damn earring means."

From Wall Street Journal, permission Cartoon Features Syndicate.

might wear an oversize graphic T-shirt, baggy shorts, and a backward ball cap when hanging out with his friends; put on khakis and a polo shirt to go to the office; and dress in a formal blue suit to make a major presentation at a professional conference. In each case, he is adjusting his look to convey appropriate personableness in different settings. As a speaker trying to build credibility with an audience, you should look for ways to adapt your personal style to one that will help the audience like you and perceive you as credible.

Besides dressing appropriately for the audience and occasion, you can increase the chances that the audience will like you by smiling at individual audience members before beginning your remarks and by looking at individuals as you speak, acknowledging them with a quick nod. You can also demonstrate personableness by using appropriate humor. By appropriate humor, we mean humor that demonstrates respect for diverse listeners by not potentially offending a particular group (e.g., sexist, ageist, racist) or the values held by them.

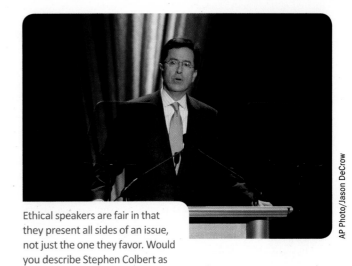

Ethical speakers are fair in that they present all sides of an issue, not just the one they favor. Would you describe Stephen Colbert as ethical in this regard?

AP Photo/Jason DeCrow

personableness: the extent to which you project an agreeable or pleasing personality

Information Comprehension and Retention

Although audience analysis helps you select a topic that is appropriate for your audience's current knowledge level, you will still need to adapt the information you present so that audience members can easily follow what you are saying and remember it when you are through. Six guidelines that can aid you are (1) appealing to diverse learning styles, (2) orienting the audience with transitions, (3) choosing specific and familiar language, (4) using vivid language and examples, (5) personalizing information, and (6) comparing unfamiliar ideas with those the audience recognizes.

Appeal to Diverse Learning Styles

A **learning style** is a person's preferred way of receiving information. Because people differ in how they prefer to learn, you should present your ideas in ways that make it easy for all audience members to understand and remember what you are saying. Models for understanding learning styles have been developed by a number of scholars across many disciplines.[3] One prominent model, called Kolb's cycle of learning, conceptualizes these preferences along four dimensions: feeling, thinking, watching, and doing.[4] Kolb's model is actually rooted in John Dewey's experiential learning theory.[5] Exhibit 5.1 illustrates the cycle.

Some people prefer to learn by "watching" and easily understand and remember things they see and hear. People who prefer to learn by watching relate to well-designed visual aids and vivid examples that they can picture. Others prefer to learn by "doing." For these people, hands-on activities aid their comprehension and memory. People who prefer to learn by doing relate well when speakers provide real-life applications and clearly state how the speech topic is relevant to their personal or professional lives.

Some people find it difficult to understand and remember factual material and learn better if their feelings are engaged. These people learn well from stories and other supporting material that appeals to their emotions or senses. Other people learn well by absorbing and considering factual material. People

learning style: a person's preferred way of receiving information

Exhibit 5.1 Kolb's cycle of learning

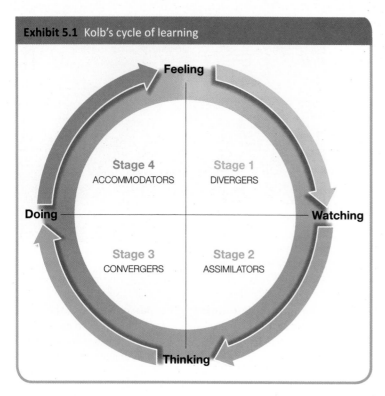

who prefer to learn by thinking connect well when your ideas are supported with detailed definitions, explanations, facts, and statistics.

Exhibit 5.1 depicts how the watching–doing and feeling–thinking dimensions of the cycle of learning theory result in four types of learners. Although each of us has a favored learning style, research reveals that all people learn most effectively when ideas are presented in ways that "round" the entire cycle of learning.[6] So as you consider what information you will provide, adapt to diverse learning styles by presenting new information in ways that appeal to watching and feeling and doing and thinking.

For example, suppose you are trying to make the point that, for the large numbers of Americans who are functionally illiterate, understanding simple directions can be a problem. Here's an illustration that develops this idea:

For instance, a person who is functionally illiterate might not be able to read or understand a label that says, "Take three times a day after eating."

Now look at how much richer this illustration becomes when we develop the statement by using supportive material that appeals to different learning styles:

A significant number of Americans are functionally illiterate. That is, about 35 million people, 20 percent of the adult population, have serious difficulties with common reading tasks (thinking). *That means that one of every five people you see today may struggle with basic reading tasks. They cannot read well enough to understand how to bake a frozen pizza, how to assemble their children's bicycle from the printed instructions, or which bus to catch from the signs at the stop* (feeling). *Many functionally illiterate people don't read well enough to follow the directions on this bottle [show an enlarged image of the label on a medicine bottle that reads, "Take three times a day after eating"]* (watching). *So the directions on a prescription bottle like this [show visual aid of enlarged prescription bottle with directions written in garbled nonsense words] are basically meaningless* (doing).

Orient the Audience with Transitions

When listeners become confused or forget basic information, they lose interest in what is being said. If your speech is more than a couple of minutes long, you can use transitions to orient your audience. A **transition** is a sentence or two that summarizes one main point and introduces the next one. Suppose your goal is to explain the three phases of clinical trial a cancer drug must pass through to earn FDA approval. After explaining the goals of the first phase, you might use a transition like this: "So the goal of the first phase is to see whether a drug that is safe in animals is also safe in humans. Phase I trials are not designed to determine whether or not the drug works; that is actually the goal in Phase II trials."

SPEECH SNIPPET

Rounding the Cycle of Learning

In her speech about hurricanes, Megan appealed to both feeling and watching by showing photos of her own hometown after it was ravaged by a hurricane She appealed to both watching and thinking by explaining hurricane categories with the help of a scale chart visual aid. And she appealed to doing by having the audience look through a box of hurricane tossed articles to search for a baby ring.

transition: a sentence or two that summarizes one main point and introduces the next one

---

To see an excellent example of orienting listeners—former President Bill Clinton's speech outlining the reasons for NATO involvement in Kosovo—go to your CourseMate for *Challenge* to access **Web Resource 5.3: Orienting Listeners**.

Choose Specific and Familiar Language

Words have many meanings, so you want to make sure your listeners understand the meaning you intend. You can do so by using specific language and choosing familiar terms. Specific words clear up the confusion caused by general words by narrowing the focus in some way. For example, saying "a banged-up 1994 baby blue Honda Civic" is more specific than "a car." Narrowing the meaning encourages your listeners to picture the same thing you are.

"To access soup, interface opener tool and rotate can to reformat container configuration."

Tedd Goff

It is also important to use familiar words. So avoid jargon and slang terms unless (1) you define them clearly the first time you use them and (2) they are central to your speech goal. For instance, in a speech on the four major problems faced by functionally illiterate people in the workplace, it will be important for your audience to understand what you mean by "functionally illiterate." So, early in the speech, you should offer your definition: "By 'functionally illiterate,' I mean people who have trouble accomplishing simple reading and writing tasks."

Use Vivid Language and Examples

Vivid examples help audience members understand and remember abstract, complex, and novel material. One vivid example can help us understand a complicated concept. So, as you prepare your speech, you will want to adapt by finding or creating real or hypothetical examples and illustrations to help your audience understand new information you present. For example, in the previous definition of functionally illiterate, the description "people who have trouble accomplishing simple reading and writing tasks" can be made more vivid by adding the following example: "For instance, a functionally illiterate person could not read and understand the directions on a prescription label that states, 'Take three times a day with a glass of water. Do not take on an empty stomach.'"

Personalize Information

We personalize information by presenting it in a frame of reference that is familiar to the audience. Devon, a student at the University of California, is to give a speech on how the Japanese economy affects U.S. markets at the student chapter of the American Marketing Association. He wants to help his audience understand geographic data about Japan. He could just quote the following statistics from the 2004 *World Almanac*:[7]

> *Japan is small and densely populated. The nation's 128 million people live in a land area of 146,000 square miles, giving them a population density of 877 persons per square mile.*

Although this would provide the necessary information, it is not adapted to an audience composed of college students in California, for example. Devon can easily adapt the information to the audience by personalizing it for this student audience.

Japan is a small, densely populated nation. Its population of 128 million is nearly half that of the United States. Yet the Japanese are crowded into a land area of only 146,000 square miles—roughly the same size as California. Just think of the implications of having half the population of the United States living here in California, where 30 million people— about one-fifth of that total—now live. In fact, Japan packs 877 persons into every square mile of land, whereas in the United States we average about 74 persons per square mile. Overall, then, Japan is about 12 times as crowded as the United States.

This revision adapts the information by personalizing it for this audience. Even though most Americans do not have the total land area of the United States on the tip of their tongue, they do know that the United States covers a great deal of territory. Likewise, a California audience would have a sense of the size of their home state compared with the rest of the nation. Personalized information is easier for audience members to understand and remember, so as you research and prepare your speech, you will want to look for ways to personalize the information. For Devon to personalize his information, he had to research the statistics on the United States and California. If Devon were speaking to an audience from another part of the country, he could adapt to them by substituting information from that state.

Compare Unknown Ideas with Familiar Ones

An easy way to adapt your material to your audience is to compare new ideas with ones the audience already understands. So, as you prepare your speech, you will want to identify places where you can use comparisons. In the speech on functional illiteracy, if you want the audience of literates to sense what functionally illiterate people experience, you might compare it to the experience of surviving in a country where one is not fluent in the language:

Many of us have taken a foreign language in school. So we figure we can visit a place where that language is spoken and "get along," right? But when we get to the country, we are often appalled to discover that even the road signs are written in this "foreign" language. And we can't quite make the signs out, at least not at sixty kilometers an hour. I was in France last summer, equipped with my three years of high school French, and I saw a sign that indicated that the train station I was looking for was "à droit"—"to the right," or is it "to the left"? I knew it was one or the other. Unfortunately, I couldn't remember and took a shot that it was to the left. Bad move. By the time I figured it out, I was ten miles in the wrong direction and ended up missing my train. At that moment, I could imagine how tough life must be for functionally illiterate people. So many "little details" of life require the ability to comprehend written messages.

Language and Cultural Differences

Western Europeans' speaking traditions inform the approach to public speaking we discuss in this book. However, public speaking is a social and cultural act, so as you would expect, public speaking practices and their

Reflect on Ethics

In an interview for an April 3, 2010, *Newsweek* magazine article, Republican Senator John McCain said, "I've never considered myself a maverick. I consider myself a person who serves the people of Arizona to the best of his abilities." This seems to be a 180-degree turn-about from what he considered himself during the 2008 presidential campaign, when he said, for example, "Sarah [Palin] and I don't agree on every issue—what do you expect of two mavericks?" His ads then touted him as "the original maverick," and he even referred to himself as a maverick when he hosted *Saturday Night Live*. Some analysts believe he may be shunning the "maverick" label now because being a

maverick doesn't play well with Republican primary voters. And he's trying—some say desperately—to retain his Senate seat. To contrast McCain's maverick image, his challenger, J. D. Hayworth, is portraying himself as the "consistent conservative."

1. Is it ethical to adapt in a way that resonates with your audience but isn't in keeping with what you really believe?

2. Could McCain achieve his current campaign goals by using different methods? If so, how?

3. What would you do if you were McCain in this situation and why?

perceived effectiveness vary. So when you address an audience composed of people from ethnic and language groups different from your own, you should make two adaptations: try to be understandable when speaking in a second language, and show respect by choosing culturally appropriate supporting material.

Work to Be Understood When Speaking in Your Second Language

When speaking to an audience in a language that is their native language but not your own, audience members may not be able to understand what you are saying because you may speak with an accent, mispronounce words, choose inappropriate words, and misuse idioms. Fear of making these mistakes can make second-language speakers self-conscious. But most audience members are more tolerant of mistakes made by a second-language speaker than they are of those made by a native speaker. Likewise, they will work hard to understand a second-language speaker.

Nevertheless, when you are speaking in a second language, you have an additional responsibility to make your speech as understandable as possible. You can help your audience by speaking more slowly and articulating as clearly as you can. By slowing your speaking rate, you give yourself additional time to pronounce difficult sounds and choose words whose meanings you know. Also, you should give your audience members additional time to adjust their ears so they can more easily process what you are saying. You can also use visual aids to reinforce key terms and concepts as you move through your speech. Doing so assures listeners that they've heard you correctly.

One of the best ways to improve is to practice the speech in front of friends and associates who are native speakers. Ask them to take note of words and phrases that you mispronounce or misuse. Then they can work with you to correct your pronunciation or help you choose other words that better express your ideas. They can also review your visual aids to make sure they

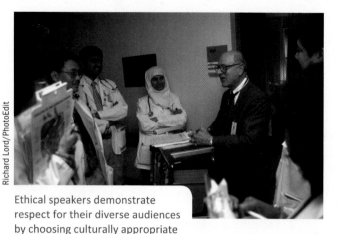

Ethical speakers demonstrate respect for their diverse audiences by choosing culturally appropriate supporting material.

are appropriate. Also, keep in mind that the more you practice speaking the language, the more comfortable you will become with it and with your ability to relate to audience members.

Choose Culturally Appropriate Supporting Material

Much of your success in adapting to the audience hinges on establishing common ground and drawing on common experiences. When you are speaking to audiences who are vastly different from you, it will take work to find out about the culture and experiences of your audience so you can adapt to them. This may mean conducting additional research to find statistics, examples, and other supporting material that will be meaningful to the audience. Or it may require you to elaborate on ideas that would be self-explanatory in your own culture. For example, suppose that Maria, a Mexican-American exchange student, was giving a narrative/personal experience speech for her speech class at Yeshiva University in Israel on the *quinceañera* party she had when she turned fifteen. Because students in Israel probably don't have any experience with the Mexican coming-of-age tradition of *quinceañera* parties, they would have trouble understanding the significance of this event unless Maria was able to use her knowledge of the bar mitzvah and bat mitzvah coming-of-age ritual celebrations in Jewish culture and relate it to them.

Forming a Specific Plan of Audience Adaptation

You now understand the challenges speakers face in developing and maintaining audience interest and understanding, and you have read about the adaptation techniques that can overcome these challenges. You have also completed your own audience analysis. So you are ready to think about the adaptation challenges you will face in your speech as well as how you might adapt to them. At this point in your preparation process, identifying the challenges you face with your audience and planning how you might meet them will provide a guide to direct your research efforts and aid you as you develop the speech. Your adaptation plan should answer the following questions:

1. **How relevant will the audience find this material?** How can I demonstrate that the material is timely, proximate, and has personal impact for audience members?

2. **What is my audience's initial disposition toward my speech topic likely to be?** What can I do to create or enhance audience interest in my topic or sympathy for my argument?

3. **What common ground do audience members share with one another and with me?** How and where can I use personal pronouns, rhetorical questions, and common experiences to enhance the perception of common ground?

4. **What can I do to enhance my credibility?** How did I develop my expertise on this topic, and how can I share that with the audience? How can I demonstrate my trustworthiness as I speak? What will I do to help the audience find me personable so they will like me?

5. **How can I make it easier for audience members to comprehend and remember the information I will share?** What types of material can I find and use to appeal to different learning style preferences? Given my topic and audience, to what ideas will the audience need to be oriented? What key terms will I need to define? What new concepts might I develop with vivid language and examples? How can I personalize the information so it is familiar to my audience? What new ideas might I want to compare to ones the audience is already familiar with?

6. **What language or cultural differences do audience members have with one another and with me?** If I will be speaking in a second language, how do I plan to increase the likelihood that the audience will understand me? What cultural differences do I need to be sensitive to, and what culturally appropriate material might I search for and use?

Speech Planning Action Step 2, Activity 2 will help you identify opportunities for audience adaptation as you develop your speeches in this course. See the Student Response box immediately following the activity for a sample of how one student completed this exercise.

SPEECH PLANNING

ACTIVITY 2

Recognizing Opportunities for Audience Adaptation

To identify opportunities for audience adaptation and lay a groundwork for applying information from the next several chapters, state your potential topic and then answer the following questions.

Potential topic: _____

1. How relevant will the audience find this material? How can I demonstrate that the material is timely, proximate, and has personal impact on the members of this audience?

2. What is my audience's initial disposition toward my speech topic likely to be?

3. What common ground do audience members share with one another and with me?

4. What can I do to enhance my credibility?

5. How can I make it easier for audience members to comprehend and remember the information I will share?

6. What language or cultural differences do audience members have with one another and with me?

CourseMate You can complete this activity online, view another student sample of this activity, and, if requested, e-mail your completed activity to your instructor. Go to your CourseMate for *Challenge* to access Action Step 2, Activity 2.

Recognizing Opportunities for Audience Adaptation

Potential topic: *The overall effects of hurricanes*

1. How relevant will the audience find this material?

Initially, since they don't live on a coast, they are not likely to see it as relevant.

How can I demonstrate that the material is timely, proximate, and has personal impact on the members of this audience?

I can make the information timely and demonstrate personal impact by talking about Hurricane Katrina, a fairly recent hurricane that most people are aware of, that affected many people, and that even affected the weather in Kentucky.

2. What is my audience's initial disposition toward my speech topic likely to be?

Most audience members will be only mildly interested in and not well informed about this topic when I begin. I hope to pique and maintain their interest by using vivid language and examples, as well as graphic photos.

3. What common ground do audience members share with one another and with me?

Because most audience members are my age and are from the same national culture, we share areas of common ground that I can draw on. First, hurricanes occur every year and affect weather patterns throughout the country when they do. I should also be able to use personal pronouns and rhetorical questions to create common ground. We are different in that I have actually lived through the devastation of a hurricane in my hometown, so I'll have to keep in mind most of my listeners have not. That means I'll have to be careful not to assume they know more than general facts about hurricanes.

4. What can I do to enhance my credibility?

I will build credibility through solid research and oral citations of sources. Early in my introduction, I'll mention where I live on the Gulf Coast and the fact that I've lived through several hurricanes.

5. How can I make it easier for audience members to comprehend and remember the information I will share?

I will round the cycle of learning by talking about my personal experiences (feeling), showing photographs (watching), offering facts and statistics about the effects of hurricanes (thinking), and providing clear instructions about how to categorize hurricanes and act appropriately to ensure safety (doing). I'll also describe the effects using vivid language and examples, and I'll compare them to other natural disasters my audience members may have experienced such as thunderstorms, tornados, and floods.

6. What language or cultural differences do audience members have with one another and with me?

I will not be speaking in a second language, but I will need to be careful not to use too many technical terms that may be "jargon" to my audience, and, when I do, I need to be sure to define them clearly. Although most audience members are U.S. nationals, there are three international students in class. I will do some research to see if any of them live in a country that experiences hurricanes, and, if so, I'll include some examples from their countries, as well.

Summary

Audience adaptation is the process of customizing your speech material to your specific audience.

One part of audience adaptation is to help the audience see the relevance of your material by demonstrating timeliness (showing how the information is useful now or in the near future), demonstrating proximity (showing relevance to personal life space), and demonstrating personal impact.

The second part of the adaptation process is to acknowledge the audience's initial disposition by framing the speech in a way that takes into account how much audience members know about your topic and what their attitudes are about it.

The third part is to develop common ground by using personal pronouns, asking rhetorical questions, and drawing from common experiences.

The fourth part is to build speaker credibility by demonstrating knowledge and expertise, establishing trustworthiness, and displaying personableness.

The fifth part is to increase audience comprehension and retention of information by creating material that appeals to diverse learning styles, orienting listeners, choosing specific and familiar language, using vivid language and examples, personalizing information, and comparing unknown ideas with familiar ones.

The sixth part is to adapt to cultural differences to be understood and demonstrate respect.

As you consider each part of audience adaptation, you can write down the specific actions you will take. This list becomes a written strategy that you can consult as you move forward in the speech-planning process. Effective speakers are able to use adaptation techniques to develop unique speeches sharing a common speech goal but tailored to the specific needs of different audiences.

Challenge Resource and Assessment Center

CourseMate Now that you have read Chapter 5, use your Speech Communication CourseMate for *The Challenge of Effective Speaking* for quick access to the electronic resources that accompany this text. These resources include the following:

- **Study tools** that will help you assess your learning and prepare for exams (*digital glossary, key term flash cards, review quizzes*).
- **Activities and assignments** that will help you hone your knowledge and build your public speaking skills throughout the course (*Speech Snippets, Speech Assignments, Action*

Step Activities). Many of these activities allow you to compare your answers with those provided by the authors, and, if requested, submit your answers to your instructor.

- **Media resources** that will help you explore communication concepts online (*Web Resources*), develop your speech outlines (*Speech Builder Express 3.0*), watch and critique videos of sample speeches (*Interactive Video Activities*), upload your speech videos for peer reviewing and critique other students' speeches (*Speech Studio online speech review tool*), and download chapter reviews so you can study when and where you'd like (*Audio Study Tools*).

This chapter's application activities and video resources are featured in this end-of-chapter section.

Applying What You've Learned

1. **Impromptu Speech Activity:** Identify a common practice that is taken for granted in your family or your community that may be an unusual or unique practice for other families or in other communities. (For example, one family celebrated Hanukkah-like birthdays where a present was received each day of the birthday week.) Prepare and present a two- to three-minute impromptu speech describing the practice in ways that employ the audience adaptation guidelines proposed in this chapter.

2. **Assessment Activity A:** Identify a cultural group in your community with which you have limited experience. Learn more about this group by (1) observing an event or other gathering, (2) participating in a cultural practice, (3) interviewing a member of the culture, as well as

(4) doing some secondary source research. Then write a two- to three-page paper in which you begin by comparing and contrasting what you have learned about this culture to your own. Then, in the second part of the paper, imagine that you were going to give a speech to an audience composed of members of this cultural group. Your assigned topic for the speech is "Reality TV." Based on what you have learned about this culture, which three of the six issues of adaptation that would be the most important for you to address, and describe how might you do that.

3. **Assessment Activity B:** Volunteer at a local service organization regularly (at least twice per week) for four weeks. Before doing so, consider some specific things you will do to seek common ground and gain credibility. Keep a journal throughout the experience, noting what worked and did not work. After four weeks, prepare a two- to three-page reflection paper regarding your adaptation experience. Focus on what you expected the experience to be like, what it was like (rewards and challenges), and what you learned about others and yourself as a result.

4. **Assessment Activity C:** Complete Action Step 2 for one of the speeches you may give this semester.

Speech-Planning Action Step

1A: Activity 2: Recognizing Opportunities for Audience Adaptation (89)

Web Resources

5.1: Demonstrating Timeliness (78)

5.2: Holistic Theory of Speaker Credibility (81)

5.3: Orienting Listeners (85)

Video Resources

1. Use your Interactive Video Activities to watch, analyze, and see the transcripts and outlines for Megan Soileau's informative speech "Understanding Hurricanes" and Tiffany Mindt's informative speech "Meat Free and Me."

2. Check out Speech Studio to see how other speakers adapted to their audiences. What did they do to demonstrate relevance, establish common ground, enhance their credibility, and adapt to cultural or language differences? Or record a speech you're working on, upload it to Speech Studio, and ask your peers for their feedback. What feedback could you use to fine-tune your audience adaptation before you give your speech in class? ✓Studio

Getty Images/BananaStock/Jupiter Images

Ethical speakers ensure that what they say is truthful by carefully researching their topic and evaluating sources for accuracy and bias.

6

gathering and evaluating information

What's the Point

QUESTIONS YOU'LL BE ABLE TO ANSWER AFTER READING THIS CHAPTER:

1. What are the differences between primary and secondary research?
2. Where can you locate information for your speech?
3. How will you evaluate information and sources?
4. How will you select and record relevant information for your speech?
5. How and why do you cite sources in a speech?

STEP 3 Gather and evaluate information

A. Examine what you know already and areas where you need additional information.

B. Locate, evaluate, and select a variety of information types and sources.

C. Prepare research cards.

D. Cite sources.

Justin was concerned. He was scheduled to give his speech in a week, but he hadn't begun to find information. A couple of months ago, he had read a magazine article about the vanishing honeybees while in the doctor's office, but he couldn't remember the name of magazine the article was in. He was still really interested in the subject. But he wondered what to do to find reliable information for a speech.

J ustin's experience is not unusual. Most of us have formed opinions about a variety of subjects based on our personal experiences, interactions with others, and things we've read or watched either online or on television. But when it comes to presenting our ideas in a public forum, we need to do research to find evidence to support them. **Evidence** is essentially any information that clarifies, explains, or otherwise adds depth or breadth to a topic. In this chapter, we explain how to locate and evaluate a variety of information types and sources, identify and select relevant information, and cite key sources appropriately in your speech.

Locate and Evaluate Information Sources

How can you quickly find the best information related to your specific speech goal? You can start by assessing your own knowledge, experience, and personal observations. Then you can move to **secondary research,** which is the process of locating information about your topic that has been discovered by other people. This includes doing Internet and library searches for relevant books, articles, general references, and websites. If the information you find from secondary sources is insufficient and doesn't answer all of the questions you are seeking answers for, you may need to conduct **primary research,** which is the process of collecting data about your topic directly from the real world.

Personal Knowledge and Experience

If you have chosen to speak on a topic you know something about, you are likely to have some personal examples and experiences you can use in your speech. For instance, musicians have special knowledge about music and instruments, entrepreneurs about starting up their own businesses, and dieticians about healthy diets. So Diane, a skilled long-distance runner, can draw on material from her own knowledge and experience for her speech on "How to Train for a Marathon." Sharing your personal knowledge and experience can also bolster your credibility if you share your **credentials**—your experiences or education that qualifies you to speak with authority on a specific subject. For Diane, establishing her credentials means briefly mentioning her training and expertise as a long-distance runner before she launches into her speech about training for a marathon.

Secondary Research

The process of locating information about your topic that has been discovered by other people is called secondary research. To conduct secondary research, you'll need to know how to locate sources and what types of sources you can draw from, as well as how to skim and evaluate them.

evidence: any information that clarifies, explains, or otherwise adds depth or breadth to a topic

secondary research: the process of locating information that has been discovered by other people

primary research: the process of conducting your own study to acquire the information you need

credentials: your experiences or education that qualifies you to speak with authority on a specific subject

SPEECH SNIPPET

Establishing Credentials

In his speech on bioluminescence—the light emitted by some living organisms, such as fireflies—Dan established his credentials by drawing on his personal knowledge as a biogenetics major and the fieldwork he had done on fireflies during an eight-week summer internship.

LOCATING SOURCES

First, you'll need to conduct a search to locate potential sources for your speech. You can do so by searching the Internet, searching online libraries and databases, and searching at a local library. Today, most of us typically begin by searching the Internet via a search engine like Google, Yahoo, or Bing. This is a great place to start because the Internet stores so much information from a variety of sources. Searching the Internet can also be overwhelming because a general search will typically reveal thousands of links. However, you can begin to collect general facts about your topic, as well as ideas as to the kinds of sources that publish material on your topic. You can also locate material on websites, blogs, YouTube, and discussion boards that might prove useful to your speech and that cannot be located elsewhere.

You can also search online libraries and databases for secondary sources about your topic. Whereas we were once limited geographically to the secondary sources housed in local libraries, we can now search hundreds of libraries across the country and the world to find material we might use in our papers and speeches. Frankly, you can often find nearly everything you need from the comfort of your own home by searching online libraries and databases. You can even search for sources at local libraries online; however, you may then want to visit the library to pick up pertinent sources such as books and articles. Visiting the library can prove helpful, too, when you get stuck trying to locate information for your speech. Although you can ask librarians for help online via an "ask the librarian" link, visiting with them face-to-face affords you their undivided attention until you are satisfied with the sources they've helped you locate. Librarians are free resources, experts who can demystify thorny research problems. Helping you is their job, so you're not imposing on them when you seek their advice.

TYPES OF SECONDARY SOURCES

As you conduct your search for secondary sources, you'll want to draw from a variety of types. You can find pertinent information in encyclopedias, books, articles in academic journals and magazines, newspapers, statistical sources, biographies, quotation books and websites, and government documents.

1. **Encyclopedias.** Encyclopedia entries can serve as a good starting point for your research. Encyclopedias give an excellent overview of many subjects and can acquaint you with the basic terminology and ideas associated with a topic. But because encyclopedias provide only overviews, they should never be the only source for your speech. General encyclopedias contain short articles about a wide variety of subjects. In addition, there are many specialized encyclopedias to choose from in areas such as art, history, religion, philosophy, and science. For instance, a college library is likely to have the *African American Encyclopedia, Latino Encyclopedia, Asian American Encyclopedia, Encyclopaedia Britannica, Encyclopedia Americana, World Book Encyclopedia, Encyclopedia of Computer Science, Encyclopedia of Women, Encyclopedia of Women in American Politics,* and many more. The online collaborative encyclopedia, Wikipedia, has become a popular research tool, but it is also a controversial source of information. Because there is no way to confirm the credibility of the people posting information in Wikipedia entries, you might use it as a starting

Someone who runs marathons would have credibility when speaking about running injuries. Can you think of topics where you would have similar credibility?

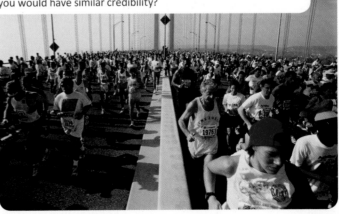
Sylvain Grandadam/Stone/Getty Images

When You're Expounding, You're Expanding

Stacey L. McKeever,
Digital Archivist
Multinational
health and nutrition
company, Los Angeles,
California

Amassing and cataloging information in digital form might evoke a vision of the cloistered librarian, but Stacey McKeever's job as a digital archivist consists of as much speech communication as it does collecting the information and artifacts associated with the company. "I'm an asset wrangler. I acquire posters, wall graphics, banners, product flyers, catalogs, and everything about the company that appears in print—as well as event photos. I convert these materials into a digital format and enter them into the database that I maintain. Since my database is available to the general public as well as company employees, I interact with a lot of people who need to access this database.

"One of my challenges is to help users of my database articulate what they need and figure out how to access it. I can talk anyone through the process of finding what he or she needs in the database. I can even do it over the phone because I'm methodical and good at giving step-by-step instructions. It's very important for me to be able to describe to users what they must do to use the database properly. I visualize what they need to do and am able to tell them what they see [on the computer screen] in front of them. I also need to be able to speak the user's language and translate highly technical language into English."

McKeever, 44, says it only took one speech class in high school "to make me realize just how much I like to talk. There were certain things about formal speaking I had to learn, but I was comfortable from the start. I tend to be a bit of a ham. I think effective speaking is also connected to whether or not you're comfortable with speaking out loud."

While getting her master's in library and information science at UCLA, Stacey worked in the departmental computer lab. "We all had to lead training sessions, and we did a lot of presentations. That's when my latent teaching gene kicked into high gear. They told us that within five years we'd all be doing public speaking of some sort."

McKeever says public speaking is easy when you are talking about "what you know." Having some attachment to the subject and being the expert allows you to have fun sharing what you know with others. McKeever doesn't over-plan her speeches, preferring to speak extemporaneously with just a few notes to remind her of her main points. "Some people write it down [word for word]. I have an idea. I mull it over. I put talking points to paper."

> **Public speaking is easy when you are talking about what you know.**

Stacy tries to make her classes and training sessions for users as inviting as possible. "I speak slowly and clearly and make sure they understand the point I'm trying to get across, and I remind them there are no stupid questions."

"Being able to speak effectively opens up doors to others. At work, I speak to coworkers, managers, and executives. Knowing how to communicate with them is exhilarating—a heady elixir. When you can speak effectively, you showcase your intelligence. And you hold court in a way that's beneficial to both your audience and yourself. Your audience gets something from what you're saying, and you get a growth moment. When you're expounding, you're expanding!"

point but not as a main source. But you can use the Notes section at the end of the articles to find links to the published sources that support and inform the entry. Then you can locate the published pieces to determine if they provide relevant and reliable evidence for your speech.

2. **Books.** If your topic has been around for more than six months, there are likely to be books written about it. Although books are excellent sources of in-depth material about a topic, most of the information in a book is likely to be at least two years old by the time it is published. So books are not a good resource if your topic is very recent or if you're looking for the latest information on a topic. You can also use the call number for one book to physically locate other books on the same subject. For example, when Diane went to the shelves to locate a book called *Improving Sports Performance in Middle and Long-Distance Running* (QT 260.5.R9 I34 1999), she discovered a number of related books located in the same area including one she would also use in her speech titled *Practical Sports Nutrition* by Louise Burke (QT 260 B959p 2007).

3. **Articles.** Articles, which may contain more current or highly specialized information on your topic than a book would, are published in **periodicals**—magazines and journals that appear at regular intervals. The information in periodical articles is often more current than that published in books because many periodicals are published weekly, biweekly, or monthly. So a periodical article is likely to be a better source if a topic is one that's "in the news." Most libraries subscribe to electronic databases that index periodical articles. Check with your librarian to learn what electronic indexes your college or university subscribes to. Four frequently available databases that index many popular magazines, such as *Time* and *Newsweek*, as well as some of the popular academic journals, such as *Communication Quarterly* and *Journal of Psychology*, are the following:

- **InfoTrac College Edition** is the electronic index that you can access from the Internet this semester through your CourseMate for *Challenge*. InfoTrac College Edition indexes millions of articles in popular magazines and academic journals.
- **InfoTrac University Library** is an expanded version of InfoTrac College Edition. Available online through most college and university libraries, it provides access to several hundred additional popular magazines and academic journals.
- **Periodical Abstract,** another electronic database available online in most college and university libraries, provides access to articles in more than 1,000 popular magazines and academic journals.
- **EBSCO,** also available online at many college and university libraries, is another database that provides access to many popular magazines and academic journals.

4. **Newspapers.** Newspaper articles are excellent sources of facts about and interpretations of both contemporary and historical issues, and they provide information about local issues and perspectives. Keep in mind, however, that most authors of newspaper articles are journalists who are not experts themselves on the topics they write about. So it is best not to rely solely on newspaper articles for your speech. Today, most newspapers are available online, which makes them very accessible. Two electronic newspaper indexes that are most useful if they are available to you are the *National Newspaper*

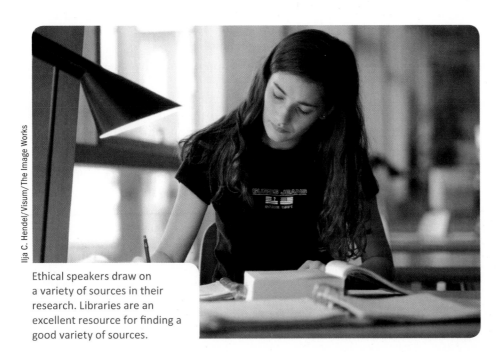

Ilja C. Hendel/Visum/The Image Works

Ethical speakers draw on a variety of sources in their research. Libraries are an excellent resource for finding a good variety of sources.

SPEECH SNIPPET

Finding Useful Information in a Book

Although Dan's speech topic, bioluminescence, was new to most of his audience, it was well studied by biogeneticists. So while an Internet search looking for "bioluminescence books" turned up several potential sources, Dan needed to use his university's online library database to locate copies of the books and then pick them up in person in order to skim them for useful information.

SPEECH SNIPPET

Finding Articles from an Online Database

Lauren typed the subject "prescription drug abuse" into the "subject" prompt on the home page of the EBSCO database. The search revealed 108 references from a variety of highly respected periodicals including the *National Review,* the *Journal of the American Medical Association,* and *American Medical News.*

SPEECH SNIPPET

Accessing Newspaper Articles

Carl wanted to give a speech on Everglades restoration efforts, so to understand how Floridians viewed this project Carl accessed the website of the *Miami Herald,* where he found 119 recent articles and more than 3,500 archived articles.

periodicals: magazines and journals that appear at fixed periods

Index, which indexes five major newspapers—the *New York Times, Wall Street Journal, Christian Science Monitor, Washington Post,* and *Los Angeles Times*—and *Newsbank,* which provides not only the indexes but also the text of articles from more than 450 U.S. and Canadian newspapers. If you don't have access to an electronic newspaper index, you may be able to access articles about your topic at the websites of specific newspapers.

5. **Statistical sources.** Statistical sources present numerical information on a wide variety of subjects. When you need facts about demography, continents, heads of state, weather, or similar subjects, access one of the many single-volume sources that report such data. *The Statistical Abstract of the United States,* which provides numerical information on various aspects of American life, is available online. For links to other web-based statistical sources, go to your CourseMate for *Challenge* to access **Web Resource 6.1: Online Statistics**. To read an interesting essay on the improper uses of statistics, access **Web Resource 6.2: Bad Uses of Statistics and Polling**.

6. **Biographies.** When you need an account of a person's life, from thumbnail sketches to reasonably complete essays, you can use a biographical reference source. Although you can access some biographical information online, you will find information of more depth and breadth by reading full-length biographies and by consulting biographical references such as *Who's Who in America* and *International Who's Who.* Your library is also likely to carry *Contemporary Black Biography, Dictionary of Hispanic Biography, Native American Women, Who's Who of American Women, Who's Who Among Asian Americans,* and many more. For links to web-based collections of biographical references, use your CourseMate for *Challenge* to access **Web Resource 6.3: Online Biographical References**.

7. **Quotation books and websites.** A good quotation can be especially provocative as well as informative, and there are times you want to use a quotation from a respected person. *Bartlett's Familiar Quotations* is a popular source of quotes from historical as well as contemporary figures. But many other collections of quotations are also available. Some others include *The International Thesaurus of Quotations; Harper Book of American Quotations; My Soul Looks Back, 'Less I Forget: A Collection of Quotations by People of Color; The New Quotable Woman;* and *The Oxford Dictionary of Quotations.* Some popular quotation websites include *The Quotations Page* and *Quoteland.com.* For links to web-based collections of quotations, go to your CourseMate for *Challenge* to access **Web Resource 6.4: Online Quotations.**

8. **Government documents.** If your topic is related to public policy, government documents may provide useful information. The *Federal Register* publishes daily regulations and legal notices issued by the U.S. executive branch and all federal agencies. It is divided into sections, such as rules and regulations and Sunshine Act meetings. Of special interest are announcements of hearings and investigations, committee meetings, and agency decisions and rulings. The *Monthly Catalog of United States Government Publications* covers publications of all branches of the federal government. It has semiannual and annual cumulative indexes by title, author/agency, and subject. For links to several frequently used U.S. federal government documents, go to your CourseMate for *Challenge* to access **Web Resource 6.5: Online Government Publications**.

SKIMMING TO DETERMINE SOURCE VALUE

skimming: a method of rapidly going through a work to determine what is covered and how

Because your search of secondary sources is likely to uncover far more information than you can use, you will want to skim sources to determine whether or not to read them in full. **Skimming** is a method of rapidly going through a work to determine what is covered and how.

If you are evaluating an article, spend a minute or two finding out whether it really presents information on the exact area of the topic you are exploring and whether it contains any documented statistics, examples, or quotable opinions. You can often do so by reading the **abstract**—a short paragraph summarizing the research findings. (We will examine the kind of information to look for in the next section.) If you are evaluating a book, read the table of contents carefully, look at the index, and skim pertinent chapters, asking the same questions as you would for a magazine article. Skimming helps you decide which sources should be read in full, which should be read in part, and which should be abandoned. Minutes spent skimming will save hours of reading.

abstract: a short paragraph summarizing the research findings

EVALUATING SOURCES

Secondary sources vary in their accuracy, reliability, and validity. Accurate sources do not distort information or demonstrate bias by not reporting conflicting pieces of information. Reliable sources can be counted on to repeatedly present accurate information. Valid sources contain information that has been demonstrated to be true. So before you use the information from a source in your speech, you will want to evaluate it. Four criteria you can use to determine the accuracy, reliability, and validity of sources are authority, objectivity, currency, and relevance.

1. **Authority.** The first test of a resource is the expertise of its author and/ or the reputation of the publishing or sponsoring organization. When an author is listed, you can check the author's credentials through biographical references or by seeing if the author has a home page listing professional qualifications. Use the electronic periodical indexes or check the Library of Congress to see what else the author has published in the field.

   On the Internet, you will find information that is anonymous or credited to someone whose background is not clear. In these cases, your ability to trust the information depends on evaluating the qualifications of the sponsoring organization. On the Internet, URLs ending in ".gov" (governmental), ".edu" (educational), and ".org" are noncommercial sites with institutional publishers. The URL ".com" indicates that the sponsor is a for-profit organization. If you do not know whether you can trust the sources, then do not use the information.

2. **Objectivity.** Although all authors have a viewpoint, you will want to be wary of information that is overly slanted. Documents that have been published by business, government, or public interest groups should be carefully scrutinized for obvious biases or good public relations fronts. To evaluate the potential biases in articles and books, read the preface or identify the thesis statement. These often reveal the author's point of view. When evaluating a website with which you are unfamiliar, look for its purpose. Most home pages contain a purpose or mission statement (sometimes in a link called "About Us"). Armed with this information, you are in a better position to recognize potential biases in the information.

3. **Currency.** In general, newer information is more accurate than older. So when evaluating your sources, be sure to consult the latest information you can find. One of the reasons for using web-based sources is that they can provide more up-to-date information than printed sources.[1] But just because a source is found online does not mean that the information is timely. To determine how current the information is, you will need to find out when the book was published, the article was written, the study was conducted, or the article was placed on the web or revised. Web page dates are usually listed at

survey: a canvassing of people to get information about their ideas and opinions, which are then analyzed for trends

ethnography: a form of primary research based on fieldwork observations

CourseMate

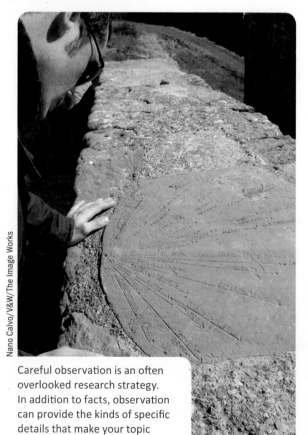

Careful observation is an often overlooked research strategy. In addition to facts, observation can provide the kinds of specific details that make your topic come alive for an audience.

Nano Calvo/V&W/The Image Works

the end of the article. If there are no dates listed, you have no way of judging how current the information is.

4. **Relevance.** During your research, you will likely come across a great deal of interesting information. Whether that information is appropriate for your speech is another matter. Relevant information is directly related to your topic and supports your main points, making your speech easier to follow and understand. Irrelevant information will only confuse listeners, so you should avoid using it no matter how interesting it is.

Web Resource 6.6: Analyzing Information Sources provides information on additional criteria you can use to evaluate your sources. Go to your CourseMate for *Challenge* to access this resource. And for more information on evaluating websites as sources of information, go to your CourseMate for *Challenge* to access **Web Resource 6.7: Evaluating Internet Sources**.

Primary Research

When there is little secondary research available on your topic or on a main idea you want to develop in your speech, or when you wonder whether what you are reading about is true in a particular setting, consider doing primary research which is conducting your own study in the real world. But keep in mind that primary research is much more labor intensive and time consuming than secondary research—and, in the professional world, much more costly. If after making an exhaustive search of secondary sources you cannot locate the information you need, try getting it by conducting fieldwork observations, surveys, interviews, original artifact or document examinations, or experiments.

FIELDWORK OBSERVATIONS

Sometimes you might question whether what you are reading in secondary research actually happens in a particular setting or with a particular group, or you might wonder whether something that was true in the past is still true today. To find out, you might conduct *fieldwork observations*, also known as **ethnography**. If, for instance, you are planning to talk about how social service agencies help the homeless find shelter and job training or the process involved in adopting a pet, you can learn more by visiting or even volunteering for a period of time at a homeless shelter or humane society. By focusing on specific behaviors and taking notes on your observations, you will have a record of specifics that you can use in your speech.

SURVEYS

A **survey** is a canvassing of people to get information about their ideas and opinions, which are then analyzed for trends. Surveys are especially effective for discovering the attitudes, values, and beliefs generally held by a group of people. Surveys may be conducted in person, over the phone or Internet, or in writing. At times, your secondary research will reveal publications that summarize findings from surveys that have been conducted by other people or organizations. At other times, you may want to conduct your own survey. If you decide to conduct your own survey, go to your

CourseMate for *Challenge* to access **Web Resource 6.8: Conducting Surveys**, which will provide you with important tips for collecting good information.

CourseMate

INTERVIEWS

Like media reporters, you may get some of your best information from an **interview**—a planned, structured conversation where one person asks questions and another answers them. To be effective, you'll want to select the best person to interview, prepare a solid **interview protocol** (the list of questions you plan to ask), and adhere to several ethical guidelines when conducting and then processing the actual interview.

1. **Selecting the best person.** Somewhere on campus or in the larger community are people who have expertise in the topic area of your speech and who can provide you with information. Usually a few telephone calls and a bit of research will lead you to the person who would be best to talk with about your topic. For instance, for a speech on "how to get a music recording contract," you might begin by asking a professor in the music department for the name of a music production agency in your community or nearby. Or you could find one by searching online. Once you find a website, you can usually find an "About Us" or "Contact Us" link on it, which will offer names, titles, e-mail addresses, and phone numbers. You should be able to find someone appropriate to your purpose from this list. Once you have identified a potential interviewee, you should contact the person to make an appointment. Today, it is generally best to do so by both e-mail and telephone if possible. Be forthright in your reasons for scheduling the interview. Whether your interview is for a class speech or for a different audience, say so. You should also tell the person how long you expect the interview to take and suggest several dates and time ranges so the person can select the date and time that works best for him or her.

At the end of the conversation to set up the interview, thank the person, repeat the date and time of the interview, and confirm the office location. If you make the appointment more than a few days in advance, it is usually wise to call the day before the interview to confirm the appointment.

Finally, before interviewing the expert, make sure that you have done other research on the topic, especially anything he or she has written about it. Likewise, do your research to understand the expert's credentials. Interviewees are more likely to talk with you if you appear informed, and being informed will ensure that you ask better questions. You don't want to waste the interviewee's time by asking questions you could find elsewhere.

2. **Preparing the interview protocol.** The heart of an effective interview is a list of good questions. How many questions you plan to ask depends on how much time you have for the interview. Keep in mind, however, that you never know how a person will respond. Some people may answer every question you were planning to ask in response to your first question; other people will answer each question with just a few words.

Early in the interview, you will want to establish rapport by asking some questions that can be answered easily and that will show your respect for the person you are interviewing. In his interview with a professor, Justin started with background questions such as, "How did you get interested in doing research on CCD?" The goal is to get the interviewee to feel at ease and talk

interview: a planned, structured conversation where one person asks questions and another answers them

interview protocol: the list of questions you plan to ask

SPEECH SNIPPET

Determining Audience Attitudes with a Survey

For her speech on prescription drug abuse, Lauren wanted to know where people in her community and students attending her school stood on the issue. So she conducted a telephone survey of the community, an Internet survey of students on campus, and a paper-and-pencil survey of her classmates, asking them whether they agreed or disagreed with the statement, "Prescription drug abuse is a real problem in our country today." She was then able to tailor her speech to address her classmates' attitudes toward the topic and use the other survey data to inform them about where the campus and community stood regarding the topic.

For his speech on the vanishing honeybees, Justin looked at the Biology Department website and discovered a faculty member who has actually published two papers on the vanishing honeybees. He read the papers and learned that the phenomenon is referred to as CCD, or Colony Collapse Disorder. He decided to try to set up an interview with the professor to learn more. He telephoned and left this message, which he followed up with an e-mail message:

Hello, my name is Justin Martin. I am preparing a classroom speech on CCD and know that you are an expert on this subject. If possible, I'd like to make an appointment to talk with you. Would you be available to talk with me for fifteen or twenty minutes during the next few days?

primary questions: questions the interviewer plans ahead of time

secondary questions: questions designed to probe the answers given to primary questions

open questions: broad-based questions that ask the interviewee to provide perspective, ideas, information, or opinions

closed questions: narrowly focused questions that require only very brief answers

freely. Then you can ask the major questions you have prepared. You may not ask all the questions you planned, but you don't want to end the interview until you have the important information you intended to get. A good interview protocol will consist of a mix of primary and secondary questions that are phrased to be neutral rather than leading.

Primary questions are the lead-in questions about one of the major topics of the interview, typically related to the main points for the speech. **Secondary questions** are follow-up questions designed to probe the answers given to primary questions. Although some follow-ups are planned ahead by anticipating possible answers, more often than not they are composed as the interview goes along. Some simply encourage the interviewee to continue ("And then?" "Is there more?"); others probe into what the person has said ("What does 'frequently' mean?" "What were you thinking at the time?"); and some probe the feelings of the interviewee ("How did it feel to win the prize?" "Were you worried when you didn't find her?").

Open questions are broad-based probes that ask the interviewee to provide perspective, ideas, information, or opinions as he or she wishes, which gives the interviewee more control, but these questions take time to answer ("Why do you think the vanishing honeybee crisis is happening so quickly and dramatically today?" "What are some kinds of behaviors you have seen bees exhibit when afflicted with this disease?" "What would you recommend people like me who aren't scientists or beekeepers do to help?" "What research studies are you working on next?").[2]

Closed questions are narrowly focused and require very brief (one- or two-word) answers. Some require a simple yes or no ("Do you believe we can stop the CCD crisis?"); others need only a short response ("What do you believe to be the most significant cause of CCD?"). By asking closed questions, interviewers can control the interview and obtain specific information quickly. But the answers cannot reveal the nuances behind responses, nor are they likely to yield much voluntary information.[3]

For the most part, questions should be phrased neutrally. **Neutral questions** are phrased in ways that do not direct a person's answers—for example, "What can you tell me about your work with Habitat for Humanity?" By contrast, **leading questions** are phrased in a way that suggests the interviewer has a preferred answer—for example, "What do you like about working for Habitat for Humanity?"

Exhibit 6.1 lists some of the questions you might ask in an interview with a music producer.

3. **Conducting the interview.** The following ethical guidelines characterize the "best practices" for ensuring an effective interview.

- **Dress professionally.** Doing so sends a message to the interviewee that you *respect* the time they are giving and take the interview seriously.
- **Be prompt.** You also demonstrate *respect* by showing up prepared to begin at the time you have agreed to. Remember to allow enough time for potential traffic or parking problems.
- **Be courteous.** Begin the interview by introducing yourself and the purpose for the interview and by thanking the person for taking the time to talk to you. Remember, although the interviewee may enjoy talking about the subject, may be flattered, and may wish to share knowledge, that person has nothing to gain from the interview. So you should let the interviewee know you are grateful to him or her for taking the time to talk with you. Most of all, *respect* what the person says regardless of what you may think of the answers.

Exhibit 6.1 Sample interview questions

Rapport-Building Opener

How did you get interested in becoming a music producer?

Major Topic Questions

Primary Question #1: How do you find artists to consider for contract?
 Secondary Question: Is this different from the methods used by other producers?
 Secondary Question: Do artists ever come to you in other ways?
Primary Question #2: Once an artist has been brought to your attention, what course of action follows?
 Secondary Question: Do you ever just see an artist or band and immediately sign them?
 Secondary Question: What's the longest period of time you "auditioned" an artist or band before signing them?
Primary Question #3: What criteria do you use in deciding to offer a contract?
 Secondary Question: How important are the artist's age, sex, or ethnicity?
Primary Question #4: Can you tell me the story of how you came to sign one of your most successful artists?
 Secondary Question: What do you think made the artist so successful?
Primary Question #5: Can you tell me the story of an artist you signed that was not successful?
 Secondary Question: Why do you think this artist failed?
 Secondary Question: Do you think it was a mistake to sign this artist?
 Secondary Question: In retrospect, what could you or the artist have done differently that might have helped him or her succeed?

SPEECH SNIPPET

Preparing Primary Questions

For his interview with a music producer, Noah prepared his primary questions around the topics of finding artists, the decision process, criteria for signing an artist, and stories of success and failure.

neutral questions: questions phrased in ways that do not direct a person's answers

leading questions: questions phrased in a way that suggests the interviewer has a preferred answer

---

- **Ask permission to record.** If you want to tape-record the interview, ask permission. If the interviewee says "no," *respect* his or her wishes and take careful notes instead.

- **Listen carefully.** At key places in the interview, repeat what the interviewee has said in your own words to ensure that you really understand him or her and to assure the interviewee that you will report the answers *truthfully* and *fairly* during your speech.

- **Keep the interview moving.** You do not want to rush the person, but you do want to behave *responsibly* by getting your questions answered during the allotted time.

- **Monitor your nonverbal reactions.** Demonstrate *integrity* when your facial expressions and your gestures match the tone you want to communicate. Maintain good eye contact with the person. Nod to show understanding, and smile occasionally to maintain the friendliness of the interview. How you look and act is likely to determine whether the person will warm up to you and give you an informative interview.

- **Get permission to quote.** Be sure to get permission for exact quotes. Doing so demonstrates that you *respect* the interviewee and want to report his or her ideas *honestly* and *fairly*. Doing so also communicates that you have *integrity* and strive to act *responsibly*. You might even offer to let the person see a copy of the formal outline for your speech before you actually give it or invite him or her to attend the presentation.

Ethical interviewers demonstrate honesty, respect, integrity, fairness, and responsibility by following several "best practices" for conducting interviews.

Rob Loud/Getty Images

Conducting Experiments for Primary Research

Justin had heard that the radio waves of cellular telephones are one reason honeybees become disoriented, cannot make it home to their hives, and then die. He followed the suggestion he read about placing a cell phone in a flower garden to observe what happens. Of course, he only did this long enough to see the bees' reaction, not long enough to cause a lasting result.

factual statements: information that can be verified

■ **Confirm credentials.** Before you leave, be sure to confirm your interviewee's professional title and the company or organization he or she works with. Doing so is acting *responsibly* because you'll need these details when explaining why you chose to interview this person.

■ **End on time.** As with arriving promptly, ending the interview when you said you would demonstrates *respect* for the interviewee and his or her valuable time and that you act *responsibly* and with *integrity*.

■ **Thank the interviewee.** Always close the interview by thanking the interviewee. This closure leads to positive rapport should you need to follow up with the interviewee later, and it demonstrates that you recognize the person gave up valuable time to visit with you. You may even follow up with a short thank you note after you leave.

4. **Processing the interview.** Because your interview notes were probably taken in an outline or shorthand form and may be difficult to translate later, sit down with your notes as soon as possible after the interview and make individual research cards of the information you may want to use in the speech. (Research cards will be discussed in detail later in this chapter.) If at any point you are not sure whether you have accurately transcribed what the person said, take a minute to telephone or e-mail the person to double-check.

ORIGINAL ARTIFACT OR DOCUMENT EXAMINATIONS

Sometimes the information you need may not have been published. Rather, it may exist in an original unpublished source, such as an ancient manuscript, a diary, personal correspondence, or company files. Or you may need to view an object to get the information you need, such as a geographic feature, a building, a monument, or an artifact in a museum.

EXPERIMENTS

You can design a study to test a hypothesis you have. Then, you can report the results of your experiment in your speech. Keep in mind that experimenting takes time, and you must understand the principles of the scientific process of experimentation to be able to trust results of a formal experiment. However, sometimes you can do an informal experiment to test the results of a study you learn about elsewhere.

Speech Planning Action Step 3, Activity 3A will help you evaluate and compile a list of potential sources for your speeches in this course. See the Student Response box immediately following the activity for a sample of how one student completed this exercise.

Each episode of the television program *MythBusters* is actually made up of a series of simple experiments.

Discovery Channel/Everett Collection

Identify and Select Relevant Information

The information you find in your sources that you will want to use in your speech may include factual statements, expert opinions, and elaborations.

Factual Statements

Factual statements are those that can be verified. "A recent study confirmed that preschoolers watch an average of twenty-eight hours of television a week" and "The microprocessor, which was

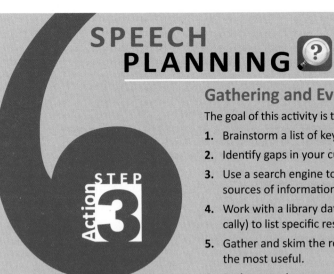

SPEECH PLANNING

STEP Action 3

Gathering and Evaluating Information Sources

The goal of this activity is to help you compile a list of potential sources for your speech.

1. Brainstorm a list of keywords that are related to your speech goal.

2. Identify gaps in your current knowledge that you would like to fill.

3. Use a search engine to identify sponsored and personal websites that may be sources of information for your speech.

4. Work with a library database (either physically located at the library or electronically) to list specific resources that appear to provide information for your speech.

5. Gather and skim the resources you have identified to decide which are likely to be the most useful.

6. Evaluate each resource to determine how much faith you can place in the information.

7. Determine what primary research you might conduct to fill gaps in the information you have collected.

CourseMate You can complete this activity online, print it, and, if requested, e-mail it to your instructor. Go to your CourseMate for *Challenge* to access Action Step 3, Activity 3A.

STUDENT RESPONSE

Gathering and Evaluating Information Sources

Speech goal: *I would like the audience to understand why honeybees are vanishing.*

1. Brainstorm a list of keywords that are related to your speech goal. *honeybees, bumblebees, beekeepers, colony collapse disorder*

2. Identify gaps in your current knowledge that you would like to fill. *Because I'm a biology major and have done an eight-week internship in the field, I am familiar with the kinds of works I'll need to seek out in order to fill any gaps in my knowledge.*

3. Use a search engine to identify sponsored and personal websites that may be sources of information for your speech. *I searched using Google and found a Wikipedia entry that I used as a starting point to locate other websites and an interview with a beekeeper I could use in my speech.*

STEP Action 3

4. Work with a library database (either physically located at the library or electronically) to list specific resources that appear to provide information for your speech. *Journal of Bee Biology, Science, Biology Quarterly, Entomol,*

5. Gather and skim the resources you have identified to decide which are likely to be the most useful.

6. Evaluate each resource to determine how much faith you can place in the information.

7. Determine what primary research you might conduct to fill gaps in the information you have collected. *I will interview my adviser, who has been studying the vanishing bees since 2006.*

invented by Ted Hoff at Intel in 1971, made the creation of personal computers possible" are both statements of fact that can be verified. One way to verify whether the information is factual is to check it against other sources on the same subject. Never use any information that is not carefully documented unless you have corroborating sources. Factual statements may come in the form of statistics or real examples.

STATISTICS

statistics: numerical facts

Statistics are numerical facts. Statistical statements, such as, "Only five of every ten local citizens voted in the last election" or "The national unemployment rate for March 2010 was 9.7 percent" can provide impressive support for a point, but when they are poorly used in a speech, they may be boring and, in some instances, downright deceiving. Here are some ethical guidelines for using statistics effectively.

1. **Use only statistics you can verify to be reliable and valid.** Taking statistics from only the most reliable sources and double-checking any startling statistics with another source will guard against the use of faulty statistics.

2. **Use only recent statistics so your audience will not be misled.**

3. **Use statistics comparatively.** By themselves, statistics are hard to interpret. When we present comparative statistics, they are easier to understand. You can show growth decline, gain, or loss by comparing two numbers. For example, according to the U.S. Department of Labor, the national unemployment rate for March 2010 was 9.7 percent. This statistic is more meaningful when you also mention that this figure has held steady for three months or when you compare it with 8.5 percent in March 2009 and with 5.1 percent in March 2008.

4. **Use statistics sparingly.** Although statistics may be an excellent way to present a great deal of material quickly, be careful not to overuse them. A few pertinent numbers are far more effective than a battery of statistics. When you believe you must use many statistics, your audience is likely to understand them better if you also show them via a chart or graph on a visual aid.

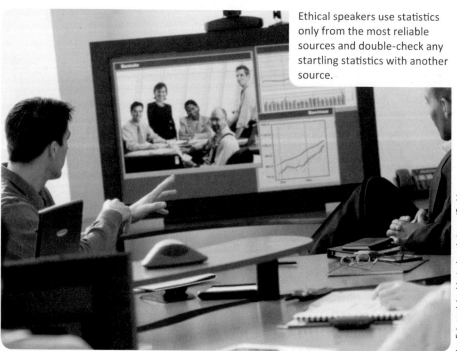

Ethical speakers use statistics only from the most reliable sources and double-check any startling statistics with another source.

Jon Feingersh/corbisstockmarket.com/Corbis

5. **Remember that statistics are biased.** Mark Twain once said there are three kinds of lies: "lies, damned lies, and statistics."[4] Not all statistics are lies, of course, but consider the source of statistics you'd like to use, what that source may have been trying to prove with these data, and how that situation might have influenced the way the data were collected and interpreted. No statistic can represent the truth perfectly, so evaluate the source thoughtfully and cross-check the method used to collect and interpret the data before using them.[4]

EXAMPLES

Examples are specific instances that illustrate or explain a general factual statement. Because you can usually find an example to make any point, ethical speakers are careful to use only examples that are typical of the more general case. One or two short examples such as the following are often enough to help make a generalization meaningful.

> *One way a company increases its power is to acquire another company. Recently, Delta bought out Northwest Airlines and is now the world's largest airline company.*

> *Professional figure skaters practice many long hours every day. 2010 Olympic Gold medalist Adam Rippon practices twenty to twenty-five hours per week.*

Examples are useful because they provide concrete details that make a general statement more meaningful to the audience.

Although most of the examples you find will be real, you may find a hypothetical example you can use or you might create one yourself. **Hypothetical examples** are specific illustrations based on reflections about future events. They develop the idea "What if . . . ?" In the following excerpt, John A. Ahladas presents some hypothetical examples of what it will be like in the year 2039 if global warming continues.

> *In New York, workers are building levees to hold back the rising tidal waters of the Hudson River, now lined with palm trees. In Louisiana, 100,000 acres of wetland are steadily being claimed by the sea. In Kansas, farmers learn to live with drought as a way of life and struggle to eke out an existence in the increasingly dry and dusty heartland. . . . And reports arrive from Siberia of bumper crops of corn and wheat from a longer and warmer growing season.[5]*

Because hypothetical examples are not themselves factual, you must be very careful to check that the facts on which they are based are accurate.

Three principles should guide your use of examples. First, the examples should be clear and specific enough to create a picture the audience can understand. Consider the following generalization and supporting example.

Generalization: Electronics is one of the few areas in which products are significantly cheaper today than they were in the 1980s.

Supporting example: In the mid-1980s, Motorola sold cell phones for $5,000 each; now a person can buy a cell phone for under $50.

With this single example, the listener has a vivid picture of the tremendous difference in about a thirty-year period.

Second, the examples you use should be representative. If cell phones were the *only* electronics product whose prices had dropped so much over that same period, this vivid example would be misleading and unethical. Any misuse of data is unethical, especially if the user knows better.

Third, use at least one example to support every generalization.

examples: specific instances that illustrate or explain a general factual statement

hypothetical examples: specific instances based on reflections about future events

DEFINITIONS

definition: a statement that clarifies the meaning of a word or phrase

A **definition** is a statement that clarifies the meaning of a word or phrase. Definitions are often used in speeches to clarify a topic or some aspect of it. Definitions serve to clarify in three ways.

First, definitions clarify the meaning of terminology that is specialized, technical, or otherwise likely to be unfamiliar to your audience. For example, when Dan talked about bioluminescence, he clarified the meaning of the word *bioluminescence* with the following definition: "According to *Encyclopaedia Britannica Online*, bioluminescence is the emission of visible light by living organisms like fireflies." Although dictionaries and encyclopedias contain definitions, your speech topic might be such that you have to find definitions through prominent researchers or professional practitioners. For example, in a speech about eating disorders, you might go to the website of the American Dietetic Association for your definition of the term *eating disorders.*

Second, definitions clarify words and terms that have more than one meaning and might be misconstrued. For example, because *child abuse* is a term that encompasses a broad range of behaviors, you might choose to define it in a way that acknowledges which behaviors you intend to focus on in your speech.

Third, particularly with controversial subjects, definitions clarify your stance on a subject in an effort to draw listeners to interpret it as you do. For example, in a speech about domestic violence against women, former U.S. Secretary of Health and Human Services Donna Shalala defined such violence as "terrorism in the home."[6]

Expert Opinions

expert opinions: interpretations and judgments made by authorities in a particular subject area

Expert opinions are interpretations and judgments made by authorities in a particular subject area. They can help explain what facts mean or put them in perspective. "Watching twenty-eight hours of television a week is far too much for young children" and "Having a firewire port on your computer is absolutely necessary" are opinions. Whether they are expert opinions or not depends on who made the statements.

How do you tell if a source is an expert? An expert is someone who has mastered a specific subject, usually through long-term study, and is recognized by other people in the field as being a knowledgeable and trustworthy authority. For instance, a history professor may be an expert in ancient Greek city-states but might know little about ancient Aztec civilization.

When you use expert opinions in your speech, you should always cite the credentials of the expert. You should also identify comments from the expert as opinions. For instance, an informative speaker might say, "Temperatures throughout the 1990s were much higher than average. Paul Jorgenson, a space biologist, believes that these higher-than-average temperatures represent the first stages of the greenhouse effect, but the significance of these temperatures is still being debated."

Elaborations

Both factual information and expert opinions can be elaborated on through anecdotes and narratives, comparisons and contrasts, or quotable explanations and opinions.

ANECDOTES AND NARRATIVES

anecdotes: brief, often amusing stories

narratives: accounts, personal experiences, tales, or lengthier stories

Anecdotes are brief, often amusing stories; **narratives** are accounts, personal experiences, tales, or lengthier stories. Because holding audience interest is important and because audience attention is likely to be captured by a story,

---

SPEECH SNIPPET

Stating the Credentials of the Person You Interviewed

Justin's adviser is a nationally known expert on colony collapse disorder and the vanishing honeybee crisis, so he chose to interview her for his speech. Justin revealed her credentials in his speech by saying, "I have the privilege of having as my adviser one of the nation's leading colony collapse disorder scholars. In an interview with Dr. Susan Stromme, I learned that the radiation emitted from cell phones is one major cause of death for the bees."

anecdotes and narratives are worth looking for or creating. In a five-minute speech, you have little time to tell a detailed story, so one or two anecdotes or a very short narrative would be preferable.

The key to using stories is to make sure that the point of the story directly states or reinforces the point you are making in your speech. In the following speech excerpt, John Howard makes a point about failure to follow guidelines.

Tim Shaffer/Reuters /Landov

When it was announced that actor and director Jodie Foster would deliver the 2006 commencement address at the University of Pennsylvania, some students were skeptical—maybe they thought she'd be boring. However, she related to her audience and held their attention with stories about her own college experiences and about the September 11 attacks on New York City—and she ended with a quote by rapper Eminem!

> *The knight was returning to the castle after a long, hard day. His face was bruised and badly swollen. His armor was dented. The plume on his helmet was broken, and his steed was limping. He was a sad sight.*
>
> *The lord of the castle ran out and asked, "What hath befallen you, Sir Timothy?"*
>
> *"Oh, Sire," he said, "I have been laboring all day in your service, bloodying and pillaging your enemies to the West."*
>
> *"You've been doing what?" gasped the astonished nobleman. "I haven't any enemies to the West!"*
>
> *"Oh!" said Timothy. "Well, I think you do now."*
>
> *There is a moral to this little story. Enthusiasm is not enough. You need to have a sense of direction.[7]*

Good stories and narratives may be humorous, sentimental, suspenseful, or dramatic.

COMPARISONS AND CONTRASTS

One of the best ways to give meaning to new ideas is through comparison and contrast. **Comparisons** illuminate a point by showing similarities. Although you can easily create comparisons using information you have found, you should still keep your eyes open for creative comparisons developed by the authors of the books and articles you have found.

comparison: illuminating a point by showing similarities

Comparisons may be literal or figurative. Literal comparisons show similarities of real things:

> *The walk from the lighthouse back up the hill to the parking lot is equal to walking up the stairs of a thirty-story building.*

Figurative comparisons express one thing in terms normally denoting another:

> *I always envisioned myself as a four-door sedan. I didn't know she was looking for a sports car!*

Comparisons make ideas both clearer and more vivid. Notice how Steven Joel Trachtenberg, in a speech to the Newington High School Scholars' Breakfast, uses a figurative comparison to demonstrate the importance of a willingness to

contrast: illuminating a point by highlighting differences

plagiarism: the unethical act of representing another person's work as your own

take risks even in the face of danger. Although the speech was given years ago, the point is timeless:

> *The eagle flying high always risks being shot at by some hare-brained human with a rifle. But eagles and young eagles like you still prefer the view from that risky height to what is available flying with the turkeys far, far below.*[8]

Whereas comparisons suggest similarities, **contrasts** highlight differences. Notice how the following humorous contrast dramatizes the difference between "participation" and "commitment."

> *If this morning you had bacon and eggs for breakfast, I think it illustrates the difference. The eggs represented "participation" on the part of the chicken. The bacon represented "total commitment" on the part of the pig!*[9]

QUOTATIONS

When you find an explanation, an opinion, or a brief anecdote that seems to be exactly what you are looking for, you may quote it directly in your speech. Because audiences want to listen to your ideas and arguments, they do not want to hear a string of long quotations. Nevertheless, a well-selected quotation may be perfect in one or two key places.

Quotations can both explain and enliven. Look for quotations that make a point in a particularly clear or vivid way. For example, in his speech "Enduring Values for a Secular Age," Hans Becherer, executive officer at Deere & Company, used this Henry Ford quote to show the importance of enthusiasm to progress:

> *Enthusiasm is at the heart of all progress. With it, there is accomplishment. Without it, there are only alibis.*[10]

Frequently, historical or literary quotations can reinforce a point vividly. Cynthia Opheim, chair of the Department of Political Science at Southwest Texas State University, in her speech "Making Democracy Work," used this quote from Mark Twain on the frustration of witnessing legislative decision making:

> *There are two things you should never watch being made: sausage and legislation.*[11]

When you use a direct quotation, you need to verbally acknowledge the person it came from. Using any quotation or close paraphrase without crediting its source is **plagiarism,** the unethical act of representing another person's work as your own.

Drawing Information from Multiple Cultural Perspectives

How we perceive facts and what opinions we hold often are influenced by our cultural background. Therefore, it is important to draw your information from culturally diverse perspectives by seeking sources that have differing cultural orientations and by interviewing experts with diverse cultural backgrounds. For example, when Carrie was preparing for her speech on proficiency testing in grade schools, she purposefully searched for articles written by noted Hispanic, Asian, and African American, as well as European American, authors. In addition, she interviewed two local school superintendents—one from an urban district and one from a suburban district. Because she consciously worked to develop diverse sources of information, Carrie had greater confidence that her speech would more accurately reflect all sides of the debate on proficiency testing.

Reflect on Ethics

In 2005 the popular British rock band Coldplay admitted to *Rolling Stone* magazine that they plagiarized from various musical sources on their 2005 album *X & Y*. After admitting it, they also admitted that the album should have included a bibliography, discography, or references for the "borrowed" material. Despite their admission, they suffered no repercussions. Then, according to a report published in the December 5, 2008, issue of *Rolling Stone,* songwriter and guitarist Joe Satriani sued the band for "ripping off his 2004 track 'If I Could Fly'" for their own Grammy-nominated hit "Viva La Vida." The case was dismissed on September 14, 2009. Although Satriani's lawyer would not say whether a financial settlement was involved, one thing was clear: "Under terms of the dismissal, Coldplay won't have to admit to any wrongdoing."[12]

1. Which ethical principles did Coldplay demonstrate or violate in 2005?

2. Which ethical principles did the band demonstrate or violate in 2008?

3. Do you think Coldplay will plagiarize from other artists again? Why or why not? Be sure to point to ethical principles in your answer.

4. Would you consider that Satriani's actions, his lawyer's actions, and the court's actions demonstrated ethical behavior? Why or why not?

5. What would you do if you were in Coldplay's position? Satriani's position?

Record Information

As you find the facts, opinions, and elaborations that you want to use in your speech, you need to record the information accurately and keep a careful account of your sources so that they can be cited appropriately during your speech. Although some people try to record information in files on their computers, we propose here a proven method for organizing your information on research cards.

Preparing Research Cards

How should you keep track of the information you plan to use? Although it may seem easier to record all material from one source on a single sheet of paper (or to photocopy source material), sorting and arranging material is much easier when each item is recorded separately. Recording each piece of information on its own research card allows you to easily find, arrange, and rearrange each item of information as you prepare your speech.

In the research card method, each factual statement, expert opinion, or elaboration, along with the bibliographical information on its source, is recorded on a four- by six-inch or larger index card containing three types of information. First, each card should have a heading or keywords that identify the subcategory to which the information belongs. Second, the specific fact, opinion, or elaboration statement should be recorded on the card. Any part of the information item that is quoted directly from the source should be enclosed in quotation marks. Third, the bibliographical publication data related to the source should be recorded.

The bibliographical information you will record depends on whether the source is a book, a periodical, a newspaper, an interview, or a website. For a book, include the names of authors, the title of the book, the place of publication and the publisher, the date of publication, and the page or pages from which the information is taken. For a periodical or newspaper, include the name of the author (if given), the title of the article, the name of the publication, the date, and the page number from which the information is taken. For online sources,

Exhibit 6.2 A sample research card

Topic: Bioluminescence

Heading: Uses

Fireflies blink to communicate, and each fly has a distinctive blink. Males and females also blink during mating season.

Kathryn Lund Johnson. "Things that go 'blink' in the night." *American Gardener,* Jul./Aug. 2006, v. 85 i.4, pp. 46–47.

include the URL for the website, the credentials of the site host, the heading under which you found the information, and the date that you accessed the site. Be sure to record enough source information so that you can relocate the material if you need to and cite the source appropriately during your speech. Exhibit 6.2 shows a sample research card.

As your stack of research cards grows, you can sort the material and place each item under the heading to which it is related. For instance, for a speech on bioluminescence, you might have a stack of research cards related to the biological process of bioluminescence, species that are bioluminescent, and causes of bioluminescence. The card in Exhibit 6.2 would be indexed under the heading "species that are bioluminescent."

The number of sources you will need depends in part on the type of speech you are giving and your own expertise. For a narrative/personal experience speech, you obviously will be the main, if not the only, source. For informative reports and persuasive speeches, however, speakers ordinarily draw from multiple sources. For a five-minute speech on Ebola in which you plan to talk about causes, symptoms, and treatment, you might have two or more research cards under each heading. Moreover, the research cards should come from at least three different sources. Avoid using only one source for your information because this often leads to plagiarism; furthermore, basing your speech on one

SPEECH PLANNING

ACTIVITY 3B

Record Relevant Information on Research Cards

The goal of this activity is to review the source material that you identified in Action Step Activity 3A and to record on research cards specific items of information that you might wish to use in your speech.

1. Carefully read all print and electronic sources (including website material) that you have identified and evaluated as appropriate sources for your speech. Review your notes and tapes from all interviews and observations.

2. As you read an item (fact, opinion, example, illustration, statistic, anecdote, narrative, comparison–contrast, quotation, definition, or description) that you think might be useful in your speech, record the item on a research card or on the appropriate electronic research card form available at your CourseMate for *Challenge*. (If you are using an article that appeared in a periodical source that you read online, use the periodical research card form.)

CourseMate You can complete this activity online and, if requested, e-mail it to your instructor. You can also use online forms to prepare your own research cards and print them for use in preparing your speech. Go to your CourseMate for *Challenge* to access Action Step Activity 3B.

ACTIVITY 3B

STUDENT RESPONSE

Record Relevant Information on Research Cards

Speech goal: *I would like the audience to agree that domestic violence is a problem, realize some of its underlying causes, and be convinced of strategies to reduce domestic violence in the United States today.*

Card 1

Topic: *The problem*

Heading: *Scope*

Three million women per year are physically abused by their husbands or boyfriends. And about 31 percent of American women report being sexually or physically abused by a male partner during her lifetime. (In other words, of the twenty women in my speech class, about six will be assaulted by a male partner during her lifetime!)

Family Violence Prevention Fund Website (2007). "Domestic violence is a serious, widespread social problem in America: The facts." http://www.endabuse.org/ resources/facts. Accessed April 17, 2007.

Card 2

Topic: *The problem*

Heading: *Severity*

There were 248,300 rapes/sexual assaults in 2007, more than 500 per day, up from 190,600 in 2005.

Goodman, A. (2010, March 2). Domestic Violence: A pre-existing condition? TruthDig.com. Retrieved on April 16, 2010, at http://www.truthdig.com/report/ item/domestic_violence_a_pre-existing_condition_20100302/

Card 3

Topic: *Causes*

Heading: *Power and control*

Men often resort to violence to gain power over women when they feel threatened and subordinate and want to maintain a sense of control.

Johnson, Michael P., and Ferraro, Kathleen J. (2000). "Research on domestic violence in the 1990s: Making distinctions." Journal of Marriage and Family, 62(4), *pp. 948–963.*

Card 4

Topic: *Causes*

Heading: *Power and control*

Most abused women would leave if human capital such as housing and employment were more readily available to them.

Christy-McMullin, K., and Shobe, M. A. (2007). "The role of economic resources and human capital with woman abuse." Journal of Policy Practice, 6(1), *pp. 3–26.*

or two sources suggests that you have not done sufficient research. Selecting and using information from several sources allows you to develop an original approach to your topic, ensure a broader research base, and make it more likely that you will have uncovered various opinions related to your topic.

Speech Planning Action Step 3, Activity 3B, will help you prepare research cards for the sources you compiled in Activity 3A. See the Student Response box immediately following the activity for a sample of how one student completed this exercise.

Citing Sources in the Speech

In your speeches, as in any communication in which you use ideas that are not your own, you need to acknowledge the sources of your ideas and statements. Specifically mentioning your sources not only helps the audience evaluate the content but also adds to your credibility. In addition, citing sources will give concrete evidence of the depth of your research. Failure to cite sources, especially when you are presenting information that is meant to substantiate a controversial point, is unethical. Furthermore, failure to cite sources orally during your speech constitutes plagiarism. Just as you would provide footnotes in a written document, you must provide oral footnotes during your speech. **Oral footnotes** are references to an original source, made at the point in the speech where information from that source is presented. The key to preparing oral footnotes is to include enough information for listeners to access the sources themselves and to offer enough credentials to enhance the credibility of the information you are citing. Exhibit 6.3 gives several examples of appropriate speech source citations.

Speech Planning Action Step 3, Activity 3C, will help you prepare oral citations for the sources you recorded in Activity 3B. See the Student Response box immediately following the activity for a sample of how one student completed this exercise.

oral footnote: reference to an original source, made at the point in the speech where information from that source is presented

---

Exhibit 6.3 Appropriate speech source citations

Books

Cite the title of the book and the name of its author. You may cite the book's publication date or the author's credentials if doing so boosts credibility.

> "Thomas Friedman, noted international editor for the *New York Times,* stated in his book *Hot, Flat, and Crowded.* . ."
> "But to get a complete picture we have to look at the statistics. According to the 2007 *Statistical Abstract,* the level of production for the European Economic Community rose from . . ."

Journal or magazine articles

Cite the name and date of the publication in which you found the article. You may cite the article's author and title if doing so adds credibility.

> "According to an article about the Federal Reserve in last week's *Newsweek* magazine . . ."
> "In the latest Gallup poll cited in the February 10 issue of *Newsweek* . . ."
> "Timothy Sellnow, professor of communication at The University of Kentucky, wrote in an article published in 2009 in the *Journal of Applied Communication* that . . ."

Newspapers

Cite the name of the newspaper and date of the article. You may cite the article's author and his or her credentials if it adds credibility.

> "According to a May 2010 article in the *Washington Post.* . ."

Interviews

Cite the name and credentials of the person interviewed and the date the interview took place. If you cite the interview more than once, you need only cite the interviewee's name in subsequent oral footnotes.

> "In an interview with *The Wall Street Journal* in February 22, 2010, Treasury Secretary Timothy Geithner stated . . ."

(continued)

Exhibit 6.3 Appropriate speech source citations *(continued)*

"In my telephone interview on September 29 with Dr. Susan Nissen, physician for physical medicine in Kansas City, Kansas, I learned that . . ."

Internet sources

Cite the website's author, his or her credentials, and the date of the site's most recent revision. If there is no author, cite the credentials of the website's sponsoring organization. Do not cite the URL as part of your oral footnote.

"According to a January 2010 posting on the official website of the American Heart Association . . ."

Television programs

Cite the name of the program and the date of the original broadcast. You may also cite the name of the reporter for news programs if it boosts credibility.

"According to an October 2009 CNN special broadcast called 'Latino in America' . . ."

Public speeches

Cite the name and credentials of the speaker, as well as the occasion and date of the speech.

"In a speech on the need for financial education during times of financial crises delivered to the Kansas City Federal Reserve Interagency Consumer Complaint Conference in April of 2009, Susan C. Keating, president of the National Foundation of Credit Counseling, stated . . ."

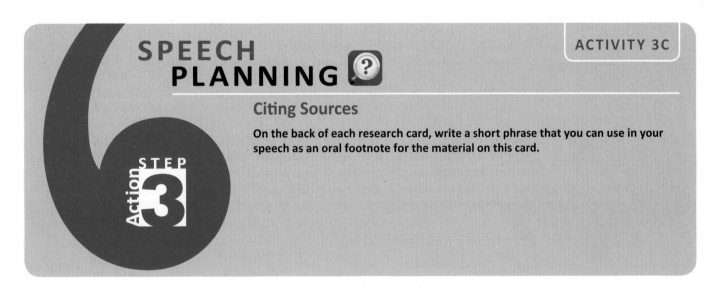

SPEECH PLANNING

ACTIVITY 3C

Action STEP 3

Citing Sources

On the back of each research card, write a short phrase that you can use in your speech as an oral footnote for the material on this card.

STUDENT RESPONSE ?

Citing Sources

According to J. S. Gordon in his book Helping Survivors of Domestic Violence: The Effects of Medial, Mental Health, and Community Services, domestic violence is the number-one reason for emergency room visits by women.

Summary

Effective speaking requires high-quality information. You need to know where to look for information, what kind of information to look for, how to record it, and how to cite sources in your speeches.

To find material, begin by exploring your personal knowledge and experience. Then, work outward by looking on the Internet for blogs, videos, and websites, as well as online and in libraries for secondary sources such as encyclopedias, books, articles, newspapers, statistical sources, biographical references, and government documents. By skimming written material, you can quickly evaluate sources to determine whether to read them in full. Four criteria for judging sources are authority, relevance, objectivity, and currency. You may also need to conduct primary research if secondary sources are insufficient. You may conduct fieldwork observations, surveys, interviews, original artifact or document examinations, or experiments. Two major types of evidence for speeches are factual statements and expert opinions. Factual statements are presented in the form of examples, statistics, and definitions. Expert opinions are interpretations of facts and judgments made by qualified authorities. Depending on your topic and speech goal, you may use facts and opinions and elaborate them with examples, anecdotes, narratives, comparisons, contrasts, and quotations.

A good method for recording material that you may want to use in your speech is to record each bit of data along with necessary bibliographical documentation on a separate research card. As your stack of information grows, sort the material under common headings. During the speech, cite the sources for the information on your research cards in the form of oral footnotes.

Challenge Resource and Assessment Center

CourseMate Now that you have read Chapter 6, use your Speech Communication CourseMate for *The Challenge of Effective Speaking* for quick access to the electronic resources that accompany this text. These resources include the following:

- **Study tools** that will help you assess your learning and prepare for exams (*digital glossary, key term flash cards, review quizzes*).
- **Activities and assignments** that will help you hone your knowledge and build your public speaking skills throughout the course (*Speech Snippets, Speech Assignments, Action Step Activities*). Many of these activities allow you to compare your answers with those provided by the authors and, if requested, submit your answers to your instructor.

- **Media resources** that will help you explore communication concepts online (*Web Resources*), develop your speech outlines (*Speech Builder Express 3.0*), watch and critique videos of sample speeches (*Interactive Video Activities*), upload your speech videos for peer reviewing and critique other students' speeches (*Speech Studio online speech review tool*), and download chapter reviews so you can study when and where you'd like (*Audio Study Tools*).

This chapter's application activities, Action Step Activities, Web Resources, and Video Activities are featured in the end-of-chapter section.

Applying What You've Learned

1. **Impromptu Speech Activity:** Draw an information source from a box in the front of the room. It might be a book; magazine or academic journal article; printout from a discussion board, blog, or website; and so forth. Read or skim the source. Then prepare a proper APA reference citation. Go to the front of the room and write the citation on the board. Then present a two- to three-minute informative speech on how well the source meets each of the four evaluation criteria for a speech on a related topic. Provide evidence for your assessments. Be sure to quote something from the information source using a proper oral footnote during the speech.

2. **Assessment Activity A:** Go to VS Video Productions website at www.vsvideoproductions.com and click on the "Video samples" link and then the "corporate" link. What kinds of information and information sources are used to compel viewers to use this company's services? Which are most compelling to you and why?

3. **Assessment Activity B:** Watch an opening story on a local or national news broadcast. Identify what information types and sources are used to support the story. Do they meet the criteria for good sources? Why or why not?

Speech-Planning Action Steps

3A: Locating and Evaluating Information Sources (105)

3B: Preparing Research Cards (112)

3C: Citing Sources (115)

Web Resources

6.1 Online Statistics (98)

6.2 Bad Uses of Statistics and Polling (98)

6.3 Online Bibliographical References (98)

6.4 Online Quotations (98)

6.5 Online Government Publications (98)

6.6 Analyzing Information Sources (100)

6.7 Evaluating Internet Sources (100)

6.8 Conducting Surveys (101)

Video Resources

1. Check out Speech Studio to watch some other students' speeches. What types of secondary and primary sources do they use? How varied are they? How relevant and timely are they? Or record a speech you're working on, upload it to Speech Studio, and ask your peers for their feedback. What feedback could you use to fine-tune your research before you give your speech in class?

2. Go to Speech Studio to see how other students cite their sources in their speeches. Or record a speech you're working on, upload it to Speech Studio, and ask your peers for their feedback. What feedback could you use to fine-tune your oral source citations before you give your speech in class?

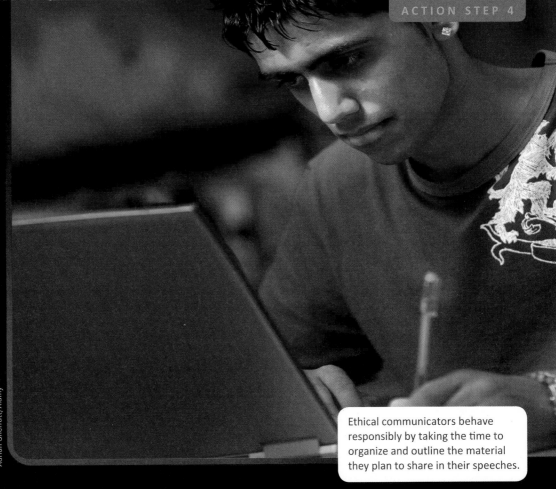

Adrian Sherratt/Alamy

7

Ethical communicators behave responsibly by taking the time to organize and outline the material they plan to share in their speeches.

"organizing and outlining the speech body"

What's the Point?

QUESTIONS YOU'LL BE ABLE TO ANSWER AFTER READING THIS CHAPTER:

1. Why is it important to limit your speech to two to four main points?

2. Why should you construct a clear thesis statement?

3. How might you arrange your points in your speech?

4. What are some types of supporting material you can use to elaborate your main points?

5. Why are transitions important?

Action STEP 4

Organize and develop ideas into a well-structured outline (the body).

A. Identify 2–4 main points.

B. Write a thesis statement with main point preview.

C. Develop your main points.

D. Outline the speech body.

"Troy, Mareka gave an awesome speech about recycling paper. I didn't realize the efforts that other universities are making to help the environment, and I haven't heard so many powerful stories in a long time."

"Yeah, Brett, I agree, the stories were interesting. But, you know, I had a hard time following the talk. I couldn't really get a hold of what the main ideas were. Did you?"

"Well, she was talking about recycling and stuff, . . . but now that you mention it, I'm not sure what she really wanted us to think or do about it. I mean, it was really interesting but kind of confusing too."

Troy and Brett's experience is not that unusual; even well-known speakers can give speeches that aren't as tightly organized as they could or should be. Yet if your speeches are well organized, you are more likely to achieve your speech goal. A well-organized speech has three identifiable parts: an introduction, a body, and a conclusion. In this chapter and the next, we explain the fourth speech plan action step: Organize and develop your ideas into a well-structured outline. This chapter focuses on developing the body of your speech by describing how to: (1) identify main points that are implied in the specific goal statement and write them into a thesis statement for the speech; (2) organize the body of your speech by carefully wording and ordering your main points, developing each main point with supporting material that is appropriate to the audience; and (3) create transitions that move the speech smoothly from one main point to the next. In the next chapter, we describe how to create introductions and conclusions that pique audience interest, aid understanding, and help the audience remember what you spoke about.

Construct a Thesis Statement

Once you have analyzed your audience, identified your general goal, created a specific goal, and assembled a body of information on your topic, you are ready to identify the main ideas you wish to present in your speech and to craft them into a well-phrased thesis statement.

Identify Main Points

main points: complete sentence statements of the two to four central ideas the audience needs to understand for your speech goal to be realized

The **main points** of a speech are complete sentence statements of the two to four central ideas the audience needs to understand if your speech goal is to be realized. You need to limit the number of main points you present so audience members can easily understand what you are saying, remember the major ideas you present, and understand the speech's importance. The difference between a five-minute speech and a twenty-five-minute speech with the same speech goal is not the number of main points, but rather, the extent to which each main point is developed.

With some speech goals, identifying the main points is easy. For example, if your goal is to demonstrate how to create a webpage, your main points will likely be the steps involved in developing it. Most times, however, you will need to do some further work to identify the main points that audience members need to understand if you are to achieve your speech goal. How can you identify these main ideas? First, begin by listing the ideas you have found that relate to your specific goal. You may be able to list as many as nine or more. Second, eliminate ideas that your audience analysis suggests this audience already understands. Third, check to see if some of the ideas can be grouped together under a broader theme. Fourth, eliminate any ideas that might be too complicated or too broad for this audience to comprehend in the time allotted for your speech. Finally, from the ideas that remain, choose two to four that are the most important for your audience to understand if you are to accomplish your specific speech goal.

Let's look at how Katie used these steps to identify the main points for a speech whose goal was to "inform my classmates of the growing problem of Adderall® use among college students." To begin, Katie listed ideas she had discovered while doing her research.

what is a prescription drug

what is Adderall

what are the ingredients in Adderall

how is Adderall made

what is the history of Adderall

who takes Adderall

why is it prescribed

benefits

risks

how many college students take Adderall without a prescription

demographics of college students who take Adderall without a prescription

why college students who don't have a prescription take it (perceived benefits)

benefit myths

actual results/consequences

Second, Katie eliminated the idea "what is a prescription drug" because she knew her audience already understood this. Third, Katie noticed that several of the ideas seemed to be related. What is Adderall, why is it prescribed, who takes it, as well as its risks and benefits seemed to go together. How many take it, demographics, and perceived benefits of college students who take Adderall without a prescription also seemed to be related. And benefit myths and actual results/consequences could be grouped together. Fourth, Katie decided the ingredients, history, and how Adderall is made were too broad to cover adequately in the time she was allotted for the speech and were not directly related to her goal. Finally, Katie decided her main points would be (1) understanding the nature and purpose of Adderall as a prescription drug, (2) its growing popularity as a study aid among college students, and (3) problems involved with using Adderall as a study aid. This process left Katie with three broad-based points that she could develop in her speech. See the figure on page 122 for what Katie's list looked like after she finished her analysis and synthesis.

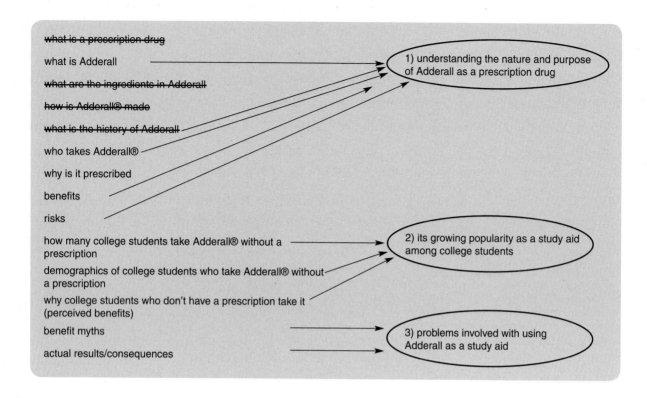

Speech Planning Action Step 4, Activity 4A, will help you identify main points to use for your speeches in this course. See the Student Response box immediately following the activity for a sample of how one student completed this exercise.

SPEECH SNIPPET

Crafting a Thesis Statement

Johanna wanted to create a memorable thesis statement for her speech whose goal was to get her classmates to commit to take action to cut the amount of solid waste they send to the landfill. So she phrased each of her main points so that they began with an "R" and used this mnemonic to help her classmates remember this thesis: "I want my classmates to commit to take action to cut their personal contributions to landfills by practicing the three R's: reduce, reuse, and recycle your waste."

Exhibit 7.1 Sample speech goals and thesis statements

General goal: I want to inform my audience.
Specific goal: I want my audience to understand how to improve their grades in college.
Thesis statement: Three proven techniques for improving test scores in college are to attend classes regularly, develop a positive attitude, and study efficiently.

General goal: I want to inform my audience.
Specific goal: I want the audience to understand the benefits of volunteering.
Thesis statement: Some important benefits of volunteering include helping underprivileged populations, supporting nonprofit organizations, and improving your own self-esteem.

General goal: I want to persuade my audience.
Specific goal: I want my audience to believe that parents should limit the time their children spend viewing television.
Thesis statement: Parents should limit the time their children spend viewing television because heavy television viewing desensitizes children to violence and increases violent tendencies in children.

General goal: I want to persuade my audience.
Specific goal: I want my audience to believe that they should learn to speak Spanish.
Thesis statement: You should learn to speak Spanish because it will benefit you personally, economically, and practically.

Write the Thesis Statement

A **thesis statement** is a one- or two-sentence summary of your speech that incorporates your general and specific goals and previews the main points of the speech. Not only will you write this sentence on your speech outline, but you will also use this sentence as a basis for the transition from the introduction to the body of your speech. Thus, your thesis statement provides a blueprint from which you will organize the body of your speech. Exhibit 7.1 provides several examples of specific speech goals and thesis statements.

Katie crafted the following thesis statement for her speech on Adderall: "I want to inform my audience about the growing problem of college students taking Adderall without a prescription by explaining the nature and purpose of Adderall as a prescription drug, its growing popularity as a study aid among college students, and problems associated with using Adderall without a prescription."

For more guidance on writing thesis statements, go to your CourseMate for *Challenge* to access **Web Resource 7.1: Writing Different Types of Thesis Statements**

Speech Planning Action Step 4, Activity 4B, will help you write a thesis statement for your speech. See the Student Response box immediately following the activity for a sample of how one student completed this exercise.

> **thesis statement:** a one- or two-sentence summary of the speech that incorporates the general and specific goals and previews the main points

> **CourseMate**

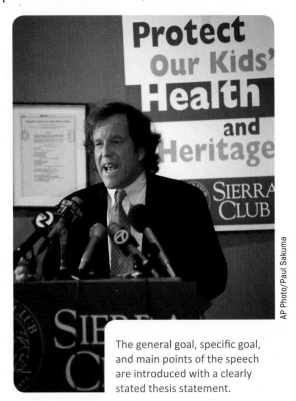

AP Photo/Paul Sakuma

The general goal, specific goal, and main points of the speech are introduced with a clearly stated thesis statement.

Outline the Body of the Speech

Once you have a thesis statement, you can begin to outline your speech. A **speech outline** is a sentence representation of the hierarchical and sequential relationships among

---

Identifying Main Points

1. List all of the ideas you have found that relate to the specific purpose of your speech.

2. If you have trouble limiting the number, do the following:

   a. Draw a line through each of the ideas that you believe the audience already understands, that you have no information to support, or that just seems too complicated.

   b. Combine ideas that can be grouped together under a single heading.

3. From those ideas that remain, choose the two to four you will use as main points in your speech.

CourseMate You can complete this activity online with Speech Builder Express and, if requested, e-mail your completed activity to your instructor. Go to your CourseMate for *Challenge* to access Action Step Activity 4A.

STUDENT RESPONSE

Identifying Main Points

General goal: *I want to inform my audience.*

Specific goal: *I want my audience to understand seasonal affective disorder (SAD).*

1. List all of the ideas you have found that relate to the specific purpose of your speech.

    What is SAD

    symptoms

    causes of SAD

    historical background

    discoverer

    types of depression

    vitamin deficiencies

    locations and prevalence

    diagnoses

    medical treatments

    organic treatments

    therapeutic treatments

    the role of sunshine

    light therapy

    myths

    realities

2. If you have trouble limiting the number, do the following:

    a. Draw a line through each of the ideas that you believe the audience already understands, that you have no information to support, or that just seems too broad or too complicated.

    b. Combine ideas that can be grouped together under a single heading.

3. From those ideas that remain, choose the two to four you will use as main points in your speech.

Main points:

What is SAD (symptoms and causes of SAD)

Misconceptions about SAD

The treatments used to combat SAD

SPEECH PLANNING

STEP Action 4

Writing a Thesis Statement

The goal of this activity is to use your general and specific goals and the main points you have identified to develop a well-worded thesis statement for your speech.

1. Write the general and specific goals you developed in Activity 4A.
2. List the main points you identified in Activity 4A.
3. Now write one or two complete sentences that combine your specific goal with your main point ideas.

CourseMate   You can complete this activity online with Speech Builder Express, view a student sample of this activity, and, if requested, e-mail your completed activity to your instructor. Go to your CourseMate for *Challenge* to access Action Step Activity 4B.

STUDENT RESPONSE

STEP Action 4

Writing a Thesis Statement

1. Write the general and specific goals you developed in Activity 4A.
   General goal: I want to inform my audience.
   Specific goal: I want my audience to enjoy symphonic music.

2. List the main points you identified in Activity 4A.
   The characteristics of symphonic music
   How to listen to symphonic music
   The influence of symphonic music on popular music

3. Now write one or two complete sentences that combine your general and specific goals with your main point ideas.
   My goal is to increase the audience's enjoyment of symphonic music by describing the characteristics of symphonies, by explaining how to listen to a symphony, and by discussing the influence that symphonic music had and continues to have on popular music.

---

the ideas presented in the speech. In a way, it is a diagram that organizes the information you will present. Your outline may have three hierarchical levels of information: main points (noted by the use of Roman numerals: I, II, III, . . .), subpoints that support a main point (noted by the use of capital letters: A, B, C,. . .), and sometimes sub-subpoints to support subpoints (noted by Arabic numerals: 1, 2, 3,. . .).

speech outline: a sentence representation of the hierarchical and sequential relationships among the ideas presented in the speech

You will want to write your main points and subpoints in complete sentences, to clarify the relationship between main points and subpoints. Exhibit 7.2 shows the general form of how a formal speech outline system looks.

Exhibit 7.2 General form for a speech outline

I. **Main point one**
   A. Subpoint A for main point one
      1. Sub-subpoint one
         a. Elaboration material (if needed)
         b. Elaboration material (if needed)
      2. Sub-subpoint two
         a. Elaboration material (if needed)
         b. Elaboration material (if needed)
   B. Subpoint B for main point one
      1. Sub-subpoint one
         a. Elaboration material (if needed)
         b. Elaboration material (if needed)
      2. Sub-subpoint two
         a. Elaboration material (if needed)
         b. Elaboration material (if needed)

II. **Main point two**
   A. Subpoint A for main point two
      1. Sub-subpoint one
         a. Elaboration material (if needed)
         b. Elaboration material (if needed)
      2. Sub-subpoint two
         a. Elaboration material (if needed)
         b. Elaboration material (if needed)
   B. Subpoint B for main point two
      1. Sub-subpoint one
         a. Elaboration material (if needed)
         b. Elaboration material (if needed)
      2. Sub-subpoint two
         a. Elaboration material (if needed)
         b. Elaboration material (if needed)
      3. Sub-subpoint three
         a. Elaboration material (if needed)
         b. Elaboration material (if needed)
   C. Subpoint C for main point two
      1. Sub-subpoint one
         a. Elaboration material (if needed)
         b. Elaboration material (if needed)
      2. Sub-subpoint two
         a. Elaboration material (if needed)
         b. Elaboration material (if needed)
      3. Sub-subpoint three
         a. Elaboration material (if needed)
         b. Elaboration material (if needed)
      . . . etc.

The length of your speech is determined not by the number of main points you have but by how thoroughly you develop each of them. The same two to four main points can be developed into a speech that will last for three to five minutes, five to seven minutes, eight to ten minutes, or even into a fifty-minute major presentation. As you will see, a complex main point may have two, three, or even more subpoints. Each subpoint will be developed through one or more sub-subpoints. And subpoints and/or sub-subpoints may be elaborated with definitions, examples, statistics, personal experiences, stories, quotations, and other items. It's often the number and length of elaborations that determine the length of the speech. In a five-minute speech, you may be limited to only two or three elaborations for each subpoint. But an hour-long speech may allow you to include more elaborations and longer ones for each subpoint.

Here is how Katie developed one of her main points. Notice that all main points, subpoints, and sub-subpoints are written in complete sentences.

I. Adderall is a psychostimulant prescribed to treat three conditions.

  A. Adderall, the brand name for amphetamikne-dextroamphetamine is a psychostimulant, one of a class of drugs intended to promote concentration, suppress hyperactivity, and promote healthy social experiences for patients.

    1. Adderall stimulates the central nervous system by increasing the amount of dopamine and norepinephrine in the brain. These chemicals are neurotransmitters that help the brain send signals between nerve cells.

    2. Mentally, Adderall brings about a temporary improvement in alertness, wakefulness, endurance, and motivation.

    3. Physically, it can increase heart rate and blood pressure and decrease perceived need for food or sleep.

  B. Adderall is prescribed for the medical treatment of attention deficit hyperactivity disorder (ADHD) in children and adults as well as for narcolepsy and clinical depression.

    1. ADHD is a neurobehavioral developmental disorder characterized by problems of attention coupled with hyperactivity.

      a. Since the mid-1990s, there has been a documented increase in the number of American children diagnosed and treated for ADHD.

      b. According to the *Diagnostic and Statistical Manual of Mental Disorders* (2000), symptoms must be present for at least six months for diagnosis, and symptoms must be excessive for medicinal treatment.

      c. The drugs Ritalin® and Dexedrine® are also used to treat ADHD. Adderall, however, remains the most widely prescribed of these drugs.

      d. According to the Centers for Disease Control and Prevention, approximately 4.4 million American children have been diagnosed with ADHD, and more than 2.5 million of those patients have been prescribed medicine to treat the condition.

    2. Adderall is also prescribed to treat narcolepsy, which occurs when the brain can't normally regulate cycles of sleep and waking, so sufferers experience excessive daytime sleepiness that results in episodes of suddenly falling asleep.

    3. Adderall can also be used to treat clinical depression, a disorder that is characterized by low mood, a loss of interest in normal activities, and low self-esteem.

SPEECH SNIPPET

Elaborating on a Subpoint

When discussing her main point on how to reuse materials as a means of reducing solid waste, Johanna planned to elaborate on her subpoint about reusing grocery bags by pointing out that "the homepage of ReusableBags.com cited an article in the *Wall Street Journal*, which reported that the United States goes through 100 billion plastic shopping bags annually. An estimated 12 million barrels of oil is required to make that many plastic bags."

The Words Are All Mine

Kendra Smith, Director of Continuing Education and Meetings American College of Osteopathic Surgeons, Alexandria, Virginia

Kendra Smith, 29, is a take-charge woman running a department in a national medical association of board-certified specialist physicians. She ensures that the osteopathic surgeons who are members of the association continually accumulate credits in their field so that they can remain certified.

Her job requires Smith to be *very* organized. "I plan the educational conferences and meetings [the surgeons] must attend to satisfy certification requirements. I do all the legwork, coordinating things like venue, accommodation, audio-visual equipment, food. At the beginning of each conference, I go over logistics with the key hotel staff." But her most time-consuming task is overseeing the osteopaths who volunteer to devise the program agendas, content, and roster of speakers for the conferences.

All of these interactions with others have given Smith a lot of experience in public speaking. She's found that she's much more comfortable speaking at work than she was in the speech class she took while earning a B.A. at the University of Mary Washington in Fredericksburg, Virginia. "In my job, speaking is okay. It's material I'm confident in. I'm explaining and pointing out. It's more of an educational type of speaking."

> **"Once, in college, I thought I was over-thinking everything, so I tried *not* preparing. When I got up [to speak], I had no idea what I wanted to talk about!"**

Smith feels more nervous about giving formal presentations, such as when she presents her department's recommendations about various issues to the board of directors. To help reduce her anxiety, she uses a simple but effective mental trick: thinking of her audience as individuals rather than as a big group. "If I were giving a presentation to them one on one, I wouldn't be nervous." She also prepares really well for these presentations. "I outline what I need to say in bullets—even full sentences sometimes. It makes me feel better that I can read [from my outline] if I need to. [But] I'm confident in the material, so I usually don't need to refer back—I've talked about it, researched it, written it. The words are all mine."

Smith helps ensure that she'll be able to speak extemporaneously by practicing her presentations multiple times. Through hard experience, she's learned that good preparation and practice can really help her give an effective speech. "Once, in college, I thought maybe I was over-thinking everything, so I tried *not* preparing. When I got up, I had no idea what I wanted to talk about! That didn't work out well."

Outline Main Points

Once you have a thesis statement, you can begin outlining the main points that will make up the body of your speech. Write out each main point using complete sentences. It is important to write main points, subpoints, and sub-subpoints as complete sentences because only complete sentences can fully express the relationship among the main points and subpoints, and between each main point and the specific speech goal. Once you have worded each main point, you will choose an organizing pattern.

WORDING MAIN POINTS

Recall that Katie determined that her main points would be understanding the nature and purpose of Adderall as a prescription drug, its growing popularity as a study aid among college students, and the risks involved in doing so, and that her thesis statement was: "Today I want to alert you to the uses and abuses of Adderall among college students. We'll do so by, first, discussing its nature and purpose as a prescription drug, then its growing popularity as a study aid among college students, and, finally, the problems associated with using Adderall without a prescription." Suppose she wrote her first draft of main points as follows:

    I. What exactly is Adderall, and why is it prescribed?
    II. College student use
  III. Risks

From this wording, Katie would have drafted some ideas of the main points she was going to talk about, which is essentially what you need to do in the preliminary draft of your formal outline. This version is also known as a **preparation outline** because it provides a starting point of main points but doesn't specify clearly how each main point is related to her goal. To make the relationships clear, Katie needs to create complete sentences for each. So she might clarify her main points like this:

preparation outline: provides a starting point of main points but doesn't specify clearly how each main point is related to the goal

    I. What exactly is Adderall?
    II. An increasing number of American college students are using Adderall.
  III. Abusing Adderall is risky.

Study these statements. Do they seem a bit vague? Notice that we have emphasized that this is a first draft. Sometimes, the first draft of a main point is well expressed and doesn't need additional work. More often, however, we find that our first attempt doesn't quite capture what we want to say. So we need to rework our points to make them clearer. Let's consider Katie's draft statements more carefully. Katie has made a pretty good start. Her three main points are complete sentences. Now let's see how Katie might use two test questions to assure herself that she has achieved the best wording for her points.

1. **Is the relationship between each main point statement and the goal statement clearly specified?** Katie's first main point statement doesn't indicate what purposes Adderall serves as a prescription medicine. So she could improve this statement by saying:

   What exactly is Adderall, and what is it prescribed for?

   Similarly, she can improve the second main point statement by saying:

   Adderall abuse is becoming increasingly popular among American college students.

   The third point might be redrafted to state:

   Abusing Adderall as a study aid is dangerous.

2. **Are the main points parallel in structure?** Main points are **parallel** to one another when their wording follows the same structural pattern, often using the same introductory words. Parallel structure is not a requirement, but it can help the audience recognize main points when you deliver your speech. Katie notices that she could make her main points parallel with a small adjustment:

parallel: when wording of points follows the same structural pattern, often using the same introductory words

    I. First, what exactly is Adderall, and why is it prescribed?
    II. Second, a growing number of American college students are using Adderall.
  III. Third, abusing Adderall as a study aid is dangerous.

Parallelism can be achieved in many ways. Katie used numbering: "first . . . second . . . third." Another way is to start each sentence with an active verb. Suppose Adam wants his audience to understand the steps involved in writing an effective job application cover letter. He might write the following first draft of his main points:

    I. Format the heading elements correctly.
    II. The body of the letter should be three paragraphs long.
  III. When concluding, use "sincerely" or "regards."
  IV. Then you need to proofread the letter carefully.

Darla worded her main points on the methods of disciplining children in this way:

I. First, the Skinner disciplinary method is based on behavioral modification.

II. Second, the Freud disciplinary method is rooted in the concepts of the id, the ego, and the superego.

III. Third, the Spock disciplinary method is based on cognitive reasoning.

time order: organizing the main points of the speech in a chronological sequence or by steps in a process

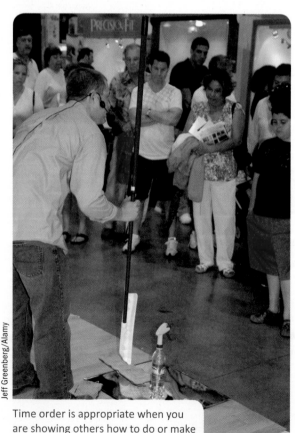

Time order is appropriate when you are showing others how to do or make something or how something works.

After further consideration, Adam might revise his main points to make them parallel in structure by using active verbs (italicized):

I. *Format the heading elements correctly.*

II. *Organize the body into three paragraphs.*

III. *Conclude the letter with "sincerely" or "regards."*

IV. *Proofread the letter carefully.*

Notice how the similarity of structure clarifies and strengthens the message. The audience can immediately identify the key steps in the process.

SELECTING AN ORGANIZATIONAL PATTERN FOR MAIN POINTS

A speech can be organized in many different ways. Your objective is to find or create the structure that will help the audience make the most sense of the material. Although speeches may follow many types of organization, beginning speakers should learn four fundamental patterns: time order, narrative order, topic order, and logical reasons order.

1. **Time order.** **Time order**, sometimes called *sequential order* or *chronological order*, is a frequently used pattern in informative speeches. When you use time order, you organize your main points in a chronological sequence or by steps in a process. Thus, time order is appropriate when you are explaining how to do something, how to make something, how something works, or how something happened. Adam's speech on the *steps* in writing a job application cover letter is an example of time order. As the following example illustrates, the order of main points is as important for audiences to remember as the ideas themselves.

   General goal: I want to inform my audience.

   Specific goal: I want the audience to understand the four steps involved in developing a personal network.

   Thesis statement: The four steps involved in developing a personal network are to analyze your current networking potential, to position yourself in places for opportunity, to advertise yourself, and to follow up on contacts.

   I. *First, analyze your current networking potential.*

   II. *Second, position yourself in places for opportunity.*

   III. *Third, advertise yourself.*

   IV. *Fourth, follow up on contacts.*

   Although the use of "first," "second," and so on, is not required when using time order, using them helps audience members understand that the *sequence* is important.

2. **Narrative order.** A second pattern for arranging your main points is narrative order. **Narrative order** conveys your ideas through a story or series of stories. Narrative order is rooted in narrative theory, which suggests that one important way people communicate is through storytelling. We use stories to teach and to learn, to entertain, and to make sense of the world around us.[1] This pattern is similar to time order because the main points are usually presented in chronological order, but with narrative order, the entire speech consists of one or more stories that include characters, settings, and plots. Narrative order is particularly effective when you tell stories that

are emotionally compelling. The goal of using this pattern is for listeners to accept your conclusion by showing them the validity of what you are saying through description rather than simply telling them. Lana shared her story about having anorexia to help listeners understand the impact of the condition on one's life.

> *General goal: I want to inform my audience.*
>
> *Specific goal: I want my audience to understand how anorexia nervosa affects the lives of its victims and their loved ones.*
>
> *Thesis statement: Today, I want to share my story as a person living with anorexia by sharing my weight obsession experiences as a high school gymnast, as a college sophomore, and as a young adult today.*
>
> > *I. I recall first becoming weight conscious when I was captain of the high school gymnastics team.*
> >
> > *II. What might have been described merely as obsessive dieting turned into full-blown anorexia during my sophomore year of college.*
> >
> > *III. Thanks to loving help from my family and friends, as well as doctors and therapists, I am alive and well today.*
> >
> > *IV. Living with anorexia nervosa means being forever cognizant of eating enough so I never go back into that horrible place where I nearly died.*

3. **Topic order.** A third often used organization for informative speeches is topic order. **Topic order** organizes the main points of the speech by categories or divisions of a subject. This is a common way of ordering main points because nearly any subject can be subdivided or categorized in many different ways. The order of the topics may go from general to specific, move from least important to most important, or follow some other logical sequence.

   In the example that follows, the topics are presented in the order that the speaker believes is most suitable for the audience and specific speech goal, with the most important point at the end.

   > *General goal: I want to inform my audience.*
   >
   > *Specific goal: I want the audience to understand three proven methods for ridding our bodies of harmful toxins.*
   >
   > *Thesis statement: Three proven methods for ridding our bodies of harmful toxins are reducing intake of animal foods, hydrating, and eating natural whole foods.*
   >
   > > *I. One proven method for ridding our bodies of harmful toxins is reducing our intake of animal products.*
   > >
   > > *II. A second proven method for ridding our bodies of harmful toxins is keeping well hydrated.*
   > >
   > > *III. A third proven method for ridding our bodies of harmful toxins is eating more natural whole foods.*

   Whereas time order suggests a sequence that must be followed, topic order suggests that, of any possible ideas or methods, two to four are particularly important, valuable, or necessary. Katie's speech on the uses and abuses of Adderall is another example of a speech using topic order.

4. **Logical reasons order.** **Logical reasons order** organizes the main points by the reasons that support the specific speech goal. It emphasizes why the audience should believe something or behave in a particular way. Logical reasons order is most appropriate for a persuasive speech.

   > *General goal: I want to persuade my audience.*
   >
   > *Specific goal: I want the audience to donate money to the United Way.*

SPEECH SNIPPET

Narrative Order

Chaz shared two stories about his friend, Garth, to help his listeners understand how Americans with disabilities were discriminated against prior to the passage of the Americans with Disabilities Act. He talked about trying to help Garth get up a flight of stairs in his wheelchair to attend classes and when Garth was told over the telephone he was the top candidate for a position but was later told the position had been eliminated when he arrived in person in his wheelchair.

narrative order: organizing the main points of the speech as a story or series of stories

topic order: organizing the main points of the speech by categories or divisions of a subject

logical reasons order: organizing the main points of a persuasive speech by the reasons that support the speech goal

Thesis statement: Donating to the United Way is appropriate because your one donation covers many charities, you can stipulate which specific charities you wish to support, and a high percentage of your donation goes to charities.

  I. *When you donate to the United Way, your one donation covers many charities.*

 II. *When you donate to the United Way, you can stipulate which charities you wish to support.*

III. *When you donate to the United Way, you know that a high percentage of your donation will go directly to the charities you've selected.*

As we mentioned earlier, these four organizational patterns are the most common. There are others, and we'll talk about some of them in later chapters. As you develop your public speaking skills, you may find that you will need to revise one of these patterns or create a totally different one to meet the needs of your particular subject matter or audience.

In summary, then, to organize the body of your speech, (1) turn your speech goal into a one- or two-sentence thesis that combines the general goal and specific goal with a preview of the main points; (2) state the main points in complete sentences that are clear, parallel, meaningful, and limited to no more than four; and (3) organize the main points in the pattern best suited to your material and the needs of your specific audience.

Exhibit 7.1, shown earlier, shows what Katie's outline would look like at this stage of preparation. Notice that her general and specific speech goals are written at the top of the page. Her thesis statement comes right after the goals because later it will become part of her introduction.

Speech Planning Action Step 4, Activity 4C, will help you develop well-written main points for your speech. See the Student Response box immediately following the activity for a sample of how one student completed this exercise.

ACTIVITY 4C

SPEECH PLANNING

Action STEP 4

Developing the Main Points of Your Speech

The goal of this activity is to help you phrase and order your main points.

1. Write your thesis statement.

2. Underline the two to four main points identified in your thesis statement.

3. For each underlined item, write one sentence that summarizes what you want your audience to know about that idea.

4. Review the main points as a group.

   a. Is the relationship between each main point statement and the goal statement clearly specified? If not, revise.

   b. Are the main points parallel in structure? If not, consider why and revise.

5. Choose an organizational pattern for your main points.

6. Identify the pattern you have used.

CourseMate You can complete this activity online with Speech Builder Express, view a student sample of this activity, and, if requested, e-mail your completed activity to your instructor. Go to your CourseMate for *Challenge* to access Activity 4C.

ACTIVITY 4C

STUDENT RESPONSE

Developing the Main Points of Your Speech

1. Write your thesis statement.

    The three tests that you can use to determine whether a diamond is real are the <u>acid test</u>, <u>the streak test</u>, and the <u>hardness test</u>.

2. <u>Underline</u> the two to four main points identified in your thesis statement.

3. For each underlined item, write one sentence that summarizes what you want your audience to know about that idea.

    I. *One way to identify a diamond is by using the acid test.*
    II. *You can also identify a diamond by using the streak test.*
    III. *You can also identify a diamond by using the hardness test.*

4. Review the main points as a group.

    a. Is the relationship between each main point statement and the goal statement clearly specified? If not, revise.

    No. Purpose of test is to identify whether the diamond is real. The following revision puts emphasis in the right place.

    Revision:

    I. *One way to identify whether a diamond is real is by using the acid test.*
    II. *You can also identify whether a diamond is real by using the streak test.*
    III. *You can also identify whether a diamond is real by using the hardness test.*

    b. Are the main points parallel in structure? If not, consider why and revise.

    Revision:

    I. *One way to determine whether a diamond is real is to use the acid test.*
    II. *A second way to determine whether a diamond is real is to use the streak test.*
    III. *A third way to determine whether a diamond is real is to use the hardness test.*

5. Choose an organizational pattern for your main points.

    I. *One way to determine whether a diamond is real is to use the acid test.*
    II. *A second way to determine whether a diamond is real is to use the streak test.*
    III. *A third way to determine whether a diamond is real is to use the hardness test.*

6. Identify the type of pattern you have used.

    Topic order

Identify and Outline Subpoints

Just as you must identify the main points of your speech, you must also identify the subpoints. One subpoint should be a **listener relevance link**, a statement alerting listeners about how this point relates to them or why they should care about this point. As we said earlier, your outline will include complete-sentence statements of each of your subpoints. A main point may have two, three, or even more subpoints depending on the complexity of the main point.

listener relevance link: a statement alerting listeners about how a main point or subpoint relates to them or why they should care about it

IDENTIFYING SUBPOINTS

You can identify subpoints by sorting the research cards you prepared earlier into piles that correspond to each of your main points. The goal at this point is to see what information you have that supports each of your main points. Once you have listed the items of information that make the point, look for relationships between and among ideas. As you analyze, you can draw lines connecting items of information that fit together logically, cross out information that seems irrelevant or doesn't really fit, and combine similar ideas using different language.

OUTLINING SUBPOINTS

Subpoints should also be represented on the outline in full sentences. Be sure to also include internal references for items of information you found in secondary sources. Doing so will remind you to cite them during the speech, which will enhance your credibility and help you avoid unintentional plagiarism. As with main points, they should be revised until they are clearly stated. The items of information listed for Katie's first main point might be grouped as follows:

I. Adderall is a psychostimulant prescribed to treat three conditions.
   Listener relevance link: Understanding the intended medical uses of the drug Adderall may help you understand why the drug is so widely abused by collegians.

   A. Adderall, the brand name for amphetamikne-dextroamphetamine is a psychostimulant, one of a class of drugs intended to promote concentration, suppress hyperactivity, and promote healthy social experiences for patients (Willis, 2001).

      1. Adderall stimulates the central nervous system by increasing the amount of dopamine and norepinephrine in the brain. These chemicals are neurotransmitters that help the brain send signals between nerve cells (Daley, 2004, April 20).
      2. Mentally, Adderall brings about a temporary improvement in alertness, wakefulness, endurance, and motivation.
      3. Physically, it can increase heart rate and blood pressure and decrease perceived need for food or sleep.

   B. Adderall is prescribed for the medical treatment of attention deficit hyperactivity disorder (ADHD) in children and adults as well as for narcolepsy and clinical depression.

      1. ADHD is a neurobehavioral developmental disorder characterized by problems of attention coupled with hyperactivity.
         a. Since the mid-1990s, there has been a documented increase in the number of American children diagnosed and treated for ADHD (McCabe, Teter, & Boyd, 2004).
         b. According to the *Diagnostic and Statistical Manual of Mental Disorders* (2000), symptoms must be present for at least six months for diagnosis, and symptoms must be excessive for medicinal treatment.
         c. The drugs Ritalin and Dexedrine are also used to treat ADHD. Adderall, however, remains the most widely prescribed of these drugs (Willis, 2001).
         d. According to the Centers for Disease Control and Prevention (2005), approximately 4.4 million American children have been diagnosed with ADHD, and more than 2.5 million of those patients have been prescribed medicine to treat the condition (2005).

2. Adderall is also prescribed to treat narcolepsy, which occurs when the brain can't normally regulate cycles of sleep and waking.

    a. Sufferers of narcolepsy experience excessive daytime sleepiness that results in episodes of suddenly falling asleep.

    b. A chronic sleep disorder, narcolepsy affects 1 in every 2,000 Americans (American Academy of Sleep Medicine, 2005).

3. Adderall can also be used to treat clinical depression, a disorder that is characterized by low mood, a loss of interest in normal activities, and low self-esteem. According to the National Institute of Mental Health, 9.5 percent of the adult population—that is, nearly 1.8 million American adults—suffer from clinical depression.

List Supporting Material

A good outline also includes short outline statements of **supporting material**— developmental material that will be used in the speech—for example, personal experiences, examples, illustrations, anecdotes, statistics, and quotations. You will choose these items to meet the needs of your specific audience. Be sure to include internal citations and develop a reference list as you go along. Doing so will help you remember what research to cite and when during your speech to enhance your credibility and to demonstrate ethical communication behavior by avoiding plagiarism.

> **supporting material:** developmental material that will be used in the speech, including personal experiences, examples, illustrations, anecdotes, statistics, and quotations

Create Transitions

Once you have outlined your main points, subpoints, and potential supporting material, you will want to consider how you will move smoothly from one main point to another. **Transitions** are words, phrases, or sentences that show the relationship between, or bridge, two ideas. Transitions act like tour guides leading the audience from point to point through the speech. There are two types of transitions: section transitions and signposts.

Section transitions are complete sentences that show the relationship between, or bridge, major parts of the speech. They typically summarize what has just been said in one main point and preview the next main idea. Essentially, section transitions are the glue that holds the macrostructure of your speech together.

For example, suppose Adam has just finished the introduction of his speech on creating a cover letter and is now ready to launch into his main points. Before stating his first main point, he might say, "Creating a good cover letter is a process that has four steps. Now let's consider the first one." When his listeners hear this transition, they are signaled to mentally prepare to listen to and remember the first main point. When he finishes his first main point, he will use another section transition to signal that he is finished speaking about step one and is moving on to discuss step two: "Now that we have seen what is involved in creating the heading elements, we can move on to the second step."

You might be thinking that this sounds repetitive or patronizing, but section transitions are important for two reasons. First, they help the audience follow the organization of ideas in the speech by signaling that you are moving to the next point. In writing, you may use verbal transitions, but you also use paragraph notation (either through indenting the first sentence of a new paragraph or double spacing between paragraphs) to indicate a change of topic. In speaking, we use section transitions and perhaps body language to signal that we are moving on to a different point. Second, section transitions help audience members to remember information. We may well remember something that was said

> **transitions:** words, phrases, or sentences that show a relationship between, or bridge, two ideas

> **section transitions:** complete sentences that show the relationship between, or bridge, major parts of a speech

> **SPEECH SNIPPET**
>
> **Using Section Transitions**
>
> In her speech about methods of disciplining children, Darla used this section transition between her first and second main point: "Certainly, the behavioral modification approach based on B. F. Skinner's work can be an effective method for disciplining children. It is not the only method, however, which leads us to a second method, based on Sigmund Freud's work."

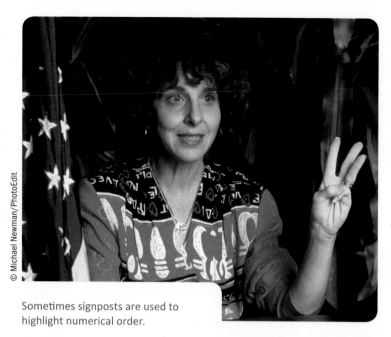
© Michael Newman/PhotoEdit

Sometimes signposts are used to highlight numerical order.

signposts: words or phrases that connect pieces of supporting material to the main point or subpoint they address

once in a speech, but our retention is likely to increase markedly if we hear something more than once. In a speech, if we preview main points, then state each main point, and also provide transitions between points, audiences are more likely to follow and remember the organization. To help you remember to use section transitions, write them in complete sentences on your speech outline.

Signposts are words or phrases that connect pieces of supporting material to the main point or subpoint they address. While section transitions are complete sentences, signposts are usually one-word references. Sometimes, signposts highlight numerical order: "first," "second," "third," or "fourth." Sometimes, they help the audience focus on a key idea: "foremost," "most important," or "above all." They can also be used to signify an explanation: "to illustrate," "for example," "in other words," "essentially," or "to clarify." Signposts can also signal that an important idea, or even the speech itself, is coming to an end: "in short," "finally," "in conclusion," or "to summarize." Just as section transitions serve as the glue that holds your macrostructure together, signposts serve as the glue that holds your subpoints and supporting material together within each main point.

Speech Planning Action Step 4, Activity 4D, will help you complete the outline for the body of your speech. See the Student Response box immediately following the activity for a sample of how one student completed this exercise.

SPEECH PLANNING

ACTIVITY 4D

Action STEP 4

Outlining the Speech Body

The goal of this exercise is to help you get started on the outline for the body of your first speech. Using complete sentences, write the following:

1. The specific speech goal you developed in Activity 4A.
2. The thesis statement you developed in Activity 4B.
3. A transition to the first main point.
4. The first main point you developed in Activity 4C.
5. The outline of the listener relevance link, subpoints, and support for your first main point, similar to the sample shown earlier, under "Outlining Subpoints."
6. A transition from your first main point to your second.
7. The other points, subpoints, support, section transitions, and signposts. Use the format for numeration, spacing, and so on shown in the Student Response to Activity 4D. (Note that the labels Introduction, Conclusion, and Sources are included just to help you understand the requirements for your final outline.) For a sample of a completed outline, see pages 162–166 of Chapter 8.

 CourseMate You can complete this activity online with Speech Builder Express and, if requested, e-mail your completed activity to your instructor. Go to your CourseMate for *Challenge* to access Activity 4D.

STUDENT RESPONSE

Outlining the Speech Body

Here is Katie's outline of her main points, including her goals, thesis statement, and section transitions.

General goal: *I want to inform my audience.*

Specific speech goal: *I would like the audience to understand the uses and abuses of Adderall.*

Thesis statement: *I want to inform my audience about the growing problem of college students taking Adderall without a prescription by explaining the nature and purpose of Adderall as a prescription drug, its growing popularity as a study aid among college students, and problems associated with using Adderall® without a prescription.*

Body

I. *Adderall is a psychostimulant prescribed to treat three conditions.*

   Listener relevance link: Understanding the intended medical uses of the drug Adderall may help you understand why the drug is so widely abused by collegians.

   A. *Adderall, the brand name for amphetamikne-dextroamphetamine, is a psychostimulant, one of a class of drugs intended to promote concentration, suppress hyperactivity, and promote healthy social experiences for patients (Willis, 2001).*

      1. *Adderall stimulates the central nervous system by increasing the amount of dopamine and norepinephrine in the brain. These chemicals are neurotransmitters that help the brain send signals between nerve cells (Daley, 2004, April 20).*

      2. *Mentally, Adderall brings about a temporary improvement in alertness, wakefulness, endurance, and motivation.*

      3. *Physically, it can increase heart rate and blood pressure and decrease perceived need for food or sleep.*

   B. *Adderall is prescribed for the medical treatment of attention deficit hyperactivity disorder (ADHD) in children and adults as well as for narcolepsy and clinical depression.*

      1. *ADHD is a neurobehavioral developmental disorder characterized by problems of attention coupled with hyperactivity.*

         a. *Since the mid-1990s, there has been a documented increase in the number of American children diagnosed with and treated for ADHD (McCabe, Teter, & Boyd, 2004).*

         b. *According to the Diagnostic and Statistical Manual of Mental Disorders (2000), symptoms must be present for at least six months for diagnosis, and symptoms must be excessive for medicinal treatment.*

         c. *The drugs Ritalin and Dexedrine are also used to treat ADHD. Adderall, however, remains the most widely prescribed of these drugs (Willis, 2001).*

         d. *According to the Centers for Disease Control and Prevention, approximately 4.4 million American children have been diagnosed with ADHD, and more than 2.5 million of those patients have been prescribed medicine to treat the condition (2005).*

(continued)

2. Adderall is also prescribed to treat narcolepsy, which occurs when the brain can't normally regulate cycles of sleep and waking.

   a. Sufferers of narcolepsy experience excessive daytime sleepiness that results in episodes of suddenly falling asleep.

   b. A chronic sleep disorder, narcolepsy affects 1 in every 2,000 Americans (American Academy of Sleep Medicine, 2005).

3. Adderall can also be used to treat clinical depression.

   a. Clinical depression is a disorder characterized by low mood, a loss of interest in normal activities, and low self-esteem.

   b. According to the National Institute of Mental Health, 9.5 percent of the adult population—that is, nearly 1.8 million American adults—suffer from clinical depression.

Transition: Now that we understand the basic properties and medical uses of the drug Adderall, let's now assess the increasing level of abuse of the drug by college students.

II. Unfortunately, Adderall has become popular among college students who use it "off label" as a study aid and for recreational purposes.

Listener relevance link: As college students, we need to be aware of what students believe about Adderall and why they are abusing it.

A. College students who don't suffer from ADHD, narcolepsy, or depression will take it with no prescription because they believe that it will improve their focus and concentration, allowing them to perform better on academic tasks (Teter, McCabe, Crandford, Boyd, & Gunthrie, 2005).

1. Adderall abuse among college students occurs especially at stressful times of the semester when students get little sleep.

   a. DeSantis, Webb, and Noar (2007) found that 72 percent of the students they surveyed reported using the drug to stay awake so that they could study longer when they had many assignments due.

   b. Katherine Stump, a Georgetown University student, reported in the school newspaper: "During finals week here at Georgetown, campus turns into an Adderall drug den. Everyone from a cappella singers to newspaper writers become addicts, while anyone with a prescription and an understanding of the free market becomes an instant pusherman" (Jaffe, 2006, January 1).

   c. Collegians report using the drug frequently during stressful times of the semester. One student said, "I use it every time I have a major paper due" (Daley, 2004, April 20).

2. Students also use Adderall for purposes other than academic ones.

   a. A survey of undergraduate and graduate students revealed that students engage in Adderall abuse for partying at a frequency just slightly less than taking the drug for academic purposes (Prudhomme White, Becker-Blease, & Grace-Bishop, 2006).

   b. DeSantis, Webb, and Noar (2007) report that students take the drug for its energizing effects. Other students report taking the drug to make them more social and outgoing at parties.

   c. Some college students, especially women, report using the drug for its use as an appetite suppressant for dieting purposes (Daley, 2004, April 20).

(continued)

STUDENT RESPONSE

B. *Adderall abuse is pervasive at the University of Kentucky, and the medication is easily obtained on campus.*

1. *I lived on campus my freshman year of college, and I currently still live in the dorms. By living in close proximity with other students, I learned a great deal about the individuals on my floor. I personally knew several students who used Adderall without a prescription. One student obtained the medication from a younger sibling diagnosed with ADHD, and another student purchased the pills from a friend on campus. The students would take the medicine to focus more intently when they had a short amount of time to complete a task. Both told me that they had used the drug as a study aid whenever they had several assignments to complete around the same time.*

2. *Adderall is easily obtained at the University of Kentucky. A male friend of mine told me that he had no problem finding someone to sell him the medication once he approached his first exam week as a college freshman. He told me that he merely had to ask around, and within no time, he was able to find a fellow student who agreed to sell him Adderall. As with any major university, the University of Kentucky is not impervious to the widespread abuse of Adderall by its students.*

Transition: **Now that we understand that Adderall abuse is prevalent on university campuses among students, it is important to understand the detrimental effects that can accompany the illegal use of Adderall.**

III. *Whether students acknowledge the dangers or not, there are great risks involved in illegally using Adderall.*

Listener relevance link: As we have now discussed the pervasiveness of Adderall abuse, statistically, it is likely that several of you have used this substance without a prescription to either enhance your academic performance or your social outings. Thus, it is important that we all recognize the adverse effects that result from taking Adderall without a prescription.

A. *Adderall abuse can cause negative health effects for individuals not diagnosed with ADHD (Daley, 2004, April 20).*

1. *Adderall is reported to cause a heightened risk for heart problems when used inappropriately. Problems include sudden heart attack or stroke, sudden death in individuals with heart conditions, and increased blood pressure and heart rate (FDA, 2010).*

2. *Adderall abuse also can result in a myriad of mental problems including manifestation of bipolar disorder, an increase of aggressive thoughts, and a heightened risk for psychosis similar to schizophrenia (FDA, 2010).*

B. *Adderall is highly addictive.*

1. *Adderall is an amphetamine, and while amphetamines were once used to treat a variety of ailments including weight loss in the 1950s and '60s, the drugs began to be much more closely regulated once their addictive nature was realized (Daley, 2004, April 20).*

2. *Adderall has similar properties to cocaine, and, as a result, abuse of the drug can lead to substance dependence (FDA, 2010).*

(continued)

C. *Though clear risks are associated with the illegal use of Adderall, unlike other drugs, collegians do not view the inappropriate use of Adderall as harmful or illegal.*

   1. *College students typically view stimulant abuse as morally acceptable and physically harmless. In a 2010 study, DeSantis and Hane found that students were quick to justify their stimulant abuse by claiming its use was fine in moderation.*

   2. *The Kentucky Kernel, the student newspaper at the University of Kentucky, published an editorial of a student who flippantly described the use of Adderall among college students. He states, "If you want to abuse ice cream, amphetamines or alcohol, then there are going to be serious problems; however, let's not pretend a person using Adderall twice a semester to help them study is in any way likely to die a horrible death or suffer terrible side effects" (Riley, 2010, May 3).*

   3. *In a study assessing the attitudes of college students toward the inappropriate use of stimulants, the authors found that "the majority of students who reported misuse or abuse were not concerned about the misuse and abuse of prescription stimulants, and a number of students thought that they should be more readily available" (Prudhomme White, Becker-Blease, & Grace-Bishop, 2006, p. 265).*

Transition: Now that we understand the risks involved in illegally using Adderall, hopefully you have a better understanding of why using the drug without a prescription is so dangerous.

Reflect on Ethics

WHAT WOULD *YOU* DO?

A SNAKE IN THE GRASS

Harriet Ziefert's children's book, *A Snake Is Totally Tail,* was to be published in early 2006 when a New York public librarian, John Peters, noticed that more than half of the text exactly matched a book by Judi Barrett. First published in 1983, Barrett's book was by then out of print. Peters posted his observation to a listserv, and Ziefert responded with, "I have no recollection of ever seeing Ms. Barrett's book—though it would be foolish of me not to consider the possibility that I might have seen it decades ago and that its structure and some of its language imprinted somewhere on my subconscious."[2] Although no formal suit was ever filed against Ziefert, the publisher decided not to publish the book after Peters's listserv posting was made public.[3]

1. Do you believe Ziefert's explanation? Why or why not?
2. Suppose that Ziefert's book did not match the earlier book word for word but instead just followed a very similar plotline that was organized the same way and used the same narrative voice. Would your opinion of Ziefert change?
3. Do you believe John Peters acted ethically? Why or why not?

Summary

A speech that is well organized is likely to achieve its goal. Speech organization begins by writing a thesis statement that articulates your specific speech goal and previews your main points.

The body of the speech includes main points and subpoints that should be written in complete sentences and checked to make sure that they are clear, parallel in structure, meaningful, and limited in number to four or fewer.

The order in which you present your main points depends on the type of speech you are giving and on the specific nature of the material you want to present. Four fundamental organizational patterns are time, narrative, topic, and logical reasons. You will want to choose an organizational pattern that best helps your audience understand and remember your main points.

The next step in organizing your speech is to choose and order material that you will use to explain each main point. To begin this process, create lists of the information you have that relates to each of your main points. Then review each list, grouping similar information under larger headings and identifying the information that is most important for helping the audience understand and remember the main point. These subpoints should be written in complete sentences and entered on your outline below the main point to which they belong. One subpoint should be a listener relevance link that indicates why or how this point relates to your specific audience. As a speaker, you will also want to consider such elements as definitions, examples, statistics, personal experiences, stories, and quotations that you can use to elaborate your key subpoints.

Section transitions bridge major parts of the speech and occur between the introduction and the body, between main points within the body, and between the body and the conclusion. Section transitions should be planned and placed in the outline as parenthetical statements where they are to occur. Whereas section transitions serve as the glue that holds together the macrostructural elements of your speech, signposts serve as the glue that holds together the subpoints and supporting material within each main point. Together, these types of transitions serve as a roadmap for listeners to follow as you present your speech.

Challenge Resource and Assessment Center

CourseMate Now that you have read Chapter 7, use your Speech Communication CourseMate for *The Challenge of Effective Speaking* for quick access to the electronic resources that accompany this text. These resources include the following:

- **Study tools** that will help you assess your learning and prepare for exams (*digital glossary, key term flash cards, review quizzes*).

- **Activities and assignments** that will help you hone your knowledge and build your public speaking skills throughout the course (*Speech Snippets, Speech Assignments, Action Step Activities*). Many of these activities allow you to compare your answers with those provided by the authors, and, if requested, submit your answers to your instructor.

- **Media resources** that will help you explore communication concepts online (*Web Resources*), develop your speech outlines (*Speech Builder Express 3.0*), watch and critique videos of sample speeches (*Interactive Video Activities*), upload your speech videos for peer reviewing and critique other students' speeches (*Speech Studio online speech review tool*), and download chapter reviews so you can study when and where you'd like (*Audio Study Tools*).

This chapter's application activities and video resources are featured in this end-of-chapter section.

1. **Impromptu Speech Activity:** Identify a favorite toy, game, food, or hobby you had as a child. Come up with a goal statement and two to four main points you could talk about concerning that toy, game, food, or hobby. Present a short speech consisting of a thesis statement as the introduction, the two to four main points linked with section transitions for the body, and a thesis restatement for the conclusion. Be sure to consider the wording of your thesis statement and the best organizational pattern for your main points. Be prepared to defend your choices if asked to do so.

2. **Assessment Activity A:** Complete Action Steps 4A, 4B, 4C, and 4D for a speech you may give this semester.

3. **Assessment Activity B:** Watch a speaker in person or on television who demonstrates how to make or do something. Try to identify the thesis statement and main points. Does the speaker use parallel phrasing, section transitions, and/or signposts? How does using or not using them influence your ability to follow along?

Speech-Planning Action Steps

4A: Identifying Main Points (122)

4B: Writing a Thesis Statement (125)

4C: Developing the Main Points of Your Speech (132)

4D: Outlining the Speech Body (136)

Web Resource

7.1 Writing Different Types of Thesis Statements (124)

Video Resources

1. Check out Speech Studio to see how other students worded their thesis statements. Or record a speech you're working on, upload it to Speech Studio, and ask your peers for their feedback. What feedback could you use to fine-tune your thesis statement before you give your speech in class?

2. Check out Speech Studio to see the transitions other students created for their speeches. Or record a speech you're working on, upload it to Speech Studio, and ask your peers for their feedback. What feedback could you use to fine-tune your transitions before you give your speech in class?

Ethical communicators demonstrate integrity when they begin and end each of their speeches with an introduction and conclusion that meets all the goals intended in them.

8

© Phil Boorman/Taxi/Getty Images

"the introduction and conclusion"

What's the Point?

QUESTIONS YOU'LL BE ABLE TO ANSWER AFTER READING THIS CHAPTER:

1. Why are solid introductions and conclusions so important to effective public speaking?

2. How can you get your audience's attention in your introduction?

3. Why should you summarize your main points again in the conclusion?

4. How might you motivate listeners to remember your speech in your conclusion?

5. How do you determine which sources to include in your outline and reference list?

STEP **Action** **4** Organize and develop ideas into a well-structured outline.

E. Create the speech introduction.

F. Create the speech conclusion.

G. Compile the list of sources used.

H. Complete the formal speech outline.

Courtney asked April to listen to her rehearse her speech. As she stood in front of the room where she was practicing, she began, "According to Merriam-Webster's online dictionary, organic food is 'relating to, yielding, or involving the use of food produced with the use of feed or fertilizer of plant or animal origin without employment of chemically formulated fertilizers, growth stimulants, antibiotics, or pesticides.' In my speech, I'd like to offer three reasons to eat organic food. First, organic food is healthier than mass produced food. Let me explain why."

"Whoa, Courtney," April said. "That's your introduction?"

"Yes," Courtney replied. "I've got a lot of information to share and don't have a lot of time to say it. So, I don't want to waste any more time than necessary on my introduction."

Courtney's response sounds reasonable at first. But what she is failing to realize is that not everyone in the audience may be ready to listen to a speech about eating organic food. People might think the topic is boring, irrelevant to them, or for some other reason not worth their time. They might also wonder what makes Courtney a credible speaker on the subject. For most speeches, how well you start the speech may determine whether most members of the audience even listen, and how well you start and finish your speech can play a major role in the speech's overall success.

One reason a speech's introduction and conclusion is so important is based on what psychologists call the **primacy-recency effect**: We are more likely to remember the first and last items conveyed orally in a series than the items in between.[1] This means listeners are more likely to remember the beginning and ending of your speech than what you say in the body. Another reason stems from the need for listeners to quickly grasp your goal and main points as they listen to your speech and to remember them after you've finished. You can give listeners a preview of the macrostructure of your speech by using the introduction to highlight your goal and preview the main points, and you can reinforce them by restating them in the conclusion.

In the previous chapter, we described the first few tasks involved in organizing the body of your speech. In this chapter, we describe how to complete the process by creating an introduction that both gets attention and leads into the body of the speech; creating a conclusion that both summarizes the material and leaves the speech on a high note; writing a title; and completing a list of the sources you used to develop the speech.

Creating the Introduction

Once you have developed the body of your speech, you can decide how to begin your speech. Because the introduction is so important to your success, you will want to develop two or three different introductions and then select the one that seems best for this particular audience. Although your introduction may be very short, it needs to motivate your audience to want to listen to what you

primacy-recency effect:
the tendency to remember the first and last items conveyed orally in a series rather than the items in between

have to say. An introduction is generally about 10 percent of the length of the entire speech, so for a five-minute speech (approximately 750 words), an introduction of about thirty seconds (approximately sixty to eighty-five words) is appropriate.

Goals of the Introduction

An effective introduction has four primary goals: to get audience attention, establish listener relevance, begin to establish speaker credibility and goodwill, and identify your thesis statement (speech goal and main point preview). In our opening scenario, Courtney didn't achieve any of these goals. Rather, she simply identified and defined the topic and then moved right into her first main point.

GET ATTENTION

An audience's physical presence does not guarantee that people will actually listen to your speech. Your first goal, then, is to create an opening that will win your listeners' attention by arousing their curiosity and motivating them to want to know more about what you have to say about your topic. Some rhetorical devices for doing so include startling statements, questions, stories, jokes, personal references, quotations, action, and suspense. You can determine which attention-getting device to use by considering what emotional tone is appropriate for your topic. A humorous attention getter will signal a lighthearted tone; a serious one signals a more thoughtful or somber tone. For instance, a speaker who starts with a funny story will put the audience in a lighthearted mood. If that speaker then says, "Now let's turn to the subject of abortion" (or nuclear war or drug abuse), the audience will be confused by the speaker's initial words, which signaled a far different type of subject.

> **SPEECH SNIPPET**
>
> **Introducing a Speech with Rhetorical Questions and a Startling Statement**
>
> Lana used a combination of rhetorical questions and a startling statement to get her listeners' attention for her speech on eating disorders: "Who are five of the most important women in your life? Your mother? Your sister? Your daughter? Your wife? Your best friend? Now which one of them has an eating disorder? Before you disregard my question, listen to what research tells us. One in every five women in the United States has an eating disorder."

1. **Make a startling statement.** A **startling statement** is a sentence or two that grabs your listeners' attention by shocking them in some way. Chris used a startling statement to get his listeners' attention for his speech about how automobile emissions contribute to global warming:

   Look around. Each one of you is sitting next to a killer. That's right. You are sitting next to a cold-blooded killer. Before you think about jumping up and running out of this room, let me explain. Everyone who drives an automobile is a killer of the environment. Every time you turn the key to your ignition, you are helping to destroy our precious surroundings.

   Once Chris's startling statement grabbed the attention of his listeners, he went on to state his speech goal and preview his main points.

2. **Ask a question.** Questions are requests for information that encourage your audience to get involved with your topic. Questions can be *rhetorical* or *direct*. A **rhetorical question** seeks a mental rather than a direct response. Notice how the following student began his speech on counterfeiting with these three short rhetorical questions:

   What would you do with this $20 bill if I gave it to you? Take your friend to a movie? Treat yourself to a pizza and drinks? Well, if you did either of these things, you could get in big trouble—this bill is counterfeit!

   Unlike a rhetorical question, a **direct question** demands an overt response from the audience, usually by a show of hands. For example, here's how author and motivational speaker Harvey Mackay started his commencement address at the University of Southern California on May 15, 2009:

   Let me start by asking all of you in the audience this question: How many people talk to themselves? Please raise your hands. I count approximately 50 percent.

startling statement: a sentence or two that grabs your listeners' attention by shocking them in some way

rhetorical question: a question that seeks a mental rather than a direct response

direct question: a question that demands an overt response from the audience, usually by a show of hands

To the other 50 percent who didn't raise your hands, I can just hear you now, saying to yourself: "Who me? I don't talk to myself!"

Well I think all of you will be talking to yourself about the day's events on your way home this evening. This is an unforgettable moment among many fine hours you will have in your career and life.[2]

Direct questions can be helpful in getting audience attention because they require a physical response. However, getting listeners to actually comply with your request can also pose a challenge.

story: an account of something that has happened (actual) or could happen (hypothetical)

SPEECH SNIPPET

Getting Attention by Telling a Story

Matt used a short story to get audience attention for his speech about spanking as a form of discipline:

One rainy afternoon, four-year-old Billy was playing "pretend" in the living room. He was Captain Jack Sparrow, staving off the bad guys with his amazing sword-fighting skills. Then it happened. Billy knocked his mother's very expensive china bowl off the table. Billy hung his head and began to cry. He knew what was coming, and sure enough it did. The low thud of his mother's hand on his bottom brought a sting to his behind and a small yelp from his mouth. Billy got a spanking.

---

3. **Tell a story.** A **story** is an account of something that has happened (actual) or could happen (hypothetical). Most people enjoy a well-told story, so it makes a good attention getter. One drawback of stories is that they are often lengthy and can take more time to tell than is appropriate for the length of your speech. Use a story only if it is short or if you can abbreviate it so that it is just right for your speech length. Yash Gupta, dean of the Carey Business School at Johns Hopkins University, used a story to get attention about assumptions, prejudices, and policies about older people:

   Imagine this.

   You are boarding a routine business flight. As you get on the plane you notice the pilot looks perhaps a bit . . . grandfatherly. In fact, he is only two years away from his FAA-mandated retirement age.

   You sit and open a magazine. You know, in advertisements flight attendants always look like the champagne they are pouring: fresh and bubbly. But looking around the cabin at the flight crew the words that instead come to mind are mature *and* no-nonsense. *All three flight attendants are in their 50s.*

   You are belted comfortably, your seat is in the upright position, and you have just felt the wheels lift off the runway from LaGuardia Airport.

   Only a couple minutes into your flight there is a loud bang, followed by another loud bang. Flames shoot out from the plane's two jet engines, and then they both go silent. Less than three minutes later, the pilot makes one terse announcement: prepare for impact.

   The next thing you know you're floating on the Hudson River and the flight crew is quickly and efficiently moving you onto the wings of the aircraft. They know their jobs.

   Flight attendant Doreen Welsh is 58. She's been flying since 1970—almost 40 years' experience. Sheila Daily is 57. She's been flying since 1980, and the other flight attendant, 51-year-old Donna Dent, has been flying since 1982.

   As you watch the rescue boats approach, one thought goes through your mind: At moments like this, who needs fresh and bubbly?

   The story of Flight 1549 suggests that in our society perhaps we have been too quick to praise youth, too ready to underestimate the value of age, wisdom and experience. One thing is certain: as we look forward to the middle years of the 21st century, we are going to have ample opportunity to discover if our assumptions, our prejudices, and our policies about older people are valid—or if perhaps we have some serious reconsidering to do.[3]

joke: an anecdote or a piece of wordplay designed to be funny and make people laugh

4. **Tell a joke.** A **joke** is an anecdote or a piece of wordplay designed to be funny and make people laugh. A joke can be used to get audience attention when it meets the *three R's test*: It must be realistic, relevant, and repeatable.[4] In other words, it can't be too far-fetched, unrelated to the speech purpose, or potentially offensive to some listeners. In his speech about

being a person of integrity, for example, an inspirational speaker offered this joke to get attention:

A lady went up to a butcher to purchase a chicken to roast for dinner. The butcher looked in the cooler and discovered he had only one left. He put it on the scale for her to consider. She said, "I think I'd like a bigger one." The butcher cleverly put the chicken back in the cooler and then took it out again. This time, he placed the chicken and his thumb on the scale to make it appear a bit heavier. After contemplating for a moment, the woman responded, "Oh heck, I'll take both of them!"

When jokes work, they adhere to the three R's test, but if you decide to use one, be sure to consider how you will handle the situation if nobody laughs.

Some speakers get attention by doing something out of the ordinary, like dressing up in traditional costume. Depending on the audience and speaking situation, this can be an effective strategy. But if the occasion doesn't call for this sort of attention-getter, you can get attention in other ways, like asking a rhetorical question, telling a joke, or reciting a quotation.

5. **Supply a personal reference.** A **personal reference** is a brief story about something that happened to you or a hypothetical situation that listeners can imagine themselves in. In addition to getting attention, a personal reference can be especially effective at engaging listeners as active participants. A personal reference like this one on exercise is suitable for a speech of any length:

Were you panting when you got to the top of those four flights of stairs this morning? I'll bet there were a few of you who vowed you'd never take a class on the top floor of this building again. But did you ever stop to think that maybe the problem isn't that this class is on the top floor? It just might be that you are not getting enough exercise.

> **personal reference:** a brief story about something that happened to you or a hypothetical situation that listeners can imagine themselves in

For longer speeches, you can build personal references that tie together the speaker, the audience, and the occasion. Let's see how Bruce Cole, chairman of the National Endowment for the Humanities, used a personal reference in the opening of his speech at New York University's "Art in an Age of Uncertainty" conference:

Good morning. It is an honor and pleasure to be here today. It's been said that a picture is worth a thousand words; as an art historian, I ardently believe this is true. And so I freely confess that nothing I say here today is as meaningful, as momentous, or as memorable as the sight of what lies nearby. We are on hallowed ground. The magnitude of the horrific events of September 11 is still being realized, the aftershocks still felt. But even in an age of uncertainty there are truths to be discovered, lessons to discern, and hope to share.

Today, I'd like to talk to you about the centrality of the humanities to democratic and civic life; the danger of American amnesia; and the possibilities of recovering our memory and protecting the best of our culture.[5]

Notice how smoothly Cole moves from personal reference into his thesis and main point preview.

6. **Recite a quotation.** A **quotation** is a comment made by and attributed to someone other than the speaker. A particularly vivid or thought-provoking quotation can make an excellent attention getter as long as

> **quotation:** a comment made by and attributed to someone other than the speaker

In her speech about binge eating and obesity, Jamie used this personal reference and startling statement to get her audience's attention: "Imagine a table full of all the food you eat in one week. *[pause]* That's a lot of food, right? Now, imagine eating all that food in one day! Believe it or not, there are people who do this. They consume many thousands of calories more than the suggested intake of 2,000 per day. This is a condition called binge eating, and it's more common than you might think."

action: an attention-getting act designed to highlight your topic or purpose

creating suspense: wording an attention getter so that what is described generates initial uncertainty or mystery and excites the audience

SPEECH SNIPPET

Using a short quotation to get attention

In a speech about the importance of courage and taking risks, Sonja began with Franklin D. Roosevelt's famous quotation, "The only thing we have to fear is fear itself."[8]

---

it relates to your topic. Although it is common to quote famous people, a good quotation from *any* source can create interest in your topic. For instance, notice how Sally Mason, provost at Purdue University, used the following quotation to get the attention of her audience, the Lafayette, Indiana, YWCA:

There is an ancient saying, "May you live in interesting times." It is actually an ancient curse. It might sound great to live in interesting times. But interesting times are times of change and even turmoil. They are times of struggle. They are exciting. But, at the same time, they are difficult. People of my generation have certainly lived through interesting times and they continue today.[6]

As the introduction progressed, she introduced her topic about the gender gap in technology.

In the following excerpt from his speech to the National Communication Association in San Diego, on November 21, 2008, Lester Olson, professor of communication at the University of Pittsburgh, began this way:

An epigram for my contribution was written by the visionary activist and internationally acclaimed poet Audre Lorde: "Unused privilege is a weapon in our enemies' hands." Lorde, you might know, was a black, lesbian, feminist, socialist, mother of two, who lived for most of her life in an interracial union. She dealt with significant biases throughout her lifetime. Yet she recognized that she could use her privileges to transform her communities. She explained, "To use privilege requires admitting to privilege, requires moving beyond guilt and accusation into creative action." Her insight helped me to form my responses to the subject of same-sex civil marriage and the discrimination afflicting this conference hotel. I hope that her words inspire you, too, as I ask each of you to reflect on your privileges and how you will use them.[7]

7. **Perform or motivate an action.** You can introduce your topic and gain attention through an **action,** an attention-getting act designed to highlight your topic or purpose. You can perform an action yourself, just as Juan did when he split a stack of boards with his hand to get attention for his speech on karate. Or you can ask volunteers from the audience to perform the action. For example, Cindria used three audience members to participate in breaking a piñata to create interest in her speech on the history of the piñata. If you choose to use audience members, consider soliciting participants ahead of time to avoid the possibility of having no volunteers when you ask during your speech. Finally, you can ask your entire audience to perform some action related to your speech topic. If you'd like to ask your whole audience to perform an action, realistically assess whether what you are asking is something your audience is likely to comply with.

8. **Create suspense.** When you **create suspense,** you word your attention getter so that what is described generates uncertainty or mystery during the first few sentences and excites the audience. When you get the audience to ask, "What is she leading up to?" you hook them for the entire speech. The suspenseful opening is especially valuable when your audience is not particularly interested in hearing about your topic. Consider this suspenseful statement:

It costs the United States more than $116 billion per year. It has cost the loss of more jobs than a recession. It accounts for nearly 100,000 deaths a year. I'm

Reflect on Ethics

On his April 2, 2010, Fox Business Network program *Imus in the Morning*, talk show host Don Imus offered humor in his introduction to colleague Stuart Varney and Varney's upcoming program, *Varney and Company*, this way:

> *It's time for* Varney and Company *here on the Fox Business Network. And the man hosting that, just emerging from the basement down there with John Batchelor, where they have been cutting up Girl Scouts . . .*

He and his two cohosts proceeded to chuckle and comment with retorts like, "What is wrong with you?" and "Maybe there's something that came before that—

cutting up Girl Scouts" and "You can do anything with a British accent." If you haven't seen the introduction, search for it on www.youtube.com.

1. Do you think Imus's use of humor was ethical? Why or why not?
2. What ethical principles did his cohosts adhere to or violate?
3. If people laugh, does that make it okay? Why or why not?
4. What would you have said in response to Imus if you were on the program? If you were Stuart Varney or John Batchelor?

---

not talking about cocaine abuse—the problem is alcoholism. Today I want to show you how we can avoid this inhumane killer by abstaining from it.

Notice that by introducing the problem, alcoholism, at the end of the statement, the speaker encourages the audience to try to anticipate the answer. And because the audience may well be thinking that the problem is narcotics, the revelation that it is alcoholism is likely to be that much more effective.

For more tips about how to use these and other types of attention getters, go to your CourseMate for *Challenge* to access **Web Resource 8.1: Strategies for Introducing Speeches**.

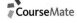
CourseMate

ESTABLISH LISTENER RELEVANCE

Even if you successfully get the attention of your listeners, to *keep* their attention you will need to motivate them to listen to your speech. You can do this by creating a clear listener relevance link, a statement of how and why your speech relates to or might affect your audience. Doing this in the introduction and again for each main point helps your audience realize its exigence.[9] Sometimes your attention-getting statement will serve this function, but if it doesn't, you will need to provide a personal connection between your topic and your audience. When creating a listener relevance link, answer these questions: Why should my listeners care about what I'm saying? In what way(s) might they benefit from hearing about it? How might my speech relate to my listeners' needs or desires for health, wealth, well-being, self-esteem, success, and so forth?

ESTABLISH YOUR CREDIBILITY AND GOODWILL

If someone hasn't formally introduced you before you speak, audience members are going to wonder who you are and why they should pay attention to what you say. So, another goal of the introduction is to begin to build your credibility. The theoretical grounding for this goal actually dates back

SPEECH SNIPPET

Getting Attention through Action

In her speech about acupressure, Andria asked her audience to perform this action as she modeled it for them

Take the thumb and index finger of your right hand and pinch the skin between the thumb and index finger of your left hand. What you've just done is stimulate a pressure point that can relieve headaches.

An effective speech introduction will not only get attention and lead into the body of the speech but will also build goodwill and set the tone for the speech. Telling a brief story is a popular and time-honored way to achieve these objectives.

Bill Aron/PhotoEdit

to ancient Greek philosophy of Aristotle in his treatise *The Rhetoric.*[10] In it, he asserted that listeners would be motivated to both listen to and believe a speaker based on their perception of his or her *ethos* (competence, good character, and goodwill), *pathos* (appeals to emotions), and *logos* (perception of truth through evidence and reasoning). To be successful, you need to begin to establish ethos during your introductory remarks. This initial ethos responds to the questions listeners may be thinking, such as: Why should I trust you? What makes you an authority on the subject? Why should I believe you? Do you seem sincere? Do you seem like a likeable person? Do your words and actions demonstrate respect for me and this occasion? Remember, though, that your goal is to highlight how you are a credible speaker on this topic, one who respects the audience and occasion, not that you are *the* or even *a* final authority on the subject. Carmen Mariano, principal of Archbishop Williams High School, established credibility and goodwill in a "welcome back, students" speech in September 2009 this way:

> *Ladies and gentlemen, you will hear one word many times this morning. That word is* welcome. *Please know how much we mean that word. Please know how much I mean that word.*
>
> *Why will we mean that word so much?*
>
> *Because without you, this is just a building on 80 Independence Avenue. And with you, this is Archbishop Williams High School. That's right. When you walked through those doors this morning, you made this building a school again.*
>
> *So welcome back.*
>
> *And welcome to your school.*[11]

STATE YOUR THESIS

Because audiences want to know what your speech is going to be about, it's important to state your thesis. Recall from Chapter 7 that your thesis statement introduces your audience to your general goal, specific goal, and main points. Thus, for his speech about romantic love, after Miguel gains attention and establishes relevance, he might draw from his thesis statement and say, "In the next five minutes, I'd like to explain to you that romantic love is composed of three elements: passion, intimacy, and commitment." Stating your main points in the introduction is necessary unless you have some special reason for not revealing the details of the thesis. For instance, after getting the attention of his audience, Miguel might say, "In the next five minutes, I'd like to explain the three aspects of romantic love," a statement that specifies the number of main points but leaves the details for a preview statement that immediately precedes the main points. Steve Jobs, in his commencement address at Stanford in 2005, did so this way: "Today I want to tell you three stories from my life. That's it. No big deal. Just three stories."[12]

Selecting the Best Introduction

Because the introduction is critical in establishing your relationship with your audience, it's worth investing the time to compare different openings. Try working on two or three different introductions; then, pick the one you believe will work best for your specific audience and speech goal.

> **SPEECH SNIPPET**
>
> **Establishing Credibility in an Introduction**
>
> In his speech about smoking in public places, Eric established his credibility by saying, "I used to smoke cigarettes and have quit, but not before I did a good deal of research about the effects of smoking and secondhand smoke."

PUTTING SPEAKING SKILLS TO WORK

Positive and Direct

Stephen Strieby, First Lieutenant, United States Marine Corps California

Courtesy of Stephen Strieby

Stephen Strieby, 25, graduated from Florida State University with a B.A. in economics and now serves as an officer in the U.S. Marine Corps. He took a public speaking class while in college and felt it was helpful, but where he really learned to speak is on the job.

One of his primary responsibilities is to inform his colleagues, defense contractors, and civilians about funding issues related to the equipment the military uses and how troops use the equipment when they're deployed. He speaks to a broad spectrum of people—sometimes an informal group of 15 to 30 Marines, other times to a more formal group of officers and civilian scientists, engineers, and researchers. He's also responsible for providing his bosses' bosses with summaries of what he learned at professional conferences he's attended. Speaking to an audience of much higher-ranking officers might seem intimidating, but he says, "The secret is, unless they were at the conference with you or have knowledge about what you're talking about, you're the resident expert. You're the one who was there."

And, of course, as an officer he is responsible for the kind of informative speaking related to training

> "The secret is, you're the resident expert."

and combat, which necessarily must be very specific and precise. "In the military," he says, "there's a very formalized way of teaching. You always introduce a training with 'Good morning, my name is so and so, and today I'll be teaching a class on whatever.' Then you go over all the main points. And you always summarize with 'In this period of instruction, you've learned x, y, and z. Are there any questions?'" This format helps his audiences fully understand the purpose of the training, maintains a momentum throughout the presentation, and leaves audience members knowing exactly what's expected of them.

Similarly, during combat Strieby must relay orders about battle plans to his troops in a highly structured way. "With that form of communication," he says, "it's incredibly important to give the correct information. If you have your times or other information wrong, things can go badly." So he's learned to keep his orders concise and direct. "Make positive and direct statements—very specific, precise, nothing fuzzy." No matter what the speaking situation, that's good advice for any speaker.

For instance, Jamie created two introductions for her speech on obesity. The first used a personal reference for an attention getter. Notice, too, how she established listener relevance and credibility by citing the U.S. Department of Health and Human Services statistic before offering her thesis statement:

Imagine a table full of all the food you eat in one week. That's a lot of food, right? Now, imagine eating all that food in one day! Believe it or not, there are people who do this. This condition, called binge eating, is contributing to a national epidemic: obesity. According to the U.S. Department of Health and Human Services, obesity may soon overtake tobacco as the leading cause of preventable death. In order to reduce obesity, let's examine the scope of the problem and its causes followed by some practical solutions. (ninety-two words)

Her second introduction used a startling statement and rhetorical question to get attention:

Tom is a 135-pound male who enjoys playing computer games and loves pizza. Sounds like an average person, right? Well, what would you think if I told you that Tom is only six years old? According to the U.S. Department of Health and Human Services, obesity may soon overtake tobacco as the leading cause of preventable death. Obesity is a serious problem in our society and warrants our attention. To prove my point, let's examine the scope of the problem and its causes followed by some practical solutions. (eighty-nine words)

Which of Jamie's introductions do you prefer? Why?

Your speech introduction should meet all four goals and be long enough to put listeners in a frame of mind that will encourage them to hear you out, without being so long that it leaves too little time to develop the substance of your speech. Of course, the shorter the speech, the shorter the introduction.

Speech Planning Action Step 4, Activity 4E, will help you develop three choices for your speech introduction. See the Student Response box immediately following the activity for a sample of how one student completed this exercise.

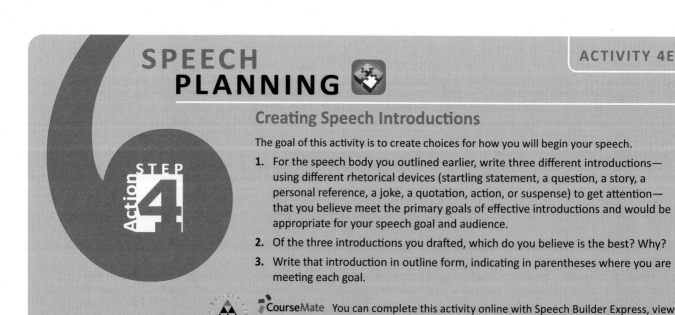

SPEECH PLANNING

ACTIVITY 4E

Action STEP 4

Creating Speech Introductions

The goal of this activity is to create choices for how you will begin your speech.

1. For the speech body you outlined earlier, write three different introductions—using different rhetorical devices (startling statement, a question, a story, a personal reference, a joke, a quotation, action, or suspense) to get attention—that you believe meet the primary goals of effective introductions and would be appropriate for your speech goal and audience.

2. Of the three introductions you drafted, which do you believe is the best? Why?

3. Write that introduction in outline form, indicating in parentheses where you are meeting each goal.

CourseMate You can complete this activity online with Speech Builder Express, view a student sample of this activity, and, if requested, e-mail your completed activity to your instructor. Go to your CourseMate for *Challenge* to access Activity 4E.

STUDENT
RESPONSE

Creating Speech Introductions

1. For the speech body you outlined earlier, write three different introductions—using different rhetorical devices (startling statement, a question, a story, a personal reference, a joke, a quotation, action, or suspense) to get attention—that you believe meet the goals of effective introductions and would be appropriate for your speech goal and audience.

   Specific goal: I would like the audience to understand the three ways to tell if a diamond is real.

   (1) *We are at an age where buying diamonds might be on our minds. I would like to tell you how you can know for sure if your diamond is real.*

   (2) *Have you ever wondered if you would know if the diamond the jeweler is trying to sell you is real? I would like to share some information that can help you.*

   (3) *Calcite, quartz, cubic zirconia, diamond. How can you tell these minerals apart? They are all colorless and can sometimes look alike. But let me tell you three ways that you can tell if you are holding a diamond.*

2. Of the three introductions you drafted, which do you believe is the best? Why?

   I believe the second one is the best because the rhetorical question is likely to motivate the audience to listen, and it leads into the body of the speech.

3. Write that introduction in outline form, indicating in parentheses where you are meeting each goal.

   I. *Have you ever wondered if you would know if the diamond that the jeweler is trying to sell you is real?*

   II. *Today, I am going to tell you three ways to identify a real diamond.*

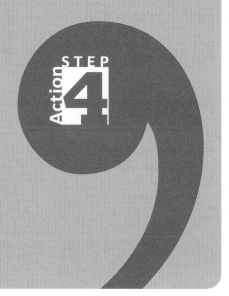

Creating the Conclusion

Shakespeare once said, "All's well that ends well." A strong conclusion can heighten the impact of a good speech. Even though the conclusion will be a relatively short part of the speech—seldom more than 5 percent (thirty-five to forty-five words for a five-minute speech)—your conclusion should be carefully planned.

Goals of the Conclusion

The conclusion of a speech has two major goals. The first is to review the goal and main points of the speech. The second is to provide a sense of closure that leaves the audience with a vivid impression of your message. Just as with your speech introduction, prepare two or three conclusions, and then choose the one you believe will be the most effective for your audience and speaking occasion.

SUMMARIZE GOAL AND MAIN POINTS

Any effective speech conclusion will include a summary of your speech goal and main points. A summary for an informative speech on how to improve your grades might be, "So I hope you now understand *[informative goal]* that three techniques for helping you improve your grades are to attend classes regularly, to develop a positive attitude toward the course, and to study systematically *[main points]*." Likewise, a short summary for a persuasive speech on why you should lift weights might be, "So remember the three major reasons why you should consider *[persuasive goal]* lifting weights are to improve your appearance, to improve your strength, and to improve your bone density *[main points]*."

> **SPEECH SNIPPET**
>
> **Summarizing Your Main Points**
>
> For her speech on the benefits of organic food, Courtney offered this summary:
>
> *So I hope you now understand how eating organically produced food contributes to physical health, a cleaner environment, and animal welfare.*

The conclusion offers you one last chance to hit home with your point. Supplementing a summary with a quote or a short anecdote is often a good way of emphasizing what you want the audience to get from the speech.

clincher: a one- or two-sentence statement in a conclusion that provides a sense of closure by driving home the importance of your speech in a memorable way

appeal to action: a statement in a conclusion that describes the behavior you want your listeners to follow after they have heard your arguments

CLINCH

Although summaries help you achieve the first goal of an effective conclusion, you'll need to develop additional material designed to achieve the second goal: leaving your audience with a vivid impression. You can achieve this second goal with a **clincher**—a one- or two-sentence statement that provides a sense of closure by driving home the importance of your speech in a memorable way. Very often, effective clinchers also achieve closure by referring back to the introductory comments in some way. Two effective strategies for developing effective clinchers are using vivid imagery and appealing to action.

To develop vivid imagery in your clincher, you can use any of the devices we discussed for getting your audience's attention: startling statement, question, story, personal reference, joke, quotation, action, or suspense. For example, in Tiffany's speech about being a vegetarian, she referred back to the personal reference she had made in her introduction about a vegetarian Thanksgiving meal:

So now you know why I made the choice to become a vegetarian and how this choice affects my life today. As a vegetarian, I've discovered a world of food I never knew existed. Believe me, I am salivating just thinking about the meal I have planned for this Thanksgiving: fennel and blood orange salad; followed by baked polenta layered with tomato, fontina, and Gorgonzola cheeses; an acorn squash tart, marinated tofu; and with what else but pumpkin pie for dessert!

Sounds good doesn't it? Clinchers that foster vivid imagery are appropriate for both informative and persuasive speeches because they leave listeners with a vibrant picture imprinted in their minds.

The appeal to action is a common way to end some persuasive speeches. The **appeal to action** describes the behavior you want your listeners to follow after they have heard your arguments. Notice how Matthew Cossolott, president and founder of Study Abroad Alumni International, concludes his speech on global awareness and responsibility with a strong appeal to action:

So, yes, you should have this re-entry program. Yes, you should network and explore international career opportunities. That's all good.

But I also encourage you to Globalize Your Locality. I urge you to Think Global. . . Act Global. . . Be Global.

This is an urgent call to action . . . for you and other study abroad alumni . . . to help us reduce the global awareness deficit.

You can do so by becoming involved with SAAI . . . and other organizations such as the National Council for International Visitors, Sister Cities, or Rotary International.

You can speak to local schools and community organizations about your study abroad experience and the need for more global awareness.

When you studied abroad, I'm sure you were told many times that you would be serving as unofficial ambassadors of the United States . . . your campus . . . and even your community back home.

Now that you're home again, I hope you'll become ambassadors for the value of the study abroad experience and for the need for greater international awareness.

In wrapping up . . . I'd like to leave you with this image . . . just picture in your mind's eye that iconic photograph of planet earth. I'm sure you've seen it. Taken over four decades ago . . . in December 1968 . . . on the Apollo 8 mission to the moon.

The photograph—dubbed Earthrise—shows our small, blue planet rising above a desolate lunar landscape. This photo was a true watershed in human history . . . marking the first time earthlings . . . fellow global citizens had traveled outside earth's orbit and looked back on our lonely planet.

The widespread publication of Earthrise had a lot to do with launching the worldwide environmental movement. It's no accident that the first Earth Day—on April 22, 1970—took place so soon after the publication of this remarkable photograph.

We're all privileged to inhabit this same planet—truly an island in space. And voices to the contrary notwithstanding . . . whether we want to admit it or not . . . we are all, undeniably and by definition, citizens of the world.

The only question is: will we accept the responsibilities of global citizenship?

Your future . . . and perhaps the survival of the planet . . . just may depend on how many of us answer yes to that question.[13]

Selecting the Best Conclusion

To determine how you will conclude your speech, create two or three conclusions; then, choose the one you believe will best reinforce your speech goal with your audience.

For her short speech on Adderall, Katie created the following three variations of summaries for consideration. Which do you like best?

Adderall is a prescription stimulant that is being used more and more among college students especially as a study aid, and there are serious risks associated with using the drug illegally. The next time you or a friend considers taking Adderall as a study aid, think again. The potential harm that the drug could cause to your body is not worth even a perfect grade point average.

Adderall is a prescription drug that is being abused by college students across the country. The stimulant is meant to treat medical conditions but is now being used illegally as a study aid. The harms in doing so are alarming. So if you've considered taking Adderall as a study aid, I hope you consider what we've talked about today before you do. Not taking it is not only better for you in the long run, just like wearing your seatbelt and not drinking and driving, but it's also obeying the law.

So, Adderall is a stimulant that is prescribed to treat real problems but is now being abused by more and more college students as a study aid, which is, quite frankly, breaking the law. I won't ask for a show of hands this time, but I will ask the question once more. If you've used Adderall illegally as a study aid, will you think twice before you do it again? If you know someone who uses it illegally as a study aid, will you share what you've learned today with that person? I sincerely hope so. It really is a matter of life and health.

For speeches that are no longer than five minutes, a one- to three-sentence conclusion is often appropriate. You're likely to need as much time as possible to do a good job presenting your main points. But as speech assignments get longer, you'll want to consider supplementing the summary to give the conclusion more impact.

Speech Planning Action Step 4, Activity 4F, will help you develop choices for your speech conclusion. See the Student Response box immediately following the activity for a sample of how one student completed this exercise.

SPEECH SNIPPET

Ending with a Clincher

Jamie drove home her point about obesity by referring back to her opening story about Tom and then offering an appeal to action:

Without doubt, obesity is a serious problem that must be addressed by examining its causes and then constructing and implementing workable solutions. Together, we can help people like Tom overcome obesity. If we can, we must—before it's too late.

SPEECH PLANNING

Action STEP 4

Creating Speech Conclusions

The goal of this activity is to help you create choices for how you will conclude your speech.

1. For the speech body you outlined earlier, write three different conclusions that review important points you want the audience to remember, and include a clincher that provides closure by leaving the audience with a vivid impression.

2. Which do you believe is the best? Why?

3. Write that conclusion in outline form.

CourseMate You can complete this activity online with Speech Builder Express, view a student sample of this activity, and, if requested, e-mail your completed activity to your instructor. Go to your CourseMate for *Challenge* to access Activity 4F.

STUDENT RESPONSE

Creating Speech Conclusions

1. For the speech body you outlined earlier, write three different conclusions that review important points you want the audience to remember, and include a clincher that provides closure by leaving the audience with a vivid impression.

   Specific goal: I would like the audience to understand the three ways to tell if a diamond is real.

   (1) So, the next time you buy or receive a diamond, you will know how to do the acid, streak, and hardness tests to make sure the diamond is real.

   (2) Before making your final diamond selection, make sure it can pass the acid test, streak test, and hardness test. Remember, you want to make sure you're buying a diamond—not paste!

   (3) You now know how to tell if your diamond is real. So, folks, if you discover that the gem you're considering effervesces in acid, has a streak that is not clear, or can be scratched, you will know that the person who tried to sell it to you is a crook!

2. Which do you believe is the best? Why?

   The third one because it restates the characteristics and leaves a vivid impression.

3. Write that conclusion in outline form.

   I. You now know how to tell if your diamond is real.

   II. If it effervesces, streaks, or scratches, the seller is a crook.

---

formal outline: A full sentence outline of your speech that includes internal references and a reference list.

Completing the Outline

At this point, you have a draft outline of your speech. To complete the **formal outline**, you will want to compile a list of the source material you will be drawing from in the speech, create a title (if required), and review your outline to make sure that it conforms to a logical structure.

Listing Sources

Regardless of the type of speech or how long or how short it will be, you'll want to prepare a list of the sources you use in it. This list will enable you to direct audience members to the specific source of the information you have used and will allow you to quickly find the information at a later date. You will also want to use internal references throughout the formal speech outline to help you remember what to cite and where during your speech. Doing so will ultimately enhance your credibility and help you avoid unintentional plagiarism. The two standard methods of organizing source lists are alphabetically by author's last name and by content category, with items listed alphabetically by author within each category. For speeches with a short list, the first method is efficient. But for long speeches with a lengthy source list, it is helpful to group sources by content categories.

Many formal bibliographical styles can be used in citing sources (for example, MLA, APA, Chicago, CBE); the "correct" form differs by professional or academic discipline. Check to see if your instructor has a preference about which style you use in class.

Regardless of the particular style, the specific information you need to record differs depending on whether the source is a book, a periodical, a newspaper, or an Internet source or website. The elements that are essential to all are author, title of article, name of publication, date of publication, and page numbers. Exhibit 8.1 gives examples of Modern Language Association (MLA) and American Psychological Association (APA) citations for the most commonly used types of sources.

Exhibit 8.1 Examples of the MLA and APA citation forms for speech sources

	MLA style	APA style
Book	Miller, Roberta B. *The Five Paths to Persuasion: The Art of Selling Your Message.* New York: Warner Business Books, 2004. Print.	Miller, R. B. (2004). *The five paths to persuasion: The art of selling your message.* New York: Warner Business Books.
Edited book	Janzen, Rod. "Five Paradigms of Ethnic Relations." *Intercultural Communication.* 10th ed. Eds. Larry Samovar and Richard Porter. Belmont, CA: Wadsworth, 2003. 36-42. Print.	Janzen, R. (2003). Five paradigms of ethnic relations. In L. Samovar & R. Porter (Eds.), *Intercultural communication* (10th ed., pp. 36–42). Belmont, CA: Wadsworth.
Academic journal	Barge, J. Kevin. "Reflexivity and Managerial Practice." *Communication Monographs* 71 (Mar. 2004): 70-96. Print.	Barge, J. K. (2004, March). Reflexivity and managerial practice. *Communication Monographs, 71,* 70–96.
Magazine	Krauthammer, Charles. "What Makes the Bush Haters So Mad?" *Time* 22 Sept. 2003: 84. Print.	Krauthammer, C. (2003, September 22). What makes the Bush haters so mad? *Time,* 84.

(continued)

	MLA style	APA style
Newspaper	Cohen, Richard. "Wall Street Scandal: Whatever the Market Will Bear." *The Cincinnati Enquirer* 17 Sept. 2003: C6. Print.	Cohen, R. (2003, September 17). Wall Street scandal: Whatever the market will bear. *The Cincinnati Enquirer,* p. C6.
Electronic article based on print source	Friedman, Thomas L. "Connect the Dots." *The New York Times.* 25 Sept. 2003. Web. 20 Aug. 2004.	Friedman, T. L. (2003, September 25). Connect the dots. *The New York Times.* Retrieved from http://www.nytimes.com/2003/09/25/opinion/25FRIED.html
Electronic article from Internet-only publication	Osterweil, Neil, and Michelle Smith. "Does Stress Cause Breast Cancer?" *Web M.D. Health.* WebMD Inc. 24 Sept. 2003. Web. 20 Aug. 2004.	Osterweil, N., & Smith, M. (2003, September 24). Does stress cause breast cancer? *Web M.D. Health.* Retrieved from http://my.webmd.com/contents/article/74/89170.htm?z3734_00000_1000_ts_01
Electronic article retrieved from database	Grabe, Mark. "Voluntary Use of Online Lecture Notes: Correlates of Note Use and Note Use as an Alternative to Class Attendance." *Computers and Education* 44 (2005): 409-21. *ScienceDirect.* Web. 28 May 2006.	Grabe, M. (2005). Voluntary use of online lecture notes: Correlates of note use and note use as an alternative to class attendance. *Computers and Education, 44,* 409–421. Retrieved from ScienceDirect.
Movie	*Pirates of the Caribbean: Dead Man's Chest.* Dir. Gore Verbinksi. Perf. Johnny Depp, Orlando Bloom, Keira Knightley. 2006. The Walt Disney Company, 2007. DVD.	Bruckheimer, J. (Producer), & Verbinksi, G. (Director). (2006). *Pirates of the Caribbean: Dead man's chest* [Motion picture]. United States: Walt Disney Pictures.
Television program episode	"Truth Be Told." *Dexter.* Showtime. 10 Dec. 2006. Television.	Gordon, K. (Director). (2006, December 10). Truth be told. [Television series episode]. In J. Manos Jr. (Executive producer), *Dexter.* New York, NY: Showtime Networks Inc.
Music recording	Nirvana. "Smells Like Teen Spirit." *Nevermind.* Geffen, 1991. CD.	Nirvana. (1991). Smells like teen spirit. On *Nevermind* [CD]. Santa Monica, CA: Geffen.
Personal interview	Mueller, Bruno. Personal interview. 19 March 2004.	APA style dictates that no personal interview is included in a reference list. Rather, cite this type of source orally in your speech, mentioning the name of the person you interviewed and the date of the interview.

Exhibit 8.2 Sample complete formal outline *(continued)*

ice cream, amphetamines or alcohol, then there are going to be serious problems; however, let's not pretend a person using Adderall twice a semester to help them study is in any way likely to die a horrible death or suffer terrible side effects" (Riley, 2010, May 3).

  3. In a study assessing the attitudes of college students toward the inappropriate use of stimulants, the authors found that "the majority of students who reported misuse or abuse were not concerned about the misuse and abuse of prescription stimulants, and a number of students thought that they should be more readily available (Prudhomme White, Becker-Blease, & Grace-Bishop, 2006, p. 265).

Transition: Now that we understand the risks involved in illegally using Adderall, hopefully you have a better understanding of why using the drug without a prescription is so dangerous.

Conclusion

  I. *Restatement of thesis:* Adderall is a prescription stimulant that is increasingly being abused by college students primarily as a study aid.
  II. *Main point review:* We have examined today what the drug Adderall is, its growing popularity among college students especially as a study aid, and the risks associated with using the drug illegally.
  III. *Clincher:* The next time you or a friend considers taking Adderall as a study aid, think again. The potential harm that the drug could cause to your body is not worth even a perfect grade point average.

References

American Psychiatric Association. *(2000). Diagnostic and statistical manual of mental disorders.* Arlington, VA: Author.

Centers for Disease Control and Prevention. (2005, September 2). *Morbidity and Mortality Weekly Report (MMWR).* Retrieved from http://www.cdc.gov

Daley, B. (2004, April 20). Perspective: Miracle drug? Adderall is prescribed for individuals with ADD and ADHD; for nonprescribed users there can be some serious risks. *Daily Pennsylvanian.* Retrieved from http://www.vpul.upenn.edu

DeSantis, A. D., & Hane, A. C. (2010). "Adderall is definitely not a drug": Justifications for the illegal use of ADHD stimulants. *Substance Use & Misuse, 45,* 31–46.

DeSantis, A. D., Webb, E. M., & Noar, S. M. (2008). Illicit use of prescription ADHD medications on a college campus: A multimethodological approach. *Journal of American College Health, 57,* 315–324.

Food and Drug Administration. (2010). *Drugs @ FDS: FDA approved drug products.* Retrieved from http://www.accessdata.fda.gov.

National Heart, Blood, and Lung Insitute (2008). "What is narcolepsy?" *National Heart, Blood, and Lung Institute Diseases and Conditions Index.* Retrieved from http://www.nhlbi.nih.gov/health/dci/Diseases/nar/nar_what.html

Jaffe, H. (2006, January 1). ADD and abusing Adderall. *The Washingtonian.* Retrieved from http://www.washingtonian.com

McCabe, S. E., Teter, C. J., & Boyd, C. J. (2004). The use, misuse and diversion of prescription stimulants among middle and high school students. *Substance Use and Misuse, 39,* 1095–1116.

Prudhomme White, B., Becker-Blease, K. A., & Grace-Bishop, K. (2006). Stimulant medication use, misuse, and abuse in an undergraduate and graduate student sample. *Journal of American College Health, 54,* 261–268.

Riley, T. (2010, May 3). Prescription drug abuse is a personal choice. *Kentucky Kernel.* Retrieved from http://kykernel.com

Exhibit 8.2 Sample complete outline *(continued)*

Substance Abuse and Mental Health Services Administration, Office of Applied Studies. (April 7, 2009). *The NSDUH Report: Nonmedical Use of Adderall among Full-Time College Students.* Rockville, MD.

Teter, J. C., McCabe, S. E., Crandford, J. A., Boyd, C. J., & Gunthrie, S. K. (2005). Prevalence and motives for illicit use of prescription stimulants in an undergraduate student sample. *Journal of American College Health, 53,* 253–262.

Willis, F. (2001). Attention deficit disorder. *Modern Drug Discovery, 4,* 84–86.

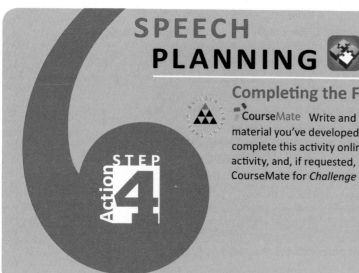

SPEECH PLANNING

ACTIVITY 4H

Action STEP 4

Completing the Formal Speech Outline

CourseMate Write and review a complete-sentence outline of your speech using material you've developed so far with the Action Steps in Chapters 4 through 8. You can complete this activity online with Speech Builder Express, view a student sample of this activity, and, if requested, e-mail your completed activity to your instructor. Go to your CourseMate for *Challenge* to access Activity 4H.

Summary

The organization process is completed by creating an introduction and a conclusion, listing the sources you used in the speech, writing a title (if required), and reviewing the formal outline. An effective speech introduction gets audience attention, establishes listener relevance, establishes credibility and goodwill, and introduces the thesis.

A well-designed speech conclusion summarizes the speech goal and main points and leaves the audience with a vivid impression. Informative and persuasive speeches may leave an impression with a clincher, a one- or two-sentence statement that provides a sense of closure by driving home the importance of your speech in a memorable way. Two strategies for effective clinchers are using vivid imagery and appealing to action.

A good formal outline also includes a list of sources compiled from the bibliographical information recorded on research cards. Short lists are alphabetized by authors' last names. Longer source lists group sources by content category before alphabetizing by author.

Although most classroom speeches may not require a title, in most speech situations outside the classroom it helps to have an informative and appealing title. Three kinds of titles are the simple statement of subject, the question, and the creative title.

You should review and revise your formal outline to make sure that you have used a standard set of symbols, used complete sentences for main points and major subdivisions, limited each point to a single idea, and related minor points to major points.

Challenge Resource and Assessment Center

CourseMate Now that you have read Chapter 8, use your Speech Communication CourseMate for *The Challenge of Effective Speaking* for quick access to the electronic resources that accompany this text. These resources include the following:

- **Study tools** that will help you assess your learning and prepare for exams (*digital glossary, key term flash cards, review quizzes*).
- **Activities and assignments** that will help you hone your knowledge and build your public speaking skills throughout the course (*Speech Snippets, Speech Assignments, Action Step Activities*). Many of these activities allow you to compare your answers to those provided by the authors and, if requested, submit your answers to your instructor.
- **Media resources** that will help you explore communication concepts online (*Web Resources*), develop your speech outlines (*Speech Builder Express 3.0*), watch and critique videos of sample speeches (*Interactive Video Activities*), upload your speech videos for peer reviewing and critique other students' speeches (*Speech Studio online speech review tool*), and download chapter reviews so you can study when and where you'd like (*Audio Study Tools*).

This chapter's application activities and Video Resources are featured in this end-of-chapter section.

Applying What You've Learned

1. **Impromptu Speech Activity:** From a basket of thesis statements provided by your instructor, create two introductions and conclusions following the guidelines offered in this chapter. (Be sure to address all the goals of an introduction and conclusion.) Deliver both versions to the class as though you were giving an actual speech on the topic. Ask for feedback regarding which version the class liked better and why.

2. **Assessment Activity A:** Attend a public presentation on campus or in your community or watch and listen to one of the speeches you'll find on your CourseMate for *Challenge*. Listen carefully to the speaker's introduction and conclusion. Did he or she address all the goals we identified in this chapter for introductions and conclusions? In your opinion, what could he or she have done differently to improve and why?

3. **Assessment Activity B:** Complete Action Step 4 for one of the speeches you may give this semester.

Speech-Planning Action Steps

4E: Create a Speech Introduction (152)

4F: Create a Speech Conclusion (156)

4G: Compile a List of Sources (159)

4H: Complete the Speech Outline (166)

Video Resources

1. Check out Speech Studio to see introductions and conclusions other students created for their speeches. Or record a speech you're working on, upload it to Speech Studio, and ask your peers for their feedback. What feedback could you use to fine-tune your introduction and conclusion before you give your speech in class?

SPEECH Studio

Web Resources

8.1 Strategies for Introducing Speeches (149)

2. To see many more examples of speech outlines, access the Interactive Videos for *Challenge* through your CourseMate. Each video features a sample student speech, including a speech transcript, complete and speaking outlines, and speaking notes. **CourseMate**

Music+Video

Ethical communicators demonstrate respect for their audiences by using presentational aids that enhance the verbal message in ways that are not likely to offend.

9

Oso Media / Alamy

"presentational aids"

What's the Point?

QUESTIONS YOU WILL BE ABLE TO ANSWER AFTER READING THIS CHAPTER:

1. Why should you incorporate presentational aids into your speech?

2. What are some types of presentational aids you can choose from?

3. What are some common mistakes speakers make when constructing and using presentational aids?

4. What are some important considerations to keep in mind when choosing presentational aids?

5. What are some important considerations to keep in mind when preparing presentational aids?

6. What are some important considerations to keep in mind when presenting with your presentational aids?

Action STEP 5 Choose, prepare, and use appropriate presentational aids.

A. Consider presentational aids that will clarify, emphasize, or dramatize your message.

B. Use another symbol system (beyond words alone) in your aids.

C. Make sure your visual aids are large enough the be seen.

D. Make sure your audio aids are loud enough to be heard.

E. Plan when to use aids and integrate them during your speech.

As Scott and Carrie drove home, Carrie exclaimed, "Wow! Dominic's speech was really great. I learned so much about what we could do to develop more sustainable electronics."

"Yeah, I know what you mean," Scott replied. "I've even got some ideas for reducing the e-waste he talked about."

"You know, what's really amazing to me is how much I learned from such a short talk!"

"I know what you mean. When I heard these were going to be PowerPoint presentations, all I could think was 'Oh no! Here we go again! Beer or no beer, it's going to be Death by PowerPoint: a darkened room and a faceless speaker talking to an oversized screen.' Thank goodness I was wrong. Dominic's visuals really helped me, but he was still the center of my focus. And the slides just helped me visualize and reinforced the important points he was making. My manager could benefit from watching someone like Dominic."

"I know. I can't believe we learned so much in five minutes! Tomorrow when I get into the office, I'm going to check out Dominic's blog."

This conversation might have occurred between two people who attended the Ignite® Seattle 6 event on April 29, 2009, when industrial designer Dominic Muren gave a five-minute PowerPoint-aided presentation titled "Humblefacturing a Sustainable Electronic Future."[1] Begun by Brady Forrest of O'Reilly Radar in 2006, Ignite has become a worldwide speaking movement. During an Ignite event, speakers give five-minute presentations, often on technical topics, aided by twenty PowerPoint slides. Unlike the "death by PowerPoint" speeches Scott alluded to and we've all had to suffer through, the speeches given at these events are adapted to people today— people for whom interacting on several different social networking sites while talking or texting on cell phones and eating dinner is the norm. We live in an era when the written, oral, visual, and digital modes of communicating are merging. Whether it is a TV news program, your professor's lecture, or a sermon you hear at a place of worship, audiences have come to expect computer-enhanced presentations. This means that when you are preparing your speech you will need to decide what presentational aids to include and how to do so in ways that will motivate your audience to both pay attention and remember your message.

A **presentational aid** is any visual, audio, audiovisual, or other sensory material used by the speaker in a speech. A **visual aid** allows the audience to see as well as hear the speaker present the information. Examples of visual aids include actual objects, models, photographs, drawings and diagrams, maps, charts, and graphs. An **audio aid** is one that enhances the speaker's verbal message with additional sound. Examples include musical clips from CDs and iTunes, and recorded clips from conversations, interviews, famous speeches, and nature sounds like bird calls. **Audiovisual aids** enhance the

presentational aid: any visual, audio, audiovisual, or other sensory material used in a speech

visual aid: a form of speech development that allows the audience to see as well as hear the speaker present the information

audio aid: a presentational aid that enhances the speaker's verbal message with additional sound

audiovisual aid: a presentational aid that enhances the speech using a combination of sight and sound

other sensory aid: a presentational aid that enhance the ideas offered verbally by appealing to smell, taste, or touch

speech using a combination of sight and sound. Examples of audiovisual aids include clips from movies and television, YouTube videos, podcasts, as well as other events or observations captured on video. **Other sensory aids** include materials that enhance the ideas offered verbally by appealing to smell, taste, or touch. For example, a verbal description of perfume's fragrance can be clarified by allowing audience members to smell it, and the flavor of a particular entrée can be clarified by allowing audience members to taste it.

There are several benefits to using presentational aids. First, they enable you to adapt to an audience's level of knowledge by clarifying and dramatizing your verbal message. Second, presentational aids help audiences retain the information they hear.[2] Third, presentational aids allow you to address the diverse learning styles of your audience.[3] Fourth, they can increase the persuasive appeal of your speech. In fact, some research suggests that speakers who use presentational aids are almost twice as likely to persuade listeners than those who do not.[4] Finally, using presentational aids may help you to feel more competent. Speakers report that, when they use presentational aids, they tend to be less anxious and have more confidence.[5]

Today, presentational aids are usually developed into computerized slide shows using presentation software such as PowerPoint®, MediaPro®, Adobe®, Acrobat®, or Photodex® and are projected onto a large screen via a computer and LCD projector. These programs allow you to embed audio and audiovisual links from local files and the Internet, which makes it fairly simple to create effective multimedia presentations. Whether creating multimedia presentations or developing simpler presentational aids, the principle is the same: effective aids enhance the speaker's message without overpowering the speaker or the verbal message. When speakers violate this principle, they end up with what Scott called "death by PowerPoint," a situation where the speaker is extraneous and the audience is overwhelmed with the technology being used. The result is that the message gets lost. In this chapter, we describe various types of presentational aids, criteria you should consider when choosing them, which and how many presentational aids to use, ways you can create aids, methods for displaying your aids to the audience, and guidelines for using them effectively when you are speaking.

Types of Presentational Aids

Before you can choose what presentational aids you might want to use for a specific speech, you need to recognize the various types of aids that you can choose from. Presentational aids range from those that are simple to use and readily available from some existing source to those that must be custom produced for your specific speech and require practice to use effectively. In this section, we describe types of presentational aids to consider using as you prepare your speech.

Visual Aids

actual object: an inanimate or animate sample of the idea you are communicating

model: a three-dimensional scaled-down or scaled-up version of an actual object

diagram: a type of drawing to show the whole and its parts

Visual aids can include actual objects and models, photographs, drawings, diagrams, maps, charts, and graphs. They enhance the verbal message by allowing audiences to see what it is you are describing or explaining in your speech.

Actual objects are inanimate or animate physical samples of the idea you are communicating. Using them allows audience members to see precisely what you are talking about. Inanimate objects make good visual aids if they are (1) large enough to be seen by all audience members, (2) small enough to carry to the site of the speech, (3) simple enough to understand visually, and (4) safe. A volleyball or Muslim prayer rug would be appropriate in size for audiences of twenty to thirty. An iPhone or Blackberry might be okay if the speech goal is simply to show what one looks like, but these would probably be too small if you want to demonstrate how to use any of their specialized functions.

Some animate objects also make effective visual aids. On occasion, *you* can be an effective visual aid. For instance, you can use descriptive gestures to show the height of a tennis net; you can use posture and movement to show the motions involved in swinging a golf club; or you can use your attire to illustrate the native dress of a particular country. Sometimes, it can be appropriate to use another person as a visual aid, such as when Jenny used a friend of hers to demonstrate the Heimlich maneuver. Animals can also be effective visual aids. For example, Josh used his AKC Obedience Champion dog to demonstrate the basics of dog training. But keep in mind that animals placed in unfamiliar settings can become difficult to control and can distract from your message.

When an object's size is inappropriate, too complex to understand visually, potentially unsafe, or uncontrollable, a model of the object can be an effective visual aid. A **model** is a three-dimensional scaled-down or scaled-up version of an actual object that may be simplified to aid understanding. In a speech on the physics of bridge construction, a scale model of a suspension bridge would be an effective visual aid. Likewise, in a speech on genetic engineering, a model of the DNA double helix might help the audience understand what happens during microscopic procedures.

If an exact reproduction of material is needed, photographs can be excellent visual aids. In a speech on "smart weapons," before and after photos of target sites would be effective in helping the audience to understand the pinpoint accuracy of these weapons. When choosing photographs, be sure that the image is large enough for the audience to see and that the object of interest in the photo is clearly identified and, ideally, in the foreground. For example, if you are giving a speech about your grandmother and show a photo of her with her college graduating class, you might circle her image so she's easily seen.

Simple drawings and **diagrams** (a type of drawing that shows how the whole relates to its parts) are easy to prepare and can be effective because you can choose how much detail to include. To make sure they look professional, you can prepare them using a basic computer software drawing program or find them already prepared using an Internet search engine like Google Images. If you do this, however, be sure to credit the source during your speech to enhance your credibility and avoid plagiarism. If you use a drawing or diagram, be sure to keep it simple so it doesn't obscure the point you wish to make. Andria's representation of the human body and its pressure points is an example of an effective diagram that clarified her message and helped her meet her speech goal (see Exhibit 9.1).

Like drawings and diagrams, maps are relatively easy to prepare or find on the Internet. Simple maps allow you to orient audiences to landmarks (mountains, rivers, and lakes), states, cities, land routes, weather systems, and

Jose Luis Pelaez Inc/Blend Images / Alamy

Using a model as a visual aid can help the audience understand your topic. This model of a wind turbine helps the speaker clarify his explanation of how it works to harness the wind and convert it into power.

Exhibit 9.1 Diagram

Accupressure Points
KEY

B	Bladder
Lu	Lung
St	Stomach

Exhibit 9.2 Map

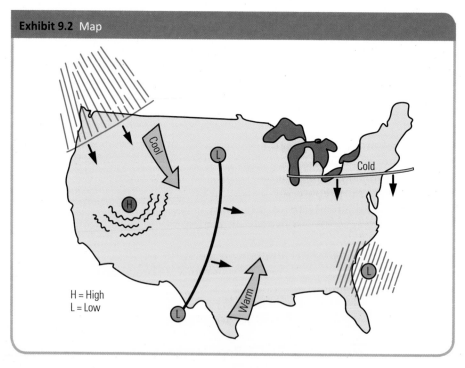

H = High
L = Low

chart: a graphic representation that distills a lot of information and presents it to an audience in an easily interpreted visual format

so on. Remember to include only the details that are relevant to your purpose. Exhibit 9.2 shows a map that focuses on weather systems.

A **chart** is a graphic representation that distills a lot of information into an easily interpreted visual format. Flowcharts, organizational charts, and pie

Reflect on Ethics

At the University of Notre Dame's 2009 commencement ceremony, President Barack Obama received an honorary law degree from the university and gave the commencement speech. In the days before and while he spoke, protests erupted on the campus and in the community of this Catholic university regarding his positions on abortion and embryonic stem cell research. Some protesters chose to use visual aids that offended some members of the community. For example, some protesters drove trucks that were covered with bloody anti-abortion images through neighborhoods. Others pushed carriages with baby dolls drenched in fake blood. These protesters maintained that they were exercising their right to free speech. But some community members were distressed because they were unable to protect their children and grandchildren from seeing the images. One concerned grandmother said, "[My granddaughter] saw one of the pictures. She's three and a half. I didn't get a chance to protect her. I didn't get a chance for her not to see it."[6]

1. Setting aside your personal beliefs regarding abortion for a moment, what if any ethical principles do these protesters violate with these images? Explain your reasoning.

2. Given that the Catholic Church is pro-life and sees abortion as sin, was it ethical for the school's administration to invite a pro-choice person to speak at commencement? Defend your answer by reviewing each of the ethical principles explaining why it was or was not violated.

3. Because the U.S. Constitution guarantees the right to free speech, the protesters were within their constitutional rights. So how do you reconcile what is ethical with what is legal? Explain.

---

charts are the most common types. A **flowchart** uses symbols and connecting lines to diagram a sequence of steps through a complicated process. Tim used a flowchart to help listeners move through the sequence of steps to assess their weight (see Exhibit 9.3 on page 174). An **organizational chart** shows the structure of an organization in terms of rank and chain of command. The chart in Exhibit 9.4 on page 175 illustrates the organization of a student union board. A **pie chart** is a diagram that shows the relationships among parts of a single unit. Ideally, pie charts have two to five "slices," or wedges—more than eight wedges clutter a pie chart. If your chart includes too many wedges, use another kind of chart unless you can consolidate several of the less important wedges into the category of "other," as Tim did to show the percentage of total calories that should come from the various components of food (see Exhibit 9.5 on page 175).

A **graph** is a diagram that presents numerical comparisons. Bar graphs and line graphs are the most common forms of graphs. A **bar graph** is a diagram that uses vertical or horizontal bars to show relationships between two or more variables. For instance, Jacqueline used a bar graph to compare the amounts of caffeine found in one serving each of chocolate, coffee, tea, and cola (see Exhibit 9.6 on page 175). A **line graph** is a diagram that indicates changes in one or more variables over time (see Exhibit 9.7 on page 176).

Audio Aids

Audio aids enhance a verbal message through sound. They are especially useful when it is difficult, if not impossible, to describe a sound in words. For example, in David's speech about the three types of trumpet mutes and how they alter the sounds a trumpet makes, he played his trumpet so listeners

flowchart: a chart that diagrams a sequence of steps through a complicated process

organizational chart: a chart that shows the structure of an organization in terms of rank and chain of command

pie chart: a diagram that shows the relationships among parts of a single unit

graph: a diagram that presents numerical comparisons

bar graph: a diagram that uses vertical or horizontal bars to show relationships between or among two or more variables at the same time or at various times on one or more dimensions

line graph: a diagram that indicates changes in one or more variables over time

Exhibit 9.3 Flowchart

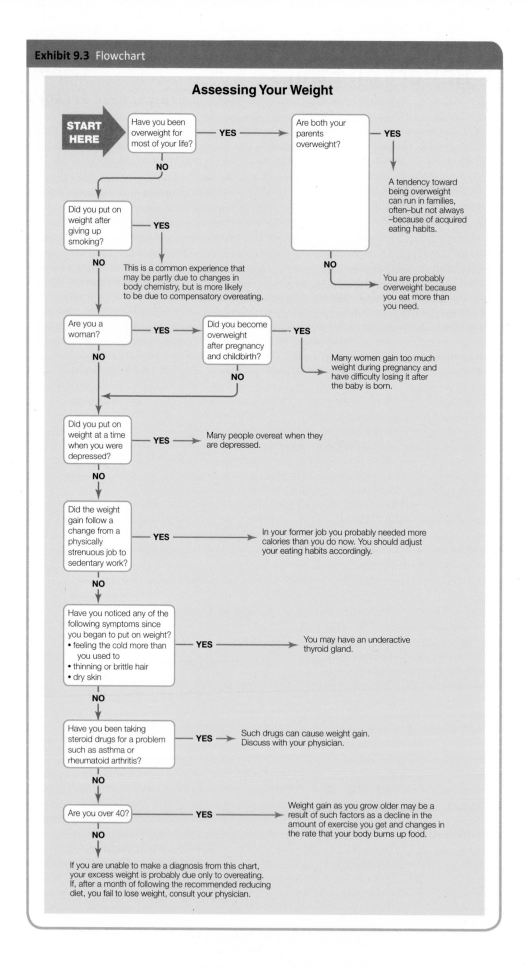

Assessing Your Weight

START HERE → Have you been overweight for most of your life? — **YES** → Are both your parents overweight? — **YES** ↓

A tendency toward being overweight can run in families, often–but not always–because of acquired eating habits.

Have you been overweight for most of your life? — **NO** ↓

Are both your parents overweight? — **NO** → You are probably overweight because you eat more than you need.

Did you put on weight after giving up smoking? — **YES** → This is a common experience that may be partly due to changes in body chemistry, but is more likely to be due to compensatory overeating.

Did you put on weight after giving up smoking? — **NO** ↓

Are you a woman? — **YES** → Did you become overweight after pregnancy and childbirth? — **YES** → Many women gain too much weight during pregnancy and have difficulty losing it after the baby is born.

Did you become overweight after pregnancy and childbirth? — **NO** ↓

Are you a woman? — **NO** ↓

Did you put on weight at a time when you were depressed? — **YES** → Many people overeat when they are depressed.

Did you put on weight at a time when you were depressed? — **NO** ↓

Did the weight gain follow a change from a physically strenuous job to sedentary work? — **YES** → In your former job you probably needed more calories than you do now. You should adjust your eating habits accordingly.

Did the weight gain follow a change from a physically strenuous job to sedentary work? — **NO** ↓

Have you noticed any of the following symptoms since you began to put on weight?
• feeling the cold more than you used to
• thinning or brittle hair
• dry skin
— **YES** → You may have an underactive thyroid gland.

Have you noticed any of the following symptoms... — **NO** ↓

Have you been taking steroid drugs for a problem such as asthma or rheumatoid arthritis? — **YES** → Such drugs can cause weight gain. Discuss with your physician.

Have you been taking steroid drugs... — **NO** ↓

Are you over 40? — **YES** → Weight gain as you grow older may be a result of such factors as a decline in the amount of exercise you get and changes in the rate that your body burns up food.

Are you over 40? — **NO** ↓

If you are unable to make a diagnosis from this chart, your excess weight is probably due only to overeating. If, after a month of following the recommended reducing diet, you fail to lose weight, consult your physician.

Exhibit 9.4 Organizational chart

Exhibit 9.5 Pie chart

could hear what he meant. If you don't want to make your own sounds, you can use recorded excerpts from sources such as famous speeches, radio programs, interviews, and recordings of music or environmental sounds, all of which may convey information better than your describing the material or

Exhibit 9.6 Bar graph

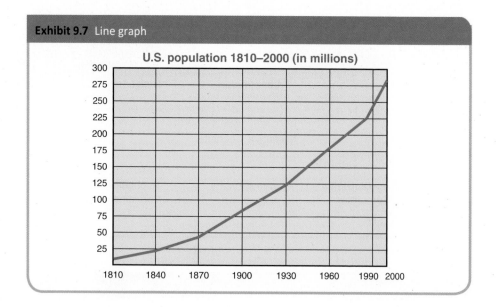

Exhibit 9.7 Line graph

U.S. population 1810–2000 (in millions)

SPEECH SNIPPET

Using Audio Aids

In her speech about whales, Emily played a recording of blue whales "singing." Playing the recording not only allowed the audience to better understand her topic, but it allowed her to present information that would have been difficult to describe with words alone.

SPEECH SNIPPET

Using Audiovisual Aids

For his speech on what happens to race horses after they retire, Paul began by playing a short clip he found on YouTube showing SuperSaver winning the 2010 Kentucky Derby.

SPEECH SNIPPET

Using Sensory Aids

For his speech on store-brand foods, Greg argued that store-brand products taste as good as their name-brand counterparts. He demonstrated his point by providing audience members with small samples of both store-brand and name-brand cereals to taste as he spoke.

reading it as a quotation. For example, Susan chose to begin her speech on the future of the NASA space program with a recording of Neil Armstrong's first words as he stepped on the surface of the moon: "That's one small step for a man, one giant leap for mankind." Before using audio material, make sure you have enough time to present it (it should make up no more than about 5 percent of your speaking time) and that you have access to a quality sound system.

Audiovisual Aids

Audiovisual aids enhance the verbal message through sight and sound. You can use short clips from films and videos to demonstrate concepts or processes and to expose audiences to important people. They are relatively easy to access on Internet sites such as YouTube. For example, during his speech about the use of robots in automobile production, Chad, who worked as a technician at the local Ford plant, showed a twenty-second video clip of a car being painted in a robotic paint booth. As with audio clips, keep video and film clips short (no more than 5 percent of your speaking time). It can be challenging to keep clips this short, particularly in short classroom speeches, so choose clips that are to the point and really enhance your message. Because computerized slide show software programs like PowerPoint make it so easy to import sounds and visual images, as well as to insert hyperlinks to websites, most effective speakers today enhance their speeches with computerized slide shows that incorporate visual, audio, and audiovisual material.

Other Sensory Aids

Depending on your topic, other sensory aids that appeal to smell, touch, or taste may effectively enhance your speech. For example, a speech about making perfume might benefit from allowing your audience to smell scented swatches as you describe the ingredients used to make the scents. In a speech about Braille, Javier handed out copies of his outline written in Braille for audience members to touch.

Criteria for Choosing Presentational Aids

Now that you understand the various types of presentational aids, you have to decide what content you want to highlight and how. Your answers to the following questions can help you make these decisions.

Celebrity chefs often ask observers to sample their product to confirm that it really tastes good.

1. **What are the most important ideas you want your audience to understand and remember?** These ideas are ones you may want to reinforce with presentational aids.

2. **Are there important ideas that are complex or difficult to explain verbally?** The old saying "One picture is worth a thousand words" is true. The same thing can be said for clarifying what you mean by letting your audience hear, taste, feel, or smell it.

3. **Is there important information in your speech that the audience may find boring?** At times you may want to use presentational aids to help your audience attend to what you are saying. For example, it's sometimes hard for the audience to pay attention to statistics, but a colorful graph can help audience members to concentrate on what you're saying.

4. **How many presentational aids should I use?** Presentational aids should supplement the oral message of your speech, not replace, overshadow, or distract from it. While the Ignite® speech referred to in the chapter opener was a five-minute speech that used twenty slides, most speakers find that about one good aid per minute of speaking time is sufficient to help audiences remember main points, clarify difficult information, and hold audience attention without becoming overly time consuming to create. So in a five-minute presentation, you might aim for between three and seven presentational aids.

5. **How large is the audience?** The kinds of presentational aids that will work for a small group of fifteen or twenty differ from the kinds that will work for an audience of a hundred or more. Presentational aids should be large enough to be seen and loud enough to be heard by those in the back and corners of the room.

6. **Are my presentational aids easy to use and transport?** Choose aids that you feel comfortable using and that are easy to transport from home to your speaking site. You want to focus on the content and delivery of your speech, not on how nervous you are using a new technology or transporting a cumbersome or fragile presentational aid.

7. **Is the necessary equipment readily available?** At times, you may be speaking in an environment that is not equipped for certain displays. In any situation in which you have scheduled equipment from an outside source, you need to prepare for the possibility that the equipment may not arrive on time or may not work the way you anticipated. Call ahead, get to your speaking location early, practice using your presentational aids with the available equipment, and have a backup plan, just in case. This is especially true when using computers and projection units from an outside source. Being prepared in this case means you might bring your own laptop and cable cords, an extra extension cord, and handouts in case the equipment still fails you. Frankly, if you do a lot of public speaking, you might invest in your own projection unit, as well.

8. **Is there sufficient time to show the aid without having it overtake the speech itself?** Remember that presentational aids are meant to supplement and enhance your speech, not replace it. If sharing the aid will take too much time, consider a different sort of aid.

9. **Is the time involved in making or getting the presentational aid and equipment cost-effective?** Presentational aids are supplements. Their goal is to supplement what you are doing verbally. If you believe that a particular aid will help you better achieve your goal, then the time spent is well worth it. Otherwise, the best advice we can offer is to "keep it simple."

Preparing Effective Presentational Aids

However simple you plan to make your presentational aids, keep in mind that you still have to take the time to design and produce them carefully. You may need to find or create charts, graphs, diagrams, maps, or drawings. You may need to search for and prepare photographs. You may choose to look for audio, video, or audiovisual clips and then need to convert them to a format that you can use at your speech site.

As you prepare, you must first determine whether you will design your aids by hand or by using computer presentation software. What you decide may depend on the resources available at your speech site. If you are artistic, can print clearly, and work neatly, then hand-designed aids would be a good choice. If you are comfortable using presentation software, then this method may be more efficient for you. The goal, however, is to prepare professional-looking presentational aids that will enhance your ethos (perceived competence, credibility, and character) in addition to clarifying your message and making it more memorable. Regardless of the method you choose, there are several guidelines you will want to follow.

1. **Limit the reading required of the audience.** The audience should not spend a long time reading your visual aid; you want them listening to you. So, write points as short phrases rather than complete sentences.

2. **Customize presentational aids from other sources.** We often get ideas and information for visual aids from other sources, and the tendency is to include everything that was in the original source. But if the original source includes information that is irrelevant to your purpose or audience, simplify your aid so that it includes only the information you want to present. For example, Jia Li was preparing a speech on alcohol abuse by young adults. During her research, she found a graph called "Current, Binge, and Heavy Alcohol Use among Persons Aged 12 or Older by Age." The graph presented information pertaining to drinkers from the ages 12 to 65+, which was much more information than Jia Li needed. So she simplified it for her presentation and used only the information for young adults ages 16 to 29.

3. **Use a photo, print, or type size that can be seen easily and a volume and sound quality that can be heard easily by your entire audience.** Regarding visual materials, check your photo, charts, and lettering for size by moving as far away from the presentational aid as the farthest person in your audience will be sitting. If you can see the image, read the lettering, and see the details from that distance, your aid is large enough; if not, create a larger draft and check it again. Check audio materials for volume and sound quality in a similar way.

4. **Use a consistent print style that is easy to read.** Avoid fancy print styles; your goal is presentational aids that are easy to read. Likewise, stick

to one print style throughout the aid or computerized slide show. In addition, some people think that printing in all capital letters creates emphasis, but the combination of uppercase and lowercase letters is easier to read than uppercase only—even when the ideas are written in short phases.

5. **Make sure information is laid out in a way that is aesthetically pleasing.** Leave sufficient white space around the whole visual so that it's easy to identify each component (white space is the areas of a page without print or pictures). Also, use typefaces and indenting to visually represent relationships between ideas.

6. **Add pictures or other visual symbols to add interest.** To truly enhance a verbal message, a presentational aid should consist of more than just words.[7] Visual symbols can increase retention by appealing to diverse learning styles.[8] If you are working with computer graphics, consider adding clip art. Most computer graphics packages have a wide variety of clip art that you can import to your document. You can also buy relatively inexpensive software packages that contain thousands of clip art images. A relevant piece of clip art can make the image look both more professional and more dramatic. Be careful, though; clip art can be overdone. Don't let your message be overpowered by unnecessary pictures or animations.

7. **Use color strategically.** Although black and white can work well for your visual aids, consider using color strategically to emphasize points. Here are some suggestions for incorporating color in your presentational aids:

   - Use the same background color for all your presentational aids and theme for the slides on your computerized slide show.
   - Use the same color to show similarities, and use opposite colors (on a color wheel) to show differences between ideas.
   - Use bright colors, such as red, to highlight important information. Be sure to avoid using red and green together, however, because audience members who are color-blind may not be able to distinguish between them.
   - Use dark colors for lettering on a white background and light colors for lettering on black or deep blue backgrounds.
   - Use no more than two or three colors on any presentational aid that is not a photograph or video clip.
   - Pretend you are your audience. Sit as far away as they will be sitting, and evaluate the colors you have chosen for their readability and appeal.

8. **Use presentation software to prepare professional-looking presentational aids. Presentation software** is a computer program that enables you to electronically prepare and store your presentational aids using a computer. Microsoft's PowerPoint®, Adobe's Captivate®, and Apple's Keynote 3® are popular commercial presentation software programs. The visuals you create on a computer can become overhead transparencies or handouts, or they can be displayed directly on a screen as a computerized slide show. Aids developed with presentation software give a very polished look to your speech and allow you to develop and deliver the complex multimedia presentations that are expected in many professional settings.

   Computerized slide shows have quickly become the presentational aid of choice today. However, too often, these shows do not adhere to the most important function of effective presentational aids, which is to enhance the verbal message, not replace it.[9] The speaker should not be

presentation software: a computer program that enables you to electronically prepare and store your visual aids using a computer relegated to the role of projectionist. Effective computerized slide shows adhere to all of the fundamental criteria we have addressed regarding presentational aids. Well-designed and well-presented computerized slide shows greatly enhance audience interest, understanding, and memory, as well as the audience's perceptions of the speaker's credibility.

Let's see if we can put all of these principles to work. Exhibit 9.8 contains a lot of important information, but notice how unpleasant it is to the eye. As you can see, this visual aid ignores all the principles we've discussed. However, with some thoughtful simplification, this speaker could produce the visual aid shown in Exhibit 9.9, which sharpens the focus by emphasizing the key words (reduce, reuse, recycle), highlighting the major details, and adding clip art for a professional touch.

Exhibit 9.8 A cluttered and cumbersome visual aid

I WANT YOU TO REMEMBER THE THREE R'S OF RECYCLING

Reduce the amount of waste people produce, like overpacking or using material that won't recycle.

Reuse by relying on cloth towels rather than paper towels, earthenware dishes rather than paper or plastic plates, and glass bottles rather than aluminum cans.

Recycle by collecting recyclable products, sorting them correctly, and getting them to the appropriate recycling agency.

Exhibit 9.9 A simple but effective visual aid

Remember the Three R's of Recycling

Reduce waste

Reuse
  cloth towels
  dishes
  glass bottles

Recycle
  collect
  sort
  deliver

Methods for Displaying Presentational Aids

Once you have decided on the specific presentational aids for your speech, you will need to choose the method to display them. Methods for displaying aids vary in the type of preparation they require, the amount of specialized training needed to use them effectively, and the professionalism they convey. Some methods, such as writing on a chalkboard, require little advance preparation. Sometimes, computerized slide shows can require extensive preparation. Finally, the quality of your presentational aid will affect your ethos. A well-run computerized slide show is impressive, but technical difficulties can make you look unprepared. Hand-drawn charts and graphs that are hastily or sloppily developed mark you as an amateur, whereas professional-looking visual aids enhance your credibility. Speakers can choose from the following methods for displaying presentational aids.

Posters

The easiest method for displaying simple drawings, charts, maps, photos, and graphs is by preparing them on or attaching them to stiff cardboard or foamcore. Then the visual can be placed on an easel or in a chalk tray when it is referred to during the speech. Because poster boards tend to be fairly small, use them only with smaller audiences (thirty people or fewer).

Whiteboards or Chalkboards

Because a whiteboard or chalkboard is a staple in every college classroom, many novice (and ill-prepared) speakers rely on this method for displaying their visual aids. Unfortunately, a whiteboard or chalkboard is easy to misuse and to overuse. Moreover, they are not suitable for depicting complex material. Writing on a whiteboard or chalkboard is appropriate only for very short items of information that can be written in a few seconds. Nevertheless, being able to use a whiteboard or chalkboard effectively should be a part of any speaker's repertoire.

Whiteboards or chalkboards should be written on prior to speaking or during a break in speaking. Otherwise, the visual is likely to be either illegible or partly obscured by your body as you write. Or you may end up talking to the board instead of to the audience. Should you need to draw or write on the board while you are talking, you should practice doing it first. If you are right-handed, stand to the right of what you are drawing. Try to face at least part of the audience while you work. Although it may seem awkward at first, your effort will allow you to maintain contact with your audience and will allow the audience to see what you are doing while you are doing it.

"Chalk talks" are easiest to prepare, but they are the most likely to result in damage to speaker credibility. It is the rare individual who can develop well-crafted visual aids on a whiteboard or chalkboard. More often, these presentations signal a lack of preparation.

Flipcharts

A **flipchart,** a large pad of paper mounted on an easel, can be an effective method for presenting visual aids. Flipcharts (and easels) are available in many sizes. For a presentation to four or five people, a small tabletop version works well; for a larger audience, a larger pad (thirty-by-forty inches) is needed.

Flipcharts are prepared before the speech using colored markers to record the information. At times, a speaker may record some of the information before the speech begins and then add information while speaking.

flipchart: a pad of paper mounted on an easel

When preparing flipcharts, leave several pages between each visual on the pad. If you discover a mistake or decide to revise, you can tear out that sheet without disturbing the order of other visuals you may have prepared. After you have the visuals, tear out all but one sheet between each chart. This blank sheet serves as both a transition page and a cover sheet. Because you want your audience to focus on your words and not on visual material that is no longer being discussed, you can flip to the empty page while you are talking about material not covered by charts. Also, the empty page between charts ensures that heavy lines or colors from the next chart will not show through.

For flipcharts to be effective, the information that is handwritten or drawn must be neat and appropriately sized. Flipchart visuals that are not neatly done detract from speaker credibility. Flipcharts can be comfortably used with smaller audiences (fewer than 100 people) but are not appropriate for larger settings. It is especially important when creating flipcharts to make sure that the information is written large enough to be easily seen by all audience members.

Handouts

At times, it may be useful for each member of the audience to have a personal copy of the visual aid. In these situations, you can prepare a handout. On the plus side, you can prepare handouts (material printed on sheets of paper) quickly, and all the people in the audience can have their own professional-quality material to refer to and take with them from the speech. On the minus side is the distraction of distributing handouts and the potential for losing audience members' attention when you want them to be looking at you.

Before you decide to use handouts, carefully consider why they would be better than some other method. Handouts are effective for information you want listeners to refer to after the speech, such as a set of steps to follow later, useful telephone numbers and addresses, or mathematical formulas.

If you do decide on handouts, distribute them at the end of the speech. If you want to refer to information on the handout during the speech, create another visual aid that you can reveal only when discussing it for use during the actual speech.

Document Cameras

Another simple way to display drawings, charts, photos, and graphs is with a document camera, such as an Elmo®. A document camera allows you to project images without transferring them to an acetate film. Transfer drawings, charts, photos, and graphs from original sources onto sheets of eight-by-eleven-inch paper so you can display them smoothly and professionally.

CD/VCR/DVD Players and LCD Projectors

LCD multimedia projector: a projection unit that connects to a VCR player, a DVD player, or a computer and projects images from them onto a screen

To show TV, film, and video clips for a classroom speech, a VCR or DVD player and a television monitor should be sufficient. For larger audiences, however, you will need multiple monitors or, ideally, an **LCD multimedia projector**. An LCD projector connects to a VCR player, a DVD player, or a computer and projects images from them onto a large screen, which makes them easy to see, even in a large auditorium. An LCD projector is also ideal for displaying computerized slide shows, such as PowerPoint® presentations.

Computerized Slide Shows

You can present computerized slide shows using an LCD projector or a large monitor connected to an onsite computer that has presentation software compatible with the software you used to make your aids. Because you can't always anticipate problems with onsite projection equipment, come with backup aids, such as handouts. When you present your slide show, ensure that the audience focuses their attention on you when you're not talking about one of your slides. To redirect their attention from your slide show to you, insert blank screens between your slides or press the B key on your computer to display a blank screen.

For more about how to use Microsoft PowerPoint, the most popular presentation software, access **Web Resource 9.1: PowerPoint Tutorial** through your CourseMate.

CourseMate

PUTTING SPEAKING SKILLS TO WORK

Read, Write, and Converse

Jaime Koepsell,
Senior Director, Retail Solutions and Project Management Office APEX Analytix, Greensboro, North Carolina

Photo courtesy of Jaime Koepsell.

Jaime Koepsell, 36, manages analysts and technologists who develop and implement custom software for profitable clients such as Wal-Mart, the world's largest retailer. She's in charge of software development, account management, and her team's training and support.

Koepsell earned a B.A. in economics from the College of William & Mary in Williamsburg, Virginia. She never took a public speaking class. "But I went to a private high school. We had small classes with a big focus on writing and being able to speak. My father was a wonderful writer and would critique my essays unmercifully! It really helped. For me there's a connection between writing and speaking. I worked on these skills when I was young and feel comfortable speaking now."

Her first job after college was writing software user manuals in a startup company. This naturally progressed to testing the software, ensuring its quality, and visiting clients where it was installed. "I had to speak in front of very important people." By the time she got her second job, in an established consulting company, she was ready for the "discipline of working with the best and the brightest. I continually focus on moving up."

Koepsell's confidence has contributed to her career growth. A routine part of her current job at APEX is speaking with and making presentations to the executives at large client companies. "It's very important that I am articulate and also compassionate about what they need." She builds on her natural confidence as a speaker by making sure she's well prepared for every

> "View presentations over the Internet. . . . Use them to craft your own style."

presentation. "I'm a stickler for preparation. I never walk into a meeting without a purpose, an agenda, notes, and a structure."

Believing as she does in the importance of preparation, Koepsell's challenge is knowing how to handle the uncertainties. "I need to be okay with it if I'm not able to prepare for every angle, for the unknowns in a situation. I used to be so nervous if I couldn't adequately prepare. I have to be able to move forward if I don't have all the answers. I need to just go in and be okay." Over time she's developed strategies that help her compensate if something comes up that she hadn't prepared for. "I use listening skills. I slowly overcame my nervousness when I trusted my own reactions. As I was continuously put in these situations, it was either sink or swim! There were times when I screwed up. But the bottom line is that you can't prepare for everything."

Koepsell also transforms any negatives to achieve an overall positive result. "There are opportunities for follow-up to regain control. I always publish minutes and outcomes, where I can correct things that might not have gone right."

Her advice to up-and-coming speakers is to "read a lot. See how concepts are written. View presentations over the Internet. You gain confidence from being exposed to things in different ways. Use them to craft your own style. Being well read increases your ability to engage in conversation. A lot of speaking is conversational. Discover ways to start conversations. Pull them from your reading."

Guidelines for Using Presentational Aids during the Speech

Many speakers think that once they have prepared good presentational aids, they will have no trouble using them in the speech. However, many speeches with good aids have become shambles because the speaker neglected to *practice with them*. You will want to make sure that you practice using presentational aids in your speech rehearsals. During practice sessions, indicate on your notes exactly when you will reveal each aid (and when you will conceal it). Work on statements for introducing the aids, and practice different ways of showing your aids until you are comfortable using them and satisfied that everyone in the audience will be able to see them. Following are several other guidelines for using presentational aids effectively in your speech.

1. **Plan carefully when to use presentational aids.** As you practice your speech, indicate on your outline when and how you will use each aid. Avoid displaying aids before you begin talking about the specific information to which they relate, as they may distract your audience's attention from important information that precedes the aid. Likewise, if you find that a presentational aid does not contribute directly to the audience's attention to, understanding of, or retention of information on your topic, then reconsider whether to use it at all.

2. **Position presentational aids and equipment before beginning your speech.** Make sure your aids and equipment are where you want them and that everything is ready and in working order. For example, check to make sure your poster boards are in sequence and positioned where all audience members will be able to see them. Test to make sure visual, audio, or audiovisual equipment works and that excerpts are cued correctly. Taking time to position your aids will make you feel more confident and look more professional and at ease.

3. **Show or play presentational aids only when talking about them.** Because presentational aids will draw audience attention, the basic rule of thumb for using them is this: When the aid is no longer the focus of attention, cover it up, remove it, turn it off, or get rid of it.

4. **Talk about the visual aid while showing it.** Because you already know what you want your audience to see in a presentational aid, tell your audience what to look for, explain the various parts of the aid, and interpret figures, symbols, and percentages. (For an audio presentational aid, point out what you want your audience to listen for before you play the aid.) When showing a visual aid, such as a transparency projected onto a screen in front of the class, use the following "turn-touch-talk" technique.

   - When you display the visual, walk to the screen—that's where everyone will look anyway. Slightly turn to the visual and touch it—that is, point to it with your arm or a pointer. (Use a pointer carefully.) Then, with your back to the screen and your body still at a slight forty-five-degree angle to the group, talk to your audience about the visual.
   - When you finish making your comments, return to the lectern or your speaking position and turn off the projector or otherwise conceal the visual.

5. **Talk to your audience, not to the presentational aid.** You may need to look at the visual aid occasionally, but it is important to maintain eye contact with your audience as much as possible—in part so that you

can gauge how they are reacting to your visual material. When speakers become too engrossed in their visual aids, looking at them instead of the audience, they tend to lose contact with the audience entirely.

6. **Display visual aids so that everyone in the audience can see them.** If you hold the visual aid, position it away from your body and point it toward the various parts of the audience. If you place your visual aid on an easel or mount it in some way, stand to one side and point with the arm nearest the visual aid. If it is necessary to roll or fold the visual aid, bring some transparent tape to mount it to the chalkboard or wall so that it does not roll or wrinkle. If the visual aid is projected onto a screen, point with your hand or a pointer to the screen.

7. **Avoid passing objects around the audience.** People look at, read, handle, and think about whatever they hold in their hands. While they are so occupied, they are not likely to be listening to you. This is why it's best to distribute a handout after your speech, not during it.

To see video clips of student speakers presenting visual aids effectively, go to your Speech Communication CourseMate for *Challenge* to access the chapter resources for Chapter 12. The speeches "U.S. Flag Etiquette," "Making Ethanol," and "The Three C's of Down Syndrome" all feature students using presentational aids. For more about how and when to use visual aids in a speech, access **Web Resource 9.2: Enhancing Written and Spoken Presentations** through your Speech Communication CourseMate.

CourseMate

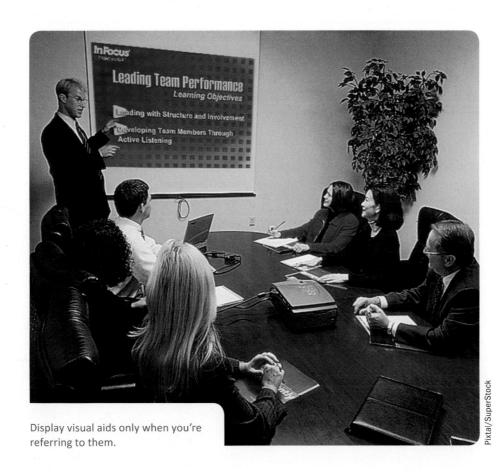

Display visual aids only when you're referring to them.

Pixtal/SuperStock

SPEECH PLANNING

Action STEP 5

Choosing, Preparing, and Using Presentational Aids

The goal of this activity is to identify information where a presentational aid would increase audience interest, understanding, and retention.

1. Identify the key ideas in your speech for which you believe a presentational aid would increase audience interest, facilitate understanding, or increase retention.

2. For each idea you have identified, list the type of presentational aid you think would be most appropriate to develop and use.

3. For each aid you have identified, decide how you will design it.

4. For each aid you have identified, decide on the method you will use to display it and how you will reference it during the speech.

CourseMate You can complete this activity online with Speech Builder Express, download a Presentational Aids Planning Chart to help you organize your aids, and, if requested, e-mail your completed activity to your instructor. Go to your Speech Communication CourseMate for *Challenge* to access Activity 5A.

STUDENT RESPONSE

Choosing, Preparing, and Using Presentational Aids

Speech goal: *I would like my audience to learn to identify common poisonous plants that grow in our area.*

1. Identify the key ideas in your speech where a presentational aid would increase audience interest, facilitate understanding, or increase retention.

   Leaf shape, size, and color; habitat; signs of contact

2. For each idea you have identified, list the type of presentational aid you think would be most appropriate to develop and use.

   I will use two color photographs of each type of plant. The first will show the entire plant; the second will be a close-up of the leaves. I will also use photos to show the habitat in which each plant is usually found. Finally, I will use photographs to show the reactions that occur as a result of contact with the plants. I will have actual plant samples available for closer inspection after my speech.

3. For each aid you have identified, decide how you will design it.

   I will use my digital camera to take photographs of each plant and the habitats in which I found them. These will be transferred to my computer, and then I will create a computerized slide show using PowerPoint. I will locate images of reactions to each plant online, download them, and add them to the computerized slide show. I will also collect samples of each type of plant and bring them with me to the speech.

4. For each aid you have identified, decide on the method you will use to display it and how you will reference it during the speech.

   I will bring a memory stick with the PowerPoint presentation on it with me and use the computer and LCD projector that is available at the speaking site. I will also have backup overheads of all my photos and slides. I will reference it using a pointer because I will be speaking to an audience of at least fifty people.

Summary

Presentational aids are useful when they help audience members understand and remember important information. The most common types of visual aids are objects, models, photographs, simple drawings and diagrams, maps, charts, and graphs. Audio aids include recordings of music, speeches, and environmental sounds. Audiovisual aids include clips from movies, television programs, commercials, and YouTube. Other sensory aids enhance the verbal message by focusing on taste, smell, or touch. Methods that speakers can use to present presentational aids include posters, flipcharts, whiteboards and chalkboards, handouts, and computerized slide shows using a computer, projector, and screen.

Before you start collecting or creating the presentational aids you plan to use, consider a number of questions. What ideas are most important in helping me achieve my speech goal? Are there ideas that are complex or difficult to explain verbally but would be easier to explain with the help of a presentational aid? How many presentational aids should I consider? How large is the audience? Is the necessary equipment readily available? Is the time involved in making or getting the visual aid or equipment cost-effective?

Take time to design your visual aids with the following principles in mind: Use a print or font size that can be seen easily by your entire audience. Use a font that is easy to read and pleasing to the eye. Use upper- and lowercase type. Try to limit the lines of type to six or fewer. Include only items of information that you will emphasize in your speech. Make sure information is laid out in a way that is aesthetically pleasing. Add clip art where appropriate. Use color strategically.

When you plan to use presentational aids in a speech, make sure you practice using them as you rehearse your speech. Keep the following suggestions in mind: Carefully plan when you will use each aid during your speech. Position the aids and equipment before beginning your speech. Show presentational aids only when talking about them; when you show a video clip or play an audio clip, talk about it before you play it. Display presentational aids so that everyone in the audience can see them. Talk to your audience, not to your presentational aid. Avoid passing objects around the audience. In short, keep your audience focused on *you* as the speaker as well as your presentational aids.

Challenge Resource and Assessment Center

CourseMate Now that you have read Chapter 9, use your Speech Communication CourseMate for *The Challenge of Effective Speaking* for quick access to the electronic resources that accompany this text. These resources include the following:

- **Study tools** that will help you assess your learning and prepare for exams (*digital glossary, key term flash cards, review quizzes*).

- **Activities and assignments** that will help you hone your knowledge and build your public speaking skills throughout the course (*Speech Snippets, Speech Assignments, Action Step Activities*). Many of these activities allow you to compare your answers to those provided by the authors, and, if requested, submit your answers to your instructor.

- **Media resources** that will help you explore communication concepts online (*Web Resources*), develop your speech outlines (*Speech Builder Express 3.0*), watch and critique videos of sample speeches (*Interactive Video Activities*), upload your speech videos for peer reviewing and critique other students' speeches (*Speech Studio online speech review tool*), and download chapter reviews so you can study when and where you'd like (*Audio Study Tools*).

This chapter's application activities and Video Resources are featured in this end-of-chapter section.

1. **Impromptu Speech Activity:** Battle of the Visual Aids. Form groups of four or five people. Your instructor will provide you with three sample visual aids that might be used in a speech. Based on the criteria and guidelines you learned in this chapter, evaluate each visual aid and select the best one. At your instructor's request, one member of each team should go to the front of the room and give a two- to three-minute speech that makes a case for why the visual aid you selected is the best of the three. After all groups have made their presentations, vote as a class on the best one and discuss why.

2. **Assessment Activity A:** Complete Action Plan Step 5 for a speech you give this semester.

3. **Assessment Activity B:** Locate a visual, audio, and audiovisual aid example that you believe represents an effective and ineffective presentational aid based on the information and guidelines offered in this chapter. Prepare a two- to three-page paper explaining why you assessed them as you did.

Speech-Planning Action Step

5A: Choosing, Preparing, and Using Presentational Aids (186)

Web Resources

9.1: PowerPoint Tutorial (183)

9.2: Enhancing Written and Spoken Presentations (185)

Video Resources

1. Use your Interactive Video Activities to watch, analyze, and see the transcript and outlines for the student speeches "U.S. Flag Etiquette," "Making Ethanol," and "The Three C's of Down Syndrome." (187)

2. Check out Speech Studio to see how other students use presentational aids in their speeches. Do any of the speeches you see give you good ideas for how to use presentational aids in your own speeches? Or record a speech you're working on, upload it to Speech Studio, and ask your peers for their feedback. What feedback could you use to fine-tune your presentational aids before you give your speech in class?

MAI /Landov

10

Ethical communicators make language choices that demonstrate respect for other individuals and groups.

language and oral style

STEP
Action 6
Practice oral language and delivery style.

A. Practice to develop an oral style using language that is appropriate, accurate, clear, and vivid.

What's the Point?
QUESTIONS YOU WILL BE ABLE TO ANSWER AFTER READING THIS CHAPTER:

1. How does oral style differ from written style?

2. How can you word your speech to avoid offending some listeners?

3. What should you do to make sure your language and style is appropriate?

4. What should you consider to make sure your word choices will be interpreted accurately by your audience?

5. What can you do to make sure your message is clear?

6. What are some strategies you can employ to make your ideas vivid?

As Rhonda replayed the recording she had made of her first speech practice session, she listened carefully to the section on the effects of Rohypnol. She stopped the tape after she heard herself saying, "Rohypnol leaves many bad effects on people. And a lot of these are really, really terrible. I mean, you can be totally out of it for a long time."

"Yuck," thought Rhonda. "That sounds so vague. I say, 'leaves bad effects,' but I don't specifically state any of the effects. And calling the effects 'really, really terrible' isn't very descriptive. What could I say instead?"

With an outline in hand and your presentational aids prepared, you are ready to practice your speech, switching your focus from the macrostructure (the overall framework you use to organize your speech content) to the microstructure (the specific language and style choices you use to frame your ideas and verbalize them to your audience). In the chapter opening, Rhonda is working on developing appropriate, accurate, clear, and vivid language for sharing her ideas. Once she does this, she will continue to rehearse until she is conversational and animated, as well as intelligible, and expressive.

In written communication, an effective style evolves through an iterative process of reading and revising. In a speech, an effective style develops through an iterative process of practicing aloud and revising. To prepare for your rehearsals, you begin by creating **speaking notes** that consist of a key-word outline adapted from your formal outline, delivery cues, and reference material you will cite as you speak. During each rehearsal, you orally elaborate on the points on your key-word outline until the finished speech is the appropriate length. With each rehearsal, you also revise your language choices until your ideas are presented appropriately, accurately, clearly, and vividly.

When a written sentence is unclear, the reader can reread it to figure out its meaning, but when a sentence in a speech is unclear, the listener cannot go back, and the meaning may be misunderstood or lost. So, as a speaker, you must focus on how to help the audience understand the meaning *as the speech is given*. In this chapter, you will learn to use the kind of language that is instantly intelligible to the *ear* so the audience receives the same meanings you intend.

Let's begin our discussion by briefly describing oral style and how it differs from written style. Then we'll offer some specific strategies you can employ to ensure that your speech is appropriate, accurate, clear, and vivid.

speaking notes: a key-word outline with delivery cues and reference citations you will use as you deliver your speech

Oral Style

Oral style refers to the manner in which one conveys messages through the spoken word. An effective oral style differs quite a bit from written style, though when giving a speech your oral style is still more formal than everyday talk. In fact, the degree of formality required to be an effective public speaker is based on the rhetorical situation. In other words, your goal is to adapt your language to the audience and occasion. For example, although

oral style: the manner in which one conveys messages through the spoken word your language when speaking to a small audience of colleagues at a business meeting will be more formal than when conversing with a friend at dinner, it will not be as formal as when speaking to an audience of 100 or more at a professional conference or workshop. As the speaker, however, your primary goal is to establish a relationship with your listeners, so your language in any of these situations should reflect a personal tone that encourages listeners to feel you are having a conversation with them. There are four primary characteristics that distinguish an effective oral style from an effective written style.

1. **An effective oral style tends toward short sentences and familiar language.** Because listeners have only one opportunity to hear your idea, work to ensure your words are ones that your audience is likely to understand.

2. **An effective oral style features plural personal pronouns.** Using personal pronouns such as "we," "us," and "our" creates a sense of relationship with the audience, showing respect for them as participants in the rhetorical situation.

3. **An effective oral style features descriptive words and phrases that appeal to the ear and are designed to sustain listener interest and promote retention.** By using colorful adjectives and adverbs, you can draw your listeners into your message and motivate them to stay focused on it.

4. **An effective oral style incorporates clear section transitions and signposts.** Because listeners hear a speaker's message only once, section transitions that verbally signal moving from one major section of the speech to the next and signposts such as "first," "second," "third," and "fourth" provide oral markers that help listeners follow your train of thought as the speech progresses.

Now, let's turn our attention to some specific things to consider when making language choices as you practice your speech. These strategies focus on speaking appropriately, accurately, clearly, and vividly.

Speaking Appropriately

Speaking appropriately means using language that adapts to the needs, interests, knowledge, and attitudes of your listeners and avoiding language that alienates any audience members. In the communication field, we use the term **verbal immediacy** to describe language used to reduce the psychological distance between you and your audience.[1] In other words, speaking appropriately means choosing words that enhance the connection between you and the members of your audience. Frankly, you want to convey positive ethos so your listeners will attend to and remember you and your message positively.

Using appropriate language makes us more effective because it demonstrates that we are adapting successfully to the rhetorical situation. It also demonstrates that we are ethical communicators who respect others, even those who differ from us. If we speak inappropriately, on the other hand, we are likely to offend some listeners and fail to achieve our speech goal. Why? Because, from that moment on, listeners are likely to shift their focus to opinions of us as people and stop listening to our message. In this section, we discuss specific strategies that will help you make appropriate language choices.

speaking appropriately: using language that adapts to the needs, interests, knowledge, and attitudes of the listener and avoiding language that alienates audience members

verbal immediacy: when the language you use reduces the psychological distance between you and your audience

Speaking appropriately by avoiding language that might offend or alienate audience members is an aspect of ethical communication. It demonstrates respect for the audience. When Olympian Shawn Johnson speaks, she does so by avoiding profanity and thanking audience members for giving her an opportunity to speak with them.

AP Photo/Kevin Sanders

Use "We" Language

"We" language, the use of plural personal pronouns like "we," "our," and "us" rather than "you" or "they," conveys a sense of connection with your listeners and involves them in the communication event. When used appropriately, "we" language fosters a sense of having a conversation *with* your audience rather than speaking or presenting *in front of* them. As a result, your audience will be more open to listening to you, believing what you say, and remembering your ideas.[2] You can easily replace "I" and "you" language with "we" language in the macrostructural elements of your speech. In your thesis statement, you can say, for example, "let's discuss..." rather than "I will inform you...," and in your section transitions, you can say "Now that we all have a clearer understanding of..." rather than "Now that I've explained..." and so on.

Use Bias-Free Language

Bias-free language (word choices that keep an ethical concern for fairness and respect with regard to race, ethnicity, gender, ability, sexual orientation, and diverse worldviews)[3] also helps create verbal immediacy.

1. **Generic language** uses words that apply only to one sex, race, or other group as though they represent everyone. In the past, English speakers used the masculine pronoun *he* to stand for all humans regardless of sex. This example of generic language excludes 50 percent of the audience. You can avoid using generic language in one of two ways. First, you can use plurals: "When people shop, they should have a clear idea of what they want to buy." Alternatively, you can use both male and female pronouns: "When a person shops, he or she should have a clear idea of what he or she wants to buy." Research shows that using "he or she," and to a lesser extent "they," helps listeners include women in their mental images, thus increasing gender balance in their perceptions.[4] The result is more accurate and bias-free language.

   A second problem of generic language results from the traditional use of *man*.[5] Consider the term *manmade*. What this really means is that a product was produced by human beings, but its underlying tone is that a *male* human being made the item. Bias-free alternatives do exist—for instance, *police officer* instead of *policeman*, *synthetic* instead of *manmade*, *humankind* instead of *mankind*, *flight attendant* instead of *stewardess*, and *server* instead of *waitress*. Bias-free language is not only more appropriate but, quite frankly, also more accurate.

2. **Nonparallel language** is when terms are changed because of the sex, race, or other group characteristics of the individual. Because it treats groups of people differently, nonparallel language is also belittling. Two common forms of nonparallelism are marking and irrelevant association.

   Marking is the *addition* of sex, race, age, or other group designations to a description. For instance, a doctor is a person with a medical degree who is licensed to practice medicine. Notice the difference between the following two sentences:

   Jones is a good doctor.
   Jones is a good black doctor.

In the second sentence, use of the marker "black" is offensive. It has nothing to do with doctoring. Marking is inappropriate because you trivialize the person's role by introducing an irrelevant characteristic.[6] The speaker may be intending to praise Jones, but listeners may interpret the sentence

---

"we" language: the use of plural personal pronouns like "we," "our," and "us" rather than "you" or "they"

bias-free language: language that demonstrates through word choices an ethical concern for fairness and respect with regard to race, ethnicity, gender, ability, sexual orientation, and diverse worldviews

generic language: language that uses words that apply only to one sex, race, or other group as though they represent everyone

nonparallel language: language in which terms are changed because of the sex, race, or other group characteristics of the individual

marking: the addition of sex, race, age, or other group designations to a description as saying that Jones is a good doctor for a black person (or a woman or an old person) but not that Jones is as good as a good white doctor (or a male doctor or a young doctor).

A second form of nonparallelism is **irrelevant association**, which is when we emphasize one person's relationship to another when that relationship is irrelevant to our point. For example, introducing a speaker as "Gladys Thompson, whose husband is CEO of Acme Inc., is the chairperson for this year's United Way campaign" is inappropriate. Mentioning her husband's status implies that Gladys Thompson is chairperson because of her *husband's* accomplishments, not her own.

Getting used to using bias-free language will be a big help to you in the workplace. Consider this audience—if you used generic or nonparallel language with them, you'd risk alienating about half of them.

Ryan McVay/Stockbyte/Getty Images

Adapt to Cultural Diversity

Verbal communication rules and expectations vary from culture to culture. One major theory used to explain similarities and differences in language and behavior is individualism versus collectivism.[7] In general, individualistic cultures emphasize individual goals more than group goals because these cultures value uniqueness. Many individualistic cultures are found in Western Europe and North America. In contrast, collectivistic cultures emphasize group goals more than individual goals because these cultures value harmony and solidarity. Many collectivistic cultures are found in Asia, Africa, and Latin America.[8]

Individualistic cultures tend to use low-context communication, in which information is (1) embedded mainly in the messages transmitted and (2) presented directly. Collectivistic cultures tend to use high-context communication, in which people (1) expect others to know how they're thinking and feeling and (2) present some messages indirectly to avoid embarrassing the other person. Thus, speakers from low-context cultures such as the United States operate on the principle of saying what they mean and getting to the point. Their approach may be characterized by such expressions as "Say what you mean" and "Don't beat around the bush."[9] In contrast, speakers from high-context cultures such as China form messages with language that is intentionally ambiguous and indirect; to interpret these messages correctly, listeners need to understand not only the message but also the context in which it is uttered.

What does this mean for public speakers? When you are a member of a cultural group that operates differently from that of the majority of your audience members, you need to adapt your language to be appropriate for your audience. If you are uncertain, then during your rehearsals ask someone from the same cultural group as the majority of your audience to listen to the parts of your speech to tell you where your wording is raising questions and to suggest ways to adapt it to be more appropriate for that audience.

To read more about how to adapt to audiences from other cultures, go to your CourseMate for *Challenge* to access **Web Resource 10.1: Speaking to International Audiences**.

Avoid Offensive Humor

Show sensitivity by avoiding offensive humor. Dirty jokes and racist, sexist, or other "-ist" remarks may not be intended to be offensive, but if some listeners are offended, you will have lost verbal immediacy. Comedian Chris Rock used offensive humor many times during his remarks as host of the 2003 MTV music awards. For example, he introduced rapper Eminem this

SPEECH SNIPPET

Using Bias-Free Language

In his speech about the Stanislavski system of method acting, Duane practiced referring to Ellen Burstyn as an "actor" rather than using "actress," which unnecessarily highlights the fact that Burstyn is a woman.

irrelevant association: emphasizing one person's relationship to another when that relationship is irrelevant to the point

CourseMate

Reflect on Ethics

On April 21, 2010, National Security Advisor James L. Jones opened his speech at the Washington Institute for Near East Policy—a pro-Israel think tank—with a joke. Many in the largely Jewish crowd laughed, while others claimed that it demonstrated a lack of sensitivity. Here's the joke:

> A member of the Taliban who gets separated from his fighting party stumbles upon a shack, which it turns out is a little store owned by a Jewish merchant.
>
> "I need water," the Taliban fighter says to the merchant. "Get me some water."
>
> "I'm sorry I don't have any water, but would you like to buy a tie?" the merchant says. "We have a nice sale of ties today."
>
> The Taliban warrior goes on a tirade against the merchant, against Jews, about Israel. "I need water; you try to sell me ties. You people don't get it."
>
> "Well, I'm sorry, I don't have water for you," the merchant says. "I forgive you for all of the insults you've levied against me, my family, my country. But I will help you out."
>
> The merchant steers the Taliban toward a restaurant two miles away.
>
> "They have all the water you'll need," the merchant says.

> The Taliban fighter walks toward the restaurant, then returns about an hour later.
>
> "Your brother tells me I need a tie to get in the restaurant," he says.
>
> Ba-dum-bum.

ABC Senior White House Correspondent Jake Tapper called it the worst kind of joke Jones could have told in trying to reach out to the Jewish community. A Jewish member of Congress responded by saying ABC News should "lighten up." General Jones later offered this statement regarding his comments: "I wish that I had not made this off the cuff joke at the top of my remarks, and I apologize to anyone who was offended by it. It also distracted from the larger message I carried that day: that the United States' commitment to Israel's security is sacrosanct."[10]

1. What ethical communication principles do you believe Jones adhered to and violated in telling this joke?
2. Would your answer change if he had been speaking to an audience not made up primarily of Jewish individuals? Why or why not?
3. How would you evaluate Jones's apology in terms of ethical communication and why?
4. What will you do regarding cultural sensitivity and humor in your speeches and why?

way: "Our next presenter saves a lot of money on Mother's Day. Give it up for Eminem!" This remark, reflecting Eminem's ongoing disputes with his mother, may have been funny to some, but it certainly offended others. Likewise, he introduced entertainment mogul P. Diddy, who had faced several lawsuits recently, as "being sued by more people than the Catholic church."[11] Again, some in his audience were probably offended. To be most effective with your formal public speeches, avoid humorous comments or jokes that may be offensive to some listeners. Being inclusive means demonstrating respect for all listeners.

Avoid Profanity and Vulgarity

Appropriate language avoids profanity and vulgar expressions. Fifty years ago, a child was punished for saying "hell" or "damn," and adults used profanity and vulgarity only in rare situations to express strong emotions. Today, "casual swearing"—profanity injected into regular conversation—is epidemic in some language communities, including college campuses.[12] In some settings, even the crudest and most offensive terms are so commonly used that speakers and (as a result) listeners alike have become desensitized, and the words have lost their ability to shock and offend.

Despite the growing, mindless use of crude speech, many people are still shocked and offended by swearing. And people who casually pepper their speech with profanity and vulgar expressions are often perceived as abrasive and lacking in character, maturity, intelligence, manners, and emotional control.[13]

Unfortunately, profanity and vulgarity are habits that are easily acquired and hard to extinguish. If you have acquired a "potty mouth," you're going to have to work very hard to clean up your act because verbal habits are hard to break. For tips on how to "tame your tongue," go to your CourseMate for *Challenge* to access **Web Resource 10.2: Cuss Control Academy**.

CourseMate

Shun Hate Speech

You've heard the old child's saying, "Sticks and stones will break my bones, but words will never hurt me." As children, we all knew that this statement was a lie. Still, it gave us psychological comfort in the face of cruel name-calling. Unfortunately, name-calling can take on even uglier forms in adult speech. Think of the damage caused by the use of words such as "nigger," "cracker," "kike," or "fag."

Hate speech is the use of words and phrases not only to demean another person or group but also to express hatred and prejudice toward that person or group. Under the U.S. Constitution, people are generally afforded free speech protection. From a communication perspective, however, hate speech is designed to be divisive rather than inclusive and demonstrates extreme lack of respect.

hate speech: the use of words and phrases to demean another person or group and to express the speaker's hatred and prejudice toward that person or group

Speaking Accurately

Using **accurate language** means using words that convey your meaning precisely. On the surface, speaking accurately seems simple enough. If you select words to represent your meaning, won't audience members understand the meaning you wish to convey? In fact, there are four reasons speaking accurately is not that simple.

accurate language: words that convey your meaning precisely

1. **Language is symbolic.** We use words to represent things, ideas, events, and so forth. Words have no tangible meanings in and of themselves; rather, we attach meaning to them.[14] In communication studies, we often simply say the *word* is not the *thing*. In their influential book, *The Meaning of Meaning: A Study of the Influence of Language upon Thought and the Science of Symbolism*, I. A. Richards and C. K. Ogden clarify this idea using the semantic triangle.[15] As depicted in Exhibit 10.1, a "referent" is the *thing* or object we refer to with a word, which is the "symbol" we use to refer to it. Our

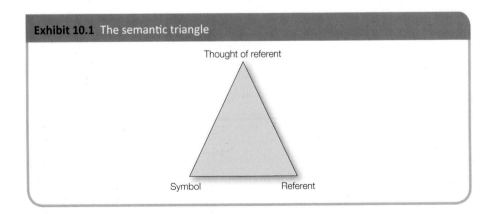

Exhibit 10.1 The semantic triangle

Thought of referent

Symbol   Referent

audience then attaches meaning to that symbol, which is what Richards and Ogden label the "thought of referent." For example, when you hear the word *dog*, what image forms in your mind? Do you visualize a poodle? A sheepdog? A mutt? There is so much variation in what the word *dog* conjures in our minds because the word *dog* is not the actual animal. The word is a symbol you use to represent the animal. So if you use the word *dog* in a speech, each member of your audience may picture something different. Because the *word* is not the *thing*, as a speaker you should use accurate words that most closely match the thing or idea you want your audience to see or understand.

2. **We are not born knowing a language; we must *learn* it.** Moreover, each generation within a language community learns the language anew. We learn much of our language early in life from our families. We then learn more in school, and we continue to learn more throughout our lives. But we do not all learn to use the same words in the same way.

3. **Although every language has a system of syntax and grammar, each utterance of a word is a creative act.** When we speak, we use language to create new sentences that represent our own personal meaning. Although on occasion we repeat other people's sentence constructions to represent what we are thinking or feeling, most of our talk is unique.

4. **Even though two people may know the same words, they may interpret the meanings of the words differently.** Thus, when James tells Chrissie that he liked going to the movies with her the previous night, what Chrissie understands James to mean by "liked" depends on how she interprets the message. For example, did James mean that he thought the movie was entertaining, or did he mean that he enjoyed spending time with Chrissie?

intelligible: capable of being understood

Using accurate language is crucial to effective speaking because it helps you be **intelligible**, or clearly understood. If listeners don't understand you or what you mean, your attempt to communicate is doomed. To help ensure that the language you use in speeches is accurate, let's take a look at three concepts that affect how words are interpreted: denotation, connotation, and dialect.

Denotation

denotation: the explicit meaning a language community formally gives a word

A word's **denotation** is its dictionary definition. So, denotatively, when Melissa said her dog died, she meant that her domesticated canine no longer demonstrates physical life. Keep in mind that in some situations the denotative meaning of a word may not be clear. Why? One reason is that dictionary definitions reflect current and past practices in the language community. Another reason is that dictionaries often offer more than one definition for a given word. And dictionaries use words to define words. The end result is that words are defined differently in various dictionaries and may include multiple meanings that also may change over time.

context: the position of a word in a sentence and its relationship to other words around it

Moreover, meaning may vary depending on the context in which the word is used. For example, the dictionary definition of *gay* includes both (1) having or showing a merry, lively mood and (2) homosexual. Thus, **context**—the position of a word in a sentence and its relationship to the other words around it—has an important effect on correctly interpreting which denotation is meant. Not only will the other words, the syntax, and the grammar of a verbal message help us understand the denotative meaning of certain words, but so will the situation in which they are spoken. For example, if you're at the beach and you say you are "surfing," you probably mean you're riding the waves. But if you're sitting at your desk in front of your computer, you probably mean you're searching the Internet for information.

Connotation

A word's **connotation** is the positive, neutral, or negative feelings or evaluations we associate with it. For example, consider how your impression of Dave would differ if someone said he was "cheap" versus "frugal." The denotative meaning of both words indicates someone who doesn't like to spend a lot of money, but for most of us "frugal" has a more positive connotation than "cheap" does. Thus, our perception of a word's connotation may be even more important than its denotation in how we interpret the meaning of the word. Connotations can be neutral, positive, or negative and can be quite different for different people. For example, the word "cop" can conjure up very different connotations for different people based on previous experiences.

Ogden and Richards were among the first scholars to consider the misunderstandings that result from the failure of communicators to realize that their subjective reactions to words are a product of their life experiences.[16] For instance, when Melissa told Trish that her dog died, Trish's understanding of the message depends on the extent to which her feelings about pets and death—her connotations of the words—correspond to the feelings Melissa has about pets and death. Whereas Melissa (who sees dogs as truly indispensable friends) may be intending to communicate her overwhelming grief, Trish (who doesn't particularly care for pets in general or dogs in particular) may miss the emotional meaning of Melissa's statement.

Connotations give emotional power to words, so much so that people will even fight and die for them. Consider the connotative meanings people assign to words like *freedom* or *honor* and *right* or *wrong*. For this reason, connotations can be used effectively to increase pathos, which you remember is the emotional appeal of your message. As you consider language options, be sure to consider how predisposed your audience may be about the words you select. Use your audience analysis to help you steer clear of words that arouse unintended connotations, or be sure to explain how you are using a word to avoid negative responses to your message.

Dialect

Dialect, a regional or ethnic variety of a language, can also affect listener understanding of your message. Dialects evolve over time, and the manner in which they differ from the "standard" of the language may be influenced by other languages spoken in the region or by the ethnic group. For instance, in her book *Chicano English in Context*, Carmen Fought details how the English spoken by some Hispanic people in the Los Angeles area differs from Standard English.[17] Regional differences are also reflected in the words used to represent common things. For example, in some places a car's turn signal is called a "blinker," a seesaw is a "teeter-totter," and a soft drink is a "pop" or a "coke." Some dialects also incorporate what is considered non-standard grammar, such as "he don't," "I says," "this here book," and "beings as how he was sick." If your audience doesn't share the dialect you normally speak, using it during your speeches can interfere with the intelligibility of your message. Not only that, it can also affect your ethos (more specifically, the audience's perception of your competence and credibility). Because most audiences are diverse, the best way to ensure being understood by all and conveying positive ethos is to use **Standard English** (which is taught in American schools and detailed in grammar handbooks like *Hodges Harbrace Handbook*, 17th ed.[18]).

connotation: the positive, neutral, or negative feelings or evaluations we associate with a word

dialect: a regional variety of a language

Standard English: form of English described in the dictionary or an English handbook

SPEECH SNIPPET

Adjusting for Dialect

As Maren, who is from Minnesota, prepared to practice her speech on the effect that drinking sugared sodas has on childhood obesity, she thought about how her roommate would tease her when she referred to "soda" as "pop." As she practiced, she made notes to always say "soda" during her speech.

Build a Bridge to Your Listener

Jon Sweeten, P.E.,
Water Resources
Consultant
Santa Monica,
California

Jon Sweeten, 54, is a water resources consultant who earned his master's degree in civil engineering from the University of Colorado at Boulder. Sweeten educates audiences worldwide about the need for using water efficiently and what people and industries can do to accomplish this goal—in California, he helped develop the first policies governing water efficiency. He routinely gives presentations to many different audiences—the public, professional organizations, city councils, and even members of Congress.

Over the years, Sweeten has learned that "to get all the stars aligned to [complete an engineering project] with public funds," you must consider more than just technical issues. "You need the ability to see, understand, and communicate all points of view to various audiences, both technical and nontechnical. The ability to build a bridge to the audience is a critically important skill. To do this you need curiosity and a willingness to learn."

Having a head for science and a heart for liberal arts helped him avoid some common public speaking pitfalls. For example, he's learned that he needs to make his key points early and to be concise because people are often busy and may even have to walk out of a speech in the middle. In addition, he's learned to keep the focus on the most important, relevant information in his speeches. "Engineers are notorious for giving horrible presentations," he says. "They want to give every detail." When he first started speaking to audiences that didn't necessarily include other engineers, "I knew I could fall into that trap. I thought about what I wanted the audience to remember at the end of my speech— what I wanted to leave people with."

He also strengthens his speech by taking advantage of one of his personal strengths—an ability to "paint pictures" for an audience. When he speaks, "I describe an image everyone can understand and share." For example, he once gave a presentation to the International Water Association on the Canary Islands to professionals from many cultures. "I needed to paint a picture of the Los Angeles they'd see if they got off an airplane—palm trees, green lawns—in order to make my point that because [L.A.] doesn't look like a desert, it's hard for the public to understand we need to conserve water."

Regardless of whether you're a novice or experienced speaker, he recommends that every speaker consider one essential point: "On the particular subject you've spent years studying, you know more than anyone else. You need to remember that and trust yourself."

> "Being brilliant technically but unable to articulate why your idea is so brilliant is a handicap."

Speaking Clearly

Speaking clearly results from reducing your use of ambiguous and confusing language. Compare the clarity of the following two descriptions of the same incident:

> *Some nut almost ran into me awhile ago.*

> *Last Saturday afternoon, an older man in a banged-up Honda Civic ran through the red light at Calhoun and Clifton and came within inches of hitting my car while I was waiting to turn left.*

Speaking clearly decreases ambiguity and audience confusion when we speak. Let's look at four strategies for improving clarity: use specific language, choose familiar terms, provide details and examples, and limit vocalized pauses.

Use Specific Language

specific language: words that clarify meaning by narrowing what is understood from a general category to a particular item or group within that category

Specific language clarifies meaning by narrowing what is understood from a general category to a particular item or group within that category. Often, as we try to express our thoughts, the first words that come to mind are general, abstract, and imprecise. The ambiguity of these words makes the listener choose from many possible images rather than picturing the precise image we have in mind. The more listeners are called on to provide their own images, the more likely they are to see meanings different from what we intend. Saying "a banged-up powder-blue 2004 Honda Civic" is more specific than saying "a car." For instance, if in her speech Nevah refers to a "blue-collar worker," you might picture any number of occupations that fall within this broad category. If, instead, she says he's a "construction worker," the number of possible images you can picture is reduced. Now you select your image from the subcategory of construction worker, and your meaning is likely to be closer to the one she intended. If she is even more specific, she may say "bulldozer operator." Now you are even clearer on the specific occupation. To see a video clip of a student speaker using specific language, go to your CourseMate for *Challenge* to access the Interactive Video Activities for Chapter 10. Select the clip called "Shakespeare."

CourseMate

Choosing specific language is easier when you have a large working vocabulary. As a speaker, the larger your vocabulary, the more choices you have from which to select the word you want. As a listener, the larger your vocabulary, the more likely you are to understand the words used by others.

One way to increase your vocabulary is to study one of the many vocabulary-building books on the shelves of almost any bookstore, such as *Word Smart: Building an Educated Vocabulary*.[19] You might also study magazine features such as "Word Power" in the *Reader's Digest*. By completing this monthly quiz and learning the words with which you are not familiar, you could increase your vocabulary by as many as twenty words per month. To take a vocabulary test online, go to your CourseMate for *Challenge* to access **Web Resource 10.3: Wordsmart Challenge**.

CourseMate

A second way to increase your vocabulary is to take note of words that you read or that people use in their conversations with you that you don't know and look them up. For instance, suppose you read or hear, "I was inundated with phone calls today!" If you wrote down *inundated* and looked it up in a dictionary later, you would find that it means "overwhelmed" or "flooded." If you then say to yourself, "She was inundated—overwhelmed or flooded—with phone calls today," you are likely to remember that meaning and apply it the next time you hear the word. If you follow this practice, you will soon notice your vocabulary increase.

A third way to increase your vocabulary is to use a thesaurus (a book of words and their synonyms) to identify synonyms that are more specific than the word you may have chosen. Most computer programs like Microsoft Word offer a thesaurus under the "Tools" option. But be careful—avoid unfamiliar words that may make you sound intelligent but could reduce your intelligibility. For example, *somnolent* is an interesting word, but most people don't know that it is a synonym for *sleepy*. Go to your CourseMate for *Challenge* to access **Web Resource 10.4: Merriam-Webster Online**.

CourseMate

Having a larger vocabulary won't help your speaking if you don't have a procedure for accessing it when you speak. So, during practice sessions, you will want to consciously experiment using specific words that precisely reflect your ideas. Suppose you were practicing a speech on registering for classes and said, "Preregistration is awful." If this word isn't quite right, you can quickly brainstorm better words, such as *frustrating, demeaning, cumbersome,* and *annoying*. Then, as you continue to practice, you might say, "Preregistration is a cumbersome process."

Some speakers think that to be effective they must impress their audience with their extensive vocabularies. As a result, instead of looking for specific and **precise words**, they use words that appear pompous, affected, or stilted to the

precise words: words that narrow a larger category

Defining Acronyms for Clarity

In her speech about STDs, Larissa first introduced the acronym this way: "According to a 2007 report by the American Social Health Association, one in every two sexually active persons will contract a sexually transmitted disease, or STD, by age twenty-five."

jargon: unique technical terminology of a trade or profession that is not generally understood by outsiders

listener. Speaking precisely and specifically does not mean speaking obscurely. The following story illustrates the problem with pretentious words:

> *A plumber wrote to a government agency, saying that he found that hydrochloric acid quickly opened drainpipes but that he wasn't sure whether it was a good thing to use. A scientist at the agency replied, "The efficacy of hydrochloric acid is indisputable, but the corrosive residue is incompatible with metallic permanence."*
>
> *The plumber wrote back thanking him for the assurance that hydrochloric acid was all right. Disturbed by this turn of affairs, the scientist showed the letter to his boss, another scientist, who then wrote to the plumber: "We cannot assume responsibility for the production of toxic and noxious residue with hydrochloric acid and suggest you use an alternative procedure."*
>
> *The plumber wrote back that he agreed. Hydrochloric acid worked fine. Greatly disturbed by this misunderstanding, the scientists took their problem to the top boss. She wrote to the plumber: "Don't use hydrochloric acid. It eats the hell out of pipes."*

So, use a more difficult word *only* when you believe that it is the very best word for a specific context. Let's suppose you wanted to use a more precise or specific word for *building*. Using the guideline of familiarity, you might select *house, apartment, high-rise,* or *skyscraper,* but you would avoid *edifice.* Each of the other choices is more precise or more specific, but *edifice* is neither more precise nor more specific, and in addition to being less well understood, it will be perceived as affected or stilted. Likewise, you would choose *clothing* instead of *apparel, bury* instead of *inter, avoid* instead of *eschew, predict* instead of *presage,* and *beauty* instead of *pulchritude.*

You will know that you have really made strides in improving specificity when you find that you can form clear messages even under the pressure of presenting your speeches.

Choose Familiar Terms

Using familiar terms is just as important as using specific words. Avoid jargon, slang, abbreviations, and acronyms unless (1) you define them clearly the first time they are used and (2) using them is central to your speech goal.

Jargon is the unique technical terminology of a trade or profession that is not generally understood by outsiders. We might forget that people who are not in our same line of work or who do not have the same hobbies may not understand the jargon that seems such a part of our daily communication. For instance, when Jenny, who is sophisticated in the use of cyberlanguage, starts talking with her computer-illiterate friend Sarah about "social MUDs based on fictional

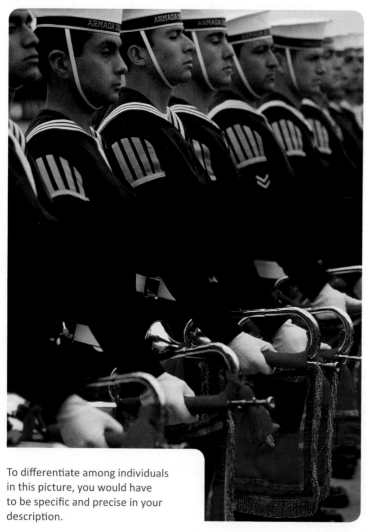

To differentiate among individuals in this picture, you would have to be specific and precise in your description.

Pablo Corral Vega/Encyclopedia/Corbis

Watterson. Reprinted with permission of Universal UCLICK

universes," Sarah is likely to be totally lost. If, however, Jenny recognizes Sarah's lack of familiarity with cyberlanguage, she can make her message clear by discussing the concepts in words her friend understands. In short, limit your use of jargon in speeches to general audiences and always define jargon in simple terms the first time you use it.

Slang refers to informal, nonstandard vocabulary and nonstandard definitions assigned to words by a social group or subculture. For example, today the word *bad*, which has a standard definition denoting something unpleasant or substandard, can mean quite the opposite in some social groups and subcultures.[20] You should generally avoid slang in your public speeches not only because you risk misunderstanding but also because slang doesn't sound professional and it can hurt your credibility (ethos). Slang is so pervasive that there are special dictionaries devoted to the specialized vocabulary of different communities. You can even find slang dictionaries online. To access one created by a former student of the University of California, Berkeley, go to your CourseMate for *Challenge* to access **Web Resource 10.5: Slang Dictionary**.

Overusing and misusing abbreviations and acronyms can also hinder clarity. Even if you think the abbreviation or acronym is a common one, to ensure intelligibility, always define it the first time you use it in the speech. For example, in a speech about NASCAR, refer to it initially by the organization's full name and then provide the acronym: "National Association for Stock Car Auto Racing, or NASCAR." Providing the full and abbreviated forms of the name will ensure clarity for all listeners. If you are assuming right now that everyone knows what NASCAR is, it might benefit you to know one of your authors had to look it up to include it in this book!

Provide Details and Examples

Sometimes, the word we use may not have a precise synonym. In these situations, clarity can be achieved by adding details or examples. For instance, Linda says, "Rashad is very loyal." The meaning of *loyal* (faithful to an idea, person, company, or other entity) is abstract, so to avoid ambiguity and confusion, Linda might add, "He defended Gerry when Sara was gossiping about her." By following up her use of the abstract concept of loyalty with this example, Linda makes it easier for her listeners to "ground" their idea of this personal quality in a "real" experience.

Likewise, providing details can clarify our messages. Saying, "He lives in a really big house" can be clarified by adding, "He lives in a fourteen-room Tudor mansion on a six-acre estate."

Limit Vocalized Pauses

Vocalized pauses are unnecessary words interjected into sentences to fill moments of silence. Words commonly used for this purpose are "like," "you know," "really," "basically," as well as "um" and "uh." We sometimes refer to vocalized pauses as "verbal garbage" because they do not serve a meaningful purpose and actually

slang: informal, nonstandard vocabulary and nonstandard definitions assigned to words by a social group or subculture

CourseMate

vocalized pause: unnecessary words interjected into sentences to fill moments of silence distract listeners from the message. Although a few vocalized pauses typically don't hinder clarity, practicing your speech aloud will help you eliminate them.

Speaking Vividly

Because listeners cannot "reread" what you have said, you must speak in ways that help them remember your message. Speaking vividly is one effective way to maintain your audience's interest and help them remember what you say. **Vivid language** is full of life—vigorous, bright, and intense. For example, a mediocre baseball announcer might say, "Jackson made a great catch," but a better commentator's vivid account might be, "Jackson leaped and made a spectacular one-handed catch just as he crashed into the center field wall." The words *leaped, spectacular, one-handed catch,* and *crashed* paint an intense verbal picture of the action. You can make your ideas come to life by using sensory language and by using rhetorical figures and structures of speech.

vivid language: language that is full of life—vigorous, bright, and intense

Use Sensory Language

Sensory language is language that appeals to the senses of seeing, hearing, tasting, smelling, and feeling. Vivid sensory language begins with vivid thought. You are much more likely to express yourself vividly if you can physically or psychologically sense the meanings you are trying to convey. If you feel the "bite of the wind" or "the sting of freezing rain," if you hear and smell "the thick, juicy sirloin steaks sizzling on the grill," you will be able to describe these sensations. Does the cake "taste good"? Or do your taste buds "quiver with the sweet double-chocolate icing and velvety feel of the rich, moist cake"?

sensory language: language that appeals to the senses of seeing, hearing, tasting, smelling, and feeling

To develop vivid sensory language, begin by considering how you can re-create what something, someone, or some place *looks like*. Consider, too, how you can help listeners imagine how something *sounds*. How can you use language to convey the way something *feels* (textures, shapes, temperatures)? How can language re-create a sense of how something *tastes* or *smells*? To achieve this in your speech, use colorful descriptors. They make your ideas more concrete and can arouse emotions. They invite listeners to imagine details. Here's an example about downhill skiing:

> *Sight:* As you climb the hill, the bright winter sunshine glistening on the snow is blinding.

Touch and feel: Just before you take off, you gently slip your goggles over your eyes. They are bitterly cold and sting your nose for a moment.

Taste: You start the descent and, as you gradually pick up speed, the taste of air and ice and snow in your mouth invigorates you.

Sound: An odd silence fills the air. You hear nothing but the swish of your skis against the snow beneath your feet. At last, you arrive at the bottom of the slope. Reality hits as you hear the hustle and bustle of other skiers and instructors directing them to their next session.

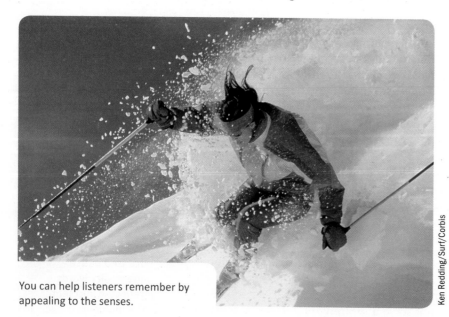

You can help listeners remember by appealing to the senses.

Ken Redding/Surf/Corbis

Smell and feel: You enter the warming house. As your fingers thaw in the warm air, the aroma from the wood stove in the corner comforts you as you drift off into sleep.

By using colorful descriptors that appeal to the senses, you arouse and maintain listener interest and make your ideas more memorable.

Use Rhetorical Figures and Structures of Speech

Rhetorical figures of speech make striking comparisons between things that are not obviously alike and so help listeners visualize or internalize what you are saying. **Rhetorical structures of speech** combine ideas in a particular way. Any of these devices can serve to make your speech more memorable as long as they aren't overused. Let's look at some examples.

A **simile** is a direct comparison of dissimilar things using the word *like* or *as.* Clichés such as "He walks like a duck" and "She's as busy as a bee" are similes. If you've seen the movie *Forrest Gump,* you might recall Forrest's use of similes: "Life is like a box of chocolates. You never know what you're going to get" and "Stupid is as stupid does." A very vivid simile was used by an elementary school teacher who said that being back at school after a long absence "was like trying to hold 35 corks under water at the same time."[21] This is a fresh, imaginative simile to describe an elementary school teacher's job. Similes can be effective because they make ideas more vivid in listeners' minds. But they should be used sparingly or they lose their appeal. Clichés should be avoided because their predictability reduces their effectiveness.

A **metaphor** is an implied comparison between two unlike things, expressed without using *like* or *as.* Instead of saying that one thing is *like* another, a metaphor says that one thing *is* another. Thus, problem cars are "lemons," and the leaky roof is a "sieve." Metaphors can be effective because they make an abstract concept more concrete, strengthen an important point, or heighten emotions. Notice how one speaker used a metaphor effectively to conclude a speech: "It is imperative that we weave our fabric of the future with durable thread."[22]

An **analogy** is an extended metaphor. Sometimes, you can develop a story from a metaphor that makes a concept more vivid. If you were to describe a family member as the "black sheep in the barnyard," that's a metaphor. If you went on to talk about the other members of the family as different animals on the farm and the roles ascribed to them, you would be extending the metaphor into an analogy. Analogies can be effective for holding your speech together in a creative and vivid way. Analogies are particularly useful to highlight the similarities between a complex or unfamiliar concept with one that is familiar.

Alliteration is the repetition of consonant sounds at the beginning of words that are near one another. Tongue twisters such as "She sells seashells by the seashore" use alliteration. In her speech about the history of jelly beans, Sharla used alliteration when she said, "And today there are more than fifty fabulous fruity flavors from which to choose." Used sparingly, alliteration can catch listeners' attention and make the speech memorable. But overuse can hurt the message because listeners might focus on the technique rather than the content of your message.

Assonance is the repetition of vowel sounds in a phrase or phrases. "How now brown cow" is a common example. Sometimes, the words rhyme, but they don't have to. Neil used assonance in his call to action this way: "Global warming is, in fact, a serious problem. I ask you to act now. Let's make a real difference for the future of our world." As with alliteration, assonance can make your speech more memorable as long as it's not overused.

---

rhetorical figures of speech: phrases that make striking comparisons between things that are not obviously alike

rhetorical structures of speech: phrases that combine ideas in a particular way

simile: a direct comparison of dissimilar things using *like* or *as*

metaphor: an implied comparison between two unlike things without using *like* or *as*

analogy: an extended metaphor

SPEECH SNIPPET

Using Metaphors

Dan decided to use a metaphor to help explain the complex concept of bioluminescence to his listeners. He said that "bioluminescence is a miniature flashlight that fireflies turn on and off at will."

alliteration: repetition of consonant sounds at the beginning of words that are near one another

assonance: repetition of vowel sounds in a phrase or phrases

onomatopoeia: words that sound like the things they stand for

personification: attributing human qualities to a concept or an inanimate object

repetition: restating words, phrases, or sentences for emphasis

Onomatopoeia is the use of words that sound like the things they stand for, such as "buzz," "hiss," "crack," and "plop." In the speech about skiing, the "swish" of the skis is an example of onomatopoeia.

Personification is attributing human qualities to a concept or an inanimate object. When Madison talked about her truck, "Big Red," as her trusted friend and companion, she used personification. Likewise, when Rick talked about flowers dancing on the front lawn, he used personification.

Repetition is restating words, phrases, or sentences for emphasis. Martin Luther King Jr.'s "I Have a Dream" speech is a classic example:

> I say to you today, my friends, so even though we face the difficulties of today and tomorrow, I still have a dream. It is a dream deeply rooted in the American dream.
>
> I have a dream that one day this nation will rise up and live out the true meaning of its creed: "We hold these truths to be self-evident: that all men are created equal."
>
> I have a dream that one day on the red hills of Georgia the sons of former slaves and the sons of former slave owners will be able to sit down together at the table of brotherhood.
>
> I have a dream that one day even the state of Mississippi, a state sweltering with the heat of injustice, sweltering with the heat of oppression, will be transformed into the oasis of freedom and justice.
>
> I have a dream that my four little children will one day live in a nation where they will not be judged by the color of their skin but by the content of their character. I have a dream today.
>
> Reprinted by arrangement with the Estate of Martin Luther King, Jr. c/o Writers House as agent for the proprietor New York, NY. Copyright 1963 Dr. Martin Luther King, Jr., copyright renewed 1991 Coretta Scott King.

antithesis: combining contrasting ideas in the same sentence

Antithesis is combining contrasting ideas in the same sentence, as when John F. Kennedy said, "Ask not what your country can do for you. Ask what you can do for your country." Likewise, astronaut Neil Armstrong used antithesis when he first stepped on the moon: "One small step for man, one giant leap for mankind." Speeches that offer antithesis in the concluding remarks are often very memorable.

Summary

Your overall language goal is to develop an oral style that captures your uniqueness and fosters a sense of positive ethos. Specific goals of oral language and style in a speech are to be appropriate, accurate, clear, and vivid.

Being appropriate means using language that adapts to the audience's needs, interests, knowledge, and attitudes and that avoids alienating or offending listeners. Appropriate language demonstrates respect for all audience members. To be appropriate, practice verbal immediacy by using "we" language and bias-free language, as well as adapting to cultural diversity and avoiding offensive humor, profanity, vulgarity, and hate speech.

Being accurate begins with a realization that words are only representations of ideas, objects, and feelings. Meaning is a product of both denotation (dictionary meaning) and connotation (positive, neutral, and negative feelings and evaluations that words evoke). To ensure that your ideas are interpreted accurately, consider denotation, connotation, and dialect.

Clear language is specific and precise. Specific language clarifies meaning. Precise words are those that narrow down a broad idea. The larger your vocabulary, the more choices you have to select a word you want. Ways to increase your vocabulary are to study vocabulary-building books, to look up meanings of words you don't understand, and to use a thesaurus to identify synonyms. Clarity can also be achieved by providing details and examples.

Vividness means full of life, vigorous, bright, and intense. Increase the vividness of your language by using sensory language as well as rhetorical figures and structures of speech.

Challenge Resource and Assessment Center

CourseMate Now that you have read Chapter 10, use your Speech Communication CourseMate for *The Challenge of Effective Speaking* for quick access to the electronic resources that accompany this text. These resources include the following:

- **Study tools** that that will help you assess your learning and prepare for exams (*digital glossary, key term flash cards, review quizzes*).
- **Activities and assignments** that will help you hone your knowledge and build your public speaking skills throughout the course (*Speech Snippets, Speech Assignments, Action Step*

Activities). Many of these activities allow you to compare your answers with those provided by the authors and, if requested, submit your answers to your instructor.

- **Media resources** that will help you explore communication concepts online (*Web Resources*), develop your speech outlines (*Speech Builder Express 3.0*), watch and critique videos of sample speeches (*Interactive Video Activities*), upload your speech videos for peer reviewing and critique other students' speeches (*Speech Studio online speech review tool*), and download chapter reviews so you can study when and where you'd like (*Audio Study Tools*).

This chapter's application activities and video resources are featured in this end-of-chapter section.

Applying What You've Learned

1. **Impromptu Speech Activity:** Draw a nonsensical word from a stack of cards created by your instructor (e.g., photomaniac, alienitus, caninicopia, aquatiphobia). Develop your own definition for this word. Then, prepare and deliver a two- to three-minute impromptu speech explaining the meaning of the word using specific language, familiar terms, details, and examples.

2. **Assessment Activity A:** Go online to the *American Rhetoric: Top 100 Speeches* website at http://www.americanrhetoric.com/top100speechesall.html. Select and listen to one of the speeches posted there. As you listen, take notes regarding the speaker's vivid language choices (sensory language and rhetorical figures and structures of speech). To what degree does

the use of them pique your interest and add to the memorability of the message? Explain.

3. **Assessment Activity B:** Select one of these popular television sitcoms: *Two and a Half Men, How I Met Your Mother, The Office, 30 Rock, Big Bang Theory,* or *Family Guy.* Watch an episode and record the following for each of the main characters: (a) use of profanity and vulgarity, (b) use of verbal immediacy, (c) use of offensive humor, and (d) use of hate speech. To what degree is each main character portrayed as a role model for viewers? Based on the kinds and number of appropriate and inappropriate language behaviors exhibited and the nature of the character as an intended role model, what message is being sent to viewers about what "appropriate" language usage is?

Web Resources

Video Resources

1. Use your Interactive Video Activities to watch, analyze, and see the transcript and outlines for Hillary Carter-Liget's informative speech "Shakespeare." (199)

2. Check out Speech Studio to see how other students use language in their speeches. Or record a speech you're working on, upload it to Speech Studio, and ask your peers for their feedback. What feedback could you use to fine-tune your language and oral style before you give your speech in class?

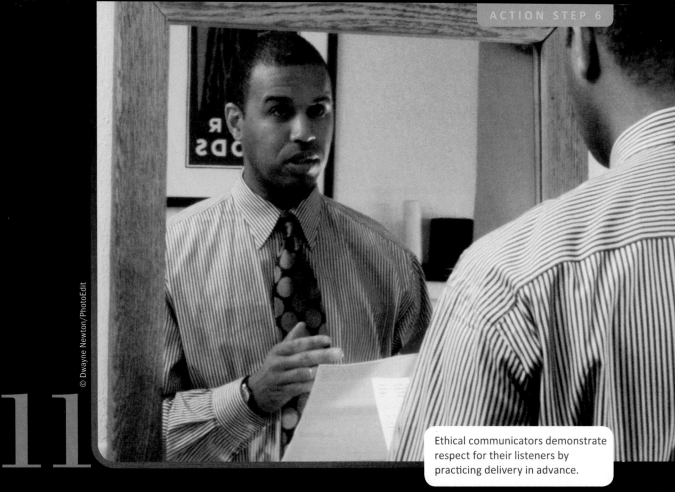

Ethical communicators demonstrate respect for their listeners by practicing delivery in advance.

© Dwayne Newton/PhotoEdit

11

'practicing delivery'

What's the Point?

QUESTIONS YOU WILL BE ABLE TO ANSWER AFTER READING THIS CHAPTER:

1. What are the characteristics of effective delivery?
2. What can you do to use your voice effectively as you deliver your speech?
3. What can you do to use your body effectively as you deliver your speech?
4. Why and how should you rehearse your speech?

Action STEP 6 Practice oral language and delivery style.

B. Practice until the delivery is conversational, intelligible, and expressive.

C. Practice integrating presentational aids until you can do so smoothly and confidently.

D. Continue practicing until you can deliver your speech extemporaneously within the time limit.

When Nadia finished speaking, everyone in the audience burst into spontaneous applause and whistles.

"I just don't get it, Maurice. My speech was every bit as good as Nadia's, but when I finished, all I got was the ordinary polite applause that everyone gets regardless of what they've done. Of course, I'm not as hot as Nadia."

"Come on, Sylvia, get off it. Yeah, Nadia's pretty, but that's not why the audience loved her. Your speech was good. You had an interesting topic, good information, and it was well organized. But when it comes to delivery, Nadia has it all over most of us, including you."

In leveling with Sylvia, Maurice recognized what has been well known through the ages: Dynamic delivery can make a mediocre speech appear good and a good speech great. Why? Delivery is important because how well the ideas are spoken can have a major impact on the audience's interest, understanding, and memory. In fact, research suggests that listeners are influenced more by delivery than by the content of speeches.[1] A speaker's delivery alone cannot compensate for a poorly researched, organized, or developed speech, but a well-delivered speech can rise above the ordinary and capture an audience. Some people, like Martin Luther King Jr. and former President Ronald Reagan, seem naturally gifted in delivering speeches. Other speakers must spend time practicing their speeches to be dynamic. Most of us will need to practice our speeches if we are to capture and hold our audience's attention.

In this chapter, we begin by talking about the characteristics of effective delivery. We then describe the elements of effective delivery: use of voice and use of body. Next, we explain the three types of speech delivery and the settings in which each is most appropriate. Finally, we suggest a process for rehearsing your speech that will prepare you to deliver it in a dynamic, conversational style. We also describe ways to adapt to your audience while giving your speech. At the end of this chapter, we have included a sample speech given by a college student.

Characteristics of an Effective Delivery Style

Think about the best speaker you have ever heard. What made this person stand out in your mind? In all likelihood, how the speaker delivered the speech had a lot to do with your evaluation. So, all the work you have done thus far to prepare your speech will be compromised if you cannot deliver it effectively.

Delivery is how a message is communicated orally and visually through your use of voice and body. Effective delivery is both conversational and animated. A conversational style allows each member of your audience to feel as if you are talking with him or her rather than speaking at the group. When your delivery is animated or lively, you create excitement about what you are saying so it is easier for your audience to pay attention. Your speech content is conveyed through language. Your delivery style, however, is conveyed through your nonverbal behaviors. **Nonverbal communication** includes all speech elements other than the words themselves.[2] These elements include your use of voice

delivery: how a message is communicated orally and visually through the use of voice and body

nonverbal communication: all speech elements other than the words themselves (e.g., pitch, volume, rate, quality, articulation, pronunciation, and pauses) and use of body (e.g., facial expressions, eye contact, gestures, body language, and even appearance).

Use a Conversational Style

You have probably witnessed speakers whose delivery was overly dramatic, too formal, or affected. And you've probably heard ineffective speakers who just read their speeches to you or sounded "canned." These delivery styles can put off an audience because the speaker appears more interested in performing or reading than in actually talking with the audience. Effective delivery reflects a **conversational style**, meaning that you sound spontaneous and relaxed, which helps your audience feel you are talking *with* them, not *at* them. The hallmark of a conversational style is spontaneity. **Spontaneity** is the ability to sound natural as you speak—as though you are really thinking about the ideas *and* getting them across to the audience as you speak. A speech with a spontaneous feel does not sound rehearsed, memorized, or read no matter how many times you've practiced it.

Speakers who try to memorize their speeches often have to struggle so hard to remember the words that their delivery becomes laborious. Although talented actors can make lines they have spoken literally hundreds of times sound spontaneous and informal, most novice public speakers cannot.

The secret to developing a conversational style is to learn the *ideas* of your speech rather than trying to memorize every *word*. Suppose someone asks you about the route you take to get to work. Because you are familiar with the route, you can present it spontaneously. You have never written out the route, and you've never memorized it—you just know it. You develop a conversational style in public speaking in the same way. Through practice, you get to know the ideas in your speech as well as you know the route you take to work. As you study your outline, you absorb the material you plan to present, and as you rehearse your speech out loud, you can focus on talking about them in an organized, professional, and natural-sounding way.

conversational style: delivery that seems spontaneous, relaxed, and informal and allows the speaker to talk *with*, not *at*, an audience

spontaneity: a naturalness of speech where what is said sounds as if the speaker is really thinking about the ideas *and* the audience as he or she speaks

Be Animated

Have you ever been bored by a professor reading a well-structured lecture while mostly looking at the lecture notes rather than at the students and making few gestures besides turning the pages of those notes? Even a well-written speech given by an expert can bore an audience unless its delivery is **animated**, lively, energetic, enthusiastic, and dynamic.

How can you be conversational and animated at the same time? The secret is to focus on conveying the passion you feel about your topic through your voice and body. In everyday life, all of us differ in how animated we are when we speak. Some of us are extroverted and naturally expressive, whereas others are introverted and more circumspect in our verbal and nonverbal expressiveness. And, of course, there are cultural differences in how much animation is appropriate when we speak. Nevertheless, when we are passionate about sharing something with someone, almost all of us become more animated in our delivery. It is this level of liveliness that you want to duplicate when you deliver your speech. To see a video clip of a student speaker with an animated delivery, go to your CourseMate for *Challenge* to access the speech "Why Pi?" in the Chapter 11 resources.

animated delivery: delivery that is lively, energetic, enthusiastic, and dynamic

Using an animated delivery helps you create a relationship with your audience and motivates them to listen to you.

Image copyright iofoto, 2010. Used under license from Shutterstock.com

For most of us, appearing conversational and animated when delivering a speech requires considerable practice. In the next two sections, we'll focus on how you can use your voice and body to deliver your speech effectively.

Effective Use of Voice

voice: the sound you produce in your larynx, or voice box, which is used to transmit the words of your speech to an audience

Your **voice** is the sound you produce using your vocal organs (including your larynx, tongue, teeth, lips, etc.). How you sound should emphasize and reinforce the meaning you intend, but sometimes it can contradict it. As a result, how you use your voice affects how successful you are in getting your ideas across. As you rehearse and deliver your speech, focus on not only *what* you say but also on *how* you sound as you say it. How your voice sounds depends on its pitch, volume, rate, and quality. Your goal is to use your voice so that what you say is both intelligible and vocally expressive. You will be better prepared to do this if you understand the characteristics of your voice.

Characteristics of Voice

The four major characteristics of voice are pitch, volume, rate, and quality.

pitch: the highness or lowness of the sounds produced in your larynx by the size and vibration of your vocal cords

Pitch is the highness or lowness of the sounds produced in your larynx by the size and vibration of your vocal cords. Just as you can change the pitch of a guitar string by making it tighter or looser, so can you change the pitch of your voice by tightening and loosening the vocal cords. Natural pitch varies from person to person, but men generally have lower pitched voices than women and children because they typically have larger vocal cords.

volume: how loudly or softly you speak

Volume is how loudly or softly you speak. You control your volume by how forcefully you expel the air through your vocal cords. When you push a lot of air through the cords, you speak loudly; when you push less air through, your volume drops.

rate: the speed at which you talk

Rate is the speed at which you talk. In normal conversations, most people speak between 130 and 180 words per minute. We generally speak faster when we are excited or fearful and slow down when we explaining difficult material or when we are sad or somber.

quality: the tone, timbre, or sound of your voice

Quality is the tone or timbre of your voice and what distinguishes it from the voices of others—it is "how you sound" to others. Voices that are nasal, breathy, harsh, or hoarse can be unpleasant to listen to and may distract from the message.

By effectively varying your pitch, volume, rate, and quality, you can achieve an animated and conversational style that is both intelligible and expressive.

Speak Intelligibly

intelligible: capable of being understood

To be **intelligible** means to be understandable. All of us have experienced situations in which we couldn't understand what was being said because the speaker was talking too softly or too quickly or had a voice that was compromised in some way. If you're not intelligible, your listeners are bound to struggle with your verbal message. By practicing using appropriate vocal pitch, volume, rate, and vocal quality, you can improve the likelihood that you will be intelligible to your audience.

Most of us speak at a pitch that is appropriate for us and intelligible to listeners. However, some people naturally have voices that are higher or lower in register or become accustomed to talking in tones that are above or below their natural pitch. Speaking at an appropriate pitch is particularly important if your audience includes people who have hearing loss because they may find it difficult to hear a pitch that is too high or too low. As overamplified music has become widespread, hearing losses, especially in the upper register, are becoming a problem even among younger people. Intelligibility is also affected by how much a speaker fluctuates his or her pitch. In normal conversation, pitch fluctuates frequently, and perhaps even a bit more during a speech. Pitch that doesn't fluctuate often hinders intelligibility. For example, in English, a sentence that is meant to be a question is vocalized with rising pitch. If pitch doesn't rise at the end of a question, listeners may interpret the sentence as a statement instead.

Appropriate volume is the key to intelligibility. You must speak loudly enough, with or without a microphone, to be heard easily by audience members seated in the back of the room but not so loudly as to bring discomfort to listeners seated near the front. In addition, you can vary your volume to emphasize important information. For example, you may speak louder as you introduce each of your main points or when imploring listeners to take action.

The rate at which you speak can determine how intelligible your message is. Speaking too slowly gives your listeners time to let their minds wander after they've processed your message. Speaking too quickly, especially when sharing complex ideas and arguments, doesn't give your listeners enough time to process the difficult information completely. Although your typical rate of speaking may be within the normal range, being nervous when giving a speech can cause you to speak more quickly or slowly. As you practice and then deliver your speech, monitor your speaking rate and slow down or speed up depending on the difficulty of the ideas and the nervousness you feel. To complete a simple test to see if your typical rate of speech is within the range that is intelligible to most people, go to your CourseMate for *Challenge* to access **Web Resource 11.1: Your Speech Rate**.

In addition to vocal characteristics, articulation, pronunciation, and accent problems can affect how intelligible your message is. **Articulation** is using the tongue, palate, teeth, jaw movement, and lips to shape vocalized sounds that combine to produce a word. Many of us suffer from minor articulation and **pronunciation** problems such as adding a sound where none appears ("athalete" for *athlete*), leaving out a sound where one occurs ("libary" for *library*), transposing sounds ("revalent" for *relevant*), and distorting sounds ("truf" for *truth*). Exhibit 11.1 on page 213 lists many common words that people are likely to mispronounce or misarticulate.

Accent is the inflection, tone, and speech habits typical of native speakers of a language. When you misarticulate or speak with a heavy accent during a conversation, your listeners can ask you to repeat yourself until they understand you. But in a speech setting, audience members are unlikely to interrupt to ask you to repeat what you have just said.

Accent is often a major concern for second language speakers or speakers from varying subcultures or geographic areas. Everyone speaks with some kind of accent, because "accent" means any tone or inflection that differs from the way others speak. Natives of a particular city or region in the United States will speak with inflections and tones that they believe are "normal" spoken English—for instance, people from the Northeast who drop the *r* sound (saying "cah" for *car*) or people from the South who elongate their vowels and "drawl." But when they visit a different city or region, they are perceived as having an accent. If your accent is "thick" or very different from that of most of your audience, practice pronouncing key words so that you are easily understood, speak slowly to allow your audience members more time to process your message, and consider using visual aids to reinforce key terms, concepts, and important points.

CourseMate

articulation: using the tongue, palate, teeth, jaw movement, and lips to shape vocalized sounds that combine to produce a word

pronunciation: the form and accent of various syllables of a word

accent: the inflection, tone, and speech habits typical of native speakers of a language

Mommy, Why Does Raj Talk Funny?

Raj Gaur, Graduate Student ABD University of Kentucky

I grew up in India. In my home we spoke Hindi, but from the time I began school at five years old, I was also taught English. So, by the time I was fourteen years old I was fluent in English—at least what I thought of at the time as English. Ten years ago, I came to the United States and have since learned that the English I speak is somewhat different from the English that is spoken here in the United States. These differences sometimes make it difficult for me to be understood by some Americans. You see, the English I learned as a child is a *nativization* of English that might more accurately be called "Indian English." What is nativization?

Nativization is the unconscious process of adapting a foreign language so it conforms to the linguistic style and rhetorical patterns of the native language spoken in a particular culture. You are familiar with the ways American English differs between regions and among groups within the United States, as well as differences between British English and American English. If there are differences among native English speakers, imagine what happens when a cultural group like Indians whose native language is Hindi adopts English as a second language! As you would probably expect, they adapt English by using some of the grammar, syntax, and pronunciation rules that characterize their first language, as well as by adopting some of the rhetorical and idiomatic expressions that they use in their mother tongue. It's not that Indians consciously decide to make these changes. Rather, the changes simply occur as the new language, in this case English, is used in everyday conversations with other Indians.

Prior to coming to the United States, most of the people I knew spoke English just like I did, and I had no problem understanding them or being understood by them. So imagine my consternation when after arriving in the United States some of my American colleagues, professors, and students had trouble understanding me when I spoke. What made this particularly interesting was that I didn't seem to have as much trouble understanding others or being understood when I wrote in English. Rather, it was when I spoke that I got quizzical looks and repeated requests to repeat myself.

What I now understand is that there are major differences between the way certain words are pronounced by those speaking American English and those speaking Indian English. Some of these differences are due to the rules each type of English uses for accenting the syllables within a word. In American English, as a general rule, words with more than one syllable alternate between accented and unaccented

> ## My friends in India complain my English is too American!

syllables. So if the first syllable is accented the second is not and vice versa. But in Hindi, whether a particular syllable is accented or not depends on the sounds in the word. Some sounds always receive an accent and others do not regardless of their position in a word. So in Indian English, "pho" is pronounced the same whether the speaker is using the word *photo* or *photography*. If you speak American English, you are used to hearing "pho·TOG·gra·phy," but when I pronounce it in Indian English, I say "PHO·to·GRAPH·y." If you're an American English speaker and you hear me say this, you may not understand me or may think, "Oh he just mispronounced that word." But to me, your pronunciation sounds just as strange because in India, that is how we pronounce the word.

There are also syntactic differences between Indian and American English. You will recall that syntax is the rules of a particular language for how words are supposed to be put together to form complete ideas. The syntactic issue that I have struggled most with is the use of articles (a, an, the, etc.). In Hindi, we may or may not use articles, and this practice also guides our Indian English. So an Indian English student may say, "I go to university in city of Mumbai," rather than "I go to *the* university in *the* city of Mumbai. Another syntactic difference that is common to speakers of Indian English is to form questions without using an auxiliary verb (do, should, can, must, etc.). In Hindi, auxiliary verbs are not required when forming an interrogatory sentence. So in Indian English I may ask: "I know you?" Rather than "*Do* I know you?" or "I finish it?" rather than "*Should* or *can* or *must* I finish it?"

Nativization of English can also be perceived at the idiomatic level when I attempt to express Indian sensibilities and Indian realities to my American friends. To clarify, as a speaker of Indian English, I sometimes exploit the syntactic structures of the language by directly translating Hindi idioms to English. For example, I might say "wheatish complexion" in Indian English to mean "not dark skinned, tending toward light." Or I might use the phrase "out of station" to mean "out of town," which has its origins to denote army officers posted to far-off places during the British rule. Indians also commonly substitute "hotel" for "restaurant," "this side" and "that side" for "here" and "there," "cent per cent" for "100 percent," and "reduce weight" for "lose weight."

Any one of these English adaptations might not pose problems, but taken together they make the brand of English that I speak very different from that of my American friends. Indian English has evolved over a long

(continued)

period of time, and English is now integrated into much of Indian culture. English is taught in schools, business is conducted in English, and English is used in government dealings. Nonetheless, the English of Delhi is not the English of London, or Berlin, or New York, or Lexington, Kentucky. And I find it ironic that after living in the United States for nearly ten years now and struggling to be understood by Americans, my friends in India now complain about my English too. They say it's too American![3]

Exhibit 11.1 Words commonly mispronounced

Word	Incorrect	Correct
arctic	ar'-tic	arc'-tic
athlete	ath'-a-lete	ath'-lete
family	fam'-ly	fam'-a-ly
February	Feb'-yu-ary	Feb'-ru-ary
get	git	get
hundred	hun'-derd	hun'-dred
larynx	lar'-nix	ler'-inks
library	ly'-ber-y	ly'-brer-y
nuclear	nu'-kyu-ler	nu'-klee-er
particular	par-tik'-ler	par-tik'-yu-ler
picture	pitch'-er	pic'-ture
recognize	rek'-a-nize	rek'-ig-nize
relevant	rev'-e-lant	rel'-e-vant
theater	thee-ay'-ter	thee'-a-ter
truth	truf	truth
with	wit or wid	with

Use Vocal Expressiveness

You achieve **vocal expressiveness** by changing your pitch, volume, and rate, stressing certain words; and using pauses strategically. These contrasts clarify the emotional meaning of your message and help animate your delivery. Generally, speeding up your rate, raising your pitch, or increasing your volume reinforces emotions such as joy, enthusiasm, excitement, anticipation, and a sense of urgency or fear. Slowing down your rate, lowering your pitch, or decreasing your volume can communicate resolution, peacefulness, remorse, disgust, or sadness.

A total lack of vocal expressiveness produces a **monotone**—a voice in which the pitch, volume, and rate remain constant, with no word, idea, or sentence differing significantly in sound from any other. Although few people speak in a true monotone, many severely limit themselves by using only two or three pitch levels and relatively unchanging volume and rate. An actual or near monotone not only lulls an audience to sleep but, more important, diminishes the chances of audience understanding. For instance, if the sentence "Congress should pass laws limiting the sale of pornography" is presented in a monotone, listeners will be uncertain whether the speaker is concerned with *who* should take action, *what* Congress *should do*, or *what* the laws should be.

Creating vocally expressive messages is a complex process. For example, Nick introduced his speech on legalizing marijuana as a painkiller this way:

> *Millions of Americans suffer needlessly each year. These people endure unbearable pain needlessly because, although our government is capable of helping them, it chooses to ignore their pain. Our government has no compassion, no*

vocal expressiveness: variety you create in your voice through changing pitch, volume, and rate, as well as stressing certain words and using pauses

monotone: a voice in which the pitch, volume, and rate remain constant, with no word, idea, or sentence differing significantly from any other *empathy, no regard for human feeling. I'm here today to convince you to support my efforts toward legalizing marijuana as a painkiller for terminally ill patients.*

To reinforce the emotional elements of anger, disgust, and seriousness, Nick gradually slowed his rate, decreased his volume, and lowered his pitch as he emphasized, "Our government has no compassion, no empathy, no regard for human feeling."

He also used **stress**, an emphasis placed on certain words by speaking them more loudly than the rest of the sentence, to shape his meaning. Read the following sentence from Nick's speech:

Millions of Americans suffer needlessly each year.

stress: emphasis placed on certain words by speaking them more loudly than the rest of the sentence

pauses: moments of silence strategically placed to enhance meaning

What did Nick intend the focus of that sentence to be? Without hearing it spoken, it is difficult to say because its focus would change depending on which word Nick chose to stress. Read the sentence aloud several times. Each time, stress a different word, and listen to how your stress changes the meaning. If you stress *millions*, the emphasis is on the number of people affected. When you stress *Americans*, the fact that the problem is on a national scale is emphasized. When you stress *suffer*, notice how much more you feel the pain. When you stress *needlessly*, you can sense Nick's frustration with how unnecessary the suffering is. And when you stress *each year*, the ongoing nature of the unnecessary suffering becomes the focus. Thus, the words you stress in a sentence affect your meaning.

Pauses, moments of silence strategically placed to enhance meaning, can also mark important ideas. If you use one or more sentences in your speech to express an important idea, pause before each sentence to signal that something important is coming up, or pause afterward to allow the ideas to sink in. Pausing one or more times within a sentence can add further impact. Nick included several short pauses within and a long pause after his line, "Our government has no compassion *(pause)*, no empathy *(pause)*, no regard for human feeling" *(longer pause)*.

SPEECH SNIPPET

Using Vocal Expressiveness

To convey a sense of urgency about prioritizing the capping of the oil leak in the Gulf of Mexico, David increased his volume and rate, and stressed words such as *now*, *today*, and *immediately*.

Effective Use of Body

Because your audience can see as well as hear you, how you use your body also contributes to how conversational and animated your audience perceives you to be. The body language elements that affect delivery are eye contact, facial expressions, gestures, movement, posture, poise, and appearance.

Eye Contact

Eye contact is looking directly at the people to whom you are speaking. In speechmaking, it involves looking at people in all parts of the room throughout a speech. As long as you are looking at someone (those in front of you, in the left rear of the room, in the right center of the room, etc.) and not at your notes or the ceiling, floor, or window, everyone in the audience will perceive you as having good eye contact with them. Generally, you should look at your audience at least 90 percent of the time, glancing at your notes only when you need a quick reference point. Maintaining eye contact is important for several reasons.

eye contact: looking directly at the people to whom you are speaking

1. **Maintaining eye contact helps audiences concentrate on the speech.** If you do not look at audience members while you talk, they are unlikely to maintain eye contact with you. This break in mutual eye contact often decreases concentration on the message.

2. **Maintaining eye contact bolsters ethos.** Just as you are likely to be skeptical of people who do not look you in the eye as they converse, so too audiences will be skeptical of speakers who do not look at them. In the United States, eye contact is perceived as a sign of sincerity. Speakers who fail to maintain eye contact with audiences are perceived almost always as ill at ease

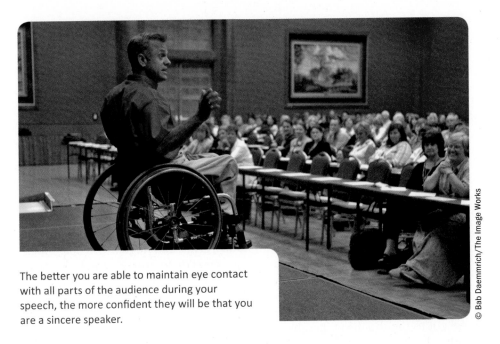

The better you are able to maintain eye contact with all parts of the audience during your speech, the more confident they will be that you are a sincere speaker.

© Bob Daemmrich/The Image Works

and often as insincere or dishonest.[4] In some cultures across the world and some subcultures within the United States, however, direct eye contact may be perceived as disrespectful. Many Native American nations, such as the Hopi, Cherokee, Navajo, and Sioux, believe indirect eye contact demonstrates humility and respect.[5] Knowing your audience becomes extremely important as you determine what kind of eye contact is most appropriate.

3. **Maintaining eye contact helps you gauge audience reaction to your ideas.** Because communication is two-way, audience members communicate with you while you are speaking to them. In conversation, the audience's response is likely to be both verbal and nonverbal; in public speaking, the audience's response is more likely shown by nonverbal cues alone. Audiences that pay attention are likely to look at you with varying amounts of intensity. Listeners who are bored may yawn, look out the window, slouch in their chairs, and even sleep. If audience members are confused, they will look puzzled; if they agree with what you say or understand it, they will nod their heads. By monitoring your audience's behavior, you can adjust by becoming more animated, offer additional examples, or move more quickly through a point. If you are well prepared, you will be better equipped to make the adjustments and adapt to the needs of your audience.

One way of ensuring eye contact during your speech is to gaze at various groups of people in all parts of the audience throughout the speech. To establish effective eye contact, mentally divide your audience into small groups scattered around the room. Then, at random, talk for four to six seconds with each group. Perhaps start with a Z pattern. Talk with the group in the back left for a few seconds, then glance at people in the far right for a few seconds, and then move to a group in the middle, a group in the front left, and then a group in the front right, and so forth. Then perhaps reverse the order, starting in the back right. Eventually, you will find yourself going in a random pattern in which you look at all groups over a period of a few minutes. Such a pattern helps you avoid spending a disproportionate amount of your time talking with those in front of you or in the center of the room.

When speaking to large audiences of 100 or more people, you must create a *sense* of looking listeners in the eye even though you actually cannot. This process is called **audience contact**. You can create audience contact using the Z pattern and four- to six-second rule as you focus on different groups of people throughout the speech.

audience contact: creating a sense of looking listeners in the eye when speaking to large audiences

SPEECH SNIPPET

Appropriate Eye Contact

As a member of the Cherokee nation, Desiree was raised to avoid direct eye contact as a sign of humility and respect. When speaking to her audience made up of people raised in the dominant American culture, however, she made a special effort to make direct eye contact with them throughout her speech.

Using Appropriate Facial Expressions

Nancy furrowed her brows and pursed her lips when she told the story of two young children who were abandoned in a parking lot—her facial expression conveyed seriousness and disgust. Thad, on the other hand, raised his eyebrows and smiled slightly as he talked about the many new forms of entertainment a domed stadium would bring to the city—his expression conveyed joy and excitement.

facial expression: eye and mouth movements that convey personableness and good character

gestures: the movements of your hands, arms, and fingers that help you remain intelligible

movement: changing the position or location of the entire body

motivated movement: movement with a specific purpose

posture: the position or bearing of the body

Facial Expressions

Your **facial expressions** are the eye and mouth movements that convey your personableness and good character (bolstering ethos) and can help you animate your speech (bolstering pathos). When you talk with friends, your facial expressions are naturally animated. Your audiences expect your expressions to be similarly animated when you give a speech. Speakers who do not vary their facial expressions during their speech and instead wear deadpan expressions, perpetual grins, or permanent scowls will be perceived as boring, insincere, or stern (hindering ethos). Audiences respond positively to natural facial expressions that appear to spontaneously reflect what you're saying and how you feel about it.

Gestures

Your **gestures**, the movements of your hands, arms, and fingers, can help intelligibility and expressiveness. You can use gestures to describe or emphasize what you are saying, refer to presentational aids, or clarify structure. For example, as Aaron began to speak about the advantages of satellite television, he said, "on one hand" and emphasized his words by lifting his right hand face up. When he got to the disadvantages, he lifted his left hand face up as he said, "on the other hand." Some of the most common gestures used by speakers are shown in Exhibit 11.2.

Some people who are nervous when giving a speech clasp their hands behind their backs, bury them in their pockets, or grip the lectern. Unable to pry their hands free gracefully, they wiggle their elbows weirdly or appear stiff, which can distract audience members from the message. As with facial expressions, effective gestures must appear spontaneous and natural even though they are carefully planned and practiced. When you practice and then deliver your speech, leave your hands free so that they will be available to gesture as you normally do.

Movement

Movement refers to changing the position or location of your entire body. During your speech, it is important to engage only in **motivated movement**, movement with a specific purpose such as emphasizing an important idea, referencing a presentational aid, or clarifying macrostructure. To emphasize a particular point, you might move closer to the audience. To create a feeling of intimacy before you tell a personal story, you might walk out from behind a lectern and sit down on a chair placed at the edge of the stage. Each time you begin a new main point, you might take a few steps to one side of the stage or the other. To use motivated movement effectively, you need to practice when and how you will move until you can do so in a way that appears spontaneous and natural. Ultimately, when you do, you bolster your ethos.

Avoid unmotivated movement such as bobbing, weaving, shifting from foot to foot, or pacing from one side of the room to the other because unplanned movements distract the audience from your message. Because many unplanned movements result from nervousness, you can minimize them by paying mindful attention to your body as you speak. At the beginning of your speech, stand up straight on both feet. Whenever you find yourself fidgeting, readjust and position your body with your weight equally distributed on both feet.

Posture

Posture refers to the position or bearing with which you hold your body. In speeches, an upright stance and squared shoulders communicate a sense of competence and confidence, which enhances your ethos. Speakers who slouch

Exhibit 11.2 Common hand gestures used by speakers

- The supine hand with palm upward to express good humor, frankness, and generalization.

- The prone hand with palm downward to show superposition or the resting of one thing upon another.

- The vertical hand with palm outward to indicate warding off, putting from, or a disagreeable thought.

- The clenched hand to reinforce anger or defiance or to emphasize an important point.

- The index finger to specialize or reinforce the first in a sequence of events.

SPEECH SNIPPET

Using Appropriate Gestures

For emphasis, Marcella repeatedly slammed her right fist into her left palm to emphasize her frustration as she said, "Over and over and over again, we have tried to stop child pornography, but to no avail."

SPEECH SNIPPET

Using Appropriate Movement

Leena ended her speech with a plea for businesses to better support parental leave to care for sick children. She decided to emphasize her call to action by moving forward toward her audience, gesturing with her palms up. Doing so emphasized the urgency of her request.

When a person speaks, we expect appropriate facial expressions, gestures, and movement.

may give an unfavorable impression of themselves, including the impression of limited self-confidence and an uncaring attitude. To read a thought-provoking discussion of how use of body may affect audience attention during a speech, go to your CourseMate for *Challenge* to access **Web Resource 11.2: Body Motions and Audience Attention**.

Poise

Poise is a graceful and controlled use of the body that gives the impression that you are self-assured, calm, and dignified. Mannerisms that convey nervousness, such as swaying from side to side, drumming fingers on the lectern, taking off or putting on glasses, jiggling pocket change, smacking the tongue, or scratching the nose, hand, or arm should be noted during practice sessions and avoided during the speech.

During speech practice sessions, try various methods to monitor or alter your bodily action. Videotape provides an excellent means of monitoring your use of body to determine whether it is enhancing the message or distracting from it. You may also want to practice in front of a mirror to see how you look to others when you speak. (Although some speakers swear by this method, others find it a traumatic experience.) Another good method is to get a willing listener to critique your use of body and help you improve. Once you have identified the behavior you want to change, tell your helper what to look for. For instance, you might say, "Raise your hand every time I begin to rock back and forth." By getting specific feedback when the behavior occurs, you can make immediate adjustments.

To see a video clip of a student speaker using effective bodily action, go to your CourseMate for *Challenge* to access the speech "No More Sugar" in the Chapter 11 resources.

CourseMate

Appearance

Some speakers think that what they wear doesn't or shouldn't affect the success of their speech. But your **appearance**, the way you look to others, does matter. Studies show that a neatly groomed and professional appearance sends important messages about a speaker's commitment to the topic and occasion, as well as the speaker's credibility (ethos).[6] Your appearance should complement your message, not detract from it. Three guidelines can help you decide how to dress for your speech.

1. **Consider the rhetorical situation.** Dress a bit more formally than you expect the members of your audience will dress. If you dress too formally, your audience is likely to perceive you as untrustworthy and insincere,[7] and if you dress too casually, the audience may view you as uncommitted to your topic or disrespectful of them or the occasion.[8]

poise: the graceful and controlled use of the body that gives the impression of self-assurance, calm, and dignity.

appearance: the way you look to others

© Bill Aron/PhotoEdit

2. **Consider your topic and purpose.** In general, the more serious your topic, the more formally you should dress. For example, if your topic is AIDS and you are trying to persuade your audience to be tested for HIV, you will want to look like someone who is an authority by dressing the part. But if your topic is spinning and you are trying to convince your audience they would enjoy taking a class at the new campus recreation center, you might dress more casually.

3. **Avoid extremes.** Your attire shouldn't detract from your speech. Avoid gaudy jewelry, over- or undersized clothing, or sexually suggestive attire. Remember, you want your audience to focus on your message, so your appearance should be neutral, not distracting.

Delivery Methods

Speeches vary in the amount of content preparation and the amount of practice you do ahead of time. The three most common delivery methods are impromptu, scripted, and extemporaneous.

Impromptu Speeches

At times, albeit at a business meeting or in a class, you may be asked to speak with little advance warning. An **impromptu speech** is one that is delivered with only seconds or minutes of advance notice for preparation and is usually presented without referring to notes of any kind. You may have already given an impromptu speech in class, so you know the kind of pressures and problems this type of speaking creates.

Because impromptu speakers gather their thoughts just before and while they speak, it is challenging to carefully organize and develop their ideas. As a result, they may leave out important information or confuse audience members. Delivery can suffer as speakers use "ah," "um," "like," and "you know" to buy time as they scramble to collect their thoughts. That's why the more opportunities you have to organize and deliver your thoughts using an impromptu method, the better you'll become at doing so.

Three of the most common rhetorical situations you may find yourself in that will require you to speak using the impromptu method are during employment and performance review interviews, at business meetings, and by the media. In each situation, having practiced organizing ideas quickly and conveying them both intelligibly and expressively will bolster your ethos and help you succeed in business and in life.

You can improve your impromptu performances by practicing "mock" impromptu speeches. For example, if you are taking a class where the professor often calls on students to answer questions, you can prepare by anticipating the questions that might be asked and by practicing giving your answers out loud. Over time, you will become more adept at quickly organizing your ideas and "thinking on your feet."

Scripted Speeches

At the other extreme, you might carefully prepare a complete written manuscript of the entire speech text and deliver it either word for word from memory or by reading the manuscript from a printed document or a teleprompter. A **scripted speech** is one that is prepared by creating a complete written manuscript and delivered by reading or memorizing a written copy.

Obviously, effective scripted speeches take a great deal of time to prepare and practice. Not only must you prepare an outline, but you must also

impromptu speech: a speech that is delivered with only seconds or minutes of advance notice for preparation and is usually presented without referring to notes of any kind

SPEECH SNIPPET

Speaking Impromptu with the News Media

Frank's efforts to stop the city from replacing a four-way stop sign with a traffic light on the street corner where he lives quickly became front-page news. As he left the city council meeting, a local TV reporter stopped him to ask him about the issue. He quickly organized his thoughts, identifying his primary reason for fighting the battle and three reasons doing so was not in the best interests of the community. Then he looked directly at the camera and shared these with the reporter.

scripted speech: a speech that is prepared by creating a complete written manuscript and delivered by reading a written copy or from memory

There are times when it's necessary to give scripted speeches, such as when there could be serious consequences if a speaker misspoke. However, it's also important to learn how to deliver a speech extemporaneously. Even world leaders, who deliver many scripted speeches, use an extemporaneous style for less formal speeches and question-and-answer sessions.

Justin Sullivan/Getty Images News / Getty Images

write out the entire speech, carefully choosing language and sentence structures that sound natural when spoken. Once you've prepared the manuscript, you memorize the script and then rehearse orally, or you rehearse with the written manuscript until you can do so without sounding like you're reading from it. When scripted speeches are memorized, you face the increased anxiety caused by fear of forgetting your lines. When they are read from a printed manuscript or from a teleprompter, you must become adept at looking at the script with your peripheral vision so that you can maintain eye contact with your audience. While politicians, talk show hosts, and television news anchors are usually good at achieving conversational style while reading from printed manuscripts and teleprompters, most speakers sound like they are reading and find it difficult to sound spontaneous and conversational.

Because of the time and skill required to effectively prepare and deliver a scripted speech, they are usually reserved for important occasions that have important consequences. Political speeches, keynote addresses at conventions, commencement addresses, and CEO remarks at annual stockholder meetings are examples of occasions when a scripted speech might be appropriate.

Extemporaneous Speeches

extemporaneous speech: a speech that is researched and planned ahead of time, but the exact wording is not scripted and will vary from presentation to presentation

Most speeches, whether in the workplace, in the community, or in class, are delivered extemporaneously. An **extemporaneous speech** is researched and planned ahead of time, but the exact wording is not scripted and will vary somewhat from presentation to presentation. When speaking extemporaneously, you refer to speaking notes reminding you of key ideas, structure, and delivery cues as you speak.

Extemporaneous speeches are the easiest to give effectively. Unlike impromptu speeches, when speaking extemporaneously, you are able to prepare your thoughts ahead of time and to have notes to prompt you. Yet unlike scripted speeches, extemporaneous speeches do not require as lengthy a preparation and practice process to be effective. In the next section, we describe how to rehearse successfully for an extemporaneous speech.

Rehearsal

rehearsing: practicing the presentation of your speech aloud

Rehearsing is the iterative process of practicing your speech aloud. Is it really necessary to practice a speech out loud? Yes. A speech that is not practiced out loud is likely to be far less effective than it would have been had you given yourself sufficient time to revise, evaluate, and mull over all aspects of the speech.[9] Inexperienced speakers often believe they are ready to present the speech once they have finished their outline. In general, try to complete the outline at least three days before you are scheduled to present it to give yourself sufficient time to practice, revise, evaluate, and practice your speech again. Exhibit 11.3 provides a useful timetable for preparing and practicing your speech.

In the sections that follow, we describe how to rehearse effectively by preparing speaking notes, handling presentational aids, and rehearsing and refining delivery.

Reflect on Ethics

During her speech at the First National Tea Party Convention in February 2010, former Alaska Governor Sarah Palin exclaimed that the Tea Party movement is "bigger than any charismatic guy with a teleprompter." She was referring to President Barak Obama, who often uses a teleprompter to deliver scripted speeches. Later, it was revealed in visual recordings of her speech and the question-and-answer session she participated in that she had relied on a "cheat sheet" of notes written on her hand. CNN political editor Mark Preston (among others) criticized Palin as a hypocrite:

Look, the fact that she wrote on her hand isn't really that big of a deal. We all work off of notes, certainly in television. But the fact that she was critical of President Obama and

called him "that charismatic guy with the teleprompter"—and as you just saw, I looked down at my notes to give that direct quote. It's very hard to be critical of one person when you yourself are using the same kind of aids when you're speaking.[10]

1. Do you agree with Preston's assessment of Palin's use of notes? Explain.
2. What, if any, ethical principles did Palin violate?
3. What, if any, ethical principles did the political media analysts violate in the way they covered this story?
4. Can you think of situations where the delivery method chosen for a speech might raise ethical questions or violate ethical principles? Explain.

Exhibit 11.3 Timetable for preparing a speech

7 days before	Select topic; begin research
6 days before	Continue research
5 days before	Outline body of speech
4 days before	Work on introduction and conclusion
3 days before	Finish outline; find additional material if needed; have all presentational aids completed
2 days before	First rehearsal session
1 day before	Second rehearsal session
Due date	Give speech

Preparing Speaking Notes

Prior to your first rehearsal session, prepare a draft of your speaking notes. **Speaking notes** are a key-word outline of your speech, including hard-to-remember information such as quotations and statistics, as well as delivery cues designed to help trigger memory. The best notes contain the fewest words possible written in lettering large enough to be seen instantly at a distance. Although some speakers do so, you should not use PowerPoint slides as speaking notes. This is bad practice because it results in you and your listeners reading from the screen rather than you communicating a message; use PowerPoint slides only as a visual enhancement.

To develop your notes, begin by reducing your speech outline to an abbreviated outline of key phrases and words. Then, if there are details you must cite exactly—such as a specific example, quotation, or set of statistics—add these in the appropriate places. You might also put these on a separate card as a "Quotation Card" you refer to when delivering direct quotations during the speech, which is what Alyssa did (see Exhibit 11.4 on page 222). Next, indicate exactly where you plan to share presentational aids. Finally, incorporate delivery cues indicating where you want to make use of your voice and body to enhance intelligibility or expressiveness. For example, indicate where you want to pause, gesture, or make a motivated movement. Capitalize or underline words you want to stress. Use slash marks (//) to remind yourself to pause. Use an upward-pointing arrow to remind yourself to increase rate or volume.

speaking notes: a key-word or phrase outline of your speech, plus hard-to-remember information such as quotations and statistics, as well as delivery cues designed to trigger memory

Exhibit 11.4 Alyssa's speaking outline on four note cards

NOTE CARD 1: Introduction

PLANT FEET….DIRECT EYE CONTACT….POISE/ETHOS! ☺

I.   Famous Indian peace activist Mahatma Gandhi: "We must become the change we seek in the world."
     Tall order….We can make a difference right here in Lexington, KY

II. Think for a moment….child/homework, neighbor/leaves, stranger/ groceries….It's easy for college students like us to get involved.

III. I volunteer at LRM and reaped benefits (Slide 1)

IV. Benefits volunteering….
     a. get acquainted
     b. responsibility & privilege
     c. resumé-building skills
     BLANK SLIDE, WALK RIGHT, EYE C.: Let's begin by explaining the ways volunteering can help us connect to our local community.

NOTE CARD 2: Body

I.   GREAT WAY to become acquainted ☺ ☺
     LR: Comforts of home….unfamiliar city….volunteering….easy and quick way….
     Natalie Cunningham—May 2nd (Q. CARD #1)
     Social issues and conditions
     Acc. to a 1991 article published in the *J. of Prevention and Intervention in the Community* by Cohen, Mowbray, Gillette, and Thompson raise awareness….
     My experience at LRM (SLIDES 2 & 3)
     BLANK SLIDE, WALK LEFT, EYE C.: Not only is volunteering important….familiar and social issues….FRANKLY….dem society….

II. Civic responsibility AND privilege….LR: We benefit college….give back.
     I agree with Wilson and Musick who said in their 1997 article in *Social Forces* **active participation or deprived.** (SLIDES 4 &5)
     Also a privilege….make a difference….feel good….self-actualization (SLIDE #6)

NOTE CARD 3: Body & Conclusion

BLANK SLIDE, WALK RIGHT, EYE C: privilege & responsibility….resume-building….

III. Life skills
     Article "Employability Credentials: A Key to Successful Youth Transition to Work" by
         I. Charner—1988 issue of the Journal of Career Development….(Q. CARD #2)
     Laura Hatfield….leadership, teamwork, and listening skills
     Andrea Stockelman, volunteer (SLIDE #7) (Q. CARD #3)
     MY RESUMÉ (SLIDE #8)
     BLANK SLIDE, WALK TO CENTER, EYE C: Today, we've discussed….get acquainted, responsibility & privilege, resumé-building life skills help after grad.
     CL: So, I'm hoping the next time you recall….not distant past. Instead, I hope you'll be thinking bout how you **ARE** being the change you seek in the world by **volunteering right here //in Lexington///right now!**
PAUSE, EYE CONTACT, POISE, NOD ☺

Quotation Card

#1: "My first group of students needed rides to all the various volunteer sites b/c they had no idea where things were in the city. It was really easy for the students who lived on campus to remain ignorant of their city, but while volunteering they become acquainted with Lexington and the important issues going on here."

#2: "Employers rely on credentials to certify that a young person will become a valuable employee. Credentials that document the experiences and employability skills, knowledge, and attitude."

#3: "I learned that there was a lot more that went into preparing food for the homeless than I ever thought possible. It was neat to be a part of that process."

Making speaking notes not only provides you with prompts when you are speaking, but it also helps in two other ways. First, the act of compiling the speaking notes helps to cement the flow of the speech's ideas in your mind. Second, as you prepare your notes, think about key ideas and phrasings. Notes don't include all the developmental material.

For a three- to five-minute speech, you will need no more than three 3- by 5-inch note cards to record your speaking notes. For longer speeches, you might need one card for the introduction, one for each main point, and one for the conclusion. If your speech contains a particularly important and long quotation or a complicated set of statistics, you can record this information in detail on a separate card. Exhibit 11.4 shows Alyssa's speaking notes for her complete outline, which is shown at the end of this chapter.

During practice sessions, use the notes you will use when you actually give the speech. If you will use a lectern, set the notes on the speaker's stand or, alternatively, hold them in one hand and refer to them only when needed. How important is it to construct good note cards? Speakers often find that the act of making a note card is so effective in helping cement ideas in the mind that during practice, or later during the speech itself, they rarely use the notes at all.

Handling Presentational Aids

Some speakers make the mistake of thinking that once they have prepared good presentational aids, they will have no trouble using them in the speech. However, many speeches with good aids have become a shambles because the aids were not well handled. You can avoid problems by following these guidelines.

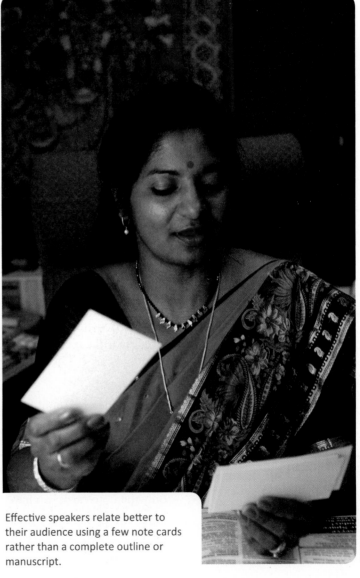

Effective speakers relate better to their audience using a few note cards rather than a complete outline or manuscript.

© Michael Newman/PhotoEdit

1. **Carefully plan when to use the presentational aids.** Indicate on your speaking notes/outline exactly when you will reveal and conceal each presentational aid.

2. **Consider audience needs carefully.** As you practice, eliminate any presentational aid that does not contribute directly to the audience's attention to, understanding of, or retention of the key ideas in your speech.

3. **Share a presentational aid only when talking about it.** Because presentational aids will draw audience attention, practice sharing them only when you are talking about them and then concealing them when they are no longer the focus of attention. Because a single presentational aid may contain several bits of information, practice only exposing the portion you are discussing. On computerized slideshows, you can do so by using the "custom animation" feature to allow only one item to appear at a time, strike the "B" key for a black screen when you aren't directly referencing the aid, and insert blank slides during the presentation when your ideas are not being supplemented by something on the slideshow.

4. **Display presentational aids so that everyone in the audience can see and hear them.** It's frustrating not to be able to see or hear an aid. If possible, practice in the space where you will give your speech so you can adjust equipment accordingly. If you cannot practice in the space ahead of time, then arrive early enough on the day of the presentation to practice quickly with the equipment you will use.

5. **Talk to your audience, not to the presentational aid.** Although you will want to acknowledge the presentational aid occasionally, it is important to keep your eye contact focused mainly on your audience. As you practice, resist the urge to stare at your presentational aid.

6. **Resist the temptation to pass objects through the audience.** People look at, read, handle, and think about whatever they hold in their hands. While they are so occupied, they are not likely to be listening to you. If you have handouts or objects, distribute them after the speech rather than during it.

Rehearsing and Refining Delivery

As with any other activity, effective speech delivery requires practice, and the more you practice, the better your speech will be. During practice sessions, you have three goals. First, you will practice language choices so they are appropriate, accurate, clear, and vivid. Second, you will practice your speech aloud until your voice and body convey your ideas conversationally, intelligibly, and expressively. Third, you will practice using presentational aids. As part of each practice, you will want to analyze how well it went and set goals for the next practice session. Let's look at how you can proceed through several practice rounds.

FIRST PRACTICE

Your initial rehearsal should include the following steps:

1. Record your practice session so you can analyze it and make improvements. You may also want to have a friend or relative sit in on your practice.

2. Read through your complete sentence outline once or twice to refresh your memory. Then, put the outline out of sight and practice the speech using only the note cards you have prepared.

3. Make the practice as similar to the public speaking situation as possible, including using the presentational aids you've prepared. Stand up and face your imaginary audience. Pretend that the chairs, lamps, books, and other objects in your practice room are people.

4. Write down the time that you begin.

5. Begin speaking. Regardless of what happens, keep going until you have presented your entire speech. If you goof, make a repair as you would if you were actually delivering the speech to an audience.

6. Write down the time you finish. Compute the length of the speech for this first rehearsal.

ANALYSIS

Watch and listen to your recorded performance while reviewing your complete outline. How did it go? Did you leave out any key ideas? Did you talk too long on any one point and not long enough on another? Did you clarify each of your points? Did you adapt to your anticipated audience? (If you had a friend or relative listen to your practices, have him or her help with your analysis.) Were your note cards effective? How well did you do with your presentational aids? Make any necessary changes before your second rehearsal.

SECOND PRACTICE

Repeat the six steps listed for the first practice. By practicing a second time right after your analysis, you are more likely to make the kind of adjustments that begin to improve the speech.

ADDITIONAL REHEARSALS TO FURTHER REFINE YOUR DELIVERY

After you have completed one full rehearsal session, consisting of two practices and an analysis in between them, put the speech away until that night or the next day. Although you should rehearse the speech at least a couple more times,

SPEECH
PLANNING

STEP
Action
6

Rehearsing Your Speech

The goal of this activity is to rehearse your speech, analyze it, and rehearse it again. One complete rehearsal includes (1) a practice, (2) an analysis, and (3) a second practice.

1. Find a place where you can be alone to practice your speech. Follow the six points of the first rehearsal.

2. Watch and listen to the recording. Review your outline as you do so and then complete a speech evaluation checklist to see how well you presented your speech during this rehearsal. (You can find the Speech Evaluation Checklist: General Criteria on page 14 in Chapter 1, a more detailed checklist in this chapter, and checklists for informative and persuasive speeches in later chapters.)

   List three specific changes you will make in your next practice session.

   One: _____

   Two: _____

   Three: _____

3. Go through the six steps outlined for the first rehearsal again. Then assess: Did you achieve the goals you set for the second rehearsal?

   Reevaluate the speech using the checklist and continue to practice until you are satisfied with all of your presentation.

   CourseMate You can complete this activity online, print copies of this rehearsal analysis sheet, see a student sample of a practice round, and, if requested, e-mail your work to your instructor. Go to your CourseMate for *Challenge* to access Activity 6.

you will not benefit if you cram all the practices into one long rehearsal time. You may find that a final practice right before you go to bed will be very helpful; while you are sleeping, your subconscious will continue to work on the speech. As a result, you are likely to find significant improvement in your mastery of the speech when you practice again the next day.

How many times you practice depends on many variables, including your experience, your familiarity with the subject, and the length of your speech. For beginning speakers, we suggest at least four rehearsal sessions.

Adapting to Your Audience as You Give Your Speech: The Rhetorical Situation

Even when you've practiced your speech to the point that you know it inside and out, you must be prepared to adapt to your audience and possibly change course a bit as you give your speech. Remember that your primary goal as a public speaker is to generate shared understanding with your listeners, so pay attention to the audience's feedback as you speak and adjust accordingly. Here are six tips for adapting to your audience.

1. **Be aware of and respond to audience feedback.** As you make eye contact with members of your audience, notice how they react to what you say. For instance, if you see quizzical looks on the faces of several listeners, you may need to explain a particular point in a different way, perhaps by providing an additional example to clarify the point. On the other hand, if you see listeners nodding impatiently, recognize that you don't need to belabor your point, and move on. If you notice that many audience members look bored, adjust your voice and try to rekindle their interest by showing your enthusiasm for what you are saying.

2. **Be prepared to use alternative developmental material.** Your ability to adjust to your audience's needs depends on how much additional alternative information you have to share. If you have prepared only one example, you wouldn't be ready if your audience is confused and needs another. If you have prepared only one definition for a term, you may be unable to rephrase an additional definition if needed. As you prepare, try to anticipate where your audience may be confused or already knowledgeable and practice adding or dropping examples and other details.

3. **Correct yourself when you misspeak.** Every speaker makes mistakes. They stumble over words, mispronounce terms, forget information, and mishandle presentational aids. So expect that you will make a few mistakes—it's normal. What's important is what you do when you make that mistake. If you stumble over a phrase or mispronounce a word, correct yourself and move on. Don't make a big deal of it by laughing, rolling your eyes, or in other ways drawing unnecessary attention to it. If you suddenly remember that you forgot to provide some information, consider how important it is for your audience to have that information. If what you forgot to say will make it difficult for your audience to understand a point that comes later, figure out how and when to provide the information later in your speech. Usually, however, information we forgot to share is not critical to the audience's understanding and its better to leave it out and move on.

    When you make a mistake, remember that your goal is to get your ideas across to the audience. If your mistake will prevent your audience from understanding what you are saying, correct it. Otherwise, go on. Your audience doesn't know what you had planned to say, so as long as what you do say makes sense, your audience won't notice the mistake.

4. **Adapt to unexpected events.** Maintain your composure if something unexpected happens, such as a cell phone ringing or someone entering the room while you're speaking. Simply pause until the disruption ceases and then move on. If the disruption causes you to lose your train of thought or has distracted the audience, take a deep breath, look at your speaking notes, and continue your speech at a point slightly before the interruption occurred. This will allow both you and your audience to refocus on your speech. You might acknowledge that you are backtracking by saying something like, "Let's back up a bit and remember where we were—."

5. **Adapt to unexpected audience reactions.** Sometimes, you'll encounter listeners who disagree strongly with your message. They might show their disagreement by being inattentive, heckling you belligerently, or rolling their eyes when you try to make eye contact with them. If these behaviors are limited to one or only a few members of your audience, ignore them and focus on the rest of your listeners. If, however, you find that your audience analysis was inaccurate and that the majority of your audience is hostile to what you are saying, try to anticipate and address their concerns. You might begin by acknowledging their feedback and then try to persuade your audience to suspend their judgment while they listen. For example, you could say something like, "I can see that most of you don't agree with my first point. But let me ask you to put aside your initial reaction and think along with me on this next point. Even if we end up disagreeing, at least you will understand my position."

6. **Handle questions respectfully.** It is rare for audience members to interrupt speakers with questions during a speech. But if you are interrupted, be prepared to deal respectfully with the question. If the question is directly related to understanding the point you are making, answer it immediately. If it is not, acknowledge the question, indicate that you will answer it later, and then do so. In most professional settings, you will be expected to answer questions when you've finished your speech. Some people will ask you to clarify information. Some will ask you for an opinion or to draw conclusions beyond what you have said.

Whenever you answer a question, it is important to be honest about what you know and don't know. If an audience member asks a question you don't know the answer to, admit it by saying something like, "That's an excellent question. I'm not sure of the answer, but I would be happy to follow up on it later if you're interested." Then move on to the next question. If someone asks you to state an opinion about a matter you haven't thought much about, it's okay to say, "You know, I don't think I have given that enough thought to have a valid opinion."

Be sure to monitor how much time you have to answer questions. When the time is nearly up, mention that you'll entertain one more question so as to warn listeners that the question-and-answer period is almost over. You might also suggest that you'll be happy to talk more with individuals one on one later—this provides your more reserved listeners an opportunity to follow up with you.

Although you cannot predict everything that could happen during your speech, you can prepare yourself to be ready for some adjustments. The most important thing to remember is that no speech is perfect. But you will succeed if your audience understands and remembers your message. That's what counts most.

SPEECH ASSIGNMENT

Presenting an Informative Speech with Presentational Aids

Based on the specific assignment of your instructor, prepare a three- to five-minute speech by completing the Speech Plan Action Step activities. You can also use Speech Builder Express as a tool to help you prepare your speech and your outline. You can see an example of Alyssa's outline and speech in the sample speech at the end of this chapter.

SPEECH EVALUATION CHECKLIST

Speech Evaluation Form

Check items that were accomplished effectively.

Content

_____ 1. Was the goal of the speech clear?

_____ 2. Did the speaker offer breadth and depth to support each main point?

_____ 3. Did the speaker have high-quality information?

_____ 4. Did the speaker use a variety of kinds of developmental material?

_____ 5. Were presentational aids appropriate?

_____ 6. Did the speaker establish common ground and adapt the content to the audience with listener relevance links?

Macrostructure

_____ 7. Did the introduction gain attention, establish credibility and listener relevance, as well as state the goal of the speech and preview the main points?

_____ 8. Were the main points clear, parallel, and meaningful complete sentences?

_____ 9. Did transitions lead smoothly from one point to another?

_____ 10. Did the conclusion tie the speech together?

Microstructure

_____ 11. Was the language appropriate?

_____ 12. Was the language accurate?

_____ 13. Was the language clear?

_____ 14. Was the language vivid?

Delivery

_____ 15. Was the speaker conversational?

_____ 16. Was the speaker intelligible?

_____ 17. Was the speaker vocally expressive?

_____ 18. Did the speaker look directly at and throughout the audience?

_____ 19. Did the speaker use appropriate facial expressions?

CONTINUED

_____ 20. Did the speaker have good posture that communicated poise and confidence?

_____ 21. Were the speaker's gestures and movement appropriate?

_____ 22. Did the speaker conceal, reveal, and reference the presentational aids effectively?

Based on these criteria, evaluate the speech as (check one):
_____ excellent _____ good _____ satisfactory _____ fair _____ poor

CourseMate   You can go to your CourseMate for _Challenge_ to access this checklist online under the resources for Chapter 11.

SAMPLE SPEECH

Informative Speech with Presentational Aids

This section presents a sample informative speech with presentational aids, given by a student and including an adaptation plan, an outline, and a transcript.

College Student Volunteering and Civic Engagement

By Alyssa Grace Millner, University of Kentucky[11]

CourseMate   Read the speech adaptation plan, outline, and transcript of a speech given by Alyssa Grace Millner. You can access a video clip of Alyssa's speech through the Chapter 11 resources of your CourseMate for _Challenge_. You can also use your CourseMate to identify some of the strengths of Alyssa's speech by preparing an evaluation checklist and an analysis. You can then compare your answers with those of the authors.

ADAPTATION PLAN

1. **Key aspects of audience.** The majority of listeners know what volunteering is in a general sense, but they probably don't know the ways it can benefit them as college students.

2. **Establishing and maintaining common ground.** I'll use personal pronouns throughout the speech, as well as specific examples about volunteering from volunteers right here in Lexington.

3. **Building and maintaining interest.** I'll insert listener relevance links in the introduction and for each main point that point out how volunteering is directly related to improving the lives of college students in some way.

4. **Building credibility.** I will point out right away that I volunteer and that I've done a good deal of research on it. I'll insert examples of my own experiences throughout the speech, as well as cite credible research to support my claims.

5. **Audience attitudes.** Some may be indifferent, but according the research I've found, most will probably be open to the idea of volunteering. They might not know how easy it can be to get started though.

6. **Adapting to audiences from different cultures and language communities.** Although most of my classmates are U.S. citizens, there are a couple of international students in the class. So, when I talk about volunteering being a civic responsibility, I'll make sure to talk about how all of us are reaping benefits of a U.S. education; that's why we are all responsible for giving back in some way. I'll talk about it as an ethical responsibility.

CONTINUED

7. **Use presentational aids.** I will show photographs of people engaged in volunteer work throughout the speech. I think this will make my ideas very concrete for the audience and will enhance pathos (emotional appeal). I'll also show some graphs about homelessness in Lexington and the percentage of college students who believe in volunteering. I think these will bolster my ethos as the audience will see I've done research. Finally, I'll show my resumé with elements highlighted that I've been able to include because I've volunteered. I think this will drive home my point about the future benefits for college students who volunteer while still in school.

FORMAL SPEECH OUTLINE

General goal: I want to inform my audience.

Specific goal: I want my audience to realize the benefits of volunteering in Lexington while we are still students at the University of Kentucky.

INTRODUCTION

Attention getter

I. The famous Indian Peace activist and spiritual leader Mahatma Gandhi is known for saying "We must become the change we seek in the world." That sounds at first like an awfully tall order, but today I'd like to show you how each of us can do just that and make a difference right here in Lexington, Kentucky.

Listener relevance link

II. Think for a moment of a time in your life when you did something kind for someone else. Maybe you helped a child do homework, or a neighbor rake leaves, or even a stranger get groceries from the store to the car. Do you remember how that made you feel? Well, that feeling can be a normal part of your week when you choose to be a volunteer. And for college students like us, it's easy to get involved as volunteers in our local community.

Speaker credibility

III. Personally, I volunteer at the Lexington Rescue Mission and have reaped many benefits by doing so. *(Show slide 1: picture of me volunteering at the Mission.)* I've also done extensive research on volunteering and civic engagement.

Thesis statement with main point preview

IV. So, let's spend the next few minutes discussing the benefits volunteering can have for us as college students by focusing on how volunteering helps us get acquainted with the local community, why civic engagement is the responsibility of every one of us, and what volunteering can do to teach us new skills and build our resumés.

Transition

Let's begin by explaining the ways volunteering can connect each of us to our local community.

Body

I. Volunteering is a great way to become acquainted with a community beyond the university campus.

Listener relevance link

Most college students move away from the comforts of home to a new and unfamiliar city. Not knowing what there is to do or even how to get around can be overwhelming and isolating. Volunteering is an easy way to quickly become familiar with and begin to feel a part of this new city in addition to the campus community.

A. Volunteering allows you to learn your way around town.
1. In an interview I had with Natalie Cunningham, the volunteer coordinator of the Lexington Rescue Mission, she said, "My first group of students needed rides to all the various volunteer sites because they

CONTINUED

had no idea where things were in the city. It was really easy for the students who lived on campus to remain ignorant of their city, but while volunteering they become acquainted with Lexington and the important issues going on here" (personal communication, May 2, 2010).

    2. It seems like a silly thing, but knowing your way around town starts to make any city feel like home. Volunteering gets you out into the local area and helps you begin to get acquainted with new people and places.

B. Volunteering can also open your eyes to local social issues and conditions.

    1. Many nonprofit organizations strive to raise awareness of important social issues, things like hunger and homelessness (Cohen, Mowbray, Gillette, & Thompson, 1991).

    2. The second time I showed up to volunteer at the Lexington Rescue Mission, I served food to the homeless. *(Show slide 2: group of volunteers in the kitchen.)*

        a. I served soup and hung out with other volunteers and local homeless people. One of the "veteran" volunteers explained to me that Lexington has approximately 3,000 homeless people. *(Show slide 3: homelessness statistics in Lexington.)*

        b. I was shocked to learn that we had such a large number of men, women, and children without a regular place to sleep. I wouldn't have known about this problem or the organizations working to end homelessness if I hadn't been a volunteer.

Not only is volunteering important because it helps us become familiar with a town and its social issues; frankly, as members of a democratic society, volunteering is our civic responsibility.	**Transition**

II. Giving back to the community through volunteer work is our civic responsibility and a privilege. Each of us in this room—whether as U.S. citizens or international students—are reaping the benefits of earning college degrees in this democratic society. With that benefit comes the responsibility and privilege of giving back. — **Listener relevance link**

A. Volunteering is our civic responsibility.

    1. Wilson and Musick (1997) explain that, without active participation in the local community, civil society becomes deprived.

    2. I agree. Giving back by volunteering helps the community in so many ways. *(Show slides 4 and 5: volunteers sorting clothes at the mission and then volunteers playing cards with people served at the shelter.)*

B. Volunteering is also a privilege. Making a difference by volunteering ends up making us feel better about ourselves and our role in the world around us.

    1. In fact, college students aged sixteen to twenty-four represent the largest growth in percentages of volunteers across the country (Corporation for National and Community Service, 2006). *(Show slide 6: bar graph of growth.)*

    2. A study of first-year college students done by the Higher Education Research Institute published in January 2009 revealed that 69.7 percent of students believe it is *essential* or *very important* to volunteer in order to help people in need (Pryor et al., 2009).

Certainly, the privilege of giving back as volunteers is our civic responsibility and helps our local community, but we can also reap valuable resumé-building life skills by volunteering.	**Transition**

III. Volunteering helps teach us new skills.

These new skills and talents can actually make us more marketable for better jobs once we graduate.	**Listener relevance link**

A. Being a consistent volunteer at a nonprofit organization while attending college can strengthen your resumé.

1. "Employers rely on credentials to certify that a young person will become a valuable employee. Credentials that document the experiences and employability skills, knowledge, and attitude" (Charner, 1988, p. 30).
2. Laura Hatfield, director of the Center for Community Outreach at the University of Kentucky, points out that volunteers can include leadership, teamwork, and listening skills on their resumés because they can document the experiences where they had to use them effectively in the real world.
3. Andrea Stockelman, another volunteer at the Lexington Rescue Mission, explained some of the new skills she picked up with volunteering. She said, "I learned that there was a lot more that went into preparing food for the homeless than I ever thought possible. It was neat to be a part of that process" (personal communication, April 28, 2010). *(Show slide 7: photo of Andrea preparing food.)*

B. Volunteering at the Lexington Rescue Mission taught me new skills that bolstered my resume. *(Show slide 8: resume with skills highlighted.)*
   1. I learned to coordinate the schedules of other volunteers.
   2. I also practiced important people skills such as teamwork, empathy, conflict management, and listening.

Conclusion

Thesis restatement with main point summary

I. Today we've discussed why volunteering is beneficial to college students by focusing on how volunteering can connect us quickly and easily to our local community, why it's both our responsibility and a privilege to do so, and how volunteering will benefit us after we graduate.

Clincher

II. So, I'm hoping the next time you recall a time you really enjoyed making a difference by helping someone, that memory won't come from the distant past. Instead, I hope you'll be thinking about how you are being the change you seek in the world by volunteering right here in Lexington right now.

References

Charner, I. (1988). Employability credentials: A key to successful youth transition to work. *Journal of Career Development, 15*(1), 30–40.

Cohen, E., Mowbray, C. T., Gillette, V., & Thompson, E. (1991). Religious organizations and housing development. *Journal of Prevention and Intervention in the Community, 10(*1), 169–185.

Corporation for National and Community Service. (2006). *College students helping America.* Washington, DC: Author.

Pryor, J. H., Hurtado, S., DeAngelo, L., Sharkness, J., Romero, L., Korn, W. S., & Tran, S. (2009). *The American freshman: National norms for fall 2008.* Los Angeles, CA: Higher Education Research Institute.

Wilson, J., & Musick, M. A. (1997). Work and volunteering: The long arm of the job. *Social Forces, 76*(1), 251–272.

SPEECH AND ANALYSIS

Speech

The famous Indian peace activist and spiritual leader Mahatma Gandhi is known for saying "We must become the change we seek in the world." That sounds at first like an awfully tall order, but today I'd like to show you how each of us can do just that and make a difference right here in Lexington, Kentucky. Think for a moment of a time in your life when you did something kind for someone else. Maybe you helped a child do homework, or a neighbor rake leaves, or even a stranger get groceries from the store to the car. Do you remember how that made you feel? Well, that feeling can be a normal part of your week when you choose to be a volunteer. And for college students like us, it's easy to get involved as volunteers in our local community. Personally, I volunteer at the Lexington Rescue Mission and have reaped many benefits by doing so. *(Show slide 1: picture of me volunteering at the Mission.)* I've also done extensive research on volunteering and civic engagement. So, let's spend the next few minutes discussing the benefits volunteering can have for us as college students by focusing on how volunteering helps us get acquainted with the local community, why civic engagement is the responsibility of every citizen, and what volunteering can do to teach us new skills and build our resumes. Let's begin by explaining the ways volunteering can connect each of us to our local community.

Volunteering is a great way to become acquainted with a community beyond the university campus. Most college students move away from the comforts of home to a new and unfamiliar city. Not knowing what there is to do or even how to get around can be overwhelming and isolating. Volunteering is an easy way to quickly become familiar with and begin to feel a part of this new city in addition to the campus community.

Volunteering allows you to learn your way around town. In an interview I had with Natalie Cunningham, the volunteer coordinator of the Lexington Rescue Mission, she said, "My first group of students needed rides to all the various volunteer sites because they had no idea where things were in the city. It was really easy for the students who lived on campus to remain ignorant of their city, but while volunteering they become acquainted with Lexington and the important issues going on here." It seems like a silly thing, but knowing your way around town starts to make any city feel like home. Volunteering gets you out into the local area and helps you begin to get acquainted with new people and places.

Volunteering can also open your eyes to local social issues and conditions. According to Cohen, Mowbray, Gillette, and Thompson, many nonprofit organizations strive to raise awareness of important social issues, things like hunger and homelessness. The second time I showed up to volunteer at the Lexington Rescue Mission, I served food to the homeless. *(Show slide 2: group of volunteers in the kitchen.)* I served soup and hung out with other volunteers and local homeless people. One of the "veteran" volunteers explained to me that

Analysis

Notice how Alyssa uses a famous quotation to get the attention of her audience in a way that also piques interest about the topic.

Here, Alyssa establishes listener relevance by pointing out that helping others makes us feel good and volunteering can be easy. Alyssa mentions that she volunteers, which bolsters ethos and establishes her credibility to speak on the topic.

Notice how Alyssa's thesis with main point preview gives us a sense of the organizational framework for her ideas.

Again, as Alyssa introduces the first main point, she gets us to tune in because we all know how overwhelming and isolating we can feel when we move to a new place.

Quoting the volunteer coordinator is a great piece of developmental material that encourages us to trust that Alyssa's message is trustworthy. (Note that interviews are not included in the reference section but are cited in the text of the outline.)

Alyssa intersperses actual photos of her and others volunteering throughout the speech. Doing so enhances her verbal message but

Lexington has approximately 3,000 homeless people. *(Show slide 3: homelessness statistics in Lexington.)* I was shocked to learn that we had such a large number of men, women, and children without a regular place to sleep. I wouldn't have known about this problem or the organizations working to end homelessness if I hadn't been a volunteer. Not only is volunteering important because it helps us become familiar with a town and its social issues; frankly, as members of a democratic society, volunteering is our civic responsibility.

Giving back to the community through volunteer work is our civic responsibility and a privilege. Each of us in this room—whether as U.S. citizens or international students—are reaping the benefits of earning college degrees in this democratic society. With that benefit comes the responsibility and privilege of giving back. Volunteering is our civic responsibility. Wilson and Musick explain that, without active participation in the local community, civil society becomes deprived. I agree. Giving back by volunteering helps the community in so many ways. *(Show slides 4 and 5: volunteers sorting clothes at the mission and then volunteers playing cards with people served at the shelter.)*

Volunteering is also a privilege. Making a difference by volunteering ends up making us feel better about ourselves and our role in the world around us. In fact, research conducted by the Corporation for National and Community Service from 2002 to 2005 shows that college students age sixteen to twenty-four represent the fastest growing demographic of volunteers in this country. *(Show slide 6: bar graph showing growth.)* Not only that, a study done by the Higher Education Research Institute published in January of 2009 shows that a whopping 69.7 percent of first-year college students believe it is essential or very important to volunteer to help people in need. Certainly, the privilege of giving back as volunteers is our civic responsibility and helps our local community, but we can also reap valuable resumé-building life skills by volunteering.

Volunteering helps teach us new skills. These new skills and talents can actually make us more marketable for better jobs once we graduate. Being a consistent volunteer at a nonprofit organization while attending college can strengthen your resume. According to Charmer, in the Journal of Career Development, "Employers rely on credentials to certify that a young person will become a valuable employee. Credentials that document the experiences and employability skills, knowledge, and attitude." Laura Hatfield, director of the Center for Community Outreach at the University of Kentucky, points out that volunteers can include leadership, teamwork, and listening skills on their resumés because they can document the experiences where they had to use them effectively in the real world. Andrea Stockelman, another volunteer at the Lexington Rescue Mission, explained some of the new skills she picked up with volunteering. She said, "I learned that there was a lot more that went into preparing food for the homeless than I ever thought possible. It was neat to be a part of that process." *(Show slide 7: photo of Andrea preparing food.)*

doesn't replace it. The photos also provide pathos, making her ideas more emotionally compelling.

Here and throughout the speech, notice how Alyssa uses effective section transitions to verbally tie the point she is wrapping up with an introduction of the point to come. This makes her speech flow smoothly so listeners can follow her train of thought and bolsters her ethos because she sounds prepared. Alyssa's careful audience analysis reveals itself here as she reminds her audience that even those who are not American citizens are benefiting as students in our educational system and, thus, have a responsibility to give back in some way.

Alyssa's choice to include national statistics of college student volunteers bolsters her credibility and provides listener relevance by reinforcing that college students are doing this, want to do this, and feel good about doing this kind of work.

Students want to know how to market themselves to get good jobs. So this main point will help maintain listener interest at a point when minds might tend to wander.

By including a quotation from another volunteer, we don't have to take Alyssa's word alone.

Volunteering at the Lexington Rescue Mission taught me new skills that bolstered my resumé. *(Show slide 8: resumé with skills highlighted.)* I learned to coordinate the schedules of other volunteers. I also practiced important people skills such as teamwork, empathy, conflict management, and listening.

Today we've discussed why volunteering is beneficial to college students by focusing on how volunteering can connect us quickly and easily to our local community, why it's both our responsibility a privilege to do so, and how volunteering will benefit us after we graduate. So, I'm hoping the next time you recall a time you really enjoyed making a difference by helping someone, that memory won't come from the distant past. Instead, I hope you'll be thinking about how you are being the change you seek in the world by volunteering right here in Lexington right now.

This very clear thesis restatement with main point summary signals a sense of closure.

Notice how Alyssa ties back to her opening quotation in her clincher. This provides a sense of wrapping up without saying thank you that helps listeners feel like the speech is complete in a memorable way.

Summary

Delivery refers to the use of voice and body to communicate the message of the speech; it is what the audience sees and hears. Effective delivery is conversational and animated.

The physical elements of delivery include the use of voice and use of body. By varying the four characteristics of voice (pitch, volume, rate, and quality) and using strategically placed pauses, you can ensure that your speech is intelligible to your audience and is vocally expressive. During a speech, you can use your body (eye contact, facial expressions, gestures, movement, posture, poise, and appearance) to convey ethos, reinforce the emotional tone of your ideas, and clarify structure.

Speeches vary in the amount of content preparation and practice done ahead of time. Speeches may be delivered impromptu (with little advanced preparation), scripted (memorized or delivered from a written manuscript or a teleprompter), or extemporaneously—researched and planned ahead of time but with the exact wording varying from presentation to presentation.

Between the time the outline is completed and the speech is given, it is important to engage in rehearsal sessions consisting of a practice, an analysis, and another practice. During these rehearsal sessions, you will work on using a key-word outline of your speaking notes, using your presentational aids effectively, and using an effective oral language and delivery style.

When you are finally ready to give your speech, remember that your goal is to have your audience understand your message, so be prepared to adapt to your audience during your speech.

Challenge Resource and Assessment Center

CourseMate Now that you have read Chapter 11, use your Speech Communication CourseMate for *The Challenge of Effective Speaking* for quick access to the electronic resources that accompany this text. These resources include the following:

- **Study tools** that will help you assess your learning and prepare for exams (*digital glossary, key term flash cards, review quizzes*).

- **Activities and assignments** that will help you hone your knowledge and build your public speaking skills throughout the course (*Speech Snippets, Speech Assignments, Action Step*

Activities). Many of these activities allow you to compare your answers with those provided by the authors and, if requested, submit your answers to your instructor.

- **Media resources** that will help you explore communication concepts online (*Web Resources*), develop your speech outlines (*Speech Builder Express 3.0*), watch and critique videos of sample speeches (*Interactive Video Activities*), upload your speech videos for peer reviewing and critique other students' speeches (*Speech Studio online speech review tool*), and download chapter reviews so you can study when and where you'd like (*Audio Study Tools*).

This chapter's application activities and video resources are featured in this end-of-chapter section.

Applying What You've Learned

1. **Impromptu Speech Activity:** Draw a slip of paper from a container provided by your instructor. The slip of paper will identify an element we've discussed about effective speech preparation (identifying a topic and writing a speech goal, audience analysis and adaptation, locating and evaluating secondary research sources, types of developmental material, conducting primary research, elements of an effective macrostructure, elements of effective microstructure, constructing presentational aids, effective delivery, use of voice, use of body, delivery methods, rehearsal sessions, and so on). Prepare and present a two- to three-minute impromptu speech explaining the element with specific examples.

2. **Assessment Activity A:** Complete Action Step 6 (Rehearsing Your Speech) for a speech you will deliver this term.

3. **Assessment Activity B:** Go to your Interactive Activities for *Challenge* through your CourseMate and select a sample speech recorded there. Using the Speech Evaluation Checklist provided in this chapter, assess the speech. After doing so, provide a brief narrative critique of the speaker's delivery (use of voice and body). Be sure to answer these questions in your assessment: (1) What did the speaker do particularly well and why? (2) What could the speaker do to improve delivery, why, and how? (3) What will you do during your own rehearsal sessions based on your critique of this speaker's delivery?

Speech Planning Action Step

6: Rehearsing Your Speech (225)

Video Resources

1. Use your Interactive Video Activities to watch, analyze, and see the transcript and outlines for the student speeches "Why Pi?" (209), "No More Sugar" (218), and "College Student Volunteering and Civic Engagement" (229)

Web Resources

11.1: Your Speech Rate (211)

11.2: Body Motions and Audience Attention (218)

2. Check out Speech Studio to see how other students deliver their speeches. Or record a speech you're working on, upload it to Speech Studio, and ask your peers for their feedback. What feedback could you use to fine-tune your delivery before you give your speech in class?

✓ SPEECH Studio

EPA/Photoshot

12

Ethical communicators demonstrate honesty and responsibility by providing listeners with the facts as they unfold during crisis events.

"informative speaking"

What's the Point?

QUESTIONS YOU'LL BE ABLE TO ANSWER AFTER READING THIS CHAPTER:

1. What is the goal of an informative speaker?
2. What are the characteristics of effective informative speaking?
3. What are the major methods of informing?
4. What are the two most common informative speech frameworks?
5. What are the major elements of process speeches?
6. What are the major types of expository speeches?

The campus had been fortunate to hear a number of excellent speakers at this year's Future of Energy *series, and tonight would be no different. Interested students, faculty, and invited guests took their seats and listened as the speaker was introduced by the director of the university's Center for the Study of the Environment. Now, Susan Cischke, vice president of Sustainability, Environment and Safety Engineering for Ford Motor Company, walked to the microphone to begin her speech titled "Sustainability, Environment, and Safety Engineering."*

T his is but one of many scenes played out every day when experts deliver speeches to help others understand complex information. In this chapter, we focus specifically on the characteristics unique to good informative speaking and the methods you can use to develop an effective informative speech.

An **informative speech** is one whose goal is to explain or describe facts, truths, and principles in a way that stimulates interest, facilitates understanding, and increases the likelihood of remembering. In short, informative speeches are designed to educate audiences. Thus, most lectures your instructors give are basically informative speeches (although, as you are aware, they may range from excellent to poor in quality). Informative speeches answer questions about a topic, such as who, when, what, where, why, how to, and how does. For example, your informative speech might describe who popular singer-songwriter Lady Gaga is, define what Scientology is, compare and contrast the similarities and differences between Twitter and Facebook, narrate the story of former *Saturday Night Live* comedian Al Franken's campaign for U.S. Senate, or demonstrate how to create and post a video on a website like YouTube. Informative speaking differs from other speech forms (such as speaking to persuade, to entertain, or to celebrate) in that your goal is simply to achieve mutual understanding about an object, person, place, process, event, idea, concept, or issue.

In this chapter, we first discuss five distinguishing characteristics of informing. Next, we discuss five methods of informing. And, finally, we discuss two common types of informative speeches and provide examples of each.

Characteristics of Effective Informative Speaking

When your goal is to inform, you face some unique challenges to gain and sustain the attention of your listeners, as well as to get them to retain the information. These can be successfully met if you attend to five characteristics of effective informative speaking and develop your speech with these in mind. An effective informative speech is intellectually stimulating, is relevant, is creative, is memorable, and addresses diverse learning styles.

Intellectually Stimulating

Your audience will perceive information to be **intellectually stimulating** when it is new to them and when it is explained in a way that piques their curiosity and excites their interest. By *new*, we mean new information that most of

informative speech: a speech whose goal is to explain or describe facts, truths, and principles in a way that stimulates interest, facilitates understanding, and increases the likelihood of remembering

intellectually stimulating: information that is new to audience members and is explained in a way that piques their curiosity

creativity: the ability to produce original, innovative ideas your audience is unfamiliar with or new insights into a topic they are already familiar with.

If your audience is unfamiliar with your topic, you should consider how you might tap their natural curiosity. Imagine you are an anthropology major who is interested in prehistoric humans, not an interest shared by most members of your audience. You know that in 1991, a 5,300-year-old man, Otzi, as he has become known, was found surprisingly well preserved in an ice field in the mountains between Austria and Italy. Even though the discovery was big news at the time, it is unlikely that your audience knows much about it. You can draw on their natural curiosity, however, as you present "Unraveling the Mystery of the Iceman," where you describe scientists' efforts to understand who Otzi was and what happened to him.[1]

If your audience is familiar with your topic, you will need to identify new insight about it. Begin by asking yourself: What about my topic do listeners probably not know? Then, consider depth and breadth as you answer the question. *Depth* has to do with going beyond people's general knowledge of the topic. If you've ever watched programs on the *Food Channel*, that's what they do. Most people know basic recipes, but these programs show new ways to cook the same foods. *Breadth* has to do with looking at how your topic relates to associated topics. Trace considered breadth when he informed listeners about Type 1 diabetes. He discussed not only the physical and emotional effects on a person with diabetes but also the emotional and relational effects on the person's family and friends, as well as the financial effects on society. As you can see, when your topic is one that the audience is familiar with, you will need to explore a new angle on it if you are going to stimulate them intellectually.

So whether your topic is familiar or unfamiliar to the audience, your special challenge is to choose a goal and develop your speech in a way that somehow makes it "new" to them. In doing so, your audience will feel informed rather than bored.

Relevant

A general rule to remember when preparing your informative speeches is this: Don't assume your listeners will recognize how the information you share is relevant to them. So to be effective at gaining and maintaining their interest, remember to incorporate **listener relevance links**—statements that clarify how a particular point may be important to a listener—throughout the speech. For example, how might the information you share during each main point make them happier, healthier, wealthier, and so forth? Another strategy is to compare an unfamiliar topic with something the audience is familiar with and that they feel is relevant to their lives. Trace did this when he compared the relational effects of living with diabetes to other chronic diseases such as heart disease and diverticulitis.

Creative

Your audience will perceive your information to be creative when it yields innovative ideas. You may never have considered yourself creative, but that may be because you have never worked to develop innovative ideas. Contrary to what you may think, **creativity** is not a gift that some have and some don't; rather, it is the result of hard work. Creativity comes from good research, time, and productive thinking.

When you speak about a familiar topic, such as how to cook a meal, your audience will be more engaged and receptive if you find a way to make the topic intellectually stimulating by describing a new technique or tool that would make a cook's life easier or a unique way to prepare a particular entree.

Steve Fenn/ABC/Getty Images

Creative informative speeches begin with good research. The more you learn about the topic, the more you will have time to think about and develop it creatively. If you have read only one story, located one set of statistics, or consulted one expert, how can you do much more than present this material? Speakers who present information creatively do so because they have given themselves lots of supporting material to work with.

For the creative process to work, you have to give yourself time. If you finish your outline an hour before you are to speak, you are unlikely to come up with creative ideas for maintaining audience interest. Rarely do creative ideas come when we are in a time crunch. Instead, they are likely to come when we least expect it—when we're driving our car, preparing for bed, or daydreaming. So a simple way to increase the likelihood that you will develop creative ideas is to give yourself time by completing your outline several days before you are to speak. Then, you will have time to consider how to present your ideas creatively.

For the creative process to work, you have to think productively. **Productive thinking** occurs when we contemplate something from a variety of perspectives. Then, with numerous ideas to choose from, the productive thinker selects the ones that are best suited to a particular audience. In the article "Thinking Like a Genius," author Michael Michalko describes eight strategies you can use to become a productive thinker. To read this article, go to your CourseMate for *Challenge* to access **Web Resource 12.1: Thinking Like a Genius**.

Now let's look at how productive thinking can help you identify different approaches to a topic. Suppose you want to give a speech on volunteering in the United States, and, in your research, you run across the data shown in Exhibit 12.1.

With productive thinking, you can identify several lines of development for your speech. For instance, notice that in roughly two-thirds of the states college students (ages sixteen to twenty-four) volunteer as much as or more than the general adult population. You could investigate why this is so and do a speech about it. Looking at the data from another perspective, you might notice that the percentage of both the general adult and college student populations that volunteer in three states (Minnesota, Nebraska, and Utah) is 40 percent or more. You might examine what types of volunteer work people do in those states and why. Looking at these data yet another way reveals that Utah ranks first for percentage of the general adult population that volunteers and Nevada ranks last. You could do a speech comparing volunteerism in those two states. Or you might notice that a majority of the states that rank lowest in terms of percentages who volunteer are in the east, and many of the states that tend to rank highest are in the Midwest and mountain west. Again, an interesting speech could be given to explain these differences.

Productive thinking can also help us find alternative ways to make the same point. Again, using the information in Exhibit 12.1, we can quickly create two ways to support the point "On average, about 30 percent of the U.S. general adult population volunteers."

Alternative A: Eighteen of the fifty states plus District of Columbia had volunteering rates between 25 and 30 percent. Twelve of them had volunteering rates between 30 and 35 percent. In other words, thirty of the fifty states plus D.C. (or 60 percent) report volunteering rates between 25 and 35 percent.

Alternative B: If we exclude Nevada with its very low volunteering rate of 18.8 percent and Utah, Nebraska, and Minnesota with very high rates of 48 percent, 42.8 percent, and 40.7 percent, respectively, then we see that most states (forty-seven) reported volunteering rates between 20 and 40 percent.

productive thinking: to contemplate something from a variety of perspectives

CourseMate

State	General adult population		College students, ages 16–24	
	Volunteering rate (in %)	State rank	Volunteering rate (in %)	State rank
Alabama	28.9	32	34.8	16
Alaska	38.9	5	40.1	7
Arizona	24.9	45	30.8	32
Arkansas	25.6	43	31.7	22
California	26.1	40	28.5	38
Colorado	32.8	17	38.3	10
Connecticut	30.8	21	31.5	23
Delaware	26.7	37	26.4	42
District of Columbia	30.8	22	31.0	30
Florida	24.1	48	25.9	43
Georgia	25.9	41	21.4	51
Hawaii	25.4	44	29.6	35
Idaho	35.5	14	44.4	2
Illinois	29.7	28	31.2	27
Indiana	29.5	29	37.3	13
Iowa	39.2	4	31.1	29
Kansas	38.6	8	31.5	24
Kentucky	29.8	27	30.4	33
Louisiana	22.7	49	27.8	40
Maine	33.2	16	31.4	25
Maryland	30.3	25	30.2	34
Massachusetts	27.0	36	24.0	47
Michigan	32.1	18	37.4	12
Minnesota	40.7	3	39.9	8
Mississippi	26.4	39	33.1	20
Missouri	31.9	20	38.9	9
Montana	37.9	10	34.6	17
Nebraska	42.8	2	41.5	5
Nevada	18.8	51	23.6	49
New Hampshire	32.0	19	32.0	21
New Jersey	26.5	38	25.0	45
New Mexico	28.5	33	31.3	26
New York	21.3	50	23.4	50
North Carolina	29.1	30	28.8	37
North Dakota	36.5	13	33.7	19
Ohio	30.7	24	34.4	18
Oklahoma	30.0	26	43.0	3
Oregon	33.6	15	31.1	28
Pennsylvania	30.8	23	35.1	15
Rhode Island	24.9	46	25.8	44
South Carolina	28.0	35	28.3	39
South Dakota	38.8	6	31.0	31
Tennessee	25.9	42	24.0	48
Texas	28.3	34	29.2	36
Utah	48.0	1	62.9	1
Vermont	38.1	9	41.5	4
Virginia	29.0	31	24.6	46
Washington	36.8	12	37.6	11
West Virginia	24.6	47	27.4	41
Wisconsin	37.0	11	36.2	14
Wyoming	38.8	7	40.3	6

Memorable

If your speech is really informative, your audience will hear a lot of new information but will need your help in remembering what is most important. Effective informative speeches emphasize the specific goal, main ideas, and key facts in ways that help audience members remember them. You can use several techniques to emphasize the material you want your audience to remember. For example, as described in Exhibit 12.2, you might use presentational aids, repetition, transitions, humor, or mnemonics. Any of these techniques can pique listener interest as you move through your informative speech.

Exhibit 12.2 Techniques for making informative speech material memorable		
Technique	**Use**	**Example**
Presentational aids	To provide the opportunity for the audience to retain a visual as well as an audio memory of important or difficult material	A diagram of the process of making ethanol.
Repetition	To give the audience a second or third chance to retain important information by repeating or paraphrasing it	"The first dimension of romantic love is passion; that is, it can't really be romantic love if there is no sexual attraction."
Transitions	To increase the likelihood that the audience will retain the relationships among the information being presented, including which information is primary and which is supporting	"So the three characteristics of romantic love are passion, intimacy, and commitment. Now let's look at each of the five ways you can keep love alive. The first is through small talk."
Humor and other emotional anecdotes	To create an emotional memory link to important ideas	"True love is like a pair of socks: you've got to have two, and they've got to match. So you and your partner need to be mutually committed and compatible."
Mnemonics and acronyms	To provide an easily remembered memory prompt or shortcut to increase the likelihood that a list is retained	"You can remember the four criteria for evaluating a diamond as the four C's: carat, clarity, cut, and color." or "As you can see, useful goals are SMART: S—Specific, M—Measurable, A—Action oriented, R—Reasonable, and T—Time bound. That's SMART."

Diverse Learning Styles

Because the members of your audience differ in how they prefer to learn, effective informative speeches are developed in ways that address diverse learning styles. You can appeal to people who prefer to learn through the feeling dimension by providing concrete, vivid images, examples, stories, and testimonials. You can address the watching dimension by using visual aids and by using appropriate facial expressions and gestures. You can address the thinking dimension through clear macrostructure as well as definitions, explanations, and statistics. Finally, you can address the doing dimension by providing your listeners with an opportunity to do something during the speech or afterward. Rounding the cycle ensures that you address the diverse learning styles of your audience and make the speech understandable, meaningful, and memorable for all. To help you round the cycle, you might even make note of where and how you address each dimension in your speech outline.

Methods of Informing

Once you have decided that the general goal of your speech will be to inform, you must decide what methods you will use to educate your audience about your topic. We can inform by describing, defining, comparing and contrasting, narrating, and demonstrating. In some cases, you might choose one method of informing as the basis for organizing your entire speech. For example, when an architect presents the plans for a new building, we expect the speech to describe what the building will look like. But in most cases, you will use different methods of informing as you develop each main point.

In this section, we explain each method of informing that you might use in developing your speeches. Later in the chapter, we will describe two of the most common organizational frameworks for informative speeches: a process (or demonstration) framework and an expository framework.

Description

Description is a method used to create an accurate, vivid, verbal picture of an object, geographic feature, setting, event, person, or image. This method usually answers an overarching "who," "what," or "where" question. If the thing to be described is simple and familiar (like a light bulb or a river), the description may not need to be detailed. But if the thing to be described is complex and unfamiliar (like a sextant or holograph), the description will be more exhaustive. Descriptions are of course easier if you have a presentational aid, but verbal descriptions that are clear and vivid can create mental pictures that are also informative. To describe something effectively, you can explain its size, shape, weight, color, composition, age, condition, and spatial organization. Although your description may focus on only a few of these, each is helpful to consider as you create your description.

You can describe size subjectively as large or small and objectively by noting the specific numerical measurements. For example, you can describe New York City subjectively as the largest city in the United States or more objectively as home to more than 8 million people with more than 26,000 people per square mile.

You can describe shape by reference to common geometric forms, such as round, triangular, oblong, spherical, conical, cylindrical, or rectangular, or by reference to common objects such as a book or a milk carton. For example, the lower peninsula of Michigan can be described as a left-handed mitten. Shape is made more vivid by using adjectives such as smooth or jagged.

You can describe weight subjectively as heavy or light and objectively by pounds and ounces or kilograms, grams, and milligrams. As with size, descriptions of weight are clarified by comparison. So you can describe a Humvee (Hummer) as weighing about 7,600 pounds, or about as much as three Honda Civics.

You can describe color as black, white, red, yellow, orange, blue, green, and brown. Because these eight basic colors will not always describe accurately, a safe way to describe color is to couple a basic color with a common familiar object. For instance, instead of describing something as puce or ocher, you might do better by describing the object as "eggplant purple" or "clay pot red."

You can describe the composition of something by indicating what it is made of, such as a building made of brick, concrete, wood, or aluminum siding.

description: the informative method used to create an accurate, vivid, verbal picture of an object, geographic feature, setting, or image

At times, you can create the most vivid image of something by describing what it seems like rather than what it is. For example, an object may best be described as "metallic" even if it is made of plastic, not metal.

You can describe something by age as old or new and by condition as worn or pristine, either of which helps the audience to visualize what is being described more clearly. Together, descriptions of age and condition can give the audience cues about the worth or value of what is being described. For example, describing a coin as old but in mint condition indicates that it may be worth far more than its face value. Similarly, describing a city as ancient and well-kept gives rise to different mental pictures than does describing a city as old and decrepit.

Finally, you can describe spatial organization, going from top to bottom, left to right, or outer to inner. A description of the Sistine Chapel might go from the floor to the ceiling; a description of a painting might proceed from foreground to background, left to right, or top to bottom; and a description of a NASCAR automobile might go from the body to the engine to the interior.

Definition

Definition is a method that explains the meaning of something. There are four ways you can explain what something means.

First, you can define a word or idea by classifying it and differentiating it from similar ideas. For example, in a speech on vegetarianism, you might use information from the Vegan Society's website (http://www.vegansociety.com) to develop the following definition of a vegan: "A vegan is a vegetarian who is seeking a lifestyle free from animal products for the benefit of people, animals, and the environment. Vegans eat a plant-based diet free from all animal products, including milk, eggs, and honey. Vegans also don't wear leather, wool, or silk and avoid other animal-based products."

Second, you can define a word by explaining its derivation or history. For instance, a vegan is a form of vegetarian who omits all animal products from his or her diet. So where did that come from? At the Vegan Society website, we learn that "the word vegan is made up from the beginning and end of the word VEGetariAN and was coined in the UK in 1944 when the Vegan Society was founded. The derivation of the word symbolizes that veganism is at the heart of vegetarianism and the logical conclusion of the vegetarian journey in pursuit of good health without the suffering or death of any animal."[3] Offering this etymology will help your audience remember the meaning of vegan.

Third, you can define a word by explaining its use or function. For example, in vegan recipes, you can use tofu or tempeh to replace meat and soy milk to replace cow's milk.

The fourth and perhaps the quickest way to define something is by using a familiar synonym or antonym. A **synonym** is a word that has the same or a similar meaning; an **antonym** is a word that is directly opposite in meaning. So, you could define a *vegan* by comparing it to the word *vegetarian*, which is a synonym, or to the word *carnivore*, which is an antonym.

You can describe a NASCAR automobile spatially proceeding from the engine to the interior.

Jason Smith/Getty Images for NASCAR

definition: a method of informing that explains something by identifying its meaning

synonym: a word that has the same or a similar meaning

antonym: a word that is directly opposite in meaning

Comparison and Contrast

Comparison and contrast is a method of informing that focuses on how something is similar to and different from other things. For example, in a speech on vegans, you might want to tell your audience how vegans are similar to and different from other types of vegetarians. You can point out that, like all vegetarians, vegans don't eat meat but that, unlike semi-vegetarians, they also do not eat fish or poultry. Like lacto-vegetarians, they don't eat eggs, but unlike this group and the lacto-ovo-vegetarians, vegans also don't use dairy products. So of all vegetarians, vegans have the most restrictive diets. As you will remember, comparisons and contrasts can be figurative or literal. So you can use metaphors and analogies in explaining your ideas as well as making actual comparisons.

Narration

Narration is a method of informing that recounts an autobiographical or biographical event, a myth, a story, or some other account. The narrative method is grounded in narrative theory, which is essentially storytelling. Stories usually have four parts. First, the narration orients the listener by describing when and where the event took place and by introducing the important people or characters. Second, the narration explains the sequence of events that led to a complication or problem, including details that enhance the development. Third, the narration discusses how the complication or problem affected key people in the narrative. Finally, the narration recounts how the complication or problem was solved. The characteristics of a good narration include a strong story line; use of descriptive language and details that enhance the plot, people, setting, and events; effective use of dialogue; pacing that builds suspense; and a strong voice.[4]

Narrations can be presented in a first-, second-, or third-person voice. When you use first person, you report what you have personally experienced or observed, using the pronouns "I," "me," and "my" as you recount the events. Your narration will be effective if your audience can identify and empathize with you and the events you describe. "Let me tell you about the first time I tried to become a vegetarian …" might be the opening for a narrative story told in first person. When you use second person, you place your audience "at the scene" and use the pronouns "you" and "your." Second-person narration can be effective because it asks the audience to recall an event that has happened to them or to become an "actor" in the story being told. "Imagine that you have just gotten off the plane in Hong Kong. You look at the signs but can't read a thing. Which way is the terminal? …" When you use third person, you describe to your audience what has happened, is happening, or will happen to other people. Third-person narration uses pronouns like "he," "her," and "they." "When the students arrived in Venice for their study-abroad experience, the first thing they saw was…." The effectiveness of third-person narration will depend on how much your audience can identify with key people in the story.

Demonstration

Demonstration is a method of informing that shows how something is done, displays the stages of a process, or depicts how something works. Demonstrations range from very simple with a few easy-to-follow steps (such as how to iron a shirt) to very complex (such as demonstrating how a nuclear reactor works). Regardless

comparison and contrast: a method of informing that explains something by focusing on how it is similar to and different from other things

> **SPEECH SNIPPET**
>
> **Informing by Comparing**
>
> In her speech about Islamic traditions, Amanda compared them to Judeo-Christian traditions that her listeners were more familiar with.

narration: a method of informing that explains something by recounting events

demonstration: a method of informing that explains something by showing how it is done by displaying the stages of a process or by depicting how something works

The TV program *How I Met Your Mother* is an example of informing using the first-person narrative method. How does it capture and maintain audience interest?

20th Century Fox/Brinton, Monty/The Kobal Collection

of whether the topic is simple or complex, effective demonstrations require expertise, a hierarchy of steps, and vivid language and presentational aids.

In a demonstration, your experience with what you are demonstrating is critical. Expertise gives you the necessary background to supplement bare-bones instructions with personally lived experience. During a demonstration, you speak from that experience as you guide your audience through the steps. Why are TV cooking shows so popular? Because the chef doesn't just read the recipe and do what it says. Rather, while performing each step, the chef shares tips about what to do that won't be mentioned in any cookbook. It is personal experience that allows the chef to say that one egg will work as well as two or that you can't substitute margarine for butter or how to tell if the cake is really done.

In a demonstration, you organize the steps from first to last so that your audience will be able to remember the sequence. Suppose you want to demonstrate the steps in using a touch-screen voting machine. If, rather than presenting fourteen separate points, you group them under four headings—(1) get ready to vote; (2) vote; (3) review your choices; (4) cast your ballot—chances are much higher that the audience will be able to remember most if not all the items in each of the four groups.

Although you could explain how to do something using only words, most demonstrations involve actually showing the audience the process or parts of the process. That's in part why TV shows like *What Not to Wear* and *Flip This House* are so popular. If what you are explaining is relatively simple, you can demonstrate the entire process from start to finish. However, if the process is lengthy or complex, you may choose to pre-prepare the material for some of the steps. Although you will show all stages in the process, you will not have to take the time for every single step as the audience watches. For example, many of the ingredients used by TV chefs are already cut up and measured into little bowls.

Effective demonstrations require practice. Remember that, under the pressure of speaking to an audience, even the simplest task can become difficult (Have you ever tried to thread a needle with twenty-five people watching you?). As you practice, you will want to consider the size of your audience and the configuration of the room. Be sure that all of your audience can see what you are doing. You may find that your demonstration takes longer than the time limit you have been given. In that case, you may want to pre-prepare a step or two.

To see a video clip of an effective demonstration from a student informative speech, go to your CourseMate for *Challenge* to access the video clip "Flag Etiquette" under the Chapter 12 resources.

Now that you understand the methods you can use when your general goal is to inform, we want to explain two speech frameworks that commonly use informative speaking: process speeches and expository speeches.

Common Informative Frameworks

Two of the most common frameworks for organizing the macrostructure of informative speech ideas are process frameworks and expository frameworks.

Process Speeches

process speech framework: a speech that explains and shows how something is done, is made, or works

The goal of a **process speech** is to demonstrate how something is done, is made, or works. Effective process speeches require you to carefully delineate the steps and the order in which they occur. The steps typically become the main points, and concrete explanations of each step become the subpoints. Most process speeches rely heavily on the demonstration method of informing.

For example, Allie is a floral designer and has been asked by her former art teacher to speak on the basics of floral arrangement to a high school art class.

Speaking of Cooking

Sean Daly, Executive Chef and Owner Hugo Restaurant, Cincinnati, Ohio

Photo courtesy of Sean Daly

When Sean Daly dreamed of being the chef of his own restaurant, he envisioned himself working in the kitchen, creating wonderful food—he never expected that so much of his time would be spent giving speeches. But the 30-year-old executive chef and owner of Hugo Restaurant, a four-star establishment in Cincinnati that serves "sophisticated southern cuisine," is in demand as a speaker. Not only does he constantly teach the other cooks and chefs who work for him, but he also promotes his restaurant by giving interviews to the media. In addition, he finds himself giving one or two cooking demonstrations a month to culinary students, serious gourmet cooks, small gatherings of his restaurant patrons, and, in the spring of 2010, as one of the featured chefs on a truffle hunting and cooking tour in France.

While a student at Johnson and Wales University in Charleston, South Carolina, Daly was required to take a public speaking class. He remembers giving a demonstration in class on how to make mozzarella cheese. One step required him to submerge his triple-gloved hand into a pot of simmering water. When the water seeped through his gloves, burning his hands, Daly gamely continued the demonstration but recalls having very red hands for a couple of days. ("For heaven sakes, there was a grade at stake!")

Daly averages one or two demonstration speeches a month. While he enjoys demonstrating his favorite recipes, he reports that it is always a challenge to figure out how to organize the speech—which parts of

> "Work hard on preparation, and then just jump in!"

the process to prepare in advance and which parts to actually demonstrate. Then, he says, he must plan to discuss the aspects of the process that are not included in the demonstration or are not obvious to the audience. For example, if he has pre-diced an onion that is to be sautéed, he needs to explain to the audience how finely diced the onion should be. Or he has to plan to explain that the skillet he is dumping ingredients into has been pre-heating for ten minutes. Failure to incorporate this information can lead audience members to experience disasters when they try to replicate his recipe.

He says he's always a bit nervous before he begins the actual demonstrations, especially if he is in someone else's kitchen or when he is demonstrating for other chefs. But he finds that his nervousness abates once he gets into the speech and focuses on completing the steps in the demonstration. Sean says it can be a challenge to remember to focus on the audience and not get lost in the creative moment of actually cooking. "It's important to keep your eyes on your audience so you can see if they really understand how to do what you are doing. Otherwise, they just get frustrated because they know they won't be able to replicate it at home—though they always enjoy eating what you've cooked!"

When asked what advice he would give to others to help them be successful in demonstrating a process, Daly cocked his head, grinned, and responded, "Work hard on preparation, and then just jump in!"

The teacher allotted five minutes for her presentation. In preparing for the speech, Allie recognized that in five minutes she could not complete arranging one floral display of any size let alone help students understand how to create various effects. So she opted to physically demonstrate only parts of the process and bring, as additional presentational aids, arrangements in various stages of completion. For example, the first step in floral arranging is to choose the right vase and frog (flower holder). So she brought in vases and frogs of various sizes and shapes to show as she explained how to choose a vase and frog based on the types of flowers used and the desired visual effect. The second step is to prepare the basic triangle of blooms, so she began to demonstrate how to place the flowers she had brought to form one triangle. Rather than hurrying and trying to get everything perfect in the few seconds she had, however, she also brought out several other partially finished arrangements that were behind a draped table. These showed other carefully completed triangles that used other types of flowers. The third step is placing additional flowers and greenery to complete an arrangement and achieve various artistic effects. Again, Allie actually demonstrated how to place several blooms, and then, as she described them, she brought out several completed arrangements that illustrated various artistic effects. Even though Allie did not physically perform all of each step, her visual presentation was an excellent demonstration of floral arranging.

Although some process speeches require you to demonstrate, others are not suited to demonstrations; instead, you can use visual aids to help the audience "see" the steps in the process. In a speech on remodeling a kitchen, it would not be practical to demonstrate the process; however, a speaker would be able to greatly enhance the verbal description by showing pictures before, during, and after the remodeling.

SPEECH ASSIGNMENT

Process Speech

Prepare a three- to six-minute speech in which you explain how something is made, how something is done, or how something works. An adaptation plan and a complete outline are required. To help you prepare your speech and your outline, go to your CourseMate for *Challenge* to access Speech Builder Express and complete the Speech Planning Action Step Activities.

Notice that the sample Process Speech Evaluation Form includes both primary criteria related to process and demonstration speeches and general criteria items that are common to all speeches.

The following topics are examples of ones that would be appropriate for a process explanation speech:

How to do it	How to make it	How it works
select running shoes	fishing flies	helicopter
install a toilet water saving device	origami birds	air bags
apply for a loan	plastic	asexual reproduction
build a compost bin	solar cells	3-D movies

SPEECH EVALUATION CHECKLIST

Process Speech Evaluation Form

You can use this form to critique a process speech that you hear in class. As you listen to the speaker, outline the speech. Then, answer the following questions.

Primary Criteria (Content)

_____ 1. Was the specific goal appropriate for a process speech?

_____ 2. Did the speaker show personal expertise with the process?

_____ 3. Did the speaker emphasize the process steps?

_____ 4. Did the speaker have good presentational aids that helped explain the process?

CONTINUED

_____ 5. If the speaker demonstrated the process, or parts of the process, was the demonstration fluid and skillful?

_____ 6. Could the audience easily see the presentational aids or demonstration?

_____ 7. Did the demonstration or presentational aids help you understand the main ideas?

_____ 8. Did the speaker adequately answer the overarching question of how to do it, how to make it, or how it works?

General Criteria (Structure and Delivery)

_____ 1. Was the specific goal clear?

_____ 2. Was the introduction effective in creating interest and introducing the process to be explained?

_____ 3. Was the macrostructure easy to follow?

_____ 4. Was the language appropriate, accurate, clear, and vivid?

_____ 5. Was the conclusion effective in summarizing the steps and clinching?

_____ 6. Was the speaker's voice conversational, intelligible, and expressive?

_____ 7. Was the speaker's use of facial expressions, gestures, and movement effective?

Based on these criteria, evaluate the speech as (check one):
_____ excellent _____ good _____ satisfactory _____ fair _____ poor

Go to your CourseMate for *Challenge* to access this checklist online under the Chapter 12 resources.

CourseMate

SAMPLE SPEECH

Sample Process Speech

This section presents a sample informative speech given by a student, including an adaptation plan, an outline, and a transcript.

Making Ethanol

By Louisa Greene[5]

CourseMate Read the speech adaptation plan, outline, and transcript of a speech given by Louisa Greene in an introductory speaking course. You can access a video clip of Louisa's speech through the Chapter 12 resources of your CourseMate for *Challenge*. You can also use your CourseMate to identify some of the strengths of Louisa's speech by preparing an evaluation checklist and an analysis. You can then compare your answers with those of the authors.

ADAPTATION PLAN

1. **Key aspects of audience.** Most people in my audience have probably heard of ethanol as an alternative to fossil fuels but don't know exactly what it is or how it's produced.

CONTINUED

2. **Establishing and maintaining common ground**. I will begin my speech by asking the audience a question. Throughout the speech, I will refer to the audience's previous knowledge and experience.

3. **Building and maintaining interest**. Because my audience is initially unlikely to be interested in how to produce ethanol, I will have to work hard to interest them and to keep their interest through the speech. I will try to gain interest in the introduction by relating the production of ethanol, the fuel, to the production of "white lightning," the illegal alcohol, which might be of more interest to the average college student. Throughout the speech, I will use common analogies and metaphors to explain the complex chemical processes. Finally, I will use a well-designed PowerPoint presentation to capture attention.

4. **Audience knowledge and sophistication**. Because most of the class is not familiar with ethanol, I will introduce them to the four-part process of making ethanol. I believe that by relating the process to that of making alcohol that people can drink, my audience will be more likely to be interested in and retain the information.

5. **Building credibility**. Early in the speech, I will tell the audience about how I got interested in ethanol when I built a still as a science fair project in high school. I will also tell them that I am now a chemical engineering major and am hoping to make a career in the alternative fuel industry.

6. **Audience attitudes**. My audience is likely to be indifferent to my topic, so I need to capture their attention by using interesting examples. I then need to keep them interested by relating the topic to things they're familiar with.

7. **Adapting to audiences from different cultures and language communities**. I will use visual and audiovisual aids in my PowerPoint presentation to help those listeners from different cultures understand what I'm talking about even though English is not their native language.

8. **Using presentational aids to enhance understanding and memory**. Throughout the speech, I will use color-coded PowerPoint slides with headers to reinforce the steps being discussed.

OUTLINE

General goal: To inform

Specific goal: I want my audience to understand the process for making ethanol from corn.

Introduction

Attention getter

I. Did you know that the first Model T cars were originally designed to run on ethanol or that Henry Ford said that ethanol was the fuel of the future? Did you know that in World War II about 75 percent of the German and American military vehicles were powered by ethanol since oil for gasoline was difficult to attain?

Listener relevance

II. The process for making ethanol is actually very similar to the process used to make moonshine, which may be why—during the first Arab oil embargo in 1978—when Robert Warren built a still to produce ethanol, he called the product "liquid sunshine" (Warren, 2006). Ethanol is an easy-to-make, inexpensive, and nearly pollution-free renewable alternative to gasoline.

CONTINUED

III. I became interested in ethanol in high school when I built a miniature ethanol still as a science fair project. I'm now a chemical engineering major and hope to make a career in the alternative fuel industry.

Speaker credibility

IV. Today, I'm going to explain the commercial process that turns corn into ethanol. The four steps include, first, preparing the corn by making a mash; second, fermenting the mash by adding yeast to make beer; third, distilling the ethanol from the beer; and fourth, processing the remaining whole stillage to produce co-products such as animal feed (Ethanol Business, 2004). *(Slide 1. Shows the four-step flow process.)*

Thesis statement with main point preview

Body

I. The first step in the commercial process of making ethanol, preparing the mash, has two parts: milling the corn and breaking the starch down into simple sugars (DENCO, n.d.). *(Slide 2. Title: Preparation. Shows corn flowing from a silo into a hammer mill and then into a holding tank where yeast is added.)*

In your saliva, you have enzymes that begin to break the bread and other starches you eat into sugar. In your stomach, you have other enzymes that finish this job of turning starch to simple sugar so your body can use the energy in the food you eat. In the commercial process of making ethanol, a similar transformation takes place.

Listener relevance

A. The corn is emptied into a bin and passes into a hammer mill, where it is ground into coarse flour.
B. After milling, the corn flour, a starch, must be broken down so that it becomes simple sugar by mixing in water and enzymes to form thick liquid called slurry.
   1. First the water and corn flour are dosed with the enzyme alpha-amylase and heated.
   2. Then the starchy slurry is heated to help the enzyme do its work.
   3. Later gluco-amylase is added to finish the process of turning the starch to simple sugar.

Once this mixture of sugar, water, and residual corn solids is turned into slurry or mash, it is ready to be fermented.

Transition

II. The second step of the commercial process for making ethanol is fermenting the slurry or mash by adding yeast (DENCO, n.d.). *(Slide 3. Title: Fermentation. Shows yeast added to the mash in a fermenter and carbon dioxide being released to form beer.)*

This step works in much the same way yeast is used to make bread dough rise. But in bread the carbon dioxide is trapped in the dough and causes it to rise, and the alcohol is burned off when the bread is baked. In making ethanol, carbon dioxide bubbles out of the mash and is released into the air.

Listener relevance

A. The mash remains in the fermenters for about fifty hours.
B. As the mash ferments, the sugar is turned into alcohol and carbon dioxide.
C. The carbon dioxide bubbles out into the air.
D. What remains after the carbon dioxide is released is called "beer."

Once the yeast has done its job and the fermentation process is complete, we move on to distillation.

Transition

III. The third step of the commercial process for making ethanol is distilling the fermented mash, now called "beer," by passing it through a series of columns where the alcohol is removed from the mash (Tham, 1997–2006). *(Slide 4. Title: Distillation of Ethanol. Animated slide showing beer flowing into distillation tank, heat being applied to the beer, and ethanol vapors being released and captured in a condenser.)*

If you've ever seen moonshine cookers in real life or in the movies, that's basically the same process as what I'm explaining here (DENCO, n.d.).

    A. Distillation is the process of boiling a liquid and then condensing the resulting vapor in order to separate out one component of the liquid.

    B. In most ethanol production, distillation occurs through the use of cooling columns.

    C. Once the ethanol has reached the desired purity or proof, it is denatured to be made undrinkable by adding gasoline to it.

    D. The ethanol is ready to be transported from the plant.

Once this step is complete, we've successfully produced ethanol, but we aren't done until we complete step 4.

IV. The fourth step in commercial production is converting the remaining whole stillage into co-products (DENCO, n.d.). *(Slide 5. Title: Co-product. Shows a tank with remaining whole solids flowing into a condenser with output flowing into a bin of animal feed.)*

Not only is ethanol a renewable resource, but even its byproducts get put to good use!

Conclusion

I. As you can see, producing ethanol is a simple four-step process: preparing the corn into a slurry or mash, fermenting the slurry into beer, distilling the beer to release the ethanol, and processing the remaining water and corn solids into co-products. *(Slide 6: Same as slide 1.)*

II. In 1980, when Robert Warren was operating his still, only 175 million gallons of ethanol were being commercially produced in the United States. Twenty-five years later, 4.85 billion gallons were produced (Renewable Fuels Association, 2007). That's a whopping 2,674 percent increase! And it is a trend that is continuing. With today's skyrocketing gasoline prices and our increasing concerns about preserving our environment, you can see why this simple process of making liquid sunshine is getting more and more popular. I don't know about you, but I'm glad it is!

References

DENCO, LLC. (n.d.) *Tour the plant.* Retrieved July 2, 2007, from http://www.dencollc.com/DENCO%20WebSite_files/Tour.htm

Ethanol Business and Industry Center. (2004, May). *Module 2: Ethanol science and technology.* Retrieved July 3, 2007, from http://www.nwicc.com/pages/continuing/business/ethanol/Module2.htm

Renewable Fuels Association. (2007). *Industry statistics: The ethanol industry.* Retrieved July 9, 2007, from http://www.ethanolrfa.org/industry/statistics/

Tham, M. T. (1997–2006). *Distillation: An introduction.* Retrieved July 5, 2007, from http://lorien.ncl.ac.uk/ming/distil/distil0.htm

Warren, R. (2006, August). *Make your own fuel.* Retrieved July 3, 2007, from http://running_on_alcohol.tripod.com/ index.html

SPEECH AND ANALYSIS

Read the following aloud at least once. Then, analyze it on the basis of the primary criteria in the checklist on pages 248–249: Process Speech Evaluation Form.

Speech

Did you know that the first Model T's were designed to run on ethanol and that Henry Ford said that ethanol was the fuel of the future? Or that in World War II about 75 percent of the German and American military vehicles were powered by ethanol since oil for gasoline was difficult to obtain? In 1978, during the first Arab oil embargo, when gas soared from 62 cents a gallon to $1.64, Californian Robert Warren and others built stills to produce what he called—no, not "white lightning"—but "liquid sunshine," which we call ethanol.

I became interested in ethanol in high school when I built a miniature ethanol still as a science fair project. I'm now a chemical engineering major and hope to make a career in the alternative fuel industry. So, today, I'm going to explain to you the simple process that takes corn and turns it into liquid sunshine. Specifically, I want you to understand the process that is used to make ethanol from corn.

According to the Ethanol Business and Industry Center at Northwest Iowa Community College, the four steps in the commercial process of making ethanol are, first, preparing the corn by making a mash; second, fermenting the mash by adding yeast to make beer; third, distilling the ethanol from the beer; and fourth, processing the remaining whole stillage to produce co-products like animal feed. *(Slide 1)*

As this slide taken from the DENCO, LCC, "Tour the Plant" website depicts, the first step in the commercial process of making ethanol, preparing the mash, has two parts: milling the corn and breaking the starch down into simple sugars. *(Slide 2)*

The corn, which has been tested for quality and stored in a silo, is emptied into a bin and passes into a hammer mill, where it is ground into coarse flour. This is done to expose more of the corn's starchy material so that these starches can be more easily broken down into sugar.

In your saliva, you have enzymes that begin to break the bread and other starches you eat into sugar. In your stomach, you have other enzymes that finish this job of turning starch to simple sugar so your body can use the energy in the food you eat. In the commercial production of ethanol, a similar transformation takes place.

To break the milled corn flour starch into sugar, the milled flour is mixed with water and alpha-amylase, the same enzyme that you have in your saliva, and is heated. The alpha-amylase acts as Pacman and takes bites out of the long sugar chains that are bound together in the starch. What results are broken bits of starch that need further processing to become glucose. So later, gluco-amylase, which is like the enzyme in your stomach, is added, and these new Pacmen bite the starchy bits into simple glucose sugar molecules.

Analysis

Louisa begins this speech with rhetorical questions designed to pique the audience's interest. At the time she prepared the speech, gasoline prices were again soaring, so these questions—coupled with the example of Warren's solution—provide a provocative introduction to her topic.

At this point, Louisa personalizes the topic with a self-disclosure that also establishes her credibility.

One thing Louisa could do better throughout the speech is to offer listener relevance links that more directly remind the audience of the speech's relevance to them whenever possible.

Notice how Louisa has nested two steps, milling and breaking starch into sugars, under the more general heading of "Preparation." This grouping keeps the main points at a manageable number and will help her audience remember the steps. Her second slide is simple but effective because it reinforces the two substeps.

Louisa helps the audience understand the unfamiliar starch-to-sugar conversion by comparing it to the familiar process of digestion.

The Pacman analogy also helps the audience visualize what occurs during the starch-to-sugar conversion.

Now this mixture of sugar, water, and residual corn solids, called slurry or mash, is ready to be fermented.

The second step in the commercial production of ethanol is to ferment the mash by adding yeast in an environment that has no oxygen and allowing the mixture to "rest" while the yeast "works." *(Slide 3)* This is accomplished by piping the slurry into an oxygen-free tank called a fermenter, adding the yeast, and allowing the mixture to sit for about fifty hours. Without oxygen, the yeast feeds on the sugar and gives off ethanol and carbon dioxide as waste products. Eventually, deprived of oxygen, the yeast dies.

This is similar to what happens when we add yeast to bread dough. But in bread the carbon dioxide is trapped in the dough and causes it to rise, while the alcohol is burned off when the bread is baked.

In ethanol production, the carbon dioxide is not trapped in the watery slurry. Because it is a gas, it bubbles out of the mixture and is captured and released into the outside air. The ethanol, however, remains in the mixture, which is now called "beer," with the water and the nonfermentable corn solids. At the end of the fermentation process, it is the ethanol in the mixture that retains much of the energy of the original sugar. At this point, we are now ready to separate or distill the ethanol from the other parts of the beer.

The third step in the commercial production of ethanol is distillation, which, according to M. T. Tham's book *Distillation: An Introduction*, is the process of purifying a liquid by heating it and then condensing its vapor. So, for example, if you boiled your tap water and condensed the steam that was produced, you would have purified water with no minerals or other impurities. But distilling ethanol is a bit more complicated since both the ethanol and the water in the beer are liquids and can be vaporized into steam by adding heat.

Luckily, different liquids boil at different temperatures, and since ethanol boils at 173°F while water boils at 212°F, we can use this boiling point difference to separate the two. So to simplify what is really a more complex process *(Slide 4)*, in the commercial distillation of ethanol, a column or series of columns are used to boil off the ethanol and the water and then to separate these vapors so that the ethanol vapors are captured and condensed back into pure liquid ethanol. The liquid ethanol is then tested to make sure that it meets the specifications for purity and proof. At this point, ethanol is drinkable alcohol and would be subject to a $20 per gallon federal excise tax. To avoid this, it is "denatured"—made undrinkable by adding gasoline to it.

After this, the ethanol is ready to be transported from the plant.

The fourth step in the commercial production process is converting the whole stillage into co-products. *(Slide 5)* One of the greatest things about producing ethanol is that the water and nonfermentable corn solids that are left after the

---

The last sentence, mentioning slurry, is an excellent transition between the two main points.

Louisa helps the audience stay with her by using the signpost "second step." Her third slide, a visual of the "fermentation equation," nicely simplifies the complex chemistry that underlies fermentation.

Here she uses an effective transition statement to signal to her audience that she will be moving to the third step.

Her fourth slide is much more elaborate than the others. The animation in the slide helps the audience visualize how distillation works. It would have been more effective had she been able to control the motion so that each stage was animated as she talked about it.

The last sentence serves as an internal conclusion to the third step.

The slide for the fourth main point is so simple that it really isn't needed to aid audience understanding, but it is a visual reinforcement of this step, and the audience has been conditioned to expect one slide per point, so it would seem odd if there were not a slide for this step.

ethanol is distilled aren't just thrown out as waste. Instead, the remaining water and nonfermentable corn solids can also be processed to make co-products that are primarily used as animal feed.

So as you have seen, the process of making ethanol is really quite simple. *(Slide 6)* One, prepare the corn by milling and breaking its starch into sugar. Two, ferment the mash using yeast. Three, distill off the ethanol from the beer, and four, process the co-products.

In 1980, when Robert Warren was operating his still, only 175 million gallons of ethanol were being commercially produced in the United States. Twenty-five years later, according to the Renewable Fuels Association, 4.85 billion gallons were produced. That's a whopping 2,674 percent increase! And it is a trend that is continuing. With today's skyrocketing gasoline prices and our increasing concerns about preserving our environment, you can see why this simple process of making liquid sunshine is getting more and more popular. I don't know about you, but I'm glad it is!

Louisa begins the conclusion with a summary of her main points. The sixth slide, a repetition of the first slide, visually "closes the loop" and reinforces the four steps.

The conclusion includes a circular reference back to Robert Warren who was introduced at the beginning of the speech. In the conclusion, she uses statistics to drive home the point that ethanol is an important fuel source and that in the near future ethanol may be a fuel used by members of the audience.

Louisa could have offered a better clincher by tying her final sentence back to her introductory comments about Henry Ford. For example, she might have said, "Almost a century later, it seems that what Henry Ford said will be coming true. Look for a green-handled pump coming soon to a gas station near you."

Expository Speeches

The goal of an **expository speech** is to provide carefully researched in-depth knowledge about a complex topic. For example, "The Origins and Classification of Nursery Rhymes," "The Sociobiological Theory of Child Abuse," and "Viewing Gangsta Rap as Poetry" are all topics on which you could give an interesting expository speech. Lengthy expository speeches are known as lectures. In this section, we describe four kinds of expository speeches.

All expository speeches require that the speaker use an extensive research base for preparing the presentation, choose an organizational pattern that helps the audience understand the material being discussed, and use a variety of informative methods to sustain the audience's attention and comprehension of the material presented.

Even college professors who are experts in their fields draw from a variety of source material when they prepare their lectures. So you will want to acquire your information from a variety of reputable sources. Then, as you are speaking, you will want to cite the sources for the information you present. You do so in the form of **oral footnotes**—oral references to the original source of particular information at the point of presenting it during a speech. In this way, you can establish the trustworthiness of the information you present as well as strengthen your own credibility.

Expository speakers also must choose an organizational pattern that is best suited to the material they will present. Different types of expository speeches are suited to different organizational patterns. It is up to the speaker to arrange the main points of the speech thoughtfully so that they flow in a manner that aids audience understanding and memory.

Finally, a hallmark of effective expository speaking is that it uses various methods of informing for developing material. Within one speech, you may hear the speaker use descriptions, definitions, comparisons and contrasts, narration, and short demonstrations to develop the main points.

expository speech framework: an informative presentation that provides carefully researched in-depth knowledge about a complex topic

oral footnote: oral reference to the original source of particular information at the point of presenting it during a speech

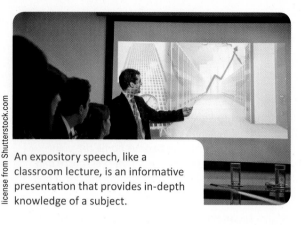

An expository speech, like a classroom lecture, is an informative presentation that provides in-depth knowledge of a subject.

Expository speeches include those that explain a political, economic, social, religious, or ethical issue; events or forces of history; a theory, principle, or law; and a creative work.

EXPOSITION OF POLITICAL, ECONOMIC, SOCIAL, RELIGIOUS, OR ETHICAL ISSUES

In an expository speech, you have the opportunity to help the audience understand the background or context of an issue, including the forces that gave rise to the issue and continue to affect it. You may also present the various positions that are held about the issue and the reasoning behind these positions. Finally, you may discuss various ways that have been presented for resolving the issue.

The general goal of your speech is to inform, not to persuade. So you will want to present all sides of controversial issues without advocating which side is better. You will also want to make sure that the sources you are drawing from are respected experts and are objective in what they report. Finally, you will want to present complex issues in a straightforward manner that helps your audience to understand while not oversimplifying knotty issues.

For example, Mahalia decided to give a speech on the issue of drilling for oil and natural gas in the Arctic National Wildlife Refuge. In doing her research, Mahalia needs to be careful that she consults articles and experts on all sides of this controversial issue and fairly incorporates their views in her outline. Because this is a very complex issue, if she has time, she will want to discuss all important aspects of the controversy, including the ecological, economic, political (national, state, and local), and technological aspects. If time is a factor, she may limit her discussion to just one or two of these aspects, but she should at least inform her audience of the other considerations that affect the issue.

You can identify an issue that you could use for an expository speech by reviewing the list of topics you brainstormed earlier in this course. The following list of topic ideas might stimulate your thinking as you work with your own list.

gay marriage	stem cell research
affirmative action	universal health care
hate speech	school vouchers
media bias	teen curfews
school uniforms	home schooling
immigration	acid rain
genetic engineering	downloading music

EXPOSITION OF HISTORICAL EVENTS AND FORCES

A second important type of expository speech is one that explains historical events or forces. It has been said that those who don't understand history may be destined to repeat it. So an expositional speech about historical events or forces can be fascinating for its own sake, but it can also be relevant for what is happening today. Unfortunately, there are people who think history is boring; we believe this is because many people have learned history from sources that are boring. As an expository speaker, you have a special obligation during your research to seek out stories and narratives that can enliven your speech. And you will want to consult sources that analyze the events you describe so

Reflect on Ethics

ETHICS OF ONLINE NEWS: "GIZMODOGATE"

Today more and more people are acquiring their news online, not only from online newspapers, but also from blogs (short for web logs) and social networking sites like Twitter and Facebook. In March 2010, one of these news sources, tech blog Gizmodo, became news itself.

Allegedly, Gizmodo paid to obtain a prototype of Apple's iPhone 4G, which an Apple employee left at a local bar and that was then picked up by someone else.[6] Nick Denton, CEO of Gizmodo's parent company, Gawker Media, admitted he paid $5,000 for the prototype, knowing the person he was paying was not the owner.[7] Gizmodo then posted photos of the prototype, without knowing whether the prototype was even real and scooping Apple, who hadn't yet made any announcements about the phone.

Gizmodo's blog posts spurred a criminal investigation, as well as a debate about the rights and responsibilities of online journalists. As part of the investigation, county prosecutors searched the home of Gizmodo's editor, Jason Chen, and seized his computers. In response, Gizmodo claimed that this seizure violated laws that limit newsroom investigations.

1. What, if any, ethical principles did Gizmodo violate by posting the photos and stories about the prototype iPhone?

2. Should online journalists who host blogs be held to the same ethical codes of fact checking and credential verification as traditional journalists? If so, how?

3. Should the laws that limit newsroom investigations also protect online journalists who work on computers in their homes? Why or why not?

---

that you can discuss what impact they had at the time they occurred and what meaning they have for us today. Although many of us are familiar with the historical fact that the United States developed the atomic bomb during World War II, an expository speech on the Manhattan Project (as it was known) that dramatized the race to produce the bomb and told the stories of the main players would add to our understanding of the inner workings of "secret" government-funded research projects. It might also place modern arms races and the fear of nuclear proliferation in their proper historical context. The following list of topic ideas might stimulate your thinking about historical topics you speak about.

slavery	Gandhi's movement
the Papacy	the colonization of Africa
Irish immigration	building the Great Pyramids
women's suffrage	the Industrial Revolution
the Olympics	the Ming Dynasty
conquering Mt. Everest	the Vietnam War
the Balfour Declaration (which laid the groundwork for creating the state of Israel)	the Crusades
	space shuttle *Challenger* explosion

EXPOSITION OF A THEORY, PRINCIPLE, OR LAW

The way we live is affected by natural and human laws and principles and explained by various theories. Yet there are many theories, principles, and laws that we do not completely understand or don't understand how they affect us. An expository speech can inform us by explaining these important phenomena. The main challenge is to find material that explains the theory, law, or principle in language that is understandable to the audience. You will want to search for or create examples and illustrations that demystify esoteric or complicated terminology. Using effective examples and comparing unfamiliar ideas with those that the audience already knows can help you explain the law. For example, in a speech on the psychological principles of operant conditioning, a speaker could help the audience understand the difference between continuous reinforcement and intermittent reinforcement with the following explanation:

When a behavior is reinforced continuously, each time people perform the behavior they get the reward, but when the behavior is reinforced intermittently, the reward is not always given when the behavior is displayed. Behavior that is learned by continuous reinforcement disappears quickly when the reward is no longer provided, but behavior that is learned by intermittent reinforcement continues for long periods of time, even when not reinforced. You can see examples of how behavior was conditioned in everyday encounters. For example, take the behavior of putting a coin in the slot of a machine. If the machine is a vending machine, you expect to be rewarded every time you "play." And if the machine doesn't eject the item, you might wonder if the machine is out of order and "play" just one more coin, or you might bang on the machine. In any case, you are unlikely to put in more than one more coin. But suppose the machine is a slot machine or a machine that dispenses instant winner lottery tickets. Now how many coins will you "play" before you stop and conclude that the machine is "out of order"? Why the difference? Because you have been conditioned to a vending machine on a continuous schedule, but a slot machine or automatic lottery ticket dispenser "teaches" you on an intermittent schedule.

The following list of topic ideas might stimulate your thinking about topics for an expository speech on a theory, principle, or law.

natural selection	diminishing returns
gravity	Boyle's law
number theory	psychoanalytic theory
global warming	intelligent design
feminist theory	Maslow's hierarchy of needs
the normal distribution	color theory: complements and contrasts

EXPOSITION OF A CREATIVE WORK

Courses in art, theater, music, literature, and film appreciation give students tools by which to recognize the style, historical period, and quality of a particular piece or group of pieces. Yet most of us know very little about how to understand a creative work, so presentations designed to explain creative works such as poems, novels, songs, or even famous speeches can be very instructive for audience members.

When developing a speech that explains a creative work or body of work, you will want to find information on the work and the artist who created it. In addition, you will want to find sources that help you understand the period in which this work was created and learn about the criteria that critics use to evaluate works of this type. So, for example, if you wanted to give an expository speech on Fredrick Douglass's Fourth of July oration of 1852 in Rochester, New York, you might need to orient your audience by first reminding them of who Douglass was. Then, you would want to explain the traditional expectation that was set for Fourth of July speakers at this point in history. After this, you might want to summarize the speech and perhaps share a few memorable quotations. Finally, you would want to discuss how speech critics view the speech and why the speech is considered "great."

The following list of topic ideas might stimulate your thinking about topics for an expository speech on a creative work.

hip-hop music	the films of Alfred Hitchcock
Impressionist painting	Lady Gaga's "Paparazzi"
salsa dancing	Kabuki theater
inaugural addresses	iconography
a postmodern critique of *A Farewell to Arms*	*Catcher in the Rye*: a coming-of-age novel
Van Gogh's *Starry Night*	Spike Lee's *Mo' Better Blues*

SPEECH ASSIGNMENT

Expository Speech

Prepare a five- to eight-minute informative speech in which you present carefully researched, in-depth information about a complex topic. To help you prepare your speech and your outline, go to your CourseMate for *Challenge* to access Speech Builder Express and complete the Speech Planning Action Step Activities.

Notice that the sample Expository Speech Evaluation Checklist that follows includes both primary criteria related to expository speeches and general criteria items that are common to all speeches.

To see sample topics that would be appropriate for this speech assignment, review the topic lists provided earlier with the descriptions of types of expository speeches.

SPEECH EVALUATION CHECKLIST

Expository Speech Evaluation Checklist

You can use this form to critique an expository speech that you hear in class. As you listen, outline the speech and identify which expository speech type it is. Then, answer the following questions.

Type of expository speech

_____ Exposition of political, economic, social, religious, or ethical issues
_____ Exposition of historical events or forces
_____ Exposition of a theory, principle, or law
_____ Exposition of a creative work

Primary Criteria (Content)

_____ 1. Was the specific goal of the speech to provide well-researched information on a complex topic?

_____ 2. Did the speaker effectively use a variety of methods to convey the information?

_____ 3. Did the speaker emphasize the main ideas and important supporting material?

CONTINUED

_____ 4. Did the speaker use high-quality sources for the information presented?

_____ 5. Did the speaker use a variety of supporting material?

_____ 6. Did the speaker present in-depth, high-quality information?

General Criteria (Structure and Delivery)

_____ 1. Was the specific goal clear?

_____ 2. Was the introduction effective in creating interest, as well as introducing the topic and main points to be explained?

_____ 3. Was the macrostructure easy to follow?

_____ 4. Was the language appropriate, accurate, clear, and vivid?

_____ 5. Was the conclusion effective in summarizing the main points and clinching?

_____ 6. Was the speaker's voice intelligible, conversational, and expressive?

_____ 7. Was the speaker's use of facial expressions, gestures, and movement appropriate?

Based on these criteria, evaluate the speech as (check one):
_____ excellent _____ good _____ satisfactory _____ fair _____ poor

CourseMate Go to your CourseMate for *Challenge* to access this checklist online under the Chapter 12 resources.

SAMPLE SPEECH

Informative Speech

This section presents a sample expository speech adaptation plan, outline, and transcript given by a student in an introductory speaking course.

Understanding Hurricanes

Adapted from a speech by Megan Soileau, University of Kentucky[8]

CourseMate Read the speech adaptation plan, outline, and transcript of a speech given by Megan Soileau in an introductory speaking course. You can access a video clip of Megan's speech, delivered by Chet Harding, through the Chapter 12 resources of your CourseMate for *Challenge*. You can also use your CourseMate to identify some of the strengths of Megan's speech by preparing the Expository Speech Evaluation Checklist and an analysis. You can then compare your answers with those of the authors.

ADAPTATION PLAN

1. **Key aspects of audience.** Because audience members have probably seen television coverage on hurricanes but don't really know much about them, I will need to provide basic information.

2. **Establishing and maintaining common ground.** My main way of establishing common ground will be by using inclusive personal pronouns (we, us, our).

3. **Building and maintaining interest.** I will build interest by pointing out how hurricanes even affect the weather in Kentucky and through the use of examples.

CONTINUED

4. **Audience knowledge and sophistication**. Because most of the class has probably not been in a hurricane, I will provide as much explanatory information as I can.

5. **Building credibility**. I will build credibility through solid research and oral citation of sources. Early on, I'll mention where I live on the Gulf Coast and the fact that I have lived through several hurricanes.

6. **Audience attitudes**. I expect my audience to be curious about hurricanes, especially since Hurricane Katrina received so much media attention. So I will give them information to help them become more knowledgeable about them.

7. **Adapt to audiences from different cultures and language communities**. Because hurricanes occur on coasts all over the world, I don't need to adapt to different cultures or language communities. However, I will consider how to make the topic relevant to people who do not live on a coast.

8. **Use presentational aids to enhance audience understanding and memory**. I will use several PowerPoint slides to highlight the effects of hurricanes.

OUTLINE

General purpose: To inform

Speech goal: In this speech, I am going to familiarize the audience with the overall effects of hurricanes: how they work, ways they affect our whole country, and the toll they take on the people who live in their direct paths.

Introduction

I. Think about a time you've been absolutely terrified (whether it was by a person, event, or situation) and all you wanted to do was go home and be with your family and friends. Now imagine the feeling you might have if you were that afraid, but you had no idea if your home would even be there when you arrived.

    Attention getter

II. This is the reality for many people living on the coastlines of the United States. Hurricanes affect the lives of those living in their direct paths, but they can also cause spin-off weather that affects the entire country.

    Listener relevance link

III. I have lived about forty-five minutes from the Gulf Coast of Texas my entire life and have seen and experienced the destruction caused by hurricanes firsthand, especially in the past three years. *(Slide 1: picture of hurricane that hit my hometown last year.)*

    Speaker credibility

IV. Today I'd like to speak with you about the way hurricanes work, the ways they affect our entire country, and, most importantly, the toll they take on the people who live in their direct paths.

    Thesis statement with main point preview

Body

I. To begin, let's discuss how hurricanes form and the varying degrees of intensity of them. That way, we can be better informed when we watch news broadcasts and read newspaper reports about them.

    Listener relevance

  A. Several basic conditions must be present for a hurricane to form.

    1. According to the award-winning Discovery Communications website HowStuffWorks.com, hurricanes form "when an area of warm low pressure air rises and cool, high pressure seizes the opportunity to move in underneath it." This causes a center to develop. This center may eventually turn into what is considered a hurricane.

2. The warm and moist air from the ocean rises up into these pressure zones and begins to form storms. As this happens, the storm continues to draw up more warm moist air, and a heat transfer occurs because of the cool air being heated, causing the air to rise again.
   3. "The exchange of heat creates a pattern of wind that circulates around a center" (the eye of the storm) "like water going down a drain" (HowStuffWorks.com).
   4. The "rising air reinforces the air that is already" being pulled up from the surface of the ocean, "so the circulation and speeds of the wind increase" (HowStuffWorks.com).

B. Classifications of these types of storms help determine their intensity so we can prepare properly for them.
   1. Winds that are less than 38 miles per hour are considered tropical depressions.
   2. Tropical storms are winds ranging from 39 to 73 miles per hour.
   3. And lastly hurricanes are storms with wind speeds of 74 miles per hour and higher.
   4. When storms become classified as hurricanes, they become part of another classification system that is displayed by the Saffir-Simpson Hurricane Scale.
      a. Hurricanes are labeled as Categories 1–5 based on their wind-intensity level or speed. *(Slide 2: hurricane scale chart)*
      b. Hurricane Ike was labeled differently at different places. *(Slide 3: map showing the different places Ike was labeled in the different categories)*

Transition   *Knowing how and where hurricanes occur helps us determine how our daily lives, even here in Kentucky, may be affected when one hits.*

II. A hurricane can affect more than just those living in its direct path.

Listener relevance   These effects can actually be seen across the country in terms of the environment and the economy.

A. Hurricanes affect wildlife in negative ways.
   1. According to the *Beaumont Enterprise* on October 7, 2008, Christine Rappleye reported that the storm surge (a wall of water) Hurricane Ike brought in was up to 14 feet of water across some parts of Southeast Texas.
   2. Dolphins were swept inland with the surge and then, when the waters flowed back out to sea, dolphins were left stranded in the marsh.
   3. Some were rescued, but not all. This dolphin was rescued from a ditch. *(Slide 4: dolphin being rescued)*
B. Hurricanes also affect the economy as prices climb close to all-time highs when hurricanes hit.
   1. According to economist Beth Ann Bovino, quoted in the September 29, 2005, issue of the *Washington Post*, gas prices skyrocket when a hurricane like Katrina, Rita, or Ike hits.
      a. Paul Davidson said, in a September 12, 2008, article in *USA Today*, that in the anticipation of Hurricane Ike, twelve refineries in Texas were shut down. "This is 17 percent of the U.S. refining capacity," he said.
      b. That's why even residents here in Lexington saw a dramatic spike in gas prices immediately following Ike's landfall.
   2. Energy costs to heat and cool our homes also rise.
      a. When we consumers have to pay more to heat and cool our homes, we also have less to spend eating out at restaurants.
      b. And we have less to spend on nonessentials at the mall.
      c. So, economically we all feel the ripple effect when hurricanes hit.

So, yes, we all feel the effects of hurricanes, but we should not overlook the dramatic ways in which people who live in the direct path of a hurricane are affected.

Transition

III. When a hurricane hits, many of these people become homeless, at least for a while, and suffer emotionally and financially as they evacuate to places all over the country.

Yes, many people relocate right here in Kentucky!

Listener relevance

    A. People who go through hurricanes suffer extreme emotional effects.
        1. Evacuation is stressful because people have to pack up what they can and have no way of knowing if their homes will still be standing or inhabitable when they return. *(Slides 5 and 6: before and after pictures from Hurricane Ike)*
        2. Even returning home is emotionally taxing because returning home means rebuilding homes, neighborhoods, and even memories.
        3. Though we try to get back to a "normal" life, it can never really be the same as it once was. Instead, it's what Silicon Valley venture capitalist and investor Roger McNamee calls the "new normal" in his book *The New Normal: Great Opportunities in a Time of Great Risk*.
    B. Because they have to rebuild their homes and lives, people also go through financial difficulties.
        1. People battle with insurance companies about whether a home has wind or water damage as they seek financial assistance. (Insurance companies will often claim that it is the one—wind or water—the homeowner is uninsured for.) (Associated Press, 2008)
        2. Price gouging is another financial challenge hurricane victims face.
            a. When families and businesses begin the process of rebuilding, people come from outside areas to help with labor and materials and will charge exorbitant fees.
            b. An example of this is when my father needed people to help remove two trees from our home in September 2005 after Hurricane Rita.

Conclusion

I. Hurricanes affect victims who live in their direct path and the country as a whole.

Goal restatement

II. To understand these effects, we talked about how hurricanes work, how they affect our country and daily lives, and the impacts they have on the lives of people who live through them.

Main point summary

III. Maybe knowing some of these facts will help each of us appreciate our homes and our families just a little bit more. *(Handout: Hurricane tracking charts)*

Clincher

References

Associated Press. (2008, October 8). Windstorm costs insurers $550M. *Newark Advocate*.

Bovino, B. A. (2005, September 29). Hurricanes impact national economy. *The Washington Post*, Retrieved from http://washingtonpost.com/wpdym/content/discussion/2005/09/28/D12005092801431.html

Davidson, P. (2008, September 12). Ike blows gasoline prices higher. *USA Today*.

Marshall, B., Freudenrich, C., & Lamb, R. (2008). *How hurricanes work*. Retrieved October 8, 2008, from http://www.howstuffworks.com/hurricanes.htm

McNamee, R. (2004). *The new normal: Great opportunities in a time of great risk*. New York, NY: Penguin.

Rappleye, C. (2008, October 7). Hurricane strands marine mammals, damages facility for the stranded. *Beaumont Enterprise*.

SPEECH AND ANALYSIS

Speech

Think about a time you've been absolutely terrified, whether it was by a person, event, or situation, and all you wanted to do was go home and be with your family and friends.

Now imagine the feeling you might have if you were that afraid, but you had no idea if your home would even be there when you arrived. This is the reality for many people living on the coastlines of the United States. Hurricanes affect the lives of those living in their direct paths, but they can also affect the entire country.

I have lived about forty-five minutes from the Gulf Coast of Texas my entire life and have seen and experienced the destruction caused by hurricanes firsthand, especially in the past three years. *(Slide 1: picture of hurricane that hit my hometown last year)* This is a picture of my hometown when a hurricane hit it last year.

Today I'd like to speak with you about the way hurricanes work, the ways they affect our whole country, and, most importantly, the toll they take on the people who live in their direct paths.

To begin, let's discuss how hurricanes form and the varying degrees of intensity of them so we can be better informed when we watch news broadcasts and read newspaper reports about them.

Several basic conditions must be present for a hurricane to form. According to the award-winning Discovery Communications website HowStuffWorks.com, hurricanes form "when an area of warm low pressure air rises and cools, high pressure seizes the opportunity to move in underneath it." This causes a center to develop. This center may eventually turn into what is considered a hurricane. The warm and moist air from the ocean rises up into these pressure zones and begins to form storms. As this happens, the storm continues to draw up more warm moist air, and a heat transfer occurs because of the cool air being heated, causing the air to rise again. "The exchange of heat creates a pattern of wind that circulates around a center" (the eye of the storm) "like water going down a drain." The "rising air reinforces the air that is already" being pulled up from the surface of the ocean, "so the circulation and speeds of the wind increase."

Classifications of these types of storms help determine their intensity so we can prepare properly for them. Winds that are less than 38 miles per hour are considered tropical depressions. Tropical storms have winds that range from 39 to 73 miles per hour. And lastly hurricanes are storms with wind speeds of 74 miles per hour and higher.

When storms become classified as a hurricane, they become part of another classification system that is displayed by the Saffir-Simpson Hurricane Scale. Hurricanes are labeled as Categories 1–5 based on their wind intensity level or speed. *(Slide 2: hurricane scale chart)* Hurricane Ike was labeled

Analysis

Megan opens by using an analogy to help get her audience emotionally involved in her speech and then quickly introduces her topic.

Notice how Megan establishes her credibility by sharing that she grew up near the Gulf Coast of Texas and has been a hurricane victim herself. The first slide adds emotional appeal to her point.

Megan concludes her introduction by previewing her main points clearly.

Megan does a nice job of incorporating a listener relevance link into her first main point statement.

Here Megan offers an oral footnote to add credibility. Noting that the website is an award-winning one helps her here.

Megan missed a great opportunity to help her audience follow what she was saying. She should have used visual aids here to depict the stages in the hurricane formation process.

Showing the hurricane scale chart and the map depicting Hurricane Ike at different categories visually reinforces what Megan describes in her verbal message.

differently at different places. *(Slide 3: map showing the different places Ike was labeled in the different categories)*

Knowing how and where hurricanes occur helps us determine how our daily lives, even here in Kentucky, may be affected when one hits.

A hurricane can affect more than just those living in its direct path, and these effects can actually be seen across the country in terms of the environment and the economy.

Hurricanes affect wildlife in negative ways. According to the *Beaumont Enterprise* on October 7, 2008, Christine Rappleye reported that the storm surge, which is basically a wall of water, that Hurricane Ike brought in across some parts of Southeast Texas was about 14 feet in some places. Dolphins were swept inland with the surge and then, when the waters flowed back out to sea, dolphins were left stranded in the marsh. Some were rescued, but not all. This dolphin was rescued from a ditch. *(Slide 4: dolphin being rescued)*

Hurricanes also affect the economy. Prices climb close to all-time highs when hurricanes hit. According to economist Beth Ann Bovino, quoted in the September 29, 2005, issue of *The Washington Post*, gas prices skyrocket when a hurricane like Katrina, Rita, or Ike hits. Paul Davidson said, in a September 12, 2008, article in *USA Today* that in the anticipation of Hurricane Ike, twelve refineries in Texas were shut down. "This is 17 percent of the U.S. refining capacity," he said. That's why even residents here in Lexington saw a dramatic spike in gas prices immediately following Ike's landfall.

Energy costs to heat and cool our homes also rise. When consumers have to pay more to heat and cool our homes, we also have less to spend eating out at restaurants. And we have less to spend on nonessentials at the mall. So economically we all feel the ripple effect when hurricanes hit.

So, yes, we all feel the effects of hurricanes, but we should not overlook the dramatic ways in which people who live in the direct path of a hurricane are affected.

When a hurricane hits, many of these people become homeless, at least for a while, and suffer emotionally and financially as they evacuate to places all over the country, including Kentucky!

People who go through hurricanes suffer extreme emotional effects. Evacuation is stressful because people have to pack up what they can and have no way of knowing if their home will still be standing or inhabitable when they return. *(Slides 5 and 6: before and after pictures from Hurricane Ike)*

Even returning home is emotionally taxing because returning home means rebuilding homes, neighborhoods, and even memories. Though we try to get back to a "normal" life, it can never really be the same as it once was. Instead, it's what Silicon Valley venture capitalist and investor Roger McNamee calls the "new normal" in his book *The New Normal: Great Opportunities in a Time of Great Risk*.

Because they have to rebuild their homes and lives, people also go through financial difficulties. People battle with insurance companies about whether a home has wind or water damage as they seek financial assistance. (Insurance

Megan does a nice job tying together the two main points, which makes for a fluent section transition.

Here Megan not only describes the 14-foot-high wall of water Hurricane Ike transported across Texas, but she also reinforces it with the picture on her PowerPoint slide.

By indicating that Beth Ann Bovino is an economist makes this oral footnote stand out as very credible.

Here Megan reminds her audience that even in Lexington, Kentucky, hurricanes have relevance, which is reflected in higher gas prices and energy costs.

Megan could have further developed her main point and maintained audience interest with an example or a concrete story.

Again, Megan offers a clear and fluent section transition.

Again, Megan makes her emotional appeal stronger by showing before and after pictures.

Megan could have developed this point a bit more, perhaps by giving a specific example of someone whose life was altered.

companies will often claim that it is the one—wind or water—the homeowner is uninsured for.)

Price gouging is another financial challenge hurricane victims face. When families and businesses begin the process of rebuilding, people come from outside areas to help with labor and materials and will charge exorbitant fees. An example of this is when my father needed people to help remove two trees from our home in September 2005 after Hurricane Rita.

To close, I'd like to remind you that hurricanes affect victims who live in their direct path and the country as a whole. To understand some of these effects, we talked about how hurricanes work, how they affect our country and daily lives, and the impacts they have on the lives of people who live through them. Maybe knowing some of these facts will help each of us appreciate our homes and our families just a little bit more. *(Handout: Hurricane tracking charts)*

Megan does a nice job concluding her speech by summarizing her main points and tying back to her introduction.

Notice how Megan waits until the end of her speech to distribute her handout. That way, she kept the focus on her message during the speech.

All in all, this is a well-presented, informative speech with sufficient documentation.

Summary

An informative speech is one whose goal is to explain or describe facts, truths, and principles in a way that stimulates interest, facilitates understanding, and increases the likelihood that audiences will remember. In short, informative speeches are designed to educate an audience.

Effective informative speeches are intellectually stimulating, relevant, creative, memorable, and address diverse learning styles. We can inform by describing something, defining it, comparing and contrasting it with other things, narrating stories about it, or demonstrating it.

Two common informative speech frameworks are process speeches, in which the steps of making or doing something are shown, and expository speeches, which are well-researched explanations of complex ideas. Types of expository speeches include those that explain political, economic, social, religious, or ethical issues; those that explain events or forces of history; those that explain a theory, principle, or law; and those that explain a creative work.

Challenge Resource and Assessment Center

CourseMate Now that you have read Chapter 12, use your Speech Communication CourseMate for *The Challenge of Effective Speaking* for quick access to the electronic resources that accompany this text. These resources include the following:

- **Study tools** that will help you assess your learning and prepare for exams (*digital glossary, key term flash cards, review quizzes*).
- **Activities and assignments** that will help you hone your knowledge and build your public speaking skills throughout the course (*Speech Snippets, Speech Assignments, Action Step*

Activities). Many of these activities allow you to compare your answers with those provided by the authors and, if requested, submit your answers to your instructor.

- **Media resources** that will help you explore communication concepts online (*Web Resources*), develop your speech outlines (*Speech Builder Express 3.0*), watch and critique videos of sample speeches (*Interactive Video Activities*), upload your speech videos for peer reviewing and critique other students' speeches (*Speech Studio online speech review tool*), and download chapter reviews so you can study when and where you'd like (*Audio Study Tools*).

This chapter's video resources are featured in this end-of-chapter section.

1. **Impromptu Speech Activity:** You will draw three slips of paper from a container offered by your instructor. Each slip will identify a historical event or historical figure on it. Select one event you'd like to experience or figure you'd like to meet if you could travel back in time. Do a two- to three-minute impromptu speech about why you'd like to experience that historical event or meet that historical figure if you could travel back in time and why.

2. **Assessment Activity A:** Select a current event that's "in the news" today. Learn more about it from three different sources (e.g., a local newspaper, a national news broadcast, and an online blog or social networking site). Compare what you learn from each source and evaluate the ways in which the source cited research, acknowledged fact checking, and established the credentials for sources. Which source seems to be most credible as a result and why? Prepare a two- to three-page reflection paper explaining your conclusion. Be sure to attach copies or transcripts of the three sources.

3. **Assessment Activity B:** Identify a celebrity (e.g., television or movie actor, sports star, singer, etc.). Learn more about the person you've identified by visiting his or her personal website or blog, a social networking site devoted to the him or her, and a celebrity gossip magazine. How does the information shared about him or her on each source differ, and how does that shape your understanding of who he or she is? Which one seems most ethical based on the ethical communication principles we discuss in this book and why? Prepare a two- to three-page paper comparing the similarities and differences and your conclusions.

Web Resource

12.1: Thinking Like a Genius (240)

Video Resources

1. Use your Interactive Video Activities to watch, analyze, and see the transcript and outlines for the informative speeches "Flag Etiquette," "Making Ethanol," and "Understanding Hurricanes." (251, 262)

2. Use Speech Studio to upload a video of your own informative speech for feedback from your instructor and classmates. Or search for other students' informative speeches—do their speeches give you ideas for how you could make your speech more effective?

✓ SPEECH Studio

Ethical communicators use logos, ethos, and pathos in ways that demonstrate honesty, fairness, and responsibility.

13

understanding persuasive messages

Rick loves his golden retriever, Trini. He lives in an apartment right downtown and enjoys taking Trini for walks twice a day, but he wishes there was a place nearby where he could let Trini off her leash to run. He decides to try to persuade the city council to fence off an area of a large inner-city park to turn it into a dog park where owners can let their dogs run free. He learned he needed to circulate a petition about the idea, get at least 500 others to sign it, and collect $1,000 in donations to help pay for the fence. Rick easily gathered more than enough signatures in a few weeks of knocking on doors, but he had raised less than half of the $1,000. He wonders what he can do to persuade more people to actually donate money for the cause.

This scenario is not unusual. As was the case with Rick and the downtown dog park, whenever we attempt to convince others to agree with our position or behave a certain way, we actually construct and present persuasive messages. How successful we are, however, depends on how effectively we employ persuasive strategies in doing so. **Persuasion** is the process of influencing people's attitudes, beliefs, values, or behaviors. **Persuasive speaking** is the process of doing so in a public speech.

Persuasive messages are pervasive. Whether we are attempting to convince others or others are attempting to influence us, we are constantly involved in influencing or being influenced. Friends persuade us to go to a particular movie or to eat at a certain restaurant, salespeople persuade us to buy a certain sweater or pair of shoes, and advertisements bombard us whenever we turn on the radio or television, or surf the Internet. It is critical to understand persuasion so you can critically examine and evaluate the persuasive messages you receive and you can create effective and ethical persuasive messages of your own.

We begin our two-chapter discussion of persuasive speaking by first describing the nature of persuasive messages and the rhetorical strategies used in them. Next, using the Elaboration Likelihood Model (ELM), we explain how people process persuasive messages. Then, we focus specifically on how to use the rhetorical strategies of logos, ethos, and pathos to develop your persuasive messages and offer guidelines for you to consider when evaluating and constructing them.

The Nature of Persuasion

We draw on the work of the Greeks and Romans to define *persuasion* as logical and well-supported arguments developed through rhetorical appeals to logos, ethos, and pathos. Argument, in this context, is not synonymous with "quarrel" as we sometimes define it today. Rather, **argument** means articulating a position with the support of logos, ethos, and pathos.[1] **Logos** is a means of persuasion in which you construct logical arguments that support your point of view. **Ethos** is the means of persuasion in which you argue that your competence, credibility, and good character should persuade others to accept your point of view. **Pathos** is a means of persuasion in which you appeal to the emotions of others so that they accept your point of view.[2]

persuasion: the process of influencing people's attitudes, beliefs, values, or behaviors

persuasive speaking: the process of influencing people's attitudes, beliefs, values, or behaviors in a public speech

argument: articulating a position with the support of logos, ethos, and pathos

logos: a means of persuasion in which you construct logical arguments that support your point of view

ethos: a means of persuasion in which you argue that your competence, credibility, and good character should persuade others to accept your point of view

pathos: a means of persuasion in which you appeal to the emotions of others so that they accept your point of view

Throughout this book, we have highlighted the roles logos, ethos, and pathos play in developing effective messages. That's because informing, which we can think of as *teaching*, and persuading, which we can think of as *leading*, are different in purpose but related in process. To remember new information, we have to believe it is factual, relevant, and important, so part of your task when giving an informative speech is to convince your audience about the truthfulness, relevance, and importance of your message. Similarly, before we will be convinced to believe or do something, we must understand (be informed about) what taking that stance or action means.

The speaker's primary goal is to differentiate persuasive messages from informative ones. For example, Susan is a petrochemical engineering student taking a speech course. Last semester, she completed a term project on the Deep Water Horizon oil spill. For the paper, she researched and reported on the errors, engineering and human, that led to the massive oil spill in the Gulf of Mexico, as well as the new regulations that have been implemented since then. So she decided to use her expertise on this topic for her speeches. For her informative speech, her goal was to explain the errors that led to the explosion and subsequent oil spill. For her first persuasive speech, her goal was to convince the class that the sequence of events that led to the Deep Water Horizon spill could not happen again, and that drilling for oil offshore in deep water is safe. In her second persuasive speech, her goal was to motivate her classmates to take action to reduce their oil dependence by recycling the plastic they use and limiting or avoiding drinks packaged in plastic bottles.

While all speakers are expected to behave ethically, persuasive speakers have an extra burden to demonstrate that what they are advocating is in the best interest of the audience. So persuasive speakers must evaluate their message strategies and eliminate those that even begin to violate the ethical principles of truthfulness, integrity, fairness, respect, and responsibility.

Now that you have a basic understanding of the nature of persuasion, let's look more closely at how people think about the persuasive messages they receive.

Reflect on Ethics

WHAT WOULD *YOU* DO?

TWITTERPATED: LOBBYING IN CYBERSPACE

In her April 25, 2010, article in the *Washington Post*, Cecilia Kang reported that "employees of companies with interests in Washington are chattering online to shape opinions in hard-to-detect ways."[3] For example, P. J. Rodriguez tweets about a variety of topics, including his opinion about Federal Communications Commission (FCC) technology policy issues. Rodriguez's Twitter profile simply says he is a "pop culture maven and cable blogger." What his profile does not say, however, is that he works for the National Cable and Telecommunications Association (NCTA) and is a public relations specialist for Comcast, Cox, and Time Warner Cable. In other words, he's a lobbyist for the telecommunications industry.

Kang goes on to report that AT&T spent 15 percent more on its lobbying budget in the first quarter of 2010 than it did in all of 2009, and Google's lobbying budget rose by 57 percent. Lobbyists once visited congressional representatives personally to make their arguments. Now they are trying to influence lawmakers in record numbers as "anyone on the Web," with no rules or regulations compelling them to disclose who they really are or whose interests they represent.

1. What, if any, ethical communication principles are lobbyists like Rodriguez violating?
2. What, if any, harm is being done by individuals who attempt to persuade others online without disclosing whose interests they represent?
3. What, if anything, should the FCC do with regard to privacy and disclosure of lobbyist interests on the Internet?
4. Where would you draw the line regarding open or restricted access to Internet users and why?

How People Process Persuasive Messages: The Elaboration Likelihood Model (ELM)

Do you remember times when you listened carefully and thought about something of which someone was trying to convince you? Do you remember consciously thinking over what had been said and making a deliberate decision? Do you remember other times when you only half listened and made up your mind quickly based on your "gut" feeling about the truthfulness of what had been said? What determines how well we listen to and how carefully we evaluate the hundreds of persuasive messages we hear each day? Richard Petty and John Cacioppo developed a model that explains how likely people are to spend time evaluating information (such as the arguments that they hear in a speech) in an *elaborate* way, using their critical thinking skills, rather than processing information in a simpler, less critical manner. Called the Elaboration Likelihood Model (ELM), this theory can be used by speakers to develop persuasive speeches that will be influential with audience members regardless of how they process.

The model suggests that people process information in one of two ways. One way is intense and more time consuming. People using this "central route" listen carefully, think about what is said, and may even mentally elaborate on the message. They base their decision to agree with and possibly take action primarily on appeals to logic and reasoning (logos). The second way, called the "peripheral route," is a shortcut that relies on simple cues such as a quick evaluation of the speaker's competence, credibility, and character (ethos) or a gut check about what the listener feels (pathos) about the message.

According to the ELM, what determines if we use the central or peripheral route is how important we perceive the issue to be for us. When we feel involved with an issue, we are willing to expend the energy necessary for processing on the central route. When the issue is less important, we take the peripheral route. So how closely your audience members will follow your arguments depends on how involved they feel with your topic. For example, if you have a serious chronic illness that is expensive to treat, you are more likely to pay attention to and evaluate for yourself any proposals to change your health-care benefits. If you are healthy, you are likely to quickly agree with whatever someone you perceive to be credible suggests or go along with a proposal that seems compassionate.

The ELM also suggests that, when we form attitudes as a result of central processing, we are less likely to change our minds than when our attitudes have been formed based on peripheral cues. You can probably remember times when in the moment you were swayed by a powerful speaker but on later reflection you regretted your action and changed your mind. Likewise, based on information you have heard and spent time thinking about, you probably have some strongly held beliefs that are not easily changed. If you'd like to learn more about ELM, and persuasion in general, use your CourseMate for *Challenge* to access **Web Resource 13.1: Elaboration Likelihood Model**.

Understanding how people process persuasive messages aids you when you are preparing your speeches. Aristotle, the Greek philosopher who wrote *The Rhetoric*, defined rhetoric as the ability to discover in a certain case the available means of persuasion.[4] Those available means of persuasion, which we call rhetorical strategies, are logos, ethos, and pathos. So, when you prepare a persuasive speech, part of your preparation will entail figuring out the logical arguments, credibility, and emotions related to your topic and fit them to the audience and occasion (rhetorical situation). Logos strategies will be used by audience members who use the central processing route to decide if they believe you. Ethos and pathos strategies will be used by listeners who process on the peripheral route. Let's now take a closer look at each of these strategies.

CourseMate

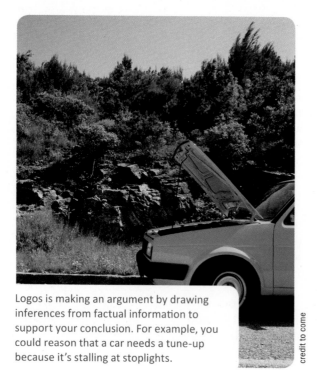

Logos is making an argument by drawing inferences from factual information to support your conclusion. For example, you could reason that a car needs a tune-up because it's stalling at stoplights.

credit to come

The Rhetorical Strategy of Logos

Audience members who process on the central route will analyze and evaluate the logic of the arguments you make. So, to frame effective arguments, you need to understand the reasoning process and how to build and test the different types of arguments.

Two Types of Reasoning

When you **reason** with an audience, you make an argument by drawing inferences from factual information to support your conclusions.[5] Thus, when you show your friend that the engine of his car is "missing" at slow speeds and stalling at stoplights, you can reason that the car needs a tune-up. You might say, "Jim, your car needs a tune-up. Why? Because the car is missing at slow speeds and stalling at stoplights." You can make arguments by reasoning inductively or deductively. **Inductive reasoning** is arriving at a general conclusion based on several pieces of specific evidence. So your argument reasons from specifics (pieces of evidence) to reach a general conclusion. When we reason inductively, how much our audience agrees with our conclusion depends on the number, quality, and typicality of each piece of evidence you offer. For Jim's car, an inductive argument might look like this:

> *Evidence: Jim's car is missing at slow speeds.*
>
> *Evidence: Jim's car is stalling at stoplights.*
>
> *Logical conclusion: Jim's car needs a tune-up.*

Whereas inductive reasoning argues from specific instances to a general conclusion, deductive reasoning argues from a generally accepted conclusion and applies it to a specific incident. **Deductive reasoning** is arguing that if something is true for everything that belongs to a certain class (**major premise**) and a specific instance is part of that class (**minor premise**), then we must conclude that what is true for all members of the class must be true in the specific instance (logical conclusion). This three-part form of deductive reasoning is called a **syllogism**. For Jim's car, a syllogism might look like this:

> *Major premise: Cars need a tune-up when the engine misses consistently at slow speeds.*
>
> *Minor premise: Jim's car is missing at slow speeds.*
>
> *Conclusion: Jim's car needs a tune-up.*

With this introduction to the two types of reasoning, let's now look at how these are used to form and test arguments.

Forming Arguments

Stephen Toulmin,[6] a philosopher and rhetorician, developed a model to explain the form of everyday arguments. His model has three major elements: the claim, the support, and the warrant.

CLAIM

The **claim** is the conclusion the speaker wants the audience to believe. In our simple example, the claim in both the inductive and deductive argument is

reasoning: the mental process of making an argument by drawing inferences from factual information to reach a conclusion

inductive reasoning: arriving at a conclusion based on a series of pieces of evidence

deductive reasoning: arriving at a conclusion based on a major premise and minor premise

major premise: a general principle that most people agree upon

minor premise: a specific point that fits within the major premise

syllogism: the three-part form of deductive reasoning

claim: the proposition or conclusion to be proven

"Jim's car needs a tune-up." A claim may ask the audience to accept what the speaker is saying as a fact, or as the best policy, or as a superior value.

SUPPORT

The **support** is the reason or evidence the speaker offers as the grounds for accepting the conclusion. You can support a claim with facts, opinions, experiences, and observations. In the car example, the support for the inductive argument includes two reasons, "missing at slow speeds" and "stalling at stoplights." But, if you look closely, you will notice that both of these reasons supporting the claim that Jim's car needs a tune-up are also claims that need to be backed up with specific evidence. For example, while the statement "The car misses at slow speeds" supports the need for a tune-up, without specific evidence, it is simply a claim that may or may not be true. So at times you will need to provide evidence for one of the grounds you have used in justifying your claim. In outline form, our inductive example looks like this:

Specific goal: I want Jim to believe that his car needs a tune-up because it fits the criteria for cars that need tune-ups. (claim)

> ***I***. *The car misses at slow speeds. (reason and claim)*
> > ***A***. *On Tuesday, it was missing when driven below 20 mph. (evidence)*
> > ***B***. *On Wednesday, it did the same thing. (evidence)*
> ***II***. *The car stalls at stoplights. (reason and claim)*
> > ***A***. *It stalled three times at lights on Monday. (evidence)*
> > ***B***. *It stalled each time I stopped at a light yesterday. (evidence)*

WARRANT

In Toulmin's model, the **warrant** is the logical statement that connects the support to the claim.[7] Sometimes, the warrant of an argument is verbalized, but other times, it is simply implied. For instance, a person who claims that "the car needs a tune-up" on the basis of "missing" and "stalling at stoplights" may verbalize the reasoning process with the warrant, "Missing at slow speeds and stalling at lights *are common indications, or signs,* that the car needs a tune-up." Or the speaker may just assume you understand that these are signs of a car that needs a tune-up.

Although you may not actually state your warrants during the speech itself, identifying the type of warrants you are planning to use will allow you to build arguments that are persuasive. Similarly, as a listener, your ability to discern warrants will help you evaluate whether or not to agree with the claim.

Using C for claim (conclusion), S for support (reasons and evidence), and W for warrant (explanation of the reasoning process), we can write the reasoning for the proposition in our example in outline form as follows:

> ***C*** *I want Jim to believe that the car needs a tune-up.*
> ***S*** *I. The engine misses at slow speeds.*
> ***S*** *II. The car stalls at stoplights.*
> ***W*** *(I believe this reasoning is sound because missing and stalling are major indicators—signs—of the need for a tune-up.) (The warrant is written in parentheses because it may not be verbalized when the speech is given.)*

Types and Tests of Arguments

Although an argument *always* includes a claim and support, different logical relationships can exist between the claim and the support on which it is based. Four types of arguments commonly used in persuasive speeches are sign, example, analogy, and causation.

ARGUING FROM SIGN

If certain events, characteristics, or situations always or usually accompany something, those events, characteristics, or situations are signs. You **argue from sign**

---

support: the reason or evidence the speaker offers as the grounds for accepting the conclusion

warrant: the logical statement that connects the support to the claim

---

SPEECH SNIPPET

Creating an Argument Using Toulmin's Model

Nathan wanted his listeners to agree that people should get six to seven hours of sleep at night. So he developed this argument:

C I want listeners to agree that we should try to get six to seven hours of sleep at night.

S Sleep produces melatonin, which can prevent cancer.

S Sleep reduces stress.

S Sleep improves mental alertness and memory.

W (I believe these benefits are *major reasons* to agree that we should strive for at least six hours of sleep at night.)

---

argue from sign: to cite information that signals the claim when you support a claim by providing evidence that the events that signal the claim have occurred. For instance, your doctor may claim that you have had an allergic reaction because you have hives and a slight fever.

The general warrant for reasoning from sign can be stated as follows: When phenomena that usually or always accompany a specific situation occur, then we can expect that specific situation is occurring (or will occur). So the warrant for the allergy argument can be stated as follows: "Hives and a slight fever are indicators (signs) of an allergic reaction."

Let's look at this argument in outline form:

    C You have had an allergic reaction.
    S A. You have hives.
        B. You have a slight fever.
    W (Hives and a slight fever are signs of an allergic reaction.)

Signs should not be confused with causes; signs accompany a phenomenon but do not bring about, lead to, or create the claim. In fact, signs may actually be the effects of the phenomenon. A rash and fever don't cause an allergic reaction; they are indications, or effects, of a reaction.

If in analyzing Juanita's campaign, you notice that she has more campaign workers than all other candidates combined and that a greater number of people from all segments of the community are wearing "Juanita for President" buttons, you may reason "Juanita's campaign has the key signs of an election victory."

A speech outline using the sign argument would look like this:

    C Juanita Martinez will be elected.
    S A. Juanita has more campaign workers than all other candidates combined.
        B. A greater number of community members are wearing her campaign buttons.
    W (The presence of a greater number of campaign workers and buttons than the opponents have is a sign/indicator of victory.)

When arguing from sign, you can make sure that your argument is valid by answering the following questions.

1. **Do the signs cited always or usually indicate the conclusion drawn?** Do large numbers of campaign workers and campaign buttons always (or usually) indicate election victory? If the data can occur independently of the conclusion, then they are not necessarily indicators. If the signs cited do not usually indicate the conclusion, then you can question the reasoning on that basis.

2. **Are a sufficient number of signs present?** Are campaign workers and buttons enough to indicate a victory? Several signs often indicate events or situations. If enough signs are not present, then the conclusion may not follow. If there are insufficient signs, then you can question the reasoning on that basis.

3. **Are contradictory signs in evidence?** Are campaign buttons thrown away in great numbers? If signs usually indicating different conclusions are present, then the stated conclusion may not be valid. If you believe that contradictory signs are evident, then you can question the reasoning on that basis.

ARGUING FROM EXAMPLE

argue from example: to support your claim by providing one or more individual examples

You **argue from example** when the support statements you use are examples of the claim you are making. For almost any topic, it is easy to find examples. So you are likely to use arguing from example quite frequently. The warrant for an argument from example—its underlying logic—is, "What is true in the examples provided is (or will be) true in general or in other instances."

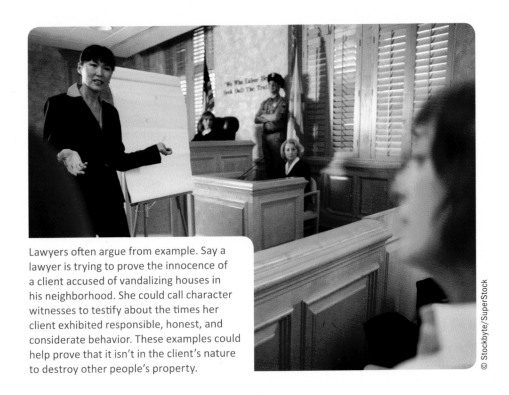

Lawyers often argue from example. Say a lawyer is trying to prove the innocence of a client accused of vandalizing houses in his neighborhood. She could call character witnesses to testify about the times her client exhibited responsible, honest, and considerate behavior. These examples could help prove that it isn't in the client's nature to destroy other people's property.

© Stockbyte/SuperStock

Suppose you are supporting Juanita Martinez for president of the local neighborhood council. One of the reasons you present is the claim that "Juanita is electable." In examining her résumé to find support for this claim, you find several examples of her previous victories. She was elected treasurer of her high school junior class, chairperson of her church youth group, and president of her college sorority. Each of these is an example that gives support to the claim. What would the warrant statement for this argument look like? You could say, "What was true in several instances (Juanita has been elected in three previous races) is true or will be true in general or in other instances (she will be electable in this situation)."

Let's look at this argument in speech analysis form:

C *Juanita Martinez is electable.*
S *Juanita has won previous elections.*
   A. *Juanita won the election for treasurer of her high school junior class.*
   B. *Juanita won the election for chairperson of her church youth group.*
   C. *Juanita won the election for president of her sorority.*
W *(Because Juanita Martinez was elected to previous offices, she is electable for this office.)*

When arguing from example, you can make sure your argument is valid by answering the following questions.

1. **Are enough examples cited?** Are three elections (junior class treasurer, youth group chairperson, and sorority president) enough examples to make your audience believe that your claim is true? Because the instances cited should represent most or all possibilities, enough must be cited to satisfy the listeners that the instances are not isolated or handpicked.

2. **Are the examples typical?** Are the three examples typical of all of Juanita's campaigns for office? Typical means that the examples cited must be similar to or representative of most or all within the category. If examples are not typical, they do not support the argument. For instance, because all three of these successes came in youth organizations, they may not be typical of

election dynamics in community organizations. If the three examples are not typical, then the logic of the argument can be questioned. As a speaker, you might search for additional examples that are typical.

3. **Are negative examples accounted for?** In searching for supporting material, we may find one or more examples that are exceptions to the argument we wish to make. If the exceptions are minor or infrequent, then they won't invalidate the argument. For instance, in college, Juanita may have run for chairperson of the Sociology Club and lost. That one failure does not necessarily invalidate the argument. If, however, negative examples prove to be more than rare or isolated instances, the validity of the argument is open to serious question. For instance, if you found that Juanita had run for office twelve times and was successful on only the three occasions cited, then the argument would be invalid.

If you believe that there are not enough examples, that the examples you have found are not typical, or that negative examples are common, then you will have only weak support for the claim and should consider making a different type of argument.

ARGUING FROM ANALOGY

You **argue from analogy** when you support a claim with a single comparable example that is so significantly similar to the subject of the claim as to be strong proof. The general statement of a warrant for an argument from analogy is, "What is true for situation A will also be true in situation B, which is similar to situation A" or "What is true for situation A will be true in all similar situations."

Suppose you wanted to argue that the Cherry Fork volunteer fire department should conduct a raffle to raise money for three portable defibrillator units. You could support the claim by analogy with a single example: Mack Fire Department conducted a raffle and raised enough money to purchase four units. The form for this argument from analogy looks like this:

   C Cherry Fork Fire Department should conduct a raffle to raise money for three portable defibrillator units.

   S Mack Fire Department, which is very similar to Cherry Fork, raised enough money through a raffle to purchase four units.

   W (What worked at a very similar volunteer fire department, Mack, will work at Cherry Fork.)

Let us return to the claim that Juanita is electable for president of the local neighborhood council to see how arguing from analogy works in a more complex situation. If you discover that Juanita has essentially the same characteristics as Paula Jefferson, who was elected president two years ago (both are very bright, both have a great deal of drive, and both have track records of successful campaigns), then you can use the single example of Paula to form a reason "Juanita has the same characteristics as Paula Jefferson, who was elected two years ago." This is analogical reasoning.

Let's look at how the Martinez argument would look in outline form:

   C Juanita Martinez is electable.

   S Juanita has the same characteristics as Paula Jefferson, who was elected two years ago. (This is also a claim, for which A, B, and C below are support.)

     A. Juanita and Paula are both very bright.

     B. Juanita and Paula both have a great deal of drive.

     C. Juanita and Paula both have won other campaigns.

   W (What was true for Paula will be true for Juanita, who is similar on the important characteristics.)

So the claim is supported through an analogy; then, additional support is offered to validate the analogy.

When arguing from analogy, you can make sure that your argument is valid by answering the following questions.

1. **Are the subjects being compared similar in every important way?** Are intelligence, drive, and track records the most important characteristics on which to determine electability? If criteria on which the subjects are being compared are not the most important ones, or if they really don't compare well, then you can question the reasoning on that basis.

2. **Are any of the ways in which the subjects are dissimilar important to the outcome?** If Paula is a native of the community, whereas Juanita has only been in the area for a year, is this dissimilarity important? When the dissimilarities outweigh the subjects' similarities, then conclusions drawn from the comparisons may be invalid.

ARGUING FROM CAUSATION

You **argue from causation** when you support a claim by citing events that have occurred that result in the claim. Reasoning from causation says that one or more of the events cited always (or almost always) brings about, leads to, or creates or prevents a predictable effect or set of effects.

argue from causation: to cite events that have occurred that result in the claim

The general warrant for arguments from causation can be stated as follows: If an event comes before another event and is associated with that event, then we can say that it is the cause of the event. "If A, which is known to bring about B, has been observed, then we can expect B to occur." For instance, you could develop a causal argument based on the relationship between mortgage interest rates and home sales: "Home sales are bound to increase during the next three months (claim) because mortgage interest rates have recently dropped markedly (causal event as support)."

Let's look at this type of argument in outline form:

   C *Home sales will increase.*
   S *Mortgage interest rates have dropped.*
   W *(Lower interest rates generally lead to higher home sales.)*

In researching Juanita's election campaign, you might discover that (1) she has campaigned intelligently and (2) she has won the endorsement of key community leaders. If these two events are usually associated with victory, then you can form the argument that Juanita has engaged in behavior that leads to campaign victories, thus supporting the claim that she is electable. The argument would look like this:

   C *Juanita Martinez will be elected.*
   S *A. Juanita has campaigned intelligently.*
      B. Juanita has key endorsements.
   W *(Intelligent campaigning and getting key endorsements lead to [cause] electoral victory.)*

When arguing from causation, you can make sure that your argument is valid by answering the following questions.

1. **Are the events alone sufficient to cause the stated effect?** Are intelligent campaigning and key endorsements important enough by themselves to result in winning elections? If the events are truly causes, it means that, if these events were eliminated, then the effect would be eliminated as well. If the effect can occur without these events occurring, then you can question the causal relationship.

2. **Do other events accompanying the cited events actually cause the effect?** Are other factors (such as luck, drive, friends) more important in determining whether a person wins an election? If the other events appear equally or more important in bringing about the effect, then you can question the causal relationship between the data cited and the conclusion. If you believe

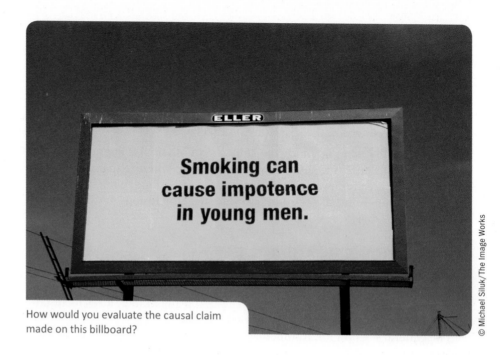

How would you evaluate the causal claim made on this billboard?

that other data caused the effect, then you can question the reasoning on that basis.

3. **Is the relationship between the causal events and the effect consistent?** Do intelligent campaigning and key endorsements always (or usually) yield electoral victories? If there are times when the effect has not followed the cause, then you can question whether a causal relationship exists. If you believe that the relationship between the cause and effect is not consistent, then you can question the reasoning on that basis.

COMBINING ARGUMENTS IN A SPEECH

An effective speech usually contains several reasons that are based on various types of arguments. For a speech with the goal "I want my audience to believe that Juanita is electable," you might choose to present three of the reasons we've been working with. Suppose you selected the following:

   I. *Juanita has run successful campaigns in the past. (argued by example)*

       A. *Juanita was successful in her campaign for treasurer of her high school class.*

       B. *Juanita was successful in her campaign for chairperson of her church youth group.*

       C. *Juanita was successful in her campaign for president of her sorority.*

   II. *Juanita has engaged in procedures that result in campaign victory. (argued by cause)*

       A. *Juanita has campaigned intelligently.*

       B. *Juanita has key endorsements.*

   III. *Juanita is a strong leader. (argued by sign)*

       A. *Juanita has more campaign workers than all other candidates combined.*

       B. *Juanita has a greater number of community members wearing her campaign buttons.*

Just as each of our reasons is presented as an argument, so too is the overall speech. So we need to determine what type of argument we are making. What relationship do all three of these reasons have with the overall claim? That is, how do running successful campaigns in the past, being engaged in procedures that result in victory, and being a strong leader relate to whether Juanita is electable? Are they examples of being electable? Do they cause one to be elected? Are they signs that usually accompany election? Do they distinguish a person who is electable from one who is not? As you study this, you will recognize that the warrant is best stated: "Running successful campaigns in the past, being engaged in procedures that result in victory, and being a strong leader are all signs of electability." Now you can test the soundness of the overall argument by using the tests of sign argument listed earlier.

Reasoning Fallacies

As you are developing your reasons and the arguments you will make, you should check to make sure that your reasoning is appropriate for the particular situation. This will allow you to avoid fallacies, or errors in reasoning. Five common fallacies to avoid are hasty generalization, false cause, either-or, straw man, and ad hominem arguments.

1. A **hasty generalization** is a fallacy that presents a generalization that is either not supported with evidence or is supported with only one weak example. Because the supporting material should be representative of all the supporting material that could be cited, enough supporting material must be presented to satisfy the audience that the instances are not isolated or hand-picked. Avoiding hasty generalizations requires you to be confident that the instances you cite as support are typical and representative of your claim. For example, someone who argued, "All Akitas are vicious dogs," whose sole piece of evidence was, "My neighbor had an Akita and it bit my best friend's sister," would be guilty of a hasty generalization. It is hasty to generalize about the temperament of a whole breed of dogs based on a single action of one dog.

    hasty generalization: a fallacy that presents a generalization that is either not supported with evidence or is supported with only one weak example

2. A **false cause** fallacy occurs when the alleged cause fails to be related to, or to produce, the effect. The Latin term for this fallacy is *post hoc, ergo propter hoc*, meaning "after this, therefore because of this." Just because two things happen one after the other does not mean that the first necessarily caused the second. Unlike people who blame monetary setbacks and illness on black cats or broken mirrors, be careful that you don't present a coincidental event as a cause unless you can prove the causal relationship. An example of a false cause fallacy is when a speaker claims that school violence is caused by television violence, the Internet, a certain song or musical group, or lack of parental involvement. When one event follows another, there may be no connection at all, or the first event might be just one of many causes that contribute to the second.

    false cause: a fallacy that occurs when the alleged cause fails to be related to, or to produce, the effect

3. An **either-or** fallacy is the argument that there are only two alternatives when, in fact, others exist. Many such cases are an oversimplification of a complex issue. For example, when Robert argued that "we'll either have to raise taxes or close the library," he committed an either-or fallacy. He reduced a complex issue to one oversimplified solution when there were many other possible solutions.

    either-or: a fallacy that argues there are only two alternatives when, in fact, there are many

4. A **straw man** fallacy is when a speaker weakens the opposing position by misrepresenting it in some way and then attacks that weaker (straw man) position. For example, in her speech advocating a seven-day waiting period to purchase handguns, Colleen favored regulation, not prohibition, of gun ownership. Bob argued against that by claiming "it is our constitutional right to bear arms." However, Colleen did not advocate abolishing the right to bear arms. Hence, Bob distorted Colleen's position, making it easier for him to refute.

    straw man: a fallacy that occurs when a speaker weakens the opposing position by misrepresenting it and then attacks that weaker position

Ad hominem arguments praise or attack a person rather than present an argument. Celebrity endorsements in advertisements are examples. This ad suggests that, if you like Jude Law, you should also like Dior cologne.

ad hominem: a fallacy that occurs when a speaker attacks or praises a person making an argument rather than addressing the argument itself

5. An **ad hominem** fallacy attacks or praises the person making the argument rather than addressing the argument itself. *Ad hominem* literally means "to the man." For example, if Jamal's support for his claim that his audience should buy an Apple computer is that Steve Jobs, the founder and current president of Apple Computer, is a genius, he is making an ad hominem argument. Jobs's intelligence isn't really a reason to buy a particular brand of computer. Unfortunately, politicians sometimes resort to ad hominem arguments when they attack their opponent's character rather than their platforms while campaigning for office. Bullying in person, over the Internet, and via text messaging is another example of ad hominem attacks that can have dire consequences. TV commercials that feature celebrities using a particular product are often guilty of ad hominem reasoning. For example, Robert De Niro and Jerry Seinfeld have both appeared in American Express commercials, and Gwyneth Paltrow has done ads for Estée Lauder. What makes any of these celebrities experts about the products they are endorsing?

Evaluating Evidence to Support Reasons

Although a reason may seem self-explanatory, before most audience members will believe it, they want to hear evidence that backs it up. As you did your research, you may have discovered more evidence to support a reason than you will be able to use in the time allotted for your speech. So you will have to choose what evidence you will present.

Verifiable factual statements are a strong type of supporting material. Suppose that, in a speech whose goal is to convince people that Alzheimer's research should be better funded, you give the reason "Alzheimer's disease is an increasing health problem in the United States." The following would be a factual statement that supported this reason: "According to a 2003 article in the *Archives of Neurology*, 4.5 million Americans had Alzheimer's in 2000 and is expected to affect 13.2 million Americans by the year 2050."

Statements from people who are experts on a subject can also be used as evidence to support a reason. For example, the statement "According to the surgeon general, 'By 2050 Alzheimer's disease may afflict 14 million people a year'" is an expert opinion.

Regardless of whether the evidence is fact based or opinion based, you will want to choose the best evidence you have found to support your point. You can use the answers to the following questions to help you select evidence that is likely to persuade your audience.

1. **Does the evidence come from a well-respected source?** This question involves both the people who offered the opinions or compiled the facts and the book, journal, or Internet source where they were reported. Just as some people's opinions are more reliable than others, so are some printed and Internet sources more reliable than others. Eliminate evidence that comes from a questionable, unreliable, or biased source.

2. **Is the evidence recent and, if not, is it still valid?** Things change, so information that was accurate for a particular time period may or may not be valid today. Consider when the evidence was gathered. Something that was true five years ago may not be true today. A trend that was forecast a year ago may have been revised since then. And a statistic that was reported last week may be based on data that were collected three years ago. So, whether it is a fact or an opinion, you want to choose evidence that is valid today.

For example, the evidence "The total cost of caring for individuals with Alzheimer's is at least $100 billion, according to the Alzheimer's Association and the National Institute on Aging"[8] was cited in a 2003 National Institutes of Health publication. But it is based on information from a study conducted using 1991 data, updated to 1994 data before being published. As a result, we can expect that annual costs would be higher today. If you choose to use this evidence, you should disclose the age of the data in the study and indicate that today the costs would be higher.

3. **Does the evidence really support the reason?** Some of the evidence you have found may be only indirectly related to the reason and should be eliminated in favor of evidence that provides more central support.

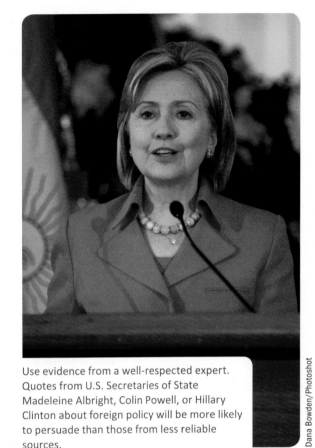

Use evidence from a well-respected expert. Quotes from U.S. Secretaries of State Madeleine Albright, Colin Powell, or Hillary Clinton about foreign policy will be more likely to persuade than those from less reliable sources.

Dana Bowden/Photoshot

4. **Will this evidence be persuasive for this audience?** Finally, you will want to choose evidence that your particular audience is likely to find persuasive. So, if you have a choice of two quotations from experts, you will want to use the one from the person your audience is likely to find more compelling.

The Rhetorical Strategy of Ethos

Not everyone will choose the central processing route to make a decision regarding a persuasive message. Some will choose to pay minimal attention to your arguments and will instead use simple cues to decide whether or not to accept your proposal. One important cue people use when they process information by the peripheral route is ethos. So, you will want to demonstrate good character via goodwill. Throughout the speech, you also will want to say and do things to convey competence and credibility.

Conveying Good Character

We turn again to the ancient Greek philosopher Aristotle (384–322 B.C.E.) who first observed that a speaker's credibility is dependent on the audience's perception of the speaker's goodwill. Today, we define **goodwill** as a perception the audience forms of a speaker who they believe understands them, empathizes with them, and is responsive to them.[9] In other words, goodwill is the audience's take on the speaker's intentions toward them. When audience members believe in the speaker's goodwill, they are willing to believe what the speaker says.

Let's take a closer look at what goodwill entails. The better you know audience members' experiences, circumstances, and desires, the better you will

goodwill: a perception the audience forms of a speaker who they believe understands them, empathizes with them, and is responsive to them formulate proposals that they will see as in their best interests. A thorough audience analysis will help you. For example, in his speech at the annual conference of the Property Casualty Insurers Association of America (PCI) on November 6, 2006, Julian James, director of Worldwide Markets for Lloyds, demonstrated understanding for the membership by referencing membership facts over the past year.

> *I would certainly contend that, following two consecutive record hurricane seasons, we have passed a key financial test. Debate after Katrina was largely about the detail of how we can do things better, and not about whether the industry could survive—as it was after 9/11. Not bad progress for an industry that faced almost double the value of claims from catastrophes in 2005 as it did for 9/11.... If we come out of this year intact, U.S. insurance industry profits in 2006 are forecast to be the best in a generation at $55 to $60 billion.*[10]

Not only must you understand your audience, but speakers who show goodwill also empathize with their audience. **Empathy** is the ability to see the world through the eyes of someone else. When we empathize, we put aside our own ideas and feelings and try to experience something from another's point of view. If you do not understand your audience, you will be unable to empathize with them. But empathizing requires you to go beyond understanding to also identify emotionally with your audience members' views.

Empathizing with the views of the audience doesn't mean that you accept their views as your own. It does mean that you acknowledge them as valid. Although your speech may be designed to change audience members' views, the sensitivity you show to audience members' feelings will demonstrate your goodwill. Julian James demonstrates empathy for the reputation of business and industry today:

> *So far the industry's finances have rarely looked better. But not everyone is celebrating. With success in business comes greater scrutiny—just ask the oil industry.*
>
> *In recent weeks we have seen a growing vilification of insurers that is unprecedented and, I believe, wholly unwarranted. Take these recent headlines I came across:*
>
> > *From* USA Today: *"Insurance rates pummel Florida homeowners."*
> > *From* Dow Jones Market Watch: *"Sweet are the uses of adversity: Are insurers reeling from disaster or reeling in the profits?" (No prizes for guessing which side the authors came down on in that one.)*
> > *And from the* Niagara Falls Reporter: *"Insurance companies real villains in Hurricane Katrina's aftermath."*
>
> *If that is the kind of press the industry is getting in Niagara Falls, in upstate New York, you might wonder how we are being portrayed in the Gulf States.*[11]

Finally, to demonstrate goodwill, you want to be responsive to the audience. Speakers who are **responsive** show that they care about the audience by acknowledging feedback, especially subtle negative cues. This feedback may occur during the presentation, but it also may have occurred prior to the speech.

For example, Julian James reminded this audience about their responses to his speech at a previous PCI convention.

> *When I spoke to you at this conference, I posed a challenge and asked, "Do you want to take control of the insurance cycle... or do you want to stay a passenger?" The reaction was very interesting. One group said, "That's so obvious, why hasn't anyone said that before?" Others said, "Ah, but you're very young, you*

don't understand, insurance cycles are a fact of life, and you can't do anything
about them.". . . Ladies and gentlemen, four years ago, it may have felt like we
were standing at the cliff edge, looking into the abyss.

The good news is that, in the intervening period, we have made important
progress. . . . But we put our future in grave danger if we stop here. . . . The chal-
lenges we face today may be different, but the message from 2002 remains the
same: "Our thinking and behaviour must change if the insurance industry is to
be a stable, secure industry for our policy holders and shareholders of the future."
Let's not mess it up again.[12]

Conveying Competence and Credibility

Not surprisingly, we are more likely to be persuaded when we perceive a speaker to be competent and credible. You want your listeners to realize you are well informed about your topic. We propose the following strategies for increasing your audience's perception of your ethos so that your **terminal credibility**, their perception of your expertise at the end of your speech, is greater than your **initial credibility**, their perception of your expertise at the beginning of your speech.

1. **Explain your competence.** Unless someone has formally introduced you and your qualifications to your audience, your initial credibility will be low, and as you speak, you will need to tell your audience about your expertise. Sending these types of messages during the speech results in your achieving a level of **derived credibility** with your audience. You can interweave comments about your expertise into introductory comments and at appropriate places within the body of the speech.[13] If you've done a good deal of research on the topic, say so. If you have personal experience, say so. It's important for the audience to know why they can trust what you are saying.

2. **Establish common ground.** Identify with the audience by talking about shared beliefs and values related to your speech topic.[14] If the topic is controversial or your target audience is opposed to your position, establish common ground by showing empathy for your audience's position before trying to convince them to change. In so doing, you will increase your derived credibility since the audience will feel respected and understood.

3. **Use evidence from respected sources.** If you are not a recognized expert on your subject, you can increase your derived credibility by using supporting material from well-recognized, unbiased, and respected sources who are experts. So, if you have a choice between using a statistic from a known partisan organization or from a dispassionate professional association, choose the professional association. Likewise, if you can quote a local expert who is well known and respected by your audience or an international scholar with limited name recognition with your audience, use the local expert's opinion.

4. **Use nonverbal elements of delivery to enhance your image.** Your audience establishes its assessment of your initial credibility not only from what it has heard about you before you begin speaking but also from what it has observed about you by looking at you prior to your speech. So how you look and what you do in the few minutes before you speak are important.

Although professional attire enhances credibility in any speaking situation, it is particularly important for persuasive speeches. Research shows that attractive people are perceived as more competent, well organized, and confident.[15] Attire contributes to this, and persuasive speakers dressed more formally are perceived as more credible than those dressed casually or sloppily.[16] So your audience will assess your physical appearance in developing its initial judgment about your credibility. That's why it is important to "dress the part."

terminal credibility: perception of a speaker's expertise at the end of the speech

initial credibility: perception of a speaker's expertise at the beginning of the speech

derived credibility: strategies employed throughout the speech that signal a speaker's expertise

SPEECH SNIPPET

Establishing Common Ground

In his speech arguing against the death penalty, Lester used the common ground technique in his introduction when he said: "I'm sure that you, like me, value human life."

The audience will also notice how confident you appear as you prepare to address them. From the moment you rise to speak, you will want to convey through your nonverbal behavior that you are competent. Plant your feet firmly, glance at your notes, and then make eye contact or audience contact with one person or group before taking a breath and beginning to speak. These simple behaviors create a perception of competence and confidence.

Likewise, pause and establish eye contact upon finishing the speech. Just as pausing and establishing eye contact or audience contact before the speech enhance credibility, doing so upon delivering the closing lines of the speech has the same result.

5. **Use vocal expression to enhance your credibility.** Research shows that credibility is strongly influenced by how you sound. Speaking fluently, using a moderately fast rate, and expressing yourself with conviction makes you appear more intelligent and competent.[17] So you will want to practice until you can smoothly and confidently deliver your speech avoiding vocal interrupters like "ums," "uhs," "you knows," and "likes," all of which make you appear unsure of what you are saying and detract from your derived credibility.

Talk to the Animals

Brittany Smith,
Licensed Veterinary
Technician
Fairfax, Virginia

Photo courtesy of Brittany Smith

Every day Brittany Smith effectively persuades, convinces, and influences a diverse audience of listeners. Her audience is so diverse, in fact, that it often consists of assorted small animals! That's because she works in a veterinary hospital, providing hands-on nursing and giving therapeutic treatments.

Of course, Smith, 23, who earned her BS in Veterinary Medical Technology at Wilson College in Chambersburg, Pennsylvania, is also called upon to converse with humans. She meets and negotiates with representatives from pharmaceutical, medical supply, and medical machinery companies. She also supervises the care provided by the veterinary assistants working under her.

One of Smith's speaking challenges on the job is reprimanding her employees. She considers herself a very passive person, which could be considered a detriment to her credibility as a supervisor. "But," she says, "I can crack down if I have to." To increase her credibility when she has to "crack down," she organizes her thoughts before she speaks. For example, when she reprimanded two people who each claimed the other wasn't working, she made sure she could communicate her expectations clearly. "I made up a list of each person's responsibilities and showed it to them individually, one on one: 'These are my expectations.' They both understood very well."

> "When you converse with people, they analyze what you say.... Animals are much better listeners."

In college, Smith was required to take a communication course, so she took Effective Speaking. "We had to come up with a few different speeches: a toast, a tribute.... I was extremely scared. I practiced millions of times. If you have a better idea of what you're going to say you're less likely to mess up, or have to look down at your notes." Although her job doesn't require her to address large public groups, Smith routinely uses the skills she learned from her college course. "That class taught me how to outline. I outline what I want to say to drug reps as well as employees. It makes the conversation fluid." She also learned to cater to specific audiences. "Knowing your audience helps you change your approach—formal versus more relaxed and friendly, for example."

One of the most useful things regarding public speaking Smith has learned on the job is that you have to figure out how to stay relaxed. She used to get really nervous about speaking. But talking with impartial listeners—the animals—has helped her learn to calm herself. "Sometimes there is no better cure for a troubled psyche than to talk to a *being* that won't judge you. When you converse with people, they analyze what you say.... Animals are much better listeners. They don't care what you're saying—they are just happy to have your company!"

The Rhetorical Strategy of Pathos

When we are involved with something, we care about it and have an emotional stake in it. **Emotions** are the buildup of action-specific energy.[18] We can see simple examples of this when we observe how people's facial expressions change as they receive good or bad news. Smiling is one way to release our built-up feelings of happiness. Crying is a way to release our built-up feelings of sadness. When people experience the tension associated with any emotion, they look for a way to release the energy. So as a speaker, if you can involve your audience (give them an emotional stake) in what you are saying, they are more likely to use their energy to listen carefully and internalize your speech.[19] Let's look at how research from Robin Nabi shows how you can increase involvement by stimulating both negative and positive emotions in your speeches.[20]

emotions: the buildup of action-specific energy

Evoking Negative Emotions

Negative emotions are disquieting, so when people experience them, they look for ways to eliminate them. During your speech, if you can help your audience experience negative emotions, they will be more involved with what you are saying. As a result, they will be motivated to use their energy to listen carefully to you to see if you give them a way to reduce their feelings of discomfort. There are numerous negative emotions you can tap; in the following discussion, we describe five of the most common.

negative emotions: disquieting feelings people experience

FEAR

We experience **fear** when we perceive that we have no control over a situation that threatens us. We may fear physical harm or psychological harm. Fear is reduced when the threat is eliminated or when we escape. If, as a speaker, you can use examples, stories, and statistics that create fear in your audience, they will be more involved in hearing how your proposal can eliminate the source of their fear or allow them to escape. For example, in a speech whose goal was to convince the audience that they were at risk of developing high blood pressure, the speaker might begin by personalizing the statistics on heart disease.

fear: perceiving no control over a situation that threatens us

> One of every three Americans aged eighteen and older has high blood pressure. It is a primary cause of stroke, heart disease, heart failure, kidney disease, and blindness. It triples a person's chance of developing heart disease, boosts the chance of stroke seven times, and the chance of congestive heart failure six times. Look at the person on your right; look at the person on your left. If they don't get it, chances are, you will. Today, I'd like to convince you that you are at risk for developing high blood pressure.

GUILT

We feel **guilt** when we personally violate a moral, ethical, or religious code that we hold dear. Guilt is especially keen in situations where the violation is associated with how we believe we should conduct ourselves in relationship to others. We experience guilt as a gnawing sensation that we have done something wrong. When we feel guilty, we are energized or motivated to "make things right" or to atone for our transgression. As a speaker, you can evoke feelings of guilt in your audience so that they pay attention to your arguments. To be effective, your proposal must provide a way for the audience to repair or atone for the damage their transgression has caused or to avoid future violations. For example, in a speech designed to motivate the audience to take their turn as designated drivers, a speaker might evoke guilt like this:

guilt: feeling when we personally violate a moral, ethical, or religious code that we hold dear

> Have you ever promised your mom that you wouldn't ride in a car driven by someone who had been drinking? And then turned around and got in the car with

your buddy even though you both had had a few? You know that wasn't right. Lying to your mother, putting yourself and your buddy at risk... (pause) but what can you do? Well, today I'm going to show you how you can avoid all that guilt, live up to your promises to mom, and keep both you and your buddy safe.

SHAME

shame: feeling when we have violated a moral code and it is revealed to someone we think highly of

We feel **shame** when we have violated a moral code and it is revealed to someone we think highly of. The more egregious our behavior or the more we admire the person who has found out, the more shame we experience. When we feel shame, we are motivated to "redeem" ourselves in the eyes of that person. Likewise, we can be convinced to refrain from doing something to avoid feelings of shame. If in your speech you can evoke feelings of shame and then demonstrate how your proposal can either redeem someone after a violation has occurred or prevent feelings of shame, then you can motivate the audience to carefully consider your arguments. For example, in a speech advocating thankfulness, the speaker might use a shame-based approach by quoting the old saying, "I cried because I had no shoes until I met a man who had no feet."

ANGER

anger: feeling when we are faced with an obstacle in the way of something we want

When we are faced with an obstacle that stands in the way of something we want, we experience **anger**. We also experience anger when someone demeans us or someone we love. As with all emotions, the intensity of what we feel varies. We can be mildly annoyed, or we can experience a level of anger that short-circuits the reasoning process and leads to blind rage. Speakers who choose to evoke anger in their audience members must be careful that they don't incite so much anger that reasoning processes are short-circuited.

When we feel anger, we want to strike back at the person or overcome the situation that is thwarting our goals or demeaning us. So in your speeches, if you can rouse your audience's anger and then show how your proposal will enable them to achieve their goals or stop or prevent the demeaning that has occurred, you can motivate them to listen to you and think about what you have said. For example, suppose you want to convince the audience to support a law requiring the active notification of a community when a sex offender is released from prison and living in the neighborhood. You might arouse the audience's anger to get their attention by personalizing the story of Megan Kanka.

She was your little girl, just seven years old, and the light of your world. She had a smile that could bring you to your knees. And she loved puppies. So when that nice man who had moved in down the street invited her in to see his new puppy, she didn't hesitate. But she didn't get to see the puppy, and you didn't ever see her alive again. He beat her, he raped her, and then he strangled her. He packaged her body in an old toy chest and dumped it in a park. Your seven-year-old princess would never dig in a toy chest again or slip down the slide in that park. And that hurts. But what makes you really angry is she wasn't his first. But you didn't know that. Because no one bothered to tell you that the guy down the street was likely to kill little girls. The cops knew it. But they couldn't tell you. You, the one who was supposed to keep her safe, didn't know. Angry? You bet. Yeah, he's behind bars again, but you still don't know who's living down the street from you. But you can. There is a law pending before Congress that will require active notification of the community when a known sex offender takes up residence, and today I'm going to tell how you can help to get this passed.[21]

SADNESS

sadness: feeling when we fail to achieve a goal or experience a loss or separation

When we fail to achieve a goal or experience a loss or separation, we experience **sadness**. Unlike other negative emotions, whose energy is projected outward, when we feel sad, we tend to withdraw and become isolated. Because sadness, like the other negative emotions, is an unpleasant feeling, we look for ways to end it. This can happen through the actions of others when they notice our withdrawal and try to comfort us. Because we withdraw when we are sad, sadness helps us to focus inward, pondering what has happened and trying to make sense of it. As a result, when we are sad, we are already "looking for answers." So speeches that help us understand and find answers for what has happened can comfort us and help relieve this unpleasant feeling. For example, after 9/11, many Americans were sad. Yes, they were also afraid and angry, but overlaying it all was profound

When motivating listeners to attend to and remember your speech by appealing to negative emotions, be sure that your choice demonstrates ethical communication.

sadness for those who had been lost and what had been lost. The questions "Why? Why did they do this? Why do they hate us so?" capture the national melancholy. So, when politicians suggest that they understand the answers to these questions and can repair the relationships that led to 9/11, Americans listen and think about what they say.

Evoking Positive Emotions

Just as evoking negative emotions can cause audience members to internalize what you are saying, so too can you increase audience involvement with your proposal by tapping **positive emotions**, which are feelings that people enjoy experiencing. With negative emotions, our goal is to show how our proposal will help the audience to reduce or avoid the feeling. With positive emotions, our goal is to help the audience sustain or develop the feeling. Five of the positive emotions that can motivate the audience to become involved in listening to your arguments are discussed next.

positive emotions: feelings that people enjoy experiencing

HAPPINESS AND JOY

Happiness or joy is the buildup of positive energy we experience when we accomplish something, when we have a satisfying interaction or relationship, or when we see or possess objects that appeal to us. Think of how you felt when you won that ribbon in grade school or when you found out that you got an "A" on that volcano project in fourth grade. Think of how you felt when you heard that special someone say "I love you" for the very first time. Or think about the birthday when you received that toy you had been dreaming about. In each of these cases, you were happy, maybe even so happy that you were joyous. As a speaker, if you can show how your proposal will lead your audience members to be happy or joyful, then they are likely to listen and to think about your proposal. For example, suppose you want to motivate your audience to attend a couples encounter weekend where they will learn how to "rekindle" their relationship with a partner. If you can remind them about how they felt early in their relationship and then suggest how the weekend can reignite those feelings, they will listen.

happiness or joy: the buildup of positive energy when we accomplish something or have a satisfying interaction or relationship

PRIDE

When you experience self-satisfaction and an increase to your self-esteem as the result of something that you have accomplished or that someone you identify with has accomplished, you feel **pride**. "We're number one! We're number one!" is the chant of the crowd feeling pride in the accomplishment of "their" team. Whereas happiness is related to feelings of pleasure, pride is related to feelings of self-worth. So, if in your speech you can demonstrate how your proposal will help your audience members to feel good about themselves, they will be more

pride: feeling of self-satisfaction and increased self-esteem as the result of an accomplishment involved in hearing what you have to say. For example, suppose you want to persuade your audience to volunteer to work on the newest Habitat for Humanity house being constructed in your community. You might involve them by alluding to the pride they will feel when they see the house they have helped to build standing where there was once a vacant lot.

RELIEF

relief: feeling when a threatening situation has been alleviated

When a threatening situation has been alleviated, we feel the positive emotion of **relief**. In relief, the emotional energy that is experienced is directed inward, and we relax and put down our guard. Thus, relief is not usually accompanied by overt action. As a speaker, if you want to use relief as a way to motivate audience members to be involved with your arguments, then you will want to combine it with the negative emotion of fear. For example, suppose your goal is to convince the audience that they are not at risk for high blood pressure. You might use the same personalization of statistics that was described in the example of fear appeals, but instead of proving that the audience is at risk, you could promise relief. Your audience would then listen and evaluate whether they believed your arguments to experience relief from the fear of high blood pressure.

HOPE

hope: emotional energy that stems from believing something desirable is likely to happen

compassion: feeling of selfless concern for the suffering of another

The emotional energy that stems from believing something desirable is likely to happen is called **hope**. When you yearn for better things, you are feeling hope. Like relief, hope is a positive emotion that has its roots in a difficult situation. Whereas relief causes you to relax and let down your guard, hope energizes you to take action to overcome the situation. Hope empowers. As with relief, hope appeals are usually accompanied by fear appeals. So you can get audience members to listen to you by showing them how your proposal provides a plan for overcoming a difficult situation. In this problem-solution organization, you can embed both fear and hope appeals. For example, if your proposal is that adopting a low-fat diet will reduce the risk of high blood pressure, you can use the same personalization of statistics that were cited in the example of fear but change the ending to state: "Today, I'm going to convince you to beat the odds by adopting a low-fat diet." This offer of hope should influence your audience to listen to and adopt your plan.

COMPASSION

When we feel selfless concern for the suffering of another person and that concern energizes us to try to relieve that suffering, we feel **compassion**. Speakers can evoke audience members' feelings of compassion by vividly describing the suffering endured by someone. The audience will then be motivated to listen to see how the speaker's proposal plans to end that suffering. For example, when a speaker whose goal is to have you donate to Project Peanut Butter displays a slide of an emaciated child, claims that 13 percent of all Malawi children die of malnutrition, and states that for $10 you can save a child, he or she is appealing to your compassion.

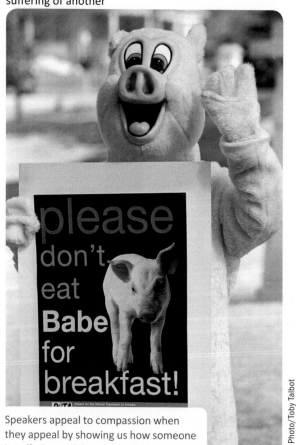

Speakers appeal to compassion when they appeal by showing us how someone is suffering and that we can help.

AP Photo/Toby Talbot

You can evoke negative emotions, positive emotions, or both as a way to encourage listeners to internalize your message. In the next section, we offer specific guidelines to do so effectively in your content, language, and delivery.

Guidelines for Appealing to Emotions

As you plan your speech, consider the following guidelines to appeal to emotions.

1. **Tell vivid stories.** Dramatize your arguments by using supporting material such as stories and testimonials that personalize the issue for listeners by appealing to specific emotions. In his speech on bone marrow donation, David Slater simply could have said, "By donating bone marrow—a simple procedure—you can save lives." Instead, he dramatized both the simplicity of the bone marrow donation procedure and the lifesaving impact with a short story designed to heighten audience members' feelings of compassion.

> *When Tricia Matthews decided to undergo a simple medical procedure, she had no idea what impact it could have on her life. But more than a year later, when she saw five-year-old Tommy and his younger brother Daniel walk across the stage of the Oprah Winfrey Show, she realized that the short amount of time it took her to donate her bone marrow was well worth it. Tricia is not related to the boys who suffered from a rare immune deficiency disorder treated by a transplant of her marrow. Tricia and the boys found each other through the National Marrow Donor Program, or NMDP, a national network which strives to bring willing donors and needy patients together. Though the efforts Tricia made were minimal, few Americans made the strides she did. Few of us would deny anyone the gift of life, but sadly, few know how easily we can help.*[22]

Notice how David used a compelling example to appeal to his listeners' emotions and personalize the information for them.

Similarly, Ryan Labor began his speech on shaken baby syndrome with the following vivid story designed to raise feelings of fear, anger, and sadness:

> *Last winter, two-year-old Cody Dannar refused to eat or play. He had a headache. Doctors said he just had the flu. After a couple weeks home with his mother, Cody felt better. Days later . . . Cody's headaches returned. Coming home from work the next afternoon, his parents found the babysitter frantically calling 911 and Cody lying rigid and unconscious on the floor. He didn't have the flu; in fact, he wasn't sick at all. The babysitter had caused his headaches. To quiet Cody down, she had shaken him, damaging the base of Cody's brain that now risked his life as he lay on the ground.*[23]

2. **Use startling statistics.** Statistics don't have to be boring; instead, when used strategically, they can evoke strong emotions. To provoke emotions, statistics need to be startling. A statistic may surprise because of its sheer magnitude. For example, in a speech urging the audience to attend a local protest march organized by the Mobilization for Global Justice, Cory used the following statistic to shame and anger his audience about the global problem of wealth distribution: "Did you know that the USA has 25.4 percent of the world's wealth? And of that, the top 10 percent of Americans control 71 percent?" Sometimes, by comparing two statistics, you can increase the emotional impact. For example, during his second main point, Cory used the following comparative statistic to highlight wealth disparity. "In the U.S., not only does the top 10 percent control 71 percent of the wealth, but the bottom 40 percent of Americans control less than 1 percent!" In Ryan's speech on shaken baby syndrome, he strengthened his emotional appeal by following his vivid story with these startling statistics:

> *Unfortunately, Cody isn't alone. Over one million infants and young children suffer from shaken baby syndrome annually while thousands die. . . . Only 15 percent survive without damage. The remaining children suffer from blindness, learning disabilities, deafness, cerebral palsy, or paralysis.*

3. **Incorporate listener relevance links.** You can also appeal to emotions by integrating listener relevance links because emotions are stronger when listeners feel personally involved. At a later point in Ryan's shaken baby syndrome speech, he appealed to emotions through listener relevance. Notice how he brings the problem close to each listener by suggesting the universality of the problem.

> *Jacy Showers, director of the first National Conference on shaken baby syndrome, says "shaking occurs in families of all races, incomes, and education levels" and "81 percent of SBS offenders had no previous history of child abuse." The reason? The offenders were so young, either babysitters or new parents.*

4. **Choose striking presentational aids.** Because "a picture is worth a thousand words," consider how you can reinforce your verbal message with dramatic presentational aids. Still pictures and short video clips at times create an emotional jolt that is difficult to achieve with words. Johnna used several before-and-after pictures of female celebrities Nicole Richie, Calista Flockhart, and Mary Kate Olsen to reinforce her point that emaciated celebrities were contributing to the eating disorder epidemic in teenage girls. Likewise, Anton used a fifteen-second video clip from the DVD *Zoned for Slavery: The Child Behind the Label*[24] to dramatize the problem of child labor in the global textile industry. His goal was to shame his audience members into sending one postcard to the manufacturer of their favorite brand of clothing asking about the working conditions of the workers who manufacture their clothing.

5. **Use descriptive and provocative language.** When developing your speech, include persuasive punch words—words that evoke emotion—where you can. Here's how Ryan used persuasive punch words to strengthen his emotional appeal:

> *The worst of all epidemics is a silent one. With the majority of all victims either infants or young children, shaken baby syndrome can be classified as a stealthy plague.... When shaken, the brain is literally ricocheted inside the skull, bruising the brain and tearing blood vessels coming from the neck... cutting off oxygen and causing the eyes to bulge.*

6. **Use nonverbal elements of delivery to reinforce your emotional appeal.** Even the most eloquently phrased emotional appeal will lose its impact unless the nonverbal parts of delivery heighten and highlight the emotional content of the message. Practice using your voice to emphasize what you are saying with the use of pauses, volume, and pitch to heighten and highlight the emotional content of your message. A dramatic pause before a startling statistic can magnify its emotional effect. Similarly, lowering or raising the volume or pitch of your voice at strategic places can create an emotional response. If you experiment as you practice out loud, you will find a combination of vocal elements that can enhance emotional appeal when delivering your speech.

7. **Use gestures and facial expressions that highlight the emotions you are conveying.** Your message will lose its emotional impact if you deliver it with a deadpan expression or if your demeanor contradicts the emotional content of your message. So, if you want your audience to feel angry, you should model this feeling by looking annoyed or livid or furious. You might clench your fists, furrow your brows, and frown. When you want to foster feelings of joy in your audience, you can smile, nod, and use other nonverbal gestures that are natural for you when you experience joy. Remember, as an ethical

speaker, you are appealing to emotions that you yourself feel about the situation, so allow yourself to experience these emotions as you practice. Then, when you give your speech, you will be more comfortable displaying your feelings for your audience.

To explore one speaker's use of emotional appeals, go to your CourseMate for *Challenge* to access **Web Resource 13.2: Terrorism and Islam: Maintaining the Faith.**

CourseMate

Summary

Persuasion is the process of influencing people's attitudes, beliefs, values, or behaviors, and persuasive speaking is doing so in a public speech. Persuasive messages differ from informative messages in that the primary goal is to seek agreement and sometimes to incite action. Because the goals of persuasion are loftier and the potential implications more acute than informing, both senders and receivers of persuasive messages must pay special attention to the ethical principles of communication when creating and interpreting them. The Elaboration Likelihood Model (ELM) describes how audiences process persuasive messages. Understanding this model helps us focus on how to use logos, ethos, and pathos appeals as we construct and delivery persuasive speeches, as well as when we evaluate the worth of the persuasive messages we encounter in our daily lives.

Logos is the means of persuasion devoted to appeals to logic and reasoning. You reason with your audience by making an argument that draws inferences from factual information to support a conclusion. You can reason inductively or deductively by addressing three basic elements of an argument. These are the claim, the support, and the warrant. Four common types of arguments used in persuasive messages are sign, example, analogy, and causation. When creating persuasive messages, it is important to avoid reasoning fallacies, and, when interpreting persuasive messages, it is important to discern them. Some common fallacies are hasty generalization, false cause, either-or, straw man, and ad hominem. Because you will rely on evidence to support your reasons, you must make sure it comes from a well-respected source, is still valid, is relevant to the argument, and is likely to persuade your audience.

Ethos is the means of persuasion devoted to conveying good character, competence, and credibility. You convey good character by demonstrating goodwill. Your goal is to encourage your audience to believe you understand them, empathize with them, and are responsive to them. You convey competence and credibility by explaining your competence, establishing common ground, using evidence from respected sources, and being nonverbally and vocally expressive in your delivery.

Pathos is the means of persuasion devoted to emotional appeals. You can appeal to negative emotions such as fear, guilt, shame, anger, and sadness. Or you can appeal to positive emotions such as happiness and joy, pride, relief, hope, and compassion. Some guidelines you can follow to appeal to emotions include telling vivid stories, using startling statistics, incorporating listener relevance links, using striking presentational aids and provocative language, and being vocally and visually expressive when delivering your message.

Employing these means of persuasion throughout your message will increase the likelihood of achieving your primary persuasive goal to seek agreement and perhaps also encourage certain actions.

Challenge Resource and Assessment Center

CourseMate Now that you have read Chapter 13, use your Speech Communication CourseMate for *The Challenge of Effective Speaking* for quick access to the electronic resources that accompany this text. These resources include the following:

- **Study tools** that will help you assess your learning and prepare for exams (*digital glossary, key term flash cards, review quizzes*).
- **Activities and assignments** that will help you hone your knowledge and build your public speaking skills throughout the course (*Speech Snippets, Speech Assignments, Action Step*

Activities). Many of these activities allow you to compare your answers with those provided by the authors and, if requested, submit your answers to your instructor.

- **Media resources** that will help you explore communication concepts online (*Web Resources*), develop your speech outlines (*Speech Builder Express 3.0*), watch and critique videos of sample speeches (*Interactive Video Activities*), upload your speech videos for peer reviewing and critique other students' speeches (*Speech Studio online speech review tool*), and download chapter reviews so you can study when and where you'd like (*Audio Study Tools*).

This chapter's video resource is featured in this end-of-chapter section.

Applying What You've Learned

1. **Impromptu Speech Activity:** Draw a common household product from a box of products your instructor provides. Some products in the box might be nonperishable foods (soup, cereal, snacks, etc.), cleaning supplies (window wash, hand soap, dishwashing liquid), and paper products (toilet paper, paper towels, napkins). Prepare a two- to three-minute speech identifying how the product you selected appeals to logos, ethos, and pathos.

2. **Assessment Activity A:** Watch a television commercial for a similar product that airs on a cable news network, sports network, and family channel. Identify similar and different rhetorical appeals used in them. Offer possible reasons

based on the ELM for using similar and different appeals. Prepare a one- to two-page reflection paper describing what you discovered and the assessment you drew from it.

3. **Assessment Activity B:** Consider an interaction you had in the last week with a friend or family member who convinced you (a) *to do something* you hadn't planned on doing (e.g., go to a movie, attend an event) or (b) *not to do something* you had intended to do (e.g., a household chore, homework). What rhetorical strategies can you identify that influenced your decision? Prepare a one- to two-page paper documenting examples of logos, ethos, and pathos that persuaded you.

Web Resources

13.1: Elaboration Likelihood Model (271)

13.2: Terrorism and Islam: Maintaining the Faith (291)

Video Resource

1. Check out Speech Studio to see how other students approach logos, ethos, and pathos in their persuasive speeches. Do any of them use logical fallacies in their speeches? Or record a speech you're working on, upload it to Speech Studio, and ask your peers for their feedback. What feedback could you use to fine-tune your persuasive speech before you give it in class?

Ted Aljibe/AFP/Getty Images

CALIFORNIA ... ON FOR
JOBS AND E... GROWTH

Ethical communicators demonstrate
responsibility by considering
implications of their persuasive
message on the audience.

14

"persuasive speaking"

What's the Point?

**QUESTIONS YOU'LL BE ABLE TO ANSWER AFTER READING
THIS CHAPTER:**

1. Why is it important to consider the initial audience attitude
   when constructing your persuasive speech goal?
2. How do you phrase a persuasive speech goal as a
   proposition?
3. What are some dispositional persuasive speech frameworks?
4. What are some actuation persuasive speech frameworks?
5. What ethical communication guidelines should you follow as
   a persuasive speaker?

As Steve finished his speech on "Taking Back the Neighborhood: Get Out the Vote!" the audience rose to their feet and began to chant, "No more! No more! No more! No more! ..." It was clear to him that he had made an impact. Not only had he convinced his audience, but he could also see that they were visibly angry and ready for action. As he was leaving the platform, he heard a member of the audience shout out, "You heard him. It's time! Voting won't do any good. Let's go take what is ours. Take to the streets! Get yours!" In the riot that ensued, three neighborhood shops were ransacked, ten cars were set on fire, and twenty-three people were arrested. The next day as he toured the neighborhood and saw firsthand the wreckage his speech had led to, all he could think was, "This wasn't what I meant. This isn't what I wanted."

In the previous chapter, we focused on how persuasive messages employ what Aristotle called the available means of persuasion (logos, ethos, and pathos) to seek agreement or to encourage action. In this chapter, we focus on how to organize those rhetorical appeals into persuasive speeches that are both effective and ethical. In the opening vignette, Steve's speech not only convinced his audience to agree with his point of view, but it also left them so emotionally agitated that when one member of the audience advocated action, the rest followed. And the actions they took went well beyond what Steve wanted the audience to do.

Recall that in the previous chapter we introduced you to the Elaboration Likelihood Model (ELM), which illustrates that there are two routes audience members use when they mentally process a persuasive message. If audience members have a personal stake in what you are saying, they are more likely to take the central route and to carefully evaluate your arguments and supporting materials. They will also be wary of overt attempts to manipulate their emotions. Audience members who are less involved with your topic—who see it as routine or unimportant—are more likely to take the peripheral route. These listeners are less critical and rely more on a quick assessment of your credibility. They are also more easily swayed by emotional appeals. To be effective with both types of audience members, you must plan your persuasive speeches carefully.

So what do you need to know in order to create effective and ethical persuasive speeches? First you need to understand where most of the audience members stand on your topic so you can identify whether a speech to convince or to actuate is most appropriate. Then you need to phrase a proposition, or persuasive speech goal, that is appropriate to the rhetorical situation and to choose a suitable persuasive organizational framework. Finally, you need to evaluate your speech plan based on the ethical guidelines you have learned, as well as additional guidelines that are specific to persuasive situations.

Audience Attitude toward Your Persuasive Topic

Because it is very difficult to convince someone to change his or her mind, what you can hope to accomplish in any one speech depends on where your audience stands on your topic. So as you begin considering your speech, you'll want to understand the current direction and strength of audience members' attitudes about your topic. An **attitude** is "a general or enduring positive or negative feeling about some person, object, or issue."[1] People express their attitudes about something when they give their opinions. So someone who claims "I think physical fitness is important" is expressing an opinion that reflects a favorable attitude about physical fitness.

Assessing your audience's attitudes is part of the audience analysis process, which is Step 2 in the speech-planning process. Recall, you can do this by surveying the audience or by referring to published surveys and extrapolating these polls to the members of your audience. So you will want to begin your persuasive speech preparation by understanding the attitudes your audience is likely to have about your topic. Audience members' attitudes can range from highly favorable to strongly opposed and can be visualized as lying on a continuum like the one pictured in Exhibit 14.1 (the numbers represent the number of audience members who fall into that category).

Even though an audience will include individuals whose opinions fall at nearly every point along the continuum, generally audience members' opinions tend to cluster in one area of it. For instance, the opinions of the audience represented in Exhibit 14.1 cluster around "mildly opposed," even though a few people are more hostile and a few have favorable opinions. That cluster point represents your **target audience**, the group of people you most want to persuade. Based on your target audience, you can classify your audience's initial attitude toward your topic as "in favor" (already supportive of a particular belief), "no opinion" (uninformed, neutral, or apathetic), or "opposed" (against a particular belief or holding an opposite point of view). Given that initial attitude, you can develop a speech goal designed to influence your audience's attitudes in the way you would like. In general, when your target audience is in favor, seek action. When your target audience has no opinion, seek agreement. When your target audience is opposed to your position, seek incremental change.

Opposed

When your target audience is opposed to your goal, it is unrealistic to believe that you will be able to change their attitude from "opposed" to "in favor" in only one short speech. Instead, when dealing with a hostile audience, seek **incremental change**, trying to move them only a small degree in your direction, hoping for further movement later. For example, if you determine that your audience is likely to be opposed to the goal "I want to convince my audience that gay marriage should be legalized," you might rephrase your goal as "I want to convince

attitude: a general or enduring positive or negative feeling about some person, object, or issue

target audience: the group of people you most want to persuade

incremental change: attempting to move your audience only a small degree in your direction

Exhibit 14.1 Sample opinion continuum

Highly opposed	Opposed	Mildly opposed	Neither in favor nor opposed	Mildly in favor	In favor	Highly in favor
2	2	11	1	2	2	0

I Speak Because There's a Need

Frances James,
Community Organizer
South Los Angeles,
California

Photo courtesy of Frances James

Decades ago Frances James decided to stand up and speak for positive change in her community. She has been using her voice to make a difference ever since.

Growing up in South Los Angeles, James played safely in the streets. But over the years the community deteriorated. "I have a lot of history in my community. I was sick and tired of nobody paying attention to it, of seeing the news talk about gang bangers and drugs. There were problems!"

Encouraged by her pastor, who lamented the area's decline, she and her mother joined a coalition of churches and schools called the South Central Organizing Committee. At the meetings James asked incisive questions. "I found my voice. Not that I couldn't speak before, but there was now a need."

The lead organizer noticed her. "He told me 'You have something. You should go to training.' I said, 'I just came here with my mother!' Why me? I was in my late thirties. I'd been working as a single parent." James asked for time off from her job in the aerospace industry, and the coalition sponsored her ten-day training in New York with the Industrial Areas Foundation. "They believe that people who live in a community can change it. That was the beginning of my twenty-five-year relationship with the IAF."

Back in Los Angeles, James led her first action to resolve the unfair deployment of police in the city—her community suffered from the lack of police protection. "We had a meeting and decided who we needed to talk to and what needed to be done." After notifying the press, James and her mother met on the steps of City Hall with a small group composed mainly of senior citizens. "The press fired questions at me. At that point I knew I could speak. I spoke with passion! I told them that [in our community,] crimes against the human person were not considered as important as property crime. Our kids were being shot while the police were out looking for stolen Mercedes."

From City Hall they marched to police headquarters in downtown Los Angeles. "By the time we got there, two hundred people had gathered. I was amazed!" James met with the deputy chief of police and handed him a report requesting a new formula for police deployment. This and subsequent actions she and her group undertook achieved just that result. "Unfairness had dictated poor peoples' lives too long. We got out and took action."

James, who took a required public speaking class in school and then received her bachelor's degree in business management from the University of Redlands, went on to rally citizens and persuade government officials. She credits one thing with helping her overcome any fear. "I focused on my eight-year-old son. He made me brave."

> "At that point I knew I could speak. I spoke with passion!"

my audience that committed gay couples should be able to have the same legal protection afforded to committed heterosexual couples through state-recognized civil unions." Begin by brainstorming objections, questions, and criticisms that might arise, and then shape your speech around them.

No Opinion

When your target audience is neutral, you can be straightforward with reasons to support your goal. Still, it might be wise for you to consider whether they are uninformed, impartial, or apathetic about your topic. If they are **uninformed**— that is, they do not know enough about the topic to have formed an opinion—you will need to provide the basic arguments and information that they require to become informed. Make sure that each of your reasons is really well supported with good information. You may find that your audience is **impartial**; that is, the target audience has some information about the topic but does not really understand why your position is preferred and so still has no opinion. In this case, they are likely to listen objectively and accept sound reasoning if you can demonstrate the superiority of your position to others. Your focus should be on presenting evidence that shows why your position is superior to others. Finally, you may find that your audience members have no opinion because they are

uninformed: the audience doesn't know enough about a topic to have formed an opinion

impartial: the audience has some information about a topic but does not really understand why one position is preferred and so still has no opinion

apathetic. An apathetic audience has no opinion because it is uninterested in, unconcerned about, or indifferent toward your topic. To convince this audience, you will need to provide strong listener relevance links and use evidence that is meaningful to them and their interests.

For more about dealing with audiences who are opposed to or have no opinion about your position, use your CourseMate for *Challenge* to access **Web Resource 14.1: Dealing with a Hostile Audience** and **Web Resource 14.2: Dealing with a Challenging Audience**.

CourseMate

In Favor

When your target audience is only mildly in favor of your proposal, your task is to reinforce and strengthen their beliefs. An audience whose attitude supports your topic will still benefit from a logical explanation of the reasons for doing so. The audience may also become further committed to an attitude, value, or belief by hearing additional or new reasons and more recent evidence that support it.

When your audience analysis reveals that your listeners strongly agree with your position on the topic, then you can consider a speech goal that moves the audience to act on it. So, for example, if the topic is gay marriage and your audience poll shows that most audience members strongly favor the idea, then your goal might be "I want my audience to write their state legislators to express their support for gay marriage."

Identifying Your Proposition

In a persuasive speech, you state you specific goal as a proposition. A **proposition** is a declarative sentence that clearly indicates the position you will advocate. For example, "I want to convince my audience that smoking causes cancer" is a proposition. From it, we know that the speaker will present arguments, reasons, and evidence to prove the validity of the proposition.

> **SPEECH SNIPPET**
>
> **Persuading an Audience in Favor of Your Proposition**
>
> Adam knew that most if not all of the people in his audience already agreed that bullying is bad, so he decided to focus on a speech that would get them to do their part to help stop it.

proposition: the specific goal of a persuasive speech stated as a declarative sentence that clearly indicates the position the speaker will advocate

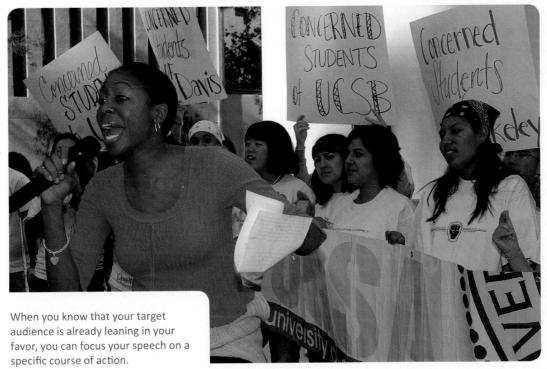

When you know that your target audience is already leaning in your favor, you can focus your speech on a specific course of action.

AP Images/Tiffany Michalka

Notice how a persuasive proposition differs from an informative speech goal on the same subject: "I want to inform my audience about the research on smoking and cancer." In the informative speech, the goal is met if the audience understands and remembers the information the speaker has shared. In the persuasive situation, however, the audience must not only understand what has been said but also agree with it and sometimes even take action. The three major types of persuasive goals are stated as propositions of fact, value, or policy.

A **proposition of fact** is a statement designed to convince your audience that something: (1) did, probably did, probably did not, or did not exist or occur; (2) is, probably is, probably is not, or is not true; or (3) will, probably will, probably will not, or will not occur. It takes a position on something that is generally not known but that can be argued for as true. Propositions of fact can concern the past, present, or future. Although propositions of fact may or may not be true—both positions are arguable—so they are stated as true. For example, whether or not Lee Harvey Oswald acted alone when he killed President Kennedy is debatable. So you could argue a proposition of fact concerning this fact in two ways: "Lee Harvey Oswald was the lone gunman who shot President John F. Kennedy" or "Lee Harvey Oswald was part of a larger conspiracy to shoot President John F. Kennedy." Examples of propositions of fact concerning the present are "I want to persuade the audience that there is a God," "I want to convince the audience that using cell phones causes brain cancer," and "I want the audience to believe that large numbers of elementary school children are illiterate." Claims of fact concerning the future are predictions. For example, "Thanks to the Internet, paperbound books will eventually cease to exist" and "E-mail will eventually replace traditional postal service" are both propositions of fact concerning the future.

A **proposition of value** is a statement designed to convince your audience that something is good, bad, desirable, undesirable, fair, unfair, moral, immoral, sound, unsound, beneficial, harmful, important, or unimportant.[2] You can convince your audience that something has more value than something else, or you can convince your audience that something meets valued standards. For instance, "I want to convince my audience that a low-fat diet is actually better than a fat-free diet" is a proposition that will require you to prove that the nutritional value of a low-fat diet meets the American Dietetic Association standards that we value better than a fat-free diet. Similarly, the proposition "I want my audience to believe that multilingual education is beneficial to children" requires you to prove that children who receive multilingual education gain specific educational rewards that we, as a society, value.

A **proposition of policy** is a statement designed to convince your audience that a particular rule, plan, or course of action

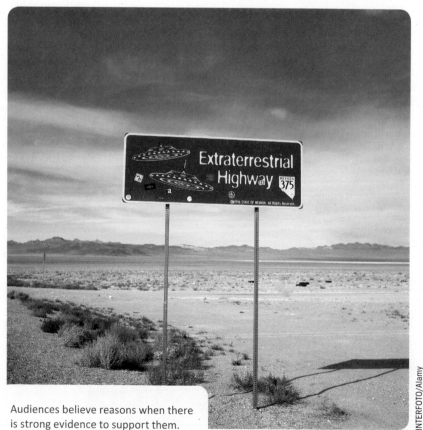

Audiences believe reasons when there is strong evidence to support them.

INTERFOTO/Alamy

proposition of fact: a statement designed to convince the audience that something did or did not exist or occur, is or is not true, or will or will not occur

proposition of value: a statement designed to convince the audience that something is good, bad, desirable, undesirable, fair, unfair, moral, immoral, sound, unsound, beneficial, harmful, important, or unimportant

proposition of policy: a statement designed to convince the audience that they should take a specific course of action should be taken. Propositions of policy will implore listeners using words such as "should/shouldn't," or "must/must not." "I want my audience to believe that a public speaking course *should* be required for all students at this university," "I want to persuade the audience that the United States *must* stop deep sea oil drilling," and "I want to convince the audience that home-schooled children *should* be afforded the opportunity to take the standardized tests required of the public school students in their district for free" are all propositions that advocate a specific policy. Similarly, "I want to convince the audience that water packaged in plastic bottles *should* be taxed to pay for the cost associated with recycling empties" and " I want to convince the audience that they *must* stop texting while driving" are propositions of policy.

Exhibit 14.2 provides several examples of how propositions of fact, value, and policy can be developed from the same topic idea.

As you begin working on your persuasive speeches, you can use the Speech Planning Action Steps and Speech Builder Express to help you organize and develop them, although some of the steps will be modified to provide you with

Exhibit 14.2 Examples of persuasive speech propositions		
Propositions of Fact	**Propositions of Value**	**Propositions of Policy**
Mahatma Gandhi was the father of passive resistance.	Mahatma Gandhi was a moral leader.	Mahatma Gandhi should be given a special award for his views on passive resistance.
Pharmaceutical advertising to consumers increases prescription drug prices.	Pharmaceutical advertising of new prescription drugs on TV is better than marketing new drugs directly to doctors.	Pharmaceutical companies should be required to refrain from advertising prescription drugs on TV.
Using paper ballots is a popular method for voting in U.S. elections.	Using paper ballots is better than using electronic voting machines.	Using paper ballots should be required for U.S. elections.

ACTIVITY 1Ep

SPEECH PLANNING

Action STEP 1

Speech Planning Action Step for Persuasive Speeches

Writing a Specific Goal as a Persuasive Proposition

1. Tentatively phrase your goal as a proposition.

2. Check whether you believe that your target audience is opposed to, has no opinion of, or is in favor of your proposition. Why?

3. Check whether you believe that the degree of your target audience's attitude makes your goal too difficult to meet or your audience is already convinced of your goal. If you've checked either of these, then rephrase your goal to adapt to that audience attitude.

4. Check whether your proposition, as stated or revised, is one of fact, value, or policy.

CourseMate You can complete this activity online with Speech Builder Express. Go to your CourseMate for *Challenge* to access Action Step Activity 1Ep.

STUDENT RESPONSE

Student Response Action Step for Persuasive Speeches

Writing a Specific Goal as a Persuasive Proposition

1. Tentatively phrase your goal as a proposition.

   I want to convince members of the audience that they should not download music from the Internet.

2. Check whether you believe that your target audience is opposed to, √ has no opinion of, or is in favor of your proposition. Why?

   Although some students may be opposed to or in favor of this proposition, I judge that the majority of the students in class are undecided.

3. Check whether you believe that the degree of your target audience's attitude makes your goal too difficult to meet or your audience is already convinced of your goal. If you've checked either of these, then rephrase your goal to adapt to that audience attitude.

   Because my audience is neutral, my goal seems achievable.

4. Check whether your proposition, as stated or revised, is one of fact, value, or √ policy.

guidance that is particular to persuasive speeches. You can use Activity 1Ep and the sample student response to help you develop a specific goal for a persuasive speech stated as a proposition.

Organizational Frameworks for Persuasive Speeches

Once you have identified your speech goal and phrased it as a proposition, you are ready to organize the main points using an appropriate persuasive speech framework. If your proposition focuses on changing or reinforcing your audience's belief or attitude toward your topic, you will give a **speech to convince**. If your proposition focuses on encouraging your audience to take action, you will give a **speech to actuate**. There are several different organizational frameworks for each of these types of persuasive speeches.

Common Organizational Frameworks for Speeches to Convince

Most speeches to convince follow one of four organizational frameworks: comparative advantages, criteria satisfaction, refutative, and statement of reasons.

COMPARATIVE ADVANTAGES

The **comparative advantages** organizational framework shows that one of two or more alternatives (which may include the status quo) is best. You show that the advantages of your alternative outweigh the disadvantages and that its advantages surpass the advantages of the other options.[3] A comparative advantages

speech to convince: a speech designed to seek agreement about a belief, value, or attitude

speech to actuate: a speech designed to incite action

comparative advantages: an organization that shows that a proposed change has more value than the status quo approach to a school tax proposition would look like this:

Proposition: I want my audience to believe that passing the school tax levy is better than not passing it. (compares the value of change to the status quo)

    I. Income from a tax levy will enable schools to reintroduce important programs that had to be cut. (advantage 1)

    II. Income from a tax levy will enable schools to avoid a tentative strike by teachers who are underpaid. (advantage 2)

    III. Income from a tax levy will enable us to retain local control of our schools, which will be lost to the state if additional local funding is not provided. (advantage 3)

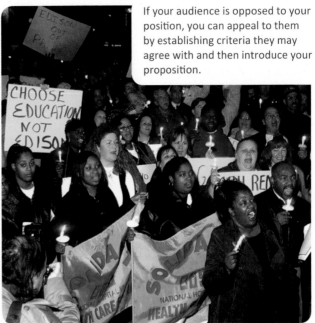

If your audience is opposed to your position, you can appeal to them by establishing criteria they may agree with and then introduce your proposition.

AP Photo/Cyrena Chang

CRITERIA SATISFACTION

The **criteria satisfaction** framework is an indirect organization that seeks audience agreement on criteria that should be considered when evaluating a particular proposition and then shows how the proposition satisfies those criteria. A criteria satisfaction framework is especially useful when your audience is opposed to your proposition because it approaches the proposition indirectly by first focusing on criteria that the audience may agree with before introducing the specific proposition. A criteria satisfaction organization for the school tax proposition would look like this:

> **Proposition:** *I want my audience to believe that passing a school tax levy is a good way to fund our schools.*
>
>   *I.* *We all can agree that a good school funding method must meet three criteria:*
>   *A. A good funding method results in the reestablishment of programs that have been dropped for monetary reasons.*
>   *B. A good funding method results in fair pay for teachers.*
>   *C. A good funding method generates enough income to maintain local control, avoiding state intervention.*
>   *II.* *Passage of a local school tax levy is a good way to fund our schools.*
>   *A. A local levy will allow us to fund important programs again.*
>   *B. A local levy will allow us to give teachers a raise.*
>   *C. A local levy will generate enough income to maintain local control and avoid state intervention.*

criteria satisfaction: an indirect organization that seeks audience agreement on criteria that should be considered when evaluating a particular proposition and then shows how the proposition satisfies those criteria

REFUTATIVE

A **refutative** framework helps you organize your main points to persuade by both challenging the opposing arguments and bolstering your own. This framework is particularly useful when the target audience opposes your position. Begin by acknowledging the merit of opposing arguments and then showing their flaws. Once listeners understand the flaws, they are more receptive to the arguments you present to support your opinion. A refutative organization for the school tax proposition might look like this:

> **Proposition:** *I want my audience to agree that a school tax levy is the best way to fund our schools.*
>
>   *I.* *Opponents of the tax levy argue that the tax increase will fall only on property owners.*
>   *A. Landlords will recoup property taxes in the form of higher rents.*
>   *B. Thus, all people will be affected.*

refutative: an organization that persuades by both challenging the opposing position and bolstering one's own

II. *Opponents of the tax levy argue that there are fewer students in the school district, so schools should be able to function on the same amount of revenue.*

   A. *Although there are fewer pupils, costs continue to rise.*

      1. *Salary cost increases*

      2. *Energy cost increases*

      3. *Maintenance cost increases*

      4. *Unfunded federal and state government mandates add to costs*

   B. *Although there are fewer pupils, there are many aging school buildings that need replacing or retrofitting for this computer age.*

III. *Opponents of the tax levy argue that parents should be responsible for the excessive cost of educating their children.*

   A. *Historically, our nation flourished under a publicly funded educational system.*

   B. *Parents today are already paying more than our parents did.*

      1. *Activity fees*

      2. *Lab fees*

      3. *Book fees*

      4. *Transportation fees*

   C. *Of school-age children today in this district, 42 percent live in families that are below the poverty line and have limited resources.*

STATEMENT OF REASONS

statement of reasons: a straightforward organization in which you present your best-supported reasons in a meaningful order

The **statement of reasons** is a form of persuasive organization used for confirming propositions of fact in which you present your best-supported reasons in a meaningful order. For a speech with three reasons or more, place the strongest reason last because this is the reason you believe the audience will find most persuasive. You will often place the second strongest reason first because you want to start with a significant point. Place the other reasons in between.

Proposition: *I want my audience to believe that passing the proposed school tax levy is necessary.*

  I. *The income will enable the schools to restore vital programs. (second strongest)*

  II. *The income will enable the schools to give teachers the raises they need to keep up with the cost of living.*

  III. *The income will allow the community to maintain local control and will save the district from state intervention. (strongest)*

SPEECH **ASSIGNMENT**

Speech to Convince

1. Prepare a four- to seven-minute speech in which you seek agreement about a belief, value, or attitude.

2. Write a persuasive plan for adapting to your specific audience that includes:

  a. How your goal stated as a proposition adapts to whether your prevailing audience attitude is in favor, has no opinion, or is opposed.

  b. What organizational framework you will use and why it is fitting for your topic and audience.

  c. What main points you will use to convince your audience to agree with your position on the topic.

3. Write a complete speech outline.

   To help you prepare your outline, go to your CourseMate for *Challenge* to access Speech Builder Express.

SPEECH EVALUATION CHECKLIST

Speech to Convince Evaluation Checklist

You can use this checklist to critique a speech to convince that you hear in class. As you listen to the speaker, outline the speech. Pay close attention to the reasoning process the speaker uses. Note the claims and supports used in the arguments, and identify the types of warrants used. Then, answer the following questions.

_____ 1. Was the introduction effective in creating interest, involving the audience in the speech, and previewing the main points?

_____ 2. Was the specific goal clear and phrased as a proposition?

_____ 3. Was the speech organized into an appropriate framework?

   Comparative advantages

   Criteria satisfaction

   Refutative

   Statement of reasons

_____ 4. Did the speaker use logos effectively?

   Strong evidence?

   Reasoning linked to claims?

   Fallacies?

_____ 5. Did the speaker use ethos effectively?

   _____ Establish expertise?

   _____ Demonstrate trustworthiness?

   _____ Convey goodwill?

_____ 6. Did the speaker use pathos effectively?

   Appeal to negative emotions? If so, check all that were tapped:
   _____ fear _____ guilt _____ anger _____ shame _____ sadness

   Appeal to positive emotions? If so, check all that were tapped:
   _____ happiness/joy _____ pride _____ relief _____ hope
   _____ compassion

   Were the appeals very effective, somewhat effective, or ineffective?

_____ 7. Was the language appropriate, accurate, clear, and vivid?

_____ 8. Was the use of voice intelligible, conversational, expressive, and convincing?

_____ 9. Was the use of body poised and expressive?

_____ 10. Did the speaker offer a compelling conclusion with thesis restatement and clincher?

Overall evaluation of the speech (check one):

   _____ excellent _____ good _____ average _____ fair _____ poor

CourseMate   Use the information from this checklist to support your evaluation. Go to your CourseMate for *Challenge* to access this checklist online under the Chapter 14 resources.

Organizational Frameworks for Speeches to Actuate

Implicit in speeches to actuate is the assumption that there is a problem that audience members can help solve by taking certain actions. As a result, most actuation persuasive speeches follow one of three organizational frameworks: problem-solution, problem-cause-solution, and the motivated sequence.

Sample Speech to Convince

This section presents a sample speech to convince given by a student, including an adaptation plan, an outline, and a transcript.

Hooking Up, Friends-with-Benefits Relationships (FWBR), or Dating: Not Really a Tough Choice

By Molly Reynolds

CourseMate Read the speech adaptation plan, outline, and transcript of a speech given by Molly Reynolds in an introductory speaking course. Access the Chapter 14 resources of your CourseMate for *Challenge* to identify some of the strengths of Molly's speech by preparing an evaluation checklist and an analysis. You can then compare your answers with those of the authors.

ADAPTATION PLAN

1. **Audience attitude**: When I asked people about their feelings concerning hookups and friends-with-benefits relationships (FWBRs), most of them regarded the practices as common and not a big deal. However, very few admitted to their own hookup or FWBRs. Instead, they talked about the involvements that "others" engaged in. Therefore, I determined that the majority of my audience is either undecided or unconcerned about the consequences.

2. **Reasons**: Dating is physically and psychologically healthier, and leads to greater relationship satisfaction.

3. **Organizational framework**: I am going to use a comparative advantages framework. This topic naturally lends itself to demonstrating the comparative advantages that dating has over both hooking up and friends-with-benefits relationships (FWBRs). The three primary advantages are physical health, psychological health, and relationship satisfaction.

OUTLINE

General goal: To persuade

Specific goal: I want to convince my audience that dating relationships are better than hooking up or friends-with-benefits relationships (FWBRs).

Introduction

Attention getter

I. *"Well you know, they travel in threes, and she was not the hot one but she wasn't the fat one either. And it was late, and if I wanted to get laid the choices were getting slim, so—"*

"We were at this party, and I was dancing with this really hot guy. One thing led to another, and I thought, what the heck. He's so hot."

"Josh and I have known each other since grade school, and I've always kind of had a thing for him. Neither one of us was seeing anyone, and one night we were

out with friends and dancing, and one thing led to another and we became, you know, 'friends with benefits.' But now I'm really hooked on him and he doesn't know it, and he's started to see someone who he thinks is special. But he wants to keep up our arrangement too because she won't sleep with him."

"I met this really cool girl in my biology class. She's really pretty and smart, and she seems to have a good sense of humor. So I broke the code and asked her out. We took a walk in the park, had dinner, and then went back to her place, and believe it or not, we just talked. It was so weird, but I really enjoyed it. So we've made plans to go to the movies on Saturday. So I won't be going out trolling for a bad girl this weekend. Who knows—I may be out of the action for a while. We'll see."

II. We have all known someone who has engaged in the above-mentioned scenarios. Which of these scenarios appeals most to you? If you had your choice of hooking up with a stranger, having sex with a friend, or going out with someone you found interesting and attractive, what would you prefer?   *Listener relevance*

III. As a member of what some call "the hookup generation," I have first-hand knowledge and some experience with the current hookup culture that is so popular on college campuses today. So I was curious about what the research says about these practices, and what I discovered might surprise you as much as it surprised me.   *Speaker credibility*

IV. Today, I'm here to convince you that hooking up and friends-with-benefits relationships (FWBRs) are poor substitutes for dating relationships.   *Thesis statement*

V. I will show why dating is the best choice by defining each relationship type and then comparing the physical risks, psychological costs, and feelings of relationship satisfaction among them.   *Preview*

Body

I. Let's begin by defining each of these three types of relationships.

I'm sure we have all known someone who hooked up and was disappointed when they didn't get a phone call the next day, and someone whose FWBR ended with no benefits and the loss of a friend. And I'm sure we have known friends who grieved the loss of what they thought was a solid dating relationship.   *Listener relevance*

  A. Before we can examine the risks, we must define what a hookup is.

    1. "Hookups are defined as a sexual encounter which may or may not include sexual intercourse, usually occurring on only one occasion between two people who are strangers or brief acquaintances." (Paul, McManus, & Hayes, 2000, p. 76)

      a. These casual sexual encounters are essentially spontaneous sex between partners who barely had contact with each other before engaging in the sexual act. (Winslow, Franzini, & Hwang, 1992)

      b. The nature of the sexual behavior involved is ambiguous and may vary from heavy kissing to intercourse.

    2. Different goals and expectations of those involved can lead to misunderstanding, dissatisfaction, and regret. (Carroll, Volk, & Hyde, 1985)

  B. Now that we understand the nature of a hookup, what exactly is a friends-with-benefits relationship (FWBR)?

    1. FWBRs are platonic friendships where partners engage in sexual behaviors ranging from kissing to sexual intercourse. (Mongeau, Shaw, & Knight, 2009)

      a. FWBRs can include numerous degrees on the intimacy spectrum.

      b. These degrees range from good friends who engage in sexual activity to individuals who engage in serial hookups but have little to no interaction beyond the hookup.

2. Despite the type of FWBR, individuals usually enter into a FWBR with no intention of it evolving into a romantic relationship. (Hughes, Morisson, & Asada, 2005)

    a. Sometimes one partner in a FWBR becomes interested in taking the relationship further, but these feelings aren't always mutual.

    b. Monica and Chandler from the show *Friends* began as friends, moved into a FWBR, and ended up married.

    c. FWBRs rarely have this fairy-tale ending in real life.

C. Now that we understand the nature of hookups and FWBRs, we must define dating relationships.

    1. In dating relationships, individuals spend time getting to know each other and enter into a sexual relationship if and when both partners feel a sense of relational intimacy.

    2. In dating relationships, both people share more intimate thoughts and feelings as trust builds.

    3. Relational success is more likely when partners know each other and date for an extended period before marriage and engage in positive communication. (Stafford, 2008)

Transition

Now that we've established a common set of definitions, let's compare these relationships according to how they affect physical health, psychological health, and relationship satisfaction.

II. Let's begin by exploring the physical risks associated with hookups, FWBRs, and dating relationships.

Listener relevance

Since most of us in this room are not married, we ought to understand the physical risks involved in engaging in these different types of relationships.

A. Because partners often fail to practice safe sex, hookups and FWBRs increase the risk of catching a sexually transmitted disease (STD).

    1. It's true that when you have sex with someone, you also have sex with everyone they have ever had sex with.

        a. Listen to the testimony of someone suffering from pelvic inflammatory disease (PID), a bacterial infection of the uterus, fallopian tubes, and ovaries:

        "I have suffered with pelvic inflammatory disease now for fifteen years. I have in the last three years had a full hysterectomy and now suffer worse pain than ever and have severe adhesions and chronic pain. My life is ruined. My PID was silent but deadly—one day no pain; next day I was crippled. PID is a horrible disease—and you don't have to be promiscuous to get it. Just sleeping with someone you don't know and whose sexual past is unknown can put you in jeopardy of this disease."

        b. PID is most frequently caused by gonorrhea and chlamydia, two common STDs.

    2. There are numerous risks associated specifically with hooking up. (Downing-Maltibag & Geisinger, 2009)

        a. Students who did not use protection often trusted that their hookup partners were STD-free based on appearance or informal character assessments.

        b. They also tended to rationalize that because there were low rates of HIV/AIDS in the region where they lived, they did not have to protect themselves against it. (p. 1204)

    3. People aren't any safer in FWBRs.

        a. People who engage in *hookups* report being more careful when engaging in sexual intercourse with unknown or lesser-known individuals than with people they already know. (Morr & Mongeau, 2004)

    b. Just because you know someone as a "friend" and have a FWBR with that person does not mean you know what he or she is doing sexually.

      i. FWBRs by their very nature are not meant to be exclusive, so he or she may have other partners who, by association, you are also sleeping with.

      ii. Even if you are both monogamous during your relationship, unless you are both tested prior to having sex, you are still at risk.

    c. In hookups and in FWBRs, the emphasis is on each partner's personal needs for sex and physical satisfaction, so the partner is an "insignificant other."

B. Because partners involved in hookups and FWBRs are less likely to practice safe sex, the likelihood of an unplanned pregnancy also increases.

    1. Listen to the experience of a woman who posted her story on Yahoo! Answers:

"I was with this guy for a very short time. It pretty much ended up being a one-night stand, even though we texted a little afterwards. When I found out I was pregnant, I decided to tell him, especially since I didn't know what I was going to do yet. But whatever I was going to do was part of his responsibility (i.e., bills for an abortion, child support, or choosing of an adoptive family). When I told him, he just begged me to get an abortion over and over until I finally agreed and told him I had gotten the abortion to get him to stop texting me every five seconds and begging while I could get some quiet time to figure out what I really wanted to do."

> Notice, guys, it was what *she* wanted to do. A man who fathers a hookup child is legally responsible for supporting that child until it is an adult. You have no say—it is her body and her decision. So, in addition to your college loans, you may have a significant financial responsibility for the next eighteen years. And every time you get a raise, your child gets part of it. It's the risk you take. And if you're morally or religiously opposed to abortion? Tough. Her body, her decision. You can try to change her mind, but if she decides on abortion, there is nothing you can do. And remember, even when condoms are used they are only 95 percent effective as a contraceptive. Think about it.

    (right margin: Listener relevance)

    2. Unintended pregnancy is a risk in any sexual relationship.

      a. But people who are dating and have built some degree of respect and intimacy are more likely to come to a mutual understanding about the woman's choice.

      b. Or they can adjust to co-parenting tasks, even if they choose to end their romantic relationship.

C. While physical risks are inherent in any sexual relationship, dating is physically healthier than either hooking up or engaging in a FWBR.

> Not only do hookups and FWBRs put you at more risk physically, but they are also more likely to do psychological damage.

    (right margin: Transition)

III. Both hooking up and engaging in FWBRs create psychological distress.

    (right margin: Listener relevance)

> How many of you know someone who says they feel more confident and have higher self-esteem following a hookup? After sleeping with their best friend? Not many, right? More often, we listen to our friends express feelings of guilt, shame, and embarrassment. People, it's called a "walk of shame" for a reason.

A. People who hook up have lower self-esteem, greater depression, and more feelings of guilt than those who don't. (Grello, et al., 2006; Sprecher, Barbee, & Schwartz, 1995)

    1. Women who engage in hooking up experience more loss of self-esteem and depression than men.

2. It is not clear whether depression leads to casual sexual behavior or whether casual sexual behavior leads to depression.

3. Women who engage in casual sex experience express feelings of good old-fashioned guilt.

4. Men don't necessarily feel guilty for hooking up with strangers, but they do feel guilty if they get drunk and hook up with a friend.

B. While breaking up a dating relationship can also lead to depression, research has found that although the first breakup can lead to depression, subsequent breakups are unlikely to do so.

1. The first act of breaking up seems to "inoculate" us, probably because we figure that there is life after a breakup.

2. The opposite seems to be true in more casual sexual relationships—the more you do it, the more guilty and depressed you become.

Transition

Because of the many negative physical and psychological consequences of hooking up and FWBRs, dating tends to produce more satisfying relationships in the end.

IV. Hooking up and FWBRs lead to less satisfying relationships than dating.

A. In a hookup, ideally neither partner wants or expects anything other than sexual satisfaction. (Grello, et al, 2006)

1. Half of all college students who engage in sexual intercourse during a hookup never see the other person again.

2. But 18 percent of women view a hookup as stepping stone to a romantic relationship.

B. In the ideal FWBR, two friends simply become "sex" or "f…ing" buddies without damaging the friendship.

C. According to that famous philosopher, Harry Burns in the 1989 movie When Harry Met Sally, "Men and women can never be friends because the sex part always gets in the way." Was Harry wrong? Yes and no.

1. In 2010 study, Lehmiller and his colleagues found yes:
   "Sex was a more common motivation for men in FWBRs, whereas emotional connection was a more common motivation for women. In addition, men were more likely to hope that the relationship stays the same over time, whereas women expressed more desire for change into either a full-fledged romance or a basic friendship."

2. This is understandable when you consider the biology of sex, according to sex therapist Dr. Ian Kerner, speaking on the Today Show in 2007:
   "During sex, women produce lots of oxytocin, a hormone that stimulates a strong emotional connection. As a result, women are more emotionally integrated when it comes to sex. That's why casual sex and hookups often backfire for lots of women. Guys produce little to no oxytocin, and can easily have sex without any sense of emotional connection. It's sex with no emotional strings attached."

3. One of the inherent problems in FWBRs is the ambiguity partners can feel about what they can expect. Euphoria posted this to the sex forum on Women's-Health.com:
   "We have a very good relationship as friends; we're very close. We've been 'talking' since November, and one night I slept over his house and it just happened. The thing that bothers me is that he didn't kiss me in the morning and didn't talk to me until the next night. And on New Year's Eve I also slept over his house, along with other people, and I was probably setting myself up for it cause it happened again. I had left early that morning, around eight, and my friend had told me later on that day that he came into the room she was sleeping in and practically woke her up to kiss her. We did agree to be friends with benefits, but I meant that I'm the only one he should doing it with. Should I say something to him, or do I have no right since we're FWB?"

4. During my research, I came upon an article by Marilyn Murphey on the Askmen.com website that talked about the pros and cons of FWBRs.
   a. Seventy-five percent of the 139 posts responding to the article talked about how a FWBR produced problems.
   b. These problems stemmed from one partner wanting the relationship to evolve into something more serious.
5. But *no*, Harry wasn't right in one sense—both men and women in a FWBR were ultimately more committed to the friendship than to the sexual aspect of the relationship. (Lehmiller et al., 2010)

D. Although not all dating relationships lead to "happily ever after," successful dating leads to more satisfactory relationships in terms of intimacy and safe sexual fulfillment.
1. Dating is the preferred type of relationship for both men and women. (Glenn & Marquardt, 2001)
   a. In a national survey of over 1,000 college women published in 2001, 83 percent agreed with the statement "Being married is very important to me."
   b. And 63 percent agreed with the statement "I would like to meet my future husband/wife in college."
   c. Yet 50 percent of the women sampled had had fewer than two dates since starting college.
   d. A 2010 study found that 87 percent of women and 64 percent of men indicated a preference for dating over hooking up, particularly when they might be interested in a long-term relationship. (Bradshaw et al.)
2. As "Bad Reputation" put it in his online post, "There are girls you date and girls you have sex with." So I ask you, ladies: Who do you want to be?

Conclusion

I. Based on analysis, I'm sure you can see that dating, while scary and angst ridden, is still superior to hooking up or having a FWBR.

II. Both hookups and FWBRs have more physical and psychological risks than dating relationships.

III. So, before you go out this weekend get smashed and find yourself looking for love in all the wrong places, consider giving that someone you've had your eye on a call and see if you can make a date for a movie, or concert, or just a cup of coffee. While it might not lead to a romantic relationship, who knows—it just might.

Thesis restatement

Main point summary

Clincher

References

Carroll, J. L., Volk, K. D., & Hyde, J. S. (1985). Differences between males and females in motives for engaging in sexual intercourse. *Archives of Sexual Behavior, 14*, 131–139.

Cohen, E. (2010). "The downside of friends with benefits." *CNN.com*. Accessed at http://www.cnn.com/2010/HEALTH/04/15/friends.benefits.stds/index.html

Downing-Maltibag, T. M., & Geisinger, B. (2009). Hooking up and sexual risk taking among college students: A health belief model perspective. *Qualitative Health Research, 19*, 1196–1204.

Glenn, N., & Marquardt, E. (2001). *Hooking up, hanging out, and hoping for Mr. Right: College women on dating and mating today.* A report conducted by the Institute for American Values for the Independent Women's Forum.

Grello, C. M., Welsh, D. P., & Harper, M. S. (2006). No strings attached: The nature of casual sex in college students. The Journal of Sex Research, 43, 255–267.

Hughes, M., Morrison, K., & Asada, K. J. K. (2005). What's love got to do with it? Exploring the impact of maintenance rules, love attitudes, and network support on friends-with-benefits relationships. *Western Journal of Communication, 69*(1), 49–66.

Kerner, I. (2007). "The biggest sex mistakes that men and women make." *The Today Show, September 27, 2007.* Accessed at http://www.today.msnbc.msn.com/id/20955254/ns/today-today_relationships//

Lehmiller, J. J., VanderDrift, L. E. & Kelly, J. R. (2010). Sex differences in approaching friends-with-benefits relationships. *Journal of Sex Research,* doi:10.1080/00224491003721694

Monroe, S. M., Rohde, P., Seeley, J. R., Lewinsohn, P. M. (Nov 1999). Life events and depression in adolescence: Relationship loss as a prospective risk factor for first onset of major depressive disorder. *Journal of Abnormal Psychology*, Vol 108(4), 606–614.

Morr, M., C., & Mongeau, P. A. (2004). First-date expectations: The impact of sex of initiator, alcohol consumption, and relationship type. *Communication Research, 31*(1), 3–35.

Murphy, M. (2009). "The pro's and con's of casual sex between friends." *Askmen.Com.* Accessed at http://www.askmen.com/includes/components/posts/postPage.php?id=910517&p=3

No name. (Nov 1, 2009). "I'm pregnant, but it was only a hookup. Should I tell him?" *Yahoo! Answers.* Accessed at http://answers.yahoo.com/questions/index?qid=20091101094838AAnz4l1

Owen, J. J., Stanley, S. M., & Fincham, F. D. (2010). "Hooking up" among college students: Demographic and psychosocial correlates. *Archives of Sexual Behavior, 39,* 653–663.

Paul, E. L., McManus, B., & Hayes, A. (2000). "Hookups": Characteristics and correlates of college students' spontaneous and anonymous sexual experiences. *Journal of Sex Research, 37,* 76–88.

Paul, E. L., & Hayes, K. A. (2002). The casualties of 'casual' sex: A qualitative exploration of the phenomenology of college students' hookups. *Journal of Social and Personal Relationships, 19,* 639–660.

Sprecher, S., Barbee, A., & Schwartz, P. (1995). "Was it good for you too?": Gender differences in first intercourse experiences. *The Journal of Sex Research, 32*(1), 3–15.

Stafford, L. (2008). Dating relationships. In Wolfgang Donsbach (Ed.), *The international encyclopedia of communication* (Vol. 3, pp. 1167–1171). Malden, MA: Blackwell Publishing Ltd.

_____. (2010). "Chalmydia CDC Fact Sheet." U.S. Department of Health and Human Services Center for Disease Control. Accessed at http://www.cdc.gov/std/chlamydia/stdfact-chlamydia.htm

_____. (2008). "Gonorrhea CDC Fact Sheet." U.S. Department of Health and Human Services Center for Disease Control. Accessed at: http://www.cdc.gov/std/Gonorrhea/STDFact-gonorrhea.htm

Winslow, R. W., Franzini, L. R., & Hwang, J. (1992). Perceived peer norms, casual sex, and AIDS risk prevention. *Journal of Applied Social Psychology, 22* (24), 1559–1816.

SPEECH AND ANALYSIS

The Speech

"Well you know, they travel in threes, and she was not the hot one but she wasn't the fat one either. And it was late, and if I wanted to get laid the choices were getting slim, so—"

"We were at this party, and I was dancing with this really hot guy. One thing led to another, and I thought, what the heck. He's so hot."

Analysis

Molly uses four hypothetical scenarios to grab her audience's attention. Doing so is particularly effective because they are scenarios that most of her classmates can probably relate to.

"Josh and I have known each other since grade school, and I've always kind of had a thing for him. Neither one of us was seeing anyone, and one night we were out with friends and dancing, and one thing led to another and we became, you know, 'friends with benefits.' But now I'm really hooked on him and he doesn't know it, and he's started to see someone who he thinks is special. But he wants to keep up our arrangement too because she won't sleep with him."

"I met this really cool girl in my biology class. She's really pretty and smart, and she seems to have a good sense of humor. So I broke the code and asked her out. We took a walk in the park, had dinner, and then went back to her place, and believe it or not, we just talked. It was so weird, but I really enjoyed it. So we've made plans to go to the movies on Saturday. So I won't be going out trolling for a bad girl this weekend. Who knows—I may be out of the action for a while. We'll see."

We have all known someone who has engaged in the above-mentioned scenarios. Which of these scenarios appeals most to you? If you had your choice of hooking up with a stranger, having sex with a friend, or going out with someone you found interesting and attractive, what would you prefer?

As a member of what some call "the hookup generation," I have first-hand knowledge and some experience with the current hookup culture that is so popular on college campuses today. So I was curious about what the research says about these practices, and what I discovered might surprise you as much as it surprised me.

Today I'm here to convince you that hooking up and friends-with-benefits relationships (FWBRs) are poor substitutes for dating relationships. I will show why dating is the best choice by defining each relationship type and then comparing the physical risks, psychological costs, and feelings of relationship satisfaction among them.

Let's begin by defining each of these three types of relationships. I'm sure we have all known someone who hooked up and was disappointed when they didn't get a phone call the next day, and someone whose FWBR ended with no benefits and the loss of a friend. And I'm sure we have known friends who grieved the loss of what they thought was a solid dating relationship. Therefore, before we can examine the associated risks, we must begin by defining what a hookup actually is.

According to Paul, McManus, and Hayes in their 2000 article "'Hookups': Characteristics and correlates of college students' spontaneous and anonymous sexual experiences," published in the *Journal of Sex Research*, "Hookups are defined as a sexual encounter which may or may not include sexual intercourse, usually occurring on only one occasion between two people who are strangers or brief acquaintances." Winslow, Franzini, and Hwang explain further in their article published in a 1992 issue of the *Journal of Applied Social Psychology* that these casual sexual encounters are essentially spontaneous sex between partners who barely had contact with each other before engaging in the sexual act. The exact nature of the sexual behavior involved during a hookup is somewhat ambiguous and may vary from heavy kissing to intercourse. Carroll, Volk, and

Here Molly establishes listener relevance by asking a series of rhetorical questions, which engages her audience from the outset.

Molly establishes credibility by pointing out her personal experience with the topic as part of the "hookup generation" and that she was surprised at what she learned from the research.

We clearly understand what Molly's proposition is and how she will organize her arguments to convince us to agree with her about this issue.

Molly realized that she couldn't succeed with her goal unless she knows that her listeners understand the nature of the different types of relationships she's discussing. So she makes this subject her first main point.

Molly bolsters her ethos by using an oral citation. Doing so enhances her credibility, telling the audience that she is informed as well as ethical.

Hyde, in their article "Differences between males and females in motives for engaging in sexual intercourse," published in a 1985 issue of the *Archives of Sexual Behavior*, report that different goals and expectations of those involved can lead to misunderstanding, dissatisfaction, and regret.

Now that we understand the nature of a hookup, what exactly is a friends-with-benefits relationship (FWBR)? Lehmiller, VanderDrift, and Kelly, in their article "Sex differences in approaching friends-with-benefits relationships," published in a 2010 issue of the *Journal of Sex Research*, explored the nature of a FWBR as platonic friendships where partners engage in sexual behaviors ranging from kissing to sexual intercourse. The authors found FWBRs can include numerous degrees on the intimacy spectrum, ranging from good friends who engage in sexual activity to individuals who engage in serial hookups but have little to no interaction beyond the hookup.

Despite the type of FWBR, Hughes, Morrison, and Asada reported in their article "What's love got to do with it," published in a 2005 issue of the *Western Journal of Communication*, individuals usually enter into a FWBR with no intention of it evolving into a romantic one. Sometimes one partner in a FWBR becomes interested in taking the relationship further. However, these feelings aren't always mutual. Some of you probably remember Monica and Chandler from the show *Friends*. They began as friends, moved into a FWBR, and ended up married. Unfortunately, FWBRs rarely have this fairy tale ending in real life.

Now that we understand the nature of hookups and FWBRs, we need to define dating relationships. In dating relationships, individuals spend time getting to know each other and enter into a sexual relationship if and when both partners feel a sense of relational intimacy. In dating relationships, both people share more intimate thoughts and feelings with each other as trust builds. In her 2008 reference in the *International Encyclopedia of Communication*, Stafford explains that relational success is more likely when partners know each other and date for an extended period before marriage and engage in positive communication.

Now that we've established a common set of definitions, let's compare these relationships according to how they affect physical health, psychological health, and relationship satisfaction. Let's begin by exploring the physical risks associated with hookups, FWBRs, and dating relationships. Since most of us in this room are not married, we ought to understand the physical risks involved in engaging in these different types of relationships.

Hookups and FWBRs increase the risk of catching an STD because partners often fail to practice safe sex. The old saying that when you have sex with someone, you also have sex with everyone they have ever had sex with is true. Listen to the testimony of someone suffering from PID (pelvic inflammatory disease), a bacterial infection of the uterus, fallopian tubes, and ovaries. PID is most frequently caused by gonorrhea and chlamydia, two common STDs that can be devastating. Listen to one sufferer's story:

Molly could have elaborated on the findings of this article. As is, listeners are left wondering what the differences are.

Molly does a nice job of using a rhetorical question to verbally tie the point she has finished talking about to the point she is introducing.

Although Molly cites a number of reputable sources for this point, she could improve by integrating a variety of types of evidence, perhaps a testimonial or a personal story.

Molly could improve by offering some kind of warrant to support this claim.
Again, Molly offers a transition that verbally ties her main points together. She also uses inclusive language when she says "we" rather than "I."

Molly could improve by elaborating on this "dating" main point. Perhaps she assumed her listeners already know what a dating relationship is.

Molly attempts to draw her listeners back in by offering an appropriate listener relevance link that proposes why her listeners ought to want to know about the physical risks.

I have suffered with pelvic inflammatory disease now for fifteen years. I have in the last three years had a full hysterectomy and now suffer worse pain than ever and have severe adhesions and chronic pain. My life is ruined. My PID was silent but deadly—one day no pain; next day I was crippled. PID is a horrible disease—and you don't have to be promiscuous to get it. Just sleeping with someone you don't know and whose sexual past is unknown can put you in jeopardy of this disease.

In their article "Hooking up and sexual risk taking among college students: A health belief model perspective," published in a 2009 issue of the *Qualitative Health Research journal*, Downing-Maltibag and Geisinger also discovered numerous risks associated with hooking up. Specifically, students who did not use protection often trusted that their hookup partners were STD-free based on appearance or informal character assessments. They also tended to rationalize that because there were low rates of HIV/AIDS in the region where they lived, they did not have to protect themselves against it.

Ironically, people aren't any safer in FWBRs. In fact, according to an article published in *Communication Research* by Morr and Mongeau in 2004, people actually report being more careful when engaging in sexual intercourse with unknown or lesser known individuals than with people they already know. Just because you know someone as a "friend" does not mean you know what they are doing sexually. FWBRs, by their very nature, are not meant to be exclusive, so while you're sleeping with your friend, he or she may also have other partners who, by association, you are also sleeping with. And even if you are both monogamous during your relationship, unless you are both tested prior to having sex, you are still at risk. In hookups and in FWBRs, the emphasis is on each partner's personal needs for sex and physical satisfaction, so the partner is an "insignificant other."

Because partners involved in hookups and FWBRs are less likely to practice safe sex, the likelihood of an unplanned pregnancy also increases. Listen to the experience of a woman who posted her story on Yahoo! Answers:

I was with this guy for a very short time. It pretty much ended up being a one-night stand, even though we texted a little afterwards. When I found out I was pregnant, I decided to tell him, especially since I didn't know what I was going to do yet. But whatever I was going to do was part of his responsibility (i.e., bills for an abortion, child support, or choosing of an adoptive family). When I told him, he just begged me to get an abortion over and over until I finally agreed and told him I had gotten the abortion to get him to stop texting me every five seconds and begging while I could get some quiet time to figure out what I really wanted to do.

Notice, guys, it was what *she* wanted to do. A man who fathers a hookup child is legally responsible for supporting that child until it is an adult. You have no say—it is her body and her decision. So, in addition to your college loans, you may have a significant financial responsibility for the next eighteen years.

Molly's decision to include a personal testimonial appeals to the feelings of listeners via a rhetorical appeal to pathos.

Some of Molly's listeners might find this fact startling, which will keep their interest focused on learning more.

Molly again uses personal testimony to appeal to pathos in her speech.

Offering this listener relevance link helps males in Molly's audience see how the story of one person's pregnancy relates to them as well.

And every time you get a raise, your child gets part of it. It's the risk you take. And if you're morally or religiously opposed to abortion? Tough. Her body, her decision. You can try to change her mind. But if she decides on abortion there is nothing you can do. And remember, even when condoms are used, they are only 95 percent effective as a contraceptive. Think about it.

While unintended pregnancy is a risk in any sexual relationship, it stands to reason that people who are dating—who have built some degree of respect and intimacy—are more likely to be equipped to come to a mutual understanding about the woman's choice and to adjust to co-parenting tasks, even if they choose to end their romantic relationship.

While physical risks are inherent in any sexual relationship, dating is physically healthier than either hooking up or engaging in a FWBR. Not only do hookups and FWBRs put you at more risk physically, but they are also more likely to do psychological damage. Both hooking up and FWB create psychological distress.

How many of you know someone who says they feel more confident and have higher self-esteem following a hookup? After sleeping with their best friend? Not many, right? More often, we listen to our friends express feelings guilt, shame, and embarrassment. People, it's called a "walk of shame" for a reason. People who hook up have lower self-esteem, as well as greater depression and feelings of guilt than those who don't. In their 2006 article "No strings attached: The nature of casual sex in college students," published in *The Journal of Sex Research*, Grello, Welsh, and Harper report that women who engage in hooking up experience more loss of self-esteem and depression than men—it is not clear whether depression leads to casual sexual behavior or casual sexual behavior leads to depression. Not only that, women who engage in casual sex experience express feelings of good old-fashioned guilt. Men, however, don't necessarily feel guilty for hooking up with strangers, but do feel guilty if they get drunk and hook up with a friend.

While breaking up a dating relationship can also lead to depression, research has found that while the first breakup of a first dating relationship can lead to depression, subsequent breakups are unlikely to do so. The first act of breaking up seems to "inoculate" us, probably because we figure that there is life after a breakup. The opposite seems to be true in more casual sexual relationships. The more you do it, the more guilty and depressed you become. Because of the many negative physical and psychological consequences of hooking up and friends-with-benefits relationships, dating tends to produce more satisfying relationships in the end.

Finally, hooking up and FWBRs lead to less satisfying relationships than dating. In a hookup, ideally neither partner wants or expects anything other than sexual satisfaction. Did you know that, according to that 2006 article by Grello, Welsh, and Harper, half of all college students who engage in sexual intercourse during a hook up never see the other person again? Not only that, 18 percent of women reported in that same study that they consider a hookup to be a stepping-stone toward developing a romantic relationship.

One thing Molly does extremely well throughout her speech is provide transitions. With each transition, she uses inclusive "we" language, which enhances a conversational style and helps listeners easily follow along.

Again, Molly uses rhetorical questions in her listener relevance link to keep listeners focused on how this message is important to them.

Here Molly failed to offer an oral citation for the Sprecher research. She missed an opportunity here to bolster her ethos, and she violated the ethic of honesty because failing to cite a source is considered plagiarism.

In the ideal FWBR, two friends simply become "sex" or "f…ing" buddies without damaging the friendship. But, according to that famous philosopher, Harry Burns in the 1989 movie *When Harry Met Sally*, "Men and women can never be friends because the sex part always gets in the way." Was Harry wrong? Well, as it turns out, yes and no.

In their 2010 study published in the *Journal of Sex Research*, Lehmiller and his colleagues found yes, and I quote:

> *Sex was a more common motivation for men to FWB relationships, whereas emotional connection was a more common motivation for women. In addition, men were more likely to hope that the relationship stays the same over time, whereas women expressed more desire for change into either a full-fledged romance or a basic friendship.*

This is understandable when you consider the biology of sex. According to sex therapist Dr. Ian Kerner, speaking on the Today Show in 2007:

> *During sex, women produce lots of oxytocin, a hormone that stimulates a strong emotional connection. As a result, women are more emotionally integrated when it comes to sex. That's why casual sex and hookups often backfire for lots of women. Guys produce little to no oxytocin, and can easily have sex without any sense of emotional connection. It's sex with no emotional strings attached.*

One of the inherent problems in FWBRs is the ambiguity partners can feel about what they can expect. Euphoria posted this to the sex forum on Women's-Health.com:

> *We have a very good relationship as friends; we're very close. We've been 'talking' since November, and one night I slept over his house and it just happened. The thing that bothers me is that he didn't kiss me in the morning and didn't talk to me until the next night. And on New Year's Eve I also slept over his house, along with other people, and I was probably setting myself up for it cause it happened again. I had left early that morning, around eight, and my friend had told me later on that day that he came into the room she was sleeping in and practically woke her up to kiss her. We did agree to be friends with benefits, but I meant that I'm the only one he should doing it with. Should I say something to him, or do I have no right since we're FWB?*

As I was researching this issue, I came upon an article by Marilyn Murphey on the Askmen.com website that talked about the pros and cons of FWBRs. What I found most interesting was that this article had 139 posts reacting to it. And when I analyzed these posts, 75 percent of them talked about how a FWBR that either the poster or a friend of the poster had been in actually produced problems stemming from one partner wanting the relationship to evolve into something more serious.

But no, Harry wasn't right in one sense. Lehmiller, Venderdrift, and Kelly, in their 2010 article in the *Journal of Sex Research*, also unexpectedly found that both men and women were ultimately more committed to the friendship than to the sexual aspect of the relationship.

Citing a quotation from popular culture—in this case the movie When Harry Met Sally—can be an effective strategy for maintaining listener attention, particularly when giving a heavy speech like this one.

Molly's speech tends to rely heavily on academic journal articles. Doing so is fine, but interjecting a few contemporary sources like this one keeps the speech from becoming too academic at the expense of intelligibility and conversationality.

Again, sources like this one—as long as they are only peppered throughout the speech— make it real and potentially more relevant to her audience.

Molly could have easily left this statement out, because it contradicts the point she is trying to make. However, including it demonstrates the ethic of fairness.

Of course, not all dating relationships lead to "happily ever after" either. However, dating leads to more satisfactory relationships since, if successful, it leads to both intimacy and safe sexual fulfillment. It should come as no surprise that it's the preferred type of relationship of both men and women. In a national survey of over 1,000 college women by Glenn and Marquardt that was published in 2001, 83 percent of them agreed with the statement "Being married is very important to me." And 63 percent agreed with the statement "I would like to meet my future husband/wife in college." Yet 50 percent of the women sampled had had fewer than two dates since starting college. Caroline Bradshaw and her colleagues reported in her 2010 study that 87 percent of women, and even 64 percent of men, indicated a preference for dating over hooking up, particularly when they might be interested in a long term relationship. As "Bad Reputation" put it in his online post, "There are girls you date and girls you have sex with." So I ask you, ladies, who do you want to be?

Based on analysis, I'm sure you can see that dating, while scary and angst ridden, is still a better choice than hooking up or having a FWBR. Both hookups and FWBRs have more physical and psychological risks than dating relationships.

So, before you go out this weekend, get smashed, and find yourself looking for love in all the wrong places, consider giving that someone you've had your eye on a call and see if you can make a date for a movie, or concert, or just a cup of coffee. While it might not lead to a romantic relationship, who knows—it just might.

This survey of both women and men is particularly compelling because it demonstrates not only that research suggests dating is preferred over hooking up or FWBRs, but also that young people themselves prefer dating for initiating long-term relationships.

Molly does a nice job of restating her proposition and providing a clincher that ties back nicely to the opening scenarios.

PROBLEM-SOLUTION

problem-solution: a persuasive organizational pattern that reveals details about a problem and poses solutions to it

A **problem-solution** framework explains the nature of a problem and proposes a solution. A problem-solution pattern can be used with any persuasive speech, but it is particularly useful when listeners may be unaware of the problem or how they personally can work toward a solution. A speech to actuate organized in this way usually has three main points. The first examines the problem, the second presents the solution(s), and the third suggests what action the listener should take.

To convince the audience that there is a problem, you will need to explore the breadth and depth of the issue, as well as provide listener relevance links. You provide breadth by showing the scope or scale of the problem, for example, giving the number of people it affects and proving upward trends over time, including forecasted trends if the problem is not solved. You might provide depth by showing the gravity of the problem. Both breadth and depth may be described through stories and startling statistics.

When you describe the solution, you should be detailed enough for the audience to understand how and why it will solve the problem. The call to action should provide your audience with specific steps that they ought to take to help implement the solution(s).

A problem-solution organization for a speech on reducing gun violence might look like this:

I. *Gun-related violence is a serious problem that affects us all.* (statement of the problem)

    A. *Gun-related violence occurs in urban, suburban, and rural communities and across the country.* (breadth)

        1. *Most recent law enforcement statistics on gun-related violence in the United States.*

        2. *Most recent law enforcement statistics on gun violence in Arizona.*

        3. *An example of gun violence right here in Tempe.* (listener relevance link)

    B. *The consequences of gun violence include injury, disability, and death.* (depth)
        1. *Statistics on gun-related injuries.*
        2. *Story of gun-related disability in a person like the audience members.*
        3. *Statistics on gun-related deaths.*
        4. *Story of local family who died in gun-related murder-suicide.*
II. *Our state legislatures and the U.S. Congress should pass measures to reduce gun violence.* (solution)
    A. *Tighten gun ownership requirements.*
        1. *Require background checks at all sales points.*
            a. *Both public and private sales.*
            b. *Checks for both criminal background and evidence of mental illness.*
        2. *Require "proof of competence" testing for gun licensure like vehicle licensure.*
            a. *Evidence of gun safety procedure knowledge.*
            b. *Evidence of marksmanship.*
        3. *Require periodic relicensing of both guns and owners.*
    B. *Increase criminal penalties associated with violation of gun laws.*
III. *You should e-mail, write, or call your state and national representatives to urge them to support measures to reduce gun violence.* (call to action)
    A. *Bills currently pending in the state legislature.*
    B. *Bills currently pending in Congress.*

PROBLEM-CAUSE-SOLUTION

The **problem-cause-solution** framework is similar to problem-solution but differs from it by adding a main point that reveals the causes of the problem and then proposes a solution designed to alleviate those causes. This pattern is particularly useful for addressing seemingly intractable problems that have been dealt with unsuccessfully in the past as a result of treating symptoms rather than underlying causes. In speeches to actuate, the problem-cause-solution main points are followed by a fourth main point that calls the audience to a specific action.

    Margaret, who lived near a landfill and was concerned about waste overflow, wanted to convince her audience that they should recycle their garbage. As she researched the problem of overflowing landfills, she noticed that recycling was catching on nationally and that, according to 2005 statistics, 32 percent of solid waste was recycled compared with 54 percent, which went into landfills, and 13 percent, which was burned.[5] She also read articles about communities whose recycling rates were higher than average and concluded that the key to increasing recycling was to make it easy and convenient. So she developed a problem-cause-solution speech to actuate that looked like this:

I. *Solid waste disposal is a problem.* (problem)
    A. *Landfills are overflowing.*
    B. *Recycling, while growing, is not widespread in our community.*
II. *Causes for recycling resistance.* (causes)
    A. *Confusion about proper recycling procedures.*
    B. *Lack of recycling containers.*
    C. *Infrequent recycling pickups.*
    D. *Inconvenience.*
III. *Solutions to overcome recycling resistance.* (solutions)
    A. *Promotional mailers and periodic reminders mailed to each residence to clarify and reinforce local recycling procedures and to communicate changes in local recycling programs.*
    B. *Grade-appropriate educational material used in local classrooms.*
    C. *Free recycling containers delivered to each residential address with additional containers available at convenient locations.*

problem-cause-solution:
a form of persuasive organization that examines a problem, its cause(s), and solutions designed to eliminate or alleviate the underlying cause(s)

When your audience agrees with you that there is a problem, but they aren't doing anything to help solve it, you might try appealing to them by identifying the reasons people don't take action and offer solutions related directly to those causes. Do you recycle? Why or why not?

motivated sequence:
a form of persuasive organization that combines a problem-solution pattern with explicit appeals designed to motivate the audience

D. *Increased frequency of pickups planned for and implemented as recycling becomes more pervasive.*

E. *No need to sort recyclables in the home.*

IV. *Audience actions.* (call to action)

  A. *Call your local waste management agency and inquire about recycling policies and procedures.*

  B. *Procure appropriate recycling containers for use in your home.*

    1. *Curbside containers.*

    2. *Containers for in-home use.*

  C. *Educate all family members on proper recycling techniques.*

  D. *Contact local school board members and urge recycling curriculum for your local school district.*

MOTIVATED SEQUENCE

The **motivated sequence** is an organizational framework that combines a problem-solution pattern with explicit appeals designed to motivate the audience. Allan Monroe articulated the motivated sequence as a distinct speech pattern in the 1930s. In the motivated sequence, the normal introduction, body, and conclusion are unified into a five-step sequence described as follows:

1. **The attention step.** The attention step replaces the traditional introduction. Like an introduction, it should begin with a statement that can generate attention. Startling statements, rhetorical questions, quotations, or short narratives will all serve this purpose. Then, you should pique the audience's curiosity by talking about the value of what you are going to say. During the attention step, you might also refer to the knowledge and experiences you have that build your credibility. Finally, just as in a traditional introduction, you will want to clearly identify your purpose stated as a proposition to preview the rest of the speech.

2. **The need step.** The need step explores the nature of the problem that gives rise to the need for change. In it, you will point out the conditions that are unsatisfactory using statistics, examples, and expert opinion to bolster your argument. Then, you will describe the implications or ramifications of this problem. What is happening because the condition is allowed to continue? Finally, you will allude to how the audience might be instrumental in changing the situation.

3. **The satisfaction step.** Having developed a rational argument that there is a need for change, in the satisfaction step you explain your solution to the problem. In this step, you will show, point by point, how what you are proposing will satisfy each of the needs that you articulated in the previous step. If there are other places where your proposal has been tried successfully, you will want to mention these. In addition, you will want to present and refute any objections to the proposal that you can anticipate.

4. **The visualization step.** In the visualization step, you ask your audience to imagine what will happen if your proposal is implemented and is successful. Alternatively, you can ask the audience to visualize how things will be if your proposal is not adopted, or you can do both and have the audience experience the comparison. Obviously, the more descriptive and graphic your visualization step, the more likely it is to have an impact on the audience.

5. **The action appeal step.** In this final step, you might quickly review your main ideas, but then you will emphasize the specific action(s) you advocate. You will also state or restate your own commitment and action that you have

Stephen Wilkes/Stone/Getty Images

taken. You also offer a direct call to action indicating what your listeners are to do and how. Finally, you will want to conclude with a quote, story, or other element that is emotionally compelling.

Let's look at a short outline of what a speech asking the audience to support a school tax levy would look like if it were organized using the motivated sequence.

Proposition: I want the audience to vote in favor of the school tax levy that is on the ballot in November.

   I. Attention step
- **A.** *Comparisons of worldwide test scores in math and science show the United States continues to lose ground.*
- **B.** *I've made an extensive study of this problem, and today I'm going to tell you how you can help stop this decline.*
- **C.** *I'll start by describing the problem; then, I will tell you what you should do and why it will help.*

  II. Need step: *The local schools are underfunded.*
- **A.** *The current funding is insufficient and has resulted in program cuts.*
- **B.** *Qualified teachers leave because of stagnant wages.*
- **C.** *A threatened state takeover of local schools would lead to more bureaucracy and less learning.*

 III. Satisfaction step: *The proposed local tax levy is large enough to solve these problems.*
- **A.** *Programs will be restored.*
- **B.** *Qualified teachers will be compensated so they will stay.*
- **C.** *We will retain local control.*
- **D.** *You'll once again have pride in your community.*

 IV. Visualization step: *Imagine the best, and imagine the worst.*
- **A.** *What it will be like if we pass the levy. How will you feel?*
- **B.** *What it will be like if we don't. How will you feel?*

  V. Action appeal step: *Vote "yes" for the levy in November.*
- **A.** *If you want to see schools improve and the United States catch up to the rest of the world, vote for the levy.*
- **B.** *Come join me. I'm registered, I'm ready, I'm voting for the levy.*
- **C.** *It costs to be the best in the world. Where there is pain, there is gain.*
- **D.** *They say it takes a village, so you can make a difference.*

SPEECH ASSIGNMENT

Actuation Persuasive Speech

1. Prepare a four- to seven-minute persuasive speech in which your goal is to persuade the audience to act. To help you prepare your speech and your outline, go to your CourseMate for *Challenge* to access Speech Builder Express and complete the Speech Planning Action Step Activities.

2. As an addendum to the outline, write a persuasive speech adaptation plan in which you describe:
   - **a.** Target audience initial attitude and background knowledge.
   - **b.** Organizational framework you will use and why.
   - **c.** Arguments you will make to support your proposition (logos).
   - **d.** How you will demonstrate competence, credibility, and good character (ethos).
   - **e.** How you will create and maintain interest (pathos).

Speech to Actuate Evaluation Checklist

_____ 1. Was the introduction effective in creating interest, involving the audience in the speech, and previewing the main points?

_____ 2. Was the specific goal clear and phrased as a proposition?

_____ 3. Was the speech organized into an appropriate actuation persuasive speech framework?

Problem solution

Problem-cause-solution

Motivated sequence

_____ 4. Did the speaker use logos effectively?

Strong evidence?

Reasoning linked to claims?

Fallacies?

_____ 5. Did the speaker use ethos effectively?

_____ Establish expertise?

_____ Demonstrate trustworthiness?

_____ Convey goodwill?

_____ 6. Did the speaker use pathos effectively?

Appeal to negative emotions? If so, check all that were tapped:
_____ fear _____ guilt _____ anger _____ shame _____ sadness

Appeal to positive emotions? If so, check all that were tapped:
_____ happiness/joy _____ pride _____ relief _____ hope
_____ compassion

Were the appeals very effective, somewhat effective, or ineffective?

_____ 7. Was the language appropriate, accurate, clear, and vivid?

_____ 8. Was the use of voice intelligible, conversational, expressive, and convincing?

_____ 9. Was the use of body poised and expressive?

_____ 10. Did the speaker offer a compelling call to action?

Based on these criteria, evaluate the speech as (check one):
_____ excellent _____ good _____ average _____ fair _____ poor

Go to your CourseMate for *Challenge* to access this checklist online under the Chapter 14 resources.

SAMPLE SPEECH

Sample Actuation Persuasive Speech

This section presents a sample speech to actuate given by a student, including an adaptation plan, an outline, and a transcript.

Together, We Can Stop Cyber-Bullying[6]
By Adam Parrish

CONTINUED

CourseMate Read the speech adaptation plan, outline, and transcript of a speech given by Adam Parrish in an introductory speaking course. You can access a video clip of Adam's speech through the Chapter 14 resources of your CourseMate for *Challenge*. You can also use your CourseMate to identify some of the strengths of Adam's speech by preparing an evaluation checklist and an analysis. You can then compare your answers with those of the authors.

ADAPTATION PLAN

1. **Target audience initial attitude and background knowledge**: My audience is composed of traditional-aged college students with varying majors and classes. Most are from middle-class backgrounds. The initial attitude about bullying for most will be to agree with me already that it's a bad thing. So I will try to get them to take action. My perception is that my audience knows about cyber-bullying but not the nuances of it.

2. **Organizational framework**: I will organize my speech using a problem-cause-solution framework because my audience already agrees that bullying is bad but may not know what they can and should do to help stop it.

3. **Arguments (logos)**: I will demonstrate what widespread (breadth) and harmful (depth of effects) cyber-bullying is and why it persists (causes). Once I've convinced my audience, I will propose solutions that must be taken and cite specifically what we must do to help stop this horrible practice.

4. **Building competence, credibility, and good character (ethos)**: I will use credible sources to support my claims and cite them using oral footnotes. I will also offer personal stories to create goodwill.

5. **Creating and maintaining interest (pathos)**: I will involve my audience by appealing to several emotions, including guilt, sadness, relief, hope, and compassion.

OUTLINE

General goal: To persuade

Specific goal: To convince my audience to take action to help stop cyber-bullying.

Introduction

I. "I'll miss just being around her." "I didn't want to believe it." "It's such a sad thing." These quotes are from the friends and family of 15-year-old Phoebe Prince, who, on January 14, 2010, committed suicide by hanging herself. Why did this senseless act occur? The answer is simple: Phoebe Prince was bullied to death.

Attention catcher

II. Many of us know someone who has been bullied in school. Perhaps they were teased in the parking lot or in the locker room. In the past, bullying occurred primarily in and around schools. However, with the advent of new communication technologies such as cell phones with text messaging capability, instant messaging, e-mails, blogs, and social networking sites, bullies can now follow their victims anywhere, even into their own bedrooms. Using electronic communications to tease, harass, threaten, and intimidate another person is called cyber-bullying.

Listener relevance

Speaker credibility	**III.** As a tutor and mentor to young students, I have witnessed cyber-bullying first-hand, and by examining current research, I believe I understand the problem, its causes, and how we can help end cyber-bullying.
Thesis statement (stated as a proposition)	**IV.** Cyber-bullying is a devastating form of abuse that must be confronted and stopped.
Preview	**V.** Today, we will examine the widespread and harmful nature of cyber-bullying, discover how and why it persists, and propose some simple solutions that we must engage in to thwart cyber-bullies and comfort their victims.
Transition	*Let's begin by tackling the problem head on.*

Body

The problem	**I.** Cyber-bullying is a pervasive and dangerous behavior.
Listener relevance	Many of us have read rude, insensitive, or nasty statements posted about us or someone we care about on social networking sites like MySpace and Facebook. Whether or not those comments were actually intended to hurt another person's feelings, they are perfect examples of cyber-bullying.

    A. Cyber-bullying takes place all over the world through a wide array of electronic media.

        1. According to an article in the winter 2005 edition of *Reclaiming Children and Youth*, 57 percent of American middle-school students have experienced instances of cyber-bullying ranging from hurtful comments to threats of physical violence (Keith & Martin, 2005).

        2. Females are just as likely as males to engage in cyber-bullying, although women are 10 percent more likely to be victimized (Li, 2007).

        3. While the number of students who are targets of cyber-bullies decreases as students age, data from the Youth Internet Safety Survey indicate that the instances of American high school students being cyber-bullied increased nearly 50 percent from 2000 to 2005 (Ybarra, Mitchell, Wolak, & Finkelhor, 2006).

        4. Quing Li (2007), a researcher of computer-mediated communication, noted that Internet and cell-phone technologies have been used by bullies to harass, torment, and threaten young people in North America, Europe, and Asia.

        5. A particularly disturbing incident occurred in Dallas, Texas, where an overweight student with multiple sclerosis was targeted on a school's social networking page. One message read, "I guess I'll have to wait until you kill yourself, which I hope is not long from now, or I'll have to wait until your disease kills you" (Keith & Martin, 2005, p. 226).

Transition	*Clearly, cyber-bullying is a widespread problem. What is most disturbing about cyber-bullying, however, is its effects upon victims, bystanders, and perhaps even upon the bullies themselves.*

    B. Cyber-bullying can lead to traumatic physical psychological injuries upon its victims.

        1. According to a 2007 article in the *Journal of Adolescent Health*, 36 percent of the victims of cyber-bullies are also harassed by their attackers in school (Ybarra, Diener-West, & Leaf, 2007).

        2. For example, the Dallas student with MS had eggs thrown at her car and a bottle of acid thrown at her house (Keith & Martin, 2005).

        3. Ybarra et al. (2007) reported that victims of cyber-bullying experience such severe emotional distress that they often exhibit behavioral problems such as poor grades, skipping school, and receiving detentions and suspensions.

        4. Smith et al. (2008) suggested that even a few instances of cyber-bullying can have these long-lasting and heartbreaking results.

5. What is even more alarming is that victims of cyber-bullying are significantly more likely to carry weapons to school as a result of feeling threatened (Ybarra et al., 2007). Obviously, this could lead to violent, and perhaps even deadly, outcomes for bullies, victims, and even bystanders.

Now that we realize the devastating nature, scope, and effects of cyber-bullying, let's look at its causes. Transition

II. Cyber-bullying is perpetuated because victims and bystanders do not report their abusers to authorities. **The cause**

Think back to a time when you may have seen a friend or loved one being harassed online. Did you report the bully to the network administrator or other authorities? Did you console the victim? I know I didn't. If you are like me, we may unknowingly be enabling future instances of cyber-bullying. **Listener relevance**

A. Cyber-bullies are cowards who attack their victims anonymously.
   1. Ybarra et al. (2007) discovered that 13 percent of cyber-bullying victims did not know who was tormenting them.
   2. This is an important statistic because, as Keith and Martin (2005) point out, traditional bullying takes place face to face and often ends when students leave school. However, today, students are subjected to bullying in their own homes.
   3. Perhaps the anonymous nature of cyber-attacks partially explains why Li (2007) found that nearly 76 percent of victims of cyber-bullying and 75 percent of bystanders never reported instances of bullying to adults.
B. Victims and bystanders who do not report attacks from cyber-bullies can unintentionally enable bullies.
   1. According to De Nies, Donaldson, and Netter of *ABCNews.com* (2010) several of Phoebe Prince's classmates were aware that she was being harassed but did not inform the school's administration.
   2. Li (2007) suggested that victims and bystanders often do not believe that adults will actually intervene to stop cyber-bullying.
   3. However, *ABCNews.com* (2010) reports that 41 states have laws against bullying in schools, and 23 of those states target cyber-bullying specifically.

Now that we realize that victims of cyber-bullies desperately need the help of witnesses and bystanders to report their attacks, we should arm ourselves with the information necessary to provide that assistance. Transition

III. Cyber-bullying must be confronted on national, local, and personal levels. **The solution**

Think about the next time you see a friend or loved one being tormented or harassed online. What would you be willing to do to help? **Listener relevance**

A. There should be a comprehensive national law confronting cyber-bullying in schools. Certain statutes currently in state laws should be amalgamated to create the strongest protections for victims and the most effective punishments for bullies as possible.
   1. According to Limber and Small's (2003) article titled *State Laws and Policies to Address Bullying in Schools*, Georgia law requires faculty and staff to be trained on the nature of bullying and what actions to take if they see students being bullied.
   2. Furthermore, Connecticut law *requires* school employees to report bullying as part their hiring contract (Limber & Small, 2003). Washington takes this a step further by protecting employees from any legal action if a reported bully is proven to be innocent (Limber & Small, 2003).
   3. When it comes to protecting victims, West Virginia law demands that schools must ensure that a bullied student does not receive additional abuse at the hands of his or her bully (Limber & Small, 2003).

4. Legislating punishment for bullies is difficult. As Limber and Small (2003) noted, zero-tolerance polices often perpetuate violence because at-risk youth (bullies) are removed from all of the benefits of school, which might help make them less abusive.

5. A comprehensive anti-cyber-bullying law should incorporate the best aspects of these state laws and find a way to punish bullies that is both punitive and has the ability to rehabilitate abusers.

B. Local communities must organize and mobilize to attack the problem of cyber-bullying.

1. According to Greene (2006), communities need to support bullying prevention programs by conducting a school-based bullying survey for individual school districts. We can't know how to best protect victims in our community without knowing how they are affected by the problem.

2. It is critical to know this information. As Greene noted, only 3 percent of teachers in the United States perceive bullying to be a problem in their schools (Greene, 2006).

3. Local school districts should create a Coordinating Committee made up of "administrators, teachers, students, parents, school staff, and community partners" to gather bullying data and rally support to confront the problem (Greene, 2006, p. 73).

4. Even if your local school district is unable or unwilling to mobilize behind this dire cause, there are some important actions you can take personally to safeguard those you love against cyber-bullying.

C. Take note of these warning signs that might indicate a friend or loved one is a victim of a cyber-bully.

1. Victims of cyber-bullies often use electronic communication more frequently than do people who are not being bullied.

2. Victims of cyber-bullies have mood swings and difficulty sleeping (Keith & Martin, 2005).

3. Victims of cyber-bullies seem depressed and/or become anxious (Keith & Martin, 2005).

4. Victims of cyber-bullies become withdrawn from social activities and fall behind in scholastic responsibilities (Keith & Martin, 2005).

D. If you see a friend or loved one exhibiting any of these signs, I implore you not to ignore them. Rather take action. Get involved. Do something to stop it.

1. According to Raskauskas and Stoltz (2007), witnesses of cyber-bullying should inform victims to take the attacks seriously, especially if the bullies threaten violence.

2. Tell victims to report their attacks to police or other authority figures (Raskauskas & Stoltz, 2007).

3. Tell victims to block harmful messages by blocking e-mail accounts and cell phone numbers (Raskauskas & Stoltz, 2007).

4. Tell victims to save copies of attacks and provide them to authorities (Raskauskas & Stoltz, 2007).

5. If you personally know the bully and feel safe confronting him or her, do so! As Raskauskas and Stoltz (2007) noted, bullies will often back down when confronted by peers.

6. By being a good friend and by giving good advice, you can help a victim report his or her attacks from cyber-bullies and take a major step toward eliminating this horrendous problem.

Transition

So, you see, we are not helpless to stop the cyber-bulling problem as long as we make the choice NOT to ignore it.

Conclusion

Thesis restatement

I. Cyber-bullying is a devastating form of abuse that must be reported to authorities.

II. Cyber-bullying is a worldwide problem perpetuated by the silence of both victims and bystanders. By paying attention to certain warning signs, we can empower ourselves to console victims and report their abusers.

III. Today, I implore you to do your part to help stop cyber-bullying. I know that you agree that stopping cyber-bullying must be a priority. First, although other states have cyber-bullying laws in place, ours does not. So I'm asking you to sign this petition that I will forward to our district's state legislators. We need to make our voices heard that we want specific laws passed to stop this horrific practice and to punish those caught doing it. Second, I'm also asking you to be vigilant in noticing signs of cyber-bullying and then taking action. Look for signs that your friend, brother, sister, cousin, boyfriend, girlfriend, or loved one might be a victim of cyber-bullying and then get involved to help stop it! Phoebe Prince showed the warning signs, and she did not deserve to die so senselessly. None of us would ever want to say, "I'll miss just being around her," "I didn't want to believe it," "It's such a sad thing" about our own friends or family members. We must work to ensure that victims are supported and bullies are confronted nationally, locally, and personally. I know that, if we stand together and refuse to be silent, we can and will stop cyber-bullying.

Main point summary

Call to action and clincher

References

De Nies, Y., Donaldson, S., & Netter, S. (2010, January 28). Mean girls: Cyberbullying blamed for teen suicides. *ABCNews.com*. Retrieved from http://abcnews.go.com/GMA/Parenting/girls-teen-suicide-calls-attention-cyberbullying/story?id=9685026

Greene, M. B. (2006). Bullying in schools: A plea for measure of human rights. *Journal of Social Issues, 62*(1), 63–79.

Keith, S., & Martin, M. (2005). Cyber-bullying: Creating a culture of respect in the cyber world. *Reclaiming Children and Youth, 13*(4), 224–228.

Li, Q. (2007). New bottle of old wine: A research of cyberbullying in schools. *Computers in Human Behavior, 23*, 1777–1791.

Limber, S. P., & Small, M. A. (2003). State laws and policies to address bullying in schools. *School Psychology Review, 32*(3), 445–455.

Raskauskas, J., & Stoltz, A. D. (2007). Involvement in traditional and electronic bullying among adolescents. *Developmental Psychology, 43*(3), 564–575.

Smith, P. K., Mahdavi, J., Carvalho, M., Fisher, S. Russel, S., & Tippett, N. (2008). Cyberbullying: Its nature and impact in secondary school pupils. *Journal of Child Psychology and Psychiatry, 49*(4), 374–385.

Ybarra, M. L., Diener-West, M., & Leaf, P. J. (2007). Examining the overlap in internet harassment and school bullying: Implications for school intervention. *Journal of Adolescent Health, 41*, S42–S50.

Ybarra, M. L., Mitchell, K. J., Wolak, J., & Finkelhor, D. (2006). Examining characteristics and associated distress related to Internet harassment: Findings from the second Youth Internet Safety Survey. *Pediatrics, 118*, 1169–1177.

SPEECH AND ANALYSIS

The Speech

"I'll miss just being around her." "I didn't want to believe it." "It's such a sad thing." These quotes are from the friends and family of 15-year-old Phoebe Prince, who, on January 14, 2010, committed suicide by hanging herself. Why did this senseless act occur? The answer is simple… Phoebe Prince was bullied to death.

Analysis

Adam uses quotes from family and friends of cyber-bullying victim Phoebe Prince to get attention and lead into his proposition.

Many of us know someone who has been bullied in school. Perhaps they were teased in the parking lot or in the locker room. In the past, bullying occurred primarily in school. However, with the advent of new communication technologies such as cell phones, text messaging, instant messaging, blogs, and social networking sites, bullies can now follow and terrorize their victims anywhere, even into their own bedrooms. Using electronic communications to tease, harass, threaten, and intimidate another person is called cyber-bullying.

Here Adam further entices his listeners to pay attention by offering listener relevance that we all can relate to.

Using the vivid term "terrorize," Adam appeals to negative emotions (pathos).

As a tutor and mentor to young students, I have witnessed cyber-bullying firsthand, and by examining current research, I believe I understand the problem, its causes, and how we can help end cyber-bullying. What I know for sure is that cyber-bullying is a devastating form of abuse that must be confronted on national, local, and personal levels.

Adam begins to establish ethos by mentioning why he has credibility about this topic. Mentioning that he is a tutor and mentor also conveys goodwill. Listeners are likely to think he must have good character if he volunteers as a tutor and mentor.

Today, we will examine the widespread and harmful nature of cyber-bulling, uncover how and why it persists, and pinpoint some simple solutions we must begin to enact in order to thwart cyber-bullies and comfort their victims. Let's begin by tackling the problem head on.

Adam does a nice job of previewing his problem-cause-solution organizational framework, but his thesis statement phrased as a proposition is somewhat lost and could be made more overtly here.

Many of us have read rude, insensitive, or nasty statements posted about us or someone we care about on social networking sites like MySpace and Facebook. Well, whether or not those comments were actually intended to hurt another person's feelings, if they did hurt their feelings, then they are perfect examples of cyber-bullying.

Again, Adam's use of a listener relevance helps keep listeners tuned in and interested in hearing more.

Cyber-bullying is a pervasive and dangerous behavior. It takes place all over the world and through a wide array of electronic media. According to Keith and Martin's article in the winter 2005 edition of *Reclaiming Children and Youth,* 57 percent of American middle-school students had experienced instances of cyber-bullying ranging from hurtful comments to threats of physical violence. Quing Li's article published in the journal *Computers in Human Behavior* noted that cyber-bullying is not gender biased. According to Li, females are just as likely as males to engage in cyber-bullying, although women are 10 percent more likely to be victimized.

Here Adam bolsters his ethos (and avoids plagiarism) by citing an oral footnote for his statistics.

While the number of students who are targets of cyber-bullies decreases as students age, data from the *Youth Internet Safety Survey* indicates that the instances of American high school students being cyber-bullied had increased nearly 50 percent from 2000 to 2005. The problem does not exist in the United States alone.

Although this statistic is interesting, it would be more compelling to know more recent statistics and the trends since 2005.

Li noted that Internet and cell-phone technologies have been used by bullies to harass, torment, and threaten young people in North America, Europe, and Asia. However, some of the most horrific attacks happen right here at home.

Notice Adam's word choices (harass, torment, threaten, horrific) to enhance pathos.

According to Keith and Martin, a particularly disturbing incident occurred in Dallas, Texas, where an overweight student with multiple sclerosis was targeted on a school's social networking page. One message read, "I guess I'll have to wait until you kill yourself which I hope is not long from now, or I'll have to wait until your disease kills you." Clearly, the cyber-bullying is a worldwide and perverse phenomenon. What is most disturbing about cyber-bullying is its effects upon victims, bystanders, and perhaps even upon bullies themselves.

This example provides an emotional appeal by offering a real example of a real victim in Dallas, Texas.

Cyber-bullying can lead to physical and psychological injuries upon its victims. According to a 2007 article in the *Journal of Adolescent Health,* Ybarra and colleagues noted that 36 percent of the victims of cyber-bullies are also harassed by their attackers in school. For example, the Dallas student with MS had eggs thrown at her car and a bottle of acid thrown at her house.

Ybarra et al. reported that victims of cyber-bullying experience such severe emotional distress that they often exhibit behavioral problems such as poor grades, skipping school, and receiving detentions and suspensions. Furthermore, Smith et al. suggested that even a few instances of cyber-bullying can have these long-lasting negative effects.

What is even more alarming is that, according to Ybarra and colleagues, victims of cyber-bullying are significantly more likely to carry weapons to school as a result of feeling threatened. Obviously, this could lead to violent outcomes for bullies, victims, and even bystanders.

Now that we have heard about the nature, scope, and effects of cyber-bullying, let's see if we can discover its causes. Let's think back to a time when we may have seen a friend or loved one being harassed online. Did we report the bully to the network administrator or other authorities? Did we console the victim? I know I didn't. If you are like me, we may unknowingly be enabling future instances of cyber-bullying.

Cyber-bullying occurs because of the anonymity offered to bullies by cell phone and Internet technologies, as well as the failure of victims and bystanders to report incidents of cyber-bullying. You see, unlike schoolyard bullies, cyber-bullies can attack their victims anonymously.

Ybarra and colleagues discovered that 13 percent of cyber-bullying victims did not know who was tormenting them. This devastating statistics is important because, as Keith and Martin noted, traditional bullying takes place face to face and often ends when students leave school. However, today, students are subjected to nonstop bullying, even when they are alone in their own homes.

Perhaps the anonymous nature of cyber-attacks partially explains why Li found that nearly 76 percent of victims of cyber-bullying and 75 percent of bystanders never reported instances of bullying to adults. Victims and bystanders who do not report attacks from cyber-bullies can unintentionally enable bullies.

According to De Nies, Donaldson, and Netter of *ABCNews.com* (2010), several of Phoebe Prince's classmates were aware that she was being harassed but did not inform the school's administration. Li suggested that victims and bystanders often do not believe that adults will actually intervene to stop cyber-bullying. However, *ABCNews.com* reports that 41 states have laws against bullying in schools, and 23 of those states target cyber-bullying specifically.

Now that we know that victims of cyber-bullies desperately need the help of witnesses and bystanders to report their attacks, we should arm ourselves with the information necessary to provide that assistance. Think about the next time you see a friend or loved one being tormented or harassed online. What would you be willing to do to help?

This vivid example enhances pathos.

Now that Adam has established the breadth of the problem as widespread, he moves into a discussion about the depth of the effects it can have on victims.

Here Adam helps pique listener interest by pointing out how bystanders could also be hurt if we don't do something to stop this form of terrorism.

Notice how Adam's transition verbally ties the point he is finishing (problem) to the next point (causes) clearly using inclusive "we" language. This, too, bolsters a sense of goodwill and uses a conversational style that keeps listeners engaged.

Again, Adam does a nice job with his transition.

Cyber-bullying must be confronted on national, local, and personal levels. There should be a comprehensive national law confronting cyber-bullying in schools. Certain statutes currently in state laws should be amalgamated to create the strongest protections for victims and the most effective punishments for bullies as possible.

According to Limber and Small's article titled *State Laws and Policies to Address Bullying in Schools*, Georgia law requires faculty and staff to be trained on the nature of bullying and what actions to take if they see students being bullied.

Furthermore, Connecticut law *requires* school employees to report bullying as part their hiring contract. Washington takes this a step further by protecting employees from any legal action if a reported bully is proven to be innocent. When it comes to protecting victims, West Virginia law demands that schools must ensure that a bullied student does not receive additional abuse at the hands of his or her bully.

Legislating punishment for bullies is difficult. As Limber and Small noted, zero-tolerance polices often perpetuate violence because at-risk youth, i.e., bullies, are removed from all of the benefits of school, which might help make them less abusive. A comprehensive anti-cyber-bullying law should incorporate the best aspects of these state laws and find a way to punish bullies that is both punitive and has the ability to rehabilitate abusers. However, for national laws to be effective, local communities need to be supportive.

Local communities must organize and mobilize to attack the problem of cyber-bullying. According to Greene's 2006 article published in the *Journal of Social Issues*, communities need to support bullying prevention programs by conducting a school-based bullying survey for individual school districts. We can't know how to best protect victims in our community without knowing how they are affected by the problem. It is critical to know this information. As Greene noted, only 3 percent of teachers in the United States perceive bullying to be a problem in their schools.

Local school districts should create a Coordinating Committee made up of administrators, teachers, students, parents, school staff, and community partners to gather bullying data and rally support to confront the problem. Even if your local school district is unable or unwilling to mobilize behind this dire cause, there are some important actions you can take personally to safeguard those you love against cyber-bullying.

There are several warning signs that might indicate a friend or loved one is a victim of a cyber-bully. If you see a friend or loved one exhibiting these signs, the decision to get involved can be the difference between life and death.

According to Keith and Martin's article *Cyber-Bullying: Creating a Culture of Respect in a Cyber World*, victims of cyber-bullies often use electronic communication more frequently than do people who are not being bullied. Victims of cyber-bullies have mood swings and difficulty sleeping. They seem depressed and/or become anxious. Victims can also become withdrawn from social activities and fall behind in scholastic responsibilities. If you witness your friends or family members exhibiting these symptoms, there are several ways you can help.

Notice how Adam gets right to the point about needing to take action on a variety of levels to stop this practice.

Adam gives credence to his policy statement by pointing to several states that have already succeeded in creating such laws.

Here Adam points to the need for consequences for bullying behavior when it is caught.

Adam offers specific action steps that communities ought to do to help stop cyber-bullying.

Here Adam gets personal, pointing out that each person in the room has an ethical responsibility to help stop cyber-bullying.

According to Raskauskas and Stoltz's 2007 article in *Developmental Psychology,* witnesses of cyber-bullying should inform victims to take the attacks seriously, especially if the bullies threaten violence. You should tell victims to report their attacks to police or other authorities, to block harmful messages by blocking e-mail accounts and cell phone numbers, and to save copies of attacks and provide them to authorities.

Adam could make this statement more compelling by offering a specific example of what one might tell the police, as well as how to install blockers on e-mail and cell phones.

If you personally know the bully and feel safe confronting him or her, do so! As Raskauskas and Stoltz noted, bullies will often back down when confronted by peers. By being a good friend and by giving good advice, you can help a victim report his or her attacks from cyber-bullies and take a major step toward eliminating this horrendous problem. So, you see, we are not helpless to stop the cyber-bulling problem as long as we make the choice NOT to ignore it.

To conclude, cyber-bullying is a devastating form of abuse that must be reported to authorities. Cyber-bullying is a worldwide problem perpetuated by the silence of both victims and bystanders. By paying attention to certain warning signs, we can empower ourselves to console victims and report their abusers.

Here Adam restates his proposition, but it actually could be more comprehensive (beyond just our need to report bullying to authorities).

Today, I'm imploring you to do your part to help stop cyber-bullying. I know that you agree that stopping cyber-bullying must be a priority. First, although other states have cyber-bullying laws in place, ours does not. So I'm asking you to sign this petition that I will forward to our district's state legislators. We need to make our voices heard that we want specific laws passed to stop this horrific practice and to punish those caught doing it.

Adam reminds us of his specific call to action and even asks listeners to sign a petition today. His approach encourages listeners to follow through with his goal, that is, to actuate.

Second, I'm also asking you to be vigilant in noticing signs of cyber-bullying and then taking action. Look for signs that your friend, brother, sister, cousin, boyfriend, girlfriend, or loved one might be a victim of cyber-bullying, and then get involved to help stop it! Phoebe Prince showed the warning signs, and she did not deserve to die so senselessly. None of us would ever want to say, "I'll miss just being around her," "I didn't want to believe it," "It's such a sad thing" about our own friends or family members. We must work to ensure that victims are supported and bullies are confronted nationally, locally, and personally.

Adam does a nice job with his clincher in terms of tying back to the Phoebe story in his attention catcher. Doing so also appeals to emotions (pathos) in a way that should make his speech very memorable.

I know that, if we stand together and refuse to be silent, we can and will stop cyber-bullying.

Ethical Guidelines for Persuasive Speeches

Throughout this book, we have discussed the fundamental behaviors of ethical communicators. At this point, we want to look at six ethical guidelines speakers should follow when their specific goal is to convince the audience to believe a certain idea or to move the audience to action.

1. **Ethical persuasive speeches aim to improve the well-being of the audience by advocating the honest belief of the speaker.** If you have reason to believe that the members of the audience will be hurt or disadvantaged if they believe what you say or do what you ask, then you should not give the speech.

At times, we can get excited about seeing what we can do as a devil's advocate—that is, argue for a belief or action that is totally counter to anything we really believe just to stir up discussion. Although this can be fun when we're dealing with a few friends who just enjoy the spirit of debate, in the real world it is unethical for you to give a speech that calls for the audience to believe something that you do not believe. So, for your persuasive speech, phrase a proposition that you enthusiastically endorse.

2. **Ethical persuasive speeches provide choice.** In any speech, you are free to provide the audience with reasoning that encourages them to evaluate what you have said before making up their own minds. Although it is possible to persuade an audience by manipulating their emotions, using smear tactics to attack opposite points of view (or advocates of those points of view), or coercing them with serious threats, it is unethical.

3. **Ethical persuasive speeches use representative supporting information.** Support your persuasive claims with evidence in the form of statistics, expert opinions, and examples. You can probably find a piece of "evidence" to support any claim, but ethical speakers make sure the evidence they cite is representative of all the evidence that might be used. Although you may use an individual item to show that something is possible, you do not want to give the impression that the item is commonplace. It is unethical to misrepresent what a *body* of evidence (as opposed to a single item) would show if all of it were presented to the audience.

4. **Ethical persuasive speeches use emotional appeals to engage the audience in the rational thought process.** Emotional appeals are a legitimate part of a persuasive speech when they are used to increase the involvement of the audience so that audience members choose the central processing route to listen to, think about, evaluate, and personally decide whether to believe or act. When excessive emotional appeals are used as the basis of persuasion instead of logical reasons, then, although the speech might be effective, it is unethical.

5. **Ethical persuasive speeches honestly present the speaker's credibility.** Because some audience members will process what you say along a peripheral route, using your credibility as the primary factor that determines what they will believe or how they will act, as an ethical speaker you will want to present your expertise and trustworthiness honestly. It is unethical to act as if you know a great deal about a subject when you do not. In fact, most people believe it is unethical to try to convince others of something on which you are not extremely well informed because you may inadvertently misrepresent the arguments and information. Finally, ethical speakers disclose interests that may have inadvertently biased their arguments and may place their interests and those of their audience at odds. You might say, for example, "I think you should know that I work for the Literacy Project as a paid intern, so even though I will do my best to give you the most accurate information possible on this subject, I may not be totally objective."

As you work on your speech, you will want to continually remind yourself of your ethical responsibilities. It's easy to get caught up in trying to build arguments and lose sight of your bigger ethical responsibility to your audience.

Ethical persuasion requires speakers to admit their expertise and trustworthiness honestly, which includes acknowledging personal values that might directly influence one's position.

Rudy K. Lawidjaja/Sipa Press /Newscom

Reflect on Ethics

GM AND THE GOVERNMENT BAILOUT LOAN: TWO SIDES OF THE SAME ISSUE

On April 20, 2010, General Motors (GM) Chairman and CEO, Ed Whitacre, announced that GM had repaid its government bailout loan in full with interest and five years ahead of schedule. His announcement was distributed publically via a piece published in *The Wall Street Journal* and a television advertisement—if you'd like to see the TV ad, you can search for it on YouTube.

The next day, the U.S. Department of the Treasury confirmed the debt as paid in full. But one week later, three congressional representatives wrote a letter to Timothy Geithner, Secretary of the Treasury, claiming the GM story was misleading. They pointed out that, although the debt was repaid, a large portion of the repayment came from the "bailout" money GM had received from the government-owned Troubled Assets

Relief Program, or TARP (P. Ryan, J. Hensarling, & S. Garrett, personal communication, April 28, 2010). Congressman Paul Ryan posted a public response to the GM advertisement, which you can also see on YouTube.

GM stopped airing the advertisement on April 27, 2010.

1 What, if any, ethical communication principles did GM violate in airing the advertisement of debt repayment as it did?

2 What, if any, ethical communication principles did Congressman Ryan violate in airing his YouTube response as he did?

3 Should limitations or regulations be placed on what may be posted on video websites such as YouTube? Explain.

Summary

Persuasive speeches are designed to influence the attitudes, beliefs, values, or behaviors of audience members. This chapter focused on creating effective and ethical persuasive speeches. The first step in preparing an effective and ethical persuasive speech is to analyze your target audience to determine where they stand with regard to your topic so you can decide whether a speech to convince or a speech to actuate is most appropriate. Then you can construct a persuasive speech goal phrased as a proposition that is based on their initial attitude toward your topic. An audience may be opposed to the proposition, have no opinion (because they are uninformed, impartial, or apathetic), or be in favor. Generally, if the target audience is opposed to your proposition, seek incremental change. If they have no opinion, seek agreement. If they are in favor, seek action.

Then, you will choose an organizational framework. If you seek agreement through a speech to convince, you will likely select from among four frameworks: comparative advantages, criteria satisfaction, refutative, or statement of reasons. If you seek action, you will likely select from among three common frameworks—problem-solution, problem-cause-solution, or motivated sequence—to organize your arguments. One important element in an effective actuation persuasive speech is a call to action that clearly describes actions you want audience members to take.

Finally, persuasive speakers must evaluate their speech plan based on the ethical guidelines you have learned as well as some additional ones that are specific to persuasive speeches. These include advocating the honest belief of the speaker, providing choice for the audience, using supporting information that is representative, using emotional appeal to engage audiences, and honestly presenting speaker credibility. Persuasive speaking is challenging but can also be extremely rewarding for those who do so effectively and ethically.

Challenge Resource and Assessment Center

CourseMate Now that you have read Chapter 14, use your Speech Communication CourseMate for *The Challenge of Effective Speaking* for quick access to the electronic resources that accompany this text. These resources include the following:

- **Study tools** that will help you assess your learning and prepare for exams (*digital glossary, key term flash cards, review quizzes*).

- **Activities and assignments** that will help you hone your knowledge and build your public speaking skills throughout the course (*Speech Snippets, Speech Assignments, Action Step*

Activities). Many of these activities allow you to compare your answers with those provided by the authors and, if requested, submit your answers to your instructor.

- **Media resources** that will help you explore communication concepts online (*Web Resources*), develop your speech outlines (*Speech Builder Express 3.0*), watch and critique videos of sample speeches (*Interactive Video Activities*), upload your speech videos for peer reviewing and critique other students' speeches (*Speech Studio online speech review tool*), and download chapter reviews so you can study when and where you'd like (*Audio Study Tools*).

   This chapter's application activities and video resources are featured in this end-of-chapter section.

Applying What You've Learned

1. **Impromptu Speech Activity:** Select an item from a box provided by your instructor. Items could be anything from a small toy to an eating utensil to a tool to a knick-knack. Prepare a two- to three-minute impromptu speech attempting to "sell" the item to the target audience using the motivated sequence organizational framework. Alternatively, groups of three students might do so in a role-play impromptu "television advertisement" selling the product as it fulfills some "unique need" for college students. The "need" might not be what the item is typically intended for.

2. **Impromptu Speech Activity:** You and a partner will draw a slip of paper from a container provided by your instructor. The paper will identify competing topics (e.g., superman versus batman, butter versus margarine, eat eggs/ don't eat eggs, fly versus drive, running versus

walking for exercise). Each of you will prepare a one- to two-minute persuasive impromptu speech advocating opposing positions as a point/ counterpoint activity.

3. **Assessment Activity A:** Watch a television commercial and identify the following: Who is the target audience for the product, and why do you believe so? What would you believe their initial attitude is for the product and why? Identify how the advertisement addresses each element of the motivated sequence and whether it does so effectively. If it does not address an element effectively, suggest how it could be modified to improve. Write up your assessment in the form of a one- to two-page reflection paper.

4. **Assessment Activity B:** Complete all the Action Step activities for a persuasive speech you will give in class.

Speech Planning Action Steps

1.Ep: Writing a Specific Goal as a Persuasive Proposition

Web Resources

14.1: Dealing with a Hostile Audience (297)

14.2: Dealing with a Challenging Audience (297)

Video Resources

1. Use your Interactive Video Activities to watch, analyze, and see the transcript and outlines for Adam's speech to actuate, "Together, We Can Stop Cyber-Bullying." (320)

2. Check out Speech Studio to see persuasive speeches to convince and to actuate given by

other students. How effective and ethical were their speeches? Or record a speech you're working on, upload it to Speech Studio, and ask your peers for their feedback. What feedback could you use to fine-tune your persuasive speech before you give it in class?

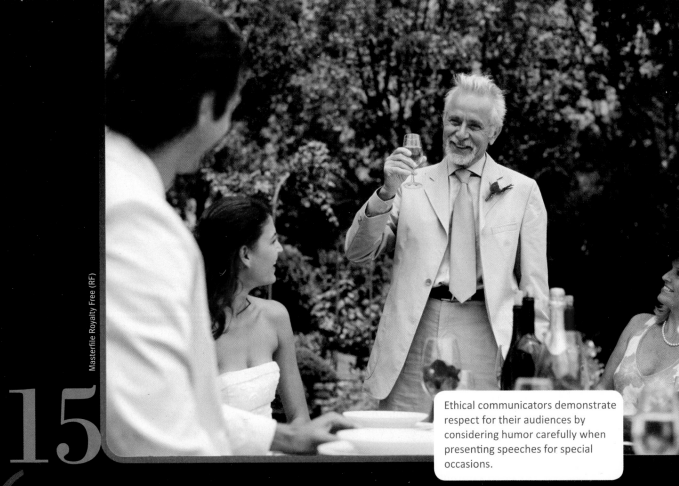

Masterfile Royalty Free (RF)

15

"ceremonial speaking: speeches for special occasions"

Ethical communicators demonstrate respect for their audiences by considering humor carefully when presenting speeches for special occasions.

What's the Point?
QUESTIONS YOU'LL BE ABLE TO ANSWER AFTER READING THIS CHAPTER:

1. What should you include in a speech of welcome?
2. Why should a speech of introduction be brief?
3. What is your goal in a speech of nomination?
4. When might you be expected to give a speech of recognition?
5. What are some common types of speeches of tribute?

Because Ben didn't know his biological father, his grandfather had been like a father to him. He and his grandfather had spent hours playing ball, fishing, or simply watching television together. Although Ben's grandfather had lived a long and fruitful life, Ben was finding it difficult to say goodbye. Still, he wanted to give the eulogy at the funeral. How could he find the right words to do justice to his grandfather's memory?

On special occasions such as weddings and funerals, we may be called on to "say a few words." On these ceremonial occasions, your audience has distinct expectations for what they will hear. So, although the speech plan action steps you have learned will help you prepare your remarks, you also need to understand how the occasion affects how you should shape your speech.

The goal of ceremonial speaking lies somewhere between informing and persuading. In ceremonial speeches, you invite listeners to agree with you about the value of the person, object, event, or place the special occasion revolves around. Another characteristic of most ceremonial speeches is brevity: They are generally—although not always—fewer than five minutes long. This chapter describes six common types of ceremonial speeches given on special occasions: speeches of welcome, introduction, nomination, recognition, acceptance, and tribute. For each speech type, we describe the typical expectations for you to keep in mind as you prepare.

Speeches of Welcome

speech of welcome: a brief, formal ceremonial address that greets and expresses pleasure for the presence of a person or an organization

master of ceremonies: an individual designated to set the mood of the program, introduce participants, and keep the program moving

A **speech of welcome** is usually a very brief, formal ceremonial address that greets and expresses pleasure for the presence of a person or an organization. A speech of welcome is generally not more than two to four minutes long. You can welcome someone on your own, but, more frequently, you will give a speech of welcome as the representative of a group. On some occasion, you may be asked to serve as **master of ceremonies**, an individual designated to welcome guests, set the mood of the program, introduce participants, and keep the program moving. (Either a woman or a man can be referred to as a master of ceremonies.) Year-end honorary banquets, corporate dinner meetings, and local charity events typically use someone in this role.

Expectations

You must be familiar with the group that you are representing and the occasion. It is surprising how little some members of an organization, a community, or a college or university really know about their organization or community. As you prepare your welcome, you may need to do some research so you can accurately describe the group and the circumstances or occasion to the person or people you are welcoming.

A speech of welcome invites listeners to agree that the occasion is friendly and their attendance is appreciated. Do this by respectfully catching their attention and, after expressing appreciation on behalf of your group for the presence of the person or people, provide a brief description of the group and setting to which they are being welcomed. The conclusion should briefly express your hope for the outcome of the visit, event, or relationship. A typical speech of welcome might be as simple as this:

> *Today, I want to welcome John Sheldon, who is joining us from the North Thurston Club. John, as you are aware, we are a newer club, having been established in 2007. At that time, we had only ten members. But we had big hopes. Today, we are 127 members strong, and we raised more than $250,000 last year to support local children's organizations. We hope that our talks here today will lead to closer cooperation between the North Thurston Club and ours here in Yelm.*

At times, you may be asked to give a speech that both welcomes and introduces a speaker. When this is the case, the speech can be a bit longer and should also include the type of information described in the next section.

Speeches of Introduction

A **speech of introduction** is a brief ceremonial speech that establishes a supportive climate for the main speaker, highlights the speaker's credibility by familiarizing the audience with pertinent biographical information, and generates enthusiasm for listening to the speaker and topic. Generally, a speech of introduction is not more than three to five minutes long.

Expectations

The goal of a speech of introduction is to establish the credibility of the main speaker by letting the audience know the education, background, and experience of the speaker related to the speech topic and to suggest why the audience should listen. At times, you will be given a résumé or brief biography of the speaker; at other times, you may need to research the speaker's background yourself. Regardless of what you learn, you should also try to contact the speaker and ask what points in the biography the speaker would like you to emphasize.

The beginning of the speech of introduction should quickly establish the nature of the occasion, the body of the speech should focus on three or four things about the person being introduced that are critical for the audience to know, and the conclusion should mention the speaker by name and briefly identify the speaker's topic or the title of the speech. If the person is well known, you might simply say something like, "Ladies and gentlemen, the president of the United States." If the person is less well known, however, then mentioning his or her name specifically during the speech of introduction and especially at the end is imperative.

Speeches of introduction should honestly represent the person being introduced. Do not hype a speaker's credentials or over-praise the speaker. If you set the audience's expectations too high, even a good speaker may have trouble living up to them. For instance, an overzealous introducer can doom a competent speaker by saying, "This man [woman] is undoubtedly one of the greatest speakers of our time. I have no doubt that what you are about to hear will change your thinking." Although this introduction is meant to be complimentary, it does the speaker a grave disservice.

A typical speech of introduction might look like the following:

> *Today, it is my pleasure to introduce our speaker, Ms. Susan Wong, the new president of the finance club. I've worked with Susan for three years and have found her to have a gift for organization, insight into the financial markets, and an interest in aligning student organizations with leaders in our community. Susan, as you may not know, has spent the past two summers working as an intern at Salomon Smith Barney and has now laid the groundwork for more*

speech of introduction: a brief ceremonial speech that establishes a supportive climate for the main speaker, highlights the speaker's credibility by familiarizing the audience with pertinent biographical information, and generates enthusiasm for listening to the speaker and topic

Speech of Introduction

Prepare a three-minute speech of introduction. Assume that you are introducing the featured speaker for a specific occasion. Criteria for evaluation include creativity in establishing speaker credibility and presenting the name of the speaker and the speech title.

college internships for students from our university. She is a finance major, with a minor in international business. Today, she is going to talk with us about the benefits of summer internships. Let's give a warm welcome to Susan Wong!

Speeches of Nomination

speech of nomination: a ceremonial presentation that proposes a nominee for an elected office, honor, position, or award

A **speech of nomination** is a ceremonial presentation that proposes a nominee for an elected office, honor, position, or award. Every four years, the Democratic and Republican parties have speeches of nomination at their national conventions. Those speeches are rather long, but most speeches of nomination are brief, lasting only about two to four minutes.

Expectations

The goal of a speech of nomination is to highlight the qualities that make this person the most credible candidate. To do so, first clarify the importance of the position, honor, or award by describing the responsibilities involved, related challenges or issues, and the characteristics needed to fulfill it. Second, list the candidate's personal and professional qualifications that meet those criteria. Doing so links the candidate with the position, honor, or award in ways that make him or her appear to be a natural choice. Finally, formally place the candidate's name in nomination, creating a dramatic climax to clinch your speech.

Speeches of nomination should be brief and should make clear that the nominee is well suited for the position, honor, or award. Moreover, the nominee is generally most well received when the nominator is a respected member of the organization. A speech of nomination could be as simple and brief as this:

> *I am very proud to place in nomination for president of our association the name of one of our most active members, Ms. Adrienne Lamb.*
>
> *We all realize the demands of this particular post. It requires leadership. It requires vision. It requires enthusiasm and motivation. And, most of all, it requires a sincere love for our group and its mission.*
>
> *Adrienne Lamb meets and exceeds each one of these demands. It was Adrienne Lamb who chaired our visioning task force. She led us to articulate the mission statement we abide by today. It was Adrienne Lamb who chaired the fund-raising committee last*

You can expect to give a speech of introduction at some point in your life, as event coordinators and sponsors often do. Here, actor Mariska Hargitay greets the crowd and introduces event co-chair Lilly Tartikoff before the beginning of the 8th Annual Revlon Run/Walk for Women.

year when we enjoyed a record drive. And it was Adrienne Lamb who acted as mentor to so many of us, myself included, when we were trying to find our place in this association and this community. This association and its members have reaped the benefits of Adrienne Lamb's love and leadership so many times and in so many ways. We now have the opportunity to benefit in even greater ways.

It is truly an honor and a privilege to place in nomination for president of our association Ms. Adrienne Lamb!

Speeches of Recognition

A **speech of recognition** is a ceremonial presentation that acknowledges someone and usually presents an award, a prize, or a gift to the individual or a representative of a group. Usually, the speech is a fairly short, formal recognition of an accomplishment. You have probably watched speeches of recognition given on awards shows such as the Academy Awards, the Grammies, or the MTV Movie Awards. Some speeches of recognition are typically quite brief (fewer than three minutes long), but occasionally they are longer.

speech of recognition: a ceremonial presentation that acknowledges someone and usually presents an award, a prize, or a gift to the individual or a representative of a group

Expectations

A speech of recognition discusses the nature of the accomplishment or award, including its history, donor, or source, and the conditions under which it is made. Although the tangible award may be a certificate, plaque, trophy, or check symbolizing an achievement, the recognition may have a long history and tradition that you are responsible for recounting.

Because the audience wants to know why the recipient is being recognized, you must know the recognition criteria and how the recipient met them. If the recognition is based on a competition, this might include the number of contestants and the way the contest was judged. If the person earned the award through years of achievement, you will want to describe the specific milestones that the person passed.

Ordinarily, the speech begins by describing what the recognition is for, then states the criteria for winning or achieving the recognition, and finally describes how the person being recognized won or achieved the award. In some cases, the recognition is meant to be a surprise, so you will deliberately omit the name of the recipient in what you say, building to a climax when the name is announced.

There are two special considerations for the speech of recognition. First, as in a speech of introduction, you should refrain from over-praising; do not explain everything in superlatives that make the presentation seem to lack sincerity and honesty. Second, in the United States, it is traditional to shake hands with recipients as awards are received. So, if you have a certificate or other tangible award that you are going to hand to the recipient, be careful to hold it in your left hand and present it to the recipient's left hand. That way, you will be able to shake the right hand in congratulations. A typical speech of recognition may look like this:

When presenting an award, discuss the nature of the award and the recipient's accomplishments. Here, Los Angeles Mayor Antonio Villaraigrosa presents an award at the 76th Annual Blessing of the Animals celebration.

I'm honored to present this year's Idea of the Year Award to Ryan Goldbloom from the installation department. As you may remember, this is an award that we have been

> *giving since 1985 to the employee who has submitted an idea that resulted in the largest first-year cost savings for the company. Ryan's idea to equip all installation trucks with prepackaged kits for each type of job has resulted in a $10,458 savings in the first twelve months. And in recognition of this contribution to our bottom line, I am pleased to share our savings with Ryan in the form of a check for $2,091.60, one-fifth of what he has saved us. Good work, Ryan.*

Speeches of Acceptance

speech of acceptance: a ceremonial speech given to acknowledge receipt of an honor or award

A **speech of acceptance** is a ceremonial speech given to acknowledge receipt of an honor or award. The goal is to sincerely convey to listeners your appreciation for the honor and the recognition and to quickly acknowledge others who have been instrumental in your success. To be effective, the speech should be brief, humble, and gracious. Generally, a speech of acceptance should be no longer than one to two minutes. Remember that the goal in a speech of acceptance is to convey appreciation in a way that makes the audience feel good about you receiving the award.

Expectations

In this speech, speakers should briefly thank the person or group bestowing the honor, acknowledge the competition, express feelings about receiving the award, and thank those who contributed to achieving the honor or award.

Most acceptance speeches are brief. Rarely, as in the case of a politician accepting a nomination, a professional accepting the presidency of a national organization, or a person receiving a prestigious award that is the focus of the gathering, an audience will expect a longer speech. If you have ever watched award programs such as the Academy Awards, MTV Music Awards, the People's Choice Awards, or Grammys, you no doubt have observed an award winner who gave an overly long or otherwise inappropriate acceptance speech. Some of the most famous of them, for instance, were when in 1985 Sally Field chose to say "you like me, right now, you really like me" rather than to humbly and graciously thank the academy for honoring her, and when in 2003 Michael Moore used the occasion to chastise the U.S. president by saying "shame on you Mr. Bush, shame on you" rather than to focus on humbly and graciously thanking the academy. So, when you have the opportunity to give an acceptance speech, you will want to practice it so that you are confident that you can accomplish your purpose quickly. It is also important that you focus your remarks on the recognition you have been given or on the position you are accepting. It is inappropriate to use an acceptance speech to advocate for an unrelated cause. The following is an example of an appropriate speech of acceptance:

> *On behalf of our board of directors, thank you for this award, the Largest Institutional Benefactor in Second Harvest's 1998 Food Drive. It is an honor to be a part of such a worthwhile cause, and it is really our board who should*

be thanking you, Second Harvest, for all the wonderful work you have done over the years. You continue to collect and distribute food to thousands of needy families and individuals, especially to our senior citizens and single mothers. Without your work, many would otherwise go hungry. You are a model of community sharing and caring.

I would also like to thank our company staff—Juanita Alverez, Su Lin, Al Pouzorek, Linda Williams, and Jesus Washington—for their efforts in organizing the collection of food and money to go to Second Harvest. They were tireless in their work, persistent in their company memos and meetings requesting donations, and consistent in their positive and upbeat attitudes throughout the drive! We could not have won this award without them! Let's give them a round of applause, too.

Finally, thank you, Second Harvest, for this honor—and we hope to be back next year to receive it again!

To see an example of an acceptance speech at a formal occasion, go to your CourseMate for *Challenge* to access **Web Resource 15.1: Martin Luther King's Nobel Prize Acceptance Speech**.

SPEECH SNIPPET

Acknowledging the Contributions of Others

When Renee accepted her award for "outstanding community service," she began by acknowledging how much she admired the work of the three other nominees before saying how honored she was to receive the award.

 CourseMate

Reflect on Ethics

WHAT WOULD *YOU* DO?

LANGUAGE OKAY FOR THE OCCASION?

On January 6, 2010, actor and comedian Steve Carell won the People's Choice Award for favorite TV comedy actor. His acceptance speech was filled with sexual innuendos. For example, he said, "Wow! I can't believe it. This is much *bigger* than I thought it would be," and "I'm going to go home, and I'm going to find a special place to *put* this," and "I'm glad I *came*." You can search for and watch Carell's speech on YouTube.

1. What, if any, expectations for an acceptance speech did Carell violate?
2. What, if any, ethical communication principles did Carell violate?
3. Do you think his speech offended any members in the live or television audience? Explain.
4. Based on your answers to questions 1, 2, and 3, do you think his speech was appropriate? Effective? Why or why not?

SPEECH ASSIGNMENT

Speech of Acceptance

This assignment can be paired with the speech of recognition assignment. Prepare a one- to two-minute speech of acceptance in response to another speaker's speech of recognition. The criteria for evaluation are how well you express your feelings about the recognition and your acknowledgment of the contribution of others.

Speeches of Tribute

speech of tribute: a ceremonial speech that praises or celebrates a person, a group, or an event

A **speech of tribute** is a ceremonial speech that praises or celebrates a person, a group, or an event. You might be asked to pay tribute to a person or persons on the occasion of their birthday, wedding, anniversary, oath of office, retirement, or funeral. There are a variety of special types based on the specific special occasion they are meant for. The goal is to invite listeners to truly appreciate the person, group, or event by arousing their sentiments. This is achieved by focusing on the most notable characteristics or achievements of the person, group, or event with vivid stories, examples, and language that arouses sentiments. Speeches of tribute can vary in length from very brief to lengthy depending on the nature of the occasion. Let's take a closer look at three types of tribute that you are likely to be asked to give.

Toasts

toast: a ceremonial speech offered at the start of a reception or meal that pays tribute to the occasion or to a person

A **toast** is a ceremonial speech offered at the start of a reception or meal that pays tribute to the occasion or to a person. On most occasions, a toast is expected to be very brief (lasting less than a minute), consisting of only a few sentences, and focusing on a single characteristic of the person or occasion. Usually, a short example is used to support or illustrate the characteristic. Wedding toasts, given at a rehearsal dinner or reception by a family member or member of the wedding party, are generally longer speeches (three to four minutes) that may use humor but should not embarrass the persons at whom they are directed.

A toast should be sincere and express a sentiment that is likely to be widely shared by those in attendance. The person giving the toast often stands or in some other way separates from the rest of the people. Generally, the person giving the toast and all other attendees have a drink in hand, which they raise and sip from at the conclusion of the toast. So, before offering a toast, it is customary to make sure that drinks are refreshed so that all can participate. If particular people are being toasted, the toast is drunk in their honor, so they do not drink.

A typical toast by a daughter given to honor her mother's college graduation might be:

> Tonight, I'd like to offer a toast to a woman I admire and respect. My mom has always supported my brother and me. So, when she told me that she wanted to go back and finish college, I was worried about how we'd all manage. But I shouldn't have worried. Mom not only finished her degree in less than two years, but she also continued to work full time, and, what's more, she's even had time to coach my brother's Little League team. Here's to you, Mom—you're amazing!

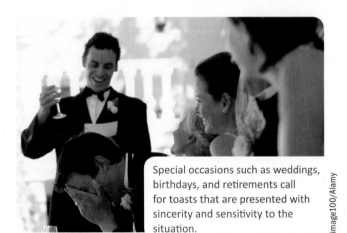

Special occasions such as weddings, birthdays, and retirements call for toasts that are presented with sincerity and sensitivity to the situation.

image100/Alamy

SPEECH ASSIGNMENT

Toast

Prepare a one-minute toast to a specific person or persons on a specific occasion. Criteria for evaluation include how well you illustrate a quality or behavior of the person you are celebrating.

Roasts

One unique type of tribute speech is given as part of a **roast**, which is an event where family and friends share short speeches in honor of one person. In these short speeches, guests might offer good-natured insults or anecdotes, heartwarming or outlandish personal stories, or uplifting accolades. Roasts became mainstream in popular culture when Dean Martin hosted a series of celebrity roasts on television during the 1970s. Some of the most famous celebrity roasts have been of William Shatner, Pamela Anderson, Frank Sinatra, Hugh Hefner, Johnny Carson, and Muhammad Ali. The key when offering a speech of recognition during a roast is to demonstrate the ethical communication principles of respect and integrity by offering only jokes, stories, and anecdotes that do not offend the featured guest by sharing stories that are too private or too vulgar for a general audience. The point, after all, is to honor and laud the guest.

Eulogies

A **eulogy** is a ceremonial speech of tribute during a funeral or memorial service that praises someone's life and accomplishments. Your goal is to comfort the mourners by focusing on positive memories of the deceased person. Based on what you know about the person, select three or four positive personal characteristics of the person to use as the main points, and then use personal stories you have collected about the person to provide support. Your audience will enjoy hearing new stories that exemplify the characteristics as well as revisiting widely shared stories. Incidents that reveal how a personal characteristic helped the person overcome adversity will be especially powerful. To see an example of a eulogy, go to your CourseMate for *Challenge* to access the Interactive Video Activities for Chapter 15. There you can see a video of Oprah Winfrey's eulogy for civil rights activist Rosa Parks. Also access **Web Resource 15.2: Bob Costas's Eulogy for Mickey Mantle.** This popular tribute speech uses language that enables audiences to understand Mantle's impact, regardless of their knowledge of baseball.

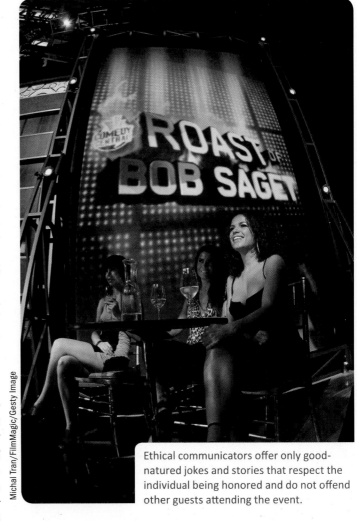

Michal Tran/FilmMagic/Gesty Image

Ethical communicators offer only good-natured jokes and stories that respect the individual being honored and do not offend other guests attending the event.

roast: an event where guests provide short speeches of tribute about the featured guests that are developed with humorous stories and anecdotes

CourseMate

eulogy: a ceremonial speech of tribute during a funeral or memorial service that praises someone's life and accomplishments

commencement address: a speech of tribute praising graduating students and inspiring them to reach for their goals

SPEECH ASSIGNMENT

Roast

Prepare a two- to three-minute roast speech. Criteria for evaluation include how well you identify and develop the person's laudable characteristics and accomplishments in the form of good-natured humorous anecdotes, stories, and examples.

Giving a Eulogy

In the eulogy for his grandfather, "Gramps," Ben highlighted three character traits in Gramps that he admired. One trait was Gramps's patience, which Ben highlighted by telling stories of how Gramps had handled Ben's mistakes during three different incidents: when he tipped the fishing boat at four years old, when he wandered away at the state fair at eight, and when he pouted about a Christmas gift at thirteen. In each instance, Gramps had taught Ben a life lesson by sharing a story from his boyhood rather than reprimanding him.

SPEECH ASSIGNMENT

Eulogy

Prepare a four- to six-minute eulogy for an important person in your life. Criteria for evaluation include how well you identify and develop the person's laudable characteristics and accomplishments.

Other Ceremonial Speeches

Other occasions that call for ceremonial speeches include graduations, holidays, anniversaries of major events, and special events. A **commencement address**, for example, is a speech of tribute praising graduating students and inspiring them to reach for their goals. A **commemorative address** is a ceremonial speech of tribute that celebrates national holidays or anniversaries of important events. A **keynote address** is a ceremonial speech that both sets the tone and generates enthusiasm for the topic of a conference or convention. A **dedication** is a speech of tribute that honors a worthy person or group by naming a structure such as a building, monument, or park after the honoree. A **farewell** is a ceremonial speech of tribute honoring someone who is leaving an organization. A **speech to entertain** is a humorous speech that makes a serious

A Smile Works Wonders

Sally A. Morrison,
Bookstore Owner
Sierra Madre,
California

Sally Morrison's first interest was education. After earning a B.A. in linguistics and an M.A. in education leadership and administration, she worked as a tutor for a private education company specializing in reading instruction. But as she moved into positions of greater responsibility, she found that she was spending 50 percent of her time traveling. That's when she knew she needed to make a change. "It was important to me to stay in one place and invest in the local community…. I looked for something my husband and I could do as a team. I loved reading. So I opened a bookstore—it brought a number of interests together."

Morrison, 35, uses the store to host a number of book-centered events—exhibits, discussions, and signings—as well as "hootenannies for kids … sing-alongs." In addition, several times a year she is asked by social and civic organizations, such as rotary clubs, to speak about the bookstore and her entrepreneurial experience. She covers everything from finding a location for her shop to choosing inventory. These types of speaking events have become natural extensions of her job. In fact, she says, when she speaks in a work context, she doesn't even realize she's doing it.

She credits her comfort in front of audiences to her experiences in Catholic school. Reading at Mass, she says, "I didn't have to say anything I'd written myself, but I was in front of people all the time. It was good preparation." She also gave presentations in class. "Some went well; some I was terrified. It all depended on how comfortable I was with my material. If I loved it, I was excited. If I was out of my depth, those were more difficult."

Like any other speaker, Morrison experiences some of the challenges of public speaking, such as getting nervous or being worried about keeping the audience interested. She relies on many common tips and techniques to help her overcome her challenges—she practices her speeches, does deep-breathing exercises, and remembers to connect with her audiences and smile. "Make eye contact with people in the room—seek out the active listeners. And smile! It makes the speaker and the audience feel better." And, if possible, incorporate something funny. "It's more appealing for the people sitting out there."

> "Smile! It makes the speaker and the audience feel better."

point. To learn more about each of these types of ceremonial speeches, go to your CourseMate for *Challenge* to access "Other Ceremonial Speeches" under the Chapter 15 resources.

Summary

In addition to informative and persuasive speeches, you are likely to have occasion to give speeches to welcome, introduce, nominate, recognize, accept, and tribute. A welcoming speech expresses pleasure at the presence of a person or an organization. A speech of introduction serves to introduce a speaker. In a speech of recognition, you present an award, a prize, or a gift to an individual or to a group. A speech of acceptance is a response to a speech of recognition. A speech of tribute celebrates an occasion, person, or event. Toasts are offered before a meal or reception to celebrate an occasion, person, or people. Roasts are events where family and friends offer short speeches of tribute developed with humorous jokes, stories, and examples about the honoree. A eulogy celebrates a person during a funeral or memorial service.

Other ceremonial speeches include commencement addresses, commemorative addresses, keynote addresses, dedications, farewells, as well as speeches to entertain.

 CourseMate

commemorative address: a speech of tribute that celebrates national holidays or anniversaries of important events

keynote address: a ceremonial speech that both sets the tone and generates enthusiasm for the topic of a conference or convention

dedication: a speech of tribute that honors a worthy person or group by naming a structure, monument, or park after them

farewell: a speech of tribute honoring someone who is leaving an organization

speech to entertain: a humorous speech that makes a serious point

Challenge Resource and Assessment Center

CourseMate Now that you have read Chapter 15, use your Speech Communication CourseMate for *The Challenge of Effective Speaking* for quick access to the electronic resources that accompany this text. These resources include the following:

- **Study tools** that will help you assess your learning and prepare for exams (*digital glossary, key term flash cards, review quizzes*).
- **Activities and assignments** that will help you hone your knowledge and build your public speaking skills throughout the course (*Speech Snippets, Speech Assignments, Action Step*

Activities). Many of these activities allow you to compare your answers with those provided by the authors and, if requested, submit your answers to your instructor.

- **Media resources** that will help you explore communication concepts online (*Web Resources*), develop your speech outlines (*Speech Builder Express 3.0*), watch and critique videos of sample speeches (*Interactive Video Activities*), upload your speech videos for peer reviewing and critique other students' speeches (*Speech Studio online speech review tool*), and download chapter reviews so you can study when and where you'd like (*Audio Study Tools*).

This chapter's application activities and video resources are featured in this end-of-chapter section.

Applying What You've Learned

1. **Impromptu Speech Activity:** Consider what you would like people to remember or know about you if you were to die tomorrow. Prepare

a two- to three-minute impromptu speech eulogy based on the expectations detailed in this chapter.

2. **Assessment Activity A:** Watch the opening segment to a popular late-night television program such as *Saturday Night Live, The Tonight Show, Late Night with David Letterman,* or *Conan* or talk show such as *Oprah, Ellen DeGeneres,* or *The View.* Consider the guidelines for a speech of welcome as described in this chapter. In what ways does the speaker follow or not follow the guidelines suggested in this chapter? How effective do you believe the speaker to be and why? Write up your assessment in the form of a one- to two-page reflection paper.

3. **Assessment Activity B:** Attend a professional public speaking event on campus or in your community. Assess the ways in which the master of ceremonies follows or does not follow the guidelines for a speech of introduction as described in this chapter. Do you believe the speech of introduction was effective in meeting the goals described in this chapter? Why or why not?

Web Resources

15.1 Martin Luther King's Nobel Prize Acceptance Speech (339)

15.2 Bob Costas's Eulogy for Mickey Mantle (341)

Video Resources

1. Use your Interactive Video Activities to watch, analyze, and see the transcript for Oprah Winfrey's eulogy for civil rights activist Rosa Parks. (343)

2. Check out Speech Studio to see other students' ceremonial speeches. Or record a speech you're working on, upload it to Speech Studio, and ask your peers for their feedback. What feedback could you use to fine-tune your ceremonial speech before you give it in class?

SPEECH Studio

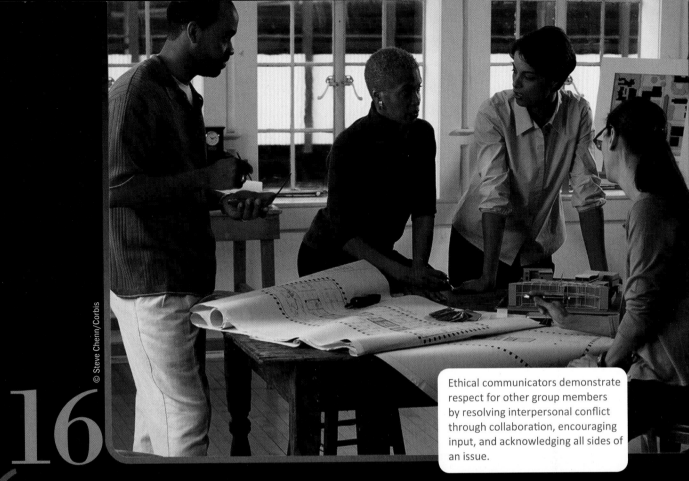

© Steve Chenn/Corbis

Ethical communicators demonstrate respect for other group members by resolving interpersonal conflict through collaboration, encouraging input, and acknowledging all sides of an issue.

16

"developing and delivering group presentations"

What's the Point?

QUESTIONS YOU'LL BE ABLE TO ANSWER AFTER READING THIS CHAPTER:

1. Why is teamwork becoming so popular as a means for solving problems?
2. What does it mean to be a responsible group member?
3. How can you solve problems effectively in groups?
4. How do you prepare a group presentation?
5. How can you evaluate group work?

WORK SESSION 1: Julio, Kristi, Luke, Bryn, and Nick have been asked to work as a small group to prepare a persuasive presentation that will count for one-third of the grade in the course. As the other members see it, Nick is a troublemaker because he has contradicted the instructor several times during previous class sessions. Their impression might be compounded by the fact that Nick wears fatigues to class and brags about being in a militia. Nick has also been absent several times and seems less than fully committed to earning a good grade. In short, the other members are worried that Nick will cause them to earn a lower grade than they would earn without him in their group.

WORK SESSION 2: After the instructor refused to move Nick to another group, Julio, Kristi, Luke, and Bryn decide to restrict Nick's participation by not asking him for substantive help even though that means he'll get a better grade than he deserves. As the full group begins discussing their topic—an assault weapons ban—Nick explains that he has a lot of material on it since he is a fairly vocal opponent of this proposal. Kristi and Luke become disgruntled because they plan to argue in support of the law, and, as they suspected, Nick opposes it. Kristi asks Bryn: "How do YOU feel about this conflict?" Much to Kristi's surprise, Bryn replies, "Actually, I'd like to hear more from Nick before I decide. Nick, tell us more." Nick goes on to share highly relevant information that would eventually be used to strengthen the group's speech. The group soon realizes the hastiness of their judgments about Nick.

Perhaps you have already been part of a group whose task was to prepare a joint presentation. If so, the opening scenario probably sounds familiar. In fact, when asked to work in small groups on a class or work project, many people respond—as Julio, Kristi, Luke, and Bryn did—with resistance. Their reasons usually focus on concerns that a few members will end up doing most of the work, that the group process will slow them down, that they'll earn a lower grade than if they worked alone, or that they will be forced to work on a topic that they aren't interested in or take a position they don't agree with.

Although working in a group to develop and deliver a presentation has its disadvantages, it is the preferred approach in business and industry.[1] These work teams begin as **problem-solving groups**: groups composed of four to seven people that are formed to carry out a specific task or solve a particular problem. Usually at the end of their deliberations, they present their findings and analysis, and recommend solutions to others in the organization. Whether you want to or not, you can expect to work in a group or on a team in your professional life, sometimes in face-to-face settings and often in virtual settings through e-mail, chat rooms, discussion boards, and video conferences.[2] Leaders in business and industry have come to realize that the advantages of

problem-solving group: four to seven people who work together to complete a specific task or solve a particular problem work teams far outweigh the disadvantages. The advantages include deeper analysis of problems, greater breadth of ideas and of potential solutions, improved group morale, and increased productivity.

You can also expect to be asked to present group findings in formal presentations whether in the form of a progress report, sales presentation, proposal, or staff report.[3] So it makes sense to learn how to work effectively in problem-solving groups and how to present your group findings orally. In this chapter, we begin by talking about the responsibilities of group members in effective problem-solving groups, paying special attention to managing conflict among members. Then we describe an effective problem-solving method described by educational philosopher John Dewey. Then we discuss how to prepare group presentations and describe five public presentation formats. Finally, we explain how you can evaluate your group's effectiveness both in terms of the group process and presentation.

Responsibilities of Group Members

When problem-solving groups work well, the product is better than what any one member could have accomplished alone. This is known as **synergy**. Your goal when working in a small group is to achieve synergy. We believe small groups usually fail when members do not understand or follow through with the ethical responsibilities shown in Exhibit 16.1. When met by all members, these five responsibilities result in shared leadership where every member and his or her contributions are valued and synergy can occur.

synergy: when the result of group work is better than what one member could achieve alone

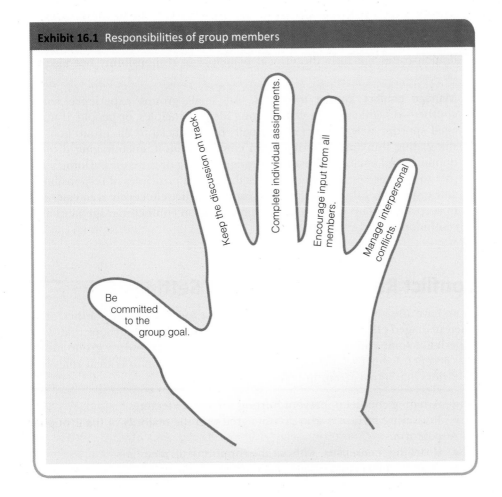

Exhibit 16.1 Responsibilities of group members

Keep the discussion on track.

Complete individual assignments.

Encourage input from all members.

Manage interpersonal conflicts.

Be committed to the group goal.

conflict: disagreement or clash among ideas, principles, or people

groupthink: when group members accept information and ideas without subjecting them to critical analysis

1. **Be committed to the group goal.** Being committed to the group goal means finding a way to align your expertise with the agreed-upon goal of the group. In addition to demonstrating responsibility, doing so also conveys both integrity and respect. So, for a class project, once your group decides on a topic, you need to be a good team member. Realize that this might mean working together on a topic that wasn't your first choice. Once the decision has been agreed upon, however, it is no longer appropriate to dredge up old issues that have already been settled.

2. **Keep discussions on track.** It is every member's responsibility to keep the discussion on track by offering only comments that are relevant and by gently reminding others to stay focused if the discussion starts to get off track. It is unproductive to talk about personal issues during the team's work time. Moreover, it is unethical to try to get the discussion off track because you disagree with what is being said.

3. **Complete individual assignments on time.** One potential advantage of group work is that tasks can be divided among members. However, each member is responsible for completing his or her tasks thoroughly and on time.

4. **Encourage input from all members.** All too often in problem-solving small groups, quiet members are overshadowed by extroverts. Sometimes, outspoken members interpret their silence as having nothing to contribute or not wanting to contribute. On the contrary, all members have valuable perspectives. If you are an extrovert, you have a special responsibility to refrain from dominating the discussion and to ask others for their opinions. Likewise, if you tend to be an introvert, make a conscious effort to express yourself. You might write down what you want to share or even raise your hand to get the attention of other members in an unobtrusive way. Doing your part to ensure that all opinions and perspectives are heard demonstrates not only the ethical principle of responsibility but also of fairness.

5. **Manage conflict among members.** All small groups experience some **conflict**—disagreement or clash among ideas, principles, or people. If managed appropriately, conflict can actually be beneficial to the group goal by stimulating thinking, fostering open communication, encouraging diverse opinions, and enlarging members' understanding of the issues.[4] Doing your part to manage conflict demonstrates the ethical principles of responsibility and respect for others. Because managing conflict effectively is so essential to successful group work, we focus specifically on conflict management and resolution in the next section.

Conflict Resolution in Group Settings

As we have already mentioned, all small groups experience some conflict, and, when managed effectively, conflict enhances synergy. In fact, groups that *don't* experience some conflict risk the problem of **groupthink**—when group members accept information and ideas without subjecting them to critical analysis.[5] Behaviors that signal groupthink include:

- Avoiding conflict to prevent hurting someone's feelings.
- Pressuring members who do not agree with the majority of the group to conform.
- Reaching "consensus" without the support of all members.
- Discouraging or ignoring disagreements.
- Rationalizing a decision without testing it.

So we know that, when groups don't experience any conflict, they run the risk of engaging in groupthink. If effective groups actually experience conflict, then how do they manage it effectively? Effective groups do so when all members understand their personal conflict management styles and follow certain guidelines when addressing potentially conflict-arousing situations. Conflict can occur over issues or personalities. Let's look at how we can effectively handle conflicts from each of these sources.

Group members demonstrate ethical communication behavior by managing conflict, collaborating, perception-checking, and paraphrasing.

diego cervo/iStockphoto.com

Conflict over Issues

Research has revealed five common conflict management styles. These are withdrawing, accommodating, forcing, compromising, and collaborating.[6]

Withdrawing involves physically or psychologically removing yourself from the conflict. For instance, in our opening scenario, if Nick decided to leave the first group session and then not show up at others because he perceived other members didn't agree with him, he would be managing conflict by withdrawing. Similarly, if he would attend the work sessions, but not share his input, he would also be withdrawing. When a group member engages in withdrawing as a conflict management style, the whole group suffers because everyone is not committed to the group goal and all members' input is not being considered.

Accommodating is a passive conflict management style of accepting others' ideas while neglecting your own, even when you disagree with their views. If we continue with the example of Nick and his group members, we could say that Nick is engaging in accommodating style if he goes along with Kristi and Luke, who want to support a ban on assault weapons, even though he personally opposes that view. When a group member engages in accommodating as a conflict management style, the whole group suffers because not all potential ideas are being weighed in the discussion.

A third style of dealing with conflict is forcing. **Forcing** means satisfying your own needs with no concern for the needs of the others and no concern for the harm it does to the group dynamics or problem-solution process of reaching the best solution. When one member dominates the group discussion by forcing his or her opinions without considering other views or even allowing them to be expressed, the whole group suffers because input from all group members is not being heard. Researchers say this results in a win-lose solution. If two or more members engage in competing forcing conflict styles, the whole group suffers, not only because all ideas are not being heard, but also because the discussion gets off track, interpersonal conflicts are not being managed, and the arguments may even impede the completion of individual assignments. If Nick and Luke engage in forcing behavior over whether or not to favor a ban on assault weapons, other input is squelched and the group process comes to a halt. Researchers say this results in a lose-lose solution.

A fourth way to manage conflict is **compromising**, which occurs when individuals give up part of what they want in order to provide at least some satisfaction to other opinions. If the group members can't find an ideal time to meet outside of class because they all have busy schedules, they might compromise on a time to meet that isn't particularly ideal for any of them. In terms of coming to a solution, one drawback of this style is that the quality of the decision is probably affected when someone "trades away" a better solution to reach a compromise.

withdrawing: a conflict management style that involves physically or psychologically removing yourself from the conflict

accommodating: a conflict management style that involves accepting others' ideas while neglecting your own, even when you disagree with their views

forcing: a conflict management style that involves satisfying your own needs with no concern for the needs of the others and no concern for the harm it does to the group dynamics or problem-solution process of reaching the best solution

compromising: a conflict management style that involves individuals giving up part of what they want in order to provide at least some satisfaction to other opinions

collaborating: a conflict management style that involves discussing the issues, describing feelings, and identifying the characteristics of an effective solution before deciding what the ultimate solution will be

A fifth style for managing conflict is collaborating. When you **collaborate**, you discuss the issues, describe feelings, and identify the characteristics of an effective solution before deciding what the ultimate solution will be. Researchers describe this as a win-win situation. Your goal in managing conflict is to achieve a win-win solution through collaborative conflict management among members. A win-win solution occurs when input from all members is heard, valued, and evaluated honestly and fairly until the group reaches consensus about how to proceed. Consider the tips in Exhibit 16.2 to achieve effective collaborative conflict management.

Exhibit 16.2 Collaborative conflict management tips

Initiating Collaboration	Responding Collaboratively
1. Identify the problem as your own using "I language." "I could really use your help here."	1. Disengage to avoid a defensive response.
2. Describe the behavior in terms of behavior, consequences, and feelings. "When I see you checking your e-mail, I feel we're missing out on your ideas for the project, and I get frustrated."	2. Respond empathically with genuine interest and concern by first describing the behavior you observe. "I see you checking your e-mail, and I wonder if you're angry or frustrated with something."
3. Refrain from blaming or accusing.	3. Paraphrase your understanding of the problem and ask questions to clarify issues. "Is there something bothering you or something we're overlooking?"
4. Find common ground. "Figuring this out is really tough. I know I feel overwhelmed about it sometimes."	4. Seek common ground. "I know that trying to come to one goal and solution seems impossible at times."
5. Mentally rehearse so you can state your request briefly.	5. Ask the other person to suggest alternative solutions. "What other ideas do you have that we might consider?"

Personality Conflicts

Sometimes we experience discord with a certain group member due to a personality conflict. The fact is we will all find ourselves working in groups where we don't necessarily see eye-to-eye with everyone or frankly even want to be friends with everyone. In these situations, manage disagreements by separating the issues from the people involved, keeping your emotions in check, and phrasing your comments descriptively, not judgmentally. Rather than calling a particular idea stupid, for example, ask for clarification about why people think or feel the way they do. Seek first to understand. To help you put aside your personal feelings and manage conflicts effectively, employ perception checking or paraphrasing, using "I language" that phrases your interpretations and opinions as your own rather than defense-arousing "you language."[7] In other words, your language needs to reflect the fact that you are responsible for your feelings.[8] Exhibit 16.3 shows some examples of how to change a "you" statement into an "I" one.

Exhibit 16.3 Reframing "you" statements into "I" statements

"You" Statement	"I" Statement
"You hurt my feelings."	"I feel hurt when you don't acknowledge what I say."
"You're so irresponsible."	"I feel my efforts don't matter when you come to the meeting unprepared."
"Don't be so critical."	"I feel disrespected when you say my opinion is stupid."
"I can't believe you said that!"	"I feel humiliated when you mention my problems in front of others."

Perception checking is a verbal statement that reflects your understanding of another's behavior. It is a two-step process: (1) In a non-evaluative way, describe what you observed or sensed from someone's behavior. (2) Add to your statement your interpretations of the behavior. **Paraphrasing** is a verbal statement that conveys your understanding of another person's verbal message. It is a four-step process: (1) Listen carefully to the message; (2) notice what images, ideas, and feelings you experience from the message; (3) determine what the message means to you; (4) create your own a message that conveys these images or feelings and asks the other person to confirm what you have understood or correct it. Exhibit 16.4 provides examples of perception checking and paraphrasing as they may be applied to avoid personality conflict.

perception checking: a verbal statement that reflects your understanding of another's behavior

paraphrasing: a verbal statement that conveys your understanding of another person's verbal message

Exhibit 16.4 Avoiding personality conflict through perception-checking and paraphrasing

Situation	Perception Check	Paraphrase
As you are offering your idea about who the group might interview to get more information on your topic, you notice that Tomika, who you see as uncommitted to the group, says, "Whatever…" and begins reading a message on her cell phone.	Tomika, when you give a dismissive response to my ideas and then start checking your messages, I sense that you don't like my suggestion. Is that an accurate read, or are you just expecting an important message, or is it something else?	From your "whatever" response, I sense that either you don't really agree with my suggestion, you aren't really committed to the project, or you just don't respect me. Or is it something else?
Over the term, Jose has been quick to volunteer for the easiest assignments and has never taken on a difficult piece of work. Today the group was finalizing who would deliver which part of the group presentation and Jose quickly volunteered, saying: "I'll be the master of ceremonies and introduce our topic and each speaker."	Jose, I have been noticing that you have been quick to volunteer and you usually choose the least time-consuming and simplest tasks, and now you're offering to take a role in the presentation that will again require little effort. Are you really overextended in your other classes or trying to take the easy way out, or is there some other explanation?	Jose, it seems to me like you are again volunteering to do the part of the presentation that will be the least amount of work. Are you really overextended with other courses or not committed to doing your share? Or is there some other reason that you want to be the master of ceremonies?
Today is the day that Madison is supposed to lead the group's discussion, as she was responsible for the research on this part of the group's project. As the group waits for her to begin, she avoids eye contact and rummages through her backpack, finally looking up and saying, "Well, I guess that you all are going to be kind of mad at me."	Madison, I'm noticing you don't seem like you want to get the meeting started, are avoiding eye contact, and have been rummaging around in your bag. I get the sense that you haven't done your homework or lost it. Am I on target, or is it something else?	Madison, from what you said, I understand that you are not prepared to lead the meeting. I'm wondering if you did your homework and lost it. Or is there something else?

Systematic Group Problem-Solving Method

When you meet with your classmates, teammates at your job, or members of community to work on a project, you will be trying to solve a problem. At school, the problem may be to develop a group presentation for which each of you will receive the same grade, depending on the total group performance. So whether you are in school, at work, or in your community, to be effective, your group will need a concrete approach that arrives at a productive solution in a short amount of time. One effective means for doing this is the **systematic problem-solving method**.[10] Although this method was created nearly a century ago, its staying power is evidenced in classrooms across the country still today.[11] The method consists of six steps.

systematic problem-solving method: an efficient six-step method for finding an effective solution to a problem

1. **Identify and define the problem.** The first step is to identify the problem or problems and define them in a way all group members understand and agree with. Groups might begin by coming up with a number of problems or needs and then narrow them to a particular one. So your class project group might identify the problems as developing an effective group presentation, identifying a topic for the presentation, fairly sharing the workload, etc. By posing questions, you can also identify and define a problem: What is the problem? What is its history? Who is affected by it, and how does it affect them? How many people are affected, in what ways, and to what degree? These questions help a group realize what kinds of information must be gathered to help define the problem. To ensure that your group is focusing on the problem itself and not just the symptoms of the problem, don't rush through this step.

2. **Analyze the problem.** To analyze the problem, you must find out as much as possible about it. Most groups begin by sharing the information individual members have acquired through their experiences. This process can be described as finding out what we already know. So in your class you may share stories you have heard from students who have already taken the class, share your ideas for topics, and share your hopes and concerns. Then the group will generate questions regarding what the group members still need

to know, which includes questions they still have and experiences they'll want to confirm or reject as typical. So the group may generate a list of questions to ask the instructor about the assignment. Once the group has identified a topic, members may need to get more information about it by doing research. You might consider using questions to guide you in analyzing the problem: Can the problem be subdivided into a series of smaller problems? Why has the problem occurred? What are the symptoms? What methods already exist for dealing with it? What are the limitations of those methods? One important element of this step when working in problem-solving small groups is to share new information with your other group members as you discover it.

3. **Determine criteria for judging solutions. Criteria** are standards used for judging the merits of proposed solutions—a blueprint for evaluating them. Without clear criteria, groups may select solutions that don't adequately address the real problem or, perhaps, solutions that create a host of new problems. Questions that might guide your thinking about criteria include the following: Exactly what must the solutions achieve? Are there any factors that might limit the choice of solutions (e.g., cost, feasibility, location, complexity, expedience, risk–benefit ratio, etc.)? Once you've established criteria, prioritize the list. Which criteria are most important? Which are least important?

4. **Generate a host of solutions.** At this point, you'll want to brainstorm for possible solutions. **Brainstorming**, you'll recall, is an uncritical, non-evaluative process of generating alternatives by being creative, suspending judgment, and combining or adapting the ideas of others. It involves verbalizing your ideas as they come to mind without stopping to evaluate their merits. At least one member should record all solutions as they are suggested. To ensure that creativity is not stifled, no solution should be ignored, and members should build on the ideas presented by others. You might come up with twenty or more solutions. As a minimum, try to come up with eight to ten solutions before moving to the next step. For more on brainstorming, go to your CourseMate for *Challenge* to access **Web Resource 16.1: Rules for Brainstorming**.

5. **Evaluate the solutions and select the best one based on the criteria.** Here you need to evaluate the merits of each potential solution based on the criteria established by the group. Consider each solution as it meets the criteria, and eliminate solutions that do not meet them adequately. In addition to applying the criteria, the group might also ask questions such as the following: How will the solution solve the problem? How difficult will it be to implement? What problems might be caused as a result of implementing the solution? Once each potential solution has been thoroughly evaluated based on the criteria, the group must select the best one(s). For more resources on evaluating solutions and making decisions, go to your CourseMate for *Challenge* to access **Web Resource 16.2: Decision Making Methods**.

6. **Implement the agreed-upon solution.** Finally, the group implements the agreed-upon solution or, if the group is presenting the solution to others for implementation, makes recommendations for how the solution should be implemented. The group has already considered implementation in terms of selecting a solution but now must fill in the details. What tasks are required by the solution(s)? Who will carry out these tasks? What is a reasonable time frame for implementation generally and for each of the tasks specifically?

Preparing Group Presentations

Once the group has worked through the systematic problem-solving method, it's time to prepare a group presentation. Doing so involves a five-step process that starts with dividing the topic into areas of responsibility and ends with practicing and then delivering the presentation.

SPEECH SNIPPET

Implementing Solutions

In their report about gang violence, Matt, Shannon, Pam, and Michelle created implementation plans for parental accountability and for the government to crack down on the illegal gun market. They also provided implementation strategies for churches, businesses, and service groups to offer alternative programs for area youth. Thus, they didn't merely offer solutions; they provided plans for implementing them.

criteria: standards used for judging the merits of proposed solutions

CourseMate

brainstorming: an uncritical, nonevaluative process of generating alternatives by being creative, suspending judgment, and combining or adapting the ideas of others

CourseMate

1. **Divide the topic into areas of responsibility.** As a group, determine the thesis and macrostructure for the presentation. Each member can then be responsible for researching and organizing the content necessary to develop a particular main point. If there are more group members than main points, assign more than one person to a main point or assign one person to develop and integrate presentational aids.

2. **Draft an outline of your topic area.** Each group member should construct an outline for his or her main point. Even though the outline is for only part of the presentation, it must still be thorough, so follow the steps for creating an outline you learned in Chapter 7.

3. **Combine member outlines to form a group outline.** Once the individual outlines are completed, the group is ready to combine them into a single outline. Members should share their individual outlines and then, as a group, develop the transitions between main points and make any other changes needed for continuity and consistency. If no member was responsible for developing the introduction and conclusion, the group should create them now. Likewise, presentational aids should be integrated at this point.

4. **Finalize the details of delivery.** Because this is a group presentation, more than the usual number of decisions must be made about delivery. For example, which presentation format will you use? (The next section in this chapter shows various presentation formats.) Who will speak when? Who will introduce the speakers and when? Where will group members sit when they are not speaking? How will presentational aids be displayed, and who will be responsible for displaying them?

5. **Practice your presentation.** It is crucial to practice both individually and as a group, using the delivery guidelines described in Chapter 11. Because group presentations pose additional complexities, there are more tasks to be done to complete the speech. As a result, there is even more need for practice if you are to succeed at conveying one seamless message to your listeners.

Public Group Presentation Formats

Although your group problem solving will be done in private—without the presence of an onlooking or participating audience—occasionally you will have the opportunity to share your issues in a public forum. At times, this means conducting your group discussion with nonparticipating observers present; at other times, it means presenting your group's conclusions to an audience. As such, public group presentations have much in common with traditional public speaking. Five common formats for public group presentations are the symposium, the panel discussion, the town hall meeting, electronic conferencing, and streaming video.

Symposium

symposium: a discussion in which a limited number of participants present individual speeches of approximately the same length dealing with the same subject and then discuss their reactions to what others have said and answer questions from the audience

A **symposium** is a discussion in which a limited number of participants (usually three to five) present individual speeches of approximately the same length dealing with the same subject. After delivering their planned speeches, the participants in the symposium respond to questions from the audience. Unfortunately, a symposium often omits the interaction necessary for a good discussion. However, if the participants make their prepared speeches short enough to allow sufficient time for questions and answers, a symposium can be interesting and stimulating.

In a symposium, all speakers typically are seated in front of the audience. One person acts as moderator, offering the introductory and concluding remarks and providing transitions between speakers. In a way, the moderator provides

It's a Different World

Rabbi Edwin C. Goldberg
Temple Judea,
Coral Gables, Florida

When he entered the University of Kansas as an undergrad, Rabbi Edwin Goldberg, 47, knew he wanted to pursue rabbinical studies, and he prepared himself in a practical and inspired way. "Rabbis write more than they speak," he says. "They also write *what* they speak. Writing and speaking have organizational similarities, so I became an English major. I learned how to write in a clear and concise way, which has helped me as a speaker ever since."

He never took formal public speaking classes, but many of his life experiences have given him opportunities to speak in front of audiences. He spent a lot of time doing theater in high school. He has served on and presided over numerous rabbinical committees, conferences, commissions, and associations. He has been an adjunct university professor. ("The best speaking experience I got was teaching at university," he says. "I had to speak in complete sentences!") And, of course, he is a rabbi and speaks in front of his congregation routinely.

> **Speaking is different nowadays. It's almost like television.**

Goldberg graduated Phi Beta Kappa in 1984, went on to attend Hebrew Union College-Jewish Institute of Religion in Cincinnati and Los Angeles, was ordained as a rabbi in 1989, and earned his doctorate in 1994. Since 1996 he has served at Temple Judea in Coral Gables, Florida. He finds that the modern world challenges speakers in many ways, even in a setting devoted to worship. "Speaking is different nowadays. A rabbi can't stand up and give the kind of sermon he used to. It has to be more conversational and matter-of-fact. . . . You're speaking in the round with a lavalier mike. You have to practice twice as hard. It's almost like television." But the modern world also provides resources that help him appeal to his audience. "There's no excuse for a bad sermon. There are so many resources available and so much you can find to jazz it up. It's easy!"

All things considered, he believes that the first *Tonight Show* host, Steve Allen, gave the best advice on public speaking: "The most important thing is practice."

the macrostructure for the group presentation. When introduced by the moderator, each speaker moves from his or her seat to the lectern to deliver a speech on the aspect of the topic he or she is covering. Although each speech can stand on its own, all fit together to present the larger picture of the issue. After all speakers have finished, the moderator returns to the lectern to offer concluding remarks and to facilitate the question-and-answer session. Questions can be directed to individuals in the group or to the group as a whole.

The way the group divides the content among speakers depends on how the material was organized. For example, each speaker might focus on one step of the problem-solving process or on one major issue related to the overall topic. If the presentation is persuasive, successive speakers might focus on the problem, the causes, and the solutions. Or one might focus on the need, another on the plan for meeting the need, another on visualization of the future, and another on a call to action. To see a sample persuasive group symposium speech, go to your CourseMate for *Challenge* to access the Interactive Video Activities for Chapter 16. There you can see the speech prepared by a group of students for their symposium "The Dirty Truth about Antibacterial Products," in which the motivated sequence organizational pattern is used to organize the order of the speeches given by each group member.

CourseMate

Panel Discussion

A **panel discussion** is a problem-solving discussion in front of an audience. After the formal discussion, the audience is often encouraged to question the participants. Perhaps you've seen or heard a panel of experts discuss a topic— for example, on radio programs like NPR or C-Span or on television programs like *SportsCenter, Meet the Press,* or *The View.* The group is typically seated in a semicircle to allow the audience to see all participants. One person serves as

panel discussion: a problem-solving discussion in front of an audience

Although panel discussions occur in face-to-face settings, they are often simultaneously delivered electronically for those who cannot attend in person.

Haider Shah/AFP/Getty Images

moderator, introduces the topic, and provides the macrostructure by asking a series of planned questions that panelists answer. Their answers and the interaction among them provide the supporting evidence. A well-planned panel discussion seems spontaneous and interactive but requires careful planning and rehearsal to ensure that all relevant information is presented and that all speakers are afforded equal speaking time.

Town Hall Meeting

A **town hall meeting** is an event in which a large number of people who are interested in a topic convene to discuss, and at times to decide, one or more issues. In the New England states, many small towns use town hall meetings of residents to decide community issues. In a town hall meeting, one person who is respected by other participants is selected to lead the discussion. The leader announces the ground rules for the discussion, introduces the issues to be discussed, calls on participants for comments, ensures that divergent opinions are expressed, periodically summarizes the discussion, and oversees the decision making. Because town hall meetings involve large numbers of people, the leader strictly controls taking turns. In your public speaking course, your instructor may have the entire class participate in a town hall meeting on a particular topic. You may be asked to consult with other students and as a group to represent a particular type of stakeholder. Your group task will be to research your stakeholder's position and then to represent these ideas in the larger forum.

town hall meeting: an event in which a large number of people who are interested in a topic convene to discuss, and at times to decide, an issue

Electronic Conference

Electronic conferencing is a widespread method for individuals to engage in live exchange in real time without being in the same room. The most common forms are **teleconferencing**, where individuals share information aurally over the telephone, and **videoconferencing**, where individuals share information aurally and visually over the Internet. Teleconferencing is the most accessible because one only needs a telephone and a group access code provided by the individual or group hosting the meeting. For a successful videoconference, on the other hand, all parties must have access to a computer, webcam, microphone, and the Internet. Many computers today come equipped with webcams and microphones, and software such as Skype, Webex, and GoToMeeting is downloadable for free or minimal cost. Electronic conferencing can be used to share formal group presentations, as well as for virtual group work sessions. You should follow a few important guidelines to be effective when engaged in electronic conferencing.

electronic conferencing: a widespread method for individuals to engage in live exchange in real time without being in the same room

teleconferencing: where a group of individuals share information aurally over the telephone

videoconferencing: where a group of individuals share information aurally and visually over the Internet

1. **Begin with a round of introductions.** Because you can't always see everyone who is present, particularly during teleconferences, a quick round of introductions provides everyone with a clear understanding of who is participating in the interaction.

2. **Reduce potential distractions.** You should turn off anything that could interrupt you or distract you from focusing on your interaction with others at the meeting. This includes radios, televisions, cell phones, e-mail, and social networking sites such as Facebook or MySpace. It is easy to get distracted by these things during face-to-face meetings, and it is even easier during electronic conferences. To resist the temptation to multitask, proper electronic conferencing etiquette is to turn them off.

3. **Be considerate.** Adhere to the five ethical responsibilities of effective group members during electronic conferences just as you would during face-to-face meetings.

4. **Keep an eye on the time.** Typically, time parameters for electronic conferences are determined in advance. And with teleconferences in particular, the conference shuts down at the predetermined end time. So, when engaged in these virtual meetings, be sure to stick to the agenda and stay on task to be most productive in achieving what needs to be done.

Streaming Videos and Slide Shows

A **streaming video** is a pre-recording that is sent in compressed form over the Internet. You are probably familiar with streaming video from popular websites such as YouTube. Streaming videos are a great way to distribute oral reports, symposiums, or panel presentations. A **streaming slide show** is a series of fifteen to twenty slides posted on the Internet, often including voice-over narration. Streaming slide shows may automatically forward after a certain number of seconds or be programmed so the viewer chooses the pace and controls when the next slide appears. Streaming videos and slide shows are useful when it is inconvenient for some or all the people who need to know the results of the group's work to meet at one time or in one place. Unlike real-time and place presentations, viewers can watch streaming videos and slide shows more than once. When preparing streaming videos and slide shows, be sure to follow all the guidelines for effective use of voice, body, and presentational aids. The same rules for effective face-to-face presentations still apply when delivering your messages online.

streaming video: a pre-recording that is sent in compressed form over the Internet

streaming slide show: a series of fifteen to twenty slides posted on the Internet sometimes narrated with a voice-over

Evaluating Group Effectiveness

Just as preparing and presenting are a bit different for group speeches than for individual speeches, so is the process of evaluating effectiveness. Evaluations should focus on group dynamics during the preparation process as well as on the effectiveness of the actual presentation.

Evaluating Group Dynamics during the Preparation Process

To be effective, groups must work together as they define and analyze a problem, generate solutions, and select a course of action. They also need to work together as they prepare their written report, which in some public speaking classrooms is a formal group outline, and practice the oral presentation.

So it is important to evaluate how effectively each member works in the group. This notion of how individuals work together as a team toward a common goal is known as **group dynamics**. You can evaluate group dynamics by judging the merit of each member's efforts in terms of the five group member responsibilities discussed earlier in this chapter. In addition, each group member could prepare a "reflective thinking process paper," which details in paragraph form what each member did well and could improve upon in terms of the five member responsibilities. In the final paragraph of the paper, each member should provide a self-evaluation of what he or she did and what he or she could do to improve the group process in future sessions. To complete a reflective thinking process paper online, go to your CourseMate for *Challenge* to access **Web Resource 16.3: Reflective Thinking Process Paper**.

Like the evaluations business managers make of employees, these evaluations serve to document the efforts of group members. They can be submitted to the instructor, just as they would be submitted to a supervisor. In business,

group dynamics: how individuals work together as a team toward a common goal

CourseMate

these documents provide a basis for determining promotion, merit pay, and salary adjustments. In the classroom, they can provide a basis for determining one portion of each member's grade.

Evaluating Effectiveness of the Group Presentation

Effective group presentations depend on quality individual presentations as well as quality overall group performance. So evaluations of group presentations should consist of both an individual and a group component. Exhibit 16.5 shows a form you can use to evaluate the effectiveness of a group presentation.

Exhibit 16.5 Sample evaluation form for group presentations

Group Member Name:_____

Critic (your name):_____

Directions: Evaluate the effectiveness of each group member according to each of the following criteria for effective presentations individually and as a group.

Rating Scale:

1 (poor)	2	3	4	5	6	7 (excellent)

INDIVIDUAL PERFORMANCE CRITIQUE

_____ **Content** (Breadth and depth and listener relevance)
(rating) Critique (Provide a rationale for the rating you gave):

_____ **Structure** (Macrostructure and microstructure/language)
(rating) Critique (Provide a rationale for the rating you gave):

_____ **Delivery** (Use of voice and use of body)
(rating) Critique (Provide a rationale for the rating you gave):

GROUP PERFORMANCE CRITIQUE

_____ **Content** (Thematic? Focused? Thorough? Construction of presentational aids?)
(rating) Critique (Provide a rationale for the rating you gave):

_____ **Structure** (Balanced? Transitions? Flow? Attn/Clincher?)
(rating) Critique (Provide a rationale for the rating you gave):

_____ **Delivery** (Teamwork? Cooperation? Fluency? Use of aids?)
(rating) Critique (Provide a rationale for the rating you gave):

Overall Comments:

_____

Evaluating Your Effectiveness

Effective group presentations depend on the combined efforts of individuals. So it's also a good idea to conduct a self-evaluation to determine whether you could be doing something better during the group problem-solving process, while preparing the group presentation, and when giving your portion of the group speech. Exhibit 16.6 is an example of a form used to evaluate your own efforts.

Exhibit 16.6 Sample self-critique form for group presentations

Directions: Complete the items below with regard to your presentation in the group symposium.

1. If I could do my portion of the oral presentation over again, I would do the following things differently:

   a.

   b.

2. In terms of content, I did the following things well in my oral presentation:

   a.

   b.

3. In terms of structure, I did the following things well in my oral presentation:

   a.

   b.

4. In terms of delivery, I did the following things well in my oral presentation:

   a.

   b.

   c.

5. In terms of my role as a group member, I am most proud of how I:

6. In terms of my role as a group member, I am least proud of how I:

7. Overall, I would give myself a grade of _____ for the group speech because:

SPEECH ASSIGNMENT

Public Group Presentation

Following your instructor's directions, form groups of four to six members. Each group will prepare a symposium or a panel discussion of a topic. Groups will use the problem-solving process to guide their work. Each group member must help identify an appropriate issue, participate in the problem-solving process, and take part in the presentation. Your instructor will provide more details of the expectations for this assignment.

Summary

Today, working and speaking in groups are popular not only in the classroom but also in business and industry. Effective problem-solving groups produce better products than individuals can do on their own. Groups are ineffective when some members fail to fulfill their responsibilities as group members. These responsibilities include being committed to the group goal, keeping the discussion on track, completing individual assignments, encouraging input from all members, and managing conflict among group members. Effective groups experience conflict but manage conflicts using collaboration and avoid personality conflict by using the skills of perception checking and paraphrasing.

One effective process for solving problems in groups is systematic problem solving. Members work together to identify and define a problem, analyze the problem, determine criteria for judging solutions, generate many solutions, evaluate solutions and select the best one based on the criteria, and implement the agreed-upon solution.

Once a group has worked through the problem-solving process, members must work together to prepare the public presentation. Groups can present their findings in a symposium, panel discussion, town hall meeting, electronic conferences, as well as streaming videos and slide shows.

Finally, evaluating group effectiveness includes an evaluation of each individual's public speaking portion of the presentation. It should also include an evaluation of group dynamics and group performance as well as self-evaluation.

Challenge Resource and Assessment Center

CourseMate Now that you have read Chapter 16, use your Speech Communication CourseMate for *The Challenge of Effective Speaking* for quick access to the electronic resources that accompany this text. These resources include the following:

- **Study tools** that will help you assess your learning and prepare for exams (*digital glossary, key term flash cards, review quizzes*).

- **Activities and assignments** that will help you hone your knowledge and build your public speaking skills throughout the course (*Speech Snippets, Speech Assignments, Action Step*

Activities). Many of these activities allow you to compare your answers to those provided by the authors and, if requested, submit your answers to your instructor.

- **Media resources** that will help you explore communication concepts online (*Web Resources*), develop your speech outlines (*Speech Builder Express 3.0*), watch and critique videos of sample speeches (*Interactive Video Activities*), upload your speech videos for peer reviewing and critique other students' speeches (*Speech Studio online speech review tool*), and download chapter reviews so you can study when and where you'd like (*Audio Study Tools*).

This chapter's application activities and video resources are featured in this end-of-chapter section.

Applying What You've Learned

1. **Impromptu Speech Activity:** Each group should brainstorm a list of at least ten topic ideas for their group presentation. Then, each member of the group should select one of the topics (no duplicates allowed) and quickly prepare a two- to three-minute impromptu speech whose goal is to convince the other group members that his or her topic should be the one the group selects for

the group's panel or symposium. After members have presented their speeches to the other group members, each member should rank order his or her preference for each topic. Groups should compile these results and use them as they decide on a topic.

2. **Assessment Activity A:** Watch a television talk show program that is presented as a panel discussion, for example, *The View, SportsCenter, Fox and Friends*, or *Morning Joe*. Evaluate the group dynamics process based on the five responsibilities of group members described in this chapter. Be sure to offer specific examples supporting your evaluation as to how each member of the panel performed and what he or

she could do to improve. Then prepare a one- to two-page reflection paper as described in **Web Resource 16.3**. 🔗CourseMate

3. **Assessment Activity B:** Assess how well your group functioned for this project by completing a one- to two-page reflection paper as described in **Web Resource 16.3**. Indicate what each member did well according to the five responsibilities and why, what each member could do to improve and why, and what your role is in that process. Also assess how well you performed according to each of the five responsibilities and why, as well as what you could do to improve, why, and how. 🔗CourseMate

Web Resources

16.1: Rules for Brainstorming (353)

16.2: Decision Making Methods (353)

16.3: Reflective Thinking Process Paper (357)

Video Resources

1. Use your Interactive Video Activities to watch, analyze, and see the transcript and outlines for the group speech "The Dirty Truth about Antibacterial Products." (355)

2. Check out Speech Studio to see group speeches given in other classes. Or record a speech your group is working on, upload it to Speech Studio, and ask your peers for their feedback. What feedback could you use to fine-tune your group speech before you give it in class? ✔Studio

notes

Chapter 1 Foundations of Public Speaking

1. Littlejohn, S. W. (2002). *Theories of human communication.*Belmont, CA: Thomson Wadsworth.

2. Kellerman, K. (1992). Communication: Inherently strategic and primarily automatic. *Communication Monographs, 59,* 288–300.

3. Ibid.

4. Knapp, M., & Daly, J. (2002). *Handbook of interpersonal communication.* Thousand Oaks, CA: Sage.

5. Poole, M. S. (1998). The small group should be the fundamental unit of communication research. In J. Trent (Ed.), *Communication: Views from the helm for the twenty-first century*(p. 94). Needham Heights, MA: Allyn & Bacon.

6. Devine, D. J., Clayton, L. D., Phillips, J. L., Dunford, B. B., & Melner, S. B. (1999). Teams in organizations: Prevalence, characteristics, and effectiveness. *Small Group Research, 30,* 678–711.

7. Morreale, S., Hugenberg, L., & Worley, D. (2006). The basic communication course at U.S. colleges and universities in the 21st century: Study VII. *Communication Education, 55*(4), 415–437.

8. Cooper, L. (1932). *The rhetoric of Aristotle.* Englewood Cliffs, NJ: Prentice-Hall.

9. Koncz, A. (2008). *Job outlook 2009.* Bethl›em, PA: National Association of Colleges and Employers.

10. Hansen, R. S., & Hansen, K. (n.d.). What do employers *really* want? Top skills and values employers se– from job-se–ers. Retrieved from http://www.quintcareers .com/job_skills_values.html

11. Das, S. K. (2003, October 20). Plagiarism in higher education: Is there a remedy? Lots of instruction and some careful vigilance could work wonders. *Scientist,* 8.

12. 2What is plagiarism? (n.d.). Retrieved from http://www.plagiarism.org/learning_ center/what_is_plagiarism.html

13. McCullen, C. (2003, November– December). Tactics and resources to help students avoid plagiarism. *Multimedia Schools,* 40–43.

14. Aristotle. (1960). *On rhetoric.* (L. Cooper, Trans.). New York: Appleton-Century-Crofts (p. 16).

15. Littlejohn, S. W., & Foss, K. A. (2008). *Theories of human communication* (9th ed.). Boston, MA: Wadsworth/Cengage.

16. Bitzer, L. F. (1995). The rhetorical situation. In Covino, W. A., Jolliffe, D. A. (Eds.), *Rhetoric: Concepts, definitions, boundaries.* Boston, MA: Allyn & Bacon.

17. Ibid.

18. Exigence. (2009). In *Microsoft Encarta world English dictionary*(North American edition). Retrieved from http://encarta.msn.com/ dictionary_1861609760/exigency.html

19. Cooper, *Rhetoric.*

20. Jensen, V. (1985). Teaching ethics in speech communication. *Communication Education, 34,* 324–330.

21. Decker, B. (1992). *You've got to be believed to be heard.* New York, NY: St. Martin's Press.

22. Treinen, K. Unpublished manuscript, delivered in speech class, North Dakota State University.

Chapter 2 Developing Confidence through the Speech-Planning Process

1. Hahner, J. C., Sokoloff, M. A., & Salisch, S. L. (2001). *Speaking clearly: Improving voice and diction*(6th ed.). New York, NY: McGraw-Hill.

2. Richmond, V. P., & McCroskey, J. C. (2000). *Communication appr›ension, avoidance, and effectiveness* (5th ed.). Scottsdale, AZ: Gorsuch Scarisbrick.

3. Phillips, G. M. (1977). Rhetoritherapy versus the medical model: Dealing with reticence. *Communication Education, 26,* 37.

4. Motley, M. (1997). COM therapy. In J. A. Daly, J. C. McCroskey, J. Ayres, T. Hopf, & D. M. Ayres (Eds.), *Avoiding communication: Shyness, reticence, and communication appr›ension* (2nd ed., p. 382). Cresskill, NJ: Hampton Press.

5. Phillips, Rhetoritherapy, 37.

6. Richmond & McCroskey, *Communication.*

7. B›nke, R. R., & Carlile, L. W. (1971). Heart rate as an index of speech anxiety. *Speech Monographs, 38,* 66.

8. Beatty, M. J., & B›nke, R. R. (1991). Effects of public speaking trait anxiety and intensity of speaking task on heart rate during performance. *Human Communication Research, 18,* 147–176.

9. Richmond & McCroskey, *Communication.*

10. Beatty, M. J., McCroskey, J. C., & Heisner, A. D. (1998, September). Communication appr›ension as temperamental expression: A communibiological paradigm. *Communication Monographs,65,* 200.

11. Richmond & McCroskey, *Communication.*

12. Bandura, A. (1973). *Social learning theory.* Englewood Cliffs, NJ: Prentice Hall.

13. Daly, J. A., Caughlin, J. P. & Stafford, L. (1997). Correlates and consequences of social-communicative anxiety. In J. A. Daly, J. C. McCroskey, J. Ayres, T. Hopf, & D. M. Ayres (Eds.), *Avoiding communication: Shyness, reticence, and communication appr›ension* (2nd ed., p. 27). Cresskill, NJ: Hampton Press.

14. White, D. (1998, September). Smile when you say that. *Working Woman*, 94–95.

15. Motley, COM therapy, 382.

16. Ibid., 380.

17. Ayres, J., & Hopf, T. S. (1990, January). The long-term effect of visualization in the classroom: A brief research report. *Communication Education, 39*, 77.

18. Scott, P. (1997, January–February). Mind of a champion. *Natural Health, 27*, 99.

19. Ayres, J., Hopf, T., & Ayres, D. M. (1994, July). An examination of whether imaging ability enhances the effectiveness of an intervention designed to reduce speech anxiety. *Communication Education, 43*, 256.

20. Bourne, E. J. (1990). *The anxiety and phobia workbook.* Oakland, CA: New Harbinger Publications.

21. Friedrich, G., & Goss, B. (1984). Systematic desensitization. In J. A. Daly & J. C. McCroskey (Eds.), *Avoiding communication.* Beverly Hills, CA: Sage.

22. Davis, M., Echelon, E., & McKay, M. (1988). *The relaxation and stress workbook.* Oakland, CA: New Harbinger Publications.

23. Richmond & McCroskey, *Communication.*

24. Ibid.

25. Griffin, K. (1995, July). Beating performance anxiety. *Working Woman*, 62–65, 76.

26. Kelly, L., Phillips, G. M., & Keaten, J. A. (1995). *Teaching people to speak well: Training and remediation of communication reticence* (p. 11). Cresskill, NJ: Hampton Press.

27. Ibid., 11–13.

28. Dwyer, K. K. (2000, January). The multidimensional model: Teaching students to self-manage high communication appr›ension by self-selecting treatments. *Communication Education, 49,* 79.

29. Richmond & McCroskey, *Communication.*

30. Study shows how sleep improves memory. (2005, June 29). *Science Daily.* Retrieved from http://www.sciencedaily.com/releases/2005/06/050629070337.htm

31. *Rhetorica ad herennium.* (1954, H. Caplan, Trans.). Cambridge, MA: Harvard University Press.

32. Bitzer, L. (1968). The rhetorical situation. *Philosophy and Rhetoric, 1*(1), 1–14.

33. Aristotle. (1960). *On rhetoric.* (L. Cooper, Trans.). New York: Appleton-Century-Crofts.

34. Fisher, W. (1987). *Human communication as narration: Toward a philosophy of reason, value, and action.*Columbia: University of South Carolina Press.

35. Associated Press. (14 December 2001). O'Leary out at Notre Dame after one we–. *Sports Illustrated.* Retrieved online at: http://sportsiullstrated.cnn.com/football/college/news/2001/12/14/oleary_notredame/

Chapter 3   Listening and Responding Effectively

1. International Listening Association. (1996). Retrieved from http://www.listen.org/

2. Janusik, L. A., & Wolvin, A. D. (2006). *24 hours in a day: A listening update to the time studies.* Paper presented at the meeting of the International Listening Association, Salem, OR.

3. International Listening Association. (2003). *Listening factoid.* Retrieved from http://www.listen.org/pages/factoids/html

4. DeWine, S., & Daniels, T. Beyond the snapshot: Setting a research agenda in organizational communication. In S. A. Deetz (Ed.), *Communication yearbook 16* (pp. 252–230). Thousand Oaks, CA: Sage.

5. Salop–, J. J. (1999). Is anyone listening? *Training and Development, 53*(9), 58–60.

6. Millar, D. P., & Irvine, R. B. (1996, November). *Exposing the errors: An examination of the nature of organizational crisis.* Paper presented at the Annual Conference of the Speech Communication Association, San Diego, CA.

7. Wolvin, A., & Coakley, C. G. (1996). *Listening*(5th ed.). New York, NY: McGraw-Hill.

8. Ibid.

9. Stephens, M. (1999). The new TV: Stop making sense. In Ray E. Hiebert (Ed.), *Impact of mass media: Current issues* (4th ed., pp. 16–22). White Plains, NY: Longman.

10. Dukette, D., & Cornish, D. (2009). *The essential 20: Twenty components of an excellent health care team* (pp. 72–73). RoseDog Books; Turning into digital goldfish. (2002, February 22). *BBC News.* Retrieved from http://news.bbc.co.uk/2/hi/science/nature/1834682.stm

11. Sharpening your listening skills. (2002, October). *Teller Vision* 0895-1039, 7.

12. Bonaguro, A. (2009, September 13). Kanye West steals Taylor Swift's thunder at MTV Video Music Awards. Retrieved from http://blog.cmt.com/2009-09-13/kanye-west-steals-taylor-swifts-thunder-at-mtv-video-music-awards/

13. Lebauer, R. S. (2000). *Learning to listen, listen to learn: Academic listening and note-taking* (2nd ed., p. 49). White Plains, NY: Longman.

14. Wolvin & Coakley, *Listening.*

15. Dunkel, P., & Pialorsi, F. (2005). *Advanced listening compr›ension: Developing aural and notetaking skills.* Boston, MA: Thomson Heinle.

16. Carnegie, D. (1936). *How to win friends and influence people.* New York: Simon and Schu ster.

Chapter 4   Selecting an Appropriate Speech Goal

1. Berger, C. R. (1988). Uncertainty reduction and information exchange in developing relationships. In S. Duck, D. Hay, S. Hobfoll, W. Ickes, & B. Montgomery (Eds.), *Handbook of interpersonal relationships: Theory, research, and interventions* (pp. 239–255). New York, NY: Wiley.

2. Callison, D. (2001). Concept mapping. *School Library Media Activities Monthly, 17*(10), 30–32.

Chapter 5   Adapting to Audiences

1. Bates, S. (2005). *Speak like a CEO: Secrets for commanding attention and getting results.* New York, NY: McGraw-Hill.

2. Blumer, H. (1969). *Symbolic interactionism.* Englewood Cliffs, NJ: Prentice-Hall.

3. Barbe, W., & Swassing, R. H. (1979). *The Swassing-Barbe Modality Index.* Columbus, OH: Waner-Bloser; Canfield, A. A. (1980). *Learning styles inventory manual.*Ann Arbor, MI: Humanics Inc.; Dunn, R., Dunn, K., & Price, G. E. (1975). *Learning styles inventory.* Lawrence, KS: Price Systems; Gardner, H. (1983). *Frames of mind: The theory of multiple intelligences.* New York, NY: Basic Books; Kolb, D. (1984). *Experiential learning: Experience as the source of learning and development.* Englewood Cliffs, NJ: Prentice Hall.

4. Kolb, *Experiential learning.*

5. Dewey, J. (1938/1997) *Experience and education.* New York, NY: Macmillan.

6. Ibid.

7. *The world almanac and book of facts* (pp. 798, 850).(2004). New York, NY: World Almanac Books.

Chapter 6 Gathering and Evaluating Information

1. Munger, D., Anderson, D., Benjamin, B., Busiel, C., & Pardes-Holt, B. (2000). *Researching online*(3rd ed.). New York, NY: Longman.

2. Tengler, C., & Jablin, F. M. (1983). Effects of question type, orientation, and sequencing in the employment screening interview. *Communication Monographs, 50,* 261.

3. Biagi, S. *Interviews that work: A practical guide for journalists* (2nd ed., p. 94). Belmont, CA: Wadsworth.

4. Frances, P. (1994). Lies, damned lies. *American Demographics, 16,* 2.

5. Ahladas, J. (1989, April 1). Global warming. *Vital Speeches,* 382.

6. Shalala, D. (1994, May 15). Domestic terrorism: An unacknowledged epidemic. *Vital Speeches,* 451.

7. Howard, J. A. (2000, August 1). Principles in default: Rediscovered and reapplied. *Vital Speeches,* 618.

8. Trachtenberg, S. (1986, August 15). Five ways in which thinking is dangerous. *Vital Speeches,* 653.

9. Durst, G. M. (1989, March 1). The manager as a developer. *Vital Speeches,*309–310.

10. Becherer, H. (2000, September 15). Enduring values for a secular age: Faith, hope and love. *Vital Speeches,* 732.

11. Opheim, C. (2000, November 1). Making democracy work: Your responsibility to society. *Vital Speeches,* 60.

12. Kreps, D. (2009, September 16). Satriani's 'Viva La Vida' copyright suit against Coldplay dismissed. *Rolling Stone.* Retrieved from http://www.rollingstone.com/rockdaily/inde.php/2009/09/16satrianis-viva-la-vida-copyright-suit-against-coldplay-dismissed/

Chapter 7 Organizing and Outlining the Speech Body

1. Fisher, W. (1987). *Human communication as narration: Toward a philosophy of reason, value, and action.* Columbia, SC: University of South Carolina Press.

2. Kids book gets pulled. (2006, January 31). *Associated Press.* Retrieved from http://www.canada.com/topics/entertainment/story.html?id=45761b54-245c-4c76-9618-212c645f9800&k=23104

3. Deahl, R. (2006, January 31). Blue Apple to cancel book. *Publishers We–ly.* Retrieved from http://www.publisherswe–ly.com/article/CA6303375.html

Chapter 8 The Introduction and Conclusion

1. Trenholm, S. (1989). *Persuasion and social influence.*New Jersey: Prentice-Hall; Crano, W. D. (1977). Primacy versus recency in retention of information and opinion change. *The Journal of Social Psychology, 101,* 87–96.

2. Mackay, H. (2009, July). Changing the world: Your future is a work in progress. *Vital Speeches,* 319–323.

3. Gupta, Y. (2010, February). Beyond wisdom: Business dimensions of an aging America. *Vital Speeches,* 69–75.

4. Humes, J. C. (1988). *Standing ovation: How to be an effective speaker and communicator.* New York: Harper & Row,.

5. Cole, B. (2002, July). The urgency of memory: The arts give us history. *Vital Speeches of the Day,* 563–565.

6. Mason, S. (2007, April). Equality will someday come. *Vital Speeches,* 159–163.

7. Olson, L. (2009, January). Same-sex marriage: Fool's gold in California. *Vital Speeches,* 41–43.

8. The Princeton Language Institute (Ed.). (1993). *21st century dictionary of quotations.*New York: Laurel.

9. Bitzer, L. F. (1995). The Rhetorical Situation. In W. A. Covino & D. A. Jolliffe (Eds.), *Rhetoric: Concepts, Definitions, Boundaries.* Boston, MA: Allyn and Bacon.

10. Aristotle. (1954). *Rhetoric* (W. Rhys Roberts, Trans.). New York: Modern Library.

11. Mariano, C. (2010, January). Unity, quality, responsibility: The real meaning of the words. *Vital Speeches,* 20–22.

12. Jobs, S. (2005, 15 June). You've got to find what you love. *Stanford University News.* Retrieved from http://news.stanford.edu/news/2005/june15/jobs-061505.html

13. Cossolotto, M. (2009, December). An urgent call to action for study abroad alumni to help reduce our global awareness deficit. *Vital Speeches,* 564–568.

Chapter 9 Presentational Aids

1. Muren, D. (2009). *Humblefacturing a sustainable electronic future.* Presentation at Ignite Seattle 6. Retrieved from http://www.youtube.com/watch?v=FIoU1pemi18

2. Tversky, B. (1997). Memory for pictures, maps, environments, and graphs.In D. G. Payne & F. G. Conrad (Eds.), *Intersections in basic and applied memory research* (pp. 257–277). Hillsdale, NJ: Erlbaum.

3. Kolb, D. (1984). *Experiential learning: Experience as the source of learning and development.* Englewood Cliffs, NJ: Prentice Hall; Gallo, C. (2006, December 5). Presentations with something for everyone. *Business We– Online.* Retrieved from http://www.businesswe–.com/smallbiz/content/dec2006/sb20061205_454055.htm

4. Hanke, J. (1998). The psychology of presentation visuals. *Presentations, 12*(5), 42–47.

5. Ayers, J. (1991). Using visual aids to reduce speech anxiety. *Communication Research Reports,* 73–79; Dwyer, K. (1991). *Conquer your speechfright.* Orlando, FL: Harcourt Brace.

6. Maun, K. (2009, May 7). Anti-abortion protesters disturbing communities: Anti-choice activists' graphic images in protests upsetting many. *Suite101.com.* Retrieved from http://activism.suite101.com/article.cfm/have_antichoice_protestors_gone_too_far_yes

7. Booher, D. D. (2003). *Speak with confidence [electronic resources]: Powerful presentations that inform, inspire, and persuade.* New York, NY: McGraw-Hill.

8. Kolb, *Experiential Learning*; Long, K. (1997). *Visual-Aids and Learning,* University of Portsmouth, http://www.mech.port.ac.uk/av/AVInfo.htm

9. Wahl, A. (2003, November 23). PowerPoint of no return. *Canadian Business, 76*(22); Brandt, J. R. (2007, January). Missing the (Power)point: When bullet points fly, attention spans die. *Industry We–.* Retrieved from http://www.industrywe–.com

Chapter 10 Language and Oral Style

1. Witt, P. L., Wheeless, L. R., & Allen, M. (2007, May). A meta-analytical review of the relationship between teacher immediacy and student learning. Paper presented at the annual meeting of the International Communication Association, San Diego. Retrieved from http://www.allacademic.com/meta/p112238_index.html

2. Edwards, C. C. (2002). Verbal immediacy and androgyny: An examination of student perceptions of college instructors. *Academic Exchange Quarterly,*6, 180–185; Gorham, J. (1998). The relationship between teacher verbal immediacy b›aviors and student learning. *Communication Education,* 37, 40–53; Powell R. G., & Harville, B. (1990). The effects of teacher immediacy and clarity on instructional outcomes: An intercultural assessment. *Communication Education,* 39, 369–379.

3. Braithwaite D., & Braithwaite, C. (1997). Viewing persons with disabilities as a culture. In L. Samovar & R. Porter (Eds.), *Intercultural communication: A reader* (8th ed., pp. 154–164). Belmont, CA: Wadsworth; Treinen, K., & Warren, J. (2001). Antiracist pedagogy in the basic course: Teaching

cultural communication as if whiteness matters. *Basic Communication Course Annual,*13, 46–75.

4. Stewart, L. P., Cooper, P. J., Stewart, A. D., & Friedley, S. A. (2003). *Communication and gender*(4th ed., p. 63). Boston, MA: Allyn & Bacon.

5. Gastil, J. (1990). Generic pronouns and sexist language: The oxymoronic character of masculine generics. *Sex Roles,* 23,629–643; Hamilton, M. C. (1991). Masculine bias in the attribution of personhood: People = male, male = people. *Psychology of Women Quarterly,* 15, 393–402; Switzer, J. W. (1990). The impact of generic word choices: An empirical investigation of age- and sex-related differences. *Sex Roles,* 22, 69–82.

6. Treinen and Warren, Antiracist pedagogy in the basic course.

7. Gudykunst, W. B., & Matsumoto, Y. (1996). Cross-cultural variability of communication in personal relationships. In W. B. Gudykunst, S. Ting-Toomey, & T. Nishida (Eds.), *Communication in personal relationships across cultures* (p. 21). Thousand Oaks, CA: Sage.

8. Hofstede, G. (1991). *Cultures and organizations: Software of the mind* (p. 67). New York, NY: McGraw-Hill.

9. Levine, D. (1985). *The flight from ambiguity*(p. 28). Chicago, IL: University of Chicago Press.

10. **Anti-Defamation League: National Security Adviser Jones told "inappropriate, stereotypic" joke about Jewish merchant (2010, April 26). ABCNews.com. Retrieved from http://blogs.abcnews.com/politicalpunch/2010/04/ antidefamation-league-national-security-adviser-jones-told-inappropriate-stereotypic-joke-about-jewi.html**

11. MTV Video Music Awards. (2003, August 28). Retrieved from http:// www.mtv.com/onair/vma/2003/

12. DuFrene D. D., & L›man, C. M. (2002, March). Persuasive appeal for clean language. *Business Quarterly,* 65, 48.

13. O'Connor, J. V. (2000). FAQs #1 Cuss Control Academy. Retrieved from http://www.cusscontrol.com/faqs.html

14. Duck, S. W. (1994). *Meaningful relationships.*Thousand Oaks, CA: Sage. See also Shotter, J. (1993). *Conversational realities: The construction of life through language.* Newbury Park, CA: Sage.

15. Richards, I. A., & Ogden, C. K. (1923) *The meaning of meaning: A study of the influence of language upon thought and the science of symbolism.* Orlando, FL: Harcourt.

16. Ibid.

17. Fought, C. (2003). *Chicano English in context*(pp. 64–78). New York, NY: Pallgrave MacMillan.

18. Glenn, C., & Gray, L. (2010). *Hodges Harbrace handbook* (17th ed.). Belmont, CA: Cengage Learning.

19. Robinson, A. (2001). *Word smart: Building an educated vocabulary* (3rd ed.). Princeton, NJ: Princeton Review.

20. Rader, W. (2007). The online slang dictionary. Retrieved from http://www.ocf.berkeley.edu/~wrader/slang/b.html

21. Hensley, C. W. (1995, September 1). Speak with style and watch the impact. *Vital Speeches of the Day,* p. 703.

22. Schertz, R. H. (1977, November 1). Deregulation: After the airlines, is trucking next? *Vital Speeches,* p. 40.

Chapter 11 Practicing Delivery

1. Decker, B. (1992). *You've got to be believed to be heard.*New York, NY: St. Martin's Press.

2. Watzlawick, P., Bavelas, J. B., & Jackson, D. D. (1967). *Pragmatics of human communication.*New York, NY: Norton.

3. Don't care for Nano or No-No: Mamta. (2009, March 23). *Hindustan Times.* Retrieved from http://www. hindustantimes.com; Kachru, B. B. (1992). *The other tongue: English across cultures.* Urbana, IL: University

of Illinois Press; Kachru, B. B. (1986). *The alchemy of English: The spread, functions, and models of non-native Englishes.* Oxford: Pergamon Press; Guj riots a national shame, not IPL going abroad: PC. (2009, March 23). *The Financial Express.* Retrieved from http://www. expressindia.com; Patrolling intensified in sea, on shores in Tamil Nadu. (2009, March 23). *Press Trust of India.* Retrieved from http://www.ptinews .com; Wiltshire, C., & Moon, R. (2003). Phonetic stress in Indian English vs. American English. *World Englishes,* 22(3), 291–303; Zardari is 5th biggest loser in world: Foreign policy magazine. (2009, March 23). *NDTV.* Retrieved from http://www .ndtv.com

4. Burgoon, J. K., Coker, D. A., & Coker, R. A. (1986). Communicative effects of gaze b›avior: A test of two contrasting explanations. *Human Communication Research,* 12, 495–524.

5. Chiang, L. H. (1993). *Beyond the language: Native Americans' nonverbal communication.*Paper presented at the Annual Meeting of the Midwest Association of Teachers of Educational Psychology, Anderson, IN (ERIC Document Services No. ED 368540).

6. Bates, B. (1992). *Communication and the Sexes.* Prospect Heights, IL: Waveland Press; Cherulnik, P. D. (1989). *Physical attractiveness and judged suitability for leadership,* Report No. CG 021 893. Paper presented at the Annual Meeting of the Midwestern Psychological Association, Chicago, IL (ERIC Document Services No. ED 310 317); Lawrence S. G., & Watson, M. (1991). Getting others to help: The effectiveness of professional uniforms in charitable fund raising. *Journal of Applied Communication Research,* 19, 170–185; Malloy, J. T. (1975). *Dress for Success.* New York, NY: Warner; and Temple, L. E., & Loewen, K. R. (1993). Perceptions of power: First impressions of a woman wearing a jacket. *Perceptual and Motor Skills,* 76, 339–348.

7. Phillips P. A., & Smith, L. R. (1992). *The effects of teacher dress on student perceptions,* Report No. SP 033 944. (ERIC Document Services No. ED 347 151).

8. Morris, T. L., Gorham, J., Cohen, S. H., & Huffman, D. (1996). Fashion in the classroom: Effects of attire on student perceptions of instructors in college classes. *Communication Education,* 45, 135–148.

9. Menzel, K. E., & Carrell, L. J. (1994). The relationship between preparation and performance in public speaking. *Communication Education,* 43, 23.

10. Palin's 'cheat sheet' on hand. *CNN.com.*Retrieved from http://www.cnn.com/video/#/video/politics/2010/02/08/ lemon.palin.cheat.sheet.cnn?iref=allsearch

11. Used with permission of Alyssa Grace Millner.

Chapter 12 Informative Speaking

1. Otzi, the ice man. (n.d.). *Dig: The archaeology magazine for kids.* Retrieved from http://www.digonsite.com/drdig/ mummy/22.html

2. Dote, L., Cramer, K., Dietz, N., & Grimm, R. Jr. (2006). *College students helping America.*Washington, DC: Corporation for National and Community Service.

3. Vegan Society website. Retrieved from http://www. vegansociety.com

4. Based on "Narrative" by Baerwald, D., & Northshore School District. Retrieved from http://ccweb.norshore.wednet.edu/ writingcorner/narrative.html

5. Used with permission of Louisa Greene.

6. Needleman, R. (Host). (2010, May 7). Reporters' roundtable: Ethics in online journalism. *CNET News.* [Audio podcast]. Retrieved from http://www.cnet .com/ 8301-30976_1-20004497-10348864.html

7. Sandoval, G. (2010, April 20). How Gizmodo got its iPhone scoop. *CNET News.*Retrieved from http://news.cnet.com/8301-31001_3-20002975-261.html?tag=mncol;txt

8. Used with permission of Megan Soileau.

Chapter 13 Understanding Persuasive Messages

1. Perloff, R. M. (1993). *The dynamics of persuasion.* Hillsdale, NJ: Erlbaum.

2. Kennedy, G. A. (1980). *Classical rhetoric and its Christian and secular tradition from ancient to modern times.* Chapel Hill, NC: The University of North Carolina Press.

3. Kang, C. (2010, April 24). Undercover persuasion by tech industry lobbyists. *The Washington Post.*Retrieved from http://www.washingtonpost.com/wp-dyn/content/article/2010/04/23/AR2010042305249.html

4. Aristotle. (1960). *On rhetoric* (L. Cooper, Trans.). New York, NY: Appleton-Century-Crofts.

5. Perloff, *Dynamics of persuasion.*

6. Toulmin, S. (1958). *The uses of argument.*Cambridge, England: Cambridge University Press.

7. Ibid.

8. Retrieved from http://www.nia.nih.gov/Alzheimers/Publications/ADProgress2005_2006/Part1/looming .htm

9. Labor, R. (1998). Shaken baby syndrome: The silent epidemic. In *Winning orations* (pp. 70–72). Mankato, MN: Interstate Oratorical Association.

10. James, J. (2007, January). No time for complacency. *Vital Speeches of the Day, 73,* 26–29.

11. Ibid.

12. Ibid.

13. Stewart, R. (1994). Perceptions of a speaker's initial credibility as a function of religious involvement and religious disclosiveness. *Communication Research Reports,* 11, 169–176.

14. Perloff, *Dynamics of persuasion,* pp. 145–149.

15. For example, see Buck, S., & Tiene, D. C. (1989). The impact of physical attractiveness, gender, and teaching philosophy on teacher evaluations. *Journal of Educational Research,* 82, 172–177; Cherulnik, P. D. (1989). *Physical attractiveness and judged stability for leadership* (Report No. CG 021 893). Chicago, IL: Annual Meeting of the Midwestern Psychological Association (ERIC Document Services No. ED 310 317); Drogosz, L. M., & Levy, P. E. (1996). Another look at the effects of appearance, gender and job type on performance-based decisions. *Psychology of Women Quarterly,* 20, 437–445.

16. Morris, T. L., Gorham, J., Cohen, S. H., & Huffman, D. (1996). Fashion in the classroom: Effects of attire on student perceptions of instructors in college classes. *Communication Education,* 45, 135–148; Treinen, K. (1998). *The effects of gender and physical attractiveness on peer critiques of a persuasive speech.* Unpublished master's thesis, North Dakota State University, Fargo, ND.

17. Perloff, *Dynamics of persuasion.*

18. Petri, H. L., & Govern, J. M. (2004). *Motivation: Theory, research, and application*(5th ed., p. 376). Belmont, CA: Wadsworth.

19. Eagly, A. H., & Chaiken, S. (1992). *The psychology of attitudes.* Fort Worth, TX: Harcourt Brace; Maloney, S. R. (1992). *Talk your way to the top.*Englewood Cliffs, NJ: Prentice Hall.

20. Nabi, R. L. (2002). Discrete emotions and persuasion. In J. P. Dillard & M. Pfau (Eds.), *The persuasion handbook: Developments in theory and practice* (pp. 291–299). Thousand Oaks, CA: Sage.

21. Megan's law. Retrieved July 25, 2007, from http://www.accessmylibrary.com/coms2/summary_0286-6368573_ITM

22. Slator, D. (1998). Sharing life. In *Winning orations* (pp. 63–66). Mankato, MN: Interstate Oratorical Association.

23. Labor, Shaken baby syndrome.

24. Ibid.

Chapter 14 Persuasive Speaking

1. Petty, R. E., & Cacioppo, J. (1996). *Attitudes and persuasion: Classic and contemporary approaches*(p. 7). Boulder, CO: Westview.

2. Hill, B., & Leeman, R. W. (1997). *The art and practice of argumentation and debate*(p. 135). Mountain View, CA: Mayfield.

3. Ziegelmueller, G. W., Kay, J., & Dause, C. A. (1990). *Argumentation: Inquiry and advocacy* (2nd ed., p. 186). Englewood Cliffs, NJ: Prentice Hall.

4. Used with permission.

5. Facts pages: History and statistics of U.S. waste production and recycling. (n.d.). *Tufts Recycles.* Retrieved June 15, 2007, from http://www.tufts.edu/tuftsrecycles/

6. Used with permission

Chapter 16 Developing and Delivering Group Presentations

1. O'Hair, D., O'Rourke, J., & O'Hair, M. (2001). *Business communication: A framework for success.* Cincinnati, OH: South-Western; Snyder, B. (2004). Differing views cultivate better decisions. *Stanford Business.*Retrieved from http://www.gsb.stanford.edu/NEWS/bmag/sbsm0405/feature_workteams_gruenfeld.shtml; Teams that succeed. (2004). *Harvard Business Review.* Boston: Harvard Business School Press.

2. Tullar, W., & Kaiser, P. (2000). The effect of process training on process and outcomes in virtual groups. *Journal of Business Communication,* 37, 408–427.

3. Lesikar, R., Pettit Jr., J., & Flately, M. (1999). *Basic business communication* (8th ed.). New York, NY: McGraw-Hill.

4. Rahim, M. A. (2001). *Managing conflict in organizations* (3rd ed.). Westport, CT: Greenwood Press.

5. Janis, I. L. (1982). *Groupthink: Psychological studies of policy decision and fiascos* (2nd ed.). Boston, MA: Houghton Mifflin.

6. Conrad, C. (1997). *Strategic organizational communication: Toward the 21*ˢᵗ*century.* Harcourt Brace.

7. Godamer, H. (1989). *Truth and method* (2nd ed.J. Weinsheimer & D. G. Marshall, Trans.). New York, NY: Crossroad.

8. Braithwaite, D. O., & Eckstein, N. (2003). Reconceptualizing supportive interactions: How persons with disabilities communicatively manages assistance. *Journal of Applied Communication Research, 31,* 1–26.

9. *The View on TV.com.* Retrieved from http://www.tv.com/the-view/show/1676/summary.html

10. Dewey, J. (1933). *How we think.* Boston: Heath.

11. Duch, B. J., Groh, S. E., & Allen, D. E. (Eds.). (2001). *The power of problem-based learning.*Sterling, VA: Stylus; Edens, K. M. (2000). Preparing problem solvers for the 21st century through problem-based learning. *College Teaching,48*(2), 55–60; Levin, B. B. (Ed.). (2001). *Energizing teacher education and professional development with problem-based learning.* Alexandria, MN: Association for Supervision and Curriculum Development.

glossary

accent the inflection, tone, and speech habits typical of native speakers of a language

accommodating a learning style preference that combines feeling and doing

accurate language words that convey your meaning precisely

action an attention-getting act designed to highlight your topic or purpose

actual object an inanimate or animate sample of the idea you are communicating

ad hominem a fallacy that occurs when a speaker attacks or praises a person making an argument rather than addressing the argument itself

adaptation phase the period during which your anxiety level gradually decreases

alliteration repetition of consonant sounds at the beginning of words that are near one another

analogy an extended metaphor

anecdotes brief, often amusing stories

anger feeling when we are faced with an obstacle in the way of something we want

animated delivery delivery that is lively, energetic, enthusiastic, and dynamic

anticipation phase the anxiety you experience prior to giving the speech, including the nervousness you feel while preparing and waiting to speak

antithesis combining contrasting ideas in the same sentence

antonym a word that is directly opposite in meaning

apathetic the audience is uninterested in, unconcerned about, or indifferent toward your topic

appeal to action a statement in a conclusion that describes the behavior you want your listeners to follow after they have heard your arguments

appearance the way you look to others

appreciative listening your goal is to enjoy the thoughts and experiences of others

argue from analogy to support a claim with a single comparable example that is significantly similar to the subject of the claim

argue from causation to cite events that have occurred that result in the claim

argue from example to support your claim by providing one or more individual examples

argue from sign to cite information that signals the claim

argument articulating a position with the support of logos, ethos, and pathos.

articulation using the tongue, palate, teeth, jaw movement, and lips to shape vocalized sounds that combine to produce a word

assonance repetition of vowel sounds in a phrase or phrases

attending paying attention to what the speaker is saying regardless of extraneous interference

attitude a general or enduring positive or negative feeling about some person, object, or issue

audience the specific group of people to whom your speech is directed

audience adaptation the process of tailoring your speech's information to the needs, interests, and expectations of your listeners

audience analysis the study of the intended audience for your speech

audience contact creating a sense of looking listeners in the eye when speaking to large audiences

audience-centered considering who your listeners are and how your message can best be tailored to their interests, desires, and needs

audio aid a presentational aid that relies on sound

audiovisual aid a presentational aid that relies on sight and sound

bar graph a diagram that uses vertical or horizontal bars to show relationships between or among two or more variables at the same time or at various times on one or more dimensions

bias-free language language that demonstrates through word choices an ethical concern for fairness and respect with regard to race, ethnicity, gender, ability, sexual orientation, and diverse worldviews

brainstorming an uncritical, nonevaluative process of generating alternatives by being creative, suspending judgment, and combining or adapting the ideas of others

canons of rhetoric five general rules for effective public speeches

channels both the route traveled by a message and the means of transportation

chart a graphic representation that distills a lot of information and presents it to an audience in an easily interpreted visual format

claim the proposition or conclusion to be proven

clincher a one- or two-sentence statement in a conclusion that provides a sense of closure by driving home the importance of your speech in a memorable way

closed questions narrow-focus questions that require only very brief answers

cognitive restructuring a process designed to help you systematically change your intrapersonal communication (self-talk) about public speaking

collaborate win-win problem solving method

commemorative address a speech of tribute that celebrates people or events

common ground the background, knowledge, attitudes, experiences, and philosophies that audience members and the speaker share

communication the process of creating shared meaning

communication orientation viewing a speech as just an opportunity to talk with a number of people about an important topic

communication orientation motivation (COM) techniques designed to reduce anxiety by helping the speaker adopt a "communication" rather than a "performance" orientation toward the speech

comparative advantages an organization that shows that a proposed change has more value than the status quo

comparison illuminating a point by showing similarities

comparison and contrast a method of informing that explains something by focusing on how it is similar to and different from other things

compassion feeling of selfless concern for the suffering of another

comprehensive listening your goal is to understand, remember, and recall what was said

compromising individuals give up part of what they want in order to provide at least some satisfaction to other opinions

concept mapping a visual means of exploring connections between a subject and related ideas

conflict disagreement or clash among ideas, principles, or people

confrontation phase the surge of anxiety you feel as you begin delivering your speech

connotation the positive, neutral, or negative feelings or evaluations we associate with a word

constructive critique an analysis of a speech or presentation that evaluates how well a speaker meets a specific speaking goal while following the norms for good speaking and that recommends how the presentation could be improved

context the position of a word in a sentence and its relationship to other words around it

contrast illuminating a point by highlighting differences

conversational style delivery that is spontaneous, relaxed, and informal and allows the speaker to talk *with*, not *at*, an audience

creating suspense wording an attention getter so that what is described generates initial uncertainty or mystery and excites the audience

creativity the ability to produce original, innovative ideas

credentials your experiences or education that qualifies you to speak with authority on a specific subject

credibility the perception that you are knowledgeable, trustworthy, and personable

criteria standards used for judging the merits of proposed solutions

criteria satisfaction an indirect organization that seeks audience agreement on criteria that should be considered when evaluating a particular proposition and then shows how the proposition satisfies those criteria

critical listening your goal is to evaluate the worth of a message

decoding the process of interpreting the verbal and nonverbal messages sent by others

dedication a speech of tribute that honors a worthy person or group by naming a structure, monument, or park after them

deductive reasoning arriving at a conclusion based on a major premise and minor premise

definition a statement that clarifies the meaning of a word or phrase

delivery how a message is communicated orally and visually through the use of voice and body

demographic diversity the range of demographic characteristics represented in an audience

demonstration a method of informing that explains something by showing how it is done by displaying the stages of a process or by depicting how something works

denotation the explicit meaning a language community formally gives a word

derived credibility strategies employed throughout the speech that signal a speaker's expertise

description the informative method used to create an accurate, vivid, verbal picture of an object, geographic feature, setting, or image

diagram a type of drawing to show the whole and its parts

dialect a regional variety of a language

direct question a question that demands an overt response from the audience, usually by a show of hands

discriminative listening your goal is to understand the speaker's meaning conveyed in other ways than the words themselves

either-or a fallacy that argues there are only two alternatives when, in fact, there are many

electronic conferencing a widespread method for individuals to engage in live exchange in real time without being in the same room

emotions the buildup of action-specific energy

empathic listening your goal is to be a sounding board to help another sort through feelings

empathy the ability to see the world through the eyes of someone else

encoding the process of putting our thoughts and feelings into words and nonverbal behaviors

ethics moral principles that a society, group, or individual holds that differentiate right from wrong and good behavior from bad behavior

ethos perceived speaker credibility consisting of competence and good character

eulogy a ceremonial speech of tribute during a funeral or memorial service that praises someone's life and accomplishments

evaluating critically analyzing what is said to determine its truthfulness, utility, and trustworthiness

evidence any information that clarifies, explains, or otherwise adds depth or breadth to a topic

examples specific instances that illustrate or explain a general factual statement

expert opinions interpretations and judgments made by authorities in a particular subject area

expository speech framework an informative presentation that provides carefully researched in-depth knowledge about a complex topic

extemporaneous speech a speech that is researched and planned ahead of time, but the exact wording is not scripted and will vary from presentation to presentation

eye contact looking directly at the people to whom you are speaking

facial expression eye and mouth movements that convey personableness and good character

factual statements information that can be verified

false cause a fallacy that occurs when the alleged cause fails to be related to, or to produce, the effect

farewell a speech of tribute honoring someone who is leaving an organization

fear perceiving no control over a situation that threatens us

feedback the reactions and responses to messages that indicate to the sender

whether and how a message was heard, seen, and interpreted

feedback messages messages sent by receivers intended to let the sender know how the receiver made sense of the original message

flipchart a pad of paper mounted on an easel

flowchart a chart that diagrams a sequence of steps through a complicated process

forcing satisfying your own needs with no concern for the needs of others

general goal the overall intent of the speech

generic language language that uses words that may apply only to one sex, race, or other group as though they represent everyone

goodwill an attitude of kindness or friendliness

graph a diagram that presents numerical comparisons

group dynamics how individuals work together as a team toward a common goal

groupthink when group members accept information and ideas without subjecting them to critical analysis

guilt feeling when we personally violate a moral, ethical, or religious code that we hold dear

happiness or joy the buildup of positive energy when we accomplish something or have a satisfying interaction or relationship

hasty generalization a fallacy that presents a generalization that is either not supported with evidence or is supported with only one weak example

hate speech the use of words and phrases to demean another person or group and to express the speaker's hatred and prejudice toward that person or group

hearing the biological process that occurs when the brain detects sound waves

hope emotional energy that stems from believing something desirable is likely to happen

hypothetical examples specific instances based on reflections about future events

impartial free from bias

impromptu speech a speech that is delivered with only seconds or minutes of advance notice for preparation and

is usually presented without referring to notes of any kind

incremental change attempting to move your audience only a small degree in your direction

inductive reasoning arriving at a conclusion based on a series of pieces of evidence

informative speech a speech whose goal is to explain or describe facts, truths, and principles in a way that stimulates interest, facilitates understanding, and increases the likelihood of remembering

initial audience disposition the knowledge of and opinions about your topic that your listeners have before they hear you speak

initial credibility perception of a speaker's expertise at the beginning of the speech

intellectually stimulating information that is new to audience members and is explained in a way that piques their curiosity

intelligible capable of being understood

interference/noise any stimulus that interferes with the process of sharing meaning

interpersonal communication communication between two people

interview a planned, structured conversation where one person asks questions and another answers them

intrapersonal communication communicating with yourself (a.k.a. self-talk)

irrelevant association inappropriate connection between items

jargon unique technical terminology of a trade or profession that is not generally understood by outsiders

joke an anecdote or a piece of wordplay designed to be funny and make people laugh

keynote address a ceremonial speech that both sets the tone and generates enthusiasm for the topic of a conference or convention

knowledge and expertise how well you convince your audience that you are qualified to speak on the topic

LCD multimedia projector a projection unit that connects to a VCR player, a DVD player, or a computer and projects images from them onto a screen

leading questions questions phrased in a way that suggests the interviewer has a preferred answer

learning style a person's preferred way of receiving information

liberal art a body of general knowledge needed to effectively participate in a democratic society

line graph a diagram that indicates changes in one or more variables over time

listener-relevance links statements of how and why the ideas you offer are of interest to your listeners

listening the process of receiving, attending to, constructing meaning from, and responding to spoken or nonverbal messages

logical reasons order organizing the main points of a persuasive speech by the reasons that support the speech goal

logos rhetorical appeals to logic and reasoning

macrostructure the overall framework you use to organize your speech content

main points complete sentence statements of the two to four central ideas that will be used in the thesis statement

major premise a general principle that most people agree upon

marginalizing ignoring the values, needs, and interests of certain audience members, leaving them feeling excluded from the speaking situation

marking the addition of sex, race, age, or other group designations to a description

mass communication communication produced and transmitted via media to large audiences

master or mistress of ceremonies an individual designated to set the mood of the program, introduce participants, and keep the program moving

meanings the interpretations participants make of the messages they send and receive

messages the verbal utterances and nonverbal behaviors to which meaning is attributed during communication

metaphor an implied comparison between two unlike things without using *like* or *as*

microstructure the specific language and style choices you use as you frame your ideas and verbalize them to your audience

minor premise a specific point that fits within the major premise

model a three-dimensional scaled-down or scaled-up version of an actual object

modeling learning by observing and then imitating those you admire or are close to

monotone a voice in which the pitch, volume, and rate remain constant, with no word, idea, or sentence differing significantly from any other

moral a life lesson about right and wrong

motivated movement movement with a specific purpose

motivated sequence a form of persuasive organization that combines a problem-solution pattern with explicit appeals designed to motivate the audience

movement changing the position or location of the entire body

multiple-response items survey items that give the respondent several alternative answers from which to choose

narration a method of informing that explains something by recounting events

narrative order organizing the main points as a story or series of stories

narrative/personal experience speech a presentation in which you recount an experience or experiences you have had and the significance you attach to it or them

narratives accounts, personal experiences, tales, or lengthier stories

negative emotions disquieting feelings people experience

neutral questions questions phrased in ways that do not direct a person's answers

nonparallel language language in which terms are changed because of the sex, race, or other group characteristics of the individual

nonverbal communication all speech elements other than the words themselves

occasion the setting, which includes the purpose, audience expectations, and location.

onomatopoeia words that sound like the things they stand for

open-ended items survey items that encourage respondents to elaborate on their opinions without forcing them to answer in a predetermined way

open questions broad-based questions that ask the interviewee to provide perspective, ideas, information, or opinions

oral footnote reference to an original source, made at the point in the speech where information from that source is presented

oral style the manner in which one conveys messages through the spoken word

organizational chart a chart that shows the structure of an organization in terms of rank and chain of command

other sensory aid presentational aids that appeal to one of the senses

panel discussion a problem-solving discussion in front of an audience

parallel when wording of points follows the same structural pattern, often using the same introductory words

paraphrase putting into your own words the meaning you have assigned to a message

participants the individuals who assume the roles of senders and receivers during an interaction

pathos rhetorical appeals to emotions

pauses moments of silence strategically placed to enhance meaning

perception checking a verbal statement that reflects your understanding of another's behavior

performance orientation viewing public speaking as a situation demanding special delivery techniques to impress an audience aesthetically or viewing audience members as hypercritical judges who will not forgive even minor mistakes

periodicals magazines and journals that appear at fixed periods

personableness the extent to which you project an agreeable or pleasing personality

personal pronouns "we," "us," and "our"—pronouns that directly link the speaker to members of the audience

personal reference a brief story about something that happened to you or a hypothetical situation that listeners can imagine themselves in

personification attributing human qualities to a concept or an inanimate object

persuasion the process of influencing people's attitudes, beliefs, values, or behaviors

persuasive speaking the process of influencing people's attitudes, beliefs, values, or behaviors in a public speech

pie chart a diagram that shows the relationships among parts of a single unit

pitch the highness or lowness of the sounds produced in your larynx by the size and vibration of your vocal cords

plagiarism the unethical act of representing another person's work as your own.

poise the graceful and controlled use of the body that gives the impression of self-assurance, calm, and dignity.

positive emotions feelings that people enjoy experiencing

posture the position or bearing of the body

precise words words that narrow a larger category

preparation outline a rough draft outline organizing the ideas you will present in your speech

presentation software a computer program that enables you to electronically prepare and store your visual aids using a computer

presentational aid any visual, audio, or audiovisual material used in a speech

pride feeling of self-satisfaction and increased self-esteem as the result of an accomplishment

primacy-recency effect the tendency to remember the first and last items conveyed orally in a series than the items in between

primary questions questions the interviewer plans ahead of time

primary research the process of conducting your own study to acquire the information you need

primary source a document that details a firsthand account

problem-cause-solution a form of persuasive organization that examines a problem, its cause(s), and solutions designed to eliminate or alleviate the underlying cause(s)

problem-solution a persuasive organizational pattern that reveals details about a problem and poses solutions to it

problem-solving group four to seven people who work together to complete a specific task or solve a particular problem

process speech framework a speech that explains and shows how something is done, is made, or works

productive thinking to think about something from a variety of perspectives

pronunciation the form and accent of various syllables of a word

proposition a declarative sentence that clearly indicates the position the speaker will advocate

proposition of fact a statement designed to convince the audience that something did or did not exist or occur, is or is not true, or will or will not occur

proposition of policy a statement designed to convince the audience that they should take a specific course of action

proposition of value a statement designed to convince the audience that something is good, bad, desirable, undesirable, fair, unfair, moral, immoral, sound, unsound, beneficial, harmful, important, or unimportant

proximity the relevance of information to personal life space

public communication communication that occurs among more than ten people where one message is presented to the participants who function as receivers whose own messages are limited to feedback

public speaking a sustained formal presentation by a speaker to an audience

public speaking apprehension the level of fear a person experiences when anticipating or actually speaking to an audience

public speaking skills training systematic practicing of the skills associated with the processes involved in preparing and delivering an effective public speech with the intention of improving speaking competence and reducing public speaking apprehension

quality the tone, timbre, or sound of your voice

quotation a comment made by and attributed to someone other than the speaker

rate the speed at which you talk

reasoning the mental process of making an argument by drawing inferences from factual information to reach a conclusion

receivers participants who interpret the messages sent by others

refutative an organization that persuades by both disproving the opposing position and bolstering one's own

rehearsing practicing the presentation of your speech aloud

reinforcement learning from personal experiences and past responses to our behavior

relaxation exercises breathing techniques and progressive muscle relaxation exercises that help reduce anxiety

relevance adapting the information in a speech so that audience members view it as important to them

relief feeling when a threatening situation has been alleviated

remembering being able to retain and recall information we have heard

repetition restating words, phrases, or sentences for emphasis

responding providing feedback to the speaker about what is being said; usually occurs for a speech in the form of nonverbal behaviors

rhetorical figures of speech phrases that make striking comparisons between things that are not obviously alike

rhetorical questions a question that seeks a mental rather than a direct response

rhetorical situation the composite of the occasion, speaker, and the audience that influences the speech that is given

rhetorical structures of speech phrases that combine ideas in a particular way

roast an event where guests provide short speeches of tribute about the featured guests that are developed with humorous stories and anecdotes

sadness feeling when we fail to achieve a goal or experience a loss or separation

scaled items survey items that measure the direction and/or intensity of an audience member's feeling or attitude toward something

scripted speech a speech that is prepared by creating a complete written manuscript and delivered by reading a written copy or from memory

secondary questions questions designed to pursue the answers given to primary questions

secondary research the process of locating information that has been discovered by other people

secondary source a document written about a topic, citing both primary sources and other secondary sources

section transitions complete sentences that show the relationship between, or bridge, major parts of a speech

self-talk intrapersonal communication regarding success or failure in a particular situation

senders participants who form and transmit messages using verbal symbols and nonverbal behaviors

sensory language language that appeals to the senses of seeing, hearing, tasting, smelling, and feeling

shame feeling when we have violated a moral code and it is revealed to someone we think highly of

signposts words or phrases that connect pieces of supporting material to the main point or subpoint they address

simile a direct comparison of dissimilar things using *like* or *as*

skimming a method of rapidly going through a work to determine what is covered and how

slang informal, nonstandard vocabulary and nonstandard definitions assigned to words by a social group or subculture

small group communication the interaction that occurs in a group of three to ten people

speaker the source or originator of the speech

speaking appropriately using language that adapts to the needs, interests, knowledge, and attitudes of the listener and avoiding language that alienates audience members

speaking notes a key-word outline with delivery cues and reference citations you will use as you deliver your speech

speaking situation the circumstances under which you deliver your speech

specific goal a single statement that identifies the exact response the speaker wants from the audience

specific language words that clarify meaning by narrowing what is understood from a general category to a particular item or group within that category

speech effectiveness the extent to which audience members listen to, understand, remember, and are motivated to act on what a speaker has said

speech goal a specific statement of what you want your listeners to know, believe, or do

speech of acceptance a ceremonial speech given to acknowledge receipt of an honor or award

speech of introduction a brief ceremonial speech that establishes a supportive climate for the main speaker, highlights the speaker's credibility by familiarizing the audience with pertinent biographical information, and generates enthusiasm for listening to the speaker and topic

speech of nomination a ceremonial presentation that proposes a nominee for an elected office, honor, position, or award

statement of reasons a straightforward organization in which you present your best-supported reasons in a meaningful order

speech of recognition a ceremonial presentation that acknowledges someone and usually presents an award, a prize, or a gift to the individual or a representative of a group

speech of tribute a ceremonial speech that praises or celebrates a person, a group, or an event

speech of welcome a brief, formal ceremonial address that greets and expresses pleasure for the presence of a person or an organization

formal speech outline a sentence representation of the hierarchical and sequential relationships among the ideas presented in the speech

speech plan a strategy for achieving your goal

speech to actuate a speech designed to incite action

speech to convince a speech designed to seek agreement about a belief, value, or attitude

speech to entertain a humorous speech that makes a serious point

spontaneity a naturalness of speech where what is said sounds as if the speaker is really thinking about the ideas *and* the audience as he or she speaks

Standard English form of English described in the dictionary or an English handbook

startling statement a sentence or two that grabs your listeners' attention by shocking them in some way

statistics numerical facts

stereotyping assuming all members of a group have similar behaviors or beliefs simply because they belong to the group

story an account of something that has happened (actual) or could happen (hypothetical)

straw man a fallacy that occurs when a speaker weakens the opposing position by misrepresenting it and then attacks that weaker position

streaming slide show a series of fifteen to twenty slides posted on the Internet sometimes narrated with a voice-over

streaming video a pre-recording that is sent in compressed form over the Internet

stress emphasis placed on certain words by speaking them more loudly than the rest of the sentence

subject a broad area of expertise, such as movies, computer technology, or the Middle East

support ideas used to develop a main idea

supporting material developmental material that will be used in the speech, including personal experiences, examples, illustrations, anecdotes, statistics, and quotations

survey a canvassing of people to get information about their ideas and opinions, which are then analyzed for trends

syllogism the three-part form of deductive reasoning

symposium a discussion in which a limited number of participants present individual speeches of approximately the same length dealing with the same subject and then discuss their reactions to what others have said and answer questions from the audience

synergy when the result of group work is better than what one member could achieve alone

synonym a word that has the same or a similar meaning

systematic desensitization a method that reduces apprehension by gradually having people visualize and perform increasingly more frightening events while remaining in a relaxed state

systematic problem-solving method an efficient six-step method for finding an effective solution to a problem

target audience the group of people you most want to persuade

teleconferencing where a group of individuals share information aurally over the telephone

terminal credibility perception of a speaker's expertise at the end of the speech

thesis statement a one- or two-sentence summary of the speech that incorporates the general and specific goals and previews the main points

time order organizing the main points of the speech in a chronological sequence or by steps in a process

timeliness showing how information is useful now or in the near future

toast a ceremonial speech offered at the start of a reception or meal that pays tribute to the occasion or to a person

topic some specific aspect of a subject

topic order organizing the main points of the speech by categories or divisions of a subject

town hall meeting an event in which a large number of people who are interested in a topic convene to discuss, and at times to decide, an issue

transition a sentence or two that summarizes one main point and introduces the next one

trustworthiness the extent to which the audience can believe that what you say is accurate, true, and in their best interests

two-sided items survey items that force the respondent to choose between two answers, such as yes/no, for/against, or pro/con

understanding the ability to assign accurate meaning to what was said

uninformed the audience doesn't know enough about a topic to have formed an opinion

verbal immediacy when the language you use reduces the psychological distance between you and your audience

videoconferencing where a group of individuals share information aurally and visually over the Internet

visual aid a form of speech development that allows the audience to see as well as hear information

visualization a method that reduces apprehension by helping speakers develop a mental picture of themselves giving a masterful speech

vivid language language that is full of life—vigorous, bright, and intense

vocal expressiveness variety you create in your voice through changing pitch, volume, and rate, as well as stressing certain words and using pauses

vocalized pause unnecessary words interjected into sentences to fill moments of silence

voice the sound you produce in your larynx, or voice box, which is used to transmit the words of your speech to an audience

volume how loudly or softly you speak

warrant the logical statement that connects the support to the claim

"we" language the use of plural personal pronouns like "we," "our," and "us" rather than "you" or "they"

withdrawing physically or psychologically removing oneself from a conflict.

index

demonstration used in, 245–246
description used in, 243–244
expository, 255–266
frameworks, 246–266
as intellectually stimulating, 238–239
learning styles and, 242–243
as memorable, 242
methods of informing, 243–246
narration used in, 245
outline of, 250–252, 261–263
overview of, 238
process, 246–255
relevance and, 239
Informative speech with aids
adaptation plan for, 229–230
analysis along with, 233–235
outline of, 230–232
InfoTrac College Edition, 97
Initial audience disposition, 78–79
Initial credibility, 283
Intellectually stimulating, 238–239
Intelligible, 198, 210–211
Interference, 4
Interpersonal communication, 4
Interview protocol, 101–102
Interviews, 101
conducting, 102–104
primary research and, 101–104
protocol, 101–102
sample questions for, 103
scheduling, 102
selecting best person for, 101
Intrapersonal communication, 4
Introduction
ask question in, 145–146
create suspense in, 148–149
creating, 144–153
establish credibility/goodwill, 149–150, 151
establish listener relevance in, 149, 150
get attention with, 145–149
goals of, 145–151
perform/motivate action in, 148, 149
personal reference for, 147, 148
to persuasive speech, 296
primacy-recency effect and, 144
quotation used in, 147–148
sample, 162
selecting best, 151–152
self, 14
speeches, 335–336
startling statement in, 145
state thesis in, 151
tell joke in, 146–147
tell story in, 146
Irrelevant association, 193
Irvine, Robert, 9

J

James, Frances, 297
Jargon, 200–201
Joke, 146–147
Jones, James L., 194
Joy, 289
Judgment, suspension of, 42–43

K

Kang, Cecilia, 270
Keynote address, 342
Knowledge, demonstration of, 81–82
Koepsell, Jaime, 183

L

Language. *See also* Accurate language; Speaking appropriately; Speaking clearly
generic, 192
nonparallel, 192–193
second, 87–88
sensory, 202–203
specific/familiar, 85
vivid, 85, 202–204
Law, expository speech and, 257–258
LCD multimedia projector, 182
Leading questions, 102
Learning cycle, 84
Learning styles
audience adaptation and, 83–84
informative speech and, 242–243
Liberal art, 5
democracies and, 5–6
freedom and, 6–7
public speaking as, 5–7
Line graph, 173, 176
Listener-relevance links, 133, 241
audience analysis and, 59
introduction and, 149, 150
Listening, 40
attending and, 42–43, 45
business success and, 40–41
constructive critiques and, 45–49
effective/ineffective behaviors of, 45
evaluating and, 44–45
responding and, 45
skills improvement, 42–45
types of, 41
understanding/remembering and, 43–44, 45
Lobbying, 272
Logical reasons order, 131–132
Logos, 11, 269
arguments and, 272–279
evaluating evidence to support, 280–281
reasoning fallacies and, 279–280
reasoning types and, 272
strategy of persuasion, 272–281

M

Macrostructure, 12
Mad Money (TV show), 68
Main points
conclusion and, 153
developing, 132–135
identifying, 120–121, 122
logical reasons order of, 131–132
narrative order of, 130–131
number of, 120
outlined example of, 137–140
outlining, 128–132
parallel structure and, 129–130
preparation outline of, 129
selecting organizational pattern for, 130–132

speech length regarding, 127
subpoint identification of, 133–134
subpoint outlining, 134–135
thesis statement and, 121–122, 123
time order of, 130
topic order of, 131
transitions for, 135–140
wording, 128–130
Major premise, 272
"Making Ethanol" (Greene), 249–255
Maps, 171–172
Marginalizing, 64
Marking, 192–193
Mass communication, 5
Master of ceremonies, 334
Maverick ethics example, 87
McCain, John, 87
McGuire, Jeff, 80
McKeever, Stacey L., 96
Meanings, 3
Memorable, 242
Messages, 3–4
Metaphor, 205
Microstructure, 12
Millner, Alyssa Grace, 229–235
Minor premise, 272
"Mirror Image" (Treinen), 15–16
Mnemonics, memorable speech and, 242
Modeling, 23
Models, as visual aids, 170
Monotone, 213
Moral, 32
Morrison, Sally A., 343
Motivate action, 148, 149
Motivated movement, 216
Motivated sequence, 318–319
Movement, 216
Multiple-response items, 61
Muren, Dominic, 169

N

Narration, 245
Narrative order, 130–131
Narrative/personal experience speech, 32, 34–35
Narratives, 108–109
Neutral questions, 102
Newsbank (newspaper source), 98
Newspapers, as research source, 97–98
Noise, 4
Nomination speeches, 336–337
Nonparallel language, 192–193
Nonverbal communication, 208–209
Note preparation, 221–223

O

Obama, Barack, 173
Objectivity, 99
Occasion, 11, 66–68
Oh, Saejean, 46
O'Leary, George, 35
Onomatopoeia, 204
Open-ended items, 62
Open questions, 102
Operant conditioning, 258
Oral footnotes, 114, 257